Alexander Bergs and Laurel J. Brinton (Eds.)
The History of English
Volume 5

The History of English

Volume 5: Varieties of English

Edited by
Alexander Bergs and Laurel J. Brinton

DE GRUYTER
MOUTON

ISBN 978-3-11-052279-2
e-ISBN (PDF) 978-3-11-052504-5
e-ISBN (EPUB) 978-3-11-052304-1

Library of Congress Cataloging-in-Publication Data
A CIP catalog record for this book has been applied for at the Library of Congress.

Bibliographic information published by the Deutsche Nationalbibliothek
The Deutsche Nationalbibliothek lists this publication in the Deutsche Nationalbibliografie;
detailed bibliographic data are available on the Internet at: http://dnb.dnb.de.

© 2017 Walter de Gruyter GmbH, Berlin/Boston
Cover image: elf0724/iStock/Thinkstock
Typesetting: jürgen ullrich typosatz, Nördlingen
Printing: CPI Books GmbH; Leck
♾ Printed on acid-free paper
Printed in Germany

www.degruyter.com

Table of Contents

Abbreviations —— VII

Laurel J. Brinton and Alexander Bergs
Chapter 1: Introduction —— 1

Richard W. Bailey
Chapter 2: Standard American English —— 9

Luanne von Schneidemesser
Chapter 3: Regional varieties of American English —— 31

Stefan Dollinger
Chapter 4: Canadian English in real-time perspective —— 53

Sonja L. Lanehart
Chapter 5: Re-viewing the origins and history of African American Language —— 80

Pam Peters
Chapter 6: Standard British English —— 96

Bernd Kortmann and Christian Langstrof
Chapter 7: Regional varieties of British English —— 121

Lynda Mugglestone
Chapter 8: Received Pronunciation —— 151

Ulrike Altendorf
Chapter 9: Estuary English —— 169

Sue Fox
Chapter 10: Cockney —— 187

Markku Filppula and Juhani Klemola
Chapter 11: Celtic and Celtic Englishes —— 210

Robert McColl Millar
Chapter 12: Scots —— 231

Jeffrey L. Kallen
Chapter 13: English in Ireland —— 244

Colin H. Williams
Chapter 14: English in Wales —— 265

Marianne Hundt
Chapter 15: Australian/New Zealand English —— 289

Devyani Sharma
Chapter 16: English in India —— 311

Rajend Mesthrie
Chapter 17: English in Africa – a diachronic typology —— 330

David Britain
Chapter 18: Diffusion —— 349

Raymond Hickey
Chapter 19: Supraregionalization —— 365

Suzanne Romaine
Chapter 20: Pidgins and creoles —— 385

Index —— 403

Abbreviations

ACC	accusative case
ACT	active
ADJ	adjective
ADV	adverb
AN	Anglo-Norman
Angl.	Anglian
AUX	auxiliary
C	consonant
COMPR	comparative
DAT	dative case
DEM	demonstrative
DU	dual
EModE	Early Modern English
EWSax.	Early West Saxon
FEM	feminine
Fr.	French
GEN	genitive case
Ger.	German
Gk.	Greek
Go.	Gothic
Grmc.	Germanic
IE	Indo-European
IMP	imperative
IND	indicative
INF	infinitive
INFL	inflected
INSTR	instrumental case
Kent.	Kentish
LAEME	*A Linguistic Atlas of Early Middle English*
LALME	*A Linguistic Atlas of Late Mediaeval English*
Lt.	Latin
LModE	Late Modern English
LWSax.	Late West Saxon
MASC	masculine
ME	Middle English
MED	*Middle English Dictionary*
ModE	Modern English
NEG	negative

NEUT	neuter
N	noun
NOM	nominative case
NP	noun phrase
O	object
OBJ	objective case
OE	Old English
OED	*Oxford English Dictionary*
OFr.	Old French
OHG	Old High German
ON	Old Norse
P	person
PASS	passive
PAST	past tense
PDE	Present-day English
PGrmc.	Proto-Germanic
PIE	Proto-Indo-European
PL	plural
PREP	preposition
PRON	pronoun
PRTC	participle
PRES	present tense
PRET	preterit
S	subject
SG	singular
SUBJ	subjunctive mood
SUP	superlative
SOV	subject-object-verb word order
SVO	subject-verb-object word order
T	tense
v	verb
v2	verb second
V	vowel
VO	verb-object word order
VP	verb phrase
WGrmc.	West Germanic
WSax.	West Saxon
>	changes to, becomes
<	derives from

Ø	no ending
*	reconstructed form, ungrammatical form
< >	spelling

Laurel J. Brinton and Alexander Bergs
Chapter 1: Introduction

1 English Language Studies —— 1
2 Description of the Series —— 2
3 Description of this Volume —— 4
4 References —— 8

1 English Language Studies

The study of the English language has a lengthy history. The second half of the 18th century saw a phenomenal increase in the number of published grammars of the vernacular language, while the field of comparative linguistics arising in the 19th century was concerned in large part with the Germanic languages, including English. Moreover, in the field of theoretical linguistics that English has played a truly central role. While there are no reliable statistics, it seems safe to say that the majority of studies in contemporary linguistics deal at least in part with English, and are also written in English.

During the 20th century, monumental works concerned with the English language, both synchronic and diachronic, were produced, following historical/comparative and more contemporary linguistic approaches. In keeping with developments on the field of general linguistics, today it is possible to find descriptions and analyses of the history and development of English from virtually any linguistic perspective: external, internal, generative, functional, sociolinguistic, pragmatic, comparative, phonological, morphological, syntactic, lexical, semantic. There are numerous "Histories of English" to cater to just about every (theoretical) taste, as well as detailed descriptions of historical periods, language levels, or theoretical frameworks of English and specialized studies of individual topics in the development of the language.

Work on the history of English has culminated most recently in the a series of edited handbooks and histories of English: the six-volume *Cambridge History of the English Language,* edited by Richard M. Hogg (1992–2001), *The Handbook of the History of English,* edited by Ans van Kemenade and Bettelou Los (2006), *The*

Laurel J. Brinton: Vancouver (Canada)
Alexander Bergs: Osnabrück (Germany)

Oxford History of English, edited by Lynda Mugglestone (2012 [2006]), *The Oxford Handbook of the History of English*, edited by Elizabeth Closs Traugott and Terttu Nevalainen (2012), the two-volume *English Historical Linguistics: An International Handbook*, edited by Alexander Bergs and Laurel J. Brinton (2012), and most recently *The Cambridge Handbook of English Historical Linguistics*, edited by Päiva Pahta and Merja Kytö (2015).

While study of the history of any language begins with texts, increasingly scholars are turning to dictionaries and corpora of English that are available online or electronically. The third edition of the *Oxford English Dictionary* online, while still undergoing revision, is now fully integrated with the *Historical Thesaurus*. The *Middle English Dictionary*, completed in 2001, is freely available online along with the *Corpus of Middle English Prose and Verse*. The pioneer historical corpus of English, *The Helsinki Corpus of English Texts*, was first released to scholars in 1991. The *Dictionary of Old English Web Corpus*, containing all Old English texts, is searchable online. ARCHER, *A Representative Corpus of English Registers 1650–1900*, accessible at a number of universities, provides a balanced selection of historical texts in electronic form. COHA, a 400-million-word, balanced *Corpus of Historical American English 1810–2009*, was launched online in 2010. Smaller corpora, such as the *Corpus of English Dialogues 1560–1760*, the *Lampeter Corpus of Early Modern English Tracts*, the *Corpus of Early English Correspondence*, the *Corpus of Early English Medical Writing*, the *Corpus of Late Modern English 3.0*, and the newly expanded *Old Bailey Corpus*, have made more specialized corpora – covering more periods and more text types – available to scholars. Archives of historical newspapers online, including the *Zurich English Newspaper Corpus* and the *Rostock Newspaper Corpus*, provide another source of electronic data. Finally, syntactically annotated corpora for historical stages of English are being produced, including *The York-Helsinki Parsed Corpus of Old English Poetry*, *The York-Toronto-Helsinki Parsed Corpus of Old English Prose*, *The Penn-Helsinki Parsed Corpus of Middle English*, and *The Penn-Helsinki Parsed Corpus of Early Modern English*. (For information on all of the corpora listed here, see http://www.helsinki.fi/varieng/CoRD/corpora/).

2 Description of the Series

The two-volume *English Historical Linguistics: An International Handbook* (Bergs and Brinton 2012) serves as the textual basis for the current five-volume reader series *The History of English*. The aim of this series is to make selected papers from this important handbook accessible and affordable for a wider audience, and in particular for younger scholars and students, and to allow their use in the classroom. Each chapter is written by a recognized specialist in the topic and includes an extensive bibliography suitable for a range of levels and interests.

While conventional histories of English (e.g., Brinton and Arnovick 2016) are almost universally organized chronologically, the six-volume *Cambridge History of English* (Hogg 1992–2001) is organized by linguistic level, as is the shortened version (Hogg and Denison 2006) and to a lesser extent *The Handbook of the History of English* (van Kemanade and Los 2006). Volumes 1 to 4 of this series likewise follow this pattern:

Volume 1: The History of English: Historical Outlines from Sound to Text provides a comprehensive overview of the history of English and explores key questions and debates. The volume begins with a re-evaluation of the concept of periodization in the history of English. This is followed by overviews of changes in the traditional areas of phonology, morphology, syntax, and semantics as well as chapters covering areas less often treated in histories of English, including prosody, idioms and fixed expressions, pragmatics and discourse, onomastics, orthography, style/register/text types, and standardization.

Volume 2: The History of English: Old English provides an in-depth account of Old English. Individual chapters review the state of the art in phonological, morphological, syntactic, and semantic studies of Old English. Key areas of debate, including dialectology, language contact, standardization, and literary language, are also explored. The volume sets the scene with a chapter on pre-Old English and ends with a chapter discussing textual resources available for the study of earlier English.

Volume 3: The History of English: Middle English provides a wide-ranging account of Middle English. Not only are the traditional areas of linguistic study explored in state-of-the-art chapters on Middle English phonology morphology, syntax, and semantics, but the volume also covers less traditional areas of study, including Middle English creolization, sociolinguistics, literary language (including the language of Chaucer), pragmatics and discourse, dialectology, standardization, language contact, and multilingualism.

Volume 4: The History of English: Early Modern English provides a comprehensive account of Early Modern English. In seventeen chapters, this volume not only presents detailed outlines of the traditional language levels, such as phonology, morphology, syntax, semantics and pragmatics, but it also explores key questions and debates, such as *do*-periphrasis, the Great Vowel Shift, pronouns and relativization, literary language (including the language of Shakespeare), and sociolinguistics, including contact and standardization.

The last volume in the series turns its attention to the spread of English worldwide. **Volume 5: The History of English: Varieties of English** is one of the first detailed expositions of the history of different varieties of English. It explores language variation and varieties of English from an historical perspective, covering theoretical topics such as diffusion and supra-regionalization as well as concrete descriptions of the internal and external historical developments of more than a dozen varieties of English including American English, African American Vernacular English, Received Pronunciation, Estuary English, and English in Canada, Africa, India, Wales, among many others.

Taking into account the important developments in the study of English effected by the availability of electronic corpora, this series of readers on *The History of English* offers a comprehensive, interdisciplinary, and theory-neutral synopsis of the field. It is meant to facilitate both research and teaching by offering up-to-date overviews of all the relevant aspects of the historical linguistics of English and by referring scholars, teachers, and students to more in-depth coverage. To that end, many articles have been updated from the 2012 edition to include more recent publications.

3 Description of this volume

Unlike the other four volumes in this series, this volume does not deal with the standard history of "English English", but rather takes a wider perspective in that it provides detailed descriptions of the histories of different major varieties of English (such as American English, Canadian English or Received Pronunciation) and of English-speaking regions (such as English in India or Africa). Moreover, it also includes some more theoretical chapters, for example on the origins of African American Language, on diffusion and on supraregionalization.

The first four chapters of this volume deal with the development of English (and its varieties) in North America.

Richard Bailey traces the history of "Standard American English". It becomes clear in his chapter that American English has a particularly dynamic history. After its emergence in the 16th century, it was recognized as such only about 200 years later. And while early observers noted a particular 'purity' of this variety, and a certain lack of dialect variation, British speakers also feared that this new variety might influence their own speech in the long run. From the 19th century onwards, however, American speakers began to worry about 'their language' as ever growing waves of immigrants brought new languages to the country. And to this day, there is still the open question whether there is something like a standard for American English. **Luanne von Schneidemesser** also discusses American English in her chapter, but she focuses on "Regional Varieties of American English". She provides a detailed outline of the various projects that led to the description of those varieties, including the *Linguistic Atlas of New*

England, the Dictionary of American Regional English and the most recent *Atlas of North American English*. She concludes with a plea that studies in regional dialectology and in social and ethnic dialects need to work more closely together in the future in order to arrive at a fuller picture of linguistic variation in North America. **Stefan Dollinger** begins his chapter on "Canadian English" with a general overview of Canada's settlement history. In his section on methodology, he emphasizes that the general lack of historical treatments of Canadian English seems to necessitate a complex combination of real-time and apparent-time perspectives. The reader is then introduced to major variables that characterize the history of Canadian English at all levels of linguistic structure. **Sonja Lanehardt** focuses in her contribution on "Re-viewing the origins and history of African American Language". After presenting some general views regarding the nature of African American language, such as the deficit position or structuralist perspectives, she gives a detailed description of the traditional big players in the debate, i.e. Anglicists versus Creolists. In a following section, Lanehardt moves beyond this and discusses four more recent positions. In conclusion, she points out that all these perspectives should be evaluated not just on the basis of their linguistic substance, but also with regard to the ideological and epistemic perspectives of the scholars involved.

The following five chapters deal with English in Britain, and varieties of British English in the widest sense. **Pam Peters** focuses on the history of Standard British English, beginning with notion of British English as a national standard language in the 16th century. She then traces this notion through the colonial period until the present day, where British English as a former international standard is challenged by American English and World English(es). The question remains open, however, what kind of role a regional, and yet pluralistic notion of British English will play in the future of a "world standard English". In their chapter on "Regional varieties of British English" **Bernd Kortmann** and **Christian Langstrof** provide detailed descriptions of the phonetic and phonological as well as morphosyntactic variation in major varieties of British English. They show that variation on the consonantal level, though rich in form, is mainly guided by socio-economic factors and style, rather than region (in contrast to what we see in the vowel system). Moreover, their section on morphosyntax clearly shows that we need to distinguish between pan-British features and regional markers.

The following chapters deal with individual varieties of English English, which have received considerable attention by the media and thus warrant separate treatments. The chapter on "Received Pronunciation" (RP) by **Lynda Mugglestone** explores the history and development of the notion of RP as a more recent, non-localized British accent. On the basis of new and hitherto unexamined archive data, Mugglestone traces the explicit fostering of the notion in institutions such as the BBC. In a final section, she investigates the present situation and critically evaluates the question of the validity of RP, either as a reality or even as an abstract notion. **Ulrike Altendorf** concentrates on a fairly new, popular variety called "Estuary English", which supposedly challenges the role of RP in certain circles. She provides a detailed description of this variety as regional in the south-east and beyond, and of social variation associated with Estuary English. Her chapter concludes with two sections on Estuary English as possibly a new style, or even a chimera based on related but divergent trends. Here we see the complex interplay of linguistic analyses and folk-linguistic or media treatments of one particular phenomenon. In her chapter on "Cockney" **Sue Fox** faces similar problems: the term itself is rather vague and is used by linguists and the media alike. Fox describes the history of the term and the development of the variety itself over time, keeping in mind individual, stylistic and social differences in speakers. Following detailed descriptions of the phonological systems, and cockney rhyming slang, she suggests that recent social and demographic developments may have rendered the term irrelevant for future generations, and that we may rather have to turn to Multicultural London English.

The next four chapters deal with what could be termed the Celtic Fringe in the widest sense. The 'Celtic Hypothesis' lies at the heart of **Markku Filppula** and **Juhani Klemola**'s paper on "Celtic and Celtic Englishes". They discuss two specific syntactic features of English, the progressive form of verbs and the *it*-cleft construction, which can be shown to be have been influenced by Celtic languages. For this, they identify two waves of English-Celtic influence: one in the early medieval period, and one in modern times. "Scots" features in **Robert McColl Millar**'s chapter. In his chapter, he focuses on the external, socio-cultural history of this dialect (or language) and shows how the turbulent history of Scots led to its special status today with frequent but apparently ineffectual attempts to re-install Scots as an official language. **Jeffrey Kallen** investigates "English in Ireland". His chapter encompasses both the early developments of English in Ireland from the 12th century onwards and the more recent developments as documented in the *International Corpus of English – Ireland*. Kallen shows that Irish English is historically characterized by a complex mixture of British English dialects, Scots, and Irish, and that its status as a national variety of English makes it comparable to other major English varieties. "English in Wales" is the topic of **Colin Williams** chapter. Just like with Ireland, the relationship between England and Wales has always been a very complex one, especially since Wales was one of the first English colonies. This chapter consequently focuses on the external, socio-cultural history of Wales and its languages. From the viewpoint of sociology of language, it primarily investigates multilingualism in Wales, as well as past and current political attempts to encourage and promote linguistic pluralism and language equality.

The following three chapters look at the history of English in three more remote regions: Australia and New Zealand, India, and Africa. **Marianne Hundt** sketches the history of English in Australia and New Zealand. She points out that despite their geographical proximity, both varieties need to be carefully distinguished, for both linguistic and political/cultural reasons. In her discussion of the various language levels, including pronunciation, lexicon, and grammar, she tries to show where these two southern-hemisphere varieties show convergence and divergence. One of the oldest (post-)colonial varieties, "English in India", is the topic of **Devyani Sharma's** chapter. Her study is structured according to four different periods of English in India: a phase of "early presence" in the 17th and 18th century, followed by a period of strong colonial language ideologies, which again was followed by the independence movement and finally an independent India. All these periods exhibit their own particularities, even though on a more general level this is a case of a prolonged and highly asymmetric contact situation. This chapter concludes with a section on current variation in Indian English. **Rajend Mesthrie** finally discusses "English in Africa – a diachronic typology". He stresses that the historical study of English in Africa has not really received a lot of attention so far, but that it can offer some very interesting insights. In his chapter, he covers the development and status of two L1 varieties (White South African English and Liberian English) and argues that these warrant typological comparisons with varieties outside Africa. In a final section, he also discusses L2 Englishes in Africa and suggests internal African comparisons in order to allow for the monitoring of possible future developments.

Three more theoretical papers conclude this volume. The "Diffusion" of innovative linguistic forms at three different levels is discussed by **David Britain**. He first alerts us to the fact that diffusion itself is not an unambiguous term and that we need to be very careful to distinguish between innovations and different types and causes of diffusion. In two separate sections, Britain critically outlines both diffusion on the social micro-level (in social networks) and on the social macro-level (in geographical pathways, for example). A final section discusses the linguistic consequences of diffusion. **Raymond Hickey** describes the process of "Supraregionalization", i.e. a process whereby varieties lose their local, specific features and become less regionally bound. Hickey discusses different phases of supraregionalization, such as actuation, propagation, and termination, and identifies possible factors and motivations for these sub-processes with an exemplary case-study of English in Ireland. Last, but not least, **Suzanne Romaine** in her chapter on "Pidgins and Creoles" focuses on the outcome of complex processes of language contact and language mixing. After a first definition of pidgins and creoles, Romaine offers some broad classification, and presents both a structural and a sociolinguistic examination of the factors and dimensions that are at work in the birth of new languages. In this discussion, it becomes clear that to this day we do not have a clear consensus on how to structurally define pidgins versus creoles in their complex relationship to the languages and circumstances that gave rise to them.

4 References

Brinton, Laurel J. and Leslie K. Arnovick. 2016. *The English Language: A Linguistic History*. 3rd edn. Toronto: Oxford University Press.
Hogg, Richard. 1992–2001. *The Cambridge History of the English Language*. 6 vols. Cambridge: Cambridge University Press.
Hogg, Richard and David Denison. 2006. *A History of the English Language*. Cambridge: Cambridge University Press.
Kemenade, Ans van and Bettelou Los. 2006. *The Handbook of the History of English*. Chichester: Wiley-Blackwell.
Kytö, Merja and Päiva Pahta. 2015. *The Cambridge Handbook of English Historical Linguistics*. Cambridge: Cambridge University Press.
Nevalainen, Terttu and Elizabeth Closs Traugott. 2012. *The Oxford Handbook of the History of English*. Oxford: Oxford University Press.
Mugglestone, Lynda. 2012. *The Oxford History of English*. Updated edn. Oxford: Oxford University Press. [First published 2006]

Richard W. Bailey
Chapter 2:
Standard American English

1 Introduction —— 9
2 The purity of American English —— 13
3 The contagion of American English —— 16
4 American voices —— 18
5 Anxiety about American English —— 21
6 What is the "standard"? —— 23
7 The future of American English —— 26
8 References —— 28

Abstract: Historically considered, American English begins to emerge in the 16th century, even before any English speakers reached the shores of the North American continent. General recognition of American English as a distinct English like that of Scotland or Ireland did not appear until the very end of the 18th century, and when it did, it was judged by both Britons and Americans to have an unusual "purity" and freedom from dialect differences. Before long, however, British speakers began to fear the effect of American English on their own usage, treating it as an "invasion" or "contagion". In the United States, people began to fear competition from first German and then Spanish and the likelihood that these languages would displace English speakers. Just what constitutes a "standard" of American speech remains a vexed question, but there is certain to be an influence on world English from America in the future.

1 Introduction

Conventional histories of English go from origins to outcomes, and in them American English begins when the first American expressions reach England or, less sensibly, when the present-day United States declares independence from the United Kingdom of England, Scotland, and Ireland. Political changes have little effect on linguistic events until the political has taken cultural hold (Bailey 2004).

Richard W. Bailey †: Michigan (USA)

In London, innovations from North America and the Caribbean were variously received, sometimes with delight and other times with disdain. In 1619, a prominent London intellectual greeted the addition of *maize* and *canoe* to English; in 1754, a reviewer puffing Samuel Johnson's forthcoming dictionary declared that the book would be of great assistance to those wishing "to ornament [their] discourse with those jewels" from North America like *calumet* 'peace pipe' and *wampum* 'belts of beads and shells' (unfortunately Johnson had not bothered to enter these words; see Read 2002: 8–9, 11–12; Bailey 2009). Objectors to such expressions singled out *ordinary* 'tavern' in 1674 and *bluff* 'precipitous descent of land' in 1735, the latter described as "barbarous English" (Read 2002: 9–10). Even so, though ignorant of many things American, George III (in 1774) knew the word *maize* (Read 2002: 39) and took no exception to it.

Despite additions to (and subtractions from) the stock of English words, America was slow to develop a distinctive linguistic identity. Part of the difficulty in determining when this evolution took place is that we are dependent upon outside observers recognizing and reporting differences. In addition, records of unselfconscious speech are uncommon and often dubiously authentic. Consider this specimen from the witch trials in Salem, Massachusetts, in the 1690s:

> Aug. the 11th, 1696. [1692]: It was asked Sarah Carrier by the Magistrates or Justices John Hawthorne Esq; and others: How long hast thou been a witch? A. Ever since I was six years old. Q. How old are you now? A. Near eight years old, brother Richard says, I shall be eight years old in November next. Q. Who made you a witch? A. My mother, she made me set my hand to a book. (Boyer and Nissenbaum 1977: 201)

What would a contemporary in England have seen in this extract that would identify Sarah Carrier as an American? Perhaps nothing. Our own American 21st-century perspective would probably single out only one sentence from this child's cross-examination as unlike our own English: "How long hast thou been a witch?" The interrogator's selection of *thou* shows that the old pronoun system was still in use. (The form *thou* was used for inferiors, like children and witches, and for selected superiors, like the deity. People on an equal footing used *you*.)

This pronoun system, however, was undergoing change. Early in the 17th century, when the New England settlers were departing for Massachusetts, upper-class speakers in London were giving up *thou* (and *thee, thyself, thine,* and *thy*) except for prayerful and solemn occasions and replacing it with *you* (and its corresponding forms) among equals. By the end of the century, *thou* had become dialectal (used in the north of England) and ideological (where it was used by Quakers to assert universal equality). Thus, "How long hast thou been a witch?"

would have been largely replaced by "How long have you been a witch?" – especially in East Anglia, the part of England where most Massachusetts colonists had their origins (Kytö 2004: 147–149).

American English, consequently, became more conservative than the prestige dialect of London and its environs, leading some historians to speak of "colonial lag", in that the transplanted variety would have seemed to contemporaries more archaic than the metropolitan dialect. Such terminology, however, oversimplifies a complex process of language change in which, in this case, prestige speakers led the way by adopting an innovation, leaving regional and lower-class groups using the traditional forms just as the colonists were doing.

Pronunciation presents similar examples of change at home and stability abroad. When North American settlements began, *bath, glass,* and *dance* all had a vowel resembling that of *hat* but during the late 18th century, upper-class British English speakers adopted pronunciations with a vowel close to that of *father*. Though at first ridiculed as foppish and affected, these new pronunciation soon became hallmarks of refined London English though not that of the northern part of the country. American English, for the most part, kept the "old" ways of speaking. Similarly, the replacement with a vowel of the consonant *r* (or the loss of *r*) after a vowel in the same phrase (or prosodic unit) was regional at the beginning of the 17th century, but the region included the home territory of many emigrants to North America. The vowel substitution in *clear* and *first*, for instance, made for language change both at home and abroad, but subsequently, in the 19th century, the vocalized alternatives became part of the English prestige dialects while at the same time being relegated to rustic speech in North America (for more details, see Bailey 2011). (The vocalized versions were used by some high-status Americans in the 20th century before finally merging with the variants with consonantal *r*.)

American English established itself as an independent variety of English in gradual and subtle ways, and the conservative ways of speaking were less noticed because Americans sounded as if they came from the "west country" or "the north" of England – not because they or their forebears had migrated from those places but because the evolution of English had taken the same course in all three regions.

In the mid-18th century, American visitors to London were prominent. Benjamin West became portrait painter to the royal family; Benjamin Franklin was celebrated as a scientist and bon-vivant. Anne Fisher, a Loyalist refugee from the Carolinas, set herself up as a schoolmistress specializing in correct English (Fisher 1788). None of these Americans was identified by his or her speech, though all three were surrounded by critics of correct English. They were Americans, to be sure, but nobody observed that they spoke American English.

High-status Americans spoke just like high-status Britons. Only on descending the social scale did observers begin to take account of North American English. Among the most distinctive of these low-status Americans were slaves, and in 1776 John Leacock published a provocative play, *The Fall of British Tyranny*. In it (as in real life) British officers recruit American slaves to military service by promising freedom: "Well, my brave blacks, are you come to list? *Cudjo:* Eas, massa Lord, you preazee. *Kidnapper*: How many are there of you? *Cudjo*: Twenty-two, massa. *Kidnapper*: Very well, did you all run away from your masters? *Cudjo*: Eas, massa Lord, eb'ry one, me too" (Leacock 1776: 46).

While probably not performed, Leacock's play was published and widely read. As a piece of propaganda, it was influential on the emerging revolution – George Washington is a prominent figure filled with patriotic zeal. As a representation of American speech, it was plausible. Cudjo and his companions speak a highly distinctive variety of American English, and if Washington's English is not distinct from the British, certainly Cudjo's is.

In his consular work in France, Thomas Jefferson was expected to supply papers to seamen: "[...] between the American and the English (unless of a particular province) there is no difference sensible even to a native [American]" (Jefferson 30 April 1791, see Jefferson 2008). Similar evidence appears in notices of runaway indentured servants where ways of speaking are often listed as an aid to identifying them. Scots and Irish are often discovered by their speech but very seldom are the regional dialects of England mentioned.

Contact between American and British soldiers in the Revolution and in the War of 1812–1814 led to more recognition of distinctions in English. A clever Briton managed to overpower an American sentry on the Niagara frontier in 1813:

> The [American] sentry, hearing some one approach, issues from his box, protrudes the upper part of his body though the doorway, and asks 'Who come there?'
> [Sgt. Andrew] Spearman, imitating the nasal twang of the American, answers, 'I guess, Mister, I come from Youngstown,' quietly introducing at the same time his left shoulder through the half open wicket.
> The sentry stares at him, perceives by his accoutrements and his actions that he is an enemy, turns round and runs inward exclaiming, 'The Brit ...!' He says no more, Spearman's bayonet is in his side. (Cruikshank 1907: 19)

Another example of colonial lag, *I guess* came to be recognized as a peculiarly American way of commencing an act of speaking. Long-established in English, this use of *guess* became a stereotype of American speech, and in recent usage *I guess* is nearly ten times more frequent in American than in British (Algeo 2006: 139).

Thus it was that by the beginning of the 19th century, American English had become a recognized variety of the language. Some of its presence was subtle in borrowed words or retention of expressions grown increasingly obsolete in Britain. Some of it was more characteristic of lower-, rather than upper-class, speakers. Some of it was culturally specific in meanings having arisen from new political institutions like *senate, president*, or *township*. Most of these were new senses of existing words, but some were not: *caucus, sachem*, or *pow-wow* (all three established in American English before the revolution).

These developments have been carefully studied and documented from early records. What is less recognized is the emergence of the meaning of "American English" as a distinct language with certain distinctive properties. The remainder of this chapter sketches ideas that are particularly important for understanding the meaning of American English in the 21st century.

2 The purity of American English

In 1799, a Scot visiting America reported, "The Anglo-Americans speak English with great classical purity. Dialect in general is there less prevalent there than in Britain, except among the poor slaves" (Read 2002: 56). In this view, he endorsed an idea that most travelers had articulated over the previous century and, indeed, was expressed by Noah Webster: "On examining the language, and comparing the practice of speaking among the yeomanry of this country, with the stile of Shakespeare and Addison, I am constrained to declare that the people of America, in particular the English descendants, speak the most *pure English* now known in the world" (Webster 1789: 288).

But what was meant by "great classical purity"? It did not mean what *purism* would later denote in discussions of language. The ideology of purism emerged in the 19th century as a result of emergent racial doctrines: that languages were "pure" insofar as they contained words historically connected to a people. Germans were leaders in developing these ideas which led, later in the 19th century, to the idea that race and nation, if not pure, could be purified by the elimination of "foreign words" (Thomas 1991). One 19th-century English writer lamented that English had been spoiled by French expressions introduced with the conquest of England in 1066, and that things would be much improved "by purging it of all words and terms of that descent" (Bailey 1991: 270). Most, however, realized that the task of "purifying" English by extirpating non-Germanic words would be impossible.

For these late 18th-century observers of America, such notions connecting etymology and race had not yet fully developed, though Webster had celebrated the fact that American English had "hardly a foreign idiom". "Great classical purity" meant that American English was easily intelligible, particularly in comparison to that of the British Isles. In part, this judgment was based on vocabulary. Americans were in the habit of adopting new expressions that were transparent – *statehouse* (instead of *capitol*), *firewater* 'liquor', and *garter snake*. Many local expressions found in Britain did not survive the migration to North America; these apparently included *frimicate* 'to put on airs' and *golder* 'to shout' (both from East Anglia, the home territory of the New England immigrants).

Noah Webster's speculations about the purity of American English were based on books. Shakespeare (writing two hundred years before Webster's time) and Addison (writing a century earlier) can hardly have provided much evidence for his claim that they and the American yeomanry spoke in the same way. Webster merely wanted to associate two of the most revered names in English literature with American practice. If spoken American sounded like written Shakespeare, all the better for America. His view was that English had declined in purity from the time between Shakespeare and Addison, and it was the good fortune of Americans that it had declined less in the United States than in the home country. That idea, one shared by many 18th-century intellectuals, was a general principle supporting the claim to the excellence of American English.

When Webster turned to more difficult questions – for instance, the pronunciation of *deaf* – his method became more particular:

> *Deaf* is generally pronounced *deef*. It is the universal practice in the eastern states; and it is general in the middle and southern; though some have adopted the English pronunciation *def*. The latter is certainly a corruption; for the word is in analogy with *leaf* and *sheaf*, and has been from time immemorial. (Webster 1789: 128)

Webster capped his argument by quoting an English poet, a contemporary of Addison's, who rhymed *deaf* with *leaf*. Here he relied on "analogy" to support his claim that *deef* was the ancient standard and *deaf* (as rhymed with *clef*) the "corruption". Remarkably, given his youth and lack of scholarly resources, Webster was right.

The Early Modern English pronunciation of *deaf* was *deef*, and it was used by the first settlers in America. A century after Webster wrote the innovative pronunciation *def* was still the predominant pronunciation among American rustic speakers all along the Atlantic coast (Kurath and McDavid 1961: 132 and Map 62), though by that time educated and urban Americans had adopted it just as had speakers of the prestige variety of British English living in south and southeast England. Webster endorsed the best of all possibilities, the pronunciation that was both old-fashioned and American: *deef*.

English had been corrupted in Britain, and Webster identified the culprits, those people called by the pronunciation specialist, Thomas Sheridan, the "well-educated natives" of London and the southeast. If those natives, Webster sneered, would pronounce words as they ought, "one half the language at least would be regular" (Webster 1789: 163). Having an obligation to slow if not prevent language change, these people allowed innovations to gain authority, and these were simply wrong:

> They are wrong, because they are opposed to national practice; they are wrong, because they are arbitrary or careless changes of the true sounds of our letters; they are wrong, because they break in upon the regular construction of the language; they are wrong, because they render the pronunciation difficult both for natives and foreigners; they are wrong, because they make an invidious distinction between the polite and common pronunciation, or else oblige a *nation* to change their general customs, without presenting to their view one *national* advantage. (Webster 1789: 169)

In this rhetorical tirade, Webster blamed corrupt innovation (like *def* for *deaf*) on the English elite that had so recently attempted to thwart American independence. Since the United States had thrown off allegiance to this foreign elite, it could well claim that it had preserved the ancient purity of English so carelessly abandoned in London.

Webster was audacious in seeking solutions to the problem of an American standard. He became famous, of course, for reformed spellings – among them, *center* for *centre*, *magic* for *magick*, *harbor* for *harbour*, *tho* for *though*, and *traveler* for *traveller*. These innovations, he argued, made English spelling more regular and less wasteful. Most of the new spellings were already used by some in Britain and so did not entirely shock readers with innovation. But these spellings did not affect the way in which the words were pronounced. He wanted to make these spellings "American," and he did.

The problem of pronunciation was separately addressed in Webster's spelling books. In them, he listed words designed to be memorized and recited chorally by children in school. Webster's lists gather together words that, for him, had the same vowel sound – for instance *fast, mast, lass,* and *grass*. Not long after Webster's book appeared, some of these words were pronounced in southeastern England with different vowels from the ones Americans continued to use. Similarly, Webster's lists show that *air* and *heir* were pronounced in the same way which was (and is) true of American English, though in Britain purists would strive to make people pronounce them differently. He warned, too, against the pronunciation *negur* instead of *negro*, suggesting an 18th-century taboo against the former (Webster 1790: 32). *Wound* has a "fashionable pronunciation" *voond*; he preferred analogy in which it rhymes with *ground* and *sound* (Webster 1790: 51). *Clomb* is listed (for *climbed*; cf. Atwood 1953: 8), and *none, stone,* and *home* are all given with "New England short *o*" (Trudgill 2002). Webster was also firm in teaching that polysyllables should be sounded without reduction or deletion:

med-i-cine, pros-per-ous, rev-er-end. It would be wrong to conclude that these pervasive lessons kept pronunciations alive that were already on the decline in both Britain and New England. However, the attention given in school to spelling and the belief promoted by Webster that spellings contained valuable information about correct pronunciation did influence American English and contribute to its reputation for purity.

Not everyone agreed with Webster's patriotic view of American English, and there was a persistent belief that Britain was the home of English and that Americans should follow the fashions of London. Writing in 1836 in the *Southern Literary Messenger*, an anonymous critic took direct issue with Webster:

> To speak of pronunciation would be endless. That of the South accords with England's best orators and dictionaries in all such words as *tutor* vice *tooter* – *path, wrath, carpet, garden.* Yet many sedulous students of Walker never find this out. Dr. Noah Webster would fain have us believe that orthoepy demands such sounds as *natur, feature, creatur.* We rejoice that even in Connecticut this barbarism is growing into discredit. The learned Doctor would also improve English so as to write *Savior* for *Saviour, Bridegoom* for *Bridegroom, Duelist* for *Duellist,* and the like. We humbly crave leave to wait until any one English work can be produced in which these elegancies shall appear. It is an *English*, not an American language which we are called upon to nurture and perfect. (Borealis 1836: 111)

Early in the 19th century, the reputation of American English had been settled – at least for some. The language was free of regional variation, at least in comparison to Great Britain. And it was remarkable for its purity which had been achieved through the preservation of the good old ways of Shakespeare and Addison and through efforts to regularize it by analogy (so *deaf* was like *leaf*), preservation (continuing to employ *air* and *heir* as homophones), or transparency (in a preference for *meeting house* rather than *auditorium*). An American reviewer, writing in 1821, could declare: "the corruption of the language has gone so far in no part of America, as in the heart of the English counties" (Everett 1821: 30).

3 The contagion of American English

While American patriots were pleasing themselves with the excellence of their English, Britons were raising alarms that American English was corrupting the excellence of English at home. Satisfied over several centuries with ridiculing the Scots and the Irish, English opinion leaders were threatened by the Americans in ways that had not raised such alarm from the English of their nearer neighbors. The Scots and Irish were merely eccentrics with odd ways of speaking, but the elite in London did not imagine that their distinctive English would alter things. There was a chance that Scots might have taken hold when James VI of Scotland became, as James I, the monarch of all of the British Isles in 1603. James and the courtiers he brought south with him sounded Scots, but they seem to have been eager to assimilate to southern ways as soon as possible. *A Counterblast to Tobacco*, James's polemic against sot weed published in 1604, shows no traces of Scots influence. The reign of the Stuarts in the 17th century seems not to have altered emerging ideas of what constituted "good" English.

The notion that American English was threatening was articulated in the early 19th century. It began with acceptance of the view that Americans had as much right to change English as anybody else. Here is an observation from the 1830s: "[...] there are many Americanisms which in the course of time will work their way into the language of England; as they have as good a right to do, as any other innovations that have force or point to recommend them" (Thompson 1833: 373n.). Doubtless this was a liberal view; the author was an English abolitionist and radical given to democratic opinions. He was a Londoner tolerant of linguistic variety.

When in 1839 a Scottish lexicographer, John Ogilvie, began to prepare a new dictionary for the British market, he offered as a justification the fact that Noah Webster's *American Dictionary* (1828) was selling well there. His patriotic effort was to "keep the field against American Dictionaries, which are introducing into this country vitiated forms of orthography, and many undesirable novelties of speech" (Ogilvie 1850: V). This anxiety about undesirable English soon hardened into orthodoxy. By the 1860s, English opinion had turned thoroughly against the innovations from across the Atlantic. "Look [...] at the process of deterioration which our Queen's English has undergone at the hands of the Americans" (Alford 1866: 6).

Documenting the sustained prejudice against American English over the past century and a half is not difficult since the only alteration in the complaint involves the particular expressions that have come to the attention of reviewers. So we will leap ahead to 21st century examples parallel to most of the complaints of the past.

In 2010, the expressions targeted for criticism included *ahead of* for 'before', *face up* 'confront', and *fess up* for *confess* (Kahn 2010). A counterargument has often been that these expressions are historically English, but the truths of historical linguistics are seldom persuasive or even seen as germane to the dispute. "Americanisms" are simply bad English in one way or another: slovenly, careless, or sloppy. In the case of these "creeping" Americanisms, they are "lazy, and not very clever", "slack lazy language", "a sad example of the desire to be 'in' and updated". "We're stuck with most of this, but we don't have to lie down prone, supplicate and accept our inevitable crushing by the juggernaut" (Khan 2010). Similar views have been expressed in India where "call centers" handling

U. S. technical support ask employees to "shed rigid language norms," which can trigger wider change: "Words like *wanna be, gotta be, as if, whatever, all that, get a life, babe*, are no longer limited to swanky MNCs [Multi-National Corporations] or call centers' offices. They are contagious and have caught the fancy of college teens these days" (Satyavada 2004). Reports like these seethe with disapproval.

The same metaphors are used elsewhere in the English-speaking world. In Australia, new forms of language believed to derive from America are seen as a contagion: "suffering the creeping American disease" is a way to describe a situation the critic deplores (Money 2010). People who fear American innovation imagine a conspiracy, suppose that expressions "creep in" when the linguistic barriers are weak, and believe that the English language as a whole is being vitiated or damaged by imports from America. These ideas were vividly articulated by Ernest Gowers, who, in the 1960s, was invited to revise the celebrated usage guide prepared by Henry Watson Fowler in the 1920s. Fowler said nothing about Americanisms, but Gowers devoted several columns to the subject: "The close association of the two countries in the second world war and the continued presence of the U. S. Air Force among us have done much to promote American linguistic infiltration [...]" (Gowers 1965: 23). The metaphors Gowers uses are military: Americanisms *infiltrate*, they gain a *foothold*, the *victory* of *aim to do* over *aim at doing*. These usages, he writes, "are cumulatively symptoms of surrender by the older competitor to the younger and more vigorous" (Gowers 1965: 23).

The expressions that give rise to such complaints are not such ordinary Americanisms as *blood type, laser*, or *minibus*. And some are not Americanisms at all. They share the quality of being racy, informal, and perhaps a little subversive. They are usages that poke fun at pretense and gibe at gentility.

4 American voices

Early Americans delighted in the various ways of speaking they heard around them. John Adams, eventually to be America's second president, created a character he called "Humphrey Ploughjogger" to express ideas that would later lead to the American Revolution. One of his letters, published in 1763, raised the issue of taxation. It begins with this sentence: "Thes fue Lins cums to let you no, that I am very wel at prisent, Thank God for it, hoping that you and the family are so too" (Ploughjogger 1763: 2).

Adams used these letters to raise other issues, for instance the appointment of clergy and the billeting of troops with the civilian population (Saltman 1980). The misspellings in this sentence were not exclusive to American English, but Adams nonetheless strove to express an American voice through the vernacular.

Among the first of these explorations of the vernacular in fiction was *The Clockmaker* (1836–40) by Thomas Chandler Haliburton, a Nova Scotian who created the character of Sam Slick, a Connecticut peddler of dubious goods whose pungent and satirical voice poked fun at Yankees. In these tales, Haliburton represented the dialects of African Americans, Native Americans, Dutch people, and others who gave the American vernacular its rich variety. Another such character was David Crockett, an actual frontiersman who was supplied with a fictional biography and a distinctive voice. A major, if forgotten, genre in 19th-century fiction involved local characters (like Hosea Biglow in New England), advocates of social change (like Marietta Holley's Semantha Allen), and critics of the spirit of the times (like Petroleum V. Nasby or Sut Lovingood). It would be a mistake to consider the mangled spelling and odd-ball grammar of such characters as reflecting real speech. Instead, they spun entertainment from stereotypes which innocent Britons imagined to represent the way Americans talk. Abraham Lincoln, one of the most eloquent Americans of the time, loved Lovingood's bigoted advocacy of the Confederate cause expressed in a poisonous vernacular. (For specimens of this literature, see Cassidy 1982.)

A similar enthusiasm for spoken American English appears in the recollections of John Forney, who served as a clerk in the House of Representatives and then as Secretary of the Senate in the decade before the outbreak of the Civil War in 1861. In recalling those days, he showed a great affection for the way Southern politicians expressed themselves, though not sharing their opinions about the issues of American unity:

> Henry Clay's dialect speaking was strongly marked by it [the Southern dialect]. James M. Mason, of Virginia, seemed to delight in the African accent. But there was no better specimen than the late Thomas H. Bayley, for many years of Representative in Congress of the Accomac district [of Virginia]. He was a man of considerable force and education, and I can easily recall his tall form, his expressive face and ringing voice, as, spectacles on nose, he would address 'Mr. Speakah', and refer to the honorable member who had just had the 'flo'. [Laurence Massilon] Kett, of South Carolina, had the same accent and pronunciation. So, too, Linn Boyd, of Kentucky, and Howell Cobb, of Georgia. (Forney 1873–81: 1.197)

The vogue for dialect reached its apex with Mark Twain, but there were lesser writers who explored the sounds of American English. *The Hoosier Schoolmaster* (1871) by Edward Eggleston dramatized the triumph of the schoolmaster over the rustic dialects of a community in southern Indiana. The prior schoolmaster had arrived knowing little of local speechways:

> Twenty year ago, when he come to these 'ere diggin's, that air Squire Hawkins was a poor Yankee school-master, that said 'pail' instead of bucket, and called a cow a '*caow*,' and that

couldn't tell to save his gizzard what was meant by 'low' and 'right smart.' But he's larnt our ways now, an' he's jest as civilized as the rest of us. You would-n know he'd ever been a Yankee. (quoted in Bailey 2006: 170)

The civilizing power of the community did not work its magic on the new schoolmaster who, with his wife, managed to convert the locals to a national standard.

The American voices of the 20th century were more austere and more serious. Sherwood Anderson's characters (in *Winesburg, Ohio*) are filled with pain and fear; they do not "talk funny". Dialect writing became a sub-literary genre, though with some popular exponents of the tradition like Montague Glass's *Potash and Perlmutter* (with Yiddish inflected characters) and Langston Hughes's *Simple* stories (expressed in an urban African American variety of English). Vaudeville thrived on characters expressing stereotypes, varied somewhat by the locale of the performances, with Swedish comedians exchanging snappy dialogue in the Upper Midwest where there were communities of immigrants from Scandinavia. Performers in this tradition found their way into broadcasting, first in radio and then in television and film. Dialect humor thus continued to explore the vernacular while high literature turned to other issues.

Television and movies are now the principal vehicles for this trend. When *Dallas* gained a worldwide audience, a new generation was exposed to American voices. Many films have done the same thing. Here, as an example, is a scene introducing the principal characters in *Valley Girl* (1983):

> An area that has numerous fast food restaurants. We FOCUS on this same group of teenaged girls. They seem to embody all the attributes of the famous "Valley Girl." JULIE RICHMAN, 15, is a pretty blonde, squeakily cute clean. At her side is her best friend, STACEY GARRISON, 15, the ultimate Valley girl. She's pretty and brunette. She dresses and is coiffed to perfection. SUZI BRENT, 15, fits right in with this pattern. The last girl friend is LORYN LICHTER, 15 going on 25. She's got a body that would arouse the terminally limp. MOVING IN on their conversation, we hear what every girl talks about and how.
> STACEY
> Barf out. Gag me. How could you?
> SUZI
> For sure!
> JULIE
> I'd be freakinggg out!
> LORYN
> It's totally outrageous! I don't want to like start a family. Like I'd get puffed out to the max and all, for sure. I'd be scarfin' up everything in sight. I don't know, like ... I'd be sooo fat and all. Like, what'd happen to my zits? They can get so grody. Besides, it's like totally gnarly birth control. (Lane and Crawford 1982: 3)

The linguistic depth sinks to the vivid language of the parents of these girls, who are unreconstructed hippies from the previous generation.

The linguistic merriment of these productions should not be confused with the actual speech of Americans. Audiences abroad presumed that Americans talked in the ways the movies depicted them. (So, for instance, in the 1990s, I was told by a young woman in South Africa that all Americans are surfers and talk like surfers. The fact that I did not use surf-speak did not shake her conviction that all Americans talk that way.)

The image of American English and the practice of Americans speaking are two quite different things.

5 Anxiety about American English

Monolingual Americans tend to believe that there is a causal connection between English and the institutions of democracy and the discoveries of science and technology. One cannot expect much, they think, from languages with a recent tradition of literacy or what are presumed to be small vocabularies. But even languages with long traditions of high literacy, like German and Spanish, are seen to fall short of the ideals expressed in English. On the basis of such ethnocentric beliefs, one would imagine that everyone speaking some language other than American English would rush to adopt it. There would be no reason to doubt the success of the language once others became aware of its magical properties.

Of course these ideas are far more complex than they at first appear. Bold assertions of the superiority of English are often accompanied by fears that immigrant groups will retain their languages and shove English aside. Such anxieties began quite early. In the 1750s, Benjamin Franklin wrote often of his concern that Pennsylvania would become more and more German, especially as prosperous German merchants in Philadelphia and nearby Germantown became economically and politically powerful:

> The Observation concerning the Importation of Germans in too great Numbers into Pennsylvania is, I believe, a very just one. This will in a few Years become a German Colony: Instead of their Learning our Language, we must learn their's [sic], or live as in a foreign Country. Already the English begin to quit particular Neighborhoods surrounded by Dutch, being made uneasy by the Disagreeableness of dissonant Manners; and in Time, Numbers will probably quit the Province for the same Reason. (Franklin, letter of James Parker, 20 March 1751, see Franklin 1988)

In 1787, when the Pennsylvania legislature ratified the federal constitution, the body ordered that three thousand copies of the document be printed in English and two thousand in German so that the delegates might distribute them in their constituencies. America seemed to be set on a course to lead to a multilingual nation.

German remained the focus of American nativists at the end of the 19th century and the expression "hyphenated Americans" was introduced in 1889. Especially in the Midwest, Germans had become successful and had established institutions to support their language and culture (for instance, newspapers, schools, and churches conducted in German). Anti-German sentiment reached a level of high intensity with the declaration of war on Germany by the United States in 1917, but the linguistic campaigns of "Americanization" were even more sweeping as all sorts of European languages were denounced in an attempt to make English prevail. Foreign language newspapers were shut down; telephone operators were told to disconnect calls where they heard a foreign language in use; and schools were prevented from offering instruction in languages other than English.

In 1919, the Nebraska legislature enacted a statute that put into law one of the practices earlier adopted by the Nebraska State Council of Defense to suppress German in religious practice and in schools. The law declared than no school, public or parochial, could permit anyone to "teach any subject to any person in any language other than the English language". The year following, a teacher, Robert T. Meyer, was discovered teaching a ten-year old to read the Bible in German; he was arrested and convicted of violating the act.

When the case reached the U. S. Supreme Court, the law was found to be unconstitutional, though it was acknowledged that such restrictions might be necessary in war time. Since 1923, the year of the decision, was a "time of peace and domestic tranquility", the law had no justification.

Meyer v. Nebraska reflected an acceleration of a trend already taking place: the shift from German to English in communities with historical German settlement. Restrictions on immigration beginning in 1919 cut off the flow of new German speakers to these communities (as well as to other European settlements by Poles and Italians, for instance), so the cultural ties to the "old country" were weakened. The loss of continuity in immigration and institutions meant that by the 1960s, when immigration restrictions were lifted, many were left with the impression that America was a monolingual country.

Starting in the last quarter of the 20th century a new fear of foreign languages arose around the increasing numbers of Spanish speakers. Political refugees from Cuba (in the late 1950s) and from Nicaragua (in the 1970s) added prominence to the migrants already present from Mexico and Puerto Rico. Just as the Germans had done earlier, these Spanish speakers settled in tight-knit communities unified by religious practice, newspapers, broadcasting, and community festivals. The response of monolingual Americans was the same: attempts to compel assimilation and force language change to English.

In 1981, Senator S. I. Hayakawa of California proposed a constitutional amendment to make English the "official language" of the United States (Baron 1990). After hearings, the Senate concluded that the matter was better treated at the state level, and many states with numerous Spanish speakers adopted such a law, whether as an amendment to the state constitution or as a statute. Most provided no penalties for using Spanish (or other languages); they typically focused on preventing bilingual information for state services such as driver's license tests or voting information. As in Meyer v. Nebraska, some attempted to limit the use of Spanish in schools, even though studies demonstrated that a bilingual approach to learning improved pupils' test scores. Since most Spanish speakers sought to learn English or to encourage their children to learn it, these laws were mostly symbolic in effect. Large numbers of undocumented aliens, however, were not allowed to assimilate, being limited in employment or housing by their lack of citizenship or residence papers.

What is significant about these fears of German or Spanish is the idea that American English is in danger. Many popular accounts celebrate the "cosmopolitan" nature of the language, with its borrowing of words from "immigrant" languages (particularly in the domain of food such as *taco, bratwurst, chow mien, spaghetti,* or *fricassee*). The idea that most people in the world are bi- or multilingual does not match the ideology of American English which celebrates a single language as a norm.

6 What is the "standard"?

A vexed question in linguistics concerns just what a "standard" language might be. Like pornography, there is a view that people know what it is when they see it. Others imagine that it is the performance of high-status speakers whose biographies show education, breeding, and civility. When asked to identify persons who speak "standard English", observers often become cagy. Daniel Jones, the phonetician who codified British Received Pronunciation, admitted that his own speech needed to be amended by certain features that were used by others.

The most thoughtful of American linguists, Edward Sapir, offered this view of the standard: "[...] that there is something like an ideal linguistic entity dominating the speech habits of each group, that the sense of almost unlimited freedom which each individual feels in the use of his language, is held in check by a tacitly directing norm" (Sapir 1949: 148). What this means is that anyone is a speaker of "standard English" who believes that he or she is. That is, if the "tacitly directing norm" tells you that *can* is "standard" in "Can I borrow the car?", then it is.

A century ago there arose the idea of "General American", the dialect that remained once the speech of New England and the southeast were subtracted. It was "General American" where the "standard" was presumed to lie (McArthur 1992, s. v. *General American*). This idea has now been discredited, though scholars abroad still make use of the term. In fact, there is no geographical center where the "standard" can be found, and even "broadcast English" (as heard in national television and radio) cannot be confidently held up as representative of the "standard". There is a "standard", of course, but it is not easy to locate in a region (though it is not in New York or Houston), register (though it is more likely to occur in writing than in speech), or race (though it is thought to be found more in white speech than in the speech of people of color).

Each speaker has an ideal of a "tacitly directing norm", and this form of English is so idealized that people often wince at the sounds of their recorded voices when their usage does not represent the ideal they imagine. We think our English is better than it is, and that is probably a good thing in helping us maintain our view of ourselves as speakers of "good English". Yet our usage is nuanced, and we have one style for reading lists of words and another in talking to those closest to us. "Standard English" is not one thing; there is a standard way to admonish children and a standard way of speaking at a memorial service. Standard English is inherently variable, and it makes no sense to ask if an expression is "standard" without considering the context. *Fishin* is not standard in written English; *fishing* is not standard among men sitting in a boat, watching their bobbers, and drinking beer.

Confusing the issue is the tendency of some critics to associate "standard" with individuals or groups. Thus teenagers are said not to speak Standard English because they are prone to innovation and informality. African Americans rightly resent the imputation that they do not speak Standard English but a dialect. Women have long been accused of garrulous speech, frivolous usage, and shrill tones. All such allegations do not describe the linguistic situation but the tendency of some opinion makers to criticize language when their real targets are groups of people. Careless scape-goating of individuals and groups has led to resentments and to angry rebuttals from critics who wish to defend their usages, often by pointing out that the English in question is used by quite respectable people or was formerly part of the prestige dialect (*akst* for *asked* is a frequently adduced example in this argument).

Not all assertions of "standardness" are bigoted, of course. The person who says "Can I borrow the car?" may well be aware that some people believe "May I borrow the car?" is seen as the standard alternative. The person may continue to say "Can I borrow the car?", not so much to *épate le bourgeois* but because it seems "natural" to do so.

In American English, the arguments over these matters have developed into acrimonious controversy between "prescriptivists" (advocating attentiveness to correctness) and "descriptivists" (arguing that if more than half the people use a particular form, it is "standard"). These disputes have done little to increase understanding of "standard" American English: prescriptivists seem preoccupied with the persnickety; descriptivists seem indifferent to the questions people have about their language.

One of the most ardent of the prescriptivists, Bryan A. Garner, has recently sought a rapprochement with descriptivists. He declares, "I am a prescriber who uses descriptivist methods – in effect, a descriptive prescriber" (Garner 2009: xliv). His approach allows him to continue denouncing nonstandard forms in no uncertain terms: "arrant mistake" (s. v., *gladiolus*) and "gross error" (s. v., *waist*). But he does far more than merely acknowledge that English changes over time: he treats expressions on a five-point scale ranging from 1 (*rejected*) to 5 (*fully accepted*). These are descriptive statements and can be tested against evidence, as he does in using the Internet to locate and enumerate competing usages. So, for instance, he describes *can* for *may* in "Can I borrow the car?" as stage 4 (*ubiquitous but* ...). Another stage 4 usage is *data* taken to be a mass noun and construed as a singular: thus *many data* (plural) and *much data* (singular) may both be used in formal contexts, though perhaps with a slight risk of censure. For *media* as a mass noun, Garner says it "must be accepted as standard": "the media are covering the trial as a scandal of great importance". *Media* in such sentences he regards as stage 5 (*fully accepted*).

Garner loves to be *persnickety*: "persnickety; *pernickety. Although the latter is the older form, *persnickety* is now about five times as common in print as *pernickety in American English" (s. v., *persnickety*). (In linguistic discourse, the asterisk is prefixed to hypothetical forms; it is not clear why the asterisk appears with *pernickety.) If Garner wished to make his prescription effective, he would appeal to Microsoft Word to spell-correct it automatically. He does pursue the persnickety: for instance, he distinguishes *piebald* and *skewbald*, a nice distinction indeed. Food magazines, he reports, prefer the spelling *pimiento* and "general interest magazines" *pimento*. These are descriptive statements and can be challenged with additional investigation into actual usage. Garner's dudgeon does not come into play here, but it can safely be ignored by those of a descriptivist bent. Of *early on*, for instance, he writes that the expression is "not the odious locution that some people think" and describes it as stage 5 (fully accepted). One can say valuable things about English without resorting to such labels as "odious locution". *Odium*, after all, lies in the mind of the beholder and not in the facts of usage.

"Standard American English" is a category that "resists easy definition". A collection of statements, both British and American, summarizing the problems of defining it has been compiled by Richard Nordquist. Nonetheless, it is a linguistic category that should command scholarly attention free from bias and prejudice. If a handful of people think ill of an expression – *hopefully* as a sentence adverb is a good example – the descriptivist has the obligation to show just how big the handful is.

The idea of an "international Standard English" is even more vexed than the one of defining "Standard British" or "Standard American". Part of the difficulty lies in the fact that nearly all speakers reveal their nationality by the way they use English. British people say *windscreen* and Americans say *windshield*. (Parallel word lists distinguishing British from American usage constitute a well-established genre – for instance, Schur 1987.) The Irish drink in a *shebeen* and Americans in a *blind pig*. Canadians say *hydro* and Americans *water bill*. Kenyans take a dented *mudguard* to the *panel beater*; Americans take a dented *fender* to the *body shop*. Indians eat *tiffin* and Americans *brunch*. South Africans say *biltong* and Americans *jerky*. Australians say *dinkum* and Americans *genuine* (sometimes pronounced *jen-ewe-wine*). Malaysians say *gostan* and Americans *back up*. New Zealand women wear *tights*, American women *pantyhose*. All of these are markers of national identity and all are standard in their national context. None of them are "international" and there is no hypernym that might encompass the pairs.

English is, in short, a constellation of distinct varieties. There is no "international standard English".

7 The future of American English

All we can do to predict the future is to project existing trends from the present. Americans revel in new words and have developed sophisticated methods for archiving them. Almost nothing that has appeared in print has been lost, and virtual texts (like blogs) preserve expressions that, in an earlier time, might have been quickly forgotten. Most new words are formed from existing usage expressing new senses: *blue state* 'state likely to vote for the Democratic party' (2000), *water-boarding* (2004) 'interrogation technique'. Often the prefixes and suffixes create novelties: *unconstitutionality* is such an Americanism, first noticed in a letter from George Washington in 1795. *Geocaching* (2000) 'a treasure hunt with clues located through a *GPS* (1974)' is another example of creation through affixing. *Podcast* (2004) is blended from *iPod* and *–cast* (<*broadcast*). Though formerly important in the creation of new expressions, borrowing from foreign languages is now relatively rare: *sudoku* (2000) is a recent example.

Grammatical preferences show an increasing shift from verbs and adjectives to nouns. Long strings of nouns are often collapsed into initialisms or acronyms: *AIDS* (1982) from 'acquired immune deficiency syndrome'; *NAFTA* (1990) from 'North American Free Trade Alliance'. Technical and scientific prose relies increasingly on such strings: "The native (pre-existing) collateral circulation minimizes tissue injury if obstructive vascular disease develops" (Chalothorn and Faber 2010: 251). Quite long noun phrases can easily be discovered: *Ford Motor Company Customer Relationship Center*. There is no loss of understanding if we append even more nouns to the series: *Office-Maintenance Contract Negotiation Dispute*. Even half a century ago, such structures were rare in American English. They are likely to become even more common in the future.

Based on the idea that English has lost inflections over the past millennium, one would expect that comparative and superlative adjectives would shift from the *-er* and *-est* suffixes to the use of *more* and *most*. That is, *more happy* would become more common and *happier* less. In general single syllable adjectives (like *blue*) take *-er* (that is, *bluer* rather than *more blue*); three-syllable adjectives take *more* (that is, *more beautiful* rather than *beautifuller*). (But *beautifuller* has a long and continuing history.) The greatest variability lies with two-syllable adjectives: *yellower* and *more yellow*, *handsomer* and *more handsome*. But the picture is muddled. *Funner*, as Garner points out, is common among young people; older people favor *more fun*: "The movie was a lot more fun than I expected". The future of this particular grammatical question in American English remains to be decided (cf. Mondorf 2009).

It is important to recognize that the future of American English will not result in greater uniformity. Pronunciation, as Luanne von Schneidemesser (Chapter 3) explains in her contribution to this volume, is not more uniform than in the past, and vanishing terms for agricultural practices that set dialects apart long ago are merely being replaced by new markers of regional and social differences.

There will be no less controversy and conflict over usages than in the past. Many parents now object to children using BE *like* or BE *all* as a generic verb for *express*: "I was like 'wow'!"; "She was all [facial expression of disgust]". Garner believes that once teenagers grow into adults, they will cease to use *like* and *all* in this way, but I suspect that these forms will endure to be part of the informal standard English of the future. Here, for instance, is the President of the United States speaking to an audience of 3,000 people: "He comes across as soft-spoken – you know, how he's all like 'well, you know'" (quoted in Shear 2010). One can be sure, however, that adults will continue to complain about the usage of teens, though the subjects of complaint will certainly change.

Text-messaging (or *txtng* or *TM*) seems to some to have the potential to change English, and it is certainly true that abbreviating to fit a message into the

160 byte screen of a cell phone requires ingenuity and stripping away irrelevancies in language. Becoming a skilled "TMer" requires knowing conventional abbreviations (like *gr8* 'great') and contriving new ones: *d&i* 'dandy'. As David Crystal (2008) persuasively argues, there is no reason to imagine that this technique will have any lasting effect on English apart from giving young people yet another outlet for linguistic creativity. In the past, technologies have influenced English: for instance, the cost-per-word charge for telegrams encouraged abbreviations and stripped-down grammar in those composing them. Yet the long-term effect on the language was negligible. Broadcasting expanded the audience's experience of English, displaying more kinds of English and more techniques for expressing oneself in it (like facial expressions and gestures). In general, technologies have made English richer, not poorer (cf. Bergs 2009).

One thing is certain: American English will continue to be influential on a worldwide scale. At the end of the 19th century some Americans speculated that their English would become the predominant variety, and by the middle of the 20th century British commentators (like R. W. Burchfield, editor of the supplements to the *Oxford English Dictionary*) acknowledged that it had already done so. As we have seen, American English is not always evaluated positively and its influence may be seen as insidious and debilitating (see Bailey 2001). Yet it is imitated in many places not necessarily aligned with the economic and political interests of the United States. Terrorists hidden in the mountains of Pakistan follow the progress of war through CNN in Atlanta, Georgia, and by listening to the voices of its American broadcasters. For the last half-century, people who use English as a second (or third) language outnumber those who acquire it as a native tongue. Since these second-language learners usually attempt what they perceive to be the most prestigious form, they are likely to ignore the racy and colloquial kinds of English used by native speakers. They may choose not to identify with a national variety: using what the British since 1975 have called a "midatlantic accent". Yet whatever variety they choose, an important ingredient will be Standard American English.

8 References

Alford, Henry. 1866. *A Plea for the Queen's English* (1863). 2nd edn. London: Strahan.
Algeo, John. 2006. *British or American? A Handbook of Word and Grammar Patterns*. Cambridge: Cambridge University Press.
Atwood, Elmer Bagby. 1953. *A Survey of Verb Forms in the Eastern United States*. Ann Arbor: The University of Michigan Press.
Bailey, Richard W. 1991. *Images of English: A Cultural History of the Language*. Ann Arbor: The University of Michigan Press.

Bailey, Richard W. 2001. American English Abroad. In: John Algeo (ed.), *The Cambridge History of the English Language: English in North America*, Vol. VI, 456–496. Cambridge: Cambridge University Press.

Bailey, Richard W. 2004. American English: Its Origins and History. In: Edward Finegan and John R. Rickford (eds.), *Language in the USA: Themes for the Twenty-first Century*, 3–17. Cambridge: Cambridge University Press.

Bailey, Richard W. 2006. Standardizing the Heartland. In: Thomas E. Murray and Beth Lee Simon (eds.), *Language Variation and Change in the American Midwest*, 165–178. Amsterdam/Philadelphia: John Benjamins.

Bailey, Richard W. 2009. Dr. Johnson and American Words. In: *Dictionaries* 30: 130–135.

Bailey, Richard W. 2011. *Speaking American*. Oxford/New York, NY: Oxford University Press.

Baron, Dennis E. 1990. *The English-Only Question: An Official Language for Americans*. New Haven: Yale University Press.

Bergs, Alexander. 2009. The linguistics of text messaging. In: Charley Rowe and Eva L. Wyss (eds.), *New media and linguistic change*, 55–74. Creskill, NJ: Hampton Press.

Borealis. 1836. English Language in America. In: *Southern Literary Messenger* 2(2): 110–111.

Boyer, Paul and Stephen Nissenbaum (eds.). 1977. *The Salem Witchcraft Papers: Verbatim Transcripts of the Legal Documents of the Salem Witchcraft Outbreak of 1792*. 3 Vols. New York: DaCapo Press.

Cassidy, Frederic G. 1982. Geographical Variation of English in the United States. In: Richard W. Bailey and Manfred Görlach (eds.), *English as a World Language*, 177–209. Ann Arbor: The University of Michigan Press.

Chalothorn, Dan and James E. Faber. 2010. *Journal of Molecular and Cellular Cardiology* 49: 151–159.

Cruikshank, Ernest A. (ed.). 1907. *The Documentary History of the Campaign upon the Niagara Frontier in the Year 1813*. Welland/Ontario: Tribune Office.

Crystal, David. 2008. *Txtng: The G48 Db8*. Oxford: Oxford University Press.

Everett, Edward. 1821. On the Complaints in America against the English Press. In: *North American Review* 13(1): 20–47.

Fisher, Anne. 1788. *An Accurate New Spelling Dictionary, and Expositor of the English Language*. 6th edn. London: G. J. and J. Robinson.

Forney, John W. 1873–81. *Anecdotes of Public Men*. 2 Vols. New York: Harper and Brothers.

Franklin, Benjamin. 1988. *The Papers of Benjamin Franklin*. http://franklinpapers.org/franklin; last accessed 14 April 2017.

Garner, Bryan A. 2009. *Garner's Modern American Usage*. 3rd edn. Oxford: Oxford University Press.

Gowers, Ernest. 1965. *A Dictionary of Modern English Usage*. First edn. by Henry Watson Fowler, 1926. Oxford: Oxford University Press.

Jefferson, Thomas. 2008. *The Papers of Thomas Jefferson*. http://rotunda.upress.virginia.edu/founders/TSJN-01-22-02-0094; last accessed 14 April 2017.

Khan, Urmee. 2010. BC Criticized for Creeping Americanisms. *The Daily Telegraph* (4 April). http://www.telegraph.co.uk/culture/tvandradio/bbc/7553057/BBC-criticised-for-creeping-Americanisms.html; last accessed 14 April 2017.

Kurath, Hans and Raven I. McDavid, Jr. 1961. *The Pronunciation of English in the Atlantic States*. Ann Arbor: The University of Michigan Press.

Kytö, Merja. 2004. The Emergence of American English: Evidence from Seventeenth-century Records in New England. In: Raymond Hickey (ed.), *Legacies of Colonial English: Studies in Transported Dialects*, 121–157. Cambridge: Cambridge University Press.
Leacock, John. 1776. *The Fall of British Tyranny*. Philadelphia: Styner and Cist.
Lane, Andrew and Wayne Crawford. 1982. *Valley Girl*. Revised draft. Los Angeles: Valley 9000 Prod. Co. Unpublished typescript, Margaret Herrick Library, Academy of Motion Picture Arts and Sciences, Beverly Hills.
McArthur, Tom (ed.). 1992. *The Oxford Companion to the English Language*. Oxford: Oxford University Press.
Mondorf, Britta. 2009. *More support for more-support*. Amsterdam/Philadelphia: John Benjamins.
Money, Lawrence. 2010. Fight Hambergerisation; Dig up some Old Aussie Lingo. *The Sidney Morning Herald* (07January).http://www.smh.com.au/opinion/contributors/fight-hamburgerisation-dig-up-some-old-aussie-lingo-20100201-n7u8.html; last accessed 14 April 2017.
Nordquist, Richard Francis. 2010. *What is Standard English?*
Ogilvie, John. 1850. *The Imperial Dictionary*. London: Blackie and Sons.
Ploughjogger, Humphrey. [John Adams] 1763. Letter. *Boston Evening-Post* (20June).
Read, Allen Walker. 2002. *Milestones in the History of English in America*. Durham, NC: Duke University Press.
Saltman, Helen Saltzberg. 1980. John Adams's Earliest Essays: The Humphrey Ploughjogger Letters. In: *William and Mary Quarterly* 37: 125–136.
Sapir, Edward [1921] 1949. *Language: An Introduction to the Study of Speech*. New York: Harcourt, Brae and World.
Satyavada, Rajeeva. 2004. U'R looking kewl dude. In: *The Times of India: Hydrabad Times* (3 September).
Schur, Norman W. 1987. *British English A to Zed*. New York: Facts on File Publications.
Shear, Michael D. 2010. Obama's Future Plans Rely on Reid's Survival. *Washington Post* (9 July).
Thomas, George. 1991. *Linguistic Purism*. London: Longman.
Thompson, T. Perronet. 1833. Review of Narrative of a Residence at the Court of London by Richard Rush. *The Westminster Review* 19: 373–374.
Trudgill, Peter. 2002. Short *o*' in East Anglia and New England (1998). In: *Sociolinguistic Variation and Change*, 16–20. Edinburgh: Edinburgh University Press.
Webster, Noah. 1789. *Dissertations on the English Language*. Boston: Isaiah Thomas for the author.
Webster, Noah. 1790. *The American Spelling Book*. 2nd edn. Boston: Isaiah Thomas and Ebenezer T. Andrews.

Luanne von Schneidemesser
Chapter 3:
Regional varieties of American English

1   Beginnings —— 32
2   The American Dialect Society and the *Linguistic Atlas of New England* —— 32
3   Further Linguistic Atlas publications and westward expansion —— 34
4   Branching out; social and ethnic dialects —— 39
5   The *Dictionary of American Regional English* —— 41
6   The *Atlas of North American English* and beyond —— 45
7   Summary —— 48
8   References —— 49

Abstract: While regional variation in the English spoken in America existed from the time of the first English speakers on the continent, considerable interest in studying American English did not develop until the late 19th and early 20th centuries, with the founding of the American Dialect Society. This overview will present major directions of research, starting with the Linguistic Atlas approach, in the development of the field of dialectology or linguistic geography, the preeminant direction in regional studies at the time. Over time, the number of studies concentrating not on regionality but on social factors grew to a critical mass in studies on American English. While such studies were always present, the mood of the country with a push toward social and racial equality, and in linguistics Labov's work in the 1960s and 70s, led researchers to turn toward studying social factors, e.g. type of community, age, education, gender, race, and ethnicity. Many turned away from dialect geography to the emerging field of sociolinguistics; the two areas drew little from each other's work. Only in the late 80s did the two areas converge, with researchers beginning to realize mutual benefit in working together, and with a push from the publication of the first volume of the *Dictionary of American Regional English*. The volumes of DARE were followed by the publication of Labov et al.'s (2006) *Atlas of North American English: Phonetics, Phonology and Sound Change,* which immediately had and continues to have a huge influence on the study of social and regional varieties of American English.

Luanne von Schneidemesser: Madison (Wisconsin, USA)

1 Beginnings

The history of American English began in the early 1600s, when Jamestown was settled by English-speaking immigrants, the first permanent settlement in the New World. The new surroundings with new objects and much that was different from their homeland required changes in the immigrants' language – new words and new meanings to old words, and at later dates words adopted from the languages of the many other immigrant groups which followed the English to the New World, for example.

Mathews, in his book *The Beginnings of American English: Essays and Comments*, collected some of the early writings, mostly from the latter part of the 1700s into the first half of the 1800s, on the impressions of the English language as it was developing in America, including, for example, passages from John Witherspoon, Noah Webster, Mrs. Anne Royall, James Fenimore Cooper, and John Russell Bartlett. Mathews says of the observations on the differences between American English and British English, the main concern of most of these writers:

> Some of the observations made by those who have dealt with the subject are quite useless, and show that their authors were not competent to pass any judgment on any phase of the subject they treated. Other observations were made by people who had the background necessary to enable them to have sensible views about the growing divergence between British and American usage. (Mathews 1931: 11)

For a thorough discussion of this early period, see Richard Bailey, Chapter 2 on American English. (American English is referring to English in the United States, for a discussion of Canadian English see Dollinger, Chapter 4.)

2 The American Dialect Society and the *Linguistic Atlas of New England*

Not until the late 1800s was there interest in seriously studying the English which had evolved in what was by then the United States, reaching from the original settlement areas on the East Coast across the land mass of the continent to the West Coast. The American Dialect Society (ADS) was founded in 1889 with the idea that something like Joseph Wright's (1895–1905) *English Dialect Dictionary* for England could be produced for the United States.

Work which had been done on regional dialects traditionally focused on geographical distribution of vocabulary and pronunciation and some points of grammar at that time, and indeed, the six volumes of the first publication of the

ADS, *Dialect Notes* (1890–1939), consisted in large part of lists of words jotted down by members, mostly professors, of the Society. With members/scholars turning from the idea of a dictionary to an atlas, the plan for *The Linguistic Atlas of the United States and Canada* was developed in the 1920s. In preparation for this, Hans Kurath, who was appointed director of the project, compiled "A Bibliography of American Pronunciation 1888–1928" in the journal *Language*, pointing out how much work remained to be done in pronunciation alone:

> This bibliography was compiled primarily for the purpose of making the rather scattered bits of more or less reliable information regarding the pronunciation of English in the various parts of the United States more readily accessible, but also to show how little actual work has been done and how much remains to be done before we shall have even an imperfect picture of American pronunciation. [...] With the exception of Nebraska, the country to the west of the states bordering on the Mississippi is entirely unexplored, and Indiana, Illinois, Michigan, Iowa, Wisconsin, and Minnesota are no better off. (Kurath 1929: 155)

Forerunners of the U.S. project included Georg Wenker in Germany, who started work in 1876 on what later became the *Deutscher Sprachatlas*, mapping the pronunciation of spoken dialects (Wrede et al. 1926–56); Wenker sent a list of 40 sentences in standardized German to schoolmasters throughout Germany, asking them to respond with (a written version of) how they would say the sentences in their local speech. This was followed by Jules Gilliéron's work, with his single trained fieldworker Edmond Edmont interviewing in 600 communities, published as the *Atlas Linguistique de la France* (Gilliéron and Edmont 1902–10); and by Karl Jaberg and Jakob Jud's (1928–40) *Sprach- und Sachatlas Italiens und der Südschweiz*. (Interestingly, Jud helped train the first group of fieldworkers for the American Linguistic Atlas project; see McDavid and O'Cain 1973: 143). The first project covering an English-speaking area, however, was not in the British Isles, but the project boldly undertaken by the members of the *Linguistic Atlas* project; it was decided to start with a scaled-down undertaking, focused on New England states.

Fieldwork for the *Linguistic Atlas of New England* (LANE) began in 1929, with the resulting volumes, focusing on lexical and phonetic information but also including morphology to a lesser extent, published in the format of large maps (Kurath et al. 1939–43). As explained in the interpretive companion volume *Handbook of the Linguistic Geography of New England*, 416 informants in 213 communities were interviewed (Kurath et al. 1939: 39). Worksheets, the contents of which are shown in Chapter V of the *Handbook*, contained 814 words and phrases which were to be elicited, but not by set questions: "The form of the questions by which these responses were to be secured was left largely to the ingenuity of the individual field workers, although the topical setting and the context provided in the work sheets often served as pointers" (Kurath et al. 1939: 148). The *Handbook* also contains extensive information on the methodology of the project and the training of the fieldworkers, background on the settlement of New England, and descriptions of the communities and the informants (see also O'Cain 1979). Social elements were included in this fieldwork: the informants were grouped by types, thus acknowledging the interaction of social class and regional variation in language use:

> Type I: Little formal education, little reading and restricted social contacts.
> Type II: Better formal education (usually high school) and/or wider reading and social contacts.
> Type III: Superior education (usually college), cultured background, wide reading and/or extensive social contacts.
> Type A: Aged, and/or regarded by the field worker as old-fashioned.
> Type B: Middle-aged or younger, and/or regarded by the field worker as more modern.
> (Kurath et al. 1939: 44)

3 Further Linguistic Atlas publications and westward expansion

Following the publication of LANE and its *Handbook*, fieldwork was done for the *Linguistic Atlas of the Middle and South Atlantic States* (LAMSAS, covering New York, Pennsylvania, New Jersey, Delaware, Maryland, District of Columbia, West Virginia, Virginia, North Carolina, South Carolina, and parts of Florida and Georgia), also under Kurath's direction. Two further major publications resulted from the data of LANE and LAMSAS. The first was *A Word Geography of the Eastern United States* (Kurath 1949), which established the dialect divisions of the Eastern U.S., both major and minor. The major regions were determined by the data collected and analyzed to be the North, the Midland, and the South, in opposition to the earlier divisions of North, South, and General American, or Eastern, Southern, and General American. Kenyon, for example, in the fourth edition of *American Pronunciation* (1930) used the term "General American" defining it as basically everything but the South and the East (Lance 1994: 346–7).

And the concept of General American did not die easily. Baugh, for example, in the 2nd edition of his *History of the English Language*, after stating in the preface that "The pages concerned with the dialect areas in the United States have been entirely rewritten, and a new map has been drawn to accompany the discussion" (Baugh 1957: vii) (which shows two-thirds of the country under the label 'General American'), states:

> Such a threefold division has the virtue of simplicity, and when the evidence is all in it may prove a valid classification for the country as far west as the Mississippi. As for the region farther west it would be rash to hazard an opinion, since this area contains a greater mixture of people from different parts of the country than does the eastern third of the United States. The classification has the weakness of suggesting a greater homogeneity for the Northern type than it has, containing as it does the dialect of eastern New England, which must be recognized as a distinct variety of American English, and that, let us say, of most of the state of New York, which on the basis of pronunciation is a part of General American. But such inconsistencies between lexical and phonological criteria are probably inevitable, since words are more easily transferred than regional types of pronunciation. (Baugh 1957: 439)

Baugh continues, "In the present state of our knowledge it seems best to recognize seven regional dialects in the United States" (he had undoubtedly become aware of Kurath's findings – see below). His list: 1. Eastern New England, 2. New York City, 3. Middle Atlantic, 4. Western Pennsylvania, 5. Southern Mountain (mostly within Southern), 6. Southern, and 7. General American (Baugh 1957: 439–42).

McDavid says of Kurath's regions:

> The concept of the Midland group of dialects, spreading westward and southward from the Philadelphia area, is perhaps the most fruitful contribution Kurath has made to the study of American dialects. The division into Northern, Midland, and Southern types is generally a better explanation of the historical facts and the present distribution of vocabulary items than the older grouping of Eastern, Southern, and 'General American,' and is at least as good a framework for an analysis on the basis of phonetic types. (McDavid 1948: 197)

Map 3.1, from *A Word Geography of the Eastern United States*, shows the subdivisions Kurath made in each of the three areas, North, Midland, and South. While these divisions were based on regional word usage, lexical items, as shown in Map 3.2 below, *creek* (which shows usage of *brook, run, branch,* and *-kill*), this map of speech areas was also found to hold true for the pronunciations in words mapped in the second publication, *The Pronunciation of English in the Atlantic States* (Kurath and McDavid 1961), where it was also published, without change. Indeed, Labov in the preface to the 2006 *Atlas of North American Phonology* says, "Almost every chapter of the Atlas refers to the work of Hans Kurath and Raven McDavid. The fundamental divisions they made into North, Midland and South and the connections they made with settlement history, stand up well in the light of current developments" (Labov et al. 2006: iv).

Map 3.3 from *The Pronunciation of English in the Atlantic States*, shows pronunciation of the vowel of the word *creek*, namely chiefly /ɪ/ in the North and the northern part of the Midland, and /i/ in the South. The maps of *The Pronunciation of English in the Atlantic States* frequently also include small-scale inserts, as in Map 3.3, showing the pronunciation of cultivated speech, or pronunciation in

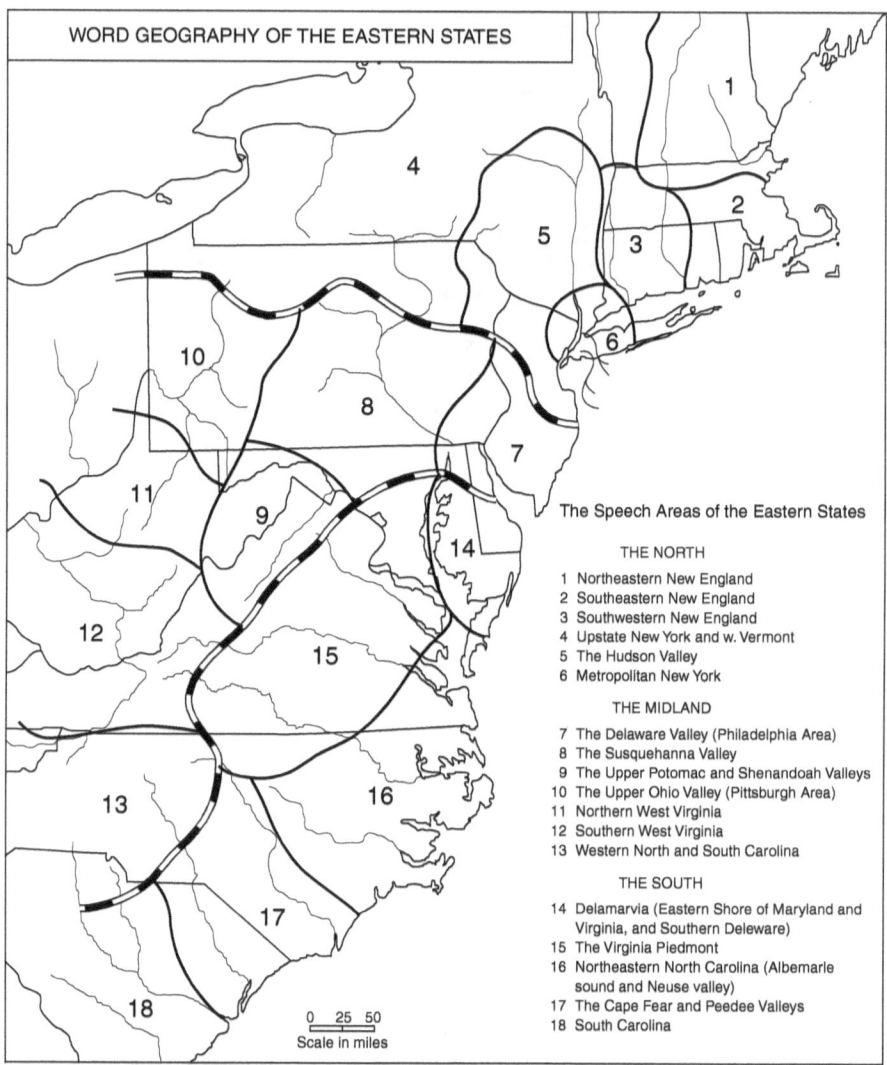

Map 3.1: The Speech Areas of the Eastern States, from *A Word Geography of the Eastern United States* (Figure 3) (Kurath 1949)

England (e.g. see figure 42 *poor* in *The Pronunciation of English in the Atlantic States*, Kurath and McDavid 1961).

While publications covering all states for a Linguistic Atlas of the United States have not been completed, fieldwork for many of the states was carried out over a 50 year period. Direct comparisons of lexical items usage or pronunciation in various parts of the country can unfortunately not be made using this data,

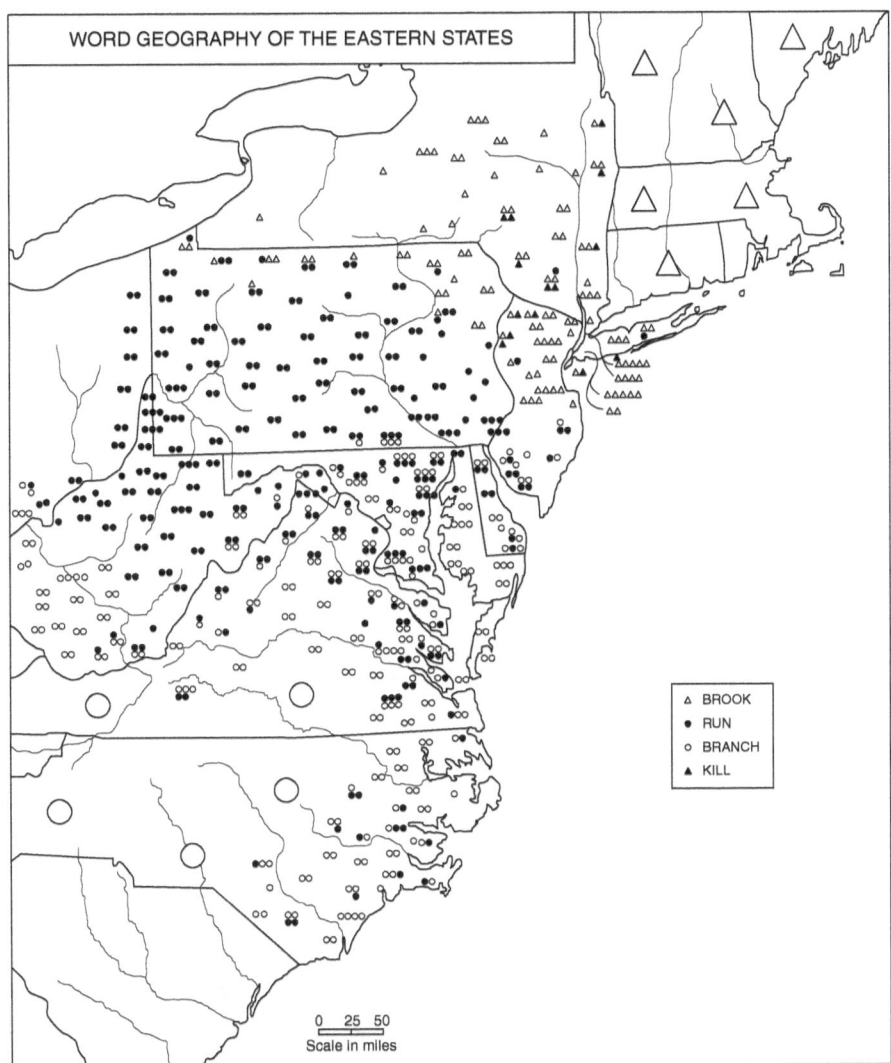

Map 3.2: *Creek* from *A Word Geography of the Eastern United States* (Figure 93) (Kurath 1949)

since the time period of collection was so extended, from the 1930s in New England, into to the 1990s in other parts of the country. Extensive material *was* published for the *Linguistic Atlas of the Upper Midwest* (Iowa, Minnesota, Nebraska, North Dakota, South Dakota) by Harold Allen (1973–76), and for the *Linguistic Atlas of the Gulf States* (Arkansas, Tennessee, Alabama, Louisiana, Mississippi, Florida, and parts of Georgia and Texas) by Lee Pederson (1988–90). For a short overview of the complete project of work done and states/regions covered, see

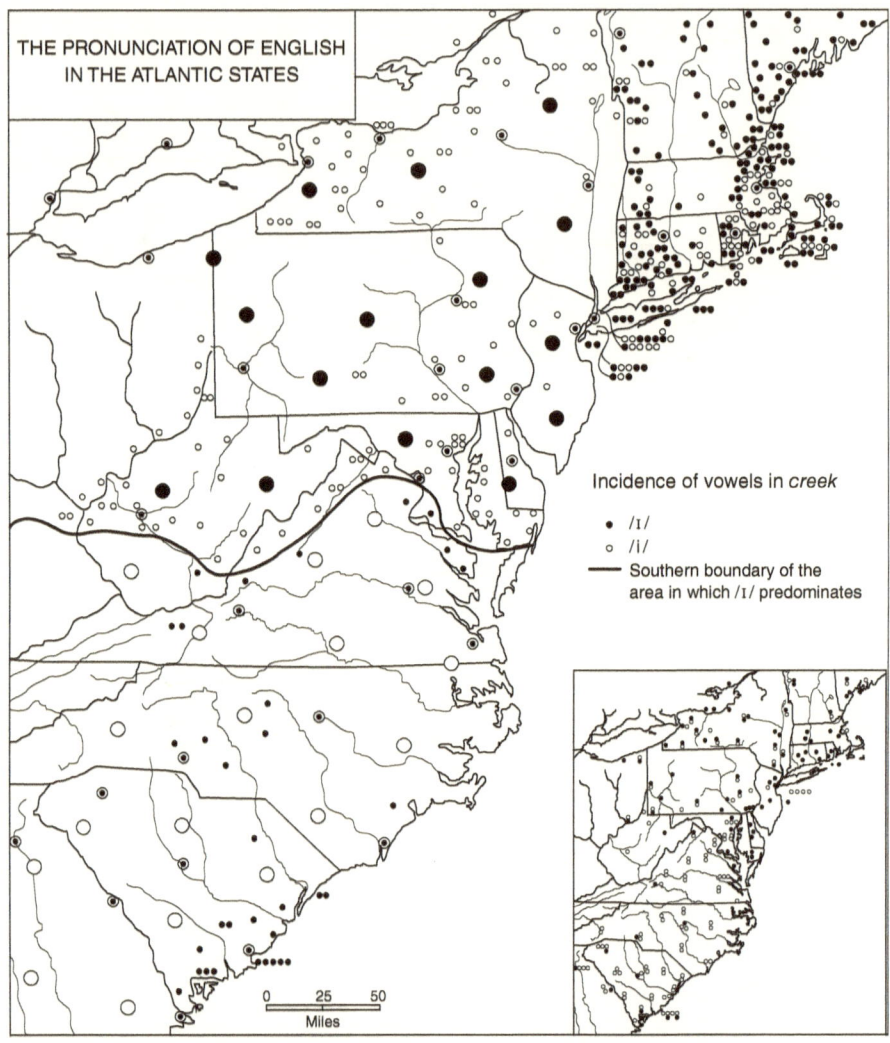

Map 3.3: *Creek* from *The Pronunciation of English in the Atlantic States* (Map 97) (Kurath and McDavid 1961), showing cultivated speakers in insert

Labov et al. (2006: 6). More detail is also provided on the Linguistic Atlas Project website, http://www.lap.uga.edu (last accessed 24 February 2017), by clicking on any of the abbreviations on the map.

Further research works based on and/or inspired by the early linguistic atlas work, leading to similar dialect fieldwork studies, are numerous, starting with E. Bagby Atwood's (1953) *A Survey of Verb Forms in the Eastern United States*, and continuing, for example, to cover parts of Texas (Atwood 1962), the Ohio River

Valley (Dakin 1966), California and Nevada (Bright 1971), and southern states (Wood 1971). Many works appeared as part of the PADS series (*Publication of the American Dialect Society*), e.g. Colorado (Hankey 1960), Illinois (Shuy 1962), and Chicago (Pederson 1965). The extension of Kurath's dialect divisions has been carried beyond the East Coast, across the country, with frequent refinements (still continuing), but his original basic boundaries remain intact and significant. (Indeed, for example, the map for the pronunciation *crick* (at the entry *creek* n¹ A) in the *Dictionary of American Regional English* (DARE) (Cassidy and Hall 1985–2012) (see Section 5) is labeled "esp Inland Nth, N Midl, West". And as *A Word Geography of the Eastern United States* showed usage of the four terms in Map 3.2 above, DARE's labeling still shows these areas of usage: *brook* is listed as "orig chiefly NEng, now widespread but esp common NEast", *run* is "scattered, but chiefly wPA, OH, WV, MD", *branch* is labeled "chiefly Sth, S Midl", and *kill* "esp NY, in Du settlement areas").

4 Branching out; social and ethnic dialects

Dialect geography, linguistic geography, dialectology – all names for working with regional varieties of a language, as discussed here of American English. Concentration was on regional variation, settlement history, older forms of the language up to the present (as witnessed in the preponderance of older informants questioned during fieldwork). But from the very beginning, social characteristics were considered, as described in Section 2.

In 1948 McDavid wrote his classic "Postvocalic /-r/ in South Carolina: A Social Analysis", which made a clear connection between pronunciation and social factors (in communities where postvocalic /r/ occurs with constriction, certain variables work against it; he shows that the more urban, younger, better educated speakers use less constriction). But it was not until the mid-1960s that such research dealing with social influences on variation became more common.

In 1963 the journal *Word* published William Labov's "The Social Motivation of a Sound Change", dealing with the shift in the phonetic position of the initial elements of /ay/ and /aw/ on the island of Martha's Vineyard, Massachusetts, where he showed that centralization had the meaning of positive orientation towards Martha's Vineyard (Labov 1963). This was the first of his many articles and books working with sound change, considering social variables such as age, occupation, ethnic group, education, and social aspirations. It was followed by *The Social Stratification of English in New York City*, published in 1966. The former and parts of the latter were published together with results of several other of Labov's studies in 1972 in *Sociolinguistic Patterns*. This was a major force in establishing research in social and ethnic dialects, indeed, in establishing the field of sociolinguistics which superseded the interest in more traditional regional dialect geography basically through the end of the century. Labov says of *Social Stratification* in the Preface to the second edition in 2006, 40 years later:

> SSENYC introduced a number of concepts that have proved useful in the study of change and variation: the linguistic variable; social and stylistic stratification; the cross-over pattern; apparent time; covert prestige. It also introduced a number of procedures that were new to linguistic studies: the creation of a representative sample; the sociolinguistic interview and the control of style-shifting within it; subjective reaction tests to measure the effect of particular linguistic variables; self-report and linguistic insecurity tests. (Labov 2006: xi)

Added to that can be listed refinements to phonological theory, the development of better tape recorders and their more refined successors, computers able to handle large amounts of data and software to analyze the data, leading to the development of acoustic analysis.

Along with many studies in urban areas (chapter 15 of Labov's 2006 2nd edition of *Social Stratification* contains a list of 37 such studies, done on speech communities world-wide 1966 to 2006), new journals sprang up starting in the 1960s, such as *Journal of English Linguistics* (1967), *Language in Society* (1972), and *Language Variation and Change* (1989). This shift in emphasis to sociolinguistics from dialect geography relegated the latter to being deemed "old-fashioned", outmoded, by many scholars during the latter part of the 20th century.

The beginnings of sociolinguistics in America had strong influence from various fields – linguistics, of course, but also anthropology, sociology – and occurrences – e.g. attention turning to social and racial equality, including attention being given to schoolchildren who speak English but a different variety than standard, and how the field of education should deal with this. In spite of the common ground – both work with language variation – relations between linguistic geography and sociolinguistics were not always smooth. McDavid and O'Cain recognized in their 1973 article the influence of linguistic geography on sociolinguistics, as well as the areas of agreement and disagreement, of common purpose and difference, in the two fields. But at that time they claimed that the information from the linguistic atlases and other linguistic geography publications, " – to say nothing of the unpublished materials in the archives which have always been open to scholars – have rarely been used in American sociolinguistics. Only Labov (1963, 1966, 1972) has made serious use of what linguistic geographers have done" (McDavid and O'Cain 1973: 139). Trudgill (1982: 237–238), in "The Contribution of Sociolinguistics to Dialectology" mentions other uses/projects, positive and negative. But there has been extensive work starting in the 1960s–1970s and still continuing on both urban and more rural dialects, on single cities and larger regions, from varieties including social and ethnic groups, and varieties of English in contact with other languages; and sociolinguistics and dialectology now realize that they can work together. See PADS *(Publication of the American Dialect Society)* and *American Speech* for many examples of such studies, as well as the much younger journals with sociolinguistics and its subfields as their main concern. Schneider says:

> Some thirty years ago, traditional camp affiliations were strong – so-called "dialect geographers" and so-called "sociolinguists" would have held conflicting opinions on questions such as principles of informant selection, the nature of reliable data, or the origin of what then was coming to be called "Black English". Today, boundaries between sub-fields have become blurred, as can be observed in matters such as attendance at meetings, data and methods chosen, or submission to journals and other publication outlets [...].What we see emerging is a complex research continuum, with sub-disciplines influencing and fertilizing each other. (Schneider 1996: 1)

See Shuy (1990) for more of an overview of the development of American sociolinguistics. Koerner also presents "a modest attempt to come to grips with the task of presenting the sources and early development of sociolinguistics, an area of research generally and erroneously thought to have arisen in the mid-1960s" (Koerner 1991: 58). He discusses earlier sources, listed as, among others, Whitney, Saussure, Meillet, Martinet, and Uriel Weinreich (the latter was Labov's major professor). Indeed, Koerner quotes Whitney from 1867: "Speech is not a personal possession, but a social; it belongs, not to the individual, but to the member of society .... The whole development of speech, though initiated by the acts of individuals, is wrought out by the community" (Koerner 1991: 59). This is most similar to Labov's comment c.140 years later: "The common understanding that unites the field – what I have called the central dogma of sociolinguistics – is that language is located in the speech community, not the individual" (Labov 2006: 380). But Koerner goes back to the scholarship and thought upon which could be and were built, culminating in the tipping point for Labov's work and influence to lead to the establishment of this new branch of linguistics.

5 The *Dictionary of American Regional English*

After the significant shift in dialectology towards social and ethnic dialects, there has more recently, chiefly in the last two decades, been a rebirth of interest in regional variation in dialects (hinted at by Schneider in Section 4), brought about especially by the publication of the volumes of the *Dictionary of American Regional English* (DARE) (Cassidy and Hall, 1985–2012) and the *Atlas of North American English: Phonetics, Phonology and Sound Change* (Labov et al. 2006), which is discussed in Section 6. (Indeed, one of the major names in sociolinguistics, who once shared the opinion that atlas-type work was a thing well-relegated to the past, told DARE staffers after publication of two volumes of DARE that he was very impressed with it and found it most useful in his work.)

The *Dictionary of American Regional English* (DARE) has finally brought to fruition the dream of the founding members of the American Dialect Society to produce a dictionary for America like Joseph Wright's *English Dialect Dictionary* (but even better, taking advantage of advances in lexicography as demonstrated by the *Oxford English Dictionary* and other dictionaries). Chief editor Frederic Cassidy was appointed in 1962. The first volume appeared in 1985, with the last text volume, Volume V, appearing in 2012 under the editorship of Joan Houston Hall. Dictionary of American Regional English Volume VI: Contrastive Maps, Index to Entry Labels, Questionnaire, and Fieldwork Data, chief editor Joan Houston Hall with Luanne von Schneidemesser, appeared in 2013, offering actual data which can be used in research, which goes beyond what is available in the first five volumes of dictionary text and explains more about DARE.

Cassidy used the *Atlas* materials, including his own fieldwork for the *Linguistic Atlas of the North Central States*; the word lists in *Dialect Notes* and the *Publication of the American Dialect Society* series; and his Wisconsin English Language Survey (see Cassidy 1948) to develop a questionnaire of over 1,600 questions (originally there were over 1,800 questions, but after a trial run in several states, over 200 questions were dropped and a handful were added) in wide-reaching semantic fields (e.g. vehicles and transportation, fishing and hunting, religion and beliefs, farm buildings, children's games, entertainments and celebrations, emotional states and attitudes, with questions on verb forms interspersed throughout). Dieth criticizes the LANE worksheets, "alarmingly modern", for containing questions on *girl friend, theater,* and *emancipated*, not real dialect words (Dieth 1948: 76–7). In contrast, these types of words and questions are indeed the strong point of DARE's questionnaire, while questions dealing with *nigh horse* or *off ox*, for example, elicited frequent answers of conflicting definition, since the terms are no longer commonly known. Used by fieldworkers who completed interviews for 1,002 questionnaires between 1965 and 1970, for which communities were chosen by settlement history and population (at least two questionnaires were done in each state, with over 80 done in a populous state such as New York), the questionnaire materials yielded an incredibly rich database of responses, including many terms which had not previously been found in written sources. This database is what makes DARE truly unique, beyond any of the earlier linguistic atlases or dictionaries. The questionnaire material was supplemented by written sources – diaries, travel reports, regional novels, government documents, biographies, donated collections, etc. – to form the basis of

Chapter 3: Regional varieties of American English — 43

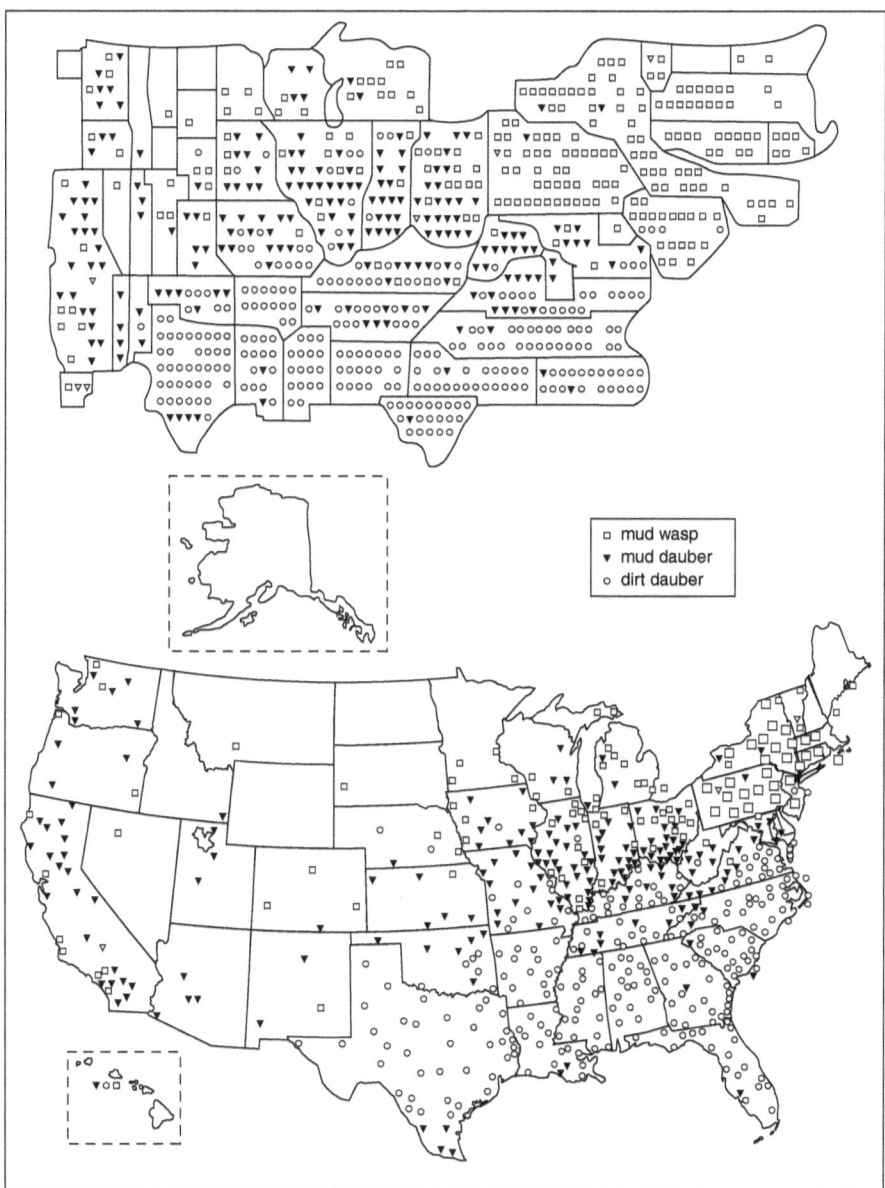

Map 3.4: Comparison of DARE (Cassidy and Hall, 1985–2012) map and conventional U.S. map, *mud wasp, mud dauber,* and *dirt dauber*. Reprinted by permission of the publisher from *Dictionary of American Regional English: Volume I – A-C*, edited by Frederick G. Cassidy, p. xxix, Cambridge, Mass.: The Belknap Press of Harvard University Press, Copyright © 1985 by the President and Fellows of Harvard College.

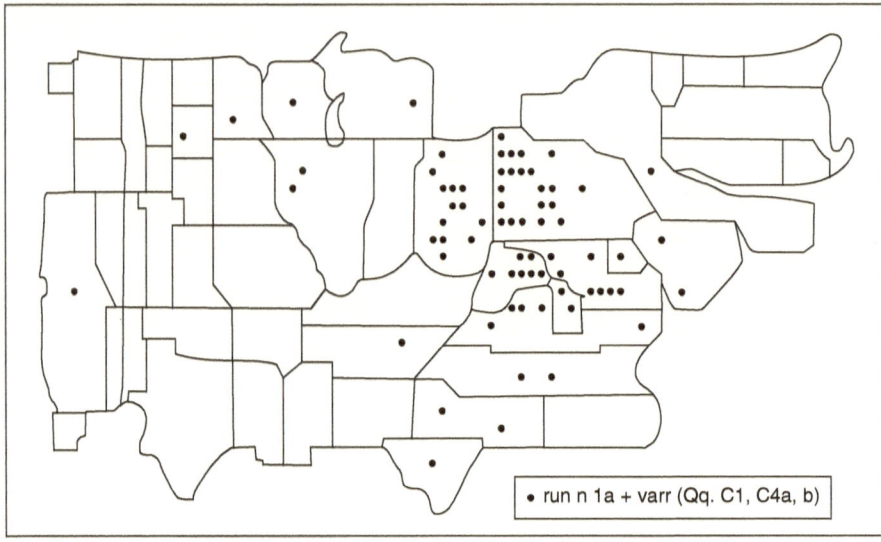

Map 3.5: *run* from DARE (Cassidy and Hall, 1985–2012). Reprinted by permission of the publisher from *Dictionary of American Regional English: Volume IV – P-Sk*, edited by Joan Houston Hall, p. 670, Cambridge, Mass.: The Belknap Press of Harvard University Press, Copyright © 2002 by the President and Fellows of Harvard College.

DARE, which as a historical dictionary shows with its citations as much is as known about the history of each word or phrase entered. In later volumes electronic sources were a rich source of additional materials. Maps, based on the responses to the questionnaires, demonstrate regionality on a proportional basis, based on population and settlement history, so that density of use in various regions can be seen, beyond what an actual geographic map would show, as shown in Map 3.4, with a comparison of a conventional U.S. map with the DARE version demonstrating usage of *mud wasp, mud dauber*, and *dirt dauber* 'wasp'. Maps are included in the text with entries, such as Map 3.5 below, the DARE map of *run* (mentioned in Section 3).

While mostly lexical, DARE also includes items on pronunciation, morphology, and syntax. Statements on usage by age, gender, education, race, and type/size of community are included in the entries where applicable (e.g. at *togs* 'clothes', "Of all Infs responding to the question, 65% were old, 60% female; of those giving this response, 83% were old, 71% female"; at *icky*, "36 of 47 total Infs female, 28 young or mid-aged"; at *waste* 'to spill', "21 of 34 total Infs Black"). And DARE provides a synchronic study of the whole nation, not only from the questionnaire materials, but from audiotapes of the informants. These tapes, now digitized, of both free conversation and a reading passage, *Arthur the Rat*, containing all phonemes of major varieties of American English, have been used in studies of various types of phonological analysis. Sound clips of 35 states from the audio files can be found at *American Languages: Our Nation's Many Voices Online*, (http://csumc.wisc.edu/AmericanLanguages/english/eng_us.htm, last accessed 24 February 2017). Over 800 clips of *Arthur the Rat* are posted at *American Languages: Our Nation's Many Voices* (https://uwdc.library.wic.edu/collections/amerlangs, last accessed 24 February 2017).

6 The *Atlas of North American English* and beyond

The publication of the *Atlas of North American English: Phonetics, Phonology and Sound Change* in 2006 was a major event in the study of regional varieties of American English (Labov et al. 2006), igniting renewed interest in linguistic geography. Indeed, a great deal of the research in regional dialects since 2006 has been inspired by this publication. Richard Bailey, in his review entitled "The Greatest Atlas Ever", starts by stating, "*The Atlas of North American English* (ANAE) is a remarkable achievement and the most important work in American linguistic geography ever published" (Bailey 2007: 292). This volume is a record of the sounds of English as spoken in urban areas of the U.S. and Canada. As Labov states in his Introduction:

> It provides the first comprehensive view of the pronunciation and phonology of English across the North American continent. The Atlas builds on the work of American dialectologists from 1933 to the present, particularly on the work of Hans Kurath and Raven McDavid in the Atlantic States. A N E A represents new departures in American dialectology in several respects: it provides information on perception as well as production, on acoustic measurements as well as impressionistic ratings, on the realization of phonemic categories as well as phonetic forms, and on phonological systems as well as individual phonemes. Most importantly, it provides a view of the systematic sound changes in progress that are responsible for increasing diversity among the regional dialects of North America. (Labov et al. 2006: 3)

The basis of the *Atlas* is a telephone survey (Telsur) carried out in (mostly) urban areas of 50,000 population or more from 1992 to 1999; "the first two local residents to answer their telephones – people who were born or raised in the speech community – could be taken to represent adequately the linguistic pattern of that community" (Labov et al. 2006: 3). Four hundred thirty-nine of 762 total samples (a total of 297 speech communities), with a somewhat elevated number of women between 20 and 40 represented, since that group has been shown to be at the forefront of change, were selected for acoustic analysis. Although not the exclusive focus, stressed vowels are primarily studied, "since it is the vowel patterns that differentiate regional dialects of English on this continent" (Labov et al. 2006: 4).

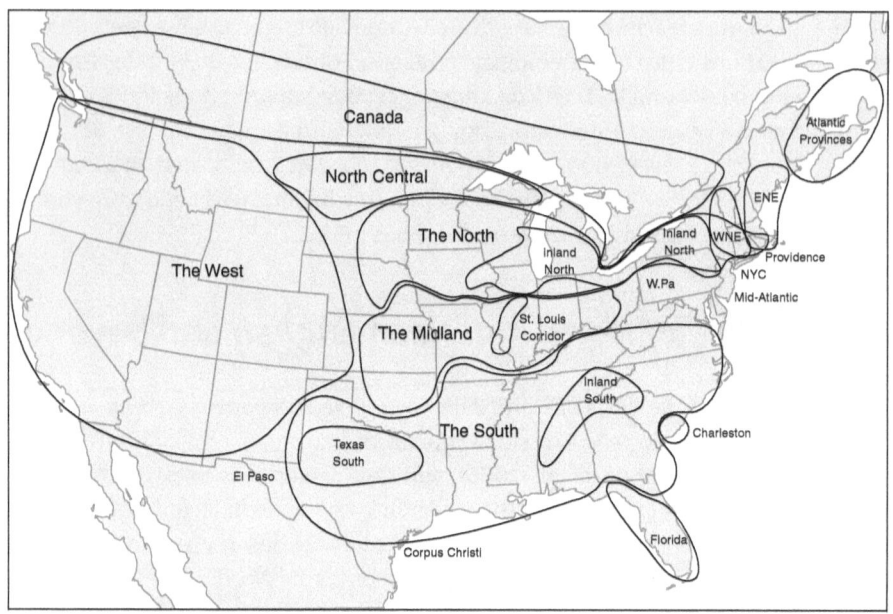

Map 3.6: *Atlas of North American English: Phonetics, Phonology and Sound Change* (Labov et al. 2006) Map 11.15, An overall view of North American dialects

The ANAE presents a discussion of its methodology, an introduction to the North American vowel system, and an overview of its dialects, based on pronunciation; after discussion of the latter, a representation is shown on its Map 11.15 "An overall view of North American dialects", reproduced here as Map 3.6, with its breakdown of regions shown. (Throughout the major reference works discussed in this article markers of the various dialect regions are discussed. Wolfram and Schilling-Estes [2005: 361–84] add as an appendix *An Inventory of Distinguishing Dialect Features*, discussing phonological and grammatical features. See also Schneider [2008] for more extensive discussions of some of the regions).

The ANAE discusses the principles of chain shifting and mergers and goes into detail on mergers and shifts presently ongoing (see below). As mentioned in Section 3 above, the fundamental divisions of dialect regions based on lexical findings from Linguistic Atlas materials by Kurath and McDavid (1961) are basically similar to what is presented in the ANAE. A work by Craig Carver in 1987, *American Regional Dialects: A Word Geography*, using materials from the *Dictionary of American Regional English*, also shows agreement of the major regional divisions for the most part. While Carver does not include the Midland, the boundary of what other studies show between the North and Midland coincides with Carver's boundary between what he terms Upper North and Lower North.

ANAE's Midland/South border is similar for most of its length to Carver's Lower North/Upper South border. See the ANAE (Labov et al. 2006: 149–151) for further analysis of agreement and differences of sub-areas, including a map of the two works superimposed on each other.

The criteria ANAE uses to establish dialect boundaries "are based on the systematic study of phonological relations in the vowel system and the activation of general principles of chain shifting". Labov continues:

> [T]here will appear a high degree of convergence between isoglosses based on regional vocabulary and the patterning of phonological isoglosses. Some major divisions will depart from those based on lexical and grammatical evidence, to a large extent the result of current changes in progress. Yet others will show a satisfying coincidence with the lexical boundaries established by the Dictionary of American Regional English [DARE] and the Linguistic Atlas studies that preceded it.
> Confidence in the phonologically based dialect boundaries displayed here is not based only on coincidence with previous studies. It is founded on two types of correlation between geography and linguistic structure. In one, isoglosses for the various elements of a chain shift coincide in an isogloss bundle, the end result of a completed series of linked changes. In the other, the successive stages of a chain shift are nested one within the other, with the oldest showing the widest domain and the most recent the most restricted application, producing a display of incomplete changes in progress. (Labov et al. 2006: 119)

Three of the sound changes which Labov considers important here are:
1) The low back merger, where the vowels of *cot* and *caught* and *Don* and *Dawn* merge; this merger has occurred in eastern New England, the West, and western Pennsylvania into Kentucky and West Virginia.
2) The Northern Cities Shift, taking place in the Inland North, first noticed in Detroit, Chicago, Syracuse, Rochester, and Buffalo; the chain shift, as shown in Figure 3.1, starts with the vowel in *bat* moving up and forward, marked with 1. At step 3, the shift presents resistance to the low back merger, since the vowels mentioned above as *caught* (*bought*) and *cot* (*pot*) must remain distinct in this system.
3) The Southern Shift shows upward and fronting movement of vowels in words like *bed* and *bid* (and the addition of a glide), movement in the opposite direction of the Northern Cities Shift (see Figure 3.2). The shift starts with the deletion of the glide in /ay/ in words like *guy, my*. The South is also resistant to the low back merger due to its vowel system.

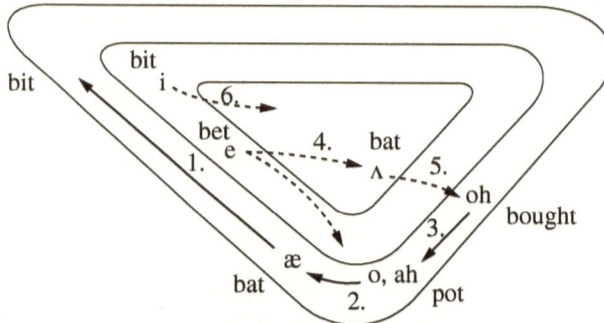

Figure 3.1: *Atlas of North American English: Phonetics, Phonology and Sound* Change (Labov et al. 2006) Northern Cities Shift

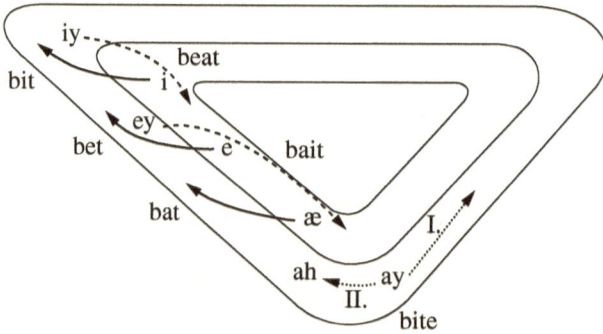

Figure 3.2: *Atlas of North American English: Phonetics, Phonology and Sound* Change (Labov et al. 2006) Southern Shift

7 Summary

The study of American regional dialects has come a long way since the founding of the American Dialect Society in 1889. Most recently, the publication of the *Atlas of North American English: Phonetics, Phonology and Sound Change* (Labov et al. 2006) was a huge advance to the field, presenting the first nationwide study of the phonology of the United States (and Canada) to complement the *Dictionary of American Regional English*'s (Cassidy and Hall 1985–2012) nationwide study of lexical items.

Labov's focus throughout his studies has been one of understanding linguistic change. The ANAE provides a view of the systematical sound changes that are in progress; it underscores the validity of the early Linguistic Atlas work of Kurath, McDavid, and others; and it helps to re-establish links between dialect geography and general linguistics.

Frequently the opinion is expressed by speakers of American English that the language is becoming more homogenous, that uniformity will take over the language. As DARE has shown with its nationwide survey of the lexicon, this is not the case. Older lexical items may be lost, such as ones queried in earlier Linguistic Atlas worksheets, but new ones develop. Labov has backed up these results with the findings of the ANAE. He says, "The most surprising finding of current studies of linguistic change in progress in North America is that regional dialects are becoming increasingly differentiated from each other". He continues:

> This increasing diversity does not apply to smaller units within the major regions. Within most of the regional boundaries, linguistic changes in progress have the effect of solidifying and developing the regional pattern. Many local dialects are indeed disappearing, but they are assimilating to larger regional patterns rather than to a national or continental model. (Labov et al. 2006: 119)

Both DARE and ANAE did nationwide surveys, as mentioned, but with DARE's 1,002 communities and ANAE's 439 acoustic samples analyzed, neither work provides a great coverage of the U.S. – certainly adequate for the purposes of each, but not a dense enough network to account for many language questions which remain. Indeed, Labov states in his introduction that the total number of speakers represented by the samples in North America is 68% (Labov et al. 2006: 3 and 149); even that 68% is covered sparsely with the low number of samples. But Labov makes it clear that the ANAE is defining regions by major urban areas; that the small towns and rural areas, as well as the transition areas, areas near borders, are where further studies are needed (Labov et al. 2006: 119, 303). This is part of the future of studies on American dialects.

8 References

Algeo, John (ed.). 2001. *English in North America. The Cambridge History of the English Language VI*. Cambridge: Cambridge University Press.

Allen, Harold B. 1973–76. *The Linguistic Atlas of the Upper Midwest*. 3 vols. Minneapolis MN: University of Minnesota Press.

Allen, Harold B. and Michael D. Linn (eds.). 1986. *Dialect and Language Variation*. Orlando FL: Academic Press.

Atwood, E. Bagby. 1953. *A Survey of Verb Forms in the Eastern United States*. Ann Arbor MI: University of Michigan Press.

Atwood, E. Bagby. 1962. *The Regional Vocabulary of Texas*. Austin: University of Texas Press.

Bailey, Richard W. 2007. The greatest atlas ever [Review of The Atlas of North American English]. *American Speech* 82: 292–300.

Baugh, Albert C. 1957. *A History of the English Language*. 2nd edn. New York: Appleton-Century-Crofts.

Bright, Elizabeth S. 1971. *A Word Geography of California and Nevada*. Berkeley: University of California Press.
Carver, Craig M. 1987. *American Regional Dialects: A Word Geography*. Ann Arbor: University of Michigan Press.
Cassidy, Frederic G. 1948. On collecting American dialect. *American Speech* 23: 185–193.
Cassidy, Frederic G. and Joan Houston Hall (eds.). 1985–2012. *Dictionary of American Regional English*. 5 vols. Cambridge, MA: Belknap Press of Harvard University Press.
Dakin, Robert Ford. 1966. *The Dialect Vocabulary of the Ohio River Valley*. Ph.D. dissertation, University of Michigan.
Davis, A. L. 1948. *A Word Atlas of the Great Lakes Region*. Ph.D. dissertation, University of Michigan.
Dieth, Eugen. 1948. Linguistic geography in New England. *English Studies* 29: 65–78.
Finegan, Edward and John R. Rickford. 2004. *Language in the USA: Themes for the Twenty-first Century*. Cambridge: Cambridge University Press.
Gilliéron, Jules, and Edmond Edmont. 1902–10. *Atlas Linguistique de la France*. Paris: Honoré Champion.
Glowka, A. Wayne and Donald M. Lance (eds.). 1993. *Language Variation in North American English: Research and Teaching*. New York: Modern Language Association of America.
Hall, Joan Houston with Luanne von Schneidemesser. 2013. *Dictionary of American Regional English Volume VI: Contrastive Maps, Index to Entry Labels, Questionnaire, and Fieldwork Data*. Cambridge, MA: Belknap Press of Harvard University Press.
Hankey, Clyde T. 1960. *A Colorado Word Geography*. Durham: Duke University Press.
Jaberg, Karl and Jakob Jud. 1928–40. *Sprach- und Sachatlas Italiens und der Südschweiz*. Zofingen: Ringier.
Koerner, Konrad. 1991. Toward a history of modern sociolinguistics. *American Speech* 66(1): 57–70.
Kretzschmar, William A. Jr., Virginia G. McDavid, Theodore K. Lerud, and Ellen Johnson. 1994. *Handbook of the Linguistic Atlas of the Middle and South Atlantic States*. Chicago: University of Chicago Press.
Kurath, Hans. 1929. A bibliography of American pronunciation 1888–1928. *Language* 5(3): 155–162.
Kurath, Hans. 1949. *A Word Geography of the Eastern United States*. Ann Arbor: University of Michigan Press.
Kurath, Hans, with the collaboration of Marcus L. Hansen, Bernard Bloch, Julia Bloch. 1939. *Handbook of the Linguistic Geography of New England*. Providence RI: Brown University. (A second edition was published by Arrangement with the American Council of Learned Societies in 1973 by AMS Press, "with a new introduction, word-index and inventory of LANE maps and commentary by Audrey R Duckert, and a reverse index of LANE maps to worksheets by Raven I McDavid, Jr.")
Kurath, Hans, dir. and ed.; Miles L. Hanley, Bernard Bloch, Guy S. Lowman, Jr. and Marcus L. Hansen. 1939–43. *The Linguistic Atlas of New England*. 3 vols. Providence RI: Brown University. Sponsored by the American Council of Learned Societies.
Kurath, Hans, and Raven I. McDavid, Jr. 1961. *The Pronunciation of English in the Atlantic States*. Ann Arbor: University of Michigan Press.
Labov, William. 1963. The social motivation of a sound change. *Word* 19: 273–309. Reprinted in *Sociolinguistic Patterns* as Chapter 1, 1–42.

Labov, William. 1966. *The Social Stratification of English in New York City*. Washington: Center for Applied Linguistics.
Labov, William. 1972. *Sociolinguistic Patterns*. Philadelphia: University of Pennsylvania Press.
Labov, William. 1994. *Principles of Linguistic Change*. Oxford: Blackwell. Vol. 1: *Internal Factors*, 1994; Vol. 2 *Social Factors*, 2000.
Labov, William. 2006. *The Social Stratification of English in New York City*. 2nd edn. New York: Cambridge University Press.
Labov, William, Sharon Ash, and Charles Boberg. 2006. *The Atlas of North American English: Phonetics, Phonology and Sound Change*. Berlin/New York: Mouton de Gruyter.
Lance, Donald M. 1994. Variation in American English. In: John Samuel Kenyon, Donald M. Lance, and Stewart A. Kingsbury (eds.), *American Pronunciation*. 12th, expanded edn. Ann Arbor MI: George Wahr Publishing Co.
Linn, Michael D. (ed.) 1998. *Handbook of Dialects and Language Variation*. 2nd edn. San Diego: Academic Press.
Mathews, Mitford M. (ed.). 1931. *The Beginnings of American English: Essays and Comments*. Chicago: University of Chicago Press.
McDavid, Raven I., Jr. 1948. Postvocalic /-r/ in South Carolina: A social analysis. *American Speech* 23: 194–203.
McDavid, Raven I., Jr. 1958. The dialects of American English. In: W. Nelson Francis (ed.), *The Structure of American English*, 480–543. New York: Ronald Press Company.
McDavid, Raven I., Jr. and Raymond K. O'Cain. 1973. Sociolinguistics and linguistic geography. *Kansas Journal of Sociology* 9(2): 137–156.
O'Cain, Raymond K. 1979. Review: Linguistic Atlas of New England. *American Speech* 54(4): 243–278.
Murray, James A. H. (eds) 1933. *Oxford English Dictionary*. 13 vols. Oxford: Clarendon Press.
Pederson, Lee A. 1965. The pronunciation of English in metropolitan Chicago. Publication of the *American Dialect Society* 44.
Pederson, Lee A. 1988–90. *Linguistic Atlas of the Gulf States [General Index, Technical Index, and Regional Matrix]*. Athens GA: University of Georgia Press.
Preston, Dennis R. (ed.). 1993. *American Dialect Research*. Amsterdam/Philadelphia: John Benjamins.
Schneider, Edgar W. (ed.). 1996. *Focus on the USA*. Amsterdam/Philadelphia: John Benjamins.
Schneider, Edgar W. (ed.). 2008. *Varieties of English 2: The Americas and the Caribbean*. Berlin/New York: Mouton de Gruyter.
Shuy, Roger W. 1962. The Northern-Midland dialect boundary in Illinois. Publication of the *American Dialect Society* 38.
Shuy, Roger W. 1990. A brief history of American sociolinguistics 1949–1989. *Historiographia Linguistica* XVII (1/2):183–209. (A shortened version is reprinted in: Christina Bratt Paulston and G. Richard Tucker (eds.). 2003. *Sociolinguistics: the Essential Readings*, 4–16. Malden, MA: Blackwell Publishing.)
Tarpley, Fred. 1970. *From Blinky to Blue-John: A Word Atlas of Northeast Texas*. Wolfe City, TX: University Press.
Trudgill, Peter. 1982. The contribution of sociolinguistics to dialectology. *Language Sciences* 4(2): 237–250.
Wolfram, Walt and Ralph W. Fasold. 1974. *The Study of Social Dialects in American English*. Englewood Cliffs, NJ: Prentice-Hall.

Wolfram, Walt and Natalie Schilling-Estes. 2005. *American English: Dialects and Variation*. 2nd edn. Malden, MA: Blackwell Publishers Inc.

Wood, Gordon R. 1971. *Vocabulary Change: A Study of Variation in Regional Words in Eight of the Southern States*. Carbondale: Southern Illinois University Press.

Wrede, Ferdinand, Walther Mitzka, and Bernard Martin. 1926–56. *Deutscher Sprachatlas: auf Grund des von George Wenker begründeten Sprachatlas des Deutschen Reiches, und mit Einschluss von Luxemburg unter Leitung von Ferdinand Wrede, fortgesetzt von Walther Mitzka und Bernhard Martin*. Marburg (Lahn): N. G. Elwert.

Wright, Joseph. 1898–1905. *The English Dialect Dictionary*. 6 vols. London: Henry Frowde.

Stefan Dollinger
Chapter 4:
Canadian English in real-time perspective

1 The study of Canadian English and historical Canadian English —— 54
2 Settlement: demographic and linguistic input —— 57
3 Evidence, data, and methods in the historical linguistics of CanE —— 60
4 Features of Canadian English in long-term perspective —— 65
5 Desiderata and outlook —— 72
6 References —— 72

Abstract: The study of Canadian English (CanE) has undergone phases of considerable activity in the 20th century and must today be considered a field in its own right. The purpose of this overview is to present the research on CanE from a diachronic, and, wherever possible, real-time perspective. Given the lack of a consistent historical research tradition in CanE linguistics, the present chapter aims to link real-time studies of CanE with the most relevant apparent-time approaches. The following pages are intended as a spring board to CanE for those approaching it from a historical and sociohistorical linguistic perspective.

The structure of this overview begins with the notions of Standard CanE and CanE regional varieties (Section 1). Section 2 provides basic demographic and settlement information over time for linguistic purposes. Section 3 introduces methods that have been applied in the study of the development of CanE varieties, while Section 4, organized along linguistic levels of description, aims to introduce the reader to major variables in historical CanE linguistics. Section 5 closes with some research desiderata. The overall focus of this chapter will give preference – in keeping with the traditions in historical English linguistics – to real-time approaches of linguistic change. This foregrounding is taken (for more synchronic summaries, see Boberg 2010; Levey 2010; Chambers 2010, 1998; Dollinger 2008a: 9–62; Bailey 1982) to highlight the historical linguistic approach to CanE.

Stefan Dollinger: Vancouver (Canada)

1 The study of Canadian English and historical Canadian English

Commencing with the foundation of the Canadian Linguistic Association in 1954, the decades since have witnessed considerable research activity. Boberg (2010: 48), in his ground-breaking monograph overview of CanE, classifies these activities into six domains, illustrated with examples below (for more detail, see Boberg 2010: 48–54; Dollinger 2008a: 23–62; Chambers 2010; Avis 1973):

1. Lexicographic work on Canadian and regional CanE (e.g. Avis et al. 1967; Story et al. 1990; Pratt 1988; Dollinger 2011b; Dollinger and von Schneidemesser 2011; Dollinger and Fee 2017)
2. Alternation among American, British, and Canadian forms, with an accompanying discussion of the historical origins and development of CanE (e.g. Avis 1954, 1955, 1956; Scargill 1977)
3. Documentation of traditional speech enclaves (e.g. Emenau 1975 [1935]; Hamilton 1975 [1958]; Paddock 1982; Clarke 1991, 1993b, 2010; Wilson 1958; Poplack and Tagliamonte 2001)
4. Microsociolinguistic studies of variation in urban Canadian English (e.g. Clarke 1982; Gregg 2004 [1984]; Woods 1999 [1979]; Walker 2007; Poplack et al. 2006; De Wolf 1992; Nylvek 1992; Childs and Van Herk 2010; Chambers and Hardwick 1986; Hoffman and Walker 2010; Tagliamonte and D'Arcy 2009; Torres Cacoullos and Walker 2009)
5. Sociophonetic research on regional and social variation in the articulation of vowels of CanE (starting with Chambers [1980] on Canadian Raising; starting with Clarke et al. 1995 on the Canadian Shift, e.g. Hoffman 2010)
6. Macrosociolinguistic studies of the use of English and other languages in Canada, particularly Quebec (e.g. Chambers 1979; Edwards 1998; Falk and Harry 1999; Heller 2010)

Boberg's domains characterize well the available work. Striking in this six-item list is the absence of a diachronic, real-time perspective. It is, with the exception of an addendum to area 2 (comparative studies), and to area 1 (lexicography), hardly present at all. Boberg (2010: 54) expressly acknowledges this desideratum and assesses that, until now, an approach that uses "historical written material for evidence of earlier stages of Canadian English […] falls outside the main traditions of work on Canadian English". The first full-length, real-time historical study (Dollinger 2008a) has since been complemented by other studies (Reuter 2017; Dollinger and Fee 2017):

While until the late 1970s the literature on CanE was "quite manageable" (Chambers 1979: 168), research output has exploded in the past two decades. The majority of contributions on the development of the variety has been carried out from five methodological perspectives:
1. language-external reasoning
2. historical lexicographical and lexicological approaches
3. self-report surveys
4. apparent-time sociolinguistic studies incorporating a long-term perspective
5. historical corpus linguistics

Studies from the first four areas are readily available, while the budding field of historical corpus linguistics is still under-developed in CanE.

1.1 Canadian English: the notion of a standard

CanE is sometimes pitted against the most distinct variety found on Canadian territory, Newfoundland English (see, for instance, Brinton and Fee 2001 and Kirwin 2001). In this chapter, CanE will be used, as it is increasingly so, as a hyperonym including Newfoundland English, Prairie English and so forth; the term "mainland CanE" (usually including Prince Edward Island) is used in opposition to Newfoundland.

The concept of *Standard Canadian English* plays a role that is somewhat different socially when compared to other standard dialects. Expanding from the original description pertaining to phonetics and phonology, "Standard Canadian English" (StCanE) is a pervasive dialect, of "urban, middle-class English as spoken by people who have been urban, middle-class, anglophone Canadians for two generations or more" (Chambers 1998c: 252). The Standard dialect, not to be confused with "General Canadian English" (in Labov et al. 2006 it is called "Canadian"), covers the entire area of mainland Canada today (Boberg 2008), and is increasingly influencing urban Newfoundland varieties (Clarke 2010, 1993).

StCanE has been the focus of most work on CanE. It is claimed to be a "uniform variety" spoken by "the majority of anglophone Canadians" (Boberg 2010: 107), i.e. by many speakers, but not necessarily a majority (Chambers 1998c: 253). Applying some social criteria for standard speakers according to Chambers (1998c: 252), those of the second generation (those born in the country), Anglophone (not Francophone), urban, and middle-class, would produce a category of speakers of more than 36%, or more than thirteen million of the population as (potential) speakers of StCanE (Dollinger 2011a: 5).

As more and more detailed studies become available (e.g. Boberg 2005a, 2008; Hoffman 2010), the focus on the standard variety, which has been considered as being remarkably homogenous across mainland Canada, from Halifax, Nova Scotia to Victoria, British Columbia since at least the 1950s (Chambers 1998c: 253; Woods 1999; Priestley 1968 [1951]), may have perhaps underplayed subtle regional variation even within StCanE (see Dollinger and Clarke 2012). The causes for this homogeneity are usually linked to the historical roots of the socially dominant Canadian dialect, which can be found in the first major immigration of English speakers in the wake of the American Revolution and the subsequent peopling of the country from Ontario westwards. With the increasing socioeconomic importance of Ontario within Canada and strong east-west links across the country Ontarian forms often provided the input for the standard (Chambers 2009: 70–73).

1.2 Regional and non-standard Canadian Englishes

Descriptions of non-standard varieties of English within Canada are faced with the lack of a complete national dialect atlas, which prevents the situating of any variety within the larger picture. This desideratum resulted in the postulation of dialect boundaries based on settlement history and geographical features. Labels such as "Prairie English", "Western Canadian English", "Saskatchewan English", "Toronto English" or "Maritimes English" are often used, but are based on pragmatic necessity rather than on linguistic data. Within these regions, research focus in general has not been evenly distributed in general. While we know a lot about Ontario English, especially its urban lects, little data exists of Maritimes English (but see, e.g. Wilson 1958; Kiefte and Kay-Raining Bird 2010) or English in Saskatchewan (but see Nylvek 1992), the English in (or close to) the territories – most likely more an ethnic than a regional variety per se – is hardly studied at all (see Ball and Bernhardt 2008).

Recent national surveys based on self-reports (see Section 3.2) allow insights into dialect boundaries based on linguistic evidence. Boberg (2005b), for instance, concludes that the traditional dialect zones, inspired by geographical units (e.g. provinces or regions) are not borne out in his lexical data set, as Table 4.1 shows (right column) – please note, however, that this study focuses on "marked" lexical items.

Boberg's study is the first quantification of isogloss strengths in CanE, both within the country and in comparison to the United States. He concludes that "[i]n Canada, the strongest lexical boundaries were found to divide the English-speaking community of Montreal from neighboring regions to the east and west,"

Table 4.1: Canadian dialect regions – three approaches

Scargill 1974 geographical	Bailey 1991 language-external reasoning	Boberg 2005b lexis (44 items)
10 Canadian provinces: Newfoundland, Prince Edward Island, Nova Scotia, New Brunswick, Quebec, Ontario, Manitoba, Saskatchewan, Alberta, British Columbia. The provinces were taken as the geographical independent variables (a choice not rationalized).	Atlantic (incl. Newfoundland)	Maritimes (Nova Scotia, New Brunswick and Prince Edward Island)
	Quebec (with Montreal and Eastern Townships as focal areas)	Newfoundland
	Ottawa Valley	Montreal (by extension Quebec)
	Toronto westwards	Central and Western Canada (Ontario, Manitoba, Saskatchewan, Alberta, British Columbia)
	West (British Columbia) Arctic North Prairies Southern Ontario	

"followed in importance by the bundle of isoglosses that divides Newfoundland from the Maritimes" (Boberg 2005b: 53).

Recent evidence suggests that CanE linguistic autonomy (Clarke et al. 1995; Boberg 2004a, 2010) is maintained, as "regional linguistic variation remains one of the few ways in which Canadians can still be reliably distinguished from Americans, at least in most parts of the continent" (Boberg 2010: 250). The evidence for dialect diversification is split, with communities in Montreal (Boberg 2005a) showing ethnic dialect features, but not in Toronto (Hoffman 2010; Hoffman and Walker 2010), which perhaps reflects different degrees of network densities.

2 Settlement: demographic and linguistic input

Settlement information is crucial for an understanding of the formation of CanE: Boberg (2010: 55–105) offers one of the best concise demographic accounts for the entire country, Clarke (2010: 10–15) describes Newfoundland and Labrador and Dollinger (2008a: 63–98) Ontario. Chambers's (1998c [first proposed in 1991]) concept of classifying immigration into four major waves, which can be supplemented with a current, ongoing fifth immigrant wave, is a useful way to present the complex settlement streams in one concise account:

I. Refugees from the Thirteen Colonies (to become the USA) entered Canada starting in 1776 and peaking in the early 1790s. These "United Empire Loyalists" moved mostly to Ontario, where more than 7,000 were counted in 1784; by 1812 there were 85,000 (Dollinger 2008a: 67–78).
II. Hundreds of thousands of immigrants from the "British Isles" (mostly Northern England, Scotland, and Ireland) arrived in Canada between 1815 and 1867, as a result of large-scale recruitment by the British government to counteract suspected pro-American sentiments.

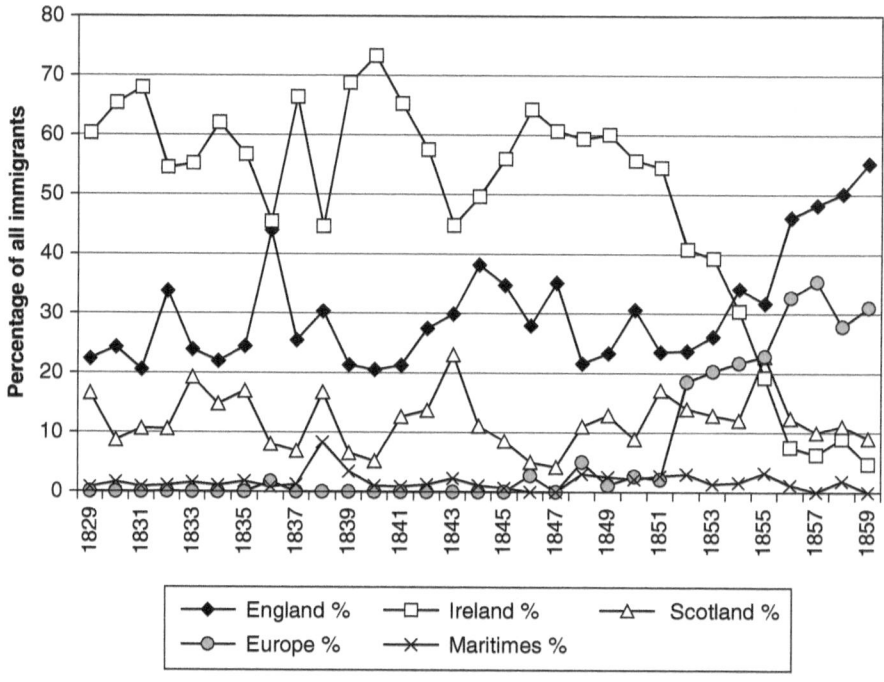

Figure 4.1: Arrivals at the Port of Quebec 1829–1859 (Dollinger 2008a: 81, based on Cowan 1961)

Figure 4.1 shows 19th-century arrivals in Quebec and their provenance. The English arrivals are, to more than 90%, from northern English areas, bringing with them a non-southern English dialect. The Scottish contingent is notable, while the Irish were the biggest group, whose role on historical CanE remains yet to be fully explored (see Clarke 1997b: 108). In total, about 470,000 Irish immigrants are counted in Figure 4.1, an average of more than 15,000 a year for the Irish alone.

III. Immigrants from diverse European homelands, such as Germany, the Austrian-Hungarian Empire, Italy, Scandinavia, the Ukraine, and including Scotland and Ireland, settled the Prairie Provinces and worked in the industrial centers in the East (c.1890–WWI).
IV. A highly diverse immigrant population of European, South-East Asian, and American provenance arrived as a result of post-World War II developments, peaking in the 1960s (Chambers 2010).
V. Ongoing immigration from all areas of the world, with a numerical focus on South-East and South Asia (China, Hong Kong, Pakistan, India), but including other areas such as Africa (e.g. Somalia), Latin America (Chile, Brazil, El Salvador), the Caribbean (e.g. Jamaica) and more recently the Middle East (e.g. Syria).

Developmental scenarios can generally be grouped in two camps: first, and representing the majority view (e.g. Bloomfield 1948; Avis 1973; Chambers 1998c; Dollinger 2008a), the first wave of immigrants are thought to have, by and large, set the speech patterns for the budding variety. This view is in accordance with the linguistic "founder principle" (Mufwene 1996). Second, an opposing view argues exclusively from numbers, maintaining that the large post-1815 British influx re-shuffled the developing speech ways and exerted linguistic influence. While the former is known as the Loyalist Base theory (Bloomfield 1948) and the more prominent theory today, the latter (Scargill 1957) is best labeled Numerical Swamping. While renewed interested has spurred work on the genesis of colonial dialects, questions of dialect formation remain disputed (see Dollinger 2008a: 122–127), with the historical role of dialect speakers (most notably the Irish, Clarke 1997b) still in need of study.

The importance of the second wave, i.e. immigration from the British Isles, is central in the Canadian context where pro-British sentiments have been felt. Today the phenomenon termed "Canadian Dainty" (Chambers 2004), i.e. the appreciation of BrE norms and fashions, including *linguistic* ones, died down after the mid-20th century (see also Section 4.6). The influence of waves III–V is of differing, but usually lesser degrees.

In connection with the second wave, the question of Canada's linguistic enclaves comes to the fore. In accordance with the founder principle, only places that were founded – in relative isolation – by second wave immigrants (and possibly later ones) preserved linguistic characteristics for some time. For the second wave, examples are found in the Ottawa Valley (Padolsky and Pringle 1981, which contains demographic information from a linguistic perspective), in Peterborough, Ontario, and in Lunenburg, Nova Scotia (Emenau 1975 [1935]; Trudgill 2001). Padolsky and Pringle (1984: 268–271), combine external information with mostly phonological variables in the Ottawa Valley, while Chambers and Lapierre (2011) use self-reports within a national sample.

Lastly, the province of Newfoundland and Labrador warrants separate treatment. Its settlement history documents an interesting mix of mostly South-East Irish and South-West English immigration (see Clarke 2010; Kirwin 2001 for an overview; Paddock 1982 for case studies). Since joining Canada in 1949, Newfoundland has undergone drastic economic changes (Clarke 2010: 9) which make it a highly interesting site for apparent-time study (e.g. Childs and Van Herk 2010; Thorburn 2011). This work is of relevance for the genesis of mainland CanE, as the relatively minor role of Irish English in CanE today needs to be explained in light of Figure 4.1 (e.g. Clarke 1997a).

3 Evidence, data, and methods in the historical linguistics of CanE

As we have seen in the previous section, there is a long tradition in developmental scenarios of CanE to argue exclusively from the external history. In the absence of real-time data, the existence of two extreme camps (M. Bloomfield 1948 and Scargill 1957) is not surprising. Early accounts were almost void of linguistic data and Scargill (1956) epitomizes the state of affairs, as his paper, entitled "Eighteenth-century English in Nova Scotia", *one* page in length, contains no linguistic analysis. The best early studies on historical data interpret literary representations, to which we turn in Section 3.1.

3.1 Literary representations of language

While a tradition exists in using literary representations to infer historical linguistic stages, this approach has fallen in disfavor given the advent of sociolinguistics. The most famous example of an early Canadian literary character is Yankee pedlar Sam Slick from Connecticut. Invented and penned by Nova Scotian judge Thomas Chandler Haliburton in the 1830s, Sam Slick's direct speech passages are fictional, contemporary representations of early 19th-century "Yankee" (New England) talk. With enormous commercial success, and a reported good ear, Haliburton depicted Eastern Seaboard dialects. Walter S. Avis studied Sam Slick novels in a historical linguistic/philological tradition and reconstructed Sam Slick's phonemic vowel system in his unpublished M.A. thesis (Avis 1950, see Avis 1969, much abbreviated), which is still of considerable interest today but underutilized. However, Bailey (1981) looks at the Nova Scotian characters in the same work, while Dollinger (2010a) uses 19th-century literary representations to trace the origin and spread of the low-back vowel merger in early Canada. Bengtsson (1956) studied Sam Slick apparently independently of Avis in the same tradition, but somewhat less innovatively.

Pringle (1981) analyzes the English depictions in early 20th-century Ontarian writer Ralph Connor for their Gaelic-influences. The use of written evidence, including literary sources, has recently seen a small revival (e.g. Hickey 2010; Minnick 2004; for CanE, see Dollinger 2010a: 192–194).

3.2 Self-report surveys

It is fair to say that Canadian dialect study has been largely carried out via self-report surveys. Starting with Avis (1954, 1955, 1956), self-reports have been used to describe CanE. In 1970, the national Survey of Canadian English (SCE) polled 16,000 grade 9 students and their parents on their use of linguistic variables. Supported by the Canadian Federation of Teachers results were published in Scargill and Warkentyne (1972), and, in slightly different form, in Scargill (1974). The SCE provides a real-time window into the early 1970s, and, via the students' parents, to the mid-1950s. As such, the SCE is an indispensible benchmark for historical comparisons. Attempts to collect *fieldwork* data for a North American linguistic atlas have usually stopped at the Canada-U.S. border, apart from early beginnings (by Henry Alexander in Nova Scotia), and occasional fieldwork in the 1930 and 1940s (in Ontario, Manitoba, Saskatchewan and New Brunswick). These unpublished data are accessible online at the Linguistic Atlas Project in Athens, Georgia, and are the best real-time data available (see Thomas 1991; Dollinger 2010a: 209–212 for details).

In sociolinguistics, Chambers (and graduate student Christine Zeller, Chambers 1994) reclaimed self-reports as a serious sociolinguistic method (Chambers 1998a; for a monograph on the method showcasing exclusively Canadian data, see Dollinger 2015a). Chambers's revival of self-reports, in his instantiation called "Dialect Topography", led to the collection of sociolinguistic self-reports from seven Canadian areas and four adjacent American locations available to everyone (The Dialect Topography data can be accessed at http://dialect.topography.chass.utoronto.ca/; last accessed 3 January 2017). A more recent application of self-reports is Boberg's (2005b) *North American Vocabulary Survey*, which used a webform to gather data on some 50 lexical items across the North American continent, allowing, for the first time in Canada, a statistically validated, data-driven establishment of dialect zones.

Self-reports are of extreme importance in CanE. They reach, via their older speakers, back to the early part of the 20th century (e.g. Chambers 2002) and can be compared to previous self-reports, such as SCE or Avis's or Gregg's surveys from the 1950s (e.g. Chambers 1998b: 20, 2002: 357; Boberg 2004b). Beyond the 1920s, however, apparent-time approaches offer no help.

3.3 Corpus linguistics

Historical corpus linguistics in the narrow sense of linguistic computing goes back to the Helsinki Corpus from the mid-1980s (Kytö 1996). This continental-European research methodology has been taken up with some delay in North America, with Canada lagging further behind. As recently as 2010, the *Corpus of Historical American English* (http://corpus.byu.edu/coha/, last accessed 14 April 2017) was made available (a large corpus from 1810 onwards). In Canada, experience with the *Corpus of Early Ontario English* (CONTE) (Dollinger 2006, corpus design in Dollinger 2008a: 99–120) has shown that some of the best material are manuscript sources which need to be transcribed manually.

The labour-intensive task of historical corpus compilation proper has not yet been addressed for CanE. There are, however, workarounds via digitized data and citations databases from lexical research. For historical CanE, a compact but tidy database is the *Bank of Canadian English* (BCE). The BCE is the online quotations database behind the revision of the *Dictionary of Canadianisms on Historical Principles* (Avis et al. 1967; Dollinger et al. 2006–) and currently comprises 2.7 million words of running text of CanE from 1555 to 2016 (Dollinger 2010b) of texts excerpts. The BCE allows the longitudinal tracing of frequent forms, such as shown in Figure 4.2.

Real-time data such as in Figure 4.2 are rare and complement existing apparent-time studies in important ways (e.g. Tagliamonte and D'Arcy 2007a for deontic modals).

CONTE (125,000 words) (http://faculty.arts.ubc.ca/sdollinger/CONTE.htm, last accessed 7 January 2017) or the BCE can be propped with other non-linguistically oriented data from print sources. Two of the best are *The Globe and Mail* (Canada's Heritage) with a range from 1844 to the present and the *Toronto Star* (Pages from the Past), from 1894 to 2004. Canadiana.org (http://www.canadiana.ca/en/home, last accessed 7 January 2017), a notable digitization project funded by the Canadian government, includes material in pdf-format throughout Canada's history until 1920, including novels, parliamentary reports, and travel reports. Recently, new historical corpora have been built with Reuter's (2017) 19th-century Ontario newspaper corpus and Meyer's (2015) 2-million word mixed corpus of three genres of 19th-century text.

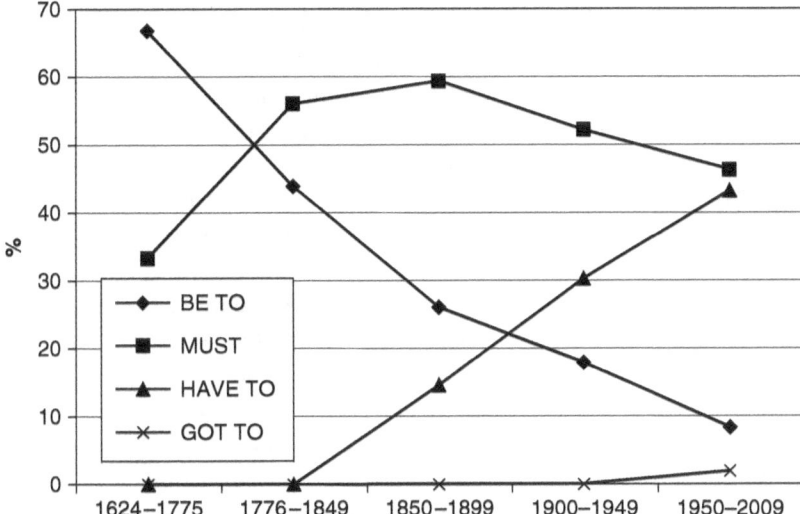

Figure 4.2: Deontic Obligation Markers (Bank of Canadian English, see Dollinger 2010c)

On the other end of the temporal spectrum, the 60 million-word the *Strathy Corpus* of present-day Canadian English (since 1985) (http://corpus.byu.edu/can/, last accessed 7 January 2017) has served as a research tool comparable in size (but not annotation) to the British National Corpus. It has been complemented by ICE Canada in 2010, a one million word corpus containing both written and spoken data from the early 1990s, edited by John Newman and Georgie Columbus.

3.4 Apparent-time approaches via sociolingustic interviews

Corpus linguistics and sociolinguistic interviews as a methodological tool dovetail in a number of areas (Dollinger 2015: 61–65). The Strathy and ICE Canada corpora are complemented by various sociolinguistic corpora of transcribed speech today, such as Tagliamonte's Toronto Corpus (e.g. Tagliamonte 2008), or Hoffman and Walker's datasets (e.g. Hoffman and Walker 2010), Poplack's Quebec English Corpus (e.g. Poplack et al. 2006), and, recently, on English in Victoria, BC.

From a historical perspective the most impressive apparent-time data is Poplack and Tagliamonte's (2001) collection for the African American diaspora in Nova Scotia, Canada (see Section 4.3).

3.5 Contact scenarios: historically-informed modeling

Recent developments in contact linguistics and the discussion around the formation of dialects in colonial settings have shifted the focus to a highly detailed integration of social history with linguistic history. One such model, Trudgill's (2004) New-Dialect Formation theory takes an extreme point of view with its focus on numerical input strength and its relegation of social factors to the sidelines in the first two generations after initial settlement. While provocative (see the discussion in, e.g., Trudgill 2008; Schneider 2008), Trudgill (2004) is a falsifiable model that can and should be put to scrutiny. Schneider (2007) is often pitted against Trudgill (2004), where, in fact, it is a model of entirely different scope. Trudgill is more specific, Schneider is more general in its focus and only superficially they seem to contradict one another. The bone of contention is the role of identity in the formation of a new dialect in new colonies (Hickey 2003; Schneider 2007: 30). Whatever the consensus will be, all approaches consider that demographic situations need to be integrated as fully as possible into linguistic modeling, addressing questions such as which groups of people, speaking which dialects, moved when to where and with what kinds of contacts with other groups.

The current discussion over the role of identity factors in the formation of postcolonial Englishes has also touched CanE (see, Schneider 2007: 238–50; Dollinger 2008a: 267–83 for two approaches). Real-time data suggests the following ranking of influences on Early Ontarian English prior to 1850: first, drift/parallel development in varieties of English; second, Loyalist base input; third, independent Canadian developments; and fourth, British influence (Dollinger 2008a: 279), while its interpretation remains open for debate.

With this renewed focus on external language history, it seems advisable to comb the archives to reconstruct the social historical record more fully. Perhaps the best resources, and best-practice example for historical linguistic work on any Canadian region can be found for Newfoundland and Labrador at the *Memorial University Folklore and Language Archive* (see http://www.mun.ca/folklore/munfla/ and http://www.mun.ca/elrc/, both last accessed 25 Jan. 2017, with some resources available online). Sister disciplines, such as rhetoric studies, offer interesting insights, e.g. Giltrow (2009) on the Hudson's Bay Company in the west, as historical census data will only be one starting point to such enquiry (see, e.g. Boberg 2010: 81; Dollinger 2007 for British Columbia).

4 Features of Canadian English in long-term perspective

In the remainder of this chapter, features of CanE that have been explored with significant diachronic data will be highlighted. Where possible, a preference will be given to real-time data. Although this section cannot claim completeness, it is hoped to reflect the state of the art of historical CanE. The situation today is significantly different to only a decade ago, when studies of the long-term development of the variety did "not yet exist" (Brinton and Fee 2001: 426).

4.1 Historical lexis

Lexis has traditionally been one of the most thoroughly studied areas in CanE. The work at Memorial University has led to the publication of a magnificent historical *Dictionary of Newfoundland English* (Story, Kirwin and Widdowson 1990, 1982), which is available online in open access (see http://www.heritage.nf.ca/dictionary/, last accessed 14 April 2017). Another project in Atlantic Canada, the *Dictionary of Prince Edward Island English* (Pratt 1988) is much smaller in scope, but equally ambitious in detail. In Canada, lexicographcial work in general has been spearheaded by the *Dictionary of Canadianisms on Historical Principles* (DCHP-1) (Avis et al. 1967; Lovell 1955), which is an early and much celebrated scholarly historical dictionary of the variety. DCHP-1, as a true milestone, triggered the first fully-Canadianized dictionary series, the Gage Canadian series, which exists to this day, inspiring later developments such as the *Canadian Oxford Dictionary* (1998, 2004) and the *ITP Nelson Canadian Dictionary* (1997). DCHP-1 is now available online for researchers (Dollinger, Brinton and Fee 2013). A Second Edition (Dollinger & Fee 2017) is now available at www.dchp.ca/dchp2 and is up-to-date till 2016, together with a host of novel features.

Overviews of Canadian lexis exist in Gregg (1993) and, more recently in Dollinger and Brinton (2008) and Dollinger and von Schneidemesser (2011). Perhaps the most striking characteristic of CanE lexis is its reliance on noun compounding, which takes a dominating role as a word-formation device. Since 1800, when the majority of Canadianisms was first formed by noun compounds, this process has been dominant. In the late 20th century, about 70% of all Candianisms are compounds, such as *grow op, seat sale, butter tart* or *video lottery terminal* (Dollinger and Brinton 2008: 52). We distinguish six basic types of Canadianisms (Dollinger & Fee 2017: Introduction), four of which are discussed below. Table 4.2 shows that the majority, or 57% of lemmas, are Type 1 Canadianisms, i.e. forms originating in Canada, which suggests a bias in the existing lists with historical and obsolete items:

Table 4.2: Types in CanE lexis (Dollinger and Brinton 2008: 52) in lemmas J, K, and L (Data analyzed by Breanna K. Laing in the spring of 2007).

Lemmas J, K, L	Type 1: Origin	Type 2: Preservation	Type 3: Semantic change	Type 4: Cultural saliency	TOTAL
Absolute	114	37	36	13	200
Relative	57 %	18.5 %	18 %	6.5 %	100 %

Table 4.2 shows a small number for Type 4, "culturally salient terms" (6.5%), such as (ice) hockey terms, forestry and mining terms. Of the 37 tokens that are Type 2, preservations from input varieties, 26 come from BrE, and 11 from AmE.

4.2 Historical phonetics and phonology

The most-widely known phenomenon of CanE is Canadian Raising (so named in Chambers 1973). Though not unique to Canada, it is a shibboleth that has found entry into popular culture. Noted in the 1930s, Canadian Raising (CR) was first described by Joos (1942), commented on by Avis (1956) and Gregg (1957), and studied by Chambers and collaborators who have traced the development of this feature over four decades, yielding a unique body of evidence in terms of diachronic real-time depth. Chambers (2006) is a summary and outlook on this phenomenon, which results in a raising of the onsets of the diphthongs /aʊ/ and /aɪ/ (Wells's MOUTH and PRICE sets) in voiceless contexts. Labov et al. (2006) identify CR as a Canadian feature, but as one whose sociophonetics are yet to be fully explored. Boberg (2010: 156–157) shows in a national sample that raised /aʊ/ (more so than raised /aɪ/) is one indicator for Canadian vowel systems when compared to American ones. Chambers and Hardwick (1986) noticed variation in raising of /aʊ/, which included a fronting process. Initially thought as declining, Canadian Raising prevails today from Toronto to Vancouver and Victoria (Hung et al. 1993; Chambers 2006: 117).

Canadian Raising has also produced a genuine real-time perspective, opening a discussion on its origins. Chambers (e.g. 1973: 122, 2006: 107) has long considered CR as a Canadian innovation, and Thomas (1991: 162), using unpublished 1930s linguistic atlas data, provides good evidence for this view, backdating CR to the 1880s. Gregg (1973: 141, 143) has argued from the background of vowel changes since the Great Vowel Shift that raising of /aɪ/ is not necessarily the result of contact phenomena in Canada, but, in the historically bigger picture, a "failure to lower" vowel onsets, which was carried out in StBrE and StAmE. Trudgill (1986: 154–156, 159), who offers the best summary on existing views on the origins of CR, proposes yet another scenario that is based on dialect mixing and reallocation of features in Canada (Trudgill 2004: 88). The majority opinion today points towards CR as a Canadian innovation, but settling this scholarly dispute is, perhaps, one of the most prized puzzles in historical CanE. Acoustic phonetics has recently provided a more precise picture of CR, which "does show clear regional differences, in terms of both its application and its phonetic output" (Boberg 2010: 204).

The sceptre of the one phonetic "pan-Canadian development" (Boberg 2008: 136), at least among middle-class speech, goes to another phonetic process, the Canadian Shift. First documented by Clarke et al. (1995), who identified it, roughly speaking, as a lowering and retraction in the front vowels, the Canadian Shift runs in the opposite direction than the American Northern Cities Shift (see Labov et al. 2006), and as such promotes the linguistic autonomy of Canada at least Canadian areas adjacent to the US "Inland North", such as southwestern Ontario (see Boberg 2008; also Roeder and Jarmasz 2010; Hoffman 2010).

Perspectives of historical phonology are also found in the literature, starting with the structuralist approaches by Avis (1956) and Gregg (1957). Labov et al. (2006) provide the continental perspective, while Boberg (2010: 125–137) assigns the CanE vowel system its place in the historical development since Middle English times, largely based on the low-back vowel merger (LOT, THOUGHT, and PALM) and the mid and low front vowel merger before /r/. The low-back vowel merger is an interesting case historically, as it is currently spreading in some parts of North America, while it has long attained categoricity in Canada, turning *cot* and *caught*, *stock* and *stalk* or *caller* and *collar* into homophones. As the phonologically most salient feature in CanE (shared with some U.S. regions), its origins are of particular interest. Chambers (1993: 11–12) from historical evidence and Dollinger (2010a: 217) with a broader database suggest its importation from merged U.S. regions prior to 1830. Boberg, however, does not rule out language contact from Scotland or Northern Ireland as a source or independent Canadian development (Boberg 2010: 128, 102). A solution of this conundrum is, just like the origin of Canadian Raising, another important desideratum.

Glide deletion, also called yod-dropping, has received substantial attention. Clarke (2006) uses data from Newfoundland from the past 30 years for comparisons with data by Woods (1999 [1979]) and Gregg (2004) to chart the highly complex picture of identity constructions of yod, whether people pronounce, e.g., *news* as /njuːz/ or /nuːz/. While these variants are, superficially, constructed as

British [yod-ful] vs. North American [yod-less] variants, Clarke (2006) disentangles such issues working with indexicalization and reindexicalization of social meaning in the Canadian and North American contexts. As a widely noticed variable, earlier reports are available (e.g. Pringle 1985). In the bigger picture of yod-dropping historically, Chambers (2002) describes the variable context in the long-term perspective.

4.3 Origins of African American English in Canada

An impressive body of research on the historical development of an ethnic variety that warrants separate treatment is the case of Nova Scotian African American speakers. Nestled in the greater discussion of the origins of African American Vernacular English (AAVE) (cf. Lanehart, Chapter 5), Poplack and Tagliamonte (e.g. 2001) gathered apparent-time data from two African communities in Nova Scotia, North Preston and Guysborough. The data are recordings of Canadian black descendants of ex-slaves who left with the "underground railway" for freedom in Canada (e.g. Poplack and Tagliamonte 1991, 2001; Poplack 2000). Dealing with morphosyntactic features that can be used as diagnostics with parallel corpora in the Caribbean and the UK, the authors reconstruct the spread of AAVE and go far beyond the usual relevance of apparent-time studies for historical linguistics. Variables include copula deletion, past tense marking (e.g. Poplack and Tagliamonte 1991), and verbal -s marking (e.g. Poplack and Tagliamonte 1994, 1989; Van Herk and Walker 2005 provide real-time, non-Canadian evidence, see Tagliamonte et al. 2005 for a methodological discussion).

4.4 Historical morphosyntax

Today, one can find an impressive range of studies from apparent-time perspectives. Studies are found for relative pronoun variation (e.g D'Arcy and Tagliamonte 2010), complementizers (e.g. Tagliamonte and Smith 2005), intensifiers (e.g. Tagliamonte 2008), non-standard -s marking (e.g. Childs and Van Herk 2010), negation (e.g. Thorburn 2011), definite article variation (Tagliamonte and Roeder 2009), past tense variation, and variation in existentials (e.g. Walker 2007) and beyond.

Five variables will be discussed representatively for similar grammatical variables: three for their importance as diagnostic features (*after* perfect, *going to* future tense and positive *anymore*) and two for their import in variationist studies (deontic modals and quotative *be like*). An interesting Irish relic feature is the *after* perfect, in sentences as *I'm after doing the dishes* for 'I (have) already finished the dishes', which is found most prominently in Newfoundland, but presumably less frequently in other parts of Canada (see Chambers 1986: 9 for some other regions). In Newfoundland, however, this construction has been spreading over the past century (Clarke 2010: 149). Another particularly interesting variable is the use of *going to* as a future marker, which can serve as a diagnostic to establish historical lineages based on English-descendant rural Nova Scotia English (Poplack and Tagliamonte 2000). *Positive anymore* has been noticed at least since the 1950s (Avis's files, Queen's University Archives, http://www.queensu.ca/strathy/, last accessed 14 April 2017), and Chambers (2007) summarizes the findings in the Ontarian context. *Anymore*, as in *Harry likes rock music anymore*, has a complex rule governing system which makes it a perfect diagnostic feature (though a near-extinct one today) for the settlement of Ontario with speakers from the American midlands (Wave I from Section 2).

Somewhat less diagnostically indicative but more widely studied are (sets of) the modal auxiliaries, with a focus on deontic markers of obligation and necessity (*must, have to, got to* and so forth, as seen in Figure 4.2 from a real-time perspective). Tagliamonte (2006b) and D'Arcy (2004), among others, approach the variables with an apparent-time approach, for which Dollinger (2006) provides a real-time component. Dollinger (2008a) is a diachronic study of 11 modal auxiliaries in real-time, tracing distributions back to the time immediately after the American Revolution in Trudgill's New-Dialect Formation theory. Jankowski (2004) also offers real-time data in a transatlantic comparison. Internationally considerable attention has been paid to quotative *be like* and Canadian data is also plentiful. Constructions as in *She's like, "Geez, what are you talking about?"* have been explored in a wide range of papers, for instance Tagliamonte and D'Arcy (2007b), Tagliamonte and Hudson (1999), which are of particular Canadian relevance. More recently, Reuter (2017) adds new historical data from Ontario confirming earlier historical work, while D'Arcy (2015) is an exploratory study of grammatical variation in early British Columbia.

Overall, the sheer multitude of variationist studies since about 1990, spearheaded by Shana Poplack, Sali Tagliamonte and their students, is staggering. Monograph-length treatments have appeared as well (e.g. Poplack and Tagliamonte 2001; Tagliamonte 2013), most of which making contributions to various aspects of historical CanE where the apparent-time data allow.

4.5 Historical pragmatics

Pragmatics as a relative newcomer has already produced a solid number of studies for CanE. Anecdotal evidence of Canadian politeness abounds and includes a number of core pragmatic phenomena. The most obvious pragmatic device associated with CanE is doubtless pragmatic marker *eh*. Occurring in sentences as diverse as *Nice day, eh?* or *What a game, eh?* or even fixed expression such as *Thanks, eh!* it has numerous meanings (Gold 2008; Columbus 2010). In an early paper on the variable, Avis (1972) took a real-time approach leading him to conclude, since *eh* had had currency in many national varieties of English, that it cannot be considered Canadian. Consequently, DCHP-1 (Avis et al. 1967) does not list it. From today's perspective, one needs to say that some Canadians have come to embrace *eh* as a linguistic identity marker. Shedding its substandard connotations since Avis carried out his studies, *eh* is today considered "a marker of both the Canadian English dialect and of Canadian national identity" (Gold and Tremblay 2006: 247).

By and large, however, work on pragmatic markers in real time has only begun. Brinton (2008) is one of the first pragmatic real-time studies that include CanE data. Based on robust quantitative data, Canadian characteristics of metalinguistic comments may appear to emerge, e.g. for *I think, if you will, as it were*, as shown in Figure 4.3:

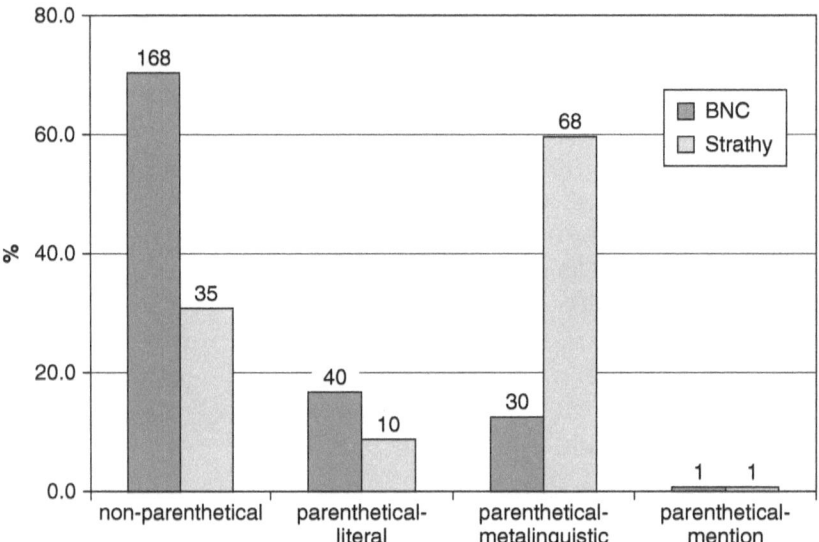

Figure 4.3: *If you will* in the British National Corpus and the CanE Strathy Corpus (percent and n) (Brinton 2008: 164)

The pragmatic uses of *if you will* in the meaning of 'if you'd like', the "parenthetical-metalinguistic" function, is used differently in terms of frequency in BrE (BNC) and CanE (Strathy, http://corpus.byu.edu/can/; last accessed 25 Jan. 2017). These solid data suggest that parenthetical *if you will* "is more fully grammaticalized as a pragmatic marker in Canadian English than in British English" (Brinton 2008: 164). Previous studies have, mostly in asides, also referred to pragmatic functions distinctive of CanE (e.g. Woods 1991: 145–147). Recent theories on the origin of the politeness marker *please*, initiated by the lower strata of society, have been corroborated for CanE data with a first attested use in 1794 (and thus 6 years after the first occurrence in BrE) by a lower-class writer (Dollinger 2008b: 275).

4.6 Historical language attitudes: Canadian Dainty and Yankee twang

Hultin (1967) opened the field with a qualitative study on Canadian attitudes toward AmE, while Chambers (1993 [1981]) is perhaps the first historical CanE attitude study. Rev. Geikie's 1857 condemnation of "Canadian English" as a "corrupt dialect" gave rise to comments, and is the first known attestation of Canadian English (Avis 1973).

An area closely linked with language attitudes is spelling. Pratt (1993) is one of the best overviews, Ireland (1979) an interesting (unpublished) monograph with both a real-time and a present-day component that shows the varying and apparently classification-defying spelling practices across the country. Gold (2004) and Dollinger (2007, 2008a: 124–127, 2015b) characterize 19th-century spelling practices. Spelling practices continue to attract attention with new analyses from various traditions, e.g. Meyer (2012).

More generally speaking, Canadian language attitudes (e.g. Warkentyne 1983) have been defined, for the longest time, by a slow emancipation of CanE in relation to the King's or Queen's English. Two phenomena are important in this context: first, Canada's slow progression toward independence (not until after World War I) and, second, one of the most profound attitude changes with the decline of "Canadian Dainty", i.e. a speaking style (until the mid-20th century) that was so Anglophile (as in *British* Standard English – cf. Peters, Chapter 120) that it made, in the joking words of Canadian poet Irving Layton, any Englishman "wince and feel/unspeakably colonial" (Layton 1992 [1956]: 87, Chambers 2004).

5 Desiderata and outlook

Throughout this short overview various desiderata have been pointed out. Two projects of prime importance come to mind, due to their potential as catalysts for historical research. A complete synchronic dialect survey of Canada would provide stimulus for diachronic research. While such a goal may be as yet illusory, more immediate and realistic aims are the creation of historical corpora that are fully stratified and thus go beyond the BCE. Theoretically, the most profound dispute in the development of CanE centers on the assessment of its input varieties and feeds into the bigger discussion of overseas dialect development. Any such approach in CanE must integrate the Loyalist Base with Numerical Swamping in the long-overdue "more balanced view" (Chambers 1975: 2), for which some suggestions have already been offered (e.g. Dollinger 2008a: 275–283).

Acknowledgements: I would like to thank an anonymous reviewer for critically reading a 2008 draft of this chapter.

6 References

Algeo, John (ed.). 2001. *The Cambridge History of the English Language*. Vol. VI: *English in North America*. Cambridge: Cambridge University Press.
Avis, Walter S. 1950. *The speech of Sam Slick*. MA Thesis, Queen's University, Kingston, Ontario.
Avis, Walter S. 1954. Speech differences along the Ontario-United States border. I: Vocabulary. *Journal of the Canadian Linguistic Association* 1: 13–18.
Avis, Walter S. 1955. Speech differences along the Ontario-United States border. II: Grammar and syntax. *Journal of the Canadian Linguistic Association* 1: 14–19.
Avis, Walter S. 1956. Speech differences along the Ontario-United States border. III: Pronunciation. *Journal of the Canadian Linguistic Association* 2: 41–59.
Avis, Walter S. 1969. A note on the speech of Sam Slick. In: Reginald E. Watters and Walter S. Avis (eds.), *The Sam Slick Anthology*, . Toronto: Clarke, Irwin & Co.
Avis, Walter S. 1972. So *Eh?* is Canadian, *Eh? Canadian Journal of Linguistics* 17(2): 89–104.
Avis, Walter S. 1973. The English language in Canada. In: Thomas Sebeok (ed.), *Current Trends in Linguistics*. Vol. 10/1, 40–74. The Hague: Mouton.
Avis, Walter S., Charles Crate, Patrick Drysdale, Douglas Leechman, Matthew H. Scargill, and Charles L. Lovell (eds.). 1967. *A Dictionary of Canadianisms on Historical Principles*. Toronto: Gage.
Bailey, Richard W. 1981. Haliburton's *eye* and *ear*. *Canadian Journal of Linguistics* 26: 90–101.
Bailey, Richard W. 1982. The English language in Canada. In: Richard W. Bailey and Manfred Görlach (eds.), *English as a World Language*, 134–176. Ann Arbor: University of Michigan Press.
Bailey, Richard W. 1991. Dialects of Canadian English. *English Today* 27: 20–25.

Ball, Jessica and Bernhardt B. May. 2008. First Nations English dialects in Canada: Implications for speech-language pathology. *Clinical Linguistics & Phonetics* 22: 570–588.
Bengtsson, Elna. 1956. *The Language and Vocabulary of Sam Slick*. Part 1. Copenhagen: Munksgaard.
Bloomfield, Morton W. 1948. Canadian English and its relation to eighteenth century American speech. *Journal of English and Germanic Philology* 47: 59–66 [reprinted in Chambers (ed.). 1975, 3–11].
Boberg, Charles. 2004a. Ethnic patterns in the phonetics of Montreal English. *Journal of Sociolinguistics* 8(4): 538–568.
Boberg, Charles. 2004b. Real and apparent time in language change: late adoption of changes in Montreal English. *American Speech* 79(3): 250–269.
Boberg, Charles. 2005a. The Canadian Shift in Montreal. *Language Variation and Change* 17(2): 133–154.
Boberg, Charles. 2005b. The North American Regional Vocabulary Survey: new variables and methods in the study of North American English. *American Speech* 80(1): 22–60.
Boberg, Charles. 2008. Regional phonetic differentiation in Standard Canadian English. *Journal of English Linguistics* 36(2): 129–154.
Boberg, Charles. 2010. *The English Language in Canada: Status, History and Comparative Analysis*. Cambridge: Cambridge University Press.
Brinton, Laurel J. 2008. *The Comment Clause in English: Syntactic Origins and Pragmatic Development*. Cambridge: Cambridge University Press.
Brinton, Laurel J. and Margery Fee. 2001. Canadian English. In: Algeo (ed.), 422–440.
Chambers, Jack K. 1973. Canadian raising. *Canadian Journal of Linguistics* 18(2): 113–135.
Chambers, Jack K. (ed.). 1975. *Canadian English: Origins and Structures*. Toronto: Methuen.
Chambers, Jack K. (ed.). 1979. *The Languages of Canada*. Montreal: Didier.
Chambers, Jack K. 1980. Linguistic variation and Chomsky's 'homogeneous speech community'. In: A. Murray Kinloch and A. B. House (eds), *Papers from the Fourth Annual Meeting of the Atlantic Provinces Linguistic Association*, 1–31. Fredericton: University of New Brunswick.
Chambers, Jack K. 1986. Three kinds of standard in Canadian English. In: William C. Lougheed (ed.), *In Search of the Standard in Canadian English*, 1–19. Kingston, Ont.: Queen's University.
Chambers, Jack K. 1993. 'Lawless and vulgar innovations': Victorian views on Canadian English. In: Sandra Clarke (ed.), 1–26.
Chambers, Jack K. 1994. An introduction to dialect topography. *English World-Wide* 15: 35–53.
Chambers, Jack K. 1998a. Inferring dialect from a postal questionnaire. *Journal of English Linguistics* 26(3): 222–246.
Chambers, Jack K. 1998b. Social embedding of changes in progress. *Journal of English Linguistics* 26(1): 5–36.
Chambers, Jack K. 1998c. English: Canadian varieties. In: John Edwards (ed.), *Language in Canada*, 252–272. Cambridge: Cambridge University Press.
Chambers, Jack K. 2002. Patterns of variation and change. In: Jack K. Chambers, Peter Trudgill, and Natalie Schilling-Estes (eds.), *The Handbook of Language Variation and Change*, 349–372. Malden, MA: Blackwell.
Chambers, Jack K. 2004. 'Canadian Dainty': the rise and decline of Briticisms in Canada. In: Raymond Hickey (ed.), *Legacies of Colonial English. Studies in Transported Dialects*, 224–241. Cambridge: Cambridge University Press.

Chambers, Jack K. 2006. Canadian Raising retrospect and prospect. *Canadian Journal of Linguistics* 51(2 and 3): 105–118.
Chambers, Jack K. 2007. A linguistic fossil: positive any more in the Golden Horseshoe. In: Peter Reich, William J. Sullivan, Arle R. Lommel, and Toby Griffen (eds.), *LACUS Forum XXXIII: Variation*, 31–44. Houston, TX: Linguistic Association of Canada and the United States.
Chambers, Jack K. 2009. *Sociolinguistic Theory*. 3rd revised edn. Malden, MA: Wiley-Blackwell.
Chambers, Jack K. 2010. English in Canada. In: Elaine Gold and Janice McAlpine (eds.), *Canadian English: A Linguistic Reader*, 1–37. Kingston, ON: Queen's University [*Strathy Language Unit Occasional Papers*, 6]. http://www.queensu.ca/strathy/apps/OP6v2.pdf; last accessed 14 April 2017.
Chambers, Jack K. and Margaret F. Hardwick. 1986. Comparative sociolinguistics of a sound change in Canadian English. *English World-Wide* 7: 124–146.
Chambers, Jack K. and André Lapierre. 2011. Dialect variants in the bilingual belt. In: France Martineau and Terry Nadasdi (eds.), *Papers in Honour of Raymond Mougeon, 35-50*. Québec: Presses de l'Université Laval.
Childs, Becky and Gerard Van Herk. 2010. Breaking old habits: Syntactic constraints underlying habitual effects in Newfoundland English. In: James A. Walker (ed.), *Linguistic Variation and Verbal Aspect*, 81–93. Amsterdam/Philadelphia: John Benjamins.
Clarke, Sandra. 1982. Sampling attitudes to dialect varieties in St. John's. In: Harold J. Paddock (ed.), *Languages in Newfoundland and Labrador*, 2nd edn., 90–105. St. John's: Memorial University of Newfoundland.
Clarke, Sandra. 1991. Phonological variation and recent language change in St. John's English. In: Jenny Cheshire (ed.), *English around the world. Sociolinguistic perspectives*, 108–122. Cambridge: Cambridge University Press.
Clarke, Sandra (ed.). 1993a. *Focus on Canada*. Amsterdam/Philadelphia: John Benjamins.
Clarke, Sandra. 1993b. The Americanization of Canadian Pronunciation: a survey of palatal glide usage. In: Sandra Clarke (ed.), 85–108.
Clarke, Sandra. 1997a. English verbal – s revisited: the evidence from Newfoundland. *American Speech* 72(3): 227–259.
Clarke, Sandra. 1997b. The role of Irish English in the formation of New Englishes: the case from Newfoundland. In: Jeffrey Kallen (ed.), *Focus on Ireland*, 207–225. Amsterdam/Philadelphia: John Benjamins.
Clarke, Sandra. 2006. *Nooz* or *nyooz*?: the complex construction of Canadian identity. *Canadian Journal of Linguistics* 51(2 and 3): 225–246.
Clarke, Sandra. 2010. *Newfoundland and Labrador English*. Edinburgh: Edinburgh University Press.
Clarke, Sandra, Ford Elms and Amani Youssef. 1995. The third dialect of English: some Canadian evidence. *Language Variation and Change* 7: 209–228.
Columbus, Georgie. 2010. 'Nice day, eh?': Canadian and New Zealand eh compared. In: Clive Upton and Barry Heselwood (eds.), *Methods in Dialectology: Proceedings of the 2008 International Conference*, 219–228. Frankfurt am Main: Peter Lang.
Cowan, Helen. 1961. *British Immigration to British North America: the First Hundred Years*. Rev. and enl. edn. Toronto: University of Toronto Press.
D'Arcy, Alexandra. 2004. Contextualizing St. John's Youth English within the Canadian quotative system. *Journal of English Linguistics* 32(4): 323–345.
D'Arcy, Alexandra. 2015. At the crossroads of change: possession, periphrasis and prescriptivism in Victoria English. In: *Grammatical Change in English World-Wide*, ed. by Peter Collins, 43–64. Amsterdam: Benjamins.

D'Arcy, Alexandra and Sali Tagliamonte. 2010. Prestige, accommodation and the legacy of relative who. *Language in Society* 39(3): 1–28.

De Wolf, Gaelan Dodds. 1992. *Social and regional factors in Canadian English: a study of phonological variables and grammatical items in Ottawa and Vancouver*. Toronto: Canadian Scholar's Press.

Dollinger, Stefan. 2006. The modal auxiliaries HAVE TO and MUST in the Corpus of Early Ontario English: gradience and colonial lag. *Canadian Journal of Linguistics* 51(2 and 3): 287–308.

Dollinger, Stefan. 2007. English-German bilingualism in British Columbia past to present: data, evidence, challenges. In: Ute Smit, Stefan Dollinger, Julia Hüttner, Gunther Kaltenböck, and Ursula Lutzky (eds.), *Tracing English through Time: Explorations in Language Variation*, 51–77. Vienna: Braumüller.

Dollinger, Stefan. 2008a. *New-Dialect Formation in Canada: Evidence from the English Modal Auxiliaries*. Amsterdam/Philadelphia: John Benjamins.

Dollinger, Stefan. 2008b. Colonial variation in the Late Modern English business letter: 'periphery and core' or 'random variation'? In: Marina Dossena and Ingrid Tieken-Boon van Ostade (eds.), *Studies in Late Modern English Correspondence: Methodology and Data*, 257–287. Bern: Lang.

Dollinger, Stefan. 2010a. Written sources of Canadian English: Phonetic Reconstruction and the Low-Back Vowel Merger. In: Raymond Hickey (ed.), *Varieties in Writing: The Written Word as Linguistic Evidence*, 197–222. Amsterdam/Philadelphia: John Benjamins.

Dollinger, Stefan. 2010b. A new historical dictionary of Canadian English as a linguistic database tool. Or, making a virtue out of necessity. In: John Considine (ed.), *Current Projects in Historical Lexicography*, 99–112. Newcastle upon Tyne: Cambridge Scholars Publishing.

Dollinger, Stefan. 2010c. The realm of deontic, dynamic and epistemic obligation/necessity in Canadian English: *must, have to, got to* and other suspects revisited. American Dialect Society, Annual Meeting. Baltimore, MD, 8 January 2010.

Dollinger, Stefan 2011a. On Standard Canadian English: notions of "standard" and the widening gap between scholarly research and public discourse. *English Today* 27(4): 3–9.

Dollinger, Stefan, Laurel J. Brinton and Margery Fee (eds.) 2013. *DCHP-1 Online: A Dictionary of Canadianisms on Historical Principles Online*. Based on Avis et al. (1967). http://dchp.ca/dchp1/ (last access 25 Jan. 2017).

Dollinger, Stefan. 2015a. *The Written Questionnaire in Social Dialectology: History, Theory, Practice*. Amsterdam: Benjamins.

Dollinger, Stefan. 2015b. Emerging standards in the colonies: variation and the Canadian letter writer. In: Anita Auer, Daniel Schreier and Richard J. Watts (eds.) *Letter Writing and Language Change*, 101–113. Cambridge: Cambridge University Press.

Dollinger, Stefan, Laurel J. Brinton and Margery Fee. 2006–. *Dictionary of Canadianisms on Historical Principles*. 2nd edn. University of British Columbia at Vancouver, Department of English. www.dchp.ca (last accessed 7 January 2012).

Dollinger, Stefan and Laurel J. Brinton. 2008. Canadian English lexis: historical and variationist perspectives. *Anglistik* 19(2): 43–64.

Dollinger, Stefan and Sandra Clarke. 2012. On the autonomy and homogeneity of Canadian English. *World Englishes* 31(4):449–466. Special issue: Autonomy and Homogeneity of Canadian English. Ed. by Stefan Dollinger and Sandra Clarke.

Dollinger, Stefan and Luanne von Schneidemesser. 2011. Canadianism, Americanism, North Americanism? A Comparison of DARE and DCHP. *American Speech* 86(2): 115–151.

Dollinger, Stefan (chief editor) and Margery Fee (associate editor). 2017. *DCHP-2: The Dictionary of Canadianisms on Historical Principles*, Second Edition. With the assistance of Baillie Ford, Alexandra Gaylie, and Gabrielle Lim. Online dictionary. Vancouver, BC: University of British Columbia. www.dchp.ca/dchp2; last accessed 17 March 2017.
Emenau, Murray B. 1975 [1935]. The dialect of Lunenburg, Nova Scotia. *Language* 11: 140–147. [reprinted in J. K. Chambers (ed.), 1975, 34–39].
Falk, Lilian and Margaret Harry (eds.). 1999. *The English Language in Nova Scotia: Essays on Past and Present Developments in English Across the Province*. Lockeport, N.S.: Roseway Publishing.
Giltrow, Janet. 2009. 'Curious gentlemen': the Hudson's Bay Company and the Royal Society, business and science in the eighteenth century. In: D. Starke- Meyerring, A. Paré, N. Artemeva, M. Horne and L. Yousoubova (eds.), *Writing (in) the Knowledge Society*. West Lafayette, IN: Parlor Press.
Gold, Elaine. 2004. Teachers, texts and Early Canadian English: Upper Canada 1791–1841. In: Sophie Burelle and Stana Somesfalean (eds.), *Proceedings of the 2003 Annual Conference of the Canadian Linguistic Association*. CD-ROM, 85–96. Montreal: Université du Québec à Montréal.
Gold, Elaine. 2008. Canadian *Eh*? From *Eh* to *Zed*. *Anglistik* 19(2): 141–156.
Gold, Elaine and Mireille Tremblay. 2006. *Eh*? and *Hein*?: Discourse particles or national icons? *Canadian Journal of Linguistics* 51(2and3): 247–264.
Gregg, Robert J. 1957. Notes on the pronunciation of Canadian English as spoken in Vancouver, British Columbia. *Journal of the Canadian Linguistic Association* 3: 20–26.
Gregg, Robert J. 1973. The diphthongs əi and ai in Scottish, Scotch-Irish and Canadian English. *Canadian Journal of Linguistics* 18(2): 136–145.
Gregg, Robert J. 1993. Canadian English lexicography. In: Sandra Clarke (ed.), *Focus on Canada*, 27–44. Amsterdam/Philadelphia: John Benjamins.
Gregg, Robert J. 2004 [1984]. The Survey of Vancouver English. A sociolinguistic study of urban Canadian English. In: Gaelan Dodds de Wolf, Margery Fee, and Janice McAlpine (eds.), *Strathy Language Unit Occasional Papers 5*. Kingston: Queen's University.
Hamilton, Donald E. 1975 [1958]. Notes on Montreal English. *Journal of the Canadian Linguistic Association* 4(1): 70–79 [reprinted in Chambers (ed.). 1975, 46–54].
Heller, Monica. 2010. *Paths to Post-Nationalism: A Critical Ethnography of Language and Identity*. Oxford: Oxford University Press.
Hickey, Raymond. 2003. How do dialects get the features they have? In: Raymond Hickey (ed.), *Motives for Language Change*, 213–239. Cambridge: Cambridge University Press.
Hickey, Raymond (ed.). 2010. *Varieties of English in Writing*. Amsterdam/Philadelphia: John Benjamins.
Hoffman, Michol F. 2010. The role of social factors in the Canadian Vowel Shift: evidence from Toronto. *American Speech* 85(2): 121–140.
Hoffman, Michol F. and James A. Walker. 2010. Ethnolects and the city: ethnic orientation and linguistic variation in Toronto English. *Language Variation and Change* 22: 37–67.
Hultin, Neil C. 1967. Canadian views of American English. *American Speech* 42: 243–260.
Hung, Henrietta, John Davison and Jack K. Chambers. 1993. Comparative sociolinguistics of (aw)-fronting. In: Sandra Clarke (ed.), 247–268.
Ireland, Robert J. 1979. *Canadian spelling. An empirical and historical survey of selected words*. PhD Thesis: York University, Toronto, Ontario.

Jankowski, Bridget. 2004. A transatlantic perspective of variation and change in English deontic modality. *Toronto Working Papers in Linguistics* 23(2): 85–113.
Joos, Martin. 1942. A phonological dilemma in Canadian English. *Language* 18: 141–144.
Kiefte, Michael and Elizabeth Kay-Raining Bird. 2010. Canadian Maritime English. In: Daniel Schreier, Peter Trudgill, Edgar W. Schneider, and Jeffrey P. Williams (eds.), *The Lesser-Known Varieties of English: An Introduction,* 59–71. Cambridge: Cambridge University Press.
Kirwin, William. 2001. Newfoundland English In: John Algeo (ed.), 441–455.
Kytö, Merja. 1996. *Manual to the Diachronic Part of the Helsinki Corpus of English Texts.* 3rd edn. Helsinki: University of Helsinki (Dept. of English).
Labov, William, Sharon Ash, and Charles Boberg. 2006. *The Atlas of North American English. Phonetics, Phonology and Sound Change.* Berlin and New York: Mouton de Gruyter.
Layton, Irving. 1992 [1956]. *Fornalutx: Selected Poems.* Montreal: McGill-Queen's University Press.
Levey, Stephen. 2010. The Englishes of Canada. In: Andy Kirkpatrick (ed.), *Routledge Handbook of World Englishes,* 113–131. New York: Routledge.
Lovell, Charles J. 1955. Whys and hows of collecting for the Dictionary of Canadian English: Part I: Scope and source material. *Journal of the Canadian Linguistic Association* 1(2): 3–8.
Meyer, Matthias L. G. 2012. The distinctiveness of Canadian English. In: Helga Bories Swala and Norbert Schaffeld (ed.). *Who Speaks Canadian?* Diversity, Identities and Language Policies, 1–24. Bochum: Brockmeyer.
Meyer, Matthias L. G. 2015. Passives of so-called 'ditransitives' in nineteenth century and present-day Canadian English. In: Peter Collins (ed.) *Grammatical Change in English World-Wide,* 147–177. Amsterdam: Benjamins.
Minnick, Lisa Cohen. 2004. *Dialect and Dichotomy: Literary Representations of African American Speech.* Tuscaloosa, AB: The University of Alabama Press.
Mufwene, Salikoko S. 1996. The founder principle in creole genesis. *Diachronica* 13: 83–134.
Nylvek, Judith A. 1992. Is Canadian English in Saskatchewan becoming more American? *American Speech* 67(3): 268–278.
Paddock, Harold J. (ed.). 1982. *Languages in Newfoundland and Labrador.* 2nd edn. St. John's, Nfld: Memorial University of Newfoundland.
Padolsky, Enoch and Ian Pringle. 1984. Demographic analysis and regional dielect surveys in Canada: data collection and use. In: Donald H. Akenson (ed.), *Canadian Papers in Rural History.* Vol. IV, 240–275. Gananoque, Ont.: Langdale Press.
Padolsky, Enoch and Ian Pringle. 1981. *A Historical Source Book for the Ottawa Valley. A Linguistic Survey of the Ottawa Valley.* Ottawa: Carelton University, Linguistic Survey of the Ottawa Valley.
Poplack, Shana (ed.). 2000. *The English History of African American English.* Malden, MA: Blackwell.
Poplack, Shana, James A. Walker, and Rebecca Malcolmson. 2006. An English "like no other"?: language contact and change in Quebec. *Canadian Journal of Linguistics* 51(2 and 3): 185–214.
Poplack, Shana and Sali Tagliamonte. 1989. There's no tense like the present: verbal -s inflection in Early Black English. *Language Variation and Change* 1: 47–84.
Poplack, Shana and Sali Tagliamonte. 1991. African American English in the diaspora: evidence from old-line Nova Scotians. *Language Variation and Change* 3: 301–339.

Poplack, Shana and Sali Tagliamonte. 1994. *-s* or nothing: marking the plural in the African-American diaspora. *American Speech* 69: 227–259.
Poplack, Shana and Sali Tagliamonte. 2000. The grammaticalization of *going to* in (African American) English. *Language Variation and Change* 11: 315–342.
Poplack, Shana and Sali Tagliamonte. 2001. *African American English in the Diaspora*. Oxford: Blackwell.
Pratt, Terrence K. (ed.). 1988. *Dictionary of Prince Edward Island English*. Toronto: University of Toronto Press.
Pratt, Terrence K. 1993. The hobglobin of Canadian English spelling. In: Sandra Clarke (ed.), *Focus on Canada*, 45–64. Amsterdam/Philadelphia: John Benjamins.
Priestley, F. R. L. 1968 [1951]. Canadian English. In: Eric Partridge and John W. Clark (eds.), *British and American English since 1900*, 72–84. New York: Greenwood Press.
Pringle, Ian. 1981. The Gaelic substratum in the English of Glengarry County and its reflection in the novels of Ralph Connor. *Canadian Journal of Linguistics* 26: 126–140.
Pringle, Ian. 1985. Attitudes to Canadian English In: Sidney Greenbaum (ed.), *The English Language Today*, 183–205. Oxford: Pergamon.
Reuter, David M. J. 2017. *Newspaper, politics, and Canadian English: a corpus-based analysis of selected linguistic variables in early nineteenth-century Ontario newspapers*. Heidelberg: Winter.
Roeder, Rebecca and Lidia-Gabriella Jarmasz. 2010. The Canadian Shift in Toronto. *Canadian Journal of Linguistics* 55(3): 387–404.
Scargill, Matthew H. 1956. Eighteenth century English in Nova Scotia. *Journal of the Canadian Linguistic Association* 2/1: 3.
Scargill, Matthew H. 1957. Sources of Canadian English. *Journal of English and Germanic Philology* 56: 611–614 [reprinted in Chambers (ed.). 1975, 12–15].
Scargill, Matthew H. 1974. *Modern Canadian English Usage: Linguistic Change and Reconstruction*. Toronto: McClelland and Stewart.
Scargill, Matthew H. 1977. *A Short History of Canadian English*. Victoria, B.C.: Sono Nis.
Scargill, Matthew H. and Henry J. Warkentyne. 1972. The Survey of Canadian English: a report. *English Quarterly* 5(3): 47–104.
Schneider, Edgar W. 2007. *Postcolonial English: Varieties Around the World*. Cambridge: Cambridge University Press.
Schneider, Edgar W. 2008. Accommodation versus identity? A response to Trudgill. *Language in Society* 37: 241–280.
Story, G. M., W. J. Kirwin and J. D. A. Widdowson (eds.) ^{2}1990 [^{1}1982] *Dictionary of Newfoundland English*. Toronto: University of Toronto Press. http://www.heritage.nf.ca/dictionary/; last accessed 14 April 2017.
Tagliamonte, Sali. 2006a. "So cool, right?": Canadian English entering the 21st century. *Canadian Journal of Linguistics* 51(2 and 3): 309–332.
Tagliamonte, Sali. 2006b. Historical change in synchronic perspective: the legacy of British dialects. In: Ans van Kemenade and Bettelou Los (eds.), *The Handbook of the History of English*, 477–506. Malden, MA: Blackwell.
Tagliamonte, Sali. 2008. So different and pretty cool: Recycling intensifiers in Toronto, Canada. *English Language and Linguistics* 12(2): 361–394.
Tagliamonte, Sali 2013. *Roots of English: Exploring the History of Dialects*. Cambridge: Cambridge University Press.

Tagliamonte, Sali and Rachel Hudson. 1999. *Be like* et al. beyond America: the quotative system in British and Canadian youth. *Journal of Sociolinguistics* 3(2): 147–172.
Tagliamonte, Sali and Jennifer Smith. 2005. No momentary fancy! The zero complementizer in English dialects. *English Language and Linguistics* 9(2): 1–12.
Tagliamonte, Sali, Jennifer Smith, and Helen Lawrence. 2005. Disentangling the roots: the legacy of British dialects in cross-variety perspective. In: Markku Filppula, Juhani Klemola, Marjattea Palander, and Esa Penttilä (eds.) *Dialects across borders: Selected papers from the 11th International Conference on Methods in Dialectology (Methods XI)*. 87–117. Joensuu: Joensuu University Press.
Tagliamonte, Sali and Alexandra D'Arcy. 2007a. The modals of obligation/necessity in Canadian perspective. *English World-Wide* 28(1): 47–87.
Tagliamonte, Sali and Alexandra D'Arcy. 2007b. Frequency and variation in the community grammar: Tracking a new change through the generations. *Language Variation and Change* 19: 199–217.
Tagliamonte, Sali and Alexandra D'Arcy. 2009. Peaks beyond phonology: adolescence, incrementation, and language change. *Language* 85(1): 58–108.
Tagliamonte, Sali and Rebecca V. Roeder. 2009. Variation in the English definite article: Sociohistorical linguistic in t'speech community. *Journal of Sociolinguistics* 13(4): 435–471.
Thomas, Eric R. 1991. The origin of Canadian Raising in Ontario. *Canadian Journal of Linguistics* 36: 147–170.
Thorburn, Jennifer. 2011. "There's no place like Petty Harbour": negation in a post-insular community. *RLS – Regional Language Studies ... Newfoundland* 22(1): 8–17.
Torres Cacoullos, Rena and James A. Walker. 2009. The present of the English future: grammatical variation and collocations in discourse. *Language* 85(2): 321–354.
Trudgill, Peter. 1986. *Dialects in Contact*. Oxford: Blackwell.
Trudgill, Peter. 2001. Sociohistorical linguistics and dialect survival: a note on another Nova Scotian enclave. In: Magnus Ljung (ed.), *Language Structure and Variation*, 195–201. Stockholm: Almqvist and Wiksell.
Trudgill, Peter. 2004. *New-Dialect Formation: the Inevitability of Colonial Englishes*. Edinburgh: Edinburgh University Press.
Trudgill, Peter. 2008. Colonial dialect contact in the history of European languages: on the irrelevance of identity to new-dialect formation. *Language in Society* 37: 241–254.
Van Herk, Gerard and James A. Walker. 2005. S marks the spot? Regional variation and early African American correspondence. *Language Variation and Change* 17: 113–131.
Walker, James A. 2007. "There's bears back there": Plural existentials and vernacular universals in (Quebec) English. *English World-Wide* 28(2): 147–166.
Warkentyne, Henry J. 1983. Attitudes and language behavior. *Canadian Journal of Linguistics* 28: 71–76.
Wilson, H. Rex. 1958. *The dialect of Lunenburg County, Nova Scotia. A study of the English of the county, with reference to its sources, preservation of relics, and vestiges of bilingualism*. PhD Thesis, University of Michigan.
Woods, Howard B. 1999 [1979]. *The Ottawa Survey of Canadian English*. Kingston: Queen's University.
Woods, Howard B. 1991. Social differentiation in Ottawa English. In: Jenny Cheshire (ed.), *English Around the World: Sociolinguistic Perspectives*, 134–152. Cambridge: Cambridge University Press.

Sonja L. Lanehart
Chapter 5:
Re-viewing the origins and history of African American Language

1   Introduction —— 81
2   Deficit position —— 82
3   Structural views of AAL —— 83
4   The big dogs in the fight: Anglicists and Creolists —— 86
5   Substratist, restructuralist, ecological, and divergence theorists —— 89
6   Summary —— 91
7   References —— 92

Abstract: This chapter reviews the differing positions concerning the history and development of African American Language (AAL), the impact of each position, and conclusions about the direction of these positions for future research in AAL and the communities involved. The positions discussed are: (1) Anglicist (aka Dialectologist), which purports that Africans in America learned regional varieties of British English dialects from British overseers with little to no influence from their own native African languages and cultures; (2) Creolist, which purports that AAL developed from a prior US creole developed by slaves that was widespread across the colonies and slave-holding areas (though Neo-Creolists acknowledge there likely was not a widespread creole but one that emerged in conditions favorable to creole development); (3) Substratist, which purports that distinctive patterns of AAL are those that occur in Niger-Congo languages such as Kikongo, Mande, and Kwa; (4) Ecological and Restructuralist, which is a perspective within the Anglicist position that acknowledges the difficulty of knowing the origins of AAL but proposes that we can say something useful about Earlier AAL (not nascent AAL) given settlement and migration patterns as well as socio-ecological issues; (5) Divergence/Convergence, which purports that AAL diverges and converges to White varieties over the course of its history with respect to changes in and degrees of racism, segregation, inequalities, and inequities that fluctuate across time and differ regionally; and (6) Deficit, which purports that AAL is based on the assumption that Africans in America and their culture are inferior to whites and their language learning as a result was imperfect and bastardized. Though the

---

Sonja L. Lanehart: San Antonio (USA)

substance of and support for each position varies, ideological and epistemological perspectives of their originators and supporters cannot go unexamined.

1 Introduction

Like most language varieties that are considered non-standard, African American Language (AAL) developed and continues to persist partly because, often, the communities that speak it do not have much contact with other ways of speaking and/or because such communities may define themselves by their speech (Ogbu 1992). According to Geneva Smitherman in *Black Talk* (1994),

> As far as historians, linguists, and other scholars go, during the first half of this [i.e., 20th] century it was widely believed that enslavement had wiped out all traces of African languages and cultures, and that Black 'differences' resulted from imperfect and inadequate imitations of European American language and culture. (Smitherman 1994: 4)

Many in the African American community share these beliefs despite their continued use of AAL. They either refuse to publicly recognize that there is a name for what they speak, besides "bad English," or they do not believe that AAL is something to be proud of and, therefore, preserved. Yet, AAL thrives due, in part, to its covert prestige – just like it always has.

In examining the origins of AAL, linguists have taken a number of different approaches to explain how it has developed historically, including considerations of Anglicist, or Dialectologist, origins (Labov 1969b; Poplack 2000; Poplack and Tagliamonte 2001; Schneider 1989; Wolfram and Thomas 2002); Creolist origins (Dillard 1972; Rickford 1998, 1999; Rickford and Rickford 2000; Smitherman 1977, 2000; Weldon 2003, 2007); Substratist connections (Dalby 1972; DeBose and Faraclas 1993; Dunn 1976); Ecological and Restructuralist factors (Mufwene 2000; Winford 1997, 1998); and Divergence/Convergence theorists (see Butters 1987). Proponents of monolithic origins hypotheses (e.g., Anglicist, Creolist, and Substratist) have compared morphosyntactic and syntactic processes in creoles, early varieties of English, and (to a limited extent) African languages to those in AAL as a means of determining the origins, development, and classification of AAL. Restructuralist and ecological theorists have also considered factors such as second language learning, social dynamics, and contact effects in explaining the evolution of AAL.

However, there is another position that, in spite of evidence to the contrary, lingers: the "Deficit" position. It has been pernicious and difficult to dismiss in the minds of those, who continue to believe that African Americans are inferior to European Americans and, as such, their language must be as well.

2 Deficit position

The Deficit position emerged in the 19th century and is based on the idea that Blacks are genetically inferior to Whites. This position posits that Africans in America were, at most, capable of imperfectly learning American English and that imperfection is what accounts for the differences between AAL and varieties of American English spoken by European Americans. Since the native languages of these slaves, were inferior and uncivilized according to the Deficit position, the slaves did the best they were capable of doing in learning English – as is seen in their "imperfect" language use.

This position endures to this day for the cultural and linguistic practices of Africans in America and reached a climax within the linguistic literature with the research of Carl Bereiter and Siegfried Englemann (1966) in *Teaching Disadvantaged Children in the Preschool* with the complicity of these and other educational psychologists in the 1960s. The publication of William Labov's (1969b) polemical *The Logic of Nonstandard English* was meant to quash the ethnocentric and racist perspectives espoused by those who used language differences as social, cultural, and linguistic (i.e., human) deficit. What made this worse was the use of so-called empirical evidence to support deficit beliefs (e.g., standardized tests), which has continued for decades since (see Farrell 1983, 1984; Hernstein and Murray 1994; Orr 1987).

This position was perpetuated in the 1980s–90s by the publication of *The Bell Curve: Intelligence and Class Structure in American Life* (1994) by Harvard psychologist Richard J. Hernstein and American Enterprise Institute political scientist Charles Murray as well as *Twice as Less: Black English and the Performance of Black Students in Mathematics and Science* (1987) by Eleanor Wilson Orr. Orr was the co-founder of the Hawthorne School in the District of Columbia. Her observations of the low-income scholarship students she admitted led her to believe that Blacks had cultural deficits that did not allow them to understand math and science in a way necessary for abstract thinking and learning. These views seem to have been re-packaged in recent years with code words such as "at risk" and "urban" to signify "deficient". Though Labov's (1969a) and John Baugh's (1988) reviews of *Twice as Less* provide substantive rebuttals of both cultural and linguistic deficit theory, the belief just will not die.

More recently, these claims are being linked to the debates in the United States about teacher and student accountability in this age of standardized testing. It is believed by some that poor students and their teachers cannot be held accountable for their poor performance because, through no fault of the children, their families are poor and deficient in providing what their children need to be successful and to be taught. While poverty is horrific and has a devastating effect on people and society, as demonstrated by the Occupy Wall Street movement in the 2011 advertising campaign by Bono where he purports that famine is the new f-word (http://www.one.org/international/blog/the-f-word/, last accessed 13 February 2017), society cannot throw up its hands and say these children cannot be saved because their families are deficient. That is unconscionable and it defies logic and humanity.

3 Structural views of AAL

Before describing the other positions about the history and development of AAL, it is important to note that most of them make their claims based on salient linguistic features of AAL (see Table 5.1 and Table 5.2) in comparison to standard American English, non-standard American English, African languages, Gullah, and Caribbean creoles. There are many characteristics of AAL just as there are for any language. However, the research literature tends to focus on a subset of those characteristics as salient linguistic features (i.e., those that define AAL). Tables 5.1 and 5.2 display a compilation of salient phonological (pronunciation), morphological (word structure and formation), and syntactic (sentence structure) AAL features as compiled from the research literature and used to support the various positions about AAL.

Table 5.1: Phonological features (features 1–6 from Bailey and Thomas 1998: 89, as cited in Mufwene et al. 1998)

1. Reduction of Final Nasal to Vowel Nasality	*bone* [bõ]
2. Final Consonant Deletion (especially affects nasals)	*save* [seː]; *sane* [seː]
3. Final Stop Devoicing (without shortening of preceding segment)	*bad* [bæt]
4. Coarticulated Glottal Stop with Devoiced Final Stop	*bad* [bætʔ]
5. Loss of /j/ after Consonants	*computer* [kəmpurə]; *Houston* [hustən]
6. Substitution of /k/ for /t/ in /str/ Clusters	*street* [skrit]; *stream* [skrim]
7. [v > b] in Word-medial Position:	*haven* [hebən]
8. Deletion of /b/, /d/, /g/ as First Consonant in Tense-Aspect marker or Auxiliary Verb	*Ah 'on know* = "I don't know"; *Ah ma do it* = "I'm gon do it"; *He ain't do it* = "He didn't do it"
9. Reduplicated Suffix *-s*:	I went and took my *tests.* [tɛsɪz]
10. Labialization of Interdental Fricatives	*bath* ⤏ [bæf]; *baths* ⤏ [bævz]

Table 5.2: Morphological and syntactic features (examples from Lanehart 2002 unless noted otherwise)

Preverbal Markers of Tense, Mood, and Aspect	
Linguistic feature	Example of feature
1. Zero Copula	He up in there talking that now.
2. *Gon*	I'm gon fix some grits.
3. Habitual Invariant *be*	He be in the house all summer. (Cukor-Avila 2001: 105)
4. Invariant *be$_2$* (*Be* + verb + *ing*)	Do they be playing all day?
5. Invariant Future *be*	He be here tomorrow. (Rickford 1999: 6)
6. Aspectual *steady*	They steady be laughing.
7. Completive, or Unstressed, *been*	It been raining ever since y'all came here.
8. Stressed *been*	I been drinking coffee.
9. Completive, or Perfective, *done*	I knew you was foolin cause I done waited on you before.
10. Future Perfective, or Sequential, *be done*	He be done left by the time we get there.
11. Future *finna* or *fitna*	He finna go. (Rickford 1999: 6)
12. Indignant *come*	He come walkin in here like he owned the damn place. (Spears 1982: 852)
13. Counterfactual *call*	They call themselves dancing. (Mufwene et al. 1998: 16)
14. *Had* + Simple Past	Today I had went to work. (Cukor-Avila 2001: 105)
15. Multiple Modals	They might should oughta do it. (Mufwene et al. 1998: 33)
16. Quasi Modals *liketa* and *poseta*	I liketa drowned. (Rickford 1999: 7); You don't poseta do it that way. (Rickford 1999: 7)
17. Zero Third Person Singular Suffix *-s*	At least he know you have a phone.
18. Generalization of *is* and *was*	They is some crazy folk. (Rickford 1999: 7)
19. Use of Past Tense Form as Past Participle	She has ran.
20. Use of Past Participle Form as Past Tense Form	She seen him yesterday.
21. Use of Verb Stem as Past Tense Form	He come down here yesterday.
22. Zero Past Tense or Past Participle Suffix *-ed*	I probably woulda end up keeping it.
23. Reduplicated Past Tense or Past Participle Suffix *-ed*	I likeded that show.
24. Aspectual Verb *-s* Suffix	I don't let it tempt me; I tempts it.
Nouns and Pronouns	
25. Zero Possessive Suffix *-s*	I ain't never seen nobody don't know they wife phone number.
26. Zero Plural Suffix *-s*	That man done changed car places since then two or three time.
27. Associative Plural (*nem* or *and (th)em*)	Larry nem lef already when I got here.
28. Pronominal Apposition	That sausage, it's nice and hot.

Table 5.2: (continued).

Preverbal Markers of Tense, Mood, and Aspect	
Linguistic feature	Example of feature
Nouns and Pronouns	
29. *They* and *Y'all* Possessive	*Who want to put on they good clothes looking like that?*
30. Use of Object Pronouns after a Verb as Personal Datives	*Ahma git me a gig.* (Rickford 1999: 8)
31. Bare Subject Relative Clause	*That's the man come here.* (Rickford 1999: 8)
32. Less Differentiated Personal Pronouns (pronouns can serve as subject and object form)	*They should do it theyselves.*
Negation	
33. Use of *ain't* as a General Preverbal Negator (includes *ain't* for *didn't*)	*He ain' here.* (Rickford 1999: 8); *He ain' do it.* (Rickford 1999: 8)
34. Negative Concord (Multiple Negation)	*I don't let myself get in no more habit than I want to get in.*
35. Negative Inversion of Auxiliary and Indefinite Pronoun Subject	*Can't nobody say nothin.* (Rickford 1999: 8)
36. But Negative (Use of *ain't but* and *don't but* for *only*)	*He ain't but fourteen years old.* (Rickford 1999: 8)
Questions	
37. Formation of Direct Questions without Inversion	*Why I can't play?* (Rickford 1999: 8)
38. Auxiliary Verb Inversion in Embedded Questions (without *if* or *whether*)	*I asked him could he go with me.* (Rickford 1999: 8)
Existential, Locative, Complementizer, Quotative, and Other Constructions	
Linguistic feature	Example of feature
39. Existential *it* instead of *there*	*It's a lot of it in there.*
40. Existential *they got* (as a Plural Equivalent of Singular *it is*, instead of *there are*)	*They got some angry women here.* (Nina Simone song, Rickford 1999: 9)
41. *Here go...* or *There go...*	*There go Mister beatin Celie again.*
42. *Tell say* Constructions	*They told me say they couldn't go.* (Rickford 1999: 9)
43. Inceptive *get/got to*	*I got to thinking about that.* (Cukor-Avila 2001: 105)

While the use of these salient linguistic features of AAL is important in AAL scholarship, we must always keep in mind that a language is more than the sum of its parts. This list can be used for good or ill – good in the advancement of our learning and understanding of AAL and language in general; bad when such things are used to further denigrate the legitimacy, logic, and value of AAL. The expectation is that we keep these features in perspective. As we will see below, the other AAL historical and developmental perspectives use these salient features for various purposes and sometimes in contradictory ways to support their arguments. This is most obvious with the research on the very contested copula in AAL. Various perspectives use the copula as a pivotal case in support of their argument. As we will see, how one is able to do that depends on the ideologies one holds about AAL from the beginning.

Of note is the intentional use of the term 'African American (Vernacular) Language' in this chapter as opposed to 'African American (Vernacular) English'. I use the former instead of the latter because the latter is fraught with connotations and assumptions that preclude certain discussions. While AA(V)L also has the ability to instigate contentious discussions, at least they have the potential to be new ones. Additionally, 'language' is less restrictive or limiting than 'English' in this situation: it allows me to be non-committal about the origins and development of AAL (which I am) and shift the focus to the social and cultural lives of those who use AAL. As we will see next, there are very strong stances with respect to the history and development of AAL that clearly draw lines in the sand.

4 The big dogs in the fight: Anglicists and Creolists

The dominant perspectives about the history and development of AAL are held by two distinctive groups: (1) Anglicists, mostly European American scholars who spend much of their time trying to support their claim that AAL is a dialect of British English and that Africans in America who created AAL forgot their native culture and language upon arrival in America; and (2) Creolists, mostly Black scholars who spend much of their time arguing for and trying to support their belief that AAL derived from contact between Blacks and Whites and the cultures and languages they brought to their contact situation. In other words, the latter group believes Africans in America maintained aspects of their languages and cultures in adapting to their oppressive environment, while the former believes Africans in America either did not value their cultures enough to preserve at least some aspects of them or they did not have the ability to do so (see Bailey 2001; Baugh 1983; Green 2002; Lanehart 2001, 2007 for an overview of the various positions regarding the origins and development of African American Language).

The Creolist position, which emerged in the 1960s in response to the Anglicist position, purports that AAL developed from a prior US creole developed by slaves that was widespread across the colonies and slave-holding areas. The Southeastern US is considered the cradle of AAL, given the large number of plantations and the Southeast's strong support of slavery and the slave trade through the Middle Passage. The economic interest in slavery increased with the dependence on cotton and other crops. Creolists tend to use morphosyntactic features (see Table 5.2), phonological features (see Table 5.1), and lexical features (see Turner 1949; Mufwene 1993; Smitherman 1994) to support their perspective on the history and development of AAL.

The most contentious feature used to support the Creolist position is the zero copula. Because many African languages, Gullah, and other Caribbean creoles do not have a copula, zero copula in AAL has been used as a primary connection to creoles. Until recently, there had been no instances of zero copula in British English varieties cited in the literature. However, Poplack (2000) and Poplack and Tagliamonte (2001) make the claim that zero copula is also present in a variety of British English. While that claim is contested, I should point out that both Creolists and Anglicists rely heavily on features to support their positions without any extensive recordings for the language of Africans in America at their inception in the Americas (i.e., nascent AAL). While Caribbean creoles are still recognizable creoles in present-day use, such is not the case for AAL – with the exception of Gullah. While there is no dispute that Gullah is a creole, its existence as being widespread in the US during slavery is disputed. Currently, Gullah is found in the islands off the coasts of Georgia and South Carolina, though its use is receding due to economic and ecological conditions. While Gullah's maintenance in the South Carolina islands seems to be better than in the Georgia islands due to infrastructural and economic supports in South Carolina that are not as prevalent in Georgia, many of the Gullah people have to leave in order to survive – which contributes to the loss of language and culture.

The existence of Gullah and the perspective of its speakers (i.e., Gullah speakers say they speak English, not a creole) is a complicating factor, but how complicating depends on how you define AAL. I choose to define AAL in agreement with Mufwene (2001: 21): "[AAE] is English as spoken by or among African Americans" because "[a] language variety is typically associated with a community of speakers and, in many communities, a language means no more than the particular way its members speak." For example, if we look up "Italian" in a dictionary, it is defined as "of or pertaining to Italy, its people, or their language; a native or inhabitant of Italy, or a person of Italian descent." (http://www.dictionary.com). Mufwene is saying that we can define AAL in the same way: "of or pertaining to African Americans; a person of African American descent." Given this definition, AAL is the umbrella term for all ways of language use of African Americans – including Gullah and African American Vernacular Language (AAVL). In my classes, I describe AAL as the umbrella covering all its varieties across the Americas where Africans in the Americans are. That means it covers West Coast AAL, East Coast AAL, Southern AAL, Gullah, AAVL, and everything in between.

The Anglicist position purports that Africans in America learned regional varieties of British English dialects from British overseers with little to no influence from their own native languages and cultures. This position emerged in the mid 20th century and is in opposition to the Creolist position. Anglicists use ex-slave recordings and texts (see Bailey et al. 1991), as well as comparisons to other historical texts, British varieties, and slave resettlement in the Americas to support their position. More current is the belief that non-standard varieties of British English are the precursors of AAL as opposed to standard ones since the Whites who slaves would have had contact with would have spoken non-standard varieties of British English instead of standard varieties (i.e., Neo-Anglicist). Anglicists, like Creolists, believe they have accounted for all salient linguistic features in some past or current variety of British English, including zero copula. According to Mufwene,

> to resolve the creolist-dialectologist debate, what is needed is convincing information regarding different kinds of plantations, their settlement history, and the pattern of Anglo-African interaction on them. Although history argues against the creole-origin hypothesis, the literature against it has done a poor job in attempting to refute it. (Mufwene 2001: 315)

He goes on to say that though Poplack (2000) did a better job of this, there are still contradictions in evidence, even with her collection of essays. One of her biggest hurdles is Samaná English, a variety used in the Spanish-speaking Dominican Republic by African Americans who sailed from Philadelphia in the 1820s (Mufwene 2001). While Poplack finds Samaná to be closer to AAL than to Caribbean English creoles, Hannah (1997) and others find that not to be the case. So the fierce debate continues.

5 Substratist, restructuralist, ecological, and divergence theorists

Substratists such as Dalby (1972), Dunn (1976), and DeBose and Faraclas (1993) purport that distinctive patterns of AAL are those that also occur in Niger-Congo languages such as Kikongo, Mande, and Kwa. In effect, the view is that AAL is structurally related to West African languages and bear only superficial similarities to general English (Green 2002: 8–9). It is so named because it is argued that the West African or substrate languages influenced the sentence and sound structures of AAL (Green 2002: 9). As Goodman (1993: 65) notes, one characteristic of a substratum "is the subordinate social or cultural status of its speakers vis-à-vis those of the reference language [i.e., English]" (see Green 2002).

Restructuralists and Ecological theorists, such as Wolfram and Thomas (2002), Bailey (2001), Cukor-Avila (2001), and Mufwene (2000), support a perspective within the Anglicist position that acknowledges the difficulty of knowing the origins of AAL but propose that we can say something useful about Earlier African American Language (not nascent AAL) given settlement and migration patterns as well as socio-ecological issues. Mufwene (2000: 234) purports:
1. The socioeconomic history of the United States does not support the hypothesis that AAVE developed from an erstwhile creole, either American or Caribbean.
2. However, this position does not preclude influence [...] from Caribbean English varieties imported with slaves in the seventeenth and eighteenth centuries on the restructuring of colonial English that produced AAVE.
3. Nor does the recognition of possible Caribbean influence entail that AAVE could not have developed into what it is now without it.
4. Closer examination of sources of the direct origins of slaves during the eighteenth century suggests that influence from African languages was perhaps more determinative than that from the Caribbean.
5. By no means should anyone overlook or downplay the nature of colonial English as spoken by both the English and the non-English in the 17th and 18th centuries, nor its central role as the target language during the development of AAVE, Gullah, and their Caribbean kin.

Restructuralists and Ecological theorists are in some ways closer to Neo-Creolist positions. As noted by Mufwene, Creolists' (namely Rickford 1998: 192)

> recognition of some merits in assuming that AAVE had an independent development [is quite noteworthy]; i.e., it did not originate as a creole nor does it simply represent 'the transfer and acquisition by Africans and African Americans of English dialects spoken by British and other white immigrants to America in earlier times.' (Mufwene 2000: 254–255)

In other words, AAL likely did not originate from or as a creole, but that absence does not then preclude the influence of native African languages in the subsequent emerging language of Africans in America.

Wolfram and Thomas (2002) and Bailey (2001) focus more on settlement patterns of European Americans in relation to settlements of Africans in America and their subsequent resettlements through migration. While no one can go back to the beginning, using these patterns provides a picture of interaction and languages in contact. Over the history of America, Europeans have settled differing areas and brought their different varieties of English and other languages with them. "Variation 101" says that separation from native language speakers and their homeland results in language variation (i.e., variation via physical separation). While the expatriate British English speakers were undergoing linguistic changes, so were the languages of the involuntary immigrants (i.e., slaves) but with a larger pool of varieties that were in contact because, as Mufwene (2000: 255) states, "all varieties of English in North America are contact-based and developed concurrently".

Also, the conditions of contact changed over time, as well as the interaction of language varieties. As such, these theorists believe that the language of Africans in America was different when compared to the 18th, 19th, 20th, and 21st centuries because the social and political and economic realities of those times differed in ways that greatly influenced language. So, for example, moving from colonial indentured servants to colonial slaves to Southern/Southeastern plantation slaves to Southern sharecroppers to Northern industrialist workers to national migrants and then to Civil Rights Activists (all the while with ideas of identity and culture waxing and waning) impacted the language of these involuntary immigrants so that the comparison is more about these factors in relation to one another than about the origin of AAL.

The Divergence/Convergence Theorists emerged in the 1980s with the work of William Labov and others. According to Labov and Harris (1986), to pursue this argument, divergence from White varieties has more recently shaped AAL. That is, AAL has diverged from varieties of American English due to racism, segregation, and inequality. As a result, African Americans are actually forming new speech communities with innovative forms, especially with a growth in urbanization (Bailey 2001). According to Labov (as cited in Butters 1987), "the more contact [B]lacks have with [W]hites, the more they move away from the vernacular side, and the more contact [W]hites have with [B]lacks, the more we observe borrowings of [B]lack forms." In other words, when inequities and inequalities in society subside and there is more contact between African Americans and Whites, AAL converges toward general American English. When there are increases in inequities and inequalities in society, AAL diverges from general American English. Too bad the same logic is not used with the Anglicists since the Divergence/Convergence theorists, by extension, imply that when people/society treat you badly, you are less inclined to want to associate with or identify with them compared to when people/society treat you humanely, thereby fostering more of an inclination to assimilate. However, persistent political, economic, and social issues (i.e., ecological issues) greatly contribute to AAL becoming more divergent instead of convergent with varieties of American English despite so-called desegregation in the 1960s to present.

Regardless of the origin of AAL, the current state of it reflects the historical ills of inequity and inequality in the US towards African Americans and their response to maintain their own distinct culture and language. Butters (1987) disputes the Divergence theory because of the few linguistic features studied, but, then again, most of this research and these theories are supported by features as opposed to the system as recommended by Lisa Green (2002) in studying AAL or any other language variety because, as noted above, a language is more than the sum of its parts.

6 Summary

My position is that we simply do not have the artifacts and hard evidence (recordings of nascent AAL) to make a definitive assessment about the origins and history of AAL. I would add that we should not rely on "salient" linguist features either since language is more than the sum of its parts or the handy grammar that we all like to turn to (clearly I do not think this point can be overstated). If language could be learned from reading a grammar book, we could all be multilingual. Yet, we consistently rely on features to make arguments about the history and origins of AAL in a way we do not for most other linguistic varieties.

As Rickford and Rickford (2000) point out, the power of culture and identity leads one to believe that no one would just forget everything about where they came from in order to learn the language of their oppressors at all cost. The work of the late linguistic anthropologist John Ogbu (1978) on involuntary minorities suggests that language and identity are powerful factors in the persistence of motherland language and culture for enslaved people like Africans in America and through the Middle Passage.

As I have stated in Lanehart (2007, 2015), when I tell people outside of linguistics about AAL, they seem dumbfounded that anyone would believe that AAL is not historically rooted to Africa since the people who speak it are, hence the African Diaspora. Yet, I have tried to convince myself that it matters whether AAL is historically a dialect of British English or an English and African creole by becoming involved in research groups and projects that engage in such questions. Scholars cannot prove that AAL is a creole or a dialect and I fundamentally do not feel the evidence exists that can support either side beyond a reasonable doubt. My point is that, today, it does not matter what the outcome of this storied debate is. I know that some believe that given current language policy it might be helpful to prove that AAL is an English and African creole so that it could be classified as a foreign language and receive bilingual education funding, but I do not buy that argument because then I remember that the Gullah speakers have not benefited much from that designation. In fact, during the Oakland Ebonics controversy of 1996–1997 (in 1996, the schoolboard in Oakland, California, passed the very controversial resolution to recognize 'Ebonics,' i.e., African American English to them, as a legitimate language), the Gullah people got no publicity at all even though there is no controversy among linguists about the origin, status, or nature of their language – it is an English and African creole.

If the "great debate" were decided without question today, how would we be better off? Would we be closer to helping AAL-speaking children to learn to read and write? Would we be closer to helping AAL-speaking children learn critical thinking and literacy skills? Would we be closer to helping AAL-speaking children have better schools with better facilities and better funding and better opportunities? I do not think so. That is a problem I cannot get past.

7 References

Bailey, Guy. 2001. The relationship between African American Vernacular English and White Vernaculars in the American South: a sociocultural history and some phonological evidence. In: Sonja L. Lanehart (ed.), *Sociocultural and Historical Contexts of African American English*, 53–92. Amsterdam/Philadelphia: John Benjamins.
Bailey, Guy, Natalie Maynor, and Patricia Cukor-Avila. 1991. *The Emergence of Black English: Text and Commentary*. Amsterdam/Philadelphia: John Benjamins.
Baugh, John. 1983. *Black Street Speech: Its History, Structure, and Survival*. Austin: University of Texas Press.
Baugh, John. 1988. Review: Twice as Less: Black English and the Performance of Black Students in Mathematics and Science, by Eleanor Wilson Orr. *Harvard Educational Review* 58(3): 395–403.

Bereiter, Carl and Siegfried Englemann. 1966. *Teaching Disadvantaged Children in the Preschool*. Englewood Cliffs, New Jersey: Prentice Hall.
Butters, Ronald R. 1987. "Are Black and White vernaculars diverging?" Papers from the NWAVE XIV Panel Discussion [by Ralph W. Fasold, William Labov, Fay Boyd Vaughn-Cooke, Guy Bailey, Walt Wolfram, Arthur K. Spears, John Rickford]. *American Speech* 62(1).
Cukor-Avila, Patricia. 2001. Co-existing grammars: The relationship between the Evolution of African American and Southern White Vernacular English in the South. In: Sonja L. Lanehart (ed.), *Sociocultural and Historical Contexts of African American English*, 93–128. Amsterdam/Philadelphia: John Benjamins.
Dalby, David. 1972. The African element in African American English. In: Thomas Kochman (ed.), *Rappin and Stylin' Out: Communication in Urban Black America*, 170–186. Urbana, Illinois: University of Illinois Press.
DeBose, Charles and Nicholas Faraclas. 1993. An Africanist approach to the linguistic study of Black English: Getting to the roots of tense-aspect modality and copula systems in Afro-American. In: Salikoko S. Mufwene (ed.), *Africanisms in Afro-American Language Varieties*, 364–387. Athens, Georgia: University of Georgia Press.
Dillard, Joe L. 1972. *Black English: Its History and Usage in the United States*. New York: Random House.
Dunn, Ernest F. 1976. Black-Southern White dialect controversy. In: Deborah S. Harrison and Tom Trabasso (eds.), *Black English: A Seminar*, 105–122. Hillsdale, NJ: Erlbaum.
Farrell, Thomas. 1983. IQ and standard English. *College Composition and Communication* 34: 470–484.
Farrell, Thomas. 1984. IQ, Orality, and literacy. *College Composition and Communication* 35: 469–478.
Goodman, Morris. 1993. African substratum: some cautionary words. In: Salikoko S. Mufwene (ed.), *Africanisms in Afro-American Language Varieties*, 64–73. Athens, Georgia: University of Georgia Press.
Green, Lisa J. 2002. *African American English: A Linguistic Introduction*. Cambridge: Cambridge University Press.
Hannah, Dawn. 1997. Copula absence in Samaná English: Implications for research on the linguistic history of African-American Vernacular English. *American Speech* 72(4): 339–372.
Hernstein, Richard J. and Charles Murray. 1996. *The Bell Curve: Intelligence and Class Structure in American Life*. New York: The Free Press.
Labov, William. 1969a. Contraction, deletion, and inherent variability in the English copula. *Language* 45: 715–776.
Labov, William. 1969b. The logic of non-standard English. In: John Alatis (ed.), *Georgetown Monograph on Languages and Linguistics* 22: 1–44.
Labov, William and Wendell Harris. 1986. DeFacto segregation of Black and White vernaculars. In: David Sankoff (ed.), *Diversity and Diachrony*, 1–24. Amsterdam/Philadelphia: John Benjamins.
Lanehart, Sonja L. 2001. *Sociocultural and Historical Contexts of African American Vernacular English*. Amsterdam/Philadelphia: John Benjamins.
Lanehart, Sonja L. 2002. *Sista, Speak! Black Women Kinfolk Talk about Language and Literacy*. Austin: University of Texas Press.
Lanehart, Sonja L. 2007. "If our children are our future, why are we stuck in the past?": Beyond the Anglicists and the Creolists, and toward social change. In: H. Samy Alim and John Baugh

(eds.), *Talkin' Black Talk: Language, Education, and Social Change*, 132–141. New York: Teachers College Press.

Lanehart, Sonja (ed.). 2015. *The Oxford Handbook of African American Language*. Oxford: Oxford University Press.

Mufwene, Salikoko S. (ed.). 1993. *Africanisms in Afro-American Language Varieties*. Athens, Georgia: University of Georgia Press.

Mufwene, Salikoko S. 2000. Some sociohistorical inferences about the development of African American English. In: Shana Poplack (ed.), *The English History of African American English*, 233–263. Malden, Massachusetts/Oxford: Blackwell.

Mufwene, Salikoko S. 2001. African-American English. In: John Algeo (ed.), *The Cambridge History of the English Language*, Vol. 6: 291–324. Cambridge: Cambridge University Press.

Mufwene, Salikoko, John R. Rickford, Guy Bailey, and John Baugh (eds.). 1998. *African American English: Structure, History, and Use*. London/New York: Routledge.

Ogbu, John U. 1978. *Minority Education and Caste: The American System in Cross-Cultural Perspective*. San Diego, California: Academic Press.

Ogbu, John U. 1992. Understanding cultural diversity and learning. *Educational Research* 21(8): 5–14.

Orr, Eleanor Wilson. 1987. *Twice as Less: Black English and the Performance of Black Students in Mathematics and Science*. New York: W.W. Norton & Co.

Poplack, Shana (ed.). 2000. *The English History of African American English*. Malden, Massachusetts/Oxford: Blackwell.

Poplack, Shana and Sali Tagliamonte. 2001. *African American English in the Diaspora*. Malden, Massachusetts/Oxford: Blackwell.

Rickford, John R. 1998. The creole origins of African American Vernacular English: Evidence from copula absence. In: Salikoko S. Mufwene, John R. Rickford, Guy Bailey, and John Baugh (eds.), *African American English: Structure, History, and Use*, 154–200. London: Routledge.

Rickford, John R. 1999. *African American Vernacular English: Features, Evolution, and Educational Implications*. New York/London: Blackwell.

Rickford, John Russell and Russell John Rickford. 2000. *Spoken Soul: The Story of Black English*. New York: John Wiley & Sons.

Schneider, Edgar W. 1989. *American Earlier Black English: Morphological and Syntactic Variables*. Tuscaloosa: University of Alabama Press.

Smitherman, Geneva. 1977. *Talkin and Testifyin: The Language of Black America*. Detroit: Wayne State University Press.

Smitherman, Geneva. 1994. *Black Talk: Words and Phrases from the Hood to the Amen Corner*. Boston: Houghton Mifflin.

Smitherman, Geneva. 2000. *Talkin that Talk: Language, Culture and Education in African America*. London/New York: Routledge.

Spears, Arthur. 1982. The Black English semi-auxiliary *come*. *Language* 58: 850–872.

Turner, Lorenzo Dow. 1949. *Africanisms in the Gullah Dialect*. Chicago: University of Chicago Press.

Winford, Donald. 1997. On the origins of African American Vernacular English – A creolist perspective. Part I: The sociohistorical background. *Diachronica* 14: 305–344.

Winford, Donald. 1998. On the origins of African American Vernacular English – A creolist perspective. Part II: Linguistic features. *Diachronica* 15: 1–55.

Wolfram, Walt and Erik R. Thomas. 2002. *The Development of African American English*. Malden, Massachusetts/Oxford: Blackwell Publishers.

Weldon, Tracey L. 2003. Revisiting the creolist hypothesis: copula variability in Gullah and southern rural AAVE. *American Speech* 78: 171–191.
Weldon, Tracey L. 2007. Gullah negation: a variable analysis. *American Speech* 82: 341–366.

Pam Peters
Chapter 6:
Standard British English

1   Introduction —— 96
2   Emergence of a national standard in England, 16th to 18th century —— 98
3   British English in the colonial and postcolonial era, 18th to
    20th century —— 102
4   Linguistic features of Standard British English in the 20th century —— 109
5   British English as an international standard —— 115
6   References —— 118

Abstract: This chapter examines the notion of "standard British English" from several perspectives. It discusses the emergence of British English as a national standard through canonical stages, like those postulated by Haugen ([1966] 1972), and by Schneider (2007) for the evolution of postcolonial Englishes. Its status as an international standard, achieved through colonial expansion, is set in counterpoint to the rise of American English in the 19th and 20th centuries. The status of "British English" as a regional standard is then discussed with reference to recent models of "world English", and contrasted with perceptions of it within Great Britain, in the tug-of-war between local identity and the ideology of the standard (Milroy 2000). Its multiple roles help to make British English linguistically more pluralistic than American English in the 21st century. How this will affect the place of British English in any putative "world standard English" remains to be seen.

1 Introduction

The term *British English* and understandings of it have both evolved over centuries. At least four different definitions were found by Hansen (1997: 59–61), all current in the last two decades of the 20th century and giving it narrower and broader scope, and a certain ambiguity in many contexts. At the narrow end of the scale it refers to (i) the language of England, or (ii) the language of Great Britain, or (iii) the language of the British Isles. At its broadest (iv) it may refer to

Pam Peters: Sydney (Australia)

the variety of English used in British Commonwealth countries where there was a sufficiently large community of British settlers to establish it as the national language (e.g. Canada, Australia). Hansen also noted (along with others e.g. McArthur 2001) the use of "British English" to refer to one of the two international standards of printed English, used in Commonwealth countries and others where English is an auxiliary official language, which makes a fifth definition (v) of "British English". In actual use there is often some indeterminacy about which meaning(s) are in play.

In this article, the second of those definitions for British English will generally be assumed: that it denotes the national language of Great Britain, without reference to dialect variation within it and as used for all government and institutional purposes. As the reference standard for education, it is associated with canonical forms used especially in writing. In these ways it meets the criteria of a national standard as articulated by Haugen ([1966] 1972: 107–110), i.e. the language with the maximal range of functions and minimal variation in form for the country. Haugen's model is useful in benchmarking the evolution of a national language, but was not designed to explain its extended jurisdiction beyond national borders. So for British English we will need to consider functions beyond the "maximal" which it envisaged.

The emergence of the national standard language in Britain can be traced back to the threshold of Early Modern English, and its codification is very clearly associated with the "age of correctness" in the 18th century. However the term "British English" was not used until the latter decades of the 19th century, with the *Oxford English Dictionary*'s first citation in 1869. Fuller recognition of the status of British English as a major regional variety of world English is a relatively recent (20th century) development. It comes from outside Britain rather than within it. In what follows we shall review the evolution of British English to the point where both at home and abroad it is perceived as a regional standard. Its wider role as an international standard (= definition (v)) will be discussed in Section 5 of the article.

The evolutionary model for new varieties of English articulated by Schneider (2007) will be used as a framework for discussing the evolution of British English below. Its five stages are: (1) Foundation, (2) Exonormative stabilization, (3) Nativization, (4) Endonormative stabilization, (5) Differentiation. Just how applicable those stages and the accompanying parameters (historical context, identity construction, sociolinguistic functions, linguistic structure) are to what is conventionally seen as the "old" variety will be explored below.

2 Emergence of a national standard in England, 16th to 18th century

2.1 Foundations

The roots of Standard English can be traced to several written dialects of late Middle English whose morphology anticipated that of the Early Modern English standard. They were the dialects of the Central Midlands, East Anglia, and the Greater London area, and then from the Midlands and North Midlands through the so-called "Chancery standard" (Smith 2008: 204–205). It originated as the medium of administrative and government writing, replacing the Latin of previous centuries. Its reach was greatly extended by the advent of Caxton's printing press (1476), set up under the walls of Westminster Abbey, a strategic location for handling government printing business. But Caxton and his 16th century successors printed a very wide range of publications, including fiction as well as nonfiction publications, so that the official variety of the language became the general medium for publishing in English. In the Tudor period, it was used in popular pamphlets as well as books in numerous technical domains: on health and medicine (Nevalainen 2008: 213), agriculture (*The Booke of Husbandry* 1598), as well as domestic topics such as cookery and carving. During the 17th century, English became the vernacular medium for science, in volumes of essays by Bacon, in Burton's *Anatomy of Melancholy* (1621), in theological treatises such as Donne's *Essays* and *Sermons*, published posthumously, and Milton's ecclesiastical pamphlets of the 1640s. The Royal Society endorsed the use of plain English for scientific purposes through Sprat's famous statement (1667), quoted below (Section 2.3).

The establishment of what had been the "Chancery standard" in all these domains of communication is analogous to the foundation of a new variety for a (colonial) nation, although the language had had a thousand years of grassroots use in England. It also represents its "acceptance" (Haugen [1966] 1972: 109–110) as the national standard for ever-increasing public and intellectual purposes. Its establishment in Tudor England coincides with that of other "vernaculars" as the official national languages elsewhere in Europe, e.g. France and Italy. Comparisons between English and French in this role were very explicitly made by contemporary men of letters: "Our tong is as copious, pithie, and significative as any other tongue in Europe [...] as fluente as the Latine, as courteous as the Spanish, as courtlike as the French [...]" (Camden 1605; quoted in Tucker 1961). Though Camden notes some criticisms of the mixed character of English and the instability of its orthography, he expresses unqualified satisfaction about it being the national language.

English reasserted itself as England's national language after centuries of displacement by Norman French and Latin. It affirmed an English national identity in tandem with the establishment of the English Church, which marked England's ecclesiastical and cultural independence from Catholic Europe and more than a millennium of Latin-based traditions. The monastic institutions which had traditionally provided lower education in Latin were dissolved; and a rising merchant class created a demand for secular schooling in English, and the development of an English curriculum. The earliest English schoolbooks-cum-dictionaries (Mulcaster's *Elementarie*, 1582; Coote's *The English Schoole-maister*, 1597) were published to meet this need.

2.2 Exonormative stabilization: the Latin component

Though Standard English gained acceptance as the national language and the medium for general and technical communication, the written language was steeped in Latin through the participation of English scholars in the European Renaissance. The rediscovery of classical scholarship took English writers back to Latin texts, on which they modeled their style (Gordon 1966: 105–111), and from which they borrowed countless words. Their use of "inkhorn terms", i.e. barely assimilated Latin words, helped to mediate newly encountered philosophical concepts and cultural values, and suggests the challenge of expressing them in ordinary contemporary English. Approximately 7,000 Latin words were added to the English language during the peak period of borrowing from 1600 to 1675 (Culpeper and Clapham 1996: 207, 215). The linguistic debt to Latin is very conspicuous on the pages of 17th century dictionaries, which are stocked with Latinisms ("inkhorn terms" and other "hard words", often technical terms) that an English person might encounter in wider reading. The practice or habit of borrowing from Latin makes an interesting analogue with the borrowing from indigenous languages by settlers in colonial territories, associated with Stage 2 of varietal evolution, although the context of lexical borrowing is intellectual rather than environmental.

Apart from this large-scale borrowing of Latin words, Latin grammar was used to frame pioneering accounts of English. Jonson's *English Grammar* (1640) uses the classifications of Latin to explain all the syntactic structures of English. The Latin paradigms are preserved for English parts of speech in later grammars by Wallis (1653) and Cooper (1685), both written in Latin under the title *Grammatica Linguae Anglicanae*. These indications of a tendency to keep referring back to Latin contrast with the general acceptance of Standard English in the 17th century, but they are analogous to the exonormativity found in the evolution of new varieties of English (Schneider 2007: 56), which looks back to the English of the mother country for linguistic benchmarks. The staple of great 17th century prose writers such as Raleigh and Milton was the Ciceronian periodic sentence (Gordon 1966: 106–107). In his poetry too, Milton makes his stylistic mark through weighty Latinate loanwords and the use of the Latin rather than English sense of words long-since assimilated into English, e.g. *respect* used in the sense "look back". The Latin language remained an exonormative reference for 17th century English literary stylists, and continued to exert its power in the 18th century, in the neoclassical prose of Johnson. It cast a long shadow even over bureaucratic/ formal English style of the 20th century, though the Latin borrowings are now thoroughly assimilated.

2.3 From nativization to codification

The polarization of English society in civil wars of the 17th century has its counterpart in contrastive movements in English prose style. In counterpoint to the humanists' preference for Latinate styles, we find communities of writers and institutions affirming the virtue of English plain style. Speech-based prose was favored by the Puritans, modeled so powerfully in Bunyan's *Pilgrim's Progress* (1676), though it was also the natural choice for everyday topics, e.g. Walton's *Compleat Angler* (1653). The movement was paralleled within the scientific community for science writing, as the Royal Society so clearly affirmed in Sprat's history of the Society (1667), preferring "a close, naked natural way of speaking" and specifically rejecting "inkhorn" terms as well as all kinds of linguistic affectation. This endorsement of plain English correlates with a radical change in English dictionary-writing tradition from the 17th to the 18th century. Mid-century dictionaries such as Blount's *Glossographia* (1656) and Phillips's *New World of English Words* (1658) consisted almost entirely of "hard words", especially Latinate ones from specialized fields such as medicine and law. In later 17th century editions, the list amounted to 17,000 words (Starnes and Noyes 1946: 56), still with little or no coverage of ordinary English words. But from the beginning of the 18th century, English dictionaries made it their business to cover everyday English as well, starting with the *New English Dictionary* (1702) attributed to Kersey, which comprised about 28,000 words, many of them everyday words extracted from lists in school books. The coverage of the "generalitie of words in the English tongue" increased with Bailey's *An Universal Etymological English Dictionary* (1721) to about 40,000 words, in keeping with the title.

The nativization of English dictionaries follows close behind the nativization of its prose style, based on English speech rather than classical rhetoric. In

Schneider's model for new Englishes, this stage normally involves consolidation of the speech community in its colonial location, which clearly does not apply to British English. Yet the beginning of the 18th century saw some kind of consolidation of British identity, through the Act of Union with Scotland in 1701, by which Great Britain itself was formed. Southern English attitudes to Scots English and Scottish mores remained rather haughty, as seen in some of Johnson's famously ironic definitions, e.g. the definition of *oats* "a grain which in England is generally given to horses but in Scotland supports the people". There was nevertheless increasing awareness in England of Scottish literature, of Burns and Scott. The later 18th century saw fresh uses of English as a literary medium, in new genres – such as novels, and discursive and lyric poetry. This coincides with the steady growth of literacy in England during the 18th century, allowing increasing proportions of the population to participate in the literary culture. The literacy rate (for women and men respectively) rose from 15% and 30% in 1660, to 50% and 67% in 1750 (McIntosh 2008: 230). With an expanding population of readers, the use of standard written English is embedded more deeply in the community.

The nativization of a new variety often ushers in a type of "sociolinguistic cleavage" between innovative and conservative users of the language (Schneider 2007: 56). This is very evident during the 18th century with conservative and frequently critical commentaries on contemporary English grammar and idiom, giving the period its byname "Age of Correctness". It reflects the then ongoing quest for a language authority, like the Academie Française and the Italian Accademia della Crusca, which had been established in France and Italy to act as arbiters on controversial aspects of the "vernacular". Though there were repeated calls for a similar language academy for English, it never quite gained sufficient support and patronage. The void was filled by many self-declared (*ipse dixit*) experts on grammars and usage, who produced 187 prescriptive grammars between 1700 and 1800 (Fitzmaurice 2000: 201). Most noteworthy were the *Short Introduction to English Grammar* published in 1762 by Lowth (bishop of London) and Murray's *English Grammar* (1795), which set out grammatical rules and illustrated them with typically negative examples from established writers and their own contemporaries (Tieken-Boon van Ostade 2010). Their commentaries form a "complaint tradition", like that associated with the nativization stage of a new variety of English (Schneider 2007: 56) – the public debate over which forms of the "standard" language were to be regarded as "correct".

Debates about correctness spring out of normative thinking about language (Cameron 1995: 7), where homogeneity is assumed, and there is little tolerance of variation. This also provides the context for the codification of a new variety (= endonormative stabilization in Schneider's model), and a key stage in the forging of a standard national language (Haugen [1966] 1972: 107–110). Typical instruments of codification are comprehensive dictionaries and grammars, some of which have already been mentioned. Large English dictionaries (such as Bailey's) appeared in the first half of the 18th century, but it was Johnson's *Dictionary of the English Language* (1755) which was accepted by British public as ultimate codification of the language. It was no doubt helped by Lord Chesterfield's declaration (1754): that he would "make a total surrender of all [his] rights and privileges in the English language [...] to Mr Johnson during the term of his dictatorship"; as well as the fact that the *Dictionary* was published without editorial change for 70 years (Reddick 1990: 176). Johnson did not identify his content in regional terms: it is projected as a reference form of English (i.e. Standard English) rather than British English. The same goes for the grammars of English published by Lowth and Murray, which were used for reference in England and the American colonies (Baron 1982: 140). In 1775, the jurisdiction of this now codified, Standard English was uncontroversial. It was the national language of Great Britain, and could also claim some sovereignty overseas (a dimension beyond Haugen's 1966 model). Its sociocultural functions were now taken for granted, in government, education, science, literature, and as the language of literacy throughout the land. English, like French and Italian, was the standardized vernacular in which the nation expressed itself, negotiated with other nations, carried on its colonial activities. It was coincidentally a regional variety, associated with Great Britain including Wales and Scotland, yet it was not seen as a local set of norms, as in stage 4 of Schneider's model for new varieties of English. For the British it was still "the English language" flagged in the title of Johnson's dictionary, not British English per se.

3 British English in the colonial and postcolonial era, 18th to 20th century

3.1 Colonial expansion and contraction

Successive waves of British settlers with their various regional dialects created an English language matrix in North America, which took on local characteristics through distinctive usages and loanwords from native American languages. The independence of American English as regional alternative was affirmed from the late 18th century by the American Philological Society in terms of "Federal English". Its principles were articulated especially by Webster in his *Dissertations on the English Language* (1789), where he urged Americans to seize the opportunity of "establishing a national language and giving it uniformity and perspicuity" (quoted in Baron 1982: 43–44). He argued for spelling to be reformed in line with common pronunciation, so as to facilitate literacy and a relatively uniform way of speaking accessible to Americans of every rank. Federal English was thus a means of avoiding the "sociolinguistic cleavage" seen in Britain, and an opportunity to create a unique American orthographic system more regular than the British. This emphasis on language reform was also a strategic defense against the persistent British view that American English was simply corrupt form of Standard English, and their disinclination to accept the "inevitability of colonial Englishes", to borrow Trudgill's (2004) title.

The American War of Independence in 1776 was the seminal event (Event X) which marked the separation of American English from the parent variety (triggering stage 4, endonormative stabilization [Schneider 2007: 274]). In fact it entailed totally new political perspectives for speakers of the old variety as well as the new. In Great Britain the impact of the war was registered immediately in terms of *realpolitik*. No longer could it take the American colonies for granted as a source of commodities or a trading partner, or as a recipient of convicts (this was the reason for turning to the newly acquired Australian territory for their resettlement). In the same way, the English implanted in the American ex-colonies could no longer be regarded as an outgrowth of universal Standard English rooted in Great Britain. Yet the reciprocal, that the reach of "British English" was now more circumscribed than before, and might indeed be more strictly identified with Great Britain (Hansen's second definition), did not come quickly.

The first recorded British use of the term "British English" occurs almost a century after the American war of Independence. The *Oxford English Dictionary* lists just two citations from the later 19th century, both from linguistic commentators: Ellis (1869), comparing British and American pronunciation, and Sweet (1892), commenting on the influence of Cockney on British and Australasian English. But neither seems to entail a conception of British English itself as a regional variety. Fowler in his *Dictionary of Modern English Usage* (1926) uses "British English" in very straightforward contrasts of usage, e.g. British v. American understanding of *billion, trillion* (page 52 column 2). But elsewhere (*-our/-or* spellings, page 415 column 1), he speaks more ironically of the British English reaction to *-or*: "'Yankee', we say, and congratulate ourselves on spelling like gentlemen". It suggests that when discussing usage differences, the British public was still inclined to foreground social rather than regional judgments.

For the British at large, the notion that the English of Great Britain might be a circumscribed regional variety was masked by fact that it was still the reference language of other settlements/colonies within British Commonwealth: Canada, Africa, and in the Asia-Pacific region. British English would therefore be understood in terms of Hansen's fourth definition (see Section 1 above). Until the later

20th century, citizens of the Commonwealth typically shared in this compact, and were themselves exonormative in thinking about Standard English. This was clearly so in case of those Australians who regarded the British Received Pronunciation (RP) accent as their model, and who even up to World War II still tended to speak of a trip to Britain as "going home", as if they were still expatriates (Moore 2008: 59). Following World War II, there was an increasingly strong sense of national identity in Australia, and the first moves to codify Australian English with Australian Government *Style Manual* (1966), and the *Macquarie Dictionary* (1981). Yet through the efforts of the British Council, British English remained the model for ESL teaching in Asia and Australia (Phillipson 1992: 173–181). This coincides with the publishing phenomenon noted by (Clyne 1992: 459–460) in connection with pluricentric languages, that the "dominant" variety (= British English) with its greater publishing resources can easily disseminate its "standard" usage within the jurisdiction of "other" varieties overseas, to challenge their regional norms. In Australia this power was reinforced by publishing cartels which were deconstructed only quite recently, with changes to the Australian Copyright Act in 1991. Until then British agencies managed the export of books to Australia (both which ones and when), and the interests of the local market/ speech community were not paramount.

3.2 New models of World English

Quasi-imperial notions of British English began to be challenged later in the 20th century in fresh descriptive models of world English, produced by speakers from the Commonwealth or outside the borders of England per se. The most influential has been Kachru's "three circles" model which created an "inner

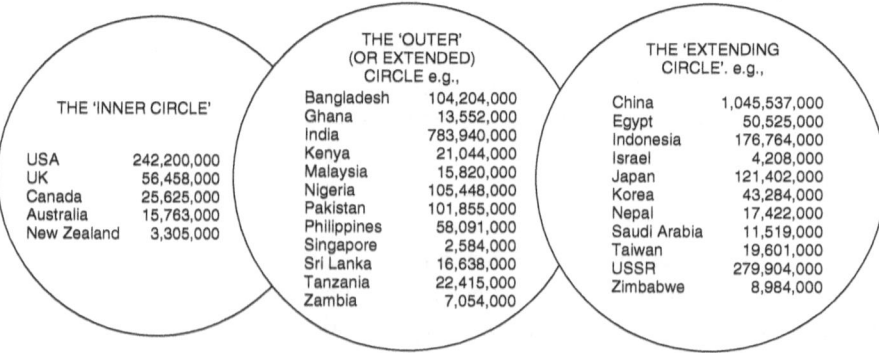

Figure 6.1: The "three circles" model, proposed by Kachru (1988)

circle" consisting of British English and American English along with Canadian, Australian, and New Zealand English. It thus accords the same status to all native-speaker varieties, whereas the newer varieties in ex-colonial regions (e.g. India, Singapore, Malaysia) spoken by indigenous people as an alternative official language, form the "outer circle". Beyond them, in the "extending" circle (now called the "expanding circle") are countries such as China, Indonesia, USSR, in which English is used for auxiliary functions which may lead to its becoming officially recognized. In Kachru's conception of world English (Figure 6.1), British English loses its historical advantage as the first form of English and the input language to the British Empire. Instead it becomes one set of native speaker varieties, each characteristic of and dominant within its region. Kachru does not apply the word "standard" to these varieties, though others such as McArthur (1987) did so. In McArthur's model, "British [Standard English]" and "American Standard English" are represented as two of a larger set of regional standards which form a ring around a notional "World Standard English", set at the heart, as shown in Figure 6.2.

McArthur's concentric circles model goes further than Kachru's in constructing regional or emerging regional standards, and in leveling the status of all varieties of English in the outermost circle, where he juxtaposes subregional "settler" varieties alongside indigenized varieties, pidgins, and creoles. Yet both models illustrate changing views about the status of British English, in a world where it and American English are seen as regional rather than world standards. Both views emanate from outside: outside Great Britain in Kachru's case, and beyond the borders of England (i.e. Scotland) in McArthur's case. They project British English within the broader notion of English as a pluricentric language, and take for granted the existence of multiple regional standards of equal status.

Less egalitarian views of world English have been projected by European commentators, including Leitner (1992: 225–227) – one of Clyne's contributors – who constructs a more abstract three-tier model for the varieties of world English. It puts the "Common Norm" on the top tier (cf. "Common English", Sections 4.2 and 5.1 below), with the British English and American English "typological clusters" of L1 Englishes on the middle tier, and individual "Englishes" on the third tier. The model privileges the British English and American English features of L1 varieties, and seems to downplay their distinctive regional properties as lower-level considerations. As sketched, the model is unclear whether (Standard) British English and American English are both supra-regional and "individual" varieties, or just the first. This is however the pervasive ambiguity affecting the status of British English over the last two centuries.

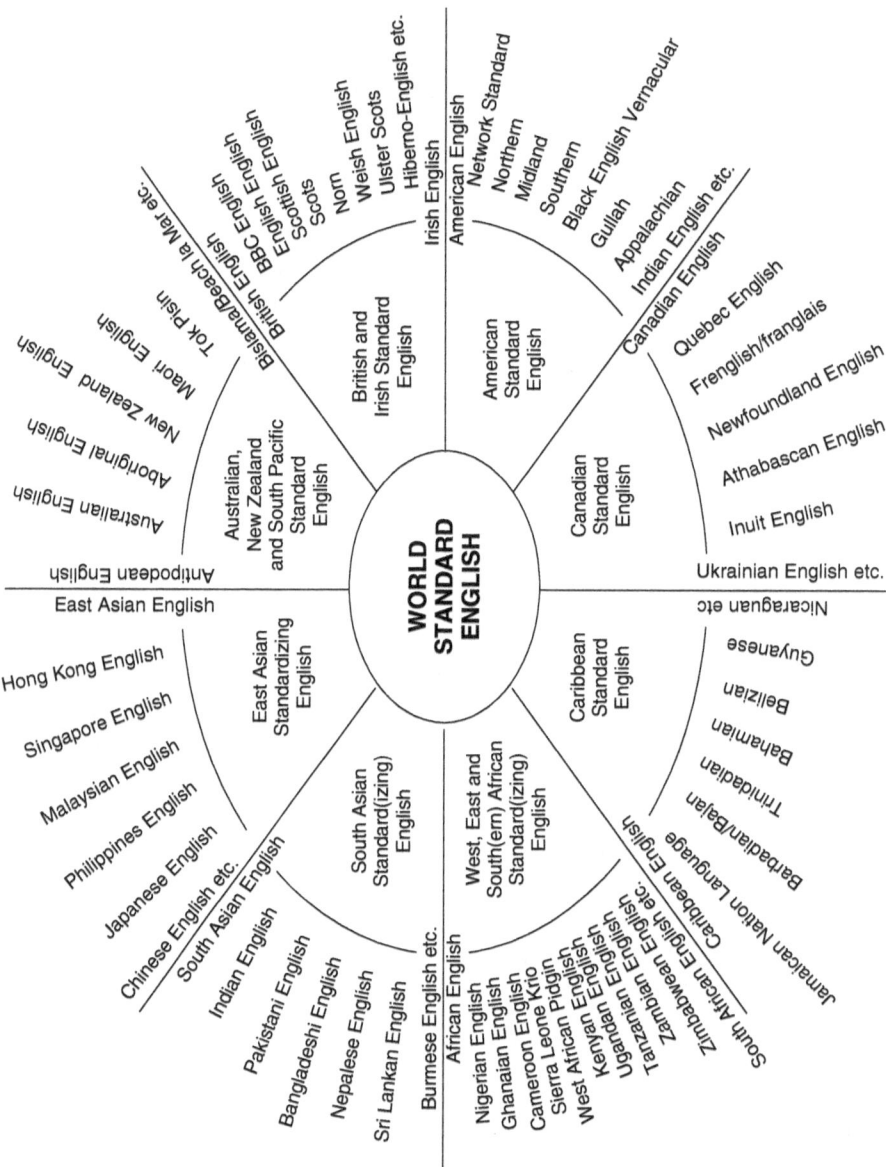

Figure 6.2: The concentric circles model of world English, proposed by McArthur (1987)

3.3 Role of British English within Great Britain

Perceptions of British English inside Great Britain and the British Isles have always been somewhat ambivalent. Though it might serve as a unifying label, British English is not universally embraced. For some British citizens, this is because it seems to imply a broader base of usage than it actually includes. The "standard" forms as written and spoken are mostly those of southern dialects: where there are contrasting regional usages, British English has tended to privilege southern usages over northern, e.g. *got* rather than *gotten* for the past participle of *get,* and the suggestion that *mad* is not properly used to mean "angry" (Peters 2004: 229, 333). Recent research (Kortmann 2008: 491–492) has identified multiple morphosyntactic features on which there is a clear North-South divide, including the lack of inversion in *wh-*questions in the North, and much higher usage of multiple negation used in the South. The southern bias of standard British English underlies the suggestion of Trudgill and Hannah (2002: 2) that it might be more aptly labeled "EngEng". Yet even "EngEng" suggests that it embraces dialectal material all the way from the West Country to the North Midlands and Tyneside, which is far from reality. Loyalty to one's local dialect is still strong within British speech communities, and the local accent, especially in Wales, Scotland, and Ireland is rated more highly than the prestige British accent (RP), in terms of prestige as well as social attractiveness (Coupland and Bishop 2007). The notion of "British English" does not yet correlate with a shared linguistic identity throughout Great Britain.

On the positive side, there is probably more acceptance of regional divergences at the turn of the millennium. Regional voices reading BBC news has helped to give them higher profile, as well as the special BBC project "Voices 2005" which produced a set of television programs featuring language diversity within Great Britain (Crystal 2006: 187–188). These developments show that RP with its exclusive overtones is no longer the prestige accent, and is probably now spoken by less than 3% of the British population (Hughes and Trudgill 1979: 3). Among younger British people of middle and higher social class, RP has been eclipsed by a London-based accent widely known as "Estuary English", which is radiating out from the Thames estuary and southeastern England to other parts of the country: "south of a line from the Wash to the Avon" (Rosewarne 1994: 4; Altendorf, Chapter 9). The centuries-old regional dialects of Britain are in decline, through their speakers' exposure to the mass media and through urbanization of much of rural England, as city workers commute long distances to and from affordable homes in the countryside. British-dialect speakers from everywhere are in daily contact with each other.

At the same time British English has been taking on new dialect elements from overseas varieties of English since World War II. American servicemen brought their alternative terms for everyday realia (e.g. *long-distance* (telephone call) for "trunk (call)", *raincoat* for "mackintosh"), and by 1970 these terms were established in Great Britain (Strang 1970: 37). Post-war consumption of American movies and other media has also familiarized the British with numerous American words and idioms now current in British English (Peters 2001: 307). The decades following World War II also saw the immigration into Britain of speakers of various Commonwealth varieties of Englishes, for example those from Pakistan into Birmingham and Bradford, and those from Jamaica creating a "British Creole" in London (Sebba 2008). There are thus ethnic dialects within the British English community, like those found within new regional varieties after endonormative stabilization (=differentiation, stage 5 in Schneider's model). The difference is that the sociolinguistic diversification within Great Britain is not self-generated, but implanted by immigrants from Commonwealth countries, especially the Caribbean islands and the Indian subcontinent, returning with their postcolonial varieties of English. There are mixed communities of both in larger cities, especially London, as conjured up by novelist Zadie Smith, author of *White Teeth* (2000). An admixture of English interlanguage, spoken by immigrants and workers from countries associated with the European Union is also increasing the diversity. Thus external varieties of English, and of English as spoken by second-language users, are new forces within British English on the threshold of the 21st century, though not canvassed within Schneider's or Haugen's models.

3.4 The ideology of the standard

With greater ethnic and social diversity in Great Britain than ever before comes the prospect of greater diversification of British English, and conservative reactions are probably to be expected. Yet public movements to defend "standard British English" in the late 20th century may have more to do with the need to reaffirm national identity than affirming the regional status of British English. The idea or *ideology* of the "standard" language (Milroy 2000: 17) was debated very publicly in Britain following the 1996 BBC Reith lectures ("The language web"), broadcast by linguist Jean Aitchison. Her strategy, to begin by discussing language prejudices, reaped the whirlwind from BBC Radio 4 listeners (Aitchison 1997: 99, 102). A vehement attack on Aitchison and other descriptive linguists was published in the same year by Honey, declaring its position upfront in the title *Language is Power: the Story of Standard English and its Enemies*. This latter-day conservative reaction in Britain reflects the same concern for authority in language as when language is codified for the first time, taking for granted the need for homogeneity in usage. It has fostered a public "grammar crusade" to maintain language standards in education, and feeds a kind of "moral panic" about the state of the language (Cameron 1995: 78–85). The humorous demagogy of Truss's very popular book on punctuation *Eats, Shoots and Leaves* (2003) capitalized on this public sentiment, especially under the emotive banner of *The Zero Tolerance Approach to Punctuation* (meaning no tolerance of incorrect punctuation, rather than no punctuation at all!). Combative publications such as those of Honey and Truss serve to fuel the ideology of the standard and enlist citizens in the "fight for English" (Crystal 2006). They reflect the "complaint tradition" noted in the nativization/codification stage (see above Section 2.3), although resurfacing at a late stage in the evolution of British English as a regional variety. It has not so far been indicated for stage 5 in the evolution of new varieties (Schneider 2007: 56).

In the development of British English before and after the American War of Independence, we see some of the sociolinguistic features associated with the evolution of new varieties of English. But they are not so strictly confined to particular stages, and the resemblances to Schneider's model are sometimes coincidental rather than intrinsic, as with the burgeoning of ethnic dialects in British English in the late 20th century. The public controversy prompted by the rhetoric of maintaining the standard may seem to reflect a kind of sociolinguistic cleavage like that of 18th century England. Yet this millennial linguistic controversy does not align itself with social class distinctions, like those against which Webster's Federal English was reacting (see above Section 3.1). That apart, the largest single difference for British English is the fact that it was (especially during the 19th and earlier 20th century) the language of empire. That international role, and the contact between it and American English, the other regional-cum-international English, have ensured that there are external forces continually impacting on British English and contributing to linguistic changes within it. These will be the focus of the following section.

4 Linguistic features of Standard British English in the 20th century

4.1 Pluralism in British English: orthography

The criteria for a national standard language, noted in the introduction, are that it may be expected to show minimal variation in form alongside a maximal range of functions (Haugen [1966] 1972). Normative processes are associated especially with Schneider's stage 4 in the evolution of new Englishes, with the emphasis on standardization and the codification of the language. They were particularly noteworthy in the formative stages of American English, with Webster's emphasis on systematizing it (see above, Section 3.1, and below), and they are part of the current controversy in British English.

Standard British English is less homogenous and less standardized than American English in its orthography – as well as its morphology and aspects of syntax, as reported in Rohdenburg and Schlüter (2009: 5–6). A plurality of grapheme-phoneme correspondences was embedded in its orthography from the start, partly because of the conservation of graphemes from Old and Middle English within Chancery English (see above, Section 2.1), and also because of interventions by Tudor orthoepists, sometimes adding diacritic letters, e.g. the *e* in the plurals of words ending in *–o*, and at other times subtracting "superfluous letters" such as the unhistorical *k* from words like *magic(k), optic(k), traffic(k)* although it returns in inflected forms such as *trafficking*. Alternation paradigms like these were added in Johnson's *Dictionary* for other words, e.g. the removal of the final *l* from *distil(l), fulfil(l), instil(l)*, which is returned to the inflected forms (*distilled*, etc.) – whereas in American English the base and inflected forms of the stem are the same. Johnson extended the practice of doubling the final *l* in suffixed forms of other verbs, e.g. *level(ler), model(ler), revel(ler)*, which by their stress on the first syllable belong to a different orthographic paradigm (cf. *differed, deferred*). These adhoc additions to modern British orthography, and the alternation between *-our* and *-or* in the *humour/humorous* paradigm were among the spelling practices which Webster sought to reform in his *American Dictionary of the English Language* (1828). For many British English users they have become the hallmarks of their variety.

Paradoxically the greater pluralism of British English orthography makes some of its England-based users more accommodating of "American" spellings than vice versa. This emerged in international surveys of spelling preferences (the Langscape surveys) conducted in 1998–2000 through the magazine *English Today*. There were marked differences in the responses of "English" and Americans on variable points of spelling and morphology, as in Table 6.1a and Table 6.1b below, extracted from Peters (1998).

Though the number of "English" respondents to this survey was larger than the American (n = 331 v. n = 56), the returns suggest that the British community is far less monolithic about these spelling and morphological variants. Users of *ae* and *e* spellings can be found in Britain, sometimes in almost equal proportions (as with *pal(a)eolithic)*, whereas the American community hardly accepts the *ae* alternative at all. Likewise the accommodation of both *-os* and *-oes* plurals by British respondents contrasts with the American commitment to the former. This

Table 6.1a: Responses by "English" and Americans on variable points of spelling and morphology, extracted from Peters (1998)

	England %	USA %
anaemia	86	0
anemia	14	100
leukaemia	73	0
leukemia	27	100
mediaeval	34	2
medieval	66	98
palaeolithic	52	2
paleolithic	48	92
septicaemia	60	2
septicemia	40	98

Table 6.1b: Responses by "English" and Americans on variable points of spelling and morphology, extracted from Peters (1998)

	England %	USA %
banjoes	24	9
banjos	76	91
flamingoes	33	5
flamingos	67	95
frescoes	37	7
frescos	63	93
haloes	25	4
halos	75	96
mottoes	17	0
mottos	83	100

pluralism allows international publishers to market American versions of books in the UK, but not British versions in the US.

British punctuation practices are also pluralistic on many points where those of American writers and publishers are unitary. One example is the regular use in American English of double quotation marks, whereas both single and double quote marks are in use in British English, depending on the publishing house and the domain of use. They differ further over the location of the final full stop relative to the quote marks (Peters 2004: 454–455). In British English punctuation subclasses of shortened forms are marked so as to distinguish "true" abbreviations from contractions (the first set are given stops and the second not: Peters 2004: 126). The fact that American punctuation practices are more standardized than British owes something to their early codification through the *Chicago*

Manual of Style (1906). There was no similar manual for British English until the first edition of Butcher's *Copy-Editing* (1975), which notes alternative practices like those just mentioned.

4.2 Pluralism in British English: grammar and corpus research

Pluralism in British English grammar can be seen from the first attempts to lay it out in the 17th century, e.g. in Wallis's (1653) alternative expressions for the future tense laid out in same paradigm, with *will* attached to second and third persons and *shall* to the first. It was probably not in line with facts of 17th century English, as Fries (1940: 153–161) found in his research on a corpus of Early Modern English drama. But it was perpetuated by 18th and 19th century grammarians, and left its mark in continuing use of *shall* as an alternative to *will* for expressing the future in current British English. Meanwhile in American English, *shall* is almost obsolete, in corpus data analysed for the *Longman Grammar* (Biber et al. 1999: 488).

Different regional patterns have emerged in modal verb negation, where once again British English is more pluralistic, using both contracted forms (*mayn't, mightn't, mustn't, needn't, shan't*) as well as the uncontracted ones (*may not, might not* etc). American English meanwhile relies very much on the latter (Algeo 2006: 22–24). The pluralism of British English usage also comes to light in the greater variety of question forms which it uses: *do you have any...?, have you any...?, have you got any ...?,* though the second and third occurred more frequently than the first in British English data from the Longman corpus used by Biber et al. (1999: 216). By contrast, *do you have any...?* predominated in all the American English data, with very low use of the others. The Longman corpus data showed that the British alternatives were in fact closely associated with particular registers and types of discourse, so that *have you got any...?* was most common in British conversation, while the more "conservative" *have you any...?* appeared most often in fiction writing. Stylistic differentiation thus helps to support alternative forms in British English.

Corpus research on collocational patterns has also confirmed the greater pluralism of British English. Comparative studies based on digital archives of newspapers (see Hundt 1998; Levin 1998) have shown this in relation to agreement with group nouns such as *government;* here British English uses both singular and plural, and American English almost always the singular. Very large heterogeneous corpora (*British National Corpus* [BNC], *The Bank of English, The Cambridge International Corpus* [CIC]) have helped to substantiate divergences in less frequent features of grammar and usage, both new arrivals and late survivals. Comparative data from the BNC and CIC showed that the recent use of *reticent* to mean "reluctant" is formulated as *reticent about* or *reticent to* in British English, but only as *reticent to* in American English (Peters 2004: 474). For other evidence of British accommodation of both older and newer usage variants, see Peters (2014; forthcoming 2017). The longer-term aspects of British English pluralism are considered below in relation to world English (Section 5.2).

4.3 Linguistic and stylistic changes in 20th century British English

Dual and divided usage is often associated with linguistic change, through changes in relative currency of the alternatives over a period of time (Aitchison 2001). This phenomenon comes to light in many longitudinal studies of British English, e.g. relative usage of the mandative subjunctive and modal paraphrases (especially with *should*) from 1900 to 1990 (Overgaard 1995). This recovery of the mandative from the brink of extinction in British English during the course of the twentieth century probably reflects American influence, as Gowers (1976: 211) noted. Changing relationships between grammatical alternatives have been found even in a 30-year period, as shown by their relative frequencies in the *Lancaster-Oslo-Bergen Corpus* (LOB) (=1960s data) and its 1990s counterpart FLOB (*Freiburg-Lancaster-Oslo-Bergen Corpus*) (Mair and Leech 2006). Among various changes to the verb phrase in British English, they noted the gradual replacement of the canonical modal verbs, e.g *must, should* with quasimodals *have to, ought to*. This too may reflect American influence on British English grammar (Collins 2009).

The grammar of speech is more pluralistic than that of writing, as the *Longman Grammar of Spoken and Written English* (1999) abundantly shows. Speech accepts variant usages more readily than writing, as with "nonstandard" uses of pronouns, including *me* in coordinated subject phrases (Quinn 2009), and *I* in coordinated non-subject phrases especially following prepositions (Peters 2009). The *Cambridge Grammar of English* (Huddleston and Pullum 2002: 463) indicates that the latter usage must now be regarded as a "standard variant". This example also suggests that spoken usages now pass more quickly into writing, helped by changing stylistic norms. Greater colloquialization of written usage has been found in relation to numerous syntactic variables, though this is typically less advanced in British English than American English (Rohdenburg and Schlüter 2009: 366–407). British English however does participate in this trend on variables such as increasing use of quasi-modals, of contractions (Mair 2006: 189–190), and of the accusative with postverbal gerunds (Peters 2006: 774). All these help to create oral effects within writing, and suggest greater acceptance of spoken usage in less formal prose. In any case, the boundaries between different registers are not immutable, but recalibrated over the course of time. Research on texts in the ARCHER corpus (Biber et al. 1994: 9–12) showed for example that journals and diaries became less information-oriented and more interactive between 1750 and 1990, and that this change was more marked in American than British texts. These changes in the character of registers take place in the context of cultural and social change, e.g. the greater or lesser value put upon formality, and on isolating formal discourse from the everyday.

A potent sociocultural force of the late 20th century is the emphasis on youth style (Mair 2006: 185–186), whose impact on British English pronunciation and usage is of no small interest. It seems likely to accelerate the take up of younger people's usage within the speech community, in advance of the natural generational change illustrated in Labov's (1972: 196–197) research on linguistic innovation in the city of New York. There were generational differences in British data returned in the Langscape survey reported above (Section 4.1), showing much greater acceptance of -*os* plurals by the younger generations, i.e. those under 25, and/or aged 25–44 (Peters 1998: 7–8), which would prefigure faster take up of the streamlined plural forms for words ending in -*o* than might otherwise happen. Likewise from the generational differences found in British National Corpus data for expressing the future, e.g. very strong endorsement by the 15–24 age group of using *gonna* for *going to* (Mair 2006: 99–100), we could predict rapid assimilation of *gonna* among the quasimodals of standard British English.

The contexts of language change in 20th century British English are essentially social – and thus broadly in keeping with the pattern for new Englishes – although the examples discussed in this section are not primarily related to the differentiation of new social groups within Great Britain. Rather they occur through the intersection of British English with external forces and external varieties of English, especially American English. This returns us to the question of how newer and older varieties relate to each other, and especially the changing role of British English as an international standard. Both these take us beyond the evolutionary model for new regional varieties to the question of supra-regional standards of English.

5 British English as an international standard

5.1 British English as a world standard alongside American English

The jurisdiction of British English as an international standard has changed continually since 1775, with the processes of colonial expansion and postcolonial contraction. This fluidity would help to explain the dearth of references to its international role before the 20th century. A rare indication is in the title chosen by Ogilvie for his two-volume *Imperial Dictionary of the English Language*, a British adaptation of a one-volume Webster's dictionary, published in Glasgow (1847–50). The *Oxford English Dictionary* (Simpson and Weiner [1884–1928] 1989) does not refer either to "British English" or "international English" in its compass-like diagram of the various types of English. Instead it uses the term "common English". Yet its positioning is essentially "Britocentric" (Simpson 2001: 276); and though it represents the "Empire of Words" (Willinsky 1994), it does not explicitly identify its content as "imperial" or "international". Meanwhile the strategic title of *Webster's New International Dictionary* (1909) flags the first linguistic challenge from American English to supply the international standard for English.

With the new mass media of the 20th century came the first opportunity to disseminate spoken British English as a reference or standard outside Great Britain. Starting in 1932, the BBC Empire Service was able to broadcast British speech in its shortwave radio programs. In its own terms it was a British *broadcasting* voice – certainly not as used socially within Great Britain, but one which could be used abroad as a reference accent (Leitner 1982: 100–104). The notion of "BBC English" as a standard form of British English is first recorded from 1932 on, according to the *Oxford Dictionary,* though its status in McArthur's model (Figure 6.2 above) is strictly regional. It was nevertheless invoked in the title of HarperCollins's *BBC English Dictionary* (1992), in a partnership between the publisher and the BBC. BBC World continues to broadcast British English voices (with a wider range of accents) in widely accessible TV newscasts. Again these initiatives have been matched for American English speech, first in radio broadcasts with *Voice of America* (from 1942 on), and from 1980 through the ubiquitous CNN, providing television news and entertainment.

In 20th century publishing, British English has shared with American English the role of being "dual" print standards (McArthur 2001: 6–7). Regional publishing cartels often require book rights to be separately negotiated for the British and American markets, and separate British English/American English versions produced for each. For example, the *Encarta World Dictionary* (1999) was published in two regional versions, one with headwords spelled as for British English (and other Commonwealth countries), the other in American English spelling. Morphological variants e.g. *dial(ling) tone*, heteronyms e.g. *duvet/comforter*, and the divergent semantics of words such as *wrangler* were indicated for the other variety within individual entries. Of course these linguistic elements are only the tip of the iceberg in terms of regionally identifiable aspects of any text. They are also embedded in regional institutions e.g. *Congress v. Parliament*, alternative measurement systems, in the geographical perspective (*east v. west*) etc., where the L1 reader's regional knowledge can be taken for granted. But the regionalized spelling, morphology, and lexicosemantics of the two "print standards" now serve to flag the publication's orientation as British or American, without explicit labeling.

The most explicit and thorough-going recognition of British English as an international language standard, in parallel with American English, can be found in the context of ELT publishing. Though the terms British English and American English are rough linguistic generalizations for their primary speech communities, they are valuable for L2s when focusing on specific learning targets – essential where spoken norms being taught, and helpful in flagging contrastive lexicogrammatical content in language teaching materials. They were used systematically in the "big four" ESL dictionaries published in 1995 (*Cambridge International Dictionary of English, Collins Cobuild Dictionary* [2nd edn.], *Longman Dictionary of Contemporary English* [3rd edn.] and the *Oxford Advanced Learners Dictionary* [5th edn.]), to alert L2 readers to British English pronunciations, spelling, morphology and usage alongside their American counterparts.

Apart from their use and application in the print medium, the terms "British English" and "American English" (or flags representing them) are now regularly used worldwide in software tools for editing, as well as in the DVD options for English-language dubbing and subtitles, and the various global positioning devices. All these examples show how recognition of British English as an international standard language has happened in tandem with the recognition of American English. There is little to document the role of British English as the sole international standard, as it might have been seen by Englishmen of the 18th and 19th century. It has effectively shared the role throughout the 20th century.

5.2 British English in the context of World Standard English

The equivalence of British English and American English as world standards is well established, allowing other nations and institutions to select one or the other for official communication and education, according to their past history and/or present *realpolitik*. British English may be preferred to American English in most of Western Europe and in academic Europe, according to Algeo (2006); whereas in Asia (apart from Hong Kong), the reverse probably holds.

Linguistic duality like this is typically asymmetrical, in Clyne's (1992: 455–457) account of the pluricentric languages of the world. It is especially so where there is no central language academy to stabilize regional variation, as in the pluricentric world of Arabic, and where a new world variety challenges that of the old world. English is more generally challenged by the now enormous numbers of L2s (Crystal 1997: 60–61). With new, economically advantaged centers of publishing in India and China, there are greater economic incentives to find an international print standard which could be used throughout the world: the "World Standard English" of McArthur's model (Figure 6.2 above). L2 writers, editors and publishers are well placed to create it, and because they do not have a particular commitment to either British or American English, it may well be an amalgam of both.

A foretaste of such amalgams can be found in the mix of regional spelling and regional usages in Chinese publications (Peters 2003: 36–37), e.g. in the *China Daily* newspaper's combination of spellings such as British English *-our* and American English *-ize* (which is used in British English in the ratio of about 2:3 alongside *-ise*, but not by the British press [Peters 2004: 298]). The Chinese use of *-ize* probably reflects American English influence in the region, as well as the fact that *-ize* is the sole American spelling. In general we might expect L2s to prefer the greater uniformity of American English orthography and morphology (see above, Section 4.1), which makes it the more straightforward reference standard. When it comes to regularity in syntactic constructions, the scales may be more evenly balanced, at least on the set of variables investigated by Rohdenburg and Schlüter (2009: 421). Yet their concluding comment is that British English seems to be more receptive to American English syntactic innovations than vice versa (Rohdenburg and Schlüter 2009: 422). Whether this take-up of American English innovations within British English will reinforce their use within a transnational "World Standard English" (Schneider 2014), or consolidate the status of American English (Mair 2013), are alternative scenarios for further research.

The future role of British English in "World Standard English" presents us with open-ended questions, yet its current status as a major regional variety of English is secure. Its role as the national language of Great Britain is not in contention, despite the counterpoint between the ideology of standard and the cultural and linguistic diversification of the British population in the 20th century. With its inherent pluralism, it readily absorbs linguistic elements from other varieties, yet maintains its own identity for its users at home in Great Britain and overseas.

6 References

Aarts, Bas and April McMahon (eds.). 2006. *Handbook of English Linguistics*. Oxford: Blackwell.
Aitchison, Jean. 1997. *The Language Web: the Power and Problem of Words*. Cambridge: Cambridge University Press.
Aitchison, Jean. 2001. *Language Change, Progress or Decay*. 3rd edn. Cambridge: Cambridge University Press.
Algeo, John. 2006. *British or American English? A Handbook of Word and Grammar Patterns*. Cambridge: Cambridge University Press.
Baron, Denis. 1982. *Grammar and Good Taste*. New Haven: Yale University Press.
Biber, Douglas, Edward Finegan, and Dwight Atkinson. 1994. ARCHER and its challenges: compiling and exploring a representative corpus of historical English registers. In: Udo Fries, Gunnel Tottie, and Peter Schneider (eds.), *Creating and Using English Language Corpora*, 1–15. Amsterdam: Rodopi.
Biber, Douglas, Geoffrey Leech, Stig Johansson, Susan Conrad, and Edward Finegan. 1999. *Longman Grammar of Spoken and Written English*. London: Longman.
Butcher, Judith. 1975. *Copy-Editing*. Cambridge: Cambridge University Press.
Cameron, Deborah. 1995. *Verbal Hygiene*. London: Routledge.
Clyne, Michael. 1992. *Pluricentric Languages: Differing Norms in Different Nations*. Berlin/New York: Mouton de Gruyter.
Collins, Peter. 2009. Modals and quasi modals. In: Pam Peters, Peter Collins, and Adam Smith (eds.), *Comparative Studies in Australian and New Zealand English. Grammar and Beyond*, 73–88. Amsterdam/Philadelphia: John Benjamins.
Coupland, Nikolas and Hywel Bishop. 2007. Ideologized values for British accents. *Journal of Sociolinguistics* 11(1): 74–103.
Crystal, David. 1997. *English as a Global Language*. Cambridge: Cambridge University Press.
Crystal, David. 2006. *The Fight for English: How the Pundits Ate, Shot and Left*. Oxford: Oxford University Press.
Culpeper, Jonathan and Phoebe Clapham. 1996. The borrowing of classical and romance words into English: a study based on the electronic *Oxford English Dictionary*. *International Journal of Corpus Linguistics* 1(2): 199–218.
Fitzmaurice, Susan. 2000. The Spectator and the politics of social networks. In: Laura Wright (ed.), 195–218.
Fowler, Henry W. 1926. *A Dictionary of Modern English Usage*. Oxford: Oxford University Press.
Fries, Charles. 1940. *American English Grammar*. New York: Appleton-Century Crofts.
Gordon, Ian. 1966. *The Movement of English Prose*. London: Longman.
Gowers, Ernest [1954] 1976. *The Complete Plain Words*. 2nd edn. Harmondsworth: Penguin.
Hansen, Klaus. 1997. *British English* and *International English* – two debatable terms. In: Edgar W. Schneider (ed.), *Englishes around the World: Studies in Honor of Manfred Goerlach*, 59–70. Vol. 2. Amsterdam/Philadelphia: John Benjamins.
Haugen, Einar [1966] 1972. Language, dialect, nation. In: John Pride and Janet Holmes (eds), 97–111.
Honey, John. 1997. *Language is Power: The Story of Standard English and its Enemies*. London: Faber and Faber.
Huddleston, Rodney D. and Geoffrey K. Pullum. 2002. *Cambridge Grammar of the English Language*. Cambridge: Cambridge University Press.

Hughes, Arthur and Peter Trudgill. 1979. *English Accents and Dialects*. London: Edward Arnold.
Hundt, Marianne. 1998. *New Zealand English Grammar: Fact or Fiction*. Amsterdam/Philadelphia: John Benjamins.
Kachru, Braj. 1988. The sacred cows of English. *English Today* 16(4): 3–8.
Kortmann, Bernd. 2008. Synopsis: morphological and syntactic variation in the British Isles. In: Bernd Kortmann and Clive Upton (eds.), 478–496.
Kortmann, Bernd and Clive Upton (eds.). 2008. *Varieties of English I: the British Isles*. Berlin/New York: Mouton de Gruyter.
Labov, William. 1972. The study of language in its social context. In: John Pride and Janet Holmes (eds.), 180–202.
Leitner, Gerhard. 1982. The consolidation of "Educated Southern English" as a model in the early 20th century. *International Review of Applied Linguistics* 20(2): 91–107.
Leitner, Gerhard. 1992. English as a pluricentric language. In: Michael Clyne (ed.), 179–237.
Levin, Magnus. 1998. Concord with collective nouns in British and American English. In: Hans Lindquist, Staffan Klintborg, Magnus Levin, and Maria Estling (eds.), *The Major Varieties of English: Papers from MAVEN 97*, 193–204. Vaxsjö: Vaxsjö University Press.
McArthur, Tom. 1987. The English Languages. *English Today* 11(3): 9–13.
McArthur, Tom. 2001. World English and world Englishes. *Language Teaching* 34:1–20.
McIntosh, Carey. 2008. British English in the Long Eighteenth Century 1660–1830. In: Haruko Momma and Michael Matto (eds.), 228–234.
Mair, Christian. 2006. *Twentieth Century English: History, Variation and Standardization*. Cambridge: Cambridge University Press.
Mair, Christian. 2013. The world system of Englishes. *English World-Wide* 34(3): 253–278.
Mair, Christian and Geoffrey Leech. 2006. Current changes in English syntax. In: Bas Aarts and April McMahon (eds.), 318–342.
Milroy, James. 2000. Historical description and the ideology of the standard language. In: Laura Wright (ed.), 11–28.
Momma, Haruko and Michael Matto (eds.). 2008. *A Companion to the History of the English Language*. Sussex, UK: Wiley-Blackwell
Moore, Bruce (ed.). 2001. *Who's Centric Now? The Present State of Post-Colonial Englishes*. Melbourne: Oxford University Press.
Moore, Bruce. 2008. *Speaking our Language: the Story of Australian English*. Melbourne: Oxford University Press.
Nevalainen, Terttu. 2008. Early Modern English (1485–1660). In: Haruko Momma and Michael Matto (eds.), 209–215.
Overgaard, Gerd. 1995. *The Mandative Subjunctive in American and British English in the 20th Century*. Uppsala: Uppsala University Press.
Peters, Pam. 1998. The extra letter: a report on the LANGSCAPE 1 questionnaire. *English Today* 14(4): 6–12.
Peters, Pam. 2001. Varietal effects: the influence of American English on Australian and British English. In: Bruce Moore (ed.), 297–309.
Peters, Pam. 2003. What is international English? In: Pam Peters (ed.), *From Local to Global English, 33–42*. Sydney: Dictionary Research Center.
Peters, Pam. 2004. *Cambridge Guide to English Usage*. Cambridge: Cambridge University Press.
Peters, Pam. 2006. English usage: description and prescription. In: Bas Aarts and April McMahon (eds.), 759–780.

Peters, Pam. 2009. Personal pronouns in spoken English grammar. In: Mats Moberg and Rhonwen Bowen (eds.), *Corpora and Discourse and Stuff. Papers in Honour of Karin Aijmer*, 253–265. Gothenburg: University of Gothenburg.

Peters, Pam. 2014. Usage Guides and Usage Trends in Australian and British English Australian. *Journal of Linguistics* 31(4): 581–598.

Peters, Pam. in press. 2017. The lexicography of English usage: describing usage variation and change. In: Ingrid Tieken-Boon van Ostade (ed.), *English Usage Guides: Usage Advice and Attitudes to Usage*, 26–44. Oxford University Press.

Peters, Pam, Peter Collins and Adam Smith (eds.). 2009. *Comparative Studies in Australian and New Zealand English: Grammar and Beyond*. Amsterdam/Philadelphia: John Benjamins.

Phillipson, Robert. 1992. *Linguistic Imperialism*. Oxford: Oxford University Press.

Pride, John and Janet Holmes (eds.). 1972. *Sociolinguistics*. Harmondsworth: Penguin.

Quinn, Heidi. 2009. Pronoun forms. In: Pam Peters, Peter Collins and Adam Smith (eds.), 31–48.

Reddick, Allen. 1990. *The Making of Johnson's Dictionary 1747–1773*. Cambridge: Cambridge University Press.

Rohdenburg, Günter and Julia Schlüter (eds.). 2009. *One Language, Two Grammars? Differences between British and American English*. Cambridge: Cambridge University Press.

Rosewarne, David. 1994. Estuary English: tomorrow's RP? *English Today* 10(1): 3–8.

Schneider, Edgar. 2007. *Postcolonial English: Varieties around the World*. Cambridge: Cambridge University Press.

Schneider, Edgar. 2014. New reflections on the evolutionary dynamics of world Englishes. *World Englishes* 33(1): 9–32.

Sebba, Mark. 2008. British Creole: morphology and syntax. In: Bernd Kortmann and Clive Upton (eds.), 463–477.

Simpson, John. 2001. Queen's English and people's English. In: Bruce Moore (ed.), 269–283.

Simpson, J.A and E.S.C. Weiner [1884–1928] 1989. *The Oxford English Dictionary*. 2nd edn. Oxford: Clarendon Press.

Smith, Jeremy. 2008. Varieties of Middle English. In: Haruko Momma and Michael Matto (eds.), 198–206.

Starnes, De Wit and Gertrude Noyes. 1946. *English Dictionaries from Cawdrey to Johnson 1604–1755*. Chapel Hill: University of North Carolina Press.

Strang, Barbara. 1970. *A History of English*. London: Methuen.

Tieken-Boon van Ostade, Ingrid. 2010. *The Bishop's Grammar*. Oxford: Oxford University Press

Trudgill, Peter. 2004. *New Dialect Formation: the Inevitability of Colonial Englishes*. Edinburgh: Edinburgh University Press.

Trudgill, Peter and Jean Hannah. 2002. *International English*. 4th edn. London: Arnold.

Truss, Lynne. 2003. *Eats, shoots and Leaves*. London: Profile Books.

Tucker, Susie. 1961. *English Examined: Two Centuries of Comment on the Mother-Tongue*. Cambridge: Cambridge University Press.

Willinsky, John. 1994. *Empire of Words: the Reign of the OED*. Princeton: Princeton University Press.

Wright, Laura (ed.). 2000. *The Development of Standard English 1300 to 1800*. Cambridge: Cambridge University Press.

Bernd Kortmann and Christian Langstrof
Chapter 7:
Regional varieties of British English

1 Introduction —— 121
2 Phonetic and phonological variation —— 122
3 Morpho-syntactic variation —— 131
4 Summary and outlook —— 145
5 References —— 147

Abstract: This chapter provides an outline of the major patterns of variation in contemporary British English on both the phonological (Section 2) and the morpho-syntactic level (Section 3). In Section 2 it will be shown that although rich patterns of variation exist on the consonant system, these are mainly a function of socioeconomic factors as well as speech style rather than regional distribution. On the other hand, major regional stratifications are found in the vowel system. On the morpho-syntactic level we can differentiate between pan-British features (outlined in Section 3.1) and regional features (Section 3.2). It will be shown that the major North-South distinction that holds in terms of the phonology of British English is also reflected in the morpho-syntactic data.

1 Introduction

Right from the beginning of dialectological studies in the 19th century there has been a strong link between historical linguistics and the study of regional variation, and up to this day it has been a fascinating enterprise within (both historical and modern) dialectology to discuss dialect features at a given stage in history from the point of view of whether they constitute continuities of older language periods or rather innovations. This is true in particular for the dialects of England which, evidently, have not only the greatest time-depth of all varieties of English around the world but which, to this day, display the richest range of structural variation (including the very number of varieties) observable across all L1, i.e. mother tongue, varieties of English. This general pattern has been pointed out

Bernd Kortmann: Freiburg (Germany)
Christian Langstrof: Paderborn (Germany)

succinctly by Schneider (2004: 1127) as a result of a large-scale comparative approach to phonological variation in the Anglophone world, and can be extended to syntactic and, especially, morphological variation:

> The amount of variability found in a given area seems to correlate with the historical depth of the independent evolution of the respective variety of English. A very large amount of minute detail characterizes the dialectal landscape of England, and the British Isles in general. In North America, there is still a fairly wide range of pronunciation details to be observed. In contrast, the pronunciations of AusE and NZE are relatively homogeneous... African and Asian varieties seem to be relatively more homogeneous [...]. (Schneider 2004: 1127)

It is the latter, large-scale perspective which will be taken in the present chapter: we will offer a snapshot of present-day structural variation, concerning both phonetics and phonology and morpho-syntax, adopting a comparative, to some extent typology-style perspective, as has become the hallmark of the Freiburg take on the mapping and study of morpho-syntactic variation among the non-standard varieties spoken in the Anglophone world, in general, and the regional dialects of the British Isles, in particular. In doing so the focus will be both on regionally most distinctive features and on dialect features with a wider, pan-Northern, pan-Southern, or even pan-British reach. We will partly draw on survey accounts (e.g. Foulkes and Docherty 1999; Kortmann and Upton 2008) and, for morpho-syntactic variation, on survey data (cf. Kortmann and Lunkenheimer 2011). Among other things, this comparative approach will allow us to identify larger geographical patterns among the grammars of regional varieties of the British Isles than previously assumed, and to put in perspective observable dialect features in the British Isles against those found in L1 varieties spoken in other parts of the Anglophone world. Given this ambitious scope, it is necessary to be selective and to dispense with in-depth discussions of individual dialects or features.

2 Phonetic and phonological variation

Regional accent variation in contemporary Britain is rather complex and has been a fruitful area of research in dialectology, sociolinguistics and sociophonetics over the last decades. In what follows, we will outline the general patterns of pronunciation differences in different areas of Britain. Note that the focus is on shibboleths distinguishing the *major* accent divisions in Britain, which implies that the list of regionally distinctive phonetic / phonological features is far from exhaustive (for more detailed overviews and feature lists of specific varieties of British Englishes, see Wells 1982; Hughes et al. 2005; Foulkes and Docherty 1999;

as well as the contributions by various authors in Kortmann and Upton 2008). Following the approach adopted in Kortmann and Upton (2008), the different "types" of British English will not be compared relative to Received Pronunciation (RP) since, on the broad level of phonological variation which we will be concerned with, RP is one of many varieties of the Southern type (cf. Mugglestone, Chapter 8).

Although there exist a number of regional differences in terms of the consonant system, the major accent divisions in contemporary Britain hold in terms of the vowel system. These differences are a matter of both the phonetic realization of specific vowels as well as the distribution of vowels across different "lexical sets" (cf. Wells 1982; his terminology will be adopted in this chapter). In very broad terms, we can identify three major areas with radically different vowel systems: Southern England, Northern England, and Scotland.

2.1 Consonants

On the whole, the English consonant inventory has remained relatively stable over the evolution of the language in terms of the overall segment inventory apart from a number of phonotactic simplifications, especially in Early Modern English, which brought about the omission of initial consonants in words such as *knight*, *pseudo*, and so on. In contemporary British English, the major patterns of variation involve the phonetic realization of intervocalic /t/, intervocalic dental fricatives /ð θ/, and the phonotactics of /r/, /h/ and /l/. However, the regional differences between some of these variables have recently blurred considerably, since the variants that were traditionally associated with the South (especially London) are now spreading to other varieties of English, as well, in the wake of the spread of so-called "Estuary English" (Rosewarne 1984; Wells 1997; Altendorf and Watt 2008; Altendorf, Chapter 9). It needs to be pointed out that there is a lively debate among scholars whether 'Estuary English' is a reality. As was pointed out by Wells (1997), the spread of features from London (working class) English to other areas in Britain has been going on for more than 500 years, so this is hardly a process that warrants the special status it has been receiving by both linguists and the media over the last decades. On the other hand, it is a convenient cover term for features that have *recently* spread across Britain so we will adhere to this terminology here. In other words, although we would agree that 'Estuary English' is inappropriate as a label covering the overall process of the spread of linguistic features originally associated with London *per se*, there is some justification in adopting it as a shorthand for the current instantiation of that process (i.e. a specific feature or feature bundle). To use a historical analogy:

just because large-scale movements of people from Asia to Europe have recurred repeatedly over the last c.5000 years doesn't invalidate the concept of 'Hungarian incursion' (i.e. a subset thereof). What needs to be demonstrated in order to invalidate the concept of 'Estuary English' as a separate identifiable subset of the overall process is not the spread per se, but a *steady rate of spread* of London features to other areas over the course of history. We are not aware that this has been empirically demonstrated.

2.1.1 /t/

To many speakers of English outside the UK, the phonetic realization of /t/ between vowels may very well be the most iconic feature of an English accent. Many speakers of contemporary British English pronounce intervocalic /t/ with a glottal stop [ʔ] in words like *butter, matter, litter*, etc. Originating in early 20th century London, the glottal stop variant has rapidly spread across England since. It is therefore arguable whether this is still a feature that in any way defines regional varieties of British English rather than a pan-British pronunciation which sets off British English from other varieties of English.

A related process, which is referred to as "glottal reinforcement", is especially prominent in the British South-West, where speakers commonly insert a glottal stop in VC transitions if the consonant is a voiceless stop in words like *sit, kick, nip*. In Tyneside English, on the other hand, glottal stops can substitute any voiceless stop in word-final position and before unstressed vowels (Foulkes and Docherty 1999).

2.1.2 /ð θ/ (th-fronting)

Similar to glottaling of medial /t/, "th-fronting" is another process which used to be strongly associated with working class London English but seems to have been spreading towards other varieties in recent decades (cf. Trudgill 1974 for an account of the rapidness of the change in Norwich). The process itself can be described as a merger between the dental fricatives and the labio-dentals on the latter, so that *thin* and *fin* are both pronounced /fɪn/. Unlike the glottalization of /t/, however, there seems to be a higher degree of stigmatisation/awareness associated with the merged variant.

2.1.3 /h/

A further feature which has traditionally been associated with urban working class London English ("Cockney") is the omission of the initial /h/ in stressed syllables. This is sometimes accompanied by a complementary process of *h*-insertion in words that have no etymological initial /h/. It should be pointed out that there is some evidence that h-dropping may be a rather old process, since we find epenthetic (i.e. non-etymological) *h* as far back as Early Middle English, e.g. in the poem "The Owl and the Nightingale", (1), which was written around 1200:

(1) Iherde ich holde grete tale
     An hule [i.e. 'owl'] and one niȝtingale (Cotton Caligula A. ix)

It has been argued (Lass 1999) that the presence of initial *h* in contemporary standard English seems to be the result of conscious restoration by language purists in Early Modern English and that the h-less pronunciation may have been present in colloquial speech from Early Middle English times onwards.

2.1.4 /l/

In "English English", there are two phonetically distinct laterals which are in complementary distribution, whereby [l] is found in syllable onsets (e.g. *lie*), whereas [ɫ] (so-called "dark l") is found in codas (e.g. *kill*). However, this phonotactic distribution seems to be restricted to England: Welsh English, Irish English (as well as Tyneside English) have [l] across the board, while Scottish English has dark *l* in all positions. In addition, Cockney English has been undergoing vocalization of coda-*l* to a mid-high back vowel [ɤ].

2.1.5 /r/

From the 18th century onwards, English underwent a sound change which dropped /r/ in pre-consonantal and word final position (in words like *car* and *cart*). This development seems to have originated in the South-East of England, and the *r*-less (also called "non-rhotic") pronunciation is now found in all of England except the South-West as well as in the late extraterritorial derivatives of English such as South African English, Australian English, and most of New Zealand English, among others. The original pronunciation is retained in the South-West of England, parts of central Lancashire, Scotland, parts of Northumberland bordering on Scotland, Ireland, and most North American varieties of English. It is worth noting that the loss of pre-consonantal /r/ had repercussions in the vowel system as well, since short vowels underwent lengthening before dropped /r/ (so-called "compensatory lengthening"), which is the only source of long /aː/ in Northern varieties of British English (the so-called START vowel, see below).

2.2 Vowels

Unlike the consonant system, the English vowel system has been subject to comprehensive changes which have affected both the phonetic realization of specific elements of the system as well as the phonological shape of the system as a whole. Examples of the former include the Great Vowel Shift as well as a number of vowel shifts affecting the short vowel system in many varieties of contemporary English. Systemic changes include the repeated allophonic readjustment of vowel length (Lass 1974) as well as a number of mergers and splits. In contemporary Britain, the most reliable phonological cues to regional origin of a given speaker stem from differences in the pronunciation and/or phonological distribution of vowels. We can discern two major isoglosses on the basis of systematic differences in the vowel system: a Southern English system, a Northern English system, and a Scottish system.

2.2.1 South vs. North – The FOOT-STRUT split and the "Broad A" rule

The main difference between the South of England and the North in terms of the distribution of vowels across different lexical sets is defined by the absence of the STRUT vowel in the Northern system, which is a result of a split of Middle English (ME) short /u/ in the South, although the change was by no means regular: in general, the relevant conditioning factor is a preceding labial stop. Examples include *push, pull, bull, bush*, etc. However, there are a number of words such as *button, putt, but*, etc., where the new variant occurs in post-labial environments. On the other hand, there are a small number of lexical items which retain the original variant in non-post-labial-stop environments (cf. *cushion* with FOOT).

Thus, it is the Northern varieties that show the more conservative system with regard to this element. In the Southern varieties, the split subsequently brought about fronting of /æ/ (i.e. TRAP) followed by lengthening of TRAP in a number of words. This so-called "broad-A rule" is to a large extent phonologically conditioned and mostly affects vowels before /s θ n f/ (e.g. *class, bath, laugh*, etc., which all have a long central/back low vowel in broad-A varieties), but shows a considerable number of lexical idiosyncrasies. For example, "flat-A" (i.e. the TRAP variant) is found in *mass, math, cancel*. Note that there are only a very small number of (near)-minimal pairs such as *ant* (with TRAP) vs. *aunt* (with START) and *math* (with TRAP) vs. *aftermath* (with START). These idiosyncrasies also hold within derivational paradigms, cf. *class* and *classy* with broad A vs. *classic* with flat A.

The lengthened allophones then underwent backing to [aː] ~ [ɑː], so that the vowel in *bath, dance, start* is usually much backer than the vowel in *trap, mass*, etc. in these varieties. In combination with the processes affecting pre-consonantal and word-final /r/ as discussed in Section 2.1.5, we arrive at a rather different distribution of /aː/ across the two systems: whereas both systems have a long low vowel, this element is restricted to formerly pre-rhotic vowels in words like *start* in the Northern varieties. In the South, on the other hand, /aː/ is also found in words like *bath* and *dance*. The overall development in the TRAP vowel in different varieties of English is shown in Figure 7.1 below. Table 7.1 shows the distribution of broad A and flat A as well as STRUT and FOOT in the two systems with American English included as a standard of comparison of a variety which has not undergone non-prevocalic *r*-dropping, but has a phonemic STRUT vowel.

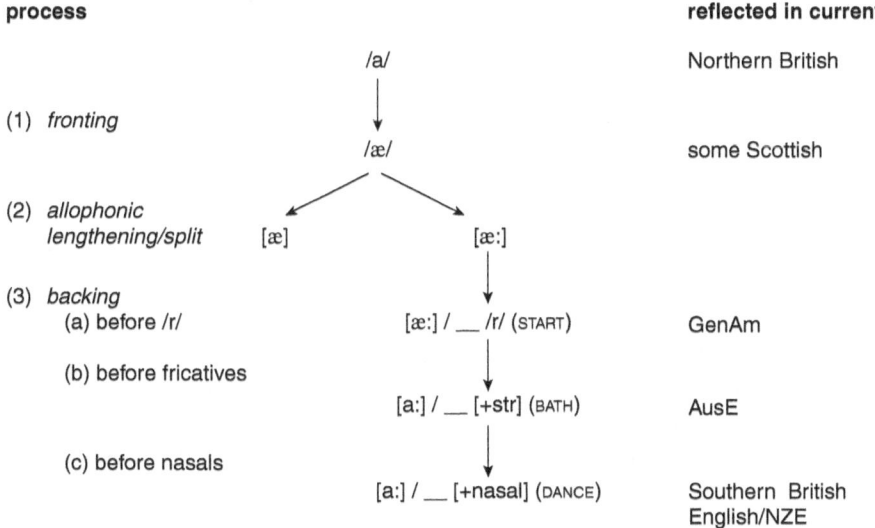

Figure 7.1: Different stages of development of Middle English short /a/ (adapted from Langstrof 2006: Chapter 5)

Table 7.1: Distribution of broad A and flat A in different varieties of English

	Southern English	Northern English	American English
strut, cut, but	/ʌ/	/ʊ/	/ʌ/
push, pull, cushion	/ʊ/	/ʊ/	/ʊ/
bad, trap	/æ/	/a/	/æ(ː)/
dance, bath	/ɑː/	/a/	/æ(ː)/

Note that the table simplifies the actual state of affairs drastically, in that the TRAP vowel is subject to complex allophonization in American English. For an in-depth discussion, see Labov (1994, 2001).

2.2.2 The Scottish Vowel Length rule

The Scottish vowel system is mainly defined on the basis of what has been termed the Scottish Vowel Length rule. In very general terms, we can say that vowel length in Scottish English is subject to allophonic conditioning not found in other varieties of English: most vowels are long before /r v ð z #/, and short otherwise ("Aitken's Law", for details see Aitken 1981; Lass 1974). This implies that, for example, the vowels in *beat* and *bit* are equally long as they occur in the same phonological environment. A further corollary of the Scottish Vowel Length rule is that there are a number of new minimal pairs not found in varieties which do not have this rule: since "morpheme boundary" (/#/) is a lengthening factor, pairs such as *heed* and *he'd* show different length in Scottish English, but not in other varieties.

It should be pointed out that all major extraterritorial varieties of English show the Southern English vowel typology rather than the Northern or the Scottish one in terms of the number of phonological contrasts, i.e. the American Englishes as well as the Southern Hemisphere varieties (South African English, Australian English, New Zealand English) have a phonemically distinct STRUT vowel. However, not all of them have undergone the broad A rule: most varieties of North American English except the New England ones retain flat A across the board, some speakers of Australian English retain flat A in pre-nasal environments.

2.2.3 Diphthong mergers

Although most varieties of British English have two phonemically distinct front centering diphthongs NEAR and SQUARE, this distinction has become neutralized in a number of varieties of English. In East Anglia there is a merger of the two vowels on the lower variant, which implies that both *cheer* and *chair* can be pronounced /tʃɛə/. In Liverpool English, SQUARE sometimes merges with NURSE.

In addition to these systemic differences, there also exist a number of phonetic differences which distinguish different varieties of British English. We will outline each of these separately.

2.2.3.1 FACE/GOAT

Another phonetic variable which stereotypically distinguishes the Northern and the Southern varieties of contemporary British English is the degree of diphthongization in the FACE and GOAT vowel. In brief, both the Northern English varieties as well as Scottish English have a monophthongal variant ([eː] and [oː], respectively), whereas the Southern varieties have an upgliding diphthong in both cases. The RP vowel is traditionally transcribed with a mid onset (/eɪ/), although more open variants are also common, especially in London English.

The history of these vowels (especially FACE) is rather complex. It should be noted that FACE derives from an Early Middle English short central low monophthong /a/ and that the lengthening, raising and diphthongization are historically disparate processes.

2.2.3.2 /æ/

The pronunciation of TRAP has been rather volatile both within and across different varieties of English showing a number of see-saw patterns and non-directionalities. In contemporary Britain, realizations ranging from a (low)-mid element [ɛ] to central [a] can be found subject to both regional variation and change in progress. In the North, the vowel seems to be relatively stable since it has never been the subject of the miniature chain shift which fronted TRAP as a result of the emergence and lowering of STRUT (see Section 2.2.1 above). In the Northern system, TRAP is realized as a low central vowel [a].

In the South, however, matters are rather more complex. The RP realization of the vowel is usually [æ], i.e. a low front vowel. Traditional Cockney (cf. Fox, Chapter 10) has a closer variant, a fact which has given rise to some debate as to whether the Cockney variant is an innovation or a retention of an earlier value (see Trudgill 2004). Nowadays, however, TRAP undergoes (re)-lowering in London

English, a process which seems to spread to "Estuary English" as well (cf. the formant frequency plots in Torgensen et al. 2006).

2.2.4 Upgliding diphthongs

The upgliding diphthongs PRICE and MOUTH are a result of the Great Vowel Shift diphthongizing Middle English high monophthongs and are usually transcribed with an identical nucleus for RP, namely a low central vowel /a/. The offglide is a high front vowel and a high back vowel, respectively. Unlike the FACE/GOAT vowels, which can be either monophthongal or diphthongal in different varieties of British English (see Section 2.2.3.1), both PRICE and MOUTH are realized as diphthongs.

However, a number of differences can be found in different accents with regard to the phonetic quality of the onset. In the South (including "Estuary English") there is a process which essentially "crosses over" the nucleus and the offglide of the two vowels in phonetic space. That is, the nucleus of the vowel with the front offglide (PRICE) undergoes backing, whereas the nucleus of MOUTH undergoes fronting. This process is especially prominent in the Southern Hemisphere varieties of English, but can be found in London English as well and has been argued to constitute a logical extension of the Great Vowel Shift (Bauer 1979).

In Scottish English, on the other hand, the nuclei of these two elements diverge from RP in the opposite direction in that they are realized with low-mid nuclei. Thus, there seems to be a correlation between the degree of diphthongization of FACE/GOAT and the diphthongization of PRICE/MOUTH: varieties such as Scottish English which have monophthongal FACE also have a PRICE nucleus that is nearer the offglide in phonetic space, and vice versa.

2.3 Summary

We have seen that the phonological variables that define the major accent divisions in contemporary Britain are found in the vowel system. Although there is a great deal of variation to be found in the consonant system as well, these differences are best defined in terms of style and sociolect rather than geographical origin of a given speaker. This is mainly due to the spread of "Estuary English", which brings about the adoption of a number of consonant variables originally restricted to London English (such as th-fronting, glottal stop) by speakers in other parts of the UK. Since the spread of these variables is a relatively recent phenomenon, we are faced with a situation where such variables can be regarded as "partially regional": if we sample older speakers born before the popularization of Estuary English, we can state a variable such as th-fronting as being defined in terms of region. However, this would not be the case in the speech of younger speakers, assuming that the sociolinguistic stratification of "Estuary English" variables is similar in different regions of Britain (which may very well be a somewhat simplistic assumption). A case in point would be the subjects sampled by Trudgill (1974) in Norwich, where th-fronting was virtually absent in the speech of subjects born before the 1960s, while there was a sharp increase in frequency of use of fronted variants in the speech of younger speakers.

If we look at the vowel system, we find rather more well-defined and less volatile accent divisions across Britain. We have seen that there are three systems that differ in terms of both the phonological inventory as well as the phonetic realization of different vowels. The Scottish system is a distinct type due to the systemic effects of the Scottish Vowel Length rule, which renders phonemic length predictable in all contexts. The Northern English system is marked by the absence of a phonemically distinct STRUT vowel. A further iconic difference between the South and the North (including Scotland) is the degree of diphthongization of the FACE/GOAT vowels where the South has a diphthong, while monophthongal realizations are the norm in the North, including Scotland. It is worth pointing out that there seems to be some super-regionalization happening with regard to the vowel system as well. For example, the typical realization of the FACE vowel in contemporary Newcastle English is a long front monophthong [eː], which has ousted the traditional variant [ɪə]. It therefore seems that different regions converge on a "pan-Northern" type in regard to the vowel system, which unlike the developments in the consonant system (where previous accent areas become increasingly blurred due to the spread of "Estuary English") serves to solidify large-scale accent divisions in Britain.

3 Morpho-syntactic variation

Especially since the turn of the 21st century there has been a rapidly growing number of studies on the dialect grammar, especially the dialect syntax, of a wide range of Romance and Germanic dialects (cf. Kortmann 2010; Murelli and Kortmann 2011), including the dialects of the British Isles (e.g. the corpus-based studies in Kortmann et al. 2005; Hernandez et al. 2011). This section will be primarily informed by the survey data of a currently ongoing dialect atlas project, the *World Atlas of Variation in English* (henceforth WAVE; Kortmann and Lunkenheimer 2011; Kortmann 2012). Its database was assembled at the University of Freiburg in a follow-up on research conducted for the *Handbook of Varieties of English* (Kortmann et al. 2004) and for the interactive CD-ROM accompanying that handbook (in some publications informally labeled WAMVE – *The World Atlas of Morpho-Syntactic Variation in English*). WAVE includes information on 235 morphosyntactic features in 74 varieties of English from eight different Anglophone world regions.

The ten regional varieties sampled from the British Isles, among them the four so-called Celtic Englishes, are the following, with the expert informants and abbreviations used in this chapter given in brackets: Channel Islands English (ChIsE; Anna Rosen), East Anglian English (EA; Peter Trudgill), Irish English (IrE; Markku Filppula), Manx English (ManxE; Jennifer Kewley Draskau), English dialects in the North of England (North; Graeme Trousdale), Orkney and Shetland English (O&SE; Gunnel Melchers), Scottish English (ScE; Jennifer Smith), English dialects in the Southeast of England (SE; Lieselotte Anderwald), English dialects in the South-West of England (SW; Susanne Wagner), and Welsh English (WelE; Robert Penhallurick). In terms of Trudgill's proposal for a new dialect typology (the "true typological split" according to Trudgill 2009), six of these qualify as low-contact L1 varieties (SW, SE, EA, North, ScE, O&SE) and four as high-contact L1 varieties (ChIsE, IrE, ManxE, WelE), with SW, EA, and the North as clearly the three English dialect areas with a time depth and, in part, feature stability dating back to medieval times. The distinction between high- and low-contact varieties, relevant as it has been shown to be for the large-scale morphosyntactic profiles of varieties and entire variety types of English around the world (cf. e.g. Szmrecsanyi and Kortmann 2009; Kortmann 2010), will not play a role in the present survey, though.

The data and informant judgments for these ten varieties form the basis of the present section. These judgments relate to the frequency with which each of the 235 features can be encountered in the relevant variety, i.e. whether the relevant feature is pervasive or obligatory (category A), neither pervasive nor extremely rare (category B), or whether it does exist, but simply is very rare (category C). The 11th British Isles variety represented in WAVE (British Creole; Mark Sebba) falls outside the scope of regional L1 varieties, even though certain South(east)ern (clearly non-creole) features have made it into this variety, as will briefly be shown in Section 3.2.

3.1 Pan-British features

In a questionnaire-based grammar survey at British schools conducted some 20 years ago, Cheshire et al. (1993) identified (out of a total of 196 features) a set of non-standard forms used by a majority of people in England (more concretely, forms which showed in 80% or more of the questionnaires returned in the survey), without displaying any regional restrictions:

(1) Top pan-British features according to Cheshire et al. (1993)
- *them* as a demonstrative (e.g. *in them days*)
- absence of plural marking on nouns of measurement (e.g. *five pound of flour*)
- *what* as subject relativizer (e.g. *The film what was on last night*)
- *never* as a past tense negator (e.g. in *No, I never did that*)
- regularized reflexive pronouns (e.g. *myself/yourself/hisself*)
- *there's/there was* with notional plural subjects (e.g. *there's three dogs in the garden*)
- perfect participles *sat* and *stood* with progressive meaning (e.g. *She was sat over there...*, *He was stood in the corner*)
- adverbs with the same form as adjectives, i.e. without *-ly* (e.g. *Come quick!*)
- indirect object preceding direct object in pronominal double object constructions (e.g. *Give me it!*)
- *ain't/in't* (e.g. *That ain't/in't working*)
- non-standard *was* (e.g. *We was singing*)

All of these clearly qualify as candidates for so-called *areoversals* (cf. Szmrecsanyi and Kortmann 2009) for the British Isles, with some of them possibly even making it into spontaneous spoken standard British English within a couple of generations. Now let us see which set of morpho-syntactic features WAVE yields as top candidates for British areoversals, defined as features which occur in at least 80% (i.e. eight of the ten) regional varieties sampled. We will first present these in three groups (according to whether they are found in all ten, in nine, or only in eight varieties), and then ask which of them can truly be called highly distinctive of the British Isles when comparing them with the most frequent non-standard morpho-syntactic features in (a) the whole Anglophone world and (b) in all mother-tongue (i.e. L1) varieties of English sampled in WAVE. The exclamation marks in (2) below indicate pan-British Isles features also included in the list by Cheshire et al. (1993) in (1) above:

(2) Candidates for areoversals of the British Isles
   a. found in all 10 regional varieties:
      - ! existential / presentational *there's/there is/there was* with plural subjects
      - ! adverbs have the same form as adjectives (i.e. no StE adverb-forming *-ly*)
      - *me* instead of *I* in coordinate subjects (*My brother and me*)
      - *myself/meself* instead of *I* in coordinate subjects (*This is Jenny and myself*).
      - *was* for conditional *were*
   b. found in 9 regional varieties:
      - ! *them* instead of demonstrative *those*
      - ! *never* as preverbal past tense negator
      - ! *was/were* generalization (*You was hungry, but he was thirsty*)
      - ! either order of pronominal objects in double object constructions (*He couldn't give her it*)
      - use of *us* + NP in subject function (*Us kids used to pinch the sweets like hell*)
      - *there* with past participle in resultative contexts (*There's sth. fallen down ...*)
      - multiple negation / negative concord (*He won't do no harm*)
      - *like* as a focusing device (*How did you get away with that like?*)
      - *she/her* used for inanimate referents (*she was burning good* [about a house])
      - leveling of past tense/past participle verb forms: regularization of irregular verb paradigms (e.g. *catch-catched-catched*)
      - leveling of past tense/past participle verb forms: unmarked forms (frequent with *give* and *run*)
      - zero-relativization in subject position (*The man Ø lives there is a nice chap*)
   c. found in 8 regional varieties:
      - ! absence of plural marking only after quantifiers (e.g. *thirteen year*)
      - ! regularized reflexives paradigm (*hisself, theirselves/theirself*)
      - no inversion/no auxiliaries in main clause *yes/no* questions (*You get the point?*)
      - *as what/than what* in comparative clauses (*He's bigger than what I am*)
      - object pronoun forms serving as base for first and/or second person reflexives (e.g. *meself* for 'myself')
      - object pronoun forms as (modifying) possessive pronouns: first person singular (*I've lost me bike*)

- forms or phrases for the 2nd person plural pronoun other than *you* (e.g. IrE *youse*)
- proximal and distal demonstratives with *here* and *there* (e.g. *this here book* vs. *them there books*)
- double comparatives and superlatives (e.g. *That is so much more easier to follow*)
- regularized comparison strategies: extension of analytic marking (e.g. *in one of the most pretty sunsets*)
- leveling of past tense/past participle verb forms: past tense replacing the past participle (e.g. *He had went*)

As we can see, there is a quite remarkable overlap between the WAVE-based feature set and the one by Cheshire et al. (1993) in (1). Eight out of the 11 features on the latter's list are among the top 80% in the British Isles sample in WAVE. In fact, did we define "pan-British" less strictly than "occurring in at least eight of all British Isles varieties in WAVE", the three remaining features of Cheshire et al.'s list ('*be sat/stood* with progressive meaning', '*ain't* as the negated form of *be*' and 'relativizer *what*') would figure as immediate runners-up in the WAVE list since they are found in seven British Isles varieties. In other words, the list of top pan-British features in morpho-syntax identified by Cheshire et al. (1993) practically turns out to be a proper subset of the corresponding WAVE set. This convergence of the survey results is reassuring given the fact that they have been arrived at by very different methodologies, with Cheshire et al.'s informants reflecting in the first place non-standard usage among adolescent native speakers.

Whichever list of widespread or even pan-British dialect features is taken, survey data as in the WAVE make it possible to put in perspective such candidates for areoversals as identified above. For it may turn out upon widening the scope to structural properties of non-standard varieties of English around the world, that what strikes us as noteworthy because a given dialect feature is found in all or most British regional varieties, should not be interpreted as a specific "dialectal Briticism", but rather as part of a larger pattern. On the one hand, the relevant feature may be found in the vast majority of all non-standard (L1, L2, Pidgin and Creole) varieties of English around the world, thus qualifying as a *vernacular angloversal* which, of course, is also found in the regional varieties of the British Isles. On the other hand, the relevant feature may be found in the vast majority of all non-standard mother-tongue varieties of English around the world, thus qualifying as an L1 *varioversal* and, again, to be expected as a pan-British feature in the regional varieties spoken in the British Isles (for a detailed discussion of (criteria for) vernacular angloversals, varioversals and areoversals, cf. Szmrecsanyi and Kortmann 2009). So what is the situation for those 28 dialect features found in a minimum of eight regional British varieties listed in (2)? To begin with, six of them turn out to be true angloversals, i.e. features attested in at least 80% of all 74 varieties sampled in WAVE. These are:

- *me* instead of *I* in coordinate subjects
- adverbs have the same form as adjectives
- multiple negation
- use of *never* as preverbal past tense negator
- no inversion rule in *yes/no* questions
- forms or phrases for the 2nd person plural pronoun other than *you* (*youse, you ones, you lot*).

Recall: the first two were found in all ten British Isles varieties, the two negation features in nine, and the last two angloversals in eight regional varieties of the British Isles. If we look at the next most widely found features in the grammars of varieties of English around the world, we immediately come across 'was for conditional *were*' (78% of 74 varieties) and 'existential/ presentational *there's/ there is/there was* with plural subjects' (72%) – the other two truly pan-British features as they are found in all ten varieties, and rather pervasively in every one of them at that. Two more "near-angloversals" listed in (2) are non-standard comparison strategies for adjectives: double comparatives and superlatives (73%), and regularized comparison strategies via the extension of analytic marking (70%). In sum, then, ten of our candidates for British Isles areoversals turn out to be vernacular angloversals or near-angloversals. What about the remaining 18 features – are they also part of a more widely occurring morpho-syntactic pattern, more concretely also regularly found in vernacular L1 varieties of English spoken outside the British Isles?

In order to answer this question, we only need to check the set of pan-British Isles features against the set of L1 varioversals, i.e. those features found in at least 80% of all 31 L1 varieties sampled WAVE. On the whole, there are 20 such features which are highly characteristic of English mother-tongue vernaculars (as compared with L2 varieties of English and English-based Pidgins and Creoles). For reasons of space the complete list cannot be given here. Suffice it to state the following: more than half (18 to be exact) of the pan-British Isles features are L1 varioversals. For instance, of those five features documented in all ten British Isles varieties, one is found in 29 (out of 31) L1 varieties of English around the world, one in 30 L1 varieties and the other three even in all (!) of the 31 L1 varieties. So this leaves us with ten candidates for, weird as it may sound, distinctively British pan-British Isles areoversals. Even of these, four lose in distinctive Britishness if we look immediately below the 80% threshold for L1 varioversals: about 75% of all L1 varieties of English worldwide exhibit regularized reflexives paradigms, *was/were* generalization, absence of plural marking after quantifiers, and leveling of past tense/past participle verb forms via the past tense replacing the past participle. Ultimately, then, we are left with the following six truly uniquely British Isles areoversals:

- object pronoun forms serving as base for first and/or second person reflexives
- proximal and distal demonstratives of the type *this here, that there*
- *there* with past participle in resultative contexts
- either order of pronominal objects in double object constructions
- zero relativization in subject position
- object pronoun forms as (modifying) possessive pronouns.

The first two of these areoversals are found in eight British Isles varieties, the other four in as many as nine of the ten British Isles varieties sampled in WAVE. Table 7.2 summarizes the discussion of pan-British Isles features presented in this section (note the following convention: '+' indicates a feature rated 'A' (= 'pervasive') in at least five British Isles varieties, and '-' a feature C-rated ('extremely rare') or non-existent in five or more British Isles varieties).

Table 7.2: The pan-British Isles features vis-à-vis (near-) angloversals and (near-) L1 varioversals

Top in WAVE (8 or more varieties)	Angloversal (≥ 80% of 74 varieties)	Near-angloversal (≥ 70% of 74 varieties)	L1 varioversal (≥ 80% of 31 varieties)	Near-L1 varioversal (≥ 70% of 31 varieties)	Also n Cheshire et al.'s (1993) top list
+ *me* instead of *I* in coordinate subjects	√		√		
+ other adverbs have the same form as adjectives	√		√		√
never as preverbal past tense negator	√		√		√
– forms or phrases for the 2nd person plural pronoun other than *you*	√		√		
multiple negation/ negative concord	√		√		

Table 7.2: (continued).

Top in WAVE (8 or more varieties)	Angloversal (≥ 80% of 74 varieties)	Near-angloversal (≥ 70% of 74 varieties)	L1 variversal (≥ 80% of 31 varieties)	Near-L1 varioversal (≥ 70% of 31 varieties)	Also in Cheshire et al.'s (1993) top list
no inversion/no auxiliaries in main clause *yes/no* questions	√		√		
+ existential / presentational *there's/there is/there was* with plural subjects		√	√		√
+ *was* for conditional *were*		√	√		
double comparatives and superlatives		√	√		
− regularized comparison strategies: extension of analytic marking		√	√		
+ *them* instead of demonstrative *those*			√		√
− *myself/meself* instead of *I* in coordinate subjects			√		
− *she/her* used for inanimate referents			√		
use of *us* + NP in subject function			√		
+ *like* as a focusing device			√		
as what/than what in comparative clauses			√		
leveling of past tense/past participle verb forms: regularization of irregular verb paradigms			√		
leveling of past tense/past participle verb forms: unmarked forms			√		
was/were generalization				√	√

Table 7.2: (continued).

Top in WAVE (8 or more varieties)	Angloversal (≥ 80% of 74 varieties)	Near-angloversal (≥ 70% of 74 varieties)	L1 varioversal (≥ 80% of 31 varieties)	Near-L1 varioversal (≥ 70% of 31 varieties)	Also in Cheshire et al.'s (1993) top list
absence of plural marking only after quantifiers				√	√
regularized reflexives paradigm				√	√
leveling of past tense/past participle verb forms: past tense replacing the past participle				√	
either order of pronominal objects in double object constructions					√
+ object pronoun forms serving as base for first and/or second person reflexives					
+ object pronoun forms as (modifying) possessive pronouns: first person singular					
zero relativization in subject position					
– proximal and distal demonstratives with *here* and *there*					
there with past participle in resultative contexts					

From a comparative perspective, it may be interesting to note at this point what the North American areoversals are according to the WAVE data (i.e. not only in the L1 varieties of English spoken in the US but also in Newfoundland English as well as in Chicano English and Gullah, the two non-L1 US varieties sampled in WAVE): special forms (e.g. *yall*) or phrases (notably *you guys*) for the second person plural, proximal, and distal demonstratives of the type *this here* vs. *that there*, invariant *don't* in the present tense, and the use of *ain't* as the negated form of *have* and *be* (*I ain't had a look at them yet; they're all in there, ain't they?*). All of these meet the hard criterion for unrestricted areoversals, i.e. they are attested in more than 90% of the non-standard varieties spoken in North America, but in no more than 60% of the varieties world-wide (cf. Szmrecsanyi and Kortmann 2009).

3.2 Regional features

For each of the ten regional varieties considered, this section lists all those features that, within the British Isles, solely occur in one variety (ordered by A, B, and C rating), or are highly distinctive of a certain regional variety and found (typically with a lower rating) in only one other British Isles variety. Irish English, the dialects of the North, and the dialect of East Anglia stand out as those with the largest number of such pervasive (i.e. A-rated) or at least moderately frequently used (i.e. B-rated) highly local features, with East Anglian English as the most distinctive of these three varieties given its high number of A-rated features. At the opposite end of these three regional varieties we find Channel Islands English and, especially, the dialect of South-East England, both of which exhibit exclusively features which are hardly used by speakers of these dialects. In general, it is interesting to note that C-rated features, which are of particular interest from the continuities vs. innovations perspective (i.e. as prime candidates for remnants of the past or spearheads of a new development) are far outnumbered in this list, showing that the vast majority of such regionally distinctive features are going strong in their homelands. When consulting the following list, the reader should keep in mind again that the WAVE set of 235 morpho-syntactic features forms the basis for this chapter. This set was selected from a total of almost 350 features which the authors and their team had compiled over the years from the dialect literature – but which can't possibly all be included in a survey questionnaire. Especially features known to be restricted to a single non-standard variety in the anglophone world (and in many cases recessive) were not included into the feature pool of WAVE. What this means is that there clearly do exist even more highly local features in the regional British varieties than those listed below.

ManxE	A-feature:	existential construction to express possessive (*a house at him*);
	B-features:	present perfect for StE simple past (*I've done it years ago*), *a*-prefixing on elements other than *ing*-forms (*and me a cuddled up*);
	C-features:	singular *it* for plural *they* in anaphoric use (with non-human referents) (*ye can get it anywhere, diseases*), attributive adjectival modifiers follow head noun (usually only in Manx words used in an English context: *they waved theer 'Oie-vies' = nights good* = 'goodnights')
O&SE	A-feature:	no number distinction in demonstratives (*dis (yon) horses pulls (poos) weel*);
	B-features:	*as/to* as comparative markers, variant forms of dummy subject *there* in existential clauses (*they were a coo lowse in the byre*)
ScE	B-features:	subject pronoun drop: dummy pronouns, *go*-based future markers, use of *gotten* and *got* with distinct meanings, *amn't* in tag questions; found in only one more regional variety: alternative forms/phrases for referential (non-dummy) *it*, plural forms of interrogative pronouns: using additional (free or bound) elements, insertion of *it* where StE favors zero, use of *gotten* and *got* with distinct meanings (dynamic vs. static);
	C-feature:	non-standard use of modals for politeness reasons
North	B-features:	subject pronoun forms as (modifying) possessive pronouns: first person plural, object pronoun forms as (modifying) possessive pronouns: first person plural, use of zero article where StE has definite article, use of zero article where StE has indefinite article, agreement sensitive to position of subject;
	C-features:	subject pronoun forms as (modifying) possessive pronouns: third person singular, object pronoun forms as (modifying) possessive pronouns: third person singular, *is* for *am/will* with 1st person singular
IrE	A-feature:	*after*-perfect (another equally distinctive IrE feature (but not part of the WAVE feature set) is subordinating *and*, as in *He seen a boat passin' along and him cuttin' oats.*);
	B-features:	emphatic reflexives with *own*, specialized plural markers for pronouns, subject pronoun drop: referential pronouns, invariant *be* as habitual marker, other non-standard habitual

markers: analytic, perfect marker *already*, present tense forms of modals used where StE has past tense forms, deletion of auxiliary *be*: before progressive, relativizer *where* or a form derived from *where*, deletion of stranded prepositions in relative clauses, deletion of *to* before infinitives, *too; too much; very much* 'very' as qualifier, other possibilities for fronting than StE, doubly filled COMP-position with *wh*-words; emphatic reflexives with *own*;

C-features: indefinite article *one/wan*, *do* as unstressed tense marker (without habitual or other aspectual meanings), superlative marker *most* occurring before head noun

SW B-features: non-coordinated subject pronoun forms in object function (*they always called I 'Willie'*), non-coordinated object pronoun forms in subject function (*us got in the train*), use of postpositions (*they'd come in dinner time*);

C-features: use of indefinite article where StE has definite article, *for*-based complementizers (*I've got a one, but 'tis a job for keep up wi' 'em* [archaic])

SE C-feature: double determiners (e.g. demonstrative/article + possessive pronoun, with possessive pronoun preposed or postposed)

EA A-features: subject pronoun forms serving as a base for reflexives (*he done it hisself*), *a*-prefixing on *ing*-forms (*where are you a-goin?*), invariant present tense forms due to zero marking for the third person singular (*he like it*), invariant *be* with non-habitual function (*there it be!*); note two further A-features which are highly regionally distinctive of East Anglian English, each of them being found only in one other regional variety of British English: alternative forms/phrases for dummy *it* (also in O&SE; *Thass raining*) and distinction between emphatic vs. non-emphatic forms of pronouns (also in SW; *I don't like it, thass no good*)

ChIsE C-features: present tense forms for neutral future reference (*I go cycling tomorrow*), invariant *don't* for all persons in the present tense (*I said I ain't go*), no subordination; chaining construction linking two main verbs (motion and activity) (*You can live here, you can live anywhere*)

WelE A-feature: other possibilities for fronting (*Singing they were*)
B-feature: substitution of *that*-clause for infinitival subclause
C-features: subject pronoun forms as (modifying) possessive pronouns: third person plural, comparatives and superlatives of parti-

ciples, zero past tense forms of regular verbs, special negative verbs in imperatives

An earlier grammar survey based on only 76 morpho-syntactic features (Kortmann 2008: 490–492) yielded a North-South divide among the regional varieties of the British Isles. It turns out that this divide also emerges, with a partially different composition of characteristically (pan-)Northern and (pan-)Southern features, when looking at the geographical patterning of the 235 WAVE features, with Scottish English, Irish English, and Manx English patterning with the North (see Table 7.3), while Welsh English patterns with the South (see Table 7.4). In both tables, features with a strong regional bias, i.e. found in four or even all five relevant regional varieties, can be distinguished from features with a weaker regional bias (found in no more than three varieties). As is easy enough to see, the number of characteristically Northern features is much longer than the corresponding one for the South. In both tables the rightmost column identifies the "outlier(s)" in the relevant other region. Here it is to be noted that it is especially the three most traditional English dialect areas which figure as outliers, i.e. the Southwest and East Anglia exhibiting the odd typical Northern feature, and the North (as well as Irish English) with the odd typical Southern feature.

3.2.1 North

Table 7.3: Morpho-syntactic features found exclusively or predominantly in the northern regional varieties of the British Isles

Feature	O&SE	ScE	North	IrE	ManxE	in South only in
wider range of uses of progressive be + v-ing than in StE: extension to stative verbs	!	!	√	√	!	WelE
use of definite article where StE has indefinite article	!	√	!	!	!	SW, WelE
be as perfect auxiliary	!	√		√	√	
agreement sensitive to subject type (nominal vs. pronominal)	!	√	√	√		
forms or phrases for the 2nd person singular pronoun other than you	!	!	√	!		SW
use of definite article where StE favors zero	√		√	!	!	ChIsE
yon/yonder indicating remoteness	!	√			√	
Northern Subject Rule	√	√	√			

Table 7.3: (continued).

Feature	O&SE	ScE	North	IrE	ManxE	in South only in
relativizer *at*	!	√	√			
loosening of sequence of tenses rule	√			√	√	
epistemic *mustn't*	√	!		√		SE
want/need + past participle	!	!		√		
relativizer *that* or *what* in non-restrictive contexts	√	√	√			EA
for (to) as infinitive marker			√	√	√	
presence of subject in imperatives	√			√	!	EA

√ attested, but not frequently used (B rating)
! pervasive (A rating)

3.2.2 South

Concerning the South, it is worth mentioning that British Creole also exhibits three of the Southern features, notably *ain't* as the negated form of *be* and the invariant non-concord tag *innit/in't it*. These two features, in particular, together with the Southeastern and East Anglian feature '*ain't* as the negated form of *have*' show the impact of intensive contact with regional Southeastern English upon British Creole, since none of these three morpho-syntactic features is to be found in Jamaican Creole or Jamaican English.

Table 7.4: Morpho-syntactic features found exclusively or predominantly in the southern regional varieties of the British Isles

Feature	SW	SE	EA	ChIsE	WelE	in North only in
as what / than what in comparative clauses	√	√	!	√	√	North, IrE
invariant non-concord tags (e.g. *innit*)	√	√		!	!	
leveling of past tense/past participle verb forms: past participle replacing the past tense form	√	√	!		√	ScE, North
gapping/zero-relativization in subject position	!	√		√		ManxE, IrE
ain't as the negated form of *be*	√	√	!			

Table 7.4: (continued).

Feature	SW	SE	EA	ChIsE	WelE	in North only In
relativizer *what* or a form derived from *what*	√	!			√	North
regularized comparison strategies: extension of synthetic marking	√	√			√	

√ attested, but not frequently used (B rating)
! pervasive (A rating)

So it looks there is sufficient evidence for claiming the existence of a morpho-syntactic counterpart of the well-known North-South split in the accents, more exactly the vowel systems, of the British Isles (recall Sections 2.2.1. and 2.3). At least there is evidence strong enough to merit further (quantitative and qualitative) exploration on the basis of a wider range of morpho-syntactic features and their use in regional British varieties (as documented, or still to be documented, in more fine-grained survey data, informant interviews, and natural discourse data).

4 Summary and outlook

Despite the descriptive nature of this chapter, it should have emerged that the scientific study of regional British varieties is very much alive and has added many fascinating new perspectives to what is typically associated with traditional English dialectology. There are many avenues along which both phonetic and phonological variation and morpho-syntactic variation are currently being pursued. In conclusion, and primarily as an appetizer for the readership, the following cursory remarks on some of the most promising of these new avenues of dialectal research shall suffice. There is, for example, the rich and sophisticated sociolinguistic take on structural variation in the British Isles (including studies on the perceptual salience of dialectal features; cf. e.g. Montgomery 2006, 2012), along with the strong interest in morpho-syntactic variation which has developed within different theoretical frameworks since the 1990s (cf. e.g. Kortmann 2010). For these approaches, and even more so for ongoing and future research most closely in line with the approach adopted in this chapter, it is obvious that they rest (or are bound to rest) in large part on the availability of new data sources (survey data like in WAVE, electronic corpora like FRED, the Freiburg English Dialect Corpus; cf. Anderwald and Wagner 2007), and the application of new or updated methodologies to large bodies of corpus or aggregated data. Take, for instance, Szmrecsanyi (2013) for what a statistically sophisticated corpus-based dialectometry for the British Isles may look like. Or consider new approaches to measuring linguistic similarities among languages and, most recently, among English dialects, in which statistical tools known from bio-informatics (phenetic networks, or phenograms) are applied to aggregated phonological and morphosyntactic data (for phonetic similarities cf. McMahon et al. 2007, 2013; for morphosyntactic similarities, cf. Wichmann and Urban 2012; or Szmreczanyi and Wolk 2013).

All of these studies help putting in perspective what we know about the regional varieties of the British Isles (and other anglophone world regions, for that matter), both from a synchronic, but also from a historical point of view. Varieties-based studies have, for example, called into question such well-entrenched claims and dictums in (English) historical and general linguistics that there is a trade-off between syntheticity and analyticity (to the effect that if a language, or variety thereof, loses in one, it necessarily gains in the other), or that all languages (and by implication also all varieties and variety types of a language) exhibit equal degrees of structural complexity (cf. Szmrecsanyi 2012; Kortmann and Szmrecsanyi 2009). Wichmann and Urban (2012), in applying their automatic similarity judgments program not just to the classification of thousands of languages, but (using the WAVE data set) also to regional British dialects, reach results confirming the existence of larger regional patterns in the British Isles and are even able to identify, via the development of statistical diversity measures, the (historical) centers of innovation and dispersal among the regional British varieties, most notably the dialects of the North of England. Finally, large survey data sets like WAVE, with the relevant small-scale and particularly large-scale patterns that they reveal, also allow us to learn more about processes and effects of language change (both in contact and non-contact situations), such as grammaticalization processes (cf. Kortmann and Schneider 2011), and thus serve as a window not only to the past, but also to the future. Angloversals and L1 varioversals – some, admittedly, more than others – are candidates for structural properties becoming part of spontaneous spoken Standard English in the long run; some areoversals may well make it into the standard variety/ies of English spoken in a given Anglophone world region (e.g. British vs. American vs. Caribbean vs. Pacific vs. Southeast Asian vs. South Asian vs. African English).

But whichever changes in English around the globe we are bound to witness, the regional varieties of the British Isles will undoubtedly continue to exhibit the largest array of (in part highly regionally restricted) distinctive phonetic/phonological and morphosyntactic features of non-standard varieties in the Anglophone world. In a continually globalizing world, there will be an increasing need for the local, not least via the vernacular variety spoken (cf. e.g. Johnstone 2010). The regional British varieties will continue to offer the richest choice in this respect. In this chapter, we barely sketched the outermost layer of the British Isles' regionalisms. Much still remains to be discovered, for example, on the level of (often highly locally restricted) syntactic, semantic and pragmatic constraints on the use of the individual WAVE features (and other features not included in WAVE).

5 References

Aitken, Adam Jack. 1981. The Scottish vowel length rule. In: Michael Benskin and Michael L. Samuels (eds.), *So meny People, Longages and Tonges: Philological Essays in Scots and Mediaeval English presented to Angus McIntosh*, 131–157. Edinburgh: The Middle English Dialect Project.

Altendorf, Ulrike and Dominic Watt. 2008. Dialects in the South of England: phonology. In: Bernd Kortmann and Clive Upton (eds.), *Handbook of Varieties of English: The British Isles*, 194–222. Berlin/New York: Mouton de Gruyter.

Anderwald, Lieselotte and Susanne Wagner. 2007. FRED – The Freiburg English Dialect corpus. In: Joan Beal, Karen Corrigan, and Hermann Moisl (eds.), *Creating and Digitizing Language Corpora*. Vol. 1: *Synchronic Corpora*, 35–53. London: Palgrave Macmillan.

Anderwald, Lieselotte and Bernd Kortmann. 2013. Typological methods in dialectology. In: Manfred Krug and Julia Schlüter (eds.), *Research Methods in Language Variation and Change*, 313–333. Cambridge: Cambridge University Press.

Bauer, Laurie. 1979. The second Great Vowel Shift? *Journal of the International Phonetic Association* 9: 57–66.

Britain, David. 2010. Grammatical variation in the contemporary spoken English of England. In: Andy Kirkpatrick (ed.), *The Routledge Handbook of World Englishes*, 30–82. London/New York: Routledge.

Cheshire, Jenny, Viv Edwards, and Pamela Whittle. 1993. Non-Standard English and Dialect Levelling. In: James Milroy and Lesley Milroy (eds.), *Real English: The Grammar of English Dialects in the British Isles*, 53–96. London/New York: Longman.

Foulkes, Paul and Gerard Docherty (eds.). 1999. *Urban Voices: Accent Studies in the British Isles*. London: Arnold.

Hernandez, Nuria, Daniela Kolbe, and Monika Schulz. 2011. *A Comparative Grammar of British English Dialects*. Vol 2: *Modals, Pronouns, Complement clauses*. Berlin/New York: Mouton de Gruyter.

Hughes, Arthur, Peter Trudgill, and Dominic Watt. 2005. *English Accents and Dialects – An Introduction to Social and Regional Varieties of English in the British Isles*. London: Arnold.

Ihalainen, Ossi. 1994. The dialects of England since 1776. In: Robert Burchfield (ed.), *The Cambridge History of the English Language*, Vol. 5: *English in Britain and Overseas: Origins and Development*, 197–274. Cambridge: Cambridge University Press.

Johnstone, Barbara. 2010. Indexing the local. In: Nicolas Coupland (ed.), *Handbook of Language and Globalization*, 386–405. Oxford: Oxford University Press.

Kortmann, Bernd. 2008. Synopsis: morphological and syntactic variation in the British Isles. In: Bernd Kortmann and Clive Upton (eds.), *Handbook of Varieties of English: The British Isles*, 478–495. Berlin/New York: Mouton de Gruyter.

Kortmann, Bernd. 2010. Variation across Englishes. In: Andy Kirkpatrick (ed.), *Routledge Handbook of World Englishes*, 400–424. London: Routledge.

Kortmann, Bernd (ed.). 2012. *World Atlas of Variation in English: Grammar*. Berlin/New York: Mouton de Gruyter.

Kortmann, Bernd and Kerstin Lunkenheimer (eds.). 2011. *The Electronic World Atlas of Variation in English: Grammar* (eWAVE). München and Berlin: Max Planck Digital Library in cooperation with Mouton de Gruyter.

Kortmann, Bernd and Agnes Schneider. 2011. Grammaticalization in non-standard varieties of English. In: Heiko Narrog and Bernd Heine (eds.), *The Oxford Handbook of Grammaticalization*, 263–278. Oxford/New York: Oxford University Press.

Kortmann, Bernd and Edgar Schneider with Kate Burridge, Rajend Mesthrie and Clive Upton (eds.). 2004. *A Handbook of Varieties of English*. Vol. 1: *Phonology*, Vol. 2: *Morphology, Syntax*. Berlin/New York: Mouton de Gruyter.

Kortmann, Bernd and Benedikt Szmrecsanyi. 2004. Global synopsis: Morphological and syntactic variation in English. In: Bernd Kortmann and Edgar Schneider with Kate Burridge, Rajend Mesthrie and Clive Upton (eds.), *A Handbook of Varieties of English*. Vol. 2: *Morphology, Syntax*, 1142–1202. Berlin/New York: Mouton de Gruyter.

Kortmann, Bernd and Benedikt Szmrecsanyi. 2009. World Englishes between simplification and complexification. In: Thomas Hoffmann and Lucia Siebers (eds.), *World Englishes: Problems – Properties – Prospects*, 265–285. Amsterdam/Philadelphia: John Benjamins.

Kortmann, Bernd and Clive Upton (eds.). 2008. *Handbook of Varieties: The British Isles*. Berlin/New York: Mouton de Gruyter.

Kortmann, Bernd and Susanne Wagner. 2005. The Freiburg English Dialect Project and Corpus. In: Bernd Kortmann, Tanja Herrmann, Lukas Pietsch, and Susanne Wagner (eds.), *A Comparative Grammar of British English Dialects: Agreement, Gender, Relative Clauses*, 1–20. Berlin/New York: Mouton de Gruyter.

Kortmann, Bernd and Susanne Wagner. 2010. Changes and continuities in dialect grammar. In: Raymond Hickey (ed.), *Eighteenth-Century English: Ideology and Change*, 269–292. Cambridge: Cambridge University Press.

Labov, William. 1994. *Principles of Linguistic Change*, Vol. 1: *Internal Factors*. Oxford: Blackwell.

Labov, William. 2001. *Principles of Linguistic Change*, Vol. 2: *Social Factors*. Oxford: Blackwell.

Langstrof, Christian. 2006. *Vowel change in New Zealand English – Patterns and Implications*. PhD thesis, University of Canterbury.

Lass, Roger. 1974. Linguistic orthogenesis? Scots vowel quantity and the English length conspiracy. In: John M. Anderson and Charles Jones (eds.), *Historical Linguistics: Proceedings of the 1st International Conference on Historical Linguistics, Edinburgh, September 1973*, 311–352. Amsterdam: North Holland.

Lass, Roger. 1999. Phonology and morphology. In: Roger Lass (ed.), *The Cambridge History of the English Language*, Vol. 3: *1476–1776*, 56–186. Cambridge: Cambridge University Press.

McMahon, April, Paul Heggarty, Robert McMahon, and Warren Maguire. 2007. The sound patterns of Englishes: representing phonetic similarity. *English Language and Linguistics* 11: 113–142.

McMahon, April. 2013. Computing linguistic distance between varieties. In: Manfred Krug and Julia Schlüter (eds.), *Research Methods in Language Variation and Change*, 421–432. Cambridge: Cambridge University Press.

Milroy, James and Lesley Milroy (eds.). 1993. *Real English: The Grammar of English Dialects in the British Isles*. London/New York: Longman.

Montgomery, Chris. 2006. *Northern English dialects: A perceptual approach*. Sheffield: University of Sheffield, Unpublished PhD Thesis.

Montgomery, Chris. 2012. Mapping the perceptions of non-linguists in Northern England. In: Sandra Hansen, Christian Schwarz, Philipp Stoeckle, and Tobias Streck (eds.), *Dialectological and Folk Dialectological Concepts of Space – Current Methods and Perspectives in Sociolinguistic Research on Dialect Change*, 164–178. Berlin and New York: Mouton de Gruyter.

Murelli, Adriano and Bernd Kortmann. 2011. Non-standard varieties in the areal typology of Europe. In: Bernd Kortmann and Johan van der Auwera (eds). *The Languages and Linguistics of Europe: A Comprehensive Guide*, 525–536. Berlin/New York: Mouton de Gruyter.

Rosewarne, David. 1984. Estuary English: David Rosewarne describes a newly observed variety of English pronunciation. *Times Educational Supplement*, 19th October 1984.

Schneider, Edgar. 2004. Global synopsis: phonetic and phonological variation in English worldwide. In: Bernd Kortmann, Edgar Schneider (eds.), Vol. 1: *Phonology*: 1111–1138.

Szmrecsanyi, Benedikt. 2012. Analyticity and syntheticity in the history of English. In: Terttu Nevalainen and Elizabeth Closs Traugott (eds.), *Handbook on the History of English: Rethinking Approaches to the History of English*, 654–665. Oxford: Oxford University Press.

Szmrecanyi, Benedikt. 2013. *Grammatical Variation in British English Dialects: A Study in Corpus-Based Dialectrometry*. Cambridge: Cambridge University Press.

Szmrecsanyi, Benedikt and Bernd Kortmann. 2009. Vernacular universals and angloversals in a typological Perspective. In: Markku Filppula, Juhani Klemola, and Heli Paulasto (eds.), *Vernacular Universals and Language Contacts: Evidence from Varieties of English and Beyond*, 33–53. London/New York: Routledge.

Szmrecsanyi, Benedikt and Christoph Wolk. 2011. Holistic corpus-based dialectology. *Brazilian Journal of Applied Linguistics*, 11(2): 561–592.

Torgersen, Eivind, Paul Kerswill and Susan Fox. 2006. Ethnicity as a source of changes in the London vowel system. In: Frans Hinskens (ed.), *Language Variation: European Perspectives*, 249–263. Amsterdam/Philadelphia: John Benjamins.

Trudgill, Peter. 1974. *The Social Differentiation of English in Norwich*. Cambridge: Cambridge University Press.

Trudgill, Peter. 2004. *New-Dialect Formation. The Inevitability of Colonial Englishes*. Edinburgh: Edinburgh University Press.

Trudgill, Peter. 2009. Vernacular universals and the sociolinguistic typology of English dialects. In: Markku Filppula, Juhani Klemola, and Heli Paulasto (eds.), *Vernacular Universals and Language Contacts: Evidence from Varieties of English and Beyond*, 304–322. London/New York: Routledge.

Upton, Clive. 2008. Synopsis: phonological variation in the British Isles. In: Bernd Kortmann and Clive Upton (eds.), *Handbook of Varieties: The British Isles*, 269–282. Berlin/New York: Mouton de Gruyter.

Wells, John C. 1982. *Accents of English*. Cambridge: Cambridge University Press.

Wells, John. 1997. What is Estuary English. *English Teaching Professional*: 46–47. www.phon.ucl.ac.uk/home/estuary/whatis.htm (last accessed 11 August 2017).

Wichmann, Søren and Matthias Urban. 2012. Towards an automated classification of Englishes. In: Terttu Nevalainen and Elizabeth Closs Traugott (eds.), *Handbook on the History of English: Rethinking Approaches to the History of English*, 676–686. Oxford: Oxford University Press.

Lynda Mugglestone
Chapter 8:
Received Pronunciation

1 Defining Received Pronunciation: an overview —— 151
2 Antecedents: supra-regional attitudes —— 154
3 Received Pronunciation: belief and behavior —— 157
4 Modern RP: the crisis of definition —— 161
5 Summary —— 165
6 References —— 166

Abstract: This chapter explores the history and identity of 'Received Pronunciation' or RP, spanning the 18th century, when comment on a non-localized British accent first appears, to contemporary discussion in terms of both usage and attitudes. Charting early attempts to disseminate and foster a reference model for spoken English, and the social meanings which could also thereby be cultivated, it also uses archive material to examine particular case-histories of its adoption and use. New archive material is also used to explore its role (and explicit fostering) in institutions such as the early BBC. Changes in modern RP (and attendant crises of definition and identity) are given careful consideration in order to evaluate the question of its continued validity, either as label or linguistic reality.

1 Defining Received Pronunciation: an overview

1.1 Controversy and consensus

Both the identity and role of Received Pronunciation (RP) have been the subject of considerable discussion. It is "an anachronism in present-day democratic society", Abercrombie (1965: 14) declared; "old-fashioned and misleading", Roach (2000: viii) later concurred. Intentionally displaced by other terms ("BBC Pronunciation" [Roach 2000], "non-regional pronunciation" [Collins and Mees 2003], "Reference Pronunciation" [Rosewarne 1984]), its claims as automatic reference model in dictionaries and in foreign language teaching have likewise been con-

Lynda Mugglestone: Oxford (UK)

tested. "If we had a completely free choice of model accent it would be possible to find more suitable ones", Roach (2000: 5) argues, advocating Scottish or Irish accents instead. Traditional images of RP nevertheless continue, foregrounding both social evaluation and supra-regionality as salient elements in its construction ("A prestige way of speaking [...] the speech of educated people, not restricted to any area of England" [Kreidler 1997: 4], "the accent spoken throughout England, by the upper-middle and upper classes [...] widely used in the private sector of the education subsystem" [Giegerich 1992: 43]). Other writers actively contest the viability of socially-orientated (and especially class-based) meanings. It is "impossible actually to identify the accent under discussion in social terms", Ramsaran (1990: 178) avers, not least since "it is no longer possible to talk in [...] clear-cut terms of social classes; nor is there any longer so straightforward a correlation between social background and profession or type of education in present-day society". Elsewhere the demise of RP is predicted – or already described – in favor of another variety of speech, widely labeled "Estuary English" (see e.g. Ballard 2001: 188). This, however, attracts its own elements of controversy: it is "a putative variety of Southern British English located in the Home Counties" (Przedlacka 2000: 19); "in reality there is no such accent, and the term should be used with care" (Roach 2000: 4).

This lack of consensus indicates something of the complexity involved in understanding RP. Like language itself, its meaning is open to flux and shift, while the socio-historical construction of this speech variety can, as we will see, still impact on how it is perceived and described, especially in attitudinal terms. History is also important in underscoring fundamental changes in its composition and identity; what "received pronunciation" signified in the 18th or 19th centuries clearly does not correspond to 21st century debates on its role and use (especially in the levels of socio-cultural resistance which such debates can reveal). Both social and linguistic changes influence what RP is, or is conceived to be. Early 20th-century definitions, for example, engaged with hierarchical and socially evaluative meanings with apparent ease; for Wyld (1934: 605), RP was "the best type of English", distinguished by the "marked distinctiveness and clarity of its sounds" and firmly embedded in models of emulation and aspiration: it was "a type of English which is neither provincial nor vulgar, a type which most people would willingly speak if they could, and desire to speak if they do not". "Received Standard Spoken English" was, moreover, the proper object of academic study ("the main object of our solicitude"); Wyld's (1914) *Short History of English* hence focused on "the origin and development of that form of English which is now spoken by educated and well-bred people" (Wyld 1914: 25), largely excluding the regional voice from consideration ("the great majority of the English Dialects are of very little importance as representatives of English speech" [Wyld 1914: 24]).

This chapter will also examine the origins and development of "received spoken English" (and its current use), if from a somewhat different perspective. Central aspects of its historical formation – in terms of both constituent features and ideological matrices – will be explored in detail (especially with reference to traditional notions of "standardness", "prestige", or "educatedness"). Emphasis will, however, be placed on its pluralism and diversity; if RP suggests, for some, a monolithic and largely invariant form, linguistic reality remains at some remove. As Trask (1996: 301) confirms, RP embraces not merely "a certain accent of British English" but "more precisely a group of closely related accents" operating along a spectrum of more or less advanced/conservative. Wells's (1982) U-RP (upper-class RP), general RP, and Adoptive RP, as well as "near-RP" confirm a similarly pluralist identity. As we will see, the precise identity of what is deemed to be "general" or mainstream RP can, however, also occasion considerable debate.

1.2 Speaking 'without an accent'

It was Alexander Ellis, dubbed "the creator of the scientific study of English phonetics" (Anon. 1890: 419), who provided the first formal specifications of RP, noting that "[i]n the present day […] we may recognise a received pronunciation all over the country" (Ellis 1869–89: Volume I: 23). Basing his comments on empirical observation (and detailed transcription), Ellis went on to explore the characteristics of speakers who typified such usage; if markers of geographical origin were absent, other associations – of education or status – were marked. "Received English pronunciation" was, for example, in evidence in the speech of "men of undoubted education" such as Benjamin Jowett (the President of Balliol College, Oxford), Sir G. B. Airy (President of the Royal Society), Dr Hooker (President of the British Association), as well as in the observed usage of politicians and "men of science" (Ellis 1869–89: Volume IV: 1208–1213).

Ellis (1869–89: Volume V: 6) was also first to deploy the initialism by which Received Pronunciation would often later be known: "rp., received pronunciation, or that of pronouncing dictionaries and educated people". It was likewise Ellis's definition of *accent* which appeared in the first fascicle of the *Oxford English Dictionary* (OED, Murray et al. 1884–1928). As Ellis explained, speaking "with an accent" was, by this time, assumed to be a signifier of regional marking (and implicit "deviation" from a norm): "This utterance consists mainly in a prevailing quality of tone, or in a peculiar alteration of pitch, but may include mispronunciation of vowels and consonants, misplacing of stress, and inflection of a sentence. The locality of a speaker is generally marked by this kind of accent". "Received pronunciation" was, in contrast, already participating in that shift by which paradoxical (if popular) images of the "accentless" – what Lippi-Green (1997: 41) terms "the myth of non-accent" – surrounded this mode of speech.

Ellis's work in the late 19th century isolated a number of distinctive features about the identity of this particular speech variety. Earlier writers had stressed that "in every province there are peculiarities of dialect, which affect (...) the pronunciation" (Campbell 1788: 353). Ellis's "received pronunciation" was significantly different, its use, as his definition of *accent* within the OED specifies, transcending regional boundaries "all over the country". Supra-local in this distributional sense, it was, Ellis makes clear, a variety which could also be defined in terms of a particular social distribution. In an era in which a general education system was instituted only in 1870, the notion of "educatedness" operated as a telling marker of status, often used with euphemistic intent (not least given the existence of non-localized models of elite education; see further Honey 1988; Mugglestone 2007: 212–257). Equally pertinent in modern attempts to define RP is therefore Ellis's (1869–89: Volume IV: 1215) assertion that "there is no such thing as educated English pronunciation. There are pronunciations of English people more or less educated in a multitude of other things, but not in pronunciation". If Ellis's "received" ("Generally adopted, accepted, approved as true or good", OED s.v.1) intentionally suggested widespread recognition (as well as a certain validation) for this form of speech in the late 19th century, his use of "educated" simultaneously confirmed its social restriction. It is, and was, the voice of a minority (usually estimated as being used by somewhere between 3–5% of the population [Trudgill 2001]).

2 Antecedents: supra-regional attitudes

2.1 'Received English' in the 18th and 19th Centuries

The idea of the "received" – and the perceived unacceptability of that not so judged – has a long history in English. "Received" English was, for example, carefully placed against that which must be "rejected" on the opening page of Johnson's *Dictionary* (1755). While Johnson's concern was with lexis and semantics (and the usage of "polite writers"), the extension of such ideas to pronunciation was apparent elsewhere. John Walker, author of a highly influential pronouncing dictionary (in print throughout the 19th century), had sought to determine what he already termed "received pronunciation". This, he stated (Walker 1774: 17), provided the best illustration of the proper enunciation of vowels in unaccented syllables. "Those sounds [...] which are the most generally received among the learned or polite [...] are the most legitimate", he added (Walker 1791: viii).

Notions of "received pronunciation" are nevertheless significantly different at this time even if, on closer examination, important continuities also emerge. The "received" English speech of the 18th century remained largely localized, though it was self-evidently part of the prescriptive purpose of many writers (including Walker) to widen access and assimilation to this chosen norm. Contemporary definitions of a reference accent at this point cluster around specifications of both geography and status – "THE PRESENT PRACTICE OF POLITE SPEAKERS IN THE CITY OF LONDON", Perry (1775: dedication) states. Evidence of language attitudes, however, reveal that regional accents were already framed in a range of supra-local evaluative paradigms. Writers such as Johnston, Walker, and Sheridan provide instructions for the "remedy" of Irish, Scots, Cockney, or southwestern pronunciation (see e.g. Johnston 1764: viii). As Buchanan (himself a Scot) noted of educational desiderata in this matter, "It ought to be, indispensably, the care of every teacher of English, not to suffer children to pronounce according to the dialect of that place of the country where they were born or reside, if it happens to be vicious" (Buchanan 1757: xli, Note). "Viciousness" was a recurrent element in such negative positioning, as was "uncouth" with its suggestion of a type of pronunciation which was literally not "known", or "received". As for Perry, "proper" pronunciation was elsewhere, founded in the "London standard" and a "metropolitan" habit of speech.

What is noteworthy is the pervasive and overt privileging of one speech variety in ways which are already (a) semantically and ideologically removed from regionality (the notion of the "provincial" and "vicious") and (b) strongly marked in social terms. The "London" speech commended is that of the upper strata: as Sheridan (1762: 30) noted, while "two different modes of pronunciation prevail" in the capital, "polite pronunciation" must be distinguished – and preferred – to that "current in the city, and [...] called the cockney". A highly specific engagement with the socio-phonetic associations of different speech varieties was also apparent: "Surely every gentleman will think it worth while, to take some pains, to get rid of such evident marks of rusticity" (Sheridan 1762: 33). "Polite pronunciation", framed by a different metalanguage ("polished", "pure"), was conversely "a sort of proof that a person has kept good company, and on that account is sought after by all, who wish to be considered as fashionable people, or members of the beau monde" (Sheridan 1762: 30). As here, social and linguistic hegemonies intentionally unite, proving a long history for the notion of an elite model in English pronunciation, as well as attendant language attitudes.

2.2 Constructing a reference model

What is revealed by such discourses is the assimilation of issues of accent within ideological manifestations of standardization, as well as the polarized social (and evaluative) meanings of different forms of speech. In essence, this already provides compelling evidence of the existence for pronunciation of what Lippi-Green (1997) terms a "language subordination model". A further important element within the ideological remit of many works on language at this time was, however, the intended supra-regional dissemination of one form of pronunciation. While contemporary dictionaries and grammars provided non-localized reference models for spelling, lexis, and grammar, the absence of a national reference model for pronunciation remained conspicuous. Buchanan's 1766 *Essay Towards Establishing a Standard for an Elegant and Uniform Pronunciation* typifies the thrust to resolve such uncertainties. Significantly unlike the meanings which later frame a supra-regional variety, however, Buchanan's ideal of a shared and "standard" mode of speech (to "obviate a vicious provincial pronunciation") also intentionally constructed a new equality of communication for all British speakers, "joining them into one social family" and aiding to "remov[e] national prejudice, which has too long subsisted, and been chiefly fostered [...] from their different forms of speech" (Buchanan 1766: xii). Sheridan, too, presented the nationwide (and top-down) assimilation of a form of speech based on a metrocentric elite as an instrument of egalitarian reform – a means by which "all natives of these realms" will, literally and metaphorically, "speak the same language":

> Thus might the rising generation, born and bred in different Countries, and Counties, no longer have a variety of dialects, but as subjects of one King, like sons of one father, have one common tongue. All native of these realms, would be restored to their birthright in commonage of language, which has been too long fenced in, and made the property of a few. (Sheridan 1761: 36)

Such texts set the ideological stage, as it were, for the notion of a supra-regional speech-variety and its stated desirability, prestige, and social value. Accent is, in effect, constructed as a commodity to be acquired or eliminated, with one accent in particular being made the focus of statusful accommodation. In terms of the establishment of a reference model for pronunciation (often seen as a salient aspect of modern RP) it is important to recognize that, at this point, it became the accepted (and "received") convention that one accent alone – founded in the discourse of a social elite, and framed by discussions of explicit and overt prestige – was codified and transcribed in the pronouncing dictionaries which, courtesy of writers such as Sheridan, Walker, and Buchanan, emerged as an important new genre. Johnson's (1755) decision to mark merely word stress was deemed inadequate; instead increasingly complex notational systems encoded, for a national audience, an /h/-full, increasingly non-rhotic accent characterized by the presence of the FOOT-STRUT split, by the phonemic (rather than allophonic) status of /ŋ/, by a clearly differentiated pattern of sounds in words such as *moor* and *more*, as well as by the (at times controversial) tendency to deploy the BATH-TRAP split.

Supra-regional in intended dissemination and use, such features also importantly confirm a localized bias for this reference model in southern rather than northern or midlands varieties of English. Transcriptions in Walker (1791) hence establish /ʌ/ rather than /ʊ/ in words such as *cut*; those whose habitual language habits were /h/-less were likewise encouraged to read relevant sections of the dictionary aloud until, as Sheridan (1762: 35) stated, "an habit is obtained of aspirating strongly". Other desirable features – the presence of the "delicate" palatal glide in words such as *garden* or *kind* (/gj-/, /kj-/) could be acquired in the same way. While the "non-localized" or "non-regional" therefore form constituent parts of many later definitions of RP, 18th-century lexicographical practice (and the early development of a supra-regional reference model for pronunciation) nevertheless already indicate certain typological problems in the unqualified use of this term.

3 Received Pronunciation: belief and behavior

3.1 Variation and norms

Case histories such as that of the scientist Michael Faraday (who shed his low-status – and "non-received" – cockney accent in a course of instruction with the elocutionist Benjamin Smart [Mugglestone 2011]) illustrate, of course, the kind of top-down modeling envisaged as salient in the establishment of a national "received" pronunciation. As Smart (1836: xl) explained, "the common standard dialect is that in which all marks of a particular place of birth are lost, and nothing appears to indicate any other habits of intercourse than with the well-bred or well-informed, wherever they may be found". Here, if the formal diction of RP is absent, the identity of this linguistic variety – defined by both supra-regional and social practice – is again unmistakable. While transcriptions within Smart's dictionary again encode this accent as a national reference model for all, issues of accent prejudice (and their consequences) are, however, palpable, displaying clear affinities with the "accent-bar" which Abercrombie (1965: 13) later censured as part of the social patterning of 20th-century RP (see further Section 4.1). "A man displaying either ["cockney" or "rustic" pronunciation] must have large portion of natural talent or acquired science, who surmounts the prejudice it creates", Smart (1836: xl) noted.

Smart, working within an often prescriptive remit, can articulate this supra-regional norm with categorical intent. Ellis, just over 20 years later, would, however, strive to engage with the same subject with descriptive clarity, and as part of the philological revolution of the late 19th century. The distance between the two is significant. Particularly important is Ellis's careful distinction between the existence of RP as part of language "belief", and as its status as an actual variety of speech (see e.g. Fabricius's [2006] similar distinction of RP as praxis and RP as ideology). "Belief", Ellis points out, underpins assumptions that RP is a "standard" of the language in evaluative and pragmatic senses:

> there prevailed, and apparently there still prevails, a belief that it is possible to erect a standard of pronunciation which should be acknowledged and followed throughout the countries where English is spoken as a native tongue, and that in fact that standard already exists, and is the norm unconsciously followed by persons who, by rank or education, have most right to establish the custom of speech. (Ellis 1869–89: Volume I: 624)

Against this, Ellis placed a more complex description which excludes the endorsement of RP as a standard of speech founded on either uniformity or "correctness": "At present there is *no* standard of pronunciation" (Ellis 1869–89: Volume I: 630). "Nothing approaching to real uniformity prevails" (Ellis 1869–89: Volume I: 626); instead "there are many ways of pronouncing English *correctly* according to the usage of large numbers of persons of either sex in different parts of the country, who have received a superior education" (Ellis 1869–89: Volume I: 630). That "educated people, born and bred in Northern England" had patterns of speech which could and did command prestige was stressed by Lloyd (1899: preface).

If RP was codified (the accent of "pronouncing dictionaries" Ellis [1869–89: Volume V: 6] specified) and was arguably a "standard" in this sense (see Milroy 2001), it was, however, the variability – as well as the social restriction – of late 19th-century RP which Ellis repeatedly emphasized. Containing within it the cross-currents of conservatism and innovation, RP was, in reality, far from uniform – age, gender, and register all impacted on the precise realizations used. Words such as *name, same, go, know* could be pronounced with monophthongs or diphthongs, the latter more apparent in younger speakers. Instability in palatal glides was widely in evidence; while the presence of /j/ in words such as *Tuesday* (/tjuːz–/), *tulip* (/tjuːlip/) was then seemingly secure, its use in words such as *kind* was "rapidly dying out"; though /gj/ (in *regarding*) was "common" (Ellis 1869–89: Volume IV: 1214). Still greater variability attended the pronunciation of vowels in words such as *fast, bath, lost, off*, revealing some of the complexity – and social undercurrents – of speech at this time. While the move away from the TRAP/CLOTH vowels is not found in regional accents north of the Trent, the fact that fully lengthened and retracted vowels in words such as *fast* were strongly associative of Cockney seems to have acted as a socio-phonetic deterrent for some RP speakers throughout the 19th and early 20th centuries; Ellis (like phoneticians such as Ripman and Ward in the early 20th century) notes a gender-specific preference within RP for /æ/ by "some ladies", as well as the use of a variety of other possible realizations (see Mugglestone 2007: 79–82). The use of a lengthened sound in words of the CLOTH set, as in *off* [ɔːf] could attract similar resistance across the RP spectrum (though it became characteristic of 20th-century U-RP). As such variabilities indicate, the fact that RP was, and is, far from monolithic remains an important – but often forgotten aspect of its identity.

Ideological and well-established associations of RP with "correctness" could, however, already lead to attitudinal resistance to certain features which were nevertheless also characteristic markers of its use. Non-rhoticity in post-vocalic and final position was, for example, popularly proscribed as well as being, in reality, a descriptive feature of a supra-regional accent in which, as Ellis (1869–89: Volume I: 593) affirmed, words such as *farther: father, stalk: stork* were regularly homophonous. Similar was the formal resistance to the shift of /hw/ to /w/ in words such as *where*. As both Ellis and Henry Sweet stressed, the presence of /hw/ confirmed the speech-conscious (and the domains of adoptive RP) rather than the speech-patterns of general RP. Ellis's "actual observations on unstudied pronunciations", as he recognized, thereby provided "a new datum in phonology, because they enable us to estimate the real amount of floating diversity of pronunciation at any time" (Ellis 1869–89: Volume IV: xvii). Scrutinizing these, we can, for instance, note the continuity within late 19th-century RP of conservative forms such as *humour* with initial /j-/ (/jumə/), the rise of diphthongal enunciations in words such as *me* /miɪ/, and, in "young educated London", the increasing consolidation of the lengthened retracted /ɑː/ in *ask*.

Improved communication – and especially the extension of a system of elite and significantly non-localized education in the form of the British public schools – led to a further strand in the supra-regional accent as a particular mark of social identity. The phonetician Daniel Jones was explicit on the socio-phonetic modeling of this form of speech; transcriptions and articulatory description in his writings from the early decades of the 20th century detail "the pronunciation […] of Southern Englishmen who have been educated as the great public boarding schools" or "that most generally heard in everyday speech in the families of Southern English persons whose men-folk have been educated at the great public boarding-schools". It was, he noted, "also used by a considerable proportion of those who do not come from the South of England but who have been educated at these schools" (Jones 1917: viii). Jones here redefined RP once more; it was now "PSP" ("Public School Pronunciation") – a term which gave a very specific social construction to the notion of "educated" speech, as well as further underpinning enduring associations of privilege, prestige, and class. Jones's influential role as probably the foremost British phonetician in the first half of the 20th century was to be of critical importance in reifying the role of RP in language teaching.

3.2 "BBC Pronunciation"

Jones had an additional role as a founder member of the BBC's Committee on Spoken English in 1926. The BBC, however, would give a new reality to the notion of "received" English. Those equipped with "receivers" (or with access to one) could now, quite literally, receive "BBC pronunciation" via this new supra-regional form of communication. While initial notions of "BBC pronunciation" were distinctly liberal in their composition, the rise of the announcer as a specialized role and, increasingly, the sense that announcers should undertake formal speech-training which, at least on the national program, meant the eradication of regionally-marked forms, meant that "BBC pronunciation" was ultimately to become yet another synonym for RP (see Mugglestone 2008). "**B.B.C. English**, standard English as maintained by B.B.C. announcers; so **B.B.C. pronunciation**", the OED later explained (s.v. *B.B.C. English*). That this notion of a "standard" was not misplaced in the interpretative slant adopted by the OED is clear from internal BBC documentation: "The B.B.C. is concerned only with questions of pronunciation, and the standard of pronunciation adopted by its official speakers is regarded more and more [...] as a standard of currency to be aimed at", one which aims "to steer a course midway between the lapses of the uneducated, and the affectations of the insufficiently educated". Moreover, "by constantly repeating one alternative it will give that one greater currency, and so tend to bring about the disuse of others. This will be a boon to many of us" (BBC Written Archives Center, WAC S259/1). In the light of recent debates on the labeling of RP, history here offers a few timely reminders of the prescriptive – and conservative – associations of "BBC Pronunciation". The first meeting of the Advisory Committee on Spoken English in 1926 discussed Item 5 extensively: "Attitude of the Committee towards the modern tendency of slovenly speech" (BBC WAC [BBC Written Archives Center, Caversham] R6/201/1: Minute Book 1926–33). Representative of such "slovenliness" were mergers resulting from non-rhoticity, the loss of distinctiveness between /hw/ and /w/, as well the on-going merger (attested already in the 19th century) by which words such as *shore : sure, more : moor* were homophones. Announcers were instructed to rectify such features in their use of English on the airwaves. Reintroducing /hw/ was deemed to be a lost cause, even in the highly idealized forms of RP endorsed in principle (even if not always adhered to in practice).

Detailed examination of the issues which surrounded broadcast English can further illuminate the divide between belief and behavior in terms of RP. While the attempt to set up a normative reference model for the nation was gradually abandoned, notions of "BBC English" as an evaluative standard remained prominent. Responses by listeners are, in this context, highly useful in indicating something of the reality of the constituent features of RP at this time. A prevalent fiction (with its legacies in modern language attitudes, as well as 19th-century comment [Mugglestone 2007: 91–94]) was the absence of intrusive /r/ from modern RP. "I know as a fact that most educated speakers of Southern English insert an *r* in *idea(r) of, India(r) Office* […] yet they all obstinately deny it", Sweet (1890: viii) had expostulated. Early listeners to the BBC maintained a healthy complaint tradition on this matter (it was a "solecism", an "abomination", a "cockney illiteracy"), though the frequency of their letters provides a useful index to the currency of the form itself. Similar resistance was directed at the smoothing evident in words such as *power*, at the loss of /ʊə/ as in *sure* (a change in progress since the mid-19th century) as well as, in an interesting precursor of what is often adjudged to be a defining feature of "estuary English", to the use of allophonic glottal stops where "proper English" demanded [t]. Such complaints also indicated the extent to which, as Cruttenden (1994: 78) confirms, RP "often became identified in the public mind with 'BBC English'". That this public – and often conservative – image (popularly bound up with notions of "correctness" and "proper standards") could conflict with the more complex reality of spoken English on the BBC (and of RP per se) should, of course, also be remembered.

4 Modern RP: the crisis of definition

4.1 Distance and resistance

By 1963, even the BBC had abandoned the "public school voice" as a sociophonetic norm; "red-brick" accents were now desirable. The BBC needed to "break away" from the "public-School voice" (BBC WAC [BBC Written Archives Center, Caversham] R34/587/4 Policy Presentation Pronunciation, 1963–64). Jones (1950: 3) too abandoned "PSP" as an accentual norm; his revised *Pronunciation of English* rejected the idea of a "standard" accent, or that speakers should strive to accommodate to this as a normative reference model. Jones stressed instead the pragmatic utility (and sense of compromise) by which he would deal with "widely understood pronunciation" or "what may be termed 'Received Pronunciation' [...] This is not a particularly good term, but it is doubtful whether a better one can be found" (Jones 1950: 4). A sense of critical unease with the connotative values – and social meanings – of RP would henceforth be a prominent strand in linguistic comment. Abercrombie (1965: 13) forcefully argued against the perpetuation of a system by which, in a form of phonetic apartheid, speakers were, in effect, segregated by an "accent-bar" which engendered both prejudice and discrimination: "your social life, your career, or both, may be affected by whether you possess [RP] or not". The analogies with race (and racism) stress the danger of distinctions founded on differences which are inherently superficial. Ideologically, the maintenance of RP was, for Abercrombie, already seen as productive of intolerance, and a dangerously subjective sense of inequality.

Subsequent decades have witnessed the further attitudinal distancing of RP – as "plummy", "lah-di-dah" or, as verified in subjective reaction tests, as resonant of coldness (if intelligence) and lack of friendliness. Many regionally marked accents have, in turn, moved into more positive attitudinal areas (trustworthiness, integrity, warmth). Sheridan's (1762: 30) selected images of regional "disgrace" would now be seen as unacceptably discriminatory while 18th-century images of a single "received" accent for all seem impossibly naïve. Popular comment has, if anything, tended to suggest that it is RP (or more particularly U-RP, "Refined RP") which is now potentially a social handicap or impediment, not least given the persuasive power of covert prestige for many speakers. Easy equations of upper class and "prestige" are also problematic. Instead, given popular modern rhetorics of equality and egalitarianism, the very notion that the speech of certain speakers is "received" and that of others not, is judged "invidious" (Lewis 2004: 223) especially when, as Milroy (2001: 17) notes, "it may not be clear exactly WHO does the permitting and receiving".

As in Ellis, however, "belief" and "behavior" must be kept apart. As a label, RP can clearly evoke a range of negative associations, bound up with traditional images of class and privilege, and uncomfortably resonant of elitism (and the validation of such). On the other hand, it has to be remembered that the essentially pyramidal image of British society remains in place, while the stratificational patterns of accent which accompany this, with those at the bottom of the social pyramid exhibiting the greatest regional marking, likewise endures. RP speakers are, conversely, still located at its apex, even if this apex in social terms now includes non-RP and especially near-RP speakers. The search for a less loaded, more neutral, designation for the speech of those who do not reveal their regional origins by means of accent has, as we have seen, prompted a proliferation of alternative labels. Some of these have already been listed (see Section 1.1), though more could be added: e.g. "BR", denoting "British English" (Upton et al. 2001), "General British" (Lewis 1972, 2004). These can, however, raise further problems, apart from the obvious lack of consensus among different writers. Can "non-regional pronunciation" serve as an effective label if the forms described still maintain a typological bias towards southern rather than northern phonologies and, indeed, as many writers argue, also reveal a far greater presence in distributional terms in southern rather than northern Britain? Likewise, in an era in which the BBC is actively extending the accents used upon the airwaves, including in authoritative domains such as the news (and the traditional bastions of RP, on BBC Radios 3 and 4), the label "BBC pronunciation" can also create problems. Given the fact that "[t]he number of native speakers of this accent who originate in Ireland, Scotland and Wales is very small and probably diminishing, and it is therefore a misnomer to call it an accent of BRITISH English" (Roach 2004: 239), Lewis's favored "GB" ("General British") is equally liable to dissent.

Controversy points in three main directions. First, the attempt to find a label with less ideological baggage remains a significant issue for many writers. Second is the precise identity of what is, in effect, being denoted by this proffered range of terminological equivalents. Outside the undeniable elements of semantic engineering ("because of the dated – and to some people objectionable – social connotations, we shall not normally use the label RP" [Collins and Mees 2003: 3]), it is, for example, clear that "BR", "GB", "Reference pronunciation" et al. all denote a supra-regional accent spectrum, operating in a continuum in the upper regions of the socio-phonetic accent pyramid. RP is also embedded in a temporal continuum. Jones (1950) and Abercrombie (1965) describe – as might be expected – what is now seen as "Conservative RP" or "Traditional RP" (Cruttenden's "Refined RP", Wells's "U-RP"). While the latter now generates perhaps the greatest degree of attitudinal resistance, modern supra-regional reference models are often located in a different generational space. Upton et al. (2001: xii) select "a younger unmarked RP [...] that accent which will be most widely acceptable as well as most intelligible to native BR speakers", stressing both its modernity and its avoidance of the negative connotations which surround "marked" or upper-class RP. A similar age-shifted preference is evident in Collins and Mees (2003: 4): "educated middle and younger generation speakers in England who have a pronunciation which cannot be pinned down to a specific area".

As the 21st century counterparts of Ellis's "young educated London", such younger speakers are in the process of redefining mainstream RP, revealing the consolidation of features which were marginal (or "advanced") within traditional and older models. "RP, unlike Standard English, appears to be changing quite rapidly", observes Kerswill (2007: 480). Age can thereby become a particularly important variable in differentiating modern trends within RP, as in the increasing use of an affricate in *tulip, Tuesday* with /tʃ-/ rather than conservative /tj/-) – a feature already detected by Ellis in his "unstudied pronunciation" of the 19th century, and condemned as a disturbing tendency in the RP of the early 20th century by the highly conservative Robert Bridges (who also chaired the BBC Advisory Committee). Here too is the increased presence of allophonic syllable-final glottals, or yod-coalescence in words such as *suit* (/suːt/ rather than /sjuːt/).

That RP changes, like all other forms of speech, is unsurprising. That a new designation is felt to be required for such changes might, however, have surprised Ellis (who stressed the importance of realising that, within "the floating diversity of pronunciation [...] the pronunciation of a future generation crystallizes, only to be dissolved by a fresh mentruum" [Ellis 1869–89: Volume IV: xvii]). As Fabricius (2006) points out, "if we start using a completely new label, we lose the link with past forms of the variety". While some linguists have advocated that this is precisely what is desired – and that a new variety is perceptible (see Milroy 2001) – others are less convinced. RP is necessarily "an evolving mode of pronunciation in its phonological system, its phonetic realization, and the incidence of its phonemes" (Cruttenden 1994: 272). Moreover, as Maidment argues with reference to "estuary English", often seen as RP's more meritocratic successor, whether this exists – or is in fact merely a more informal and advanced RP – is a further important consideration. Features such as [l-] vocalization (as in *milk*), once categorized as "near-RP" or "non-RP" (Wells 1997) and often used to hallmark "Estuary English" (see Altendorf, Chapter 122), can readily be located in the supra-regional speech of younger RP-speakers. Notions of RP (and the accent spectrum it encompasses) in this sense need to keep pace with change in progress, and the import of both situational and speaker variation.

The third aspect of controversy centers on the desirability of retaining RP as a reference accent for English as a foreign language (EFL), given its minority status in terms of speaker demographics. Counterarguments here tend to stress RP's status as the most fully documented accent of English, as well as the importance of a teaching a realistic, and modern, set of features (and awareness of concurrent variants). The conflicted sense of what RP is – ideologically and phonetically – can nevertheless be disturbingly prominent in this context. As Collins and Mees (2003: 179) note, in words such as *tune, duke* the presence of /tʃ/ and /dʒ/ is widespread though this "still starts alarm bells ringing for many speakers of traditional RP". "I like to think of the avoidance of this development as a touchstone of RP (as against Estuary English (EE), which clearly accepts it); but I am not sure that this claim can really be maintained", Wells (1997) admits, likewise revealing the legacies of RP as model of correctness versus RP as evolving language practice. What, precisely, the learner should acquire can thereby be open to dispute. If intrusive /r/ is "disliked and disapproved of" by the "speech-conscious" while also "objectively [...] part of RP", should this too be endorsed or avoided? "For EFL we might [...] agree that the learner should be aware of it receptively, but ignore it in production" (Wells 1997), Wells tentatively concludes, though this too, in reality, merely affirms the divide between what RP is in objective or, conversely, in subjective/ ideological senses.

5 Summary

5.1 RP in the 21st-century: ideology, identity, and language praxis

These levels of ongoing controversy confirm that, as yet, there are no easy solutions to issues of this kind. Whatever RP is, it is clearly not neutral in social terms, and its supra-regional use permeates the upper levels of society. Near-RP can, Upton (2004) argues, moreover be seen to characterize an expanding social base (even if one which remains to be quantitively confirmed). The fact that RP was not, and is not, monolithic means nevertheless that a certain polysemy in its definition(s) is, of course, to be expected; it operates in a continuum within which, as many phoneticians have concurred, discrete boundaries are ultimately impossible, not least perhaps between "RP" and "Near-RP". Important here is, however, the need to distinguish ideological meanings from linguistic – or sociolinguistic – ones (and ideological reservations from linguistic fact). Notions of the "best" English, the most "correct", the "most acceptable" or "the most widely understood" are, in their lack of quantification, all subjective. Socially constructed euphemisms ("educated accent") are, as Ellis indicated so long ago, by no means satisfactory (and arguably now even less so, given that university education extends to almost 50% of school leavers). Social labels are also open to contention; "class" permits no easy definition and social boundaries ("upper", "middle", "upper-middle" encompass a wide range of permutations). The fact that "class" is formally an economic determinant leads to further disparities; shared levels of income may co-exist with very different socio-linguistic identities. Models of definition based on "prestige" may fare no better; like "received", this too now tends to generate unease, especially given the fact that prestige is by no means unilinear, is covert as well as overt, and can certainly no longer be unquestionably assumed for conservative models of RP. "You can tell the Receivers where to go (and not aspirate it)", as Tony Harrison (1984: 123) famously declared.

On the plus side, RP can no longer be defined by its participation in an "accent-bar". Non-RP and especially Near-RP speakers now frequently appear in prominent public roles (a feature which seems, in fact, to have contributed to assumptions that RP is itself in decline [see Trudgill 2001: 10]). "It is nowadays necessary to define RP in a rather broader way than was once customary", states Wells (2000: xiii). Some level of semantic – and definitional – splitting ("refined" or Wells'"U-RP"; "general" or "mainstream"; "advanced") is nevertheless clearly essential in order to engage with the polysemies, and fuzziness which "RP" embraces, especially if "Regional RP" is also to come within this umbrella-term (see Cruttenden 1994 and, for counterarguments, Trudgill 2001). How "broad" this definition will need to be in future years remains an interesting – and undoubtedly challenging – proposition. Even the Royal Family exhibits a spectrum of accents (with Prince Harry often convicted as an "estuary speaker", though, in reality, merely exhibiting the features of a younger and more advanced RP). Beal's (2008) evidence of a resurgence in demand for "accent reduction" offers, however, a timely reminder of the continued significance of the supra-regional voice in both socio-phonetic and linguistic terms, while headlines such as "Brummie accent worse than silence" (*The Times*, 04/04/08) suggest that models of negative accent evaluation – as well as accommodation to supra-regional models – can remain prominent, as in the recommendation that "ambitious West Midlanders may want to consider losing their accent if they want to get on in life" (*The Times*, 04/04/08).

Acknowledgements: I would like to thank the BBC written Archives Center for permission to cite archival material within this chapter.

6 References

6.1 Unpublished Archival Material

BBC Written Archives Center (WAC), Caversham
WAC/R6/201/1 Advisory Committees. Spoken English Advisory Committee Minute Book 1926–33
WAC/R34/587/4 Policy Presentation Pronunciation (1963–64)
WAC/5259/1 Special collections: Lloyd James, 1934–40

6.2 General References

Abercrombie, David. 1965. *Studies in Phonetics and Linguistics*. London: Oxford University Press.
Anon. 1890. 'Alexander J. Ellis'. *The Academy* 38: 419–420.
Ballard, Kim. 2001. *The Frameworks of English*. Houndmills: Palgrave.

Beal, Joan. 2008. "Shamed by your English?": the Market Value of a "Good" Pronunciation. In: Joan Beal, Carmela Nocera, and Massimo Sturiale (eds.), *Perspectives on Prescriptivism*, 21–40. Bern: Peter Lang.

Buchanan, James. 1757. *Linguae Britannicae vera Pronunciatio: or, a New English Dictionary*. London: A. Millar.

Buchanan, James. 1766. *An Essay Towards Establishing a Standard for an Elegant and Uniform Pronunciation of the English Language*. London: Edward and Charles Dilly.

Campbell, George. 1788. *The Philosophy of Rhetoric*. London: W. Strahan.

Collins, Beverley and Inger Mees. 2003. *Practical Phon Phonol*. London: Routledge.

Cruttenden, Alan (ed.). 1994. *Gimson's Pronunciation of English*. Rev.edn. London: Edwin Arnold.

Ellis, Alexander. 1869–89. *On Early English Pronunciation*. 5 Vols. Vol. I: 1869; Vol. III: 1871; Vol. IV: 1875; Vol. V: 1889. London: Trübner.

Fabricius, Anne. 2006 "What is *Modern RP?*". Unpublished ms.

Giegerich, Heinz. 1992. *English Phonology*. Cambridge: Cambridge University Press.

Harrison, Tony. 1984. "Them & [uz]". In: *Selected Poems*. London: Penguin.

Honey, John. 1988. "Talking Proper"; Schooling and the Establishment of English "Received Pronunciation". In: Graham Nixon and John Honey (eds.), *An Historic Tongue: Studies in English Linguistics in Memory of Barbara Strang*, 209–227. London: Routledge.

Johnston, William. 1764. *A Pronouncing Spelling Dictionary*. London: W. Johnston.

Jones, Daniel. 1917. *An English Pronouncing Dictionary*. 4th edn. London: Dent.

Jones, Daniel. 1950. *The Pronunciation of English*. Rev. 3rd edn. Cambridge: Cambridge University Press.

Kerswill, Paul. 2007. Standard and Non-Standard English. In: David Britain (ed.), *Language in the British Isles*, 34–51. Cambridge: Cambridge University Press.

Kreidler, Charles. 1997. *Describing Spoken English. An Introduction*. London: Routledge.

Lewis, Jack. 1972. *A Concise Pronouncing Dictionary of British and American English*. London: Oxford University Press.

Lewis, Jack. 2004. Review of Upton, Clive, Kretzschmar, William, and Konopka, Rafa (2001). *The Oxford Dictionary of Pronunciation for Current English*. Oxford: Oxford University Press. *The Journal of the International Phonetic Association* 34: 220–226.

Lippi-Green, Rosina. 1997. *English with an Accent: Language, Ideology, and Discrimination in the United States*. London: Routledge.

Lloyd, Richard. 1899. *Northern English*. Leipzig: B. G. Teubner.

Milroy, James. 2001. Received Pronunciation: who "receives" it and how long will it be "received"? *Studia Anglia Posnaniensia* 36: 15–34.

Mugglestone, Lynda. 2007. *Talking Proper. The Rise of Accent as Social Symbol*. 2nd edn. Oxford: Oxford University Press.

Mugglestone, Lynda. 2008. BBC English. In the Beginning. In: Jürg Rainer Schwyter, Didier Maillat, and Christian Mair (eds.), *Broadcast English*, 197–215. Tübingen: G. Narr.

Mugglestone, Lynda. 2011. Benjamin Smart and Michael Faraday; The Principles and Practice of Talking Proper in Nineteenth-Century England. In: Michael Adams and Anne Curzan (eds.), *Contours of English and English Language Studies: In Honor of Richard W. Bailey*, 87–107. Ann Arbor: University of Michigan Press.

Murray, James A.H., Henry Bradley, William Craigie, and Charles Talbut Onions (eds.). 1884–1928. *The Oxford English Dictionary*. 1st edn. Oxford: Clarendon.

Perry, William. 1775. *The Royal Standard English Dictionary*. Edinburgh: David Willison.

Przedlacka, Joanna. 2000. Estuary English: Glottaling in the Home Counties. *Oxford University Working Papers in Linguistics, Philology, & Phonetics* 5: 19–24.

Ramsaran, Susan. 1990. RP: fact and fiction. In: Susan Ramsaran (ed.), *Studies in the Pronunciation of English: A Commemorative Volume in Honour of A. C. Gimson*, 178–190. London: Routledge.

Roach, Peter. 2000. *English Phoetics and Phonology*. 3rd edn. Cambridge: Cambridge University Press.

Roach, Peter. 2004. British English: Received Pronunciation. *Journal of the International Phonetic Association* 34: 239–245.

Rosewarne, David. 1984. Estuary English. *Times Educational Supplement*. 19 October 1984 http://www.phon.ucl.ac.uk/home/estuary/rosew.htm; last accessed 14 April 2017.

Sheridan, Thomas. 1761. *A Dissertation on the Causes of Difficulties, Which Occur, in Learning the English Tongue*. London: R. and J. Dodsley.

Sheridan, Thomas. 1762. *A Course of Lectures on Elocution*. London: W. Strahan.

Smart, Benjamin. 1836. *Walker Remodelled. A New Critial Pronouncing Dictionary*. London: T. Cadell.

Sweet, Henry. 1890. *A Primer of Spoken English*. Oxford: Clarendon Press.

Trask, Robert. 1996. *A Dictionary of Phonetics and Phonology*. London: Routledge.

Trudgill, Peter. 2001. Received Pronunciation: Sociolinguistic Aspects. *Studia Anglica Posnaniensa* 36: 3–13.

Upton, Clive. 2004. Received pronunciation. In: Edgar Schneider and Clive Upton (eds.), *A Handbook of Varieties of English*. Vol. I: *Phonology*, 217–230. Berlin/New York: Mouton de Gruyter.

Upton, Clive, William Kretzschmar, and Rafal Konopka. 2001. *The Oxford Dictionary of Pronunciation for Current English*. Oxford: Oxford University Press.

Walker, John. 1774. *A General Idea of a Pronouncing Dictionary of the English Language on a Plan Entirely New*. London: T. Becket.

Walker, John. 1791. *A Critical Pronouncing Dictionary and Expositor of the English Language*. London: G. G. J. and J. Robinson.

Wells, John. 1982. *Accents of English*. 3 vols. Cambridge: Cambridge University Press.

Wells, John. 1997. *"Whatever happened to Received Pronunciation?"* http://www.phon.ucl.ac.uk/home/wells/rphappened.htm; last accessed 14 April 2017.

Wells, John. 2000. *Longman Pronunciation Dictionary*. Harlow: Pearson.

Wyld, Henry. 1914. *A Short History of English*. London: John Murray.

Wyld, Henry. 1934. *The Best English. A Claim for the Superiority of Received Standard English S. P. E. Tract No. XXXIX*. Oxford: Clarendon Press.

Ulrike Altendorf
Chapter 9:
Estuary English

1   The early years of Estuary English —— 170
2   Regional variation of variants associated with EE in the south-east (trend 1) —— 173
3   Regional variation of variants associated with EE beyond the south-east (trend 5) —— 176
4   Social variation of variants associated with EE (trend 2) —— 178
5   Estuary English as a style (trend 3 and 4) —— 180
6   What is EE? —— 181
7   References —— 185

Abstract: The present chapter reviews the different stages in the history of research into the notoriously difficult notion of Estuary English. It begins with the classic texts by the first authors, the founder of the term and concept David Rosewarne (1984) and the author of the first book(let) on Estuary English, Paul Coggle (1993). The chapter goes on to discuss the dissemination of the term by journalists and literary authors and then proceeds to look at the work of expert linguists on Estuary English itself and related issues. It is argued that the popularity of the term with non-linguists is one of the major reasons for the skepticism with which linguists view both term and concept. Another reason for this skepticism is the rather indiscriminate use of the term as a shorthand for a number of related but divergent trends. The chapter explores the results of linguistic research into these trends and relates them to the notion of 'Estuary English', even if the researchers themselves refrain from mentioning the term.

Ulrike Altendorf: Hannover (Germany)

DOI 10.1515/9783110525045-009

1 The early years of Estuary English

1.1 David Rosewarne and Paul Coggle on Estuary English

Estuary English (henceforth referred to as EE) has by now become a term with a history. This history bears all the hallmarks of miscommunication between experts and the public. In the case of EE, the two opposing camps have mainly been expert linguists and the media. As if in accordance with this pattern, the first article ever published on EE appeared in the London edition of *The Times Educational Supplement* (see Rosewarne 1984) and not in a renowned linguistic journal. To make matters worse from an academic point of view, the concept was rather loosely defined as an accent somewhere between Cockney and Received Pronunciation (henceforth referred to as RP): "*Estuary English* is a variety of modified regional speech. It is a mixture of non-regional and local south-eastern English pronunciation and intonation. If one imagines a continuum with RP and London speech at either end, *Estuary English* speakers are to be found grouped in the middle ground" (Rosewarne 1984: 29, 1994: 5).

This definition raises a number of questions that will be discussed in the course of this chapter. The two major problems from the very beginning have been (a) to determine the defining characteristics of EE and (b) to justify coining a new name.

Rosewarne himself characterizes the difference among EE, Cockney, and RP as one of frequency or degree: "As would be expected, an *Estuary English* speaker uses fewer glottal stops for t and d than a *London* speaker, but more than an RP speaker. Vowel qualities in *Estuary English* are a compromise between unmodified regional forms and those of general RP" (Rosewarne 1984: 29).

As to the necessity of coining a new name, Rosewarne does not address this question directly. It is possible that he derives this necessity from the increasing currency of what he identifies as EE variants: "For large and influential sections of the young, the new model for general imitation may already be *Estuary English*, which may become the RP of the future" (Rosewarne 1984: 30).

The term and concept of EE was taken up several years later by Paul Coggle, a senior lecturer in German at the University of Canterbury. Coggle's (1993) booklet, titled *Do you Speak Estuary? The New Standard English – How to Spot it and Speak it*, presents the topic in an entertaining way but is far from what linguists consider to be a serious study in social dialectology. Nevertheless Coggle addresses some of the major problems, among them the problem of varietal distinction. Even less so than Rosewarne, he does not consider EE to be a clearly delineated variety but rather a continuum on a continuum. Like Rosewarne, he is still optimistic that EE speakers can be clearly identified, in his case on the basis of a characteristic combination of uncharacteristic variants:

It should now be clear that Estuary English cannot be pinned down to a rigid set of rules regarding specific features of pronunciation, grammar and special phrases. A speaker at the Cockney end of the spectrum is not so different from a Cockney speaker. And similarly, a speaker at the RP end of the spectrum will not be very different from an RP speaker. Between the two extremes is quite a range of possibilities, many of which, in isolation, would not enable us to identify a person as an Estuary speaker, but which when several are present together mark out Estuary English distinctively. (Coggle 1993: 70)

Although this approach may be more realistic, it does call into question the status of EE as a "variety" in the linguistic sense of the term (for a more detailed discussion, see Sections 2 and 6).

As to coining a new name, Coggle does not address this question either. Like Rosewarne, he stresses the increasing currency of EE ("The New Standard English") but also its limitations: "I was told in no uncertain terms by an informant that he would not allow brain surgery to be performed on himself by an Estuary English speaker" (Coggle 1993: 74).

1.2 Journalists and literary authors on Estuary English

A new stage in the history of EE began when newspaper journalists and occasionally novel writers picked up the term. In particular in the 1990s, these writers used EE as a shorthand for a number of different and divergent trends:
(1) socio-phonetic changes within the accents of south-eastern England in the direction of a supra-local regional accent: "His wasn't a Suffolk voice, rather the accent dubbed in the eighties Estuary English". (Vine 1998: 155)
(2) the social spread of London working-class variants into higher social classes, including the advanced version of RP: "'Got friends', Leo said to his milk glass. He said it in that irritating Estuary English that was becoming so fashionable, a glottal stop in place of the *t* in *got*. Thank God public school would soon breed that out of him as well". (George 1996: 244)
(3) the situation-related use of London working-class variants by speakers who are otherwise speakers of RP: "It's the way he tells 'em. Prime Minister wades into Estuary English for O'Connor chat show". (Ward 1998)
(4) the retention of south-eastern regional accent features by speakers who would otherwise have been expected to become speakers of adoptive RP: "Among those who speak it [Estuary English] are Lord Tebbit, a Conservative member of the House of Lords and a leading Euroskeptic, and Ken Livingstone, who as a Labor Member of Parliament is on the opposite end of the political spectrum". (Darnton 1993)

(5) the occurrence of variants which are – rightly or wrongly – associated with with south-eastern accents in accents in which they had not been used before: "Estuary English has taken the high road. A new form of Glaswegian dialect which borrows from the television soap *EastEnders* is flourishing in Scotland". (Corbidge 1998)

The trends described in these excerpts – with the exception of (5) – are in principle not disputed by linguists. What linguists object to is the indiscriminate use of the same term for phenomena as different as the occasional (over-)use of the glottal stop by Tony Blair in a London chat show and the regular use of the labio-dental instead of the dental fricative by young speakers in Glasgow. In addition, it is the popular origin of these theories that has been detrimental to their image and the image of EE. After all, expert linguists do not like laypersons, including journalists, to do their work for them. Apart from hurting their professional pride, journalists have a reputation of not applying as much precision to their work as academics. The following mutation of EE-founder David Rosewarne into the teacher Rose Warne can be cited as evidence supporting this concern: "Ten years later, in 1984, an English teacher called Rose Warne would find a name for this hybrid southern speak: *Estuary English*, after the Thames Estuary" (Smith 2000).

1.3 John Wells on Estuary English

Among the first to take a linguistically informed look at EE was John Wells. His handout for a talk given in 1992 and posted on his webpage on EE in 1998 was the first attempt to "pin down" EE in terms of linguistic variants and varietal distinction. Unlike Rosewarne (1984) and Coggle (1993), Wells (1998) defines EE as an accent and thus excludes allegedly EE-related variation at the level of lexis and morpho-syntax. He also cuts down on the list of variants proposed by Rosewarne and Coggle and attempts to define the boundaries between EE on the one hand and RP and Cockney on the other. Table 9.1 provides an overview of Wells's working definition of EE as an accent.

The variables identified by Wells were to become the point of departure of many linguistic studies of EE when the academic discussion finally set in the late 1990s. It was probably inspired and certainly accompanied by the EE webpage run by John Wells at http://www.phon.ucl.ac.uk/home/estuary (last accessed 14 April 2017).

Table 9.1: Phonetic and phonological features of EE according to Wells (1998) – the terms used in this table were adapted to those used throughout the chapter

Variable (Wells 1998)	Example	RP	EE	Cockney
H Dropping	[and] for *hand*	–	–	+
TH Fronting	[fɪŋk] for *think*	–	–	+
MOUTH vowel monophthong	[maːf] for *mouth*	–	–	+
T Glottalling in intervocalic position	[ˈbʌʔə] for *butter*	–	–	+
HAPPY Tensing	[ˈhæpi] for *happy*	–	+	+
T Glottalling finally etc.	[ˈðæʔˈɪz] for *that is*	–	+	+
L Vocalization	[miok] for *milk*	–	+	+
Yod Coalescence (in stressed syllables)	[ˈtʃuːzdeɪ] for *Tuesday*	–	+	+
(?) diphthong shift in FACE, PRICE, GOAT	[fʌɪs], [prɑɪs], [gʌʊʔ]	–	+	+
(?) striking allophony (phoneme split?) in *sold*	[gʌʊt] vs. [gɒʊɫ] for *goat* vs. *goal*	–	+	+

2 Regional variation of variants associated with EE in the south-east (trend 1)

The majority of empirical studies of EE set out to investigate the claim that EE was a supra-local south-eastern regional variety (see Section 1.2, trend 1). From a theoretical and methodological point of view, most of these studies followed the Labovian sociolinguistic approach. Many of them were MA theses, such as Torgersen (1997), Parsons (1998), Haenni (1999) and Hilgers (2000), a great number of which are published on Wells's UCL webpage on EE. Around the same time Ann Williams and Paul Kerswill conducted two research projects on dialect leveling in the south-east of England, the *Milton Keynes Project* on "A new dialect in a new city: children's and adult's speech in Milton Keynes" (e.g. Kerswill 1996) and the *Dialect Levelling* project on "The role of adolescents in dialect levelling" (Williams and Kerswill 1999). They were followed by the publication of two PhD theses on EE by Joanna Przedlacka (2002) and the author of this chapter (Altendorf 2003). It is these four latter studies that will be discussed in more detail in the following. Tables 9.2 and 9.3 provide an overview of the extra-linguistic and linguistic variables investigated in these studies.

Williams and Kerswill (1999: 149) as well as Przedlacka (2002: 94, 97) conclude from their results that convergence has indeed been taking place in the south-east of England. However, they consider local variation to be still too marked to justify subsuming local accents under the same regional variety. Kerswill (1996: 299) finds a different situation in Milton Keynes but draws the same conclusion. He

Table 9.2: Extralinguistic variables

Town/County	Age of speakers/ number of speakers	Social class	Gender	Style
Milton Keynes, Buckinghamshire (Kerswill 1996)	4, 8, 12 yo/ 48 speakers	working class	male and female	informal to formal
Milton Keynes and Reading (Williams and Kerswill 1999)	14 to15 yo/ 64 speakers	working and middle class	male and female	informal to formal
Buckinghamshire, Kent, Essex and Surrey (Przedlacka 2002)	14 to 16 yo/ 16 speakers	working and middle class	male and female	word elicitation modeled on the SED questionnaire
London, Colchester, Canterbury (Altendorf 2003)	16 to 17 yo/ 6 speakers	middle class	female	interview style, reading styles, word list style

points out that in Milton Keynes "every one of the Milton Keynes children's pronunciation features, both old and more recent, is also found in London and elsewhere in the south-east" (Kerswill 1996: 295) and concedes that it is "tempting to suppose that what we have observed in Milton Keynes is a form of Estuary English" (Kerswill 1996: 299). However, he considers this to be "misleading" (Kerswill 1996: 299) since the sociolinguistic situation in a new town, such as Milton Keynes, involves "much more intensive dialect contact than in other parts of the south-east" (Kerswill 1996: 299). The *Dialect Levelling Project* and Prezdlacka's study provide evidence for this hypothesis.

My own research does not point in the same direction. The female middle-class speakers from London, Colchester, and Canterbury show a high degree of similarity with regard to the majority of my linguistic variables (see Altendorf 2003: Chapter V.). The discrepancy between the results of my study and those of the three other studies may be due to the small number of speakers in my sample. The results reported by Przedlacka (2002: 60–65) show a high degree of variation in each cell that I may have missed because of the small size of the sample. On the other hand, the number of tokens for each speaker in my study is high since the interviews took up to one hour and have the advantage of covering three different styles. The results for stylistic variation, in turn, show a similarly high degree of variability within each cell. In addition, it is often not possible to identify a pattern of variation which would be in line with any of the patterns known from other sociolinguistic studies. Such deviations from identifiable patterns are also reported by Przedlacka for correlation by gender and class. Only very few variables were significant by class (2 out 14) followed by gender (7 out of 14). The clearest correlation in her study is correlation by county (8 out 13). However, with 8 out of 13 variables, we are still left with 5 variables for which such a correlation cannot be shown. It seems that the patterns of variation found in the south-east with regard to variables associated with EE are "diffuse" rather than "focussed" (Le Page and Tabouret-Keller 1985). For a discussion of the implications of these findings see Sections 6.2–6.3.

Table 9.3: Linguistic variables

	Kerswill 1996	Williams and Kerswill 1999	Przedlacka 2002	Altendorf 2003	Britain 2005
H Dropping	+	+	−	+	−
TH Fronting	+	+	+	+	+
L Vocalization	+	+	+	+	+
T Glottalling	+	+	+	+	−
P, K Glottalling	+	+	−	−	−
ST Palatalization	−	−	−	+	−
STR Palatalization	−	−	+	+	−
Yod Dropping	−	−	+	+	−
R: labio-dental [ʋ]	+	+	−	−	+
MOUTH	+	+	+	+	−
FLEECE	+	+	+	+	−
GOOSE (Fronting): [ü: ~ ʉ: ~ i: ~ ɪ:]	+	+	+	+	+
SCHOOL	−	−	−	+	−
GOAT	+	+	+	+	+
GOAL	+	+	−	−	−
FOOT (Fronting) [ɵ]	+	+	−	+	+
TRAP	+	+	+	−	−
STRUT	+	+	+	−	+
THOUGHT	+	+	+	−	−
FACE	+	+	+	−	−
PRICE	+	+	+	−	+
KIT, DRESS, CLOTH, BATH, NURSE, PALM, CHOICE, NEAR, SQUARE, START, NORTH, FORCE, CURE, HAPPY, LETTER, COMMA, HORSES	+	+	−	−	−

3 Regional variation of variants associated with EE beyond the south-east (trend 5)

There are a number of studies on socio-phonetic changes in accents outside the south-east (see Section 1.2, trend 5). From a theoretical and methodological point of view, these studies follow the Labovian sociolinguistic approach. Few of them explicitly refer to EE but many include or focus on variables that are classified as characteristics of EE, such as TH Fronting, T Glottalling, L Vocalization and GOOSE Fronting (for a more detailed discussion of these variables, see Altendorf 2003: Chapter IV). In the late 1990s, a number of these studies were assembled in *Urban Voices – Accent Studies in the British Isles*, edited by Paul Foulkes and Gerard Docherty (1999). One of them is the *Dialect Levelling Project* by Ann Williams and Paul Kerswill, already cited above, which also includes data on Hull as an example of a town outside the south-east. A study of regional accents outside the south-east that explicitly refers to EE is David Britain's (2005) study of dialects in the Fen country. These two studies and two studies on the spread of T Glottalling and L Vocalization in Scotland will be discussed in more detail in the following. An overview of the extra-linguistic variables in these studies can be found in Table 9.4. The linguistic variables investigated by Williams and Kerswill (e.g. 1999) in Hull and Britain (2005) in the Fens can also be found in Table 9.3 above.

Williams and Kerswill (1999: 149) as well as Britain (2005: 1016) conclude from their results that convergence has indeed been taking place between accents in and beyond the south-east of England, in particular with regard to those variables associated with EE. However, they consider the local characteristics of the accents spoken outside the south-east as too distinct to even contemplate classifying these non-south-eastern accents as instances of EE. Williams and Kerswill (1999: 157–158) report that young speakers in Hull differ from their counterparts in Milton Keynes and Reading by retaining H Dropping and an allophonic split of the PRICE vowel (Williams and Kerswill 1999: 157–158). Britain (2005: 1016) reports that young speakers in the three different Fen towns differ from each other and from their southern counterparts by retaining, for example, the MOAN-MOWN Split in Terrington, "Canadian Raising" in Wisbech and the quasi-absence of the FOOT-STRUT Split in Spalding (Britain 2005: 1016). However, some variants associated with EE have either been recently introduced to or are on the increase in both Hull and the Fens, in particular TH Fronting, intervocalic T Glottalling and labio-dental [ʋ] (for Hull, see Williams and Kerswill 1999: 160, 147; for the Fens, see Britain 2005: 1016). L Vocalization is on the increase in the Fens (Britain 2005: 1009), but not in Hull (Williams and Kerswill 1999: 148).

Table 9.4: Extralinguistic variables

Town/County	Age of speakers/ Number of speakers	Social class	Gender	Style
Milton Keynes, Reading and Hull (Williams and Kerswill 1999)	14 to 15 yo/ 96 speakers (32 speakers in Hull)	working and middle class	male and female	informal to formal
The Fens: Spalding, Wisbech/March and Terrington (Britain 2005)	14 to 17 yo/ 6 speakers	0	0	elicitation
Huntley (Marshall 2003)	8 to 60+ yo, subdivided in four age groups	0	male and female	interview style, narrative and elicitation
Glasgow (Stuart-Smith 2006)				
• corpus 1984/1985	10 to 66+ yo, subdivided in five age groups/ 62 speakers	working class	male and female	0
• corpus 1997	13 to 14 yo 40 to 60 yo/ 32 speakers	working and middle class	male and female	spontaneous conversation, word-list style

The spread of these variants beyond the south-east has also been reported for many other towns and areas. Marshall (2003: 97), for example, shows that T Glottalling has increased dramatically among 14- to 17-year-old speakers in the north-eastern Scottish town of Huntley. For Glasgow, Stuart-Smith (1999: 209) reports a "significant increase in glottalling" and – more recently – the "incorporation of innovative L-vocalization" of the London type which coexists and continues to increase alongside the old "Scots L-vocalization" (Stuart-Smith 2006: 71).

These and other studies have empirically corroborated the claim made in the media (see Section 1.2 trend 5) that some variants associated with EE are indeed on the increase outside the south-east of England. However, this is not true for all alleged EE variants but only for a recurring set, mostly TH Fronting, T Glottalling and labio-dental [ʊ] and to a lesser extent L Vocalization and GOOSE Fronting. In addition, these variants do no necessarily co-occur in the accents affected by this development. As to whether they have actually "taken the high road" from London and were "borrowed from the television soap EastEnders", as Corbidge (1998) and other journalists claim, is still unclear and subject to considerable debate (see e.g. Williams and Kerswill 1999: 161–162; Stuart-Smith and Timmins 2002–05).

4 Social variation of variants associated with EE (trend 2)

Only very few empirical studies dealing with socio-phonetic changes extend them to changes affecting RP. Fewer still explicitly refer to EE (see Section 1.2, trend 2). As a result there is little empirical evidence for or against the claim made by Rosewarne (1984: 29) that EE "may now and for the foreseeable future be the strongest native influence on RP", indeed "may become the RP of the future" (Rosewarne 1984: 30). In an article titled *The Cockneyfication of RP?*, Wells (1994) discusses a similar hypothesis and shows to which extent variants associated with non-standard London English are now "resisted by" and "accepted into" RP. In their work on EE, Przedlacka (2002) and Altendorf (2003) provide a small-scale empirical investigation of the same question. In addition, they take a closer look at the social accent continuum in London and the south-east in order to investigate the state of social differentiation in this area. A third empirical study by Fabricius (2000) differs from these two studies in that the author confines herself to T Glottalling and RP. She does, however, provide an in-depth study of the status of the glottal variant in the speech of RP speakers from London, the Home Counties, and the rest of England. A synopsis of the extralinguistic variables investigated in the three empirical studies can be found in Table 9.5. The linguistic variables studied by Przedlacka (2002) and Altendorf (2003) were listed in Table 9.3.

Table 9.5: Extralinguistic variables

Town/County	Age of speakers/ number of speakers	Social class	Gender	Style
London, Home Counties, rest of England (Fabricius 2000)	24 speakers	upper middle class	male and female	interview style, reading style, discrimination test similar to a word list style
Eton College (Przedlacka 2002, 2001)	13 yo/ 2 speakers	students of Eton College	male	word elicitation modeled on the SED questionnaire
London (Altendorf 2003)	16 to 17 yo/ 6 speakers	working class, middle class, upper middle class	female	interview style, reading style, word list style

As in the case of accent convergence in and beyond the south-east, the results of the three empirical studies show that convergence has been taking place across the social accent continuum ranging from Cockney to RP. However, the authors agree that the accents are (still) too distinct to be subsumed under the same regional variety, called "Estuary English". Although results for the individual variables are complex and diverse, certain trends can be identified:

(1) There are variants which are confined to the lowest of the three classes investigated in these studies. In accordance with Wells (1998), H Dropping and the MOUTH vowel monophthong, for example, are confined to working class London English (Przedlacka 2002: 63; Altendorf 2003: 79, 102).

(2) Some variants are on the verge of "seeping" into middle-class and even upper-middle-class English in London and the south-east. Members of this group are in particular TH Fronting and intervocalic T Glottalling. Wells (1998) classifies them as Cockney variants which are not part of EE let alone of RP. With regard to TH Fronting, the results of my study are in line with this prediction. TH Fronting is confined to my London working-class speakers (Altendorf 2003: 81). However, in an earlier pilot study a few instances of TH Fronting were found in the speech of a different set of middle-class and upper-middle-class speakers (Altendorf 1999: 10). A similar result is reported by Przedlacka (2002: 59), who has found instances of TH Fronting in the speech of one of her two Eton informants. Intervocalic T Glottalling has also spread further than Wells (1998) suggests. In my data, it occurs in the speech of middle-class speakers in London as well as in Colchester and Canterbury (Altendorf 2003: 86). However, intervocalic T Glottalling still displays the distributional pattern of a vernacular variant in that it is absent from the more formal reading style (Altendorf 2003: 84, 87). As to RP, intervocalic T Glottalling is absent from the upper-middle-class data of all three studies.

(3) A number of variants follow Rosewarne's prediction in that they occur in all classes but differ with regard to relative frequency and degree. This is in particular true for L Vocalization and non-intervocalic T Glottalling. In my own data, the glottal and the vocalized variant occur in all three classes with decreasing frequency from the working to the upper middle class (Altendorf 2003: 83, 91). Przedlacka (2002: 59, 60) has also found non-intervocalic T Glottalling and L Vocalization in the speech of her Eton informants. Although her overall scores are lower, her results confirm that non-intervocalic T Glottalling and L Vocalization have entered "young RP".

5 Estuary English as a style (trend 3 and 4)

The situation-related use of London working-class variants by speakers who are otherwise speakers of RP (see Section 1.2, trend 3) is frequently mentioned in the media but not yet the object of serious linguistic research. The same is true for trend 4, the retention of south-eastern regional accent features by speakers who would otherwise have been expected to become speakers of adoptive RP. One of the reasons for this "neglect" may be that these two trends are often hard to separate from each other and from trend 2, the social spread of London working-class variants into higher social classes, including the advanced version of RP. In order to be able to do so, one would have to know the speaker's vernacular. Outside this particular situation, the speaker may be a speaker of (mainstream) RP (trend 3) or of advanced RP (trend 2) or actually a speaker with a London or south-eastern accent (trend 4). In the latter two cases, situational EE may be the public version of the speakers' vernacular, modified to fit the occasion but not totally "out of character". In the following example it is, for instance, hard to decide whether the speakers in question are putting on a show (trend 3), are simply indulging in their advanced version of RP (trend 2) or both (trend 2 and 3):

> They [the stage, television] are now the careers of choice for legions of well-brought-up, well-educated, well-born young things. Every branch of the media now boasts more silver spoons than the Harrods cutlery department, and a private education is fast replacing an Equity card as the guarantor of a show-business career. [...] They may speak in the everyman argot now called Estuary English and dress in ubiquitous and genderless urban baggies, but these are people who, 30 years ago, would have been expected to trade in their expensive education for the professional security of law or medicine. (O'Brien 1999: 11)

Instead of trying to separate these three trends, researchers follow a different policy. They study the presence of variants associated with EE in the speech of those who appear in the media. Hilgers (2000), for example, investigates, as part of his MA thesis, the occurrence of EE variants in the news presented on different British radio stations, BBC Radio 1, Radio 4 and Radio 5 as well as Virgin Radio. He concludes that EE variants occur frequently, in particular on stations addressed to young people, such as BBC Radio 1 and Virgin Radio. They also occur in the news of the most prestige-oriented station BBC Radio 4 but are less frequent here (Hilgers 2000: 93).

The project *Is television a contributory factor in accent change in adolescents?* by Stuart-Smith and Timmins (2002–05) is another example of a study which does not explicitly refer to EE but investigates aspects of language use which are at least indirectly relevant to EE. In the context of their project, Stuart-Smith and Timmins (2005) also look at "Media Cockney", i.e. the use of variants associated with London and the south-east (EE), such as T Glottalling, L Vocalization and GOOSE/FOOT Fronting, in the speech of actors in soap operas, such as *EastEnders* and *The Bill*. Results are complex. They show, for example, that the language used in contemporary drama is "more like Southeast England" than Cockney "even in the soap supposedly set in the East End of London" (Stuart-Smith and Timmins 2005: 49). In addition, the "most popular characters" in *EastEnders* "also have the frontest GOOSE/FOOT vowels" (Stuart-Smith and Timmins 2005: 42). Providing that one accepts the existence of EE, this could be interpreted as an argument to support its prevalence in the popular media. Note, however, that Stuart-Smith and Timmins do not draw this conclusion.

6 What is EE?

6.1 What EE cannot be

Despite the many studies on EE or EE-related aspects of language use and change in London, the south-east of England and beyond, linguists have not yet been able to agree on a definition of the concept and on assigning a linguistic category to the phenomenon. They have, however, been prolific in describing what EE cannot be:

(1) Most linguists agree that EE is not a south-eastern variety. Their major argument is that a variety needs to display a sufficient degree of internal homogeneity and external distinction. This is seen as not to be true for EE. Internally, the local accents of the south-east have been shown to be too heterogeneous to form a common variety (see Section 2). Externally, many of the core variants ascribed to EE, such as TH Fronting, T Glottalling and L Vocalization, are too wide-spread to mark the external boundaries of a putative south-eastern variety (see Section 3).

(2) Most linguists also agree that EE is not a new phenomenon and that coining a new name is therefore not justified (e.g. Wells 1997: 47; Kerswill 1996: 299; Trudgill 1999: 80). Trudgill (1999: 80) is even of the opinion that "Estuary English" is the wrong name. The following short comment on EE summarizes the major misgivings expressed by the majority of linguists: "This ['Estuary English'] is an inappropriate term which, however, has become widely accepted. It is inappropriate because it suggests that we are talking about a new variety, which we are not; and because it suggests that this is a variety of English confined to the banks of the Thames Estuary, which it is not" (Trudgill 1999: 80).

On the plus side, most linguists accept the existence of two trends that are, rightly or wrong, associated with EE:
(1) They accept that there is a group of variants, such as TH Fronting, T Glottalling, L Vocalization and GOOSE Fronting, that are growing more frequent in Great Britain and even beyond (see Section 3).
(2) Some linguists also accept that these formerly non-standard variants are socially more acceptable than they used to be (see Sections 4 and 5).

These two trends, on which most linguists have come to agree, should be taken as a point of departure for a definition of EE. Przedlacka (2002) takes the first step in this direction when she remarks that EE is not a variety but a more general trend:

> The extent of geographical variation alone allows us to conclude that we are dealing with a number of distinct accents, not a single and definable variety [...] At the same time, what is known as "Estuary English" appears to be part of more general changes. Thus, the tendencies observed in the present study (the fronting of GOOSE and GOAT vowels, *l*-vocalisation as well as *th*-fronting) are not confined to the Home Counties, their appearance having been reported in other areas of Britain. (Przedlacka 2002: 97)

In my opinion this remark contains the heart of the matter. One could rephrase it by saying that EE is less and more than a variety. Thus it is the (traditional) concept of "variety" which is not suitable to categorize EE.

6.2 Traditional sociolinguistic conceptualization as a problem for EE

So far linguists have considered EE to be a problem because it does not fit the established sociolinguistic and dialectological categories. However, one could also take the opposite view and consider the established sociolinguistic and dialectological categories to be the problem. After all, if a phenomenon that exists cannot be described in academic terms, the problem needs to be solved at the level of the academic discipline. The phenomenon cannot be changed to fit the existing conceptualization. It cannot be abolished either. At best its existence can be ignored or deplored, which some linguists have been trying to do since 1984. Hence the rare occurrence of the term 'EE' in studies on EE-related topics (see Sections 2, 3, 4 and 5). However, the term keeps coming back, which speaks for the existence of the phenomenon. Wells, for example, grudgingly concedes:

> Many of our native-speaker undergraduates use a variety of English that I suppose we have to call Estuary English, following Rosewarne 1984, 1994, Coggle 1993, and many recent reports on press and television [...] This means that their accent is located somewhere in the continuum between RP and broad Cockney [...] As with the equally unsatisfactory term *Received Pronunciation*, we are forced to go along. (Wells 1995: 261)

Instead of feeling "forced to go along" with this unsatisfactory term, I propose to reconsider the sociolinguistic concepts applied to EE. It is not EE but the concept of "variety" and the theory of variation behind it that constitute the problem.

The concept of "variety" is a system-based ideal. In requiring varieties to be sufficiently internally homogeneous and externally distinct, theorists of language variation ideally aim at categorical variation or at least at a categorical co-occurrence of less categorical variants. Although they concede that in linguistic reality such categorical variation is hard to encounter (e.g. Berruto 1987: 265; Wunderli 1992: 182), they still require as much internal homogeneity as possible as "Verdichtungspunkte in einem Kontinuum" ['centers of gravity on the continuum'] in Berruto's (1987: 265) terminology, and as "centers ou points de gravitation" ['centers or points of gravity'] in Wunderli's (1992: 182) terms.

If the theorists are sociolinguists, they are prepared to accept more quantitative variation as long as it yields quantitatively significant patterns. Hence the significance tests in many sociolinguistic studies, including Przedlacka's study of EE (see Section 2). Behind this search lies a dichotomous theory of language and a system-based ideal. Even though Labov (e.g. 1972: 186) claims to have overcome the Saussurian notion of *langue*, his approach and the approach of those who work within his paradigm is still rather system-oriented. It is true that his methodological approach is "the direct study of language in its social context" (Labov 1972: 202). However, at the theoretical level, he aims at abstracting away from individual language use to the language system. It is at this level that sociolinguists are to "be concerned with the forms of linguistic rules, their combination into systems, the coexistence of several systems, and the evolution of these rules and systems with time" (Labov 1972: 184). In order to deserve a place at this abstract level of the system, patterns of variation need to be relatively robust. This is why current studies of the social dialectology of English accents, whether they mention the term EE or not, keep identifying the same variables, i.e. TH Fronting, T Glottalling, L Vocalization, labio-dental [ʋ] and more recently GOOSE and FOOT Fronting. The new variants have become frequent enough to "survive" abstraction to the system. It is also with regard to these "youth norms" (Williams and Kerswill 1999: 159) that some linguists now seem to find it easier to accept the existence of EE (see Przedlacka 2002: 97).

However, EE is more than a few "youth norms" that have been "taking the high road" (Corbidge 1998). It is a complex result of complex processes which consist in the reallocation of stigma and prestige as shown by Fabricius (2000) for T Glottalling in RP. These sophisticated processes are small-scale and often performance-related and therefore do not fit into the classic conceptualization of the Labovian approach. This is also one of the reasons why EE-related patterns of variation sometimes seem "diffuse" (see Section 2). And they are not alone. The quantitative-correlational approach in the Labovian tradition has problems accommodating small-scale and performance-related patterns of variation. Mair (2003) provides an in-depth discussion of this problem in general and with regard to the international variation of English in particular.

6.3 In search of a new sociolinguistic conceptualization

It would go beyond the scope of this chapter to develop a new or thoroughly revised theory of variation although such a theory would be necessary to do justice to different types of variation including EE (for a revised notion of "variety", see Altendorf 2013 and 2016). Mair (2003: xiii) suggests a "discourse-based and dynamic model". As a first step in this direction, he draws attention to the model of variation proposed by Le Page and Tabouret-Keller (1985) and their notion of "acts of identity". Although I agree with Mair (2003: xii) that the authors "have fallen short of providing a fully elaborated theoretical model", their notion of "acts of identity" is already a helpful tool to describe EE-related patterns of variation that often seem "chaotic" from a traditional sociolinguistic point of view. It would be a step forward to accept that we cannot account for EE within our established quantitative-correlational sociolinguistic framework. As an interim solution I propose to consider EE as "a pool of variants" from which speakers select different variables in different ways to express different "acts of identity". These acts of identity are complex processes of affiliation and distancing which have to be identified for each variable (see Altendorf 2003: Chapter VII) and for each trend ascribed to EE (see Section 1). It is also possible that there is a motivational common core for all variables and trends, as for example finding a balance between tradition and modernity as suggested by Altendorf (2004) and between stigma and prestige as suggested by Fabricius (2000) for T Glottalling in RP. The pool-of-variants approach would also be able to account for the high degree of internal variability and the lack of external distinction, which is otherwise cited as counter-evidence for classifying EE as a variety (for a perceptual approach to EE, see Altendorf 2016).

7 References

Altendorf, Ulrike. 1999. Estuary English: Is English going Cockney? *Moderna Språk* XCII(1): 1–11. www.phon.ucl.ac.uk/home/estuary/altendf.pdf (last accessed 20 March 2011).

Altendorf, Ulrike. 2003. *'Estuary English': levelling at the interface of RP and south-eastern British English.* Tübingen: Narr.

Altendorf, Ulrike. 2004. Language change and changing ideologies in and around RP. In: Martin Pütz, JoAnne Neff van-Aertselaer, and Teun A. van Dijk (eds.), *Communicating Ideologies: Language, Discourse and Social Practice*, 203–225. Frankfurt am Main/New York/Paris/Bern: Peter Lang.

Altendorf, Ulrike. 2013. „Where does the notion of 'variety' start and end? – A proposal for a prototype approach to language variation." In: Monika Reif, Justyna A. Robinson and Martin Pütz (eds.), *Variation in Language and Language Use: Linguistic, Socio-Cultural and Cognitive Perspectives*, 299–326. Frankfurt am Main: Peter Lang.

Altendorf, Ulrike. 2016. Caught between Aristotle and Miss Marple ... – A proposal for a perceptual prototype approach to "Estuary English". *Complutense Journal of English Studies* 24: 129–152.

Berruto, Gaetano. 1987. Varietät. In: Ulrich Ammon, Norbert Dittmar, and Klaus J. Mattheier (eds.), *Sociolinguistics/Soziolinguistik*, 263–267. Berlin/New York: De Gruyter.

Britain, David. 2005. 'Estuary English' and local dialect differentiation: the survival of Fenland Englishes. *Linguistics* 43(5): 995–1022.

O'Brien, James. 1999. The popping up of class acts: James O'Brien spots a hitherto unnoticed trend in mass entertainment. *The Spectator*, 29th May 1999: 11–12.

Coggle, Paul. 1993. *Do you Speak Estuary? The New Standard English – How to Spot it and Speak it.* London: Bloomsbury.

Corbidge, Rob. 1998. It's the way you tell 'em, me old Jock sparrer. *Sunday Times*, 29th March 1998: 3.

Darnton, John. 1993. The English are talking funny again. *The New York Times*, 21st December 1993.

Fabricius, Anne. 2000. *T-glottalling between stigma and prestige: a sociolinguistic study of modern RP.* PhD thesis, Copenhagen Business School.

Foulkes, Paul and Gerard Docherty (eds.). 1999. *Urban Voices–Accent Studies in the British Isles.* London: Arnold.

George, Elizabeth. 1996. *In the Presence of the Enemy.* London/New York/Toronto: Bentam.

Haenni, Ruedi. 1999. *The case of Estuary English: supposed evidence and perceptual approach.* University of Basel Dissertation; last accessed 14 April 2017.

Hilgers, Lothar. 2000. *Estuary English – Entwicklung, linguistische Beschreibung und sozialer Hintergrund.* University of Trier Master's Dissertation.

Kerswill, Paul. 1996. Milton Keynes and dialect levelling in south-eastern British English. In: David Graddol, Dick Leith, and Joan Swann (eds.), *English: history, diversity and change*, 292–300. London/New York: Routledge.

Labov, William. 1972. *Sociolinguistic Patterns.* Oxford: Blackwell.

Le Page, Robert B. and Andrée Tabouret-Keller. 1985. *Acts of identity. Creole-based Approaches to Language and Ethnicity.* Cambridge: CUP.

Mair, Christian. 2003. Linguistics, literature and the Postcolonial Englishes: an Introduction. In: Christian Mair (ed.), *The Politics of English as a World Language. New Horizons in Postcolonial Cultural Studies*, ix–xxi. (ASNEL Papers 7). Amsterdam/New York: Rodopi.

Marshall, Jonathan. 2003. The changing sociolinguistic status of the glottal stop in northeast Scottish English. *English World-Wide* 24(1): 89–108.
Parsons, Gudrun. 1998. *From "RP" to "Estuary English": the concept of "received" and the debate about British pronunciation standards*. University of Hamburg.
Przedlacka, Joanna. 2001. Estuary English and RP: some recent findings. *Studia Anglia Posnaniensia* 36: 35–50.
Przedlacka, Joanna. 2002. *Estuary English? A socio-phonetic study of teenage speech in the Home Counties*. Frankfurt/Berlin/Bern: Peter Lang.
Rosewarne, David. 1984. Estuary English: David Rosewarne describes a newly observed variety of English pronunciation. *Times Educational Supplement*, 19th October 1984.
Rosewarne, David. 1994. Estuary English: tomorrow's RP? *English Today* 37 10(1): 3–8.
Smith, Andrew. 2000. Where did you find that voice? *The Observer*, 12th March 2000.
Stuart-Smith, Jane. 1999. Glasgow: Accent and voice quality. In: Paul Foulkes and Gerard Doherty (eds.), *Urban Voices: Accent Studies in the British Isles*, 201–222. London: Arnold.
Stuart-Smith, Jane and Claire Timmins. 2002–2005. Is accent a contributory factor in accent change in adolescents?
Stuart-Smith, Jane and Claire Timmins. 2005. *Analysing the language of television: the case of media-Cockney*. Paper presented as part of Seminar für Medienlinguistik, University of Hanover, 15th November 2004.
Stuart-Smith, Jane, Claire Timmins, and Fiona Tweedie. 2006. Conservation and innovation in a traditional dialect: L Vocalization in Glaswegian. *English World-Wide* 27(1): 71–87.
Torgersen, Eivind 1997. *Some phonological innovations in south-eastern British English*. Unpublished MA Dissertation, Department of English, University of Bergen.
Trudgill, Peter. 1999 [1990]. *The Dialects of England*. Oxford: Blackwell.
Vine, Barbara. 1998. *The Chimney Sweeper's Boy*. London: Penguin.
Ward, Lucy. 1998. It's the way he tells 'em. Prime Minister wades into Estuary for O'Connor chat show. *The Guardian*, 15th June 1998.
Wells, John. 1994. The cockneyfication of RP? In: Gunnel Melchers and Nils-Lennart Johannesson (eds.), *Nonstandard Varieties of Language*, 198–205. Stockholm: Amquist & Wiksell.
Wells, John. 1995. Transcribing Estuary English: a discussion document. *Speech Hearing & Language* 8: 261–267.
Wells, John. 1997. What is Estuary English. *English Teaching Professional*: 46–47.
Wells, John. 1998. Estuary English?!? http://www.phon.ucl.ac.uk/home/estuary/ee-screech.pdf; last accessed 14 April 2017.
Williams, Ann and Paul Kerswill. 1999. Dialect levelling: change and continuity in Milton Keynes, Reading and Hull. In: Paul Foulkes and Gerard Docherty (eds.), *Urban Voices: Accent Studies in the British Isles*, 141–162. London: Arnold.
Wunderli, Peter. 1992. Le problème des entités diastratiques. *Communication et Cognition* 25(2–3): 171–190.

Sue Fox
Chapter 10: Cockney

1 Introduction —— 187
2 The vowel system —— 191
3 Consonants —— 198
4 Beyond phonology —— 201
5 Cockney rhyming slang —— 205
6 Summary —— 207
7 References —— 208

Abstract: There is no homogeneous speech form to which Cockney refers. There have always been slight regional differences as well as specific local variants used by some speakers and of course there have also always been social and stylistic differences among individuals. Nevertheless, Cockney is a term which has a long history and, even if its application has been rather vague, has traditionally been associated with the speech of the lower social groups in London, particularly in the "East End". However, like any variety, it has been subject to change over time and recent sociolinguistic research shows that socio-economic and demographic changes to the area may render the term Cockney irrelevant to the majority of people now living in the traditional homeland of the variety. This chapter will give an overview of the traditional aspects of the London dialect while at the same time taking into account some of the recent changes described as Multicultural London English.

1 Introduction

What is Cockney? Who speaks Cockney? Where is Cockney spoken? These seemingly simple questions have become increasingly difficult to answer within "the world in a city" (Greater London Authority 2005) and "super-diversity" (Vertovec 2007) that is London's population in the 21st century. The term Cockney has traditionally been applied to the broadest form of the working class dialect of the innermost suburbs of East London (the "East End"), the area contained within the

Sue Fox: Bern (Switzerland)

modern day borough of Tower Hamlets. Speakers of this dialect have also been referred to as "Cockneys". Today, however, references to the East End tend to cover the whole area east and north-east of the city of London, spreading into much of urbanized south Essex (light shaded areas of the map in Figure 10.1 below). The reason for this change in perception of what constitutes the East End is connected to large scale population movements since the 1950s. As a consequence, this has also had implications for a change in perception of what it means to be a Cockney.

As with any variety which has a label attached to it, there is no homogeneous speech form to which Cockney refers. There have always been slight regional differences as well as specific local variants used by some speakers. There have of course also been social and stylistic differences among speakers. Also, as with any other variety, Cockney has been subject to change over time. Nevertheless, Cockney is a term which has a long history and, even if its application has been rather vague, it has come to be associated with the speech of the lower social groups in London. We can find evidence of this as far back as John Walker's *A Critical Pronouncing Dictionary and Expositor of the English Language*, 1791, in which he describes Cockney as "native of London" and to which description he adds, in 1806, "any effeminate, low citizen". In that same publication he refers to "that feeble, cockney pronunciation which is so disagreeable to a correct ear" (Walker 1806: lxxxxv). It has, since that time, become synonymous with the furthest point away from the standard on the London accent continuum and has arguably been associated with the dense, working class Anglo kinship networks for which the East End was renowned before the movement of those families from urban to suburban social housing in the post-war redevelopment of east London (Young and Willmott 1957).

Since the 1950s there has been a vast amount of out-migration of the white working class families which predominated in the East End in the early part of the 20th century. This was due mainly to the policy of "decentralizing" the population during the post-war construction of London (Abercrombie and Forshaw 1943) and as part of this plan, many families were moved to areas further east, outlined on the map (Figure 10.1), as well as to other surrounding areas of London. Coupled with this, the London docks (mainly situated in east London) closed during the period between 1967 and 1981, causing thousands of job losses and a decline of the dockland area. Many more families, whose livelihood depended on the docks, were forced to move east to the only remaining open docks on the River Thames, which were (and still are) based at Tilbury in the county of Essex. Census figures show that the population of Tower Hamlets declined from 600,000 in 1901 to just 140,000 in 1981 (Forman 1989: 7).

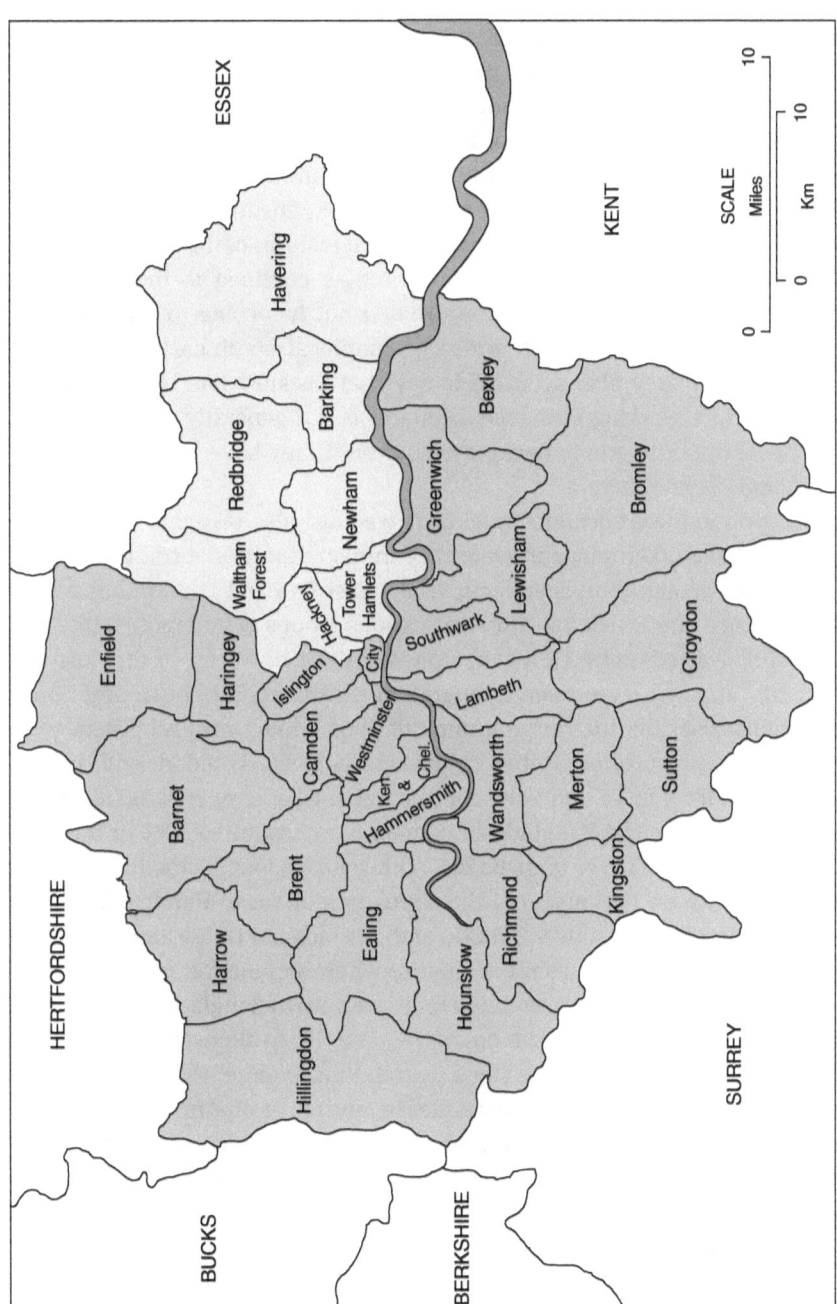

Figure 10.1: Map of London Boroughs (adapted from www.cityoflondon.gov.uk/Corporation/maps/london_map.htm, last accessed 11 January 2012)

Faced with these historical facts, it is not surprising that the areas shaded on the map (Figure 10.1), some of which were once part of rural Essex but are now urbanized and filled with "Eastenders" and their descendants, are presently known and understood to be part of East London. The sheer number of people who moved from the traditional East End into the surrounding areas of London, and in particular moved east towards and into Essex, ensured that the influence of Cockney was exerted and it is in these areas that features of the Cockney dialect can still be heard. Cockney is therefore no longer confined to the traditional dialect area with which it has been associated but has come to represent the working class dialect of a much wider geographical south-eastern region of England. It is probably also accurate to say that Cockney has become synonymous with white working class speakers and is not generally a term applied to speakers of minority ethnic backgrounds even if they have been born within the traditional Cockney area.

In addition to these sociohistorical facts we must also take into account the changes that have taken place in respect of in-migration to the traditional East End. Of course, immigration is endemic to the East End and London has a long history of being a city which has attracted various groups of immigrants (see Fox 2015 for a fuller discussion). However, from the 1950s onwards, in the post-war era, London attracted large-scale immigration of African-Caribbean and South Asian communities, the first large groups of "non-white" peoples. There were large inflows from the former British colonies of Jamaica, Trinidad, and Guyana alongside those from India and Pakistan (including what is now Bangladesh). In Tower Hamlets alone, the Bangladeshi community constituted 32% of the total population at the 2011 Census (Census 2011: Office for National Statistics), and it is still growing. Between 1981 and 2011 the population of Tower Hamlets increased from around 140,000 to just over 254,000 and this increase is due almost entirely to the growth of the Bangladeshi community whose population increased from around 9,800 (this figure only accounted for those born in Bangladesh and did not include those of Bangladeshi origin but born in the UK) to almost 66,000 (Census data 1981, 1991, 2001, 2011) in the same period. Furthermore, there has been an increase over the past two decades of smaller immigrant groups from more diverse places of origin, with London at the present time being home to people from no less than 179 countries (Vertovec 2007). Note that many of these newcomers came during the period when many of the traditional Cockney working class families were leaving, allowing little chance of interaction between the outgoing and ingoing groups. In this multicultural situation language contact abounds and it is therefore perhaps unsurprising to learn of rapid changes to the dialect of the area traditionally associated with Cockney. It also casts doubt on whether, in the present day, speakers in the innermost suburbs of the East End can reasonably be referred to as Cockneys anymore. Recent sociolinguistic research, rather more accurately it would seem, points to a "Multicultural London English" (Cheshire et al. 2011) used by speakers from many different linguistic backgrounds.

This chapter aims to give an overview of the traditional aspects of the London dialect while at the same time taking into account some of the recent changes described as Multicultural London English (MLE). There is no doubt that traditional Cockney forms do still exist but they are maybe less apparent in the innermost suburbs than they once were. Cockney, as an identity marker, is perhaps more restricted to those of a white working class background and would include those living further east of the traditional East End.

2 The vowel system

There are several studies which have focused on London English, notably Sivertsen (1960), Hurford (1967), Beaken (1971), Hudson and Holloway (1977) and Tollfree (1999), all of which are impressionistic descriptions. Overall reviews of the variety can also be found in Wells (1982) and Hughes and Trudgill (1996). The most recent works describe the vowel system in London using instrumental acoustic measurements of the vowel qualities (Torgersen et al. 2006; 2008). These latter studies also describe differences between inner London and the outermost eastern suburbs taking into account the demographic changes outlined in the previous section.

Descriptions of the qualities for many of the short vowels do not differ much from those described for Received Pronunciation (RP) and are therefore not discussed here. Where they do differ from RP to any extent they are described in the following sections and, following Wells (1982), the concept of standard lexical sets is used to refer to large groups of words which tend to share the same vowel. Vowel plots for monophthongs are shown in Figure 10.2 (inner East London) and Figure 10.3 (outermost suburb of East London).

2.1 KIT

The quality of Cockney (and London generally) KIT is said to be more central than RP at times [ɪ ~ ï] (Wells 1982; Tollfree 1999). This is confirmed for present day speakers in inner and outer London by Kerswill at al. (2008) who show that there are no generational differences between elderly speakers (aged 70–85) and adolescent speakers (aged 16–19) in the quality of this vowel (see Figures 10.2 and 10.3).

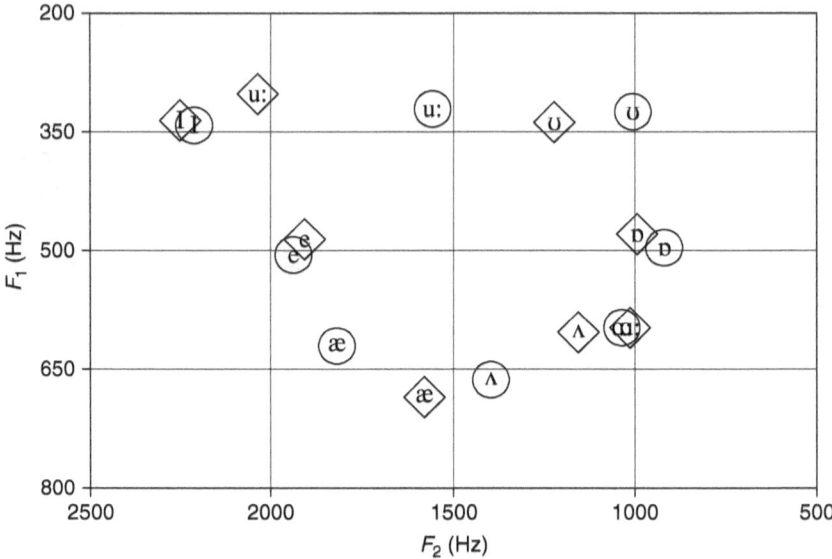

Figure 10.2: Vowel plots for elderly speakers (circles) and young speakers (diamonds) in inner East London (adapted from Kerswill et al. 2008).

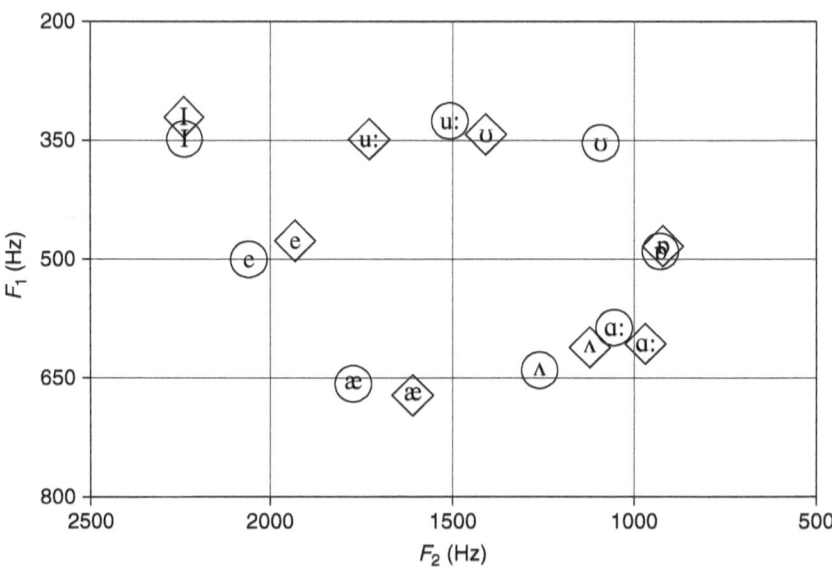

Figure 10.3: Vowel plots for elderly speakers (circles) and young speakers (diamonds) in outer East London (adapted from Kerswill et al. 2008).

2.2 DRESS

Sivertsen (1960) and Wells (1982) describe DRESS as having the same quality as RP [e] but more recent reports suggest that there has been a shift towards a more open variant. Tollfree (1999) states that [ɛ] variants are more common in her dataset and, in line with these findings, Kerswill et al. (2008) report that DRESS has the more open [ɛ] quality and is used by both older (aged 70–85) and younger (aged 16–19) speakers.

2.3 TRAP

Wells (1982: 304) reports that the TRAP vowel in Cockney is [ɛ] and therefore less open than RP [æ]. Tollfree (1999: 166) however finds [æ], sometimes lengthened to [æː], for all speakers. A traditional fully front vowel [ɛ ~ æ] is shown to be the variant favored by elderly inner London speakers but among young speakers in both inner and outer areas of London TRAP is more open and more centralized, [ɐ]. This is a change in quality much in line with the rest of south-east England (Torgersen and Kerswill 2004).

2.4 STRUT

Rather than RP [ʌ] the STRUT vowel in traditional Cockney is a front vowel ranging from a fronted [ɐ] to [a] (Wells 1982: 305) or [æ] (Hughes and Trudgill 1996: 70). However, recent developments show that adolescents in both inner and outer London have a more back and less open STRUT [ʌ] vowel in comparison to older speakers (shown in Figures 10.2 and 10.3). There were also significant differences reported in inner London between Anglo (white speakers whose families have relatively local roots) and non-Anglo (children/grandchildren of immigrants from less developed countries) adolescent speakers, with non-Anglo speakers having a less open STRUT [ʌ̝] vowel and thus leading this change. The Anglo adolescents were more likely to have a back STRUT vowel if they belonged to a multi-ethnic friendship network (Kerswill et al. 2008: 6).

2.5 FOOT

Sivertsen (1960: 79) describes the Cockney FOOT vowel as being a little more fronted than RP [ʊ]. Tollfree reports some variation in the quality of this vowel. Older speakers and some younger speakers maintain [ʊ] but for younger speakers under c.30, who use what she describes as South East London Regional Standard, the typical variant is an unrounded and centralized [ÿ̞] (Tollfree 1999: 166). Kerswill et al. (2008: 6) also report differences between older and adolescent speakers in outer London, with FOOT fronting / centring [ö] for adolescent speakers. Like TRAP this development is consistent with a southeastern trend (Torgersen and Kerswill 2004: 45). It is also in evidence to some extent in inner London but here the FOOT vowel is less central [ʊ].

2.6 START

The long monophthong START is generally much the same in London as RP [ɑː]. No generational changes are reported for this vowel in the most recent study of the London vowel system (Kerswill et al. 2008: 5).

2.7 GOOSE

Wells (1982) describes GOOSE as being slightly more fronted [ʉː] than RP [uː], with his notation covering a range of phonetic realizations. He also reports a diphthongal quality to this vowel [ʊʉ ~ əu], the latter starting point being "the most Cockney-flavoured" (Wells 1982: 304) and this accords with older descriptions of Cockney (Sivertsen 1960: 81). Tollfree (1999: 168) also reports variants which are not fully back [u̟ː], [ʉ̈ː] or [ʉː] and which may be accompanied by strong labialization in open syllables [u̟ːʷ]. However, like STRUT, recent developments of the GOOSE vowel show that it has not only undergone generational change but that there is also regional difference between inner and outer London. Adolescent speakers in both locations of London follow the trend reported by Tollfree (1999) of not using fully back variants. Figures 10.2 and 10.3 show that young speakers have a substantially more front GOOSE than older speakers. Furthermore, the fronting of this vowel is more extreme among MLE speakers in inner London, [yː]. There are significant differences between Anglo and non-Anglo speakers, with non-Anglos leading in the fronting of this vowel. Anglo speakers were more likely to have a front GOOSE vowel if they belonged to a multi-ethnic friendship network (Kerswill et al. 2008: 6). These realizations do not have a diphthongal quality (Kerswill et al. 2008: 466).

2.8 FLEECE

Older descriptions of Cockney report that the FLEECE vowel differs from RP [iː] in that it is strongly diphthongized (Sivertsen 1960; Wells 1982), having an open starting point of [ɪ], [ə] or even [ɐ]. The vowel plot of a 23 year-old male Londoner recorded in 1968 shows a diphthongized vowel with extreme lowering of the onset (Labov 1994: 210). In South-east London [iː] is typical for older and younger speakers with some broader varieties having [iːə] or [əiː] with schwa-like on- or off-glides for all speakers (Tollfree 1999: 166). The most recent study of London English describes the FLEECE vowel as near-monophthongal (Kerswill et al. 2008: 466).

2.9 MOUTH

Wells describes the London MOUTH vowel as ranging from a monophthong [æː] to a closing-backing diphthong [æʊ], the former characterizing "true Cockney" (Wells 1982: 309). The monophthongal variant is reported by Sivertsen (1960: 66) as [aː] but found "only among boys and men of a less polished type", with diphthongal variants of [ɛə] and [ɛʊ] being most common. The Cockney MOUTH diphthong, ending as it does with a mid or open offset, has been observed to attract intrusive /r/ when followed by a vowel, as in the phrase *now and then* [næʊɹənðɛn]. Cockney variants of the MOUTH vowel are reported for Labov's London speakers recorded in 1968 (Labov 1994), and elderly speakers from inner London recorded in 2004/5 are also shown to have traditional fronted and near-monophthongal MOUTH vowels (Kerswill et al. 2008: 457–458).

Younger, adolescent MLE speakers in inner London, however, use a monophthongal variant but one which is lowered from a mid-front position. Furthermore, this is used alongside an innovative back diphthong [ɑʊ], with non-Anglo speakers leading in the use of this variant. There is also some evidence of the lowering of this vowel in the outer eastern suburb of East London but less so than in the inner suburbs (Kerswill et al. 2008: 487–488).

2.10 FACE

The onset of the London/Cockney FACE vowel traditionally has a much more open and more central onset than the corresponding RP [eɪ], with [æɪ ~ aɪ] being common Cockney variants (Beaken 1971; Hughes and Trudgill 1996; Sivertsen 1960; Wells 1982). Open onsets for FACE are shown in vowel plots for male and female speakers recorded in London by Labov in 1968 (Labov 1994: 169, 210). These descriptions are also confirmed in vowel plots for older speakers recorded in 2004/5 – a male speaker born in inner London in 1938 and a female speaker born in inner London in 1928 – both of whom have very open onsets for FACE (Kerswill et al. 2008: 458).

The FACE vowel, however, has undergone change in recent developments of London English among adolescents. Fox's (2015) investigation of young speakers of Bangladeshi and white British origin in Tower Hamlets, recorded in 2001, reported that many of the young speakers used variants of [e̞ɪ] [eɪ] [ɛɪ] (sometimes with monophthongal qualities) in addition to the more traditional variants of [æɪ] and [aɪ]. The use of the newer variants was led by speakers of Bangladeshi origin and among young white British people, by boys, suggesting that their origin may lie in language and dialect contact (Fox 2015: 139). Similarly, Kerswill et al. (2008: 488) reported that the FACE vowel in inner London has changed to a narrow diphthong [e̞ɪ] or [e̞ɪ̝] among MLE speakers, with non-Anglo boys leading the change. This change is also found, albeit to a lesser extent, in the outer eastern suburb of London.

2.11 PRICE

In comparison to RP [aɪ], the Cockney PRICE vowel is described as [ɑɪ] with a "truly back initial element" that is generally unrounded (Sivertsen 1960: 64). Wells (1982: 308) states that the onset may also be rounded to [ɒ] and that the second element is sometimes reduced or absent, giving rise to variants such as [ɑː]. Realizations such as [ɑɪ] are captured in Labov's vowel plots for the male and female speakers he recorded in 1968 (Labov 1994: 169, 210) and by the 2004/5 recordings of two elderly speakers in London (Kerswill et al. 2008: 458).

However, like FACE, the PRICE vowel has also undergone recent change in London. Fox's (2015) investigation of young speakers in Tower Hamlets points to changes in the pronunciation of the PRICE vowel towards narrow diphthongs [aɪ] or [ɐɪ] where the offsets might be weakened or even a monophthongal [æ] in some cases. These changes have seemingly been initiated and are being led by speakers of Bangladeshi origin but are also being adopted by young white (predominantly male) British speakers. Fox's findings are corroborated by (Kerswill et al. 2008: 488) who report that PRICE has a "fully open central onset with variable monophthongization" among MLE speakers in inner London and that the change is led by non-Anglo speakers. The same process is observed in the outer suburb of east London but to a lesser extent. In outer London the more traditional Cockney variants are also found to be used by some speakers.

2.12 GOAT

The Cockney GOAT vowel is generally described as a diphthong but with a more front onset than that of RP [əʊ]. Sivertsen (1960: 88) reports [œʊ], Wells (1982: 308) reports [æ̈ ~ ɐ] moving towards [ÿ] and Hughes and Trudgill (1996: 71) report [æʉ]. Traditional Cockney/London diphthongal variants can be seen in the vowel plots of two speakers recorded by Labov in 1968 (Labov 1994: 169, 210) and in the vowel plots of two elderly speakers recorded in 2004/5 (Kerswill et al. 2008: 457–458).

In comparison to elderly speakers, Kerswill et al. (2008) found that adolescents in the inner and outer suburbs of London use a more raised onset to the diphthong, [ə]. Additionally, the adolescents in the outer eastern suburb tended to have a more fronted offset, [əʉ ~ əʏ], in line with speakers of a wider southeastern England area (Kerswill and Williams 2005). In the inner suburb there is a further development of this vowel in that there is a newer variant among MLE speakers which involves raising and backing of the onset, leading to monophthongization, [oʊ ~ oː]. This new variant is found mainly, but not exclusively, among non-Anglo speakers, indicating the likelihood that this innovation has come about because of the contact situation that prevails in London (Kerswill et al. 2008).

The monophthongization of FACE, PRICE and GOAT all seem to follow the same pattern. The changes appear to be innovations emerging in the inner London suburb among MLE speakers. Leading the changes in each case are speakers of non-Anglo origin. Those speakers of Anglo origin who belong to multi-ethnic friendship networks also use more of the innovative variants than those who have mainly Anglo friendship networks (Kerswill et al. 2008: 483).

2.13 lettER/commA

The use of very open realizations [ɐ] of schwa in final position (Wells 1982: 305) is still commonly found in and around London.

2.14 happY

The Cockney vowel at the end of words like *city* and *happy* is reported to be realized with the FLEECE vowel, unlike RP which is realized with a KIT vowel. Hughes and Trudgill (1996: 70) give [i] for Cockney, Wells (1982: 319) finds a range of diphthongal realizations from [əɪ] to [ɪi] through to monophthongal [i] and

Tollfree (1999: 169) reports [i] and [iː] as the preferred realizations for speakers of all ages in her study of south-east London. The latter would appear to accord with the more recent reports of FLEECE monophthongization in London (Kerswill et al. 2008).

3 Consonants

3.1 Plosives /p, t, k/

In writing about Cockney, Matthews (1938: 80) wrote that the "chief consonantal feature of the dialect is the prevalence of the glottal stop". He refers to the glottal stop replacing /t/ and /k/ in intervocalic contexts, for example in words such as *butter* [bʌʔə] and *packer* [pæʔə], with a "growing tendency" for it to also replace /p/ in words such as *paper* [paɪʔə]. Glottalization accompanying intervocalic /p/ is also referred to by Hughes and Trudgill (1996: 70). Beaken (1971) finds almost invariable glottalization of /p, t, k/ in final position. Glottalization to accompany or replace /t/ is of course common to many varieties of English, particularly in pre-consonantal and pre-pausal environments. Perhaps, though, a bare [ʔ] in intervocalic position is a feature which is commonly cited as a stereotypical characteristic of Cockney (Wells 1982: 324). Sivertsen (1960: 113) reports that intervocalic /t/ glottalization does occur but that it is more frequently used among men than women and that it is considered a little "rough". She refers to an alveolar flap [t̮] in this context as being the norm at that time (Sivertsen 1960: 119). Hughes and Trudgill, (1996: 70), however, report that [ʔ] representing /t/ is extremely common between vowels and before a pause, although of course they are reporting almost 40 years later than Sivertsen.

The most recent study to cover the realizations of these stops is Tollfree's (1999) study of south-east London. She reports glottal reinforcement/replacement of /p/ and /k/ in both pre-consonantal and pre-pausal positions as in *stopcock* [stɒʔpkɒʔk] and *keep* [kʰiːʔp], also intervocalically as in *hacker* [hæʔkɐ] and before a nasal as in *happen* [hæʔn]. The most widespread use of glottal reinforcement/replacement, however, is found in the representation of /t/. She finds widespread use of /t/ glottalling in pre-consonantal and pre-pausal positions, which is almost categorical for some speakers. There is also a high incidence, among some speakers, of /t/ glottalization in word-final pre-vocalic position and in word-internal intervocalic position. More generally though, there is variation among speakers between /t/ glottalling, the more prestigious variants of plosive [t] or aspirated [tˢ]. She also reports a tapped variant [ɾ] which may occur across word boundaries such as *lot of, get a, what is* and word internally in certain items e.g. *better, getting*

(Tollfree 1999: 170). There is no glottalization when /t/ occurs in foot-initial onset position, i.e. when it occurs word initially, e.g. *tiny,* or word-internally, e.g. *attend* (Tollfree 1999: 171).

Another development in the use of /k/ is an innovation which has been termed "K-backing" (Kerswill et al. 2008: 6). K-backing is the use of a retracted voiceless velar plosive in word-initial position before non-high back vowels, so that words such as *cousin, car, cot, caught* are pronounced with something approaching [q] rather than the usual [k]. This recent innovation is found in the speech of adolescents in inner London and to a lesser extent in outer London as shown in Tables 10.1 and 10.2.

3.2 TH

TH-fronting, the realization of the dental fricatives /θ/ and /ð/ as [f] and [v] respectively, has long been considered to be a feature of Cockney and London English generally. Matthews (1938: 80) reports variable pronunciations as does Sivertsen (1960: 122). The replacement of [f] for /θ/ can occur word-initially e.g. [fɪn] for *thin,* word-medially e.g. [ɜːfi] for *earthy* or word-finally e.g. [bɑːf] for *bath.* The replacement of [v] for /ð/ usually only occurs word-medially e.g. [fɑːvə] for *father* and word-finally e.g. [smuːv] for *smooth.* Word-initial [v] for /ð/ was also common-place in the past (Matthews 1938), and Tollfree (1999: 172) finds several instances of [vis] for *this* in her south-east London data. In word-initial position, Hughes and Trudgill (1996: 71) report that /ð/ can be replaced with [d] or even zero e.g. [də] for *the* or [ei] for *they.* Hudson and Holloway (1977) also provide evidence of initial [d] as a variant used by working class boys. Wells (1982: 329) states that in previous centuries Cockney exhibited stopping of both /θ/ and /ð/ evidenced by such spellings as *Tursday* 'Thursday' and *furder* 'further' and suggests that word-initial [d] stopping of /ð/ is a remnant of that system and therefore recessive.

Given that TH-fronting is a feature which has spread and is used widely (particularly by young speakers) in many varieties of British English (Kerswill 2003: 12), it is perhaps not surprising that the results from the most recent study of London English show a huge increase in the use of this feature among adolescents relative to the elderly speakers in the study. Tables 10.1 and 10.2 show percentage frequencies for seven consonantal variables in the outer and inner East London suburbs. In Tables 10.1 and 10.2 the term TH-fronting refers to the use of [f] for /θ/ and DH-fronting refers to the use of word-medial or word-final [v] for /ð/ (Kerswill et al. 2008: 6).

Table 10.1: Percentage frequencies for seven consonantal variables among elderly and adolescent speakers – inner London (taken from Kerswill et al. 2008)

	H-dropping	K-backing	TH-fronting (initial)	TH-fronting (final)	DH-fronting	DH-stopping	Labio-dental /r/
Elderly	58.1		29.7	39.0	19.4	1.9	0
Young	11.0	67.8	86.5	95.3	74.1	58.0	35.5
Sig.	p<0.001	N/A	p<0.001	p<0.001	p<0.001	p<0.001	N/A

There has, however, also been a huge increase in DH-stopping, involving the use of word-initial [d] for [ð]. Rather than it being a resurgence of a traditional Cockney feature, its emergence seems to have arisen due to the high contact situation in inner London. Kerswill et al. (2008: 14–15) show that there is a significant difference between Anglo and non-Anglo speakers in the use of this feature with non-Anglo speakers in the lead. Anglo MLE speakers in inner London use this feature to a greater extent than Anglo speakers in outer London. Kerswill et al. (2008: 7) suggest that this is an innovation which has arisen in inner London and that the channels for the diffusion of such innovations are mobile non-Anglo speakers.

Table 10.2: Percentage frequencies for seven consonantal variables among elderly and adolescent speakers – outer eastern London (taken from Kerswill et al. 2008)

	H-dropping	K-backing	TH-fronting (initial)	TH-fronting (final)	DH-fronting	DH-stopping	Labio-dental /r/
Elderly	25.6	0	1.2	2.4	0	0	0
Young	32.2	50.6	83.1	83.6	68.6	30	22
Sig.	p<0.05	N/A	p<0.001	p<0.001	N/A	N/A	N/A

3.3 H

The tradition of not producing [h] in stressed contexts e.g. [æmə] for *hammer*, [ænd] for *hand* and [ed] for *head*, has been a long-standing feature of English in England and has been particularly common in Cockney and popular London speech. Matthews (1938: 80) remarks on the "general agreement among Cockneys to neglect initial *h*" and Sivertsen (1960: 141) reports "great inconsistency" in the use of "pre-peak [h]". Hughes and Trudgill (1996: 70) state that "/h/ is almost invariably lost". The use of this feature has been subject to strong stigmatization and possibly for this reason its use has begun to decline recently in the south-east

(Williams and Kerswill 1999). Tollfree (1999: 173) reports a "slowly progressing or stabilising sound change which has not gone to completion". Kerswill et al. (2008: 7) confirm low use of H-dropping, with usage among adolescents considerably less than among elderly speakers in inner London (see Tables 10.1 and 10.2). There seem to be two factors to consider in the recession of this feature. Firstly, the low usage among young people follows the general trend of the south-east of England but secondly, this change appears to be being propelled by non-Anglo adolescent speakers, who do not seem to have adopted this traditional Cockney feature and have relatively little H-dropping (there are significant differences between non-Anglos and Anglos who have 4% and 18% H-dropping respectively in inner London and in outer London 9.5% and 40% respectively).

3.4 R

The use of a labiodental or bilabial approximant [ʋ] ~ [β̞] for /r/ is a form thought to be diffusing throughout Britain from London (Foulkes and Docherty 2000). This is not a feature mentioned in older reports of Cockney but appears to be a recent innovation and indeed Tollfree (1999: 174) finds variable use of a labiodental approximant [ʋ] for /r/ among some individuals in her south-east London data and consistent use of this variant among four of her informants. Tables 10.1 and 10.2 show that there is no use of such variants among elderly speakers in inner or outer East London but substantial evidence of use among adolescents and that it is seemingly diffusing from inner London given its higher use in that location.

4 Beyond phonology

4.1 Indefinite and definite articles

A recent innovation to have been reported is the move towards simplification in the indefinite and definite article allomorphy system. Many young speakers in inner London do not make the distinction that the indefinite article in standard British English is *a* [ə] before consonant-initial words and *an* [ən] before vowel-initial words, as in examples (1a) and (1b), nor do they distinguish between the two standard British English pronunciations of the definite article, *the* [ðə] when it occurs before a consonant-initial word and *the* [ði] when it occurs before a vowel-initial word, as in examples (1c) and (1d). Note that in examples (1b) and (1d) the change in form/pronunciation prevents hiatus across the vowel-vowel (V#V) context.

(1) a. *a pear* [ə pɛə]
    b. *an apple* [ənæpɫ]
    c. *the pear* [ðəpɛə]
    d. *the apple* [ði⁽ʲ⁾æpɫ]

Instead, many young speakers use *a* [ə] and *the* [ðə] categorically before consonant-initial words (as in standard British English) but also variably before vowel-initial words. The consequence of these pronunciations in pre-vocalic environments is that there is then potential for V#V hiatus. In many (non-rhotic) varieties of English (including Cockney and London English generally), in contexts where the vowel /ɔː/, /ɑː/, /ə/ or /ɜː/ is followed by another vowel the potential hiatus is overcome by the insertion of linking or intrusive /r/ e.g. [pɔːɹaʊʔ] *pour out* or [aɪdiəɹɒv] *idea of*. It might be expected then that intrusive /r/ would be triggered where *a* [ə] or *the* [ðə] is used before vowel-initial words. However, this is not the case. The young speakers do not insert intrusive /r/ to avoid vowel hiatus but instead use a glottal stop, for example *a apple* [əʔæpl] and *the apple* [ðəʔæpl]. In an investigation of young speakers of Bangladeshi and white British origin, Fox (2015) found high frequency of the use of *a* [ə] and *the* [ðə] before vowel-initial words among Bangladeshi male adolescents in Tower Hamlets, London, and to a lesser extent in the speech of their white Anglo male peers. All speakers used glottal stop to resolve hiatus in the V#V context. Multi-ethnic friendship networks were shown to play a key role in the diffusion of these features. Similarly, Gabrielatos et al. (2010) found that non-Anglo males in inner London had the highest use of indefinite article *a* before vowel-initial words in their analysis of London adolescents.

4.2 Negation

4.2.1 *ain't*

The use of *ain't* for present tense negative forms of *be* and *have* is widespread in London and the south-east generally and used with all subjects, e.g. *he ain't scared anyway, you ain't getting rid of me, she ain't got any money*.

4.2.2 Negative concord

As in many other varieties in Britain the use of negative concord is widespread, resulting in expressions such as *she can't say nothing, no-one else has to do nothing, you ain't moving me nowhere.* Recent trends indicate a huge increase in the use of negative concord among adolescent speakers (particularly in inner London) relative to elderly speakers and to wider south-east England varieties (Kerswill et al. 2008: 10).

4.2.3 *never* as past tense negator

In contrast to standard English, *never* can refer to a single occasion and has the same meaning as *didn't*, e.g. *I never done nothing* meaning *I didn't do anything* (referring to a single specific occasion).

4.3 Past tense of *be*

Recent research of this feature has shown that *was/were* variation in London is a complex phenomenon. In the outer eastern suburbs of London, leveling to a *was/weren't* pattern attested in the south-east of England generally (as well as in many other varieties of English in the UK) is well underway and can be attributed to dialect leveling. Following this pattern, speakers variably use *was* in positive contexts for all persons and *weren't* in negative contexts for all persons, as in examples (2a) and (2b).

(2) a. *they* was *coming back*
 b. *I* weren't *gonna take the risk*
 c. *we* wasn't *allowed to wear hats*

In inner London, however, both *was* and *weren't* leveling were less in evidence. Adolescents were found to use nonstandard *was* in positive contexts less frequently than elderly speakers, and there was a mixed pattern of both nonstandard *weren't* and nonstandard *wasn't* (example 2c) in negative contexts. Speaker ethnicity in inner London was highly significant. Bangladeshi adolescents generally used standard English past *be* forms, and Afro-Caribbeans led the trend towards a leveled *was/wasn't* system. It is assumed that Anglo speakers have been affected by both leveling trends, reflecting the nature of individual speakers' friendship groups (Cheshire and Fox 2009: 30).

4.4 Relative pronouns

The traditional feature of non-standard *what* usage as in, for example, *he's the one what done it* or *the car what she drives*, is declining in London and its use among adolescents is negligible. Across London (inner and outer) there is more extreme leveling to *that* than is reported elsewhere in the UK, including its use with the word *people* as in, for example, *the people that came to the party*, which elsewhere correlates with *who*. The most frequent users of *that* in inner London are speakers from minority ethnic groups and it is assumed that they have perhaps extended the use of *that* as a marker of subordinate clauses. This is conceivably an example of language contact reinforcing leveling of the relative pronoun system and the loss of non-standard *what* (Kerswill et al. 2008: 9–10).

4.5 The quotative system

As elsewhere in many other English varieties around the world there is robust use of the quotatives *be like* (3a) and *go* (3b) among young speakers in London. Furthermore, a recent innovation has been the introduction of a new quotative *this is + speaker* (3c) to the London system found only in the more multicultural inner London area and used only by young speakers (Kerswill et al. 2008: 10).

(3) a. I'm like *'go and get them'*
    b. she went *'I was only joking'*
    c. this is them *'what area are you from?'*

4.6 Pragmatic markers

The use of *innit* is an established pragmatic marker among young speakers in London. It is used as a derivation of *isn't it*, as a tag that matches the subject and verb form of the preceding clause (4a), and also in non-paradigmatic contexts, where the subject of the preceding form is not *it* and the verb is not *is* (4b) and where there is therefore no grammatical relationship between *innit* and the preceding clause.

(4) a. *it's like an act,* innit?
    b. *alright I'll give you the four pound today,* innit?

Its use was first documented in the 1980s when Hewitt (1986) stated that the use of *innit* as invariant tag was one of the most frequent forms of Jamaican Creole found in the speech of white adolescents in London, particularly in high-contact areas and in ethnically mixed conversation. Andersen (2001: 110) also argues that *innit* developed in high-contact communities, with non-Anglo speakers and adolescents in general in the lead. Today, however, its use has spread throughout the community and there is little difference between Anglo and non-Anglo speakers in the frequency of *innit* use (Torgersen et al. 2011).

Hewitt (1986: 133) also commented on the use of *you know what I mean* (5a) as an agreement-marker as "a very recent idiomatic innovation, and one which appears to be developed within the London English of black adolescents but derived from a Caribbean source". The use of *you know what I mean* has declined in inner London but appears to have spread to the outer eastern suburbs and in its place in inner London is the innovative *you get me* (5b). The latest innovation *you get me* is also led by the non-Anglo group and clearly indexes ethnicity (Torgersen et al. 2011), following the pattern of both *innit* and *you know what I mean* as well as other phonological and grammatical innovations discussed in the previous sections.

(5) a. *falling on the floor laughing* you know what I mean?
    b. *music calms me down* you get me

Briefly, other innovations found among young speakers in London include the following some of which have not yet been quantified (Kerswill et al. 2008: 8) and some may well be more widespread than London:
- pronoun *youse* (2nd person plural): *and then youse can start talking that way*
- indefinite pronoun *man*: *it's her personality man's looking at* (Cheshire 2013)
- absence of preposition *to*: *I'm going countryside*
- plural *-dem*: *one of the boydem then went <sound effect>*
- *-why ... for* question frame: *I said "why you searching my jacket for?"*
- *-enough* (and *nuff*) as intensifier: *his mum looks nuff young though*

5 Cockney rhyming slang

Finally, no chapter on Cockney would seem to be complete without some reference to Cockney rhyming slang. Cockney rhyming slang is the practice of using an expression which rhymes with a word and then using that expression instead of the word. For example, the expression "dog and bone" refers to a "phone". More commonly, the rhyming word itself is omitted so it is more likely to hear someone say "I was on the *dog* to my mate yesterday". Many people not familiar with the dialect often have the perception that this is part of the daily repertoire for speakers of this variety. In fact, this is not generally the case and it seems doubtful whether it was ever used for more than playful effect. Its origins are not clear but one of the first documented accounts of rhyming slang is contained in *The Vulgar Tongue. A Glossary of Slang, Cant, and Flash Phrases, used in London from 1839 to 1859* (Ducange 1859). It is true that some expressions have found their way into common usage e.g. *use your loaf* (loaf of bread = head), *cup of rosie* (rosie lee = tea), *mi ol' china* (china plate = mate), *to rabbit* (rabbit and pork = talk) and it is also true that new expressions spring up, but like many other street terms they emerge quickly and are short-lived. New expressions also tend to revolve around media/celebrity culture. Nevertheless, its cultural specificity is captured in Figures 10.4, 10.5 and 10.6, advertising hoardings which were displayed at the entrance of a shopping retail park. Interestingly, these were not situated in the traditional Cockney East End (where it is questionable whether they would be understood by the majority of the present day population) but in an area further east in the borough of Newham (see map in Figure 10.1). As discussed in the introduction to this chapter, this is a clear example which demonstrates that Cockney now belongs to areas outside its traditional homeland.

Fig. 10.4: Lucy Locket ('pocket')

Fig. 10.5: Jam Jars ('cars')

Fig. 10.6: Hank Marvin ('starving')

6 Summary

In the last five decades Cockney has probably undergone more rapid change than at any time in its long history. This is not surprising given the vast social and economic redevelopment of the traditional dialect area outlined in the introduction to this chapter (see also Fox 2015 for a fuller discussion). Without doubt the speech forms associated with Cockney can still be heard but predominantly among speakers from a wide geographical area around London. Within the inner suburbs of London, with its multicultural diversity, the Cockney label would seem to be becoming less and less relevant to the people living there and to the variety of English spoken by them.

Acknowledgement: I am grateful to Eivind Torgersen, Jenny Cheshire and an anonymous reviewer for helpful comments on an earlier draft of this chapter. Any errors or shortcomings are, of course, my own.

7 References

Abercrombie, Patrick and John H. Forshaw. 1943. *County of London Plan*. London: Macmillan.
Andersen, Gisle. 2001. *Pragmatic Markers and Sociolinguistic Variation*. Amsterdam/Philadelphia: John Benjamins.
Beaken, Michael A. 1971. *A Study of Phonological Development in a Primary School Population in East London*. Ph.D. Thesis, University of London.
Cheshire, Jenny. 2013. Grammaticalisation in social context: The emergence of a new English pronoun. *Journal of Sociolinguistics* 17(5): 608–633.
Cheshire, Jenny and Sue Fox. 2009. *Was/were* variation: A perspective from London. *Language Variation and Change* 21: 1–38.
Cheshire, Jenny, Paul Kerswill, Susan Fox, and Eivind Torgersen. 2011. Contact, the feature pool and the speech community: The emergence of Multicultural London English. *Journal of Sociolinguistics* 15(2): 151–196.
Ducange, Anglicus. 1859. *The Vulgar Tongue. A Glossary of Slang, Cant, and Flash phrases, used in London from 1839 to 1859*. London: B. Quaritch.
Forman, Charlie. 1989. *Spitalfields: A Battle for Land*. London: Hilary Shipman.
Foulkes, Paul and Gerard Docherty. 2000. Another chapter in the story of /r/: 'Labiodental' variants in British English. *Journal of Sociolinguistics* 4: 30–59.
Fox, Susan. 2015. *The New Cockney: New Ethnicities and Adolescent Speech in the Traditional East End of London*. Basingstoke: Palgrave Macmillan.
Gabrielatos, Costas, Eivind Torgersen, Sebastian Hoffmann, and Susan Fox. 2010. A corpus-based sociolinguistic study of indefinite article forms in London English. *Journal of English Linguistics* 38: 297–334.
Greater London Authority (eds.). 2005. *London – the World in a City: An Analysis of the 2001 Census Results*. London: Greater London Authority Data Management and Analysis Group Briefing 2005/6.
Hewitt, Roger. 1986. *White Talk, Black Talk*. Cambridge: Cambridge University Press.
Hudson, Richard and Anne Holloway. 1977. *Variation in London English*. Final report submitted to the Social Science Research Council.
Hughes, Arthur and Peter Trudgill. 1996. *English Accents and Dialects*. 3rd edn. London: Hodder Arnold.
Hurford, James. 1967. *The speech of one family: A phonetic comparison of the speech of three generations in a family in East London*. Unpublished Ph.D. dissertation. London: University College London.
Kerswill, Paul. 2003. Dialect levelling and geographical diffusion in British English. In: David Britain and Jenny Cheshire (eds.), *Social Dialectology. In Honour of Peter Trudgill*, 223–243. Amsterdam/Philadelphia: John Benjamins.

Kerswill, Paul, Jenny Cheshire, Sue Fox, and Eivind Torgersen. 2008. *Linguistic Innovators: the English of adolescents in London*. Final report submitted to the Economic and Social Research Council, February 2008.

Kerswill, Paul, Eivind Torgersen, and Susan Fox. 2008. Reversing "drift": Innovation and diffusion in the London diphthong system. *Language Variation and Change* 20: 451–491.

Kerswill, Paul and Ann Williams. 2005. New towns and koineisation: Linguistic and social correlates. *Linguistics* 43(5): 1023–1048.

Labov, William. 1994. *Principles of Linguistic Change: Internal Factors*. Oxford: Blackwell.

Matthews, William. 1938. *Cockney Past and Present: A Short History of the Dialect of London*. London: Routledge.

Sivertsen, Eva. 1960. *Cockney Phonology*. Oslo: Oslo University Press.

Tollfree, Laura. 1999. South East London English: discrete versus continuous modelling of consonantal reduction. In: Paul Foulkes and Gerry Docherty (eds.), *Urban Voices: Accent Studies in the British Isles*,163–184. London: Hodder Arnold.

Torgersen, Eivind and Paul Kerswill. 2004. Internal and external motivation in phonetic change: dialect levelling outcomes for an English vowel shift. *Journal of Sociolinguistics* 8: 23–53.

Torgersen, Eivind, Paul Kerswill, and Susan Fox. 2006. Ethnicity as a source of changes in the London vowel system. In: Frans Hinskens (ed.), *Language Variation – European Perspectives. Selected Papers from the Third International Conference on Language Variation in Europe (ICLaVE3), Amsterdam, June 2005*, 249–263. Amsterdam/Philadelphia: John Benjamins.

Torgersen, Eivind, Costas Gabrielatos, Sebastian Hoffmann, and Susan Fox. 2011. A corpus-based study of pragmatic markers in London English. *Corpus Linguistics and Linguistic Theory* 7(1): 93–118.

Vertovec, Stephen. 2007. Super-diversity and its implications. *Ethnic and Racial Studies*, 29(6): 1024–1054.

Walker, John. 1791 (revised 1806). *A Critical Pronouncing Dictionary and Expositor of the English Language*.

Wells, John. 1982. *Accents of English*. Vols. 1–3. Cambridge: Cambridge University Press.

Williams, Ann and Paul Kerswill. 1999. Dialect levelling: Change and continuity in Milton Keynes, Reading and Hull. In: Paul Foulkes and Gerard Docherty (eds.), *Urban Voices: Accent Studies in the British Isles*, 141–162. London: Hodder Arnold.

Young, Michael and Peter Willmott. 1957. *Family and Kinship in East London*. London: Routledge.

Markku Filppula and Juhani Klemola
Chapter 11:
Celtic and Celtic Englishes

1 Introduction —— 210
2 The progressive or "expanded" form of verbs —— 212
3 The *it*-cleft construction —— 219
4 Summary —— 226
5 References —— 227

Abstract: It has generally been assumed that Celtic influences in English grammar over the centuries have been minimal. The last couple of decades, however, have witnessed a continuing rise of interest in the 'Celtic Hypothesis', which argues for a need to reassess the role of the Celtic languages in the development of English. In this chapter we explicate the Celtic Hypothesis through a discussion of two syntactic features which in our view are likely to have arisen as a result of either direct or indirect (reinforcing) Celtic influence, leaving its mark on English grammar in two waves: first in the early medieval period, and later in the modern contact periods. These features are the progressive or 'expanded' form of verbs and the *it*-cleft construction. We argue that the commonalities between the histories and later developments of these features are such that they provide evidence for continued contact influences between Celtic and English.

1 Introduction

The history of any language is bound to contain areas which, despite the best efforts of generations of linguists, still remain more or less controversial or open to debates. In the history of English, the question of Celtic influences in English grammar is one such area. What has in recent discussions been termed the "Celtic Hypothesis" (CH) has preoccupied the minds of both Anglicists and Celticists for well over a century now, but no consensus has yet been reached about the nature and extent of Celtic influences. There is of course the "traditional" view, according to which such influences are minimal especially in the domain of the grammar

---

Markku Filppula: Joensuu (Finland)
Juhani Klemola: Tampere (Finland)

and phonology of English. The same view, often repeated in textbooks on the history of English, holds that apart from place- and river-names Celtic elements in English are limited to about a dozen loanwords. Otto Jespersen, who can be considered one of the first and most eminent exponents of this view, explained the paucity of Celtic influence in English through the social, political, and cultural supremacy of the Anglo-Saxons over the conquered Britons; this meant that the ruling classes had no need to learn Celtic, whereas the Celts had to learn English – and according to him, very well – in order to serve their Anglo-Saxon masters (Jespersen 1905: 39).

Although Jespersen's view has gone almost unchallenged, with a few well-known exceptions, for well over a century now, the last couple of decades have witnessed a new rise of interest in the CH. It can be said to have started with a study by Patricia Poussa (see Poussa 1990) on the possible contact origin of so-called "periphrastic DO". This was followed by a host of other studies on this and several other phonological or syntactic features by a steadily increasing number of scholars. To give but some examples, Hickey (1995) discusses some possible Celtic "low-level" phonological and syntactic contact influences, while Tristram (1999) provides a more extensive survey of the general typological influence of Celtic on English syntax and morphophonology (e.g. loss of inflections). These were followed by an edited collection of articles in Filppula et al. (2002), which sought to address the issue of Celtic influences from various linguistic and historical perspectives. At about the same time, a series of articles appeared on specific features of English grammar. For example, Mittendorf and Poppe (2000) and Poppe (2003) consider possible Brythonic influence on the English progressive; Vennemann (2001) the so-called internal possessor construction; and van der Auwera and Genee (2002) periphrastic DO. The special issue of *English Language and Linguistics* (13[2]) guest-edited by Markku Filppula and Juhani Klemola and published in 2009 then opened the debate on a wider basis and contained several important articles on a wide range of syntactic and phonological features which can be argued to have their origins in early contacts between English and Celtic.

Yet another step in trying to find out the nature and extent of Celtic influences in English was the monograph *English and Celtic in Contact*, jointly authored by Markku Filppula, Juhani Klemola and Heli Paulasto (Filppula et al. 2008). Here for the first time the possible connections between the early medieval and early modern and modern Celtic influences were given a detailed treatment. Particularly noteworthy is their finding that, despite obvious problems involved in comparing grammatical systems across different time periods, it is the same kind of structures that seem to come up for discussion whether we are dealing with the earliest or the modern Celtic influences. As far as the latter are concerned, these influences are most manifest in what have in the literature come to be called the "Celtic Englishes" (CE). These are varieties of English that have arisen as a result of language shift in the formerly Celtic-speaking areas in Ireland, (some parts of) Scotland, Wales, and the Isle of Man. They are not by any means homogeneous but display so many similarities – and dissimilarities, for that matter – that can be explained by contacts with the respective Celtic languages that the term "Celtic English" is justified as a broad cover term for Celtic-influenced varieties of English. Indeed, it seems evident that the vigorous study of the CEs in the last couple of decades has greatly contributed to the recent rise of interest in the medieval contacts between English and Celtic, as well.

In this chapter, we discuss two syntactic features which in our view are likely to have arisen as a result of either direct or indirect (reinforcing) Celtic influence leaving its mark on English grammar in two waves, as it were: first in the early medieval period, and then in the modern contact periods. These features are the so-called progressive or "expanded" form of verbs (PF) and the so-called *it*-cleft construction. The commonalities between the histories and later developments of these features are such that they provide evidence for continued contact influences between Celtic and English.

2 The progressive or "expanded" form of verbs

2.1 Progressives in Celtic Englishes

Frequent use of the progressive form (PF) in contexts where Standard British English (StE) and most other varieties of English would opt for a simple present or past tense form of verbs is a characteristic feature of all the major varieties of Celtic Englishes today. Thus, in Celtic Englishes the PF can occur with so-called stative verbs, such as verbs of "cognition", "emotion", "inert perception", and "stance", as well as "relational" verbs of "being" and "having". Examples (1)–(7) are drawn from databases representing vernacular varieties of Irish English (IrE), Welsh English (WE), Hebridean English (HebE), and Manx English (MxE). All illustrate the use of the PF with verbs denoting states of affairs rather than dynamic activities in these contexts:

(1) *There was a lot about fairies long ago [...] but I'm thinkin' that most of 'em are vanished.*
'...but I think that most of them have vanished.' (IrE; cited in Filppula 1999: 89)

(2) *I think two of the lads was lost at sea during the War. They* were belonging *to the, them men here.* (IrE; cited in Filppula 2003: 162)

(3) *I'm* not thinking *much of it.*
'I'm not impressed by it.' (WE; cited in Parry 1999: 111)

(4) *They're* keeping *hens.* (WE; cited in Parry 1999: 111)

(5) *No, people don't need the weather like what they did then – they* were depending *on the weather.*
'…they depended on the weather.' (HebE; cited in Sabban 1982: 276)

(6) *And the people then* were having *plenty of potatoes and meal of their own.* (HebE; cited in Sabban 1982: 275)

(7) *It* was meaning *right the opposite.* (MxE; cited in Preuß 1999: 111)

Secondly, the PF is commonly used in these varieties with dynamic verbs to express present or past *habitual* activities or states of affairs. This is particularly common in some WE dialects but occurs in IrE and MxE as well, as seen in (8)–(10):

(8) [Interviewer: How, if you want to know how heavy a thing is, *> you must…]
[Informant:] *Yes, yes, <* we are- we are takin' it to the barn to weigh them.* (WE; cited in Paulasto 2006: 219)

(9) *…but there, there's no bogland here now.*
[Interviewer: Yeah. = And do people go up there to cut turf?]
They were going *there long ago but the roads got the, like everything else, they got a bit too-o rich and […].* (IrE; cited in Filppula 2003: 162)

(10) *I remember my grandfather and old people that lived down the road here, they* be *all* walking *over to the chapel of a Sunday afternoon and they* be going *again at night.* (MxE; cited in Preuß 1999: 112)

Thirdly, the PF frequently combines with the auxiliaries *would/'d/ used [to]* to indicate habitual activity. In other regional varieties of the British Isles Englishes, the simple infinitive is clearly preferred in these contexts. The following, (11) and (12), are IrE examples of this usage:

(11) *So, when the young lads'd be going to bathing, like, they'd have to go by his house, and they used to all, he u', he loved children.* (IrE; cited in Filppula 2003: 163)

(12) *But they, I heard my father and uncle saying they used be dancing there long ago, like, you know.* (IrE; cited in Filppula 2003: 163)

Fourthly, the PF can, depending on the variety, also be used with other auxiliaries, such as *do/does* and *will/'ll*. The former, exemplified in (13), is restricted to the Irish dialects of English, where it is used to express habitual events or states, while the latter, illustrated in (14), is common in other varieties, too, including StE and other "mainstream" Englishes. Its main function is to denote future events or states of affairs.

(13) *Yeah, that's, that's the camp. Military camp they call it [...] They do be shooting there couple of times a week or so.* (Wicklow: D.M.)

(14) *[T]his fellow now, Jack Lynch, that's going to come into power now, that he'll, he'll be forgetting the North.* (Wicklow: M.K.)

Wider use of the PF is also a feature of at least some educated CE varieties. Kirk et al. (2008) examined selected aspects of the use of the PF based on the spoken components of two of the so-called *International Corpus of English* corpora: one representing British Standard English (called ICE-GB), the other Irish Standard English (ICE-IRL). Although the frequencies of the PF with stative verbs in general were rather similar in these two varieties, there emerged some lexically based differences. Thus, statively used verbs such as *live* (in the sense 'reside') and *expect* (denoting probable or likely occurrence or appearance of something) turned out to occur more commonly with the PF in educated IrE than in BrE. Another striking difference was the more frequent use of the combination WILL/WOULD + *be* v-*ing* in IrE than in BrE. Filppula (2012) extends the quantitative study of these phenomena to cover the vernacular regional varieties of IrE, on the one hand, and similar varieties of traditional English English (EngE), on the other. This study reveals an even more marked difference between the two varieties not only with respect to WILL/WOULD + *be* v-*ing* but more generally with the use of the PF with modal auxiliaries.

The distinctiveness of the Irish varieties and other CEs *vis-à-vis* traditional regional varieties spoken in England seems clear enough but that does not in itself suffice to show that wider use of the PF has been set off by contacts with Celtic languages, or that Celtic contact is the sole explanatory factor. After all, it is well known that the rates of use of the PF have increased even in StE from the early Modern English period onwards, leading to a relaxing of some of the semantic constraints on its use (see Elsness 1994; Mair and Hundt 1995; Mair 2006). The same has happened in other varieties, e.g. in AmE, where this tendency is more pronounced than in BrE (see Śmiecińska 2002/2003). Some English-based creoles and various African and Asian varieties of English also seem to follow suit (see Gachelin 1997; Kortmann and Szmrecsanyi 2004). It is quite possible, then, that the high incidence of the PF in all these varieties is part of a more general cross-varietal (perhaps universal?) trend towards uses which are less sensitive to contextual constraints. However, as Thomason (2001: 92) points out, even similar linguistic outcomes may have different origins, and it would not be justified to rule out contact-induced change just because similar changes are found in other languages or varieties. Whether or not a given change is contact-induced depends on a number of both linguistic and language-external factors which can help us to differentiate between contact-induced and internally motivated linguistic change (for further discussion, see Thomason 2001: 91–95).

In the context of the British Isles, the shared linguistic characteristics of the varieties spoken in the formerly Celtic-speaking areas and the similarities in their genesis lead one to assume that the more extensive use of the PF in the CEs as compared with BrE has some connection with the corresponding Celtic systems. These favor the so-called "verbal noun construction", very similar in function to the English *-ing* form, in these kinds of context. Welsh, as Parry (1999: 111) explains, has a parallel construction consisting of YR + BOD 'be' + subject + YN 'in' + verb-noun, e.g. *Y mae ef yn canu pob dydd* 'He sings [literally: is [he] in sing/ singing] every day'. This according to Parry lies behind the tendency of some dialects of WE to use the PF to indicate habitual activity (see also Thomas 1994; Penhallurick 1996; Pitkänen 2003). Irish, too, has a verbal-noun construction which provides a model for some of the IrE usages (see Filppula 2003), and the same is true of Scottish Gaelic and Manx, which have most probably then led to parallel features in the corresponding local varieties of English (for HebE and its Gaelic heritage in this respect, see Sabban 1982; for Scots and Scottish English in general, Macafee and Ó Baoill 1997; for MxE, Barry 1994 [1984]; Broderick 1997; Preuß 1999). It is interesting to note that Celtic influence on all of these varieties is also supported by Mossé (1938), who is otherwise very critical towards the idea of early Celtic influence on English syntax. Having discarded the Celtic hypothesis with regard to the earliest, medieval, forms of the English PF, he states that the abundant use of the PF in the English of Ireland, Scotland, and Wales in the modern period probably derives from the parallel tendency in Insular Celtic (Mossé 1938, II Section 106). Mossé's view invites us to look closer into the early medieval situation and the emergence of the PF.

2.2 The rise of the progressive form in early English

Although Mossé's scepticism over the possibility of early Celtic influence on the PF in medieval English has been shared by many Anglicists (cf. Mustanoja 1960; Nickel 1966), there are a number of scholars who have suggested that the rise of the PF in Middle English is due to contacts with the Celtic languages. Some of the earliest and most influential studies exploring the Celtic connection of the English PF are Keller (1925), Dal (1952), Preusler (1956), Wagner (1959), and Braaten (1967). According to Keller (1925), the use of the verbal noun as the predicate of the verb *be* gradually led to the emergence of the so-called progressive form during the ME period. As a further factor speaking for Celtic influence on the English PF Keller observes that the English progressive form *to be (a) doing* has no parallels in the other Germanic languages, except for the Low German dialect of Westfalish and Dutch folk-speech, which, however, rely on the infinitive instead of the verbal noun or the *-ing* form.

Writing both before and after World War II, Walther Preusler (our source here Preusler 1956) follows in Keller's footsteps, and generally speaking, concurs with Keller's account. As new evidence speaking for Celtic influence on the English PF, he mentions the early attestation of the verbal-noun construction in northern English and Scottish dialects and also draws attention to the strong preservation of this construction in Scottish English even today. According to him, this regional distribution pattern undermines the plausibility of the rival explanations based on either independent development (the stand adopted, e.g. in Curme 1912), French influence (Einenkel 1914), or Latin/Greek influence (Mossé 1938). Dal (1952) continues the line of inquiry opened by Keller and Preusler. Like Keller, Dal notes the verbal-noun characteristics shared by the English PF and the Celtic periphrastic constructions, and the unique nature of the English construction among Germanic languages. However, unlike Keller, who posits a rather late date for the development of the English PF, Dal traces its origins much further back, arguing that the verbal noun already emerged as a grammatical category in the OE period under the influence of the Celtic periphrastic constructions. According to her, the OE "verbal abstract" ending *-ung/-ing* had been used in especially some northern OE texts as a verbal noun, preceded by the verb *be*, and also governed by a preposition; in other words, in periphrastic constructions which resemble the progressive form. As an illustration, Dal cites the sentence *cwæð sum hālig biscop, þa he wæs on sāwlunga*, '... when he was on the point of expiring', from an early Mercian text (*Old English Martyrology* 124.21; cited in Dal 1952: 37). Although there are differing views on the progressive interpretation of this example (see Braaten 1967: 176 for discussion), Dal takes it to indicate that already in OE the *-ung/-ing*-form had started to encroach on the territory of the present participle, realised by *-ande/-ende*, and was in fact beginning to merge with it, especially in texts written in northern areas which were not so strongly dominated by the West-Saxon literary tradition.

Writing much later, Braaten (1967) follows up the line of argumentation put forward in the previous research and especially in that by Dal. Like Dal, he argues that, when the English PF (or "continuous tense", as he calls it) began to develop, it was based on the type *wæs on sāwlunga* rather than the type **wæs sāwlende*. He emphasizes, however, that the "progressive" meaning of the OE construction could hardly have been as precise as that of the present-day PF (Braaten 1967: 176). In conclusion, Braaten provides a summary of the most important factors which according to him show that the ModE PF could not have developed out of the OE present participle construction and cannot be properly explained without assuming some degree of Celtic influence:

(i) Modern English continuous tenses are clearly durative, while the OE phrase could be used to replace either a durative or a perfective verb – probably for dramatic effect.
(ii) The Modern English *-ing* participle (originally a verbal abstract) is different in nature from the OE *-ende* participle.
(iii) In other Germanic languages, the construction *be* + present participle never developed into anything like continuous tense.
(iv) The similarity between Modern English continuous tenses and corresponding constructions in Cymric is too striking to be purely coincidental.
(v) Continuous tenses tend to be used more in bilingual or formerly Celtic-speaking areas than in other parts of the country. (Braaten 1967: 180)

While surprisingly few Anglicists have given serious attention to the Celtic hypothesis, it is perhaps more understandable that very few scholars on the Celticist side have touched on the similarities between the Celtic and the English periphrastic progressive constructions and their possible common roots. Wagner (1959) must be mentioned as one of the first who explicitly discusses these commonalities in terms of some kind of contact effects. According to him, the rise of the English PF marks a typological change from the Anglo-Saxon and Germanic verbal system and has to be seen in the context of parallel developments in the Celtic languages. Indeed, he considers these developments to have led to the emergence of a typically British verbal type, where the term "British" embraces both the Celtic languages and English (Wagner 1959: 150–51).

Wagner's view, which can be regarded as a forerunner of present-day "areal linguistics", has become an object of fresh interest in recent years, both among Anglicists or general linguists and Celticists (see Tristram 1999; Vennemann 2001;

Filppula 2002; Mittendorf and Poppe 2000; Poppe 2003). While Tristram is content to note the possible connection between the rise of the English PF and its parallels in Welsh, pending more detailed work on it (Tristram 1999: 23), Vennemann is convinced that the former cannot be explained without assuming influence from the parallel Welsh constructions (Vennemann 2001: 355). Filppula (2002) considers Celtic substratum influence likely but wants to keep open the possibility that the PF and its Celtic parallels are, as suggested by Wagner, a result of adstratal developments shared by English and the Celtic languages.

Yet, by far the most thorough treatments of the subject on the Celticist side are those provided by Mittendorf and Poppe (2000), Poppe (2002) and Poppe (2003), who examine the putative Celtic and especially Middle Welsh parallels to the English PF against the background of their syntactic and functional features. They conclude that there are "striking formal similarities between the Insular Celtic and English periphrastic constructions" and, even more importantly, establish that "striking similarities also exist between their functional ranges in the medieval languages" (Mittendorf and Poppe 2000: 139). This last statement refers to the uses of the periphrastic constructions to express not only processivity, the basic function of the periphrastic constructions, but also what these authors call "expressivity" or "foregrounding" in narrative discourse and "habituality". Poppe (2002) elaborates on the possibility of semantic influence from Celtic and suggests that, if there was any such influence, it would stem from the imperfective meaning inherent to the Celtic progressive construction. In his subsequent work (Poppe 2003), he investigates in some detail the oft-mentioned putative parallels in Germanic dialects and also discusses the progressive constructions in Greek, Latin, and Romance languages. Although the results of these three studies generally point to at least some degree of Celtic contact influences, the authors formulate their conclusions in rather cautious terms. Poppe (2003) considers language contact to be a possible explanation for the rise of the English progressive, given the formal and functional parallels between English and the Celtic languages and the co-existence of the Celtic and English populations in the British Isles over a long period of time. However, he adds that it is not a necessary explanation because of the various types of more or less similar progressive constructions in many other Germanic languages or dialects (Poppe 2003: 84).

It is obvious that there is no simple answer to the question of the nature and extent of Celtic influences on the English PF. However, on the basis of our survey of the existing evidence, the following emerge as established facts that can be used to support the Celtic hypothesis (see also Filppula 2003):

(i) Of all the suggested parallels to the English PF, the Celtic (Brythonic) ones are clearly the closest, and hence, the most plausible ones, whether one thinks of

the OE periphrastic constructions or those established in the ME and modern periods, involving the *-ing* form of verbs. This fact has not been given due weight in some of the earlier work on this subject.
(ii) The chronological precedence of the Celtic constructions is beyond any reasonable doubt, which also enhances the probability of contact influence from Celtic on English.
(iii) The socio-historical circumstances of the Celtic–English interface cannot have constituted an obstacle to Celtic substratum influences in the area of grammar, as has traditionally been argued especially on the basis of the paucity of lexical borrowings from Celtic languages. On the contrary, recent research (and some of the earlier, too) has shown that the language shift situation in the centuries following the settlement of the Germanic tribes in Britain was most conducive to such influences. Again, this aspect has been ignored or not properly understood in some of the research which has tried to play down the role of Celtic influence in the history of English.
(iv) The Celtic–English contacts in the modern period have resulted in a similar tendency for some regional varieties of English to make extensive use of the PF, which lends indirect support to the Celtic hypothesis with regard to early English.
(v) The typological shift of English towards analytical structures, which it shares with its Celtic neighbors, increases the likelihood of Celtic influences on English grammar in general, and on the development of the PF, in particular.

3 The *it*-cleft construction

3.1 The rise of the *it*-cleft construction in English

Like the progressive construction discussed in the previous section, the *it*-cleft construction or "*it*-clefting" for short is a robust feature of some varieties of the Celtic Englishes, especially those spoken in Ireland, the Isle of Man, and the Hebrides, while in Welsh English the same tendency is realized by "simple" fronting or "(focus) topicalization" (see the discussion in Section 3.2). This commonality between the Celtic Englishes may therefore be of some interest from the point of view of the earliest contacts between English and the Celtic languages, too. As will be shown in the following discussion, the earliest examples of the *it*-cleft construction are found in the Old English (OE) period, but what is significant from the point of view of possible contact effects is its rather late emergence, as compared with that of its Celtic counterparts. Let us first briefly survey the history of the *it*-cleft construction in English. This should give us a better basis for considering the possible role of language contact here and its implications for the modern contacts, as well.

In some traditional accounts of the history of English syntax, *it*-clefts have been described as having been almost non-existent in the OE period. For example, Mitchell (1985: Section 1486) states *tout court* that the OE texts contain no examples of constructions with anticipatory *it* similar to the ModE *It's food that I want (not something else)*. He discusses Visser's (1963–73: Section 63) examples with *þæt* as the introductory pronoun in cleft-type constructions but does evidently not consider them examples of genuine clefts. Visser, however, provides several instances of clefted structures from OE onwards under the heading "It is father who did it". He notes that in OE introductory *hit* is sometimes omitted or, in some cases, replaced by *þæt* (Visser 1963–73: Section 63), which probably explains why Mitchell does not accept them as clefts. Traugott (1992), on her part, mentions Mitchell's negative stand on the existence of *hit*-clefting in OE but draws attention to Visser's examples with anticipatory *þæt*. However, she leaves open the question whether Visser's examples should be considered similar to the structures introduced by anticipatory *it* in later English (Traugott 1992: 280).

By far the most thorough treatment of clefts in OE and ME is Ball (1991), who presents a detailed analysis of "cleft-like" constructions from their earliest beginnings. Her discussion confirms that the cleft construction is a feature of OE but that its frequencies remain very small in that period. In other words, it can be considered an innovation in OE. Like Mitchell (1985), she finds no *hit*-clefts which would perfectly match the stereotypical Modern English *it*-cleft with specificational reading, and especially of the "stressed-focus" type (Ball 1991: 45) where the focus of the cleft construction is presented as "new" information, while the *that*-clause represents presupposed or "given" information (see Prince 1978 for this distinction). She does, however, note one possible exception, which according to her could be considered an instance of *it*-clefting in this sense. This is the example, (15), cited, but discarded, by Mitchell (1985: Section 2135) from Ælfric.

(15) *þa cwædon þa geleafullan,*
    '*Nis   hit   na   Petrus   þæt   þær   cnucað,   ac   is   his   ængel.*'
    not-is it-n. not Peter-m. REL-n. there knocks but is his angel-m.
    'Then the faithful said: It isn't Peter who is knocking there, but his angel.'
    (ÆCHom I.517–18.1; here cited from Ball 1991: 39–40)

Ball's study also reveals differences in the dates of appearance of different syntactic types of *it*-clefts: for example, pronoun-focus *hit*-clefts are not attested until the early 13th century (Ball 1991: 45). The so-called "informative-presupposition" *hit*-clefts (in which it is the relative clause rather than the focus constituent that represents new information; see Prince 1978 for this term) are even later according to Ball (1991).

Another study seeking to trace the development of *it*-clefting in English is Filppula (2009), which is based on *The York-Toronto-Helsinki Corpus of Old English Prose* (YCOE) and *The Penn-Helsinki Parsed Corpus of Middle English*, second edition (PPCME2). Both are syntactically-annotated using the same form of annotation and can be accessed by the same search engine, called Corpus-Search. YCOE consists of 1.5 million words, while PPCME2 has approximately 1.2 million words of running text.

Filppula's searches through these corpora showed that, much in line with Ball (1991) but contrary to especially Mitchell (1985), both OE and ME texts contain a wide range of clefted structures displaying different kinds and orders of the key constituents but sharing the same basic structure and semantic properties. In YCOE, the corpus search yielded a total of 89 instances of structures parsed by the compilers of this corpus as clefts; this gives a normalized frequency of 5.9 instances per 100,000 words of text. Clefts were found in 17 out of the 108 text samples in the corpus. Semantically and pragmatically, the clefts found in YCOE represent, in modern terms, either stressed-focus or informative-presupposition clefts, and hence, are functionally rather versatile. From the contact-linguistic point of view it is interesting to note that, although the majority of instances were found in texts based on Latin originals (mainly because of the predominance of "time-clefts" in Bede), as many as 15 occurred in non-translations and were spread over six different texts.

A similar search run on the PPCME2 corpus produced 96 tokens of clefts, which means a normalized frequency of 8.0 per 10,000 words. This indicates a noticeable rise n the frequencies of clefts from OE to ME and confirms that clefts are, indeed, an innovation in the OE period and gain momentum in ME. Another factor supporting this view is the more even distribution of clefted structures across text samples in PPCME2 as compared with YCOE. This, too, suggests a general increase in the rates of use of clefting in the ME period. Some quantitative and qualitative differences also emerged between the clefts in YCOE and PPCME2 that suggest a more advanced stage in the grammaticalization of this feature in the latter period. Thus, ME clefts seem to be syntactically less constrained than their OE counterparts. For examples, pronouns often occur in the focus position, and the same holds for objects and adverbial prepositional phrases which are more frequent in these positions than in OE. In most other respects, the ME clefts found in PPCME2 exhibit the same essential characteristics as their OE counterparts. The dialectal distribution of the occurrences does not allow any straightforward conclusions, but it is of some interest to note that as many as 24 were found in texts from the West Midlands or the northern areas, with many of these dating to the early part of the 13th century.

As mentioned above, one of the major factors suggesting contact-influences between Celtic and English with respect to clefting is the chronological precedence of the Celtic parallel constructions. Clefting has a long history in the Celtic languages, reaching most probably further back than their recorded history. Our sources for Old Welsh syntax and word order patterns are rather scanty as compared with those for Old Irish, (see Willis 1998: 7–11), but there is enough evidence to show that clefting has been a characteristic feature of the Brythonic branch of Celtic from very early on. Pedersen (1913: Section 547, p. 239) writes that both Irish and British (i.e. the ancestor of Welsh) use what he calls "relative inversion" (German *Umschreibung*) for the purposes of emphasis. In more recent work, Tristram (2002: 132, 134) cites examples of clefting from the 10th-century prose work entitled the *Computus Fragment*, e.g. *is did ciman ha c(e)i* (Comp. 2) 'it is a full day that thou wilt get', *Is Aries isid in arcimeir [.e.]* (Comp. 9) 'It is Aries that is opposite [e]'.

In Irish, there is no shortage of evidence for clefting from early on. Thus, Mac Eoin (1993: 137) states that clefting is "a very common construction [...] at all periods". Thurneysen (1975: 492–494) cites several examples from the mid-8th century Würzburg Glosses, and similar constructions are found in the somewhat later Milan Glosses. Similar findings are available in more recent research, e.g. Mac Cone (1979: 13–14) presents evidence showing that the use of cleft sentences for marking a constituent arose even before the generalisation of the initial verbal complex. Another detailed study is Mac Coisdealbha (1998), which provides ample evidence to demonstrate the prominent role of the cleft sentence in Old Irish syntax. For example, in the Würzburg material alone, the number of instances of clefts turns out to be "an imposing ca. 300" (Mac Coisdealbha 1998: 143), divided between several formal classes depending on the type of constituent put in the focus position: nominal or pronominal phrase (both in subject or object position), prepositional phrase, adjective, adverb, subordinate clause, etc.

Besides the chronological precedence of Celtic clefts, another factor speaking for Celtic contacts is that the Celtic clefts are both structurally and functionally close enough to their English counterparts to make them likely sources of syntactic transfer in an intense language contact situation like the one which in all probability existed for the first few centuries after the Germanic invasions of Britain began in the mid-5th century CE (for illustration, see Filppula 2009). In this respect, and despite the changes in the grammatical systems of both Celtic and English over the centuries, the situation in the early periods of contact closely resembles that witnessed in the emergence of the modern-day Celtic Englishes.

A third type of evidence strongly suggesting contact influences is areal and typological in nature. One of the first to discuss the cleft construction from this perspective is the Celticist Heinrich Wagner (1959), who notes what he calls a "geolinguistic connection" (*ein sprach-geographischer Zusammenhang*) between the French *mise en relief* construction (*c'est*-clefting) and its Insular Celtic parallels. According to Wagner, in both Celtic and French the *mise en relief* construction is an established part of the grammatical system and is closely connected with other systems, most notably those for forming questions in both of these (groups of) languages (Wagner 1959: 173–175). Wagner does not comment on the rise of the English cleft construction in this connection, but mentions the frequent use of clefts in Hiberno-English (i.e. Irish English), which according to him depends on the corresponding Irish usage. This tendency is, incidentally, also noted by Visser (1963–73: Section 64), although he, too, stops short of passing judgment on the possible implications of the modern contacts for the explaining of the early medieval ones. These will be discussed further in Section 3.2.

Besides Wagner, many others have since commented on the areal and typological dimensions of the question at hand. Thus, Ahlqvist (1977) sees such a connection between the Celtic languages, English and French, all of which have grammaticalized the cleft construction. He suggests that the CC in these languages may ultimately derive from Celtic where it has been attested earlier than in any other of these languages. Wehr (2001) goes even farther to propose that there is what she terms a *westlich-atlantischer Sprachbund*, involving the Celtic languages, French, and Portuguese as its "extreme types", while English represents a more "moderate" type. A central diagnostic feature of this *Sprachbund* according to Wehr is the weakening of the individual word, a tendency which involves several phonological processes such as sandhi phenomena, *enchaînement*, *liaison*, elision, and fusion. It is this loss of autonomy of the individual word which then explains the prominent status of clefting in these languages. English, according to Wehr, is an interesting "halfway house" in this respect: it preserves the possibility of "word accent" and can thus use prosodic means for emphasis, yet it has developed the cleft construction, unlike German, which is not part of Wehr's *Sprachbund*. The fact that English has in this respect diverged from its other Germanic sisters strongly suggests external, i.e. contact-based, influences, where Celtic and French are the two possible main sources. Of these, Celtic can be considered the more likely source because of the much earlier attestation of clefts there than in French texts. In fact, even certain types of English clefts (such as those with pronoun foci) antedate their French counterparts according to Ball (1991), who does not therefore consider French to have been the source of clefts in English (1991: 280).

To sum up so far, major factors speaking for Celtic contact influence on English are chronological precedence of Celtic clefts and closer resemblance between the English cleft construction and the Brythonic ones than the French or Latin ones. A third factor is prominence of clefting in present-day and earlier Celtic-influenced varieties of English, which is the topic of Section 3.2.

3.2 *It*-clefts in the modern-day "Celtic Englishes"

As already noted, many scholars have observed the frequent use of the *it*-cleft construction in especially modern Irish English in contexts in which speakers of other varieties of English would use sentence stress or other means of emphasis. Of course, this construction is, and has for a long time, been part of Standard English (StE) grammar, but what gives Irish English and some of the other Celtic Englishes a distinctive flavor is that the uses of the *it*-cleft construction are both functionally and syntactically less restricted than in StE, in particular. In this respect, they behave much like their Celtic counterparts, which is a major factor speaking for Celtic substratum influence. A detailed and corpus-based study of clefts in spoken dialects of IrE was given in Filppula (1986) where clefts were found to be the most frequent and functionally as well as syntactically most varied in those dialects which were closest to Irish-speaking areas in the west and south-west of Ireland. The following examples from Filppula (1986) and a somewhat later study of south-western IrE dialects by Ó hÚrdail (1997) illustrate the relative syntactic freedom of IrE from some of the syntactic constraints of StE and of most other varieties of English, for that matter. Thus, a part of a verb phrase, as in (16) and (17), an adverb of manner, as in (18), or a reflexive pronoun, as in (20) further below, can occur in the focus position of clefts in these varieties:

(16) *It is* looking *for more land they are.* (Filppula 1986: 136)

(17) *Tis* joking *you are, I suppose.* (Ó hÚrdail 1997: 190)

(18) *Tis* well *you looked.* (Ó hÚrdail 1997: 190)

In this connection it is important to note that these types of *it*-clefts have evidently been part of vernacular IrE grammar from early on, as is shown by (19) from a 17th-century depiction of an Irish sermon by John Dunton, and by (20), which is from a 19th-century letter written by a member of the Oldham family from West Cork:

(19) *Dear Catolicks, you shee here de cause dat is after bringing you to dis plaace: 'tis come bourying you are de corp, de cadaver, of a verie good woman, ...* (John Dunton, *Report of a Sermon*, 1698; quoted here from Bliss 1979: 133)

(20) *Don't blame me for Robert's not going out lastyear [last year] It was himself that would not go and the reason he gave was...* (*The Oldham Papers*, No. 8, 1854; Trinity College MS 10,435/8; cited in Filppula 1999: 256)

The Celtic connection of IrE clefts is also confirmed by very similar evidence from some other Celtic Englishes, most notably Hebridean English (HebE). The following examples recorded from local speakers in Tiree and Skye, both part of the Inner Hebrides off the west coast of Scotland, illustrate the close affinity between these varieties, as in (21) and (22):

(21) *And this day I happened to be doing something, I think it was* painting *I was*. (Odlin 1997: 40)

(22) *Och, it's* myself *that's glad to see you* [...]. (Sabban 1982: 374)

Welsh varieties of English (cf. Williams, Chapter 126), collectively known as "Welsh English" (WE), differ from IrE and HebE (or Manx English, for that matter) in that there instead of *it*-clefts the preferred means of expressing emphasis is a simple word order shift, or more precisely, "fronting" of the constituent to be highlighted. Other terms for this phenomenon include "predicate fronting" (see Williams 2000) or "focus fronting" (see Paulasto 2006). The following examples, (23) and (24), from WE illustrate this usage:

(23) Welsh *we are, see*. (Williams 2000: 224)
   '[Explanation of speaker's and husband's slightly eccentric behavior]'

(24) *... we were sitting up just there just the two of us* [...] *and er*, chatting *we were and I said...* (Paulasto 2006: 162)

Though formally distinct from the *it*-cleft construction, the WE usage reflects the same tendency for the most prominent and focal items in an utterance to be placed at the beginning of the utterance as in the other CEs. The Welsh background is evident: as Thomas (1994: 37) writes, the corresponding Welsh structures rely "universally" on fronting of a constituent rather than clefting. What is presented as "new" or otherwise prominent information by the speaker can readily be put in clause-initial position, a practice which is characteristic of Welsh and the other Celtic languages (see also Williams 2000).

4 Summary

In this chapter we have discussed the emergence and later developments of two syntactic features of English which, as we have tried to argue, have a "Celtic connection" reaching over a time-span of one and a half millennia, viz. the progressive or "expanded" form of verbs and the *it*-cleft construction.

Our method has been bidirectional, as it were: for the progressive our starting-point was the uses of the PF in the modern-day Celtic Englishes, from which we worked our way backwards to the emergence of the progressive in the earliest periods of contact between English and Celtic. Like Braaten (1967) referred to in Section 2.2, we believe that the similarities between the outcomes of the Celtic–English contacts in the modern period can be used as an indirect piece of evidence speaking for Celtic contact influence in the early medieval contact situation. The functional range of the PF as it is used in the varieties of English spoken in the (earlier or present-day) Celtic-speaking areas of the British Isles is strikingly similar to that of the respective Celtic languages, which then provides a plausible explanation for the more extensive use of the PF in the CEs as compared especially with the traditional EngE dialects. However, as noted above, Celtic influence need not be the sole explanation for the more extensive use of the PF in these varieties. Another factor to be considered is the current trend in many other varieties of English beyond the British Isles and Ireland towards uses which are less sensitive to contextual constraints. Turning back to the early contacts, functional similarity between the corresponding constructions in the medieval languages is also so obvious, as Mittendorf and Poppe (2000) have shown, that Celtic contact influence is quite possible. Areal and typological considerations give additional weight to this line of reasoning: the development of the PF in English follows a path which is not found in other Germanic languages, especially standard German. It is true that there are partial parallels to the English PF in some German and Dutch dialects, but they involve an infinitive rather than a verbal noun type of construction and hence are not based on the same kind of merger of the present participle and gerund as is the case with the English construction.

In our discussion of the *it*-cleft construction, we have used the opposite method of starting off with the first appearances of this construction and proceeding thence in the "normal" manner from the past to the present. As in the case of the PF, the *it*-cleft construction belongs to the set of syntactic features which is shared by English and Celtic, but not by most other Germanic sisters of English. It is also a salient feature of most Celtic Englishes (with some formal variations, though), which suggests external, i.e. contact-based, influences in both periods. The evidence for Celtic contact influence on early English is stronger here than in the case of the PF. The chronological precedence of the corresponding Celtic constructions is well documented, and the structural parallelism is very obvious. There is also sufficient data available in early English texts, which makes it possible to trace the development and gradual formal and functional diversification of the *it*-cleft construction in the later centuries.

5 References

Ahlqvist, Anders. 1977. Typological notes on Irish word-order. In: Paul J. Hopper (ed.), *Studies in Descriptive and Historical Linguistics. Festschrift for Winfred P. Lehmann*, 267–281. Amsterdam/Philadelphia: John Benjamins.
van der Auwera, Johan and Inge Genee. 2002. English *do*: on the convergence of languages and linguists. *English Language and Linguistics* 6.2: 283–307.
Ball, Catherine N. 1991. *The Historical Development of the* it-*cleft*, University of Pennsylvania Dissertation in Linguistics. Ann Arbor, MI: University Microfilms International.
Barry, Michael V. 1994 [1984]. Manx English. In: Peter Trudgill (ed.), *Language in the British Isles*, 167–177. Cambridge: Cambridge University Press.
Bliss, Alan J. 1979. *Spoken English in Ireland 1600–1740*. Dublin: The Dolmen Press.
Braaten, Bjorn. 1967. Notes on continuous tenses in English. *Norsk Tidsskrift for Sprogvidenskap* XXI: 167–180.
Broderick, George. 1997. Manx English: An overview. In: Hildegard L.C. Tristram (ed.), *Celtic Englishes*, 123–134. Heidelberg: Winter.
Burchfield, Robert (ed.). 1994. *The Cambridge History of the English Language*. Vol. 5: *English in Britain and Overseas. Origins and Development*. Cambridge: Cambridge University Press.
Curme, George O. 1912. History of the English gerund. *Englische Studien* 45: 349–380.
Dal, Ingerid. 1952. Zur Entstehung des englischen Participium Praesentis auf -*ing*. *Norsk Tidsskrift for Sprogvidenskap* 16: 5–116.
Einenkel, Eugen. 1914. Die Entwickelung des englischen Gerundiums. *Anglia* 38: 1–76.
Elsness, Johan. 1994. On the progression of the progressive in early Modern English. *ICAME Journal* 18: 5–25.
Filppula, Markku. 1986. *Some Aspects of Hiberno-English in a Functional Sentence Perspective*. Joensuu: University of Joensuu.
Filppula, Markku. 1999. *The Grammar of Irish English. Language in Hibernian Style*. London: Routledge.
Filppula, Markku. 2002. *The English progressive on the move*. Paper presented at the 12th International Conference on English Historical Linguistics, Glasgow, 22–26 August 2002.
Filppula, Markku. 2003. More on the English progressive and the Celtic connection. In: Hildegard L.C. Tristram (ed.), 150–168.
Filppula, Markku. 2009. The rise of it-clefting in English: areal-typological and contact-linguistic considerations. *English Language and Linguistics* 13(2): 267–293.

Filppula, Markku 2012 Exploring grammatical differences between Irish and British English. In: Bettina Migge and Máire Ní Chíosáin (eds.), *New Perspectives on Irish English*, 85–100. Amsterdam/Philadelphia: John Benjamins.

Filppula, Markku and Juhani Klemola (eds.). 2009. *Re-evaluating the Celtic Hypothesis: A Special Issue of English Language and Linguistics* 13(2).

Filppula, Markku, Juhani Klemola, and Heli Pitkänen (eds.). 2002. *The Celtic Roots of English*. Joensuu: University of Joensuu.

Filppula, Markku, Juhani Klemola, and Heli Paulasto. 2008. *English and Celtic in Contact*. New York/London: Routledge.

Gachelin, Jean-Marc. 1997. The progressive and habitual aspects in non-standard Englishes. In: Edgar W. Schneider (ed.), *Englishes Around the World*, Vol. 2: *Caribbean, Africa, Asia, Australasia. Studies in Honour of Manfred Görlach*, 33–46. Amsterdam/Philadelphia: John Benjamins.

Hickey, Raymond. 1995. Early contact and parallels between English and Celtic. *Vienna English Working Papers* 4: 87–119.

Jespersen, Otto. 1905. *Growth and Structure of the English Language*. Leipzig: B.G. Teubner.

Keller, Wolfgang. 1925. Keltisches im englischen Verbum. In: *Anglica: Untersuchungen zur englischen Philologie, Bd. 1: Sprache und Kulturgeschichte*, 55–66. Leipzig: Mayer and Müller.

Kirk, John M., Jeffrey L. Kallen, and Markku Filppula. 2008. *The Progressive in British and Irish Standard English*. Paper read at Methods XIII, Leeds, August 2008.

Klemola, Juhani, Merja Kytö, and Matti Rissanen (eds.). 1996. *Speech Past and Present. Studies in English Dialectology in Memory of Ossi Ihalainen*. Frankfurt am Main: Peter Lang.

Kortmann, Bernd and Benedikt Szmrecsanyi. 2004. Global synopsis: morphological and syntactic variation in English. In: Bernd Kortmann, Kate Burridge, Rajend Mesthrie, Edgar W. Schneider, and Clive Upton (eds.), *A Handbook of Varieties of English*, Vol. 2: *Morphology and Syntax*, 1142–1202. Berlin/New York: Mouton de Gruyter.

Macafee, Caroline and Colm Ó Baoill. 1997. Why Scots is not a Celtic English. In: Hildegard L. C. Tristram (ed.), 245–286.

Mac Coisdealbha, Pádraig. 1998. *The syntax of the sentence in Old Irish: Selected studies from a descriptive, historical and comparative point of view*. Tübingen: Niemeyer.

Mac Cone, Kim Robert. 1979. Pretonic preverbs and the absolute verbal endings in Old Irish. *Ériu* 30: 1–34.

Mac Eoin, Geroid. 1993. Irish. In: Martin J. Ball (ed.), *The Celtic Languages*, 101–144. London: Routledge.

Mair, Christian. 2006. *Twentieth-century English*. Cambridge: Cambridge University Press.

Mair, Christian and Marianne Hundt. 1995. Why is the progressive becoming more frequent in English? *Zeitschrift für Anglistik und Amerikanistik* XLIII: 111–122.

Mitchell, Bruce. 1985. *Old English Syntax*, Vol. 1. Oxford: Clarendon Press.

Mittendorf, Ingo and Erich Poppe. 2000. Celtic contacts of the English progressive? In: Hildegard L.C. Tristram (ed.), 117–145.

Mossé, Fernand. 1938. *Histoire de la Forme Périphrastique Être + Participe Présent en Germanique. Deuxième Partie: Moyen-Anglais et Anglais Moderne*. Paris: Librairie C. Klincksieck.

Mustanoja, Tauno F. 1960. *A Middle English Syntax, Part I: Parts of Speech*. Helsinki: Société Néophilologique.

Nickel, Gerhard. 1966. *Die Expanded Form im Altenglischen: Vorkommen, Funktion und Herkunft der Umschreibung 'beon/wesan' + Partizip Präsens*. Neumünster: Karl Wachholtz Verlag.

Odlin, Terence. 1997. Bilingualism and substrate influence: a look at clefts and reflexives. In: Jeffrey L. Kallen (ed.), *Focus on Ireland*, 35–50. Amsterdam/Philadelphia: John Benjamins.
Ó hÚrdail, Roibeárd. 1997. Hiberno-English: historical background and synchronic features and variation. In: Hildegard L. C. Tristram (ed.), 180–200.
Parry, David. 1999. A Grammar and Glossary of Conservative Anglo-Welsh Dialects of Rural Wales. *NATCECT, Occasional Publications*, No. 8: University of Sheffield.
Paulasto, Heli. 2006. *Welsh English Syntax: Contact and Variation*. Joensuu: Joensuu University Press.
Pedersen, Holger. 1913. *Vergleichende Grammatik der keltischen Sprachen*. Göttingen: Vandenhoeck and Ruprecht.
Penhallurick, Robert. 1996. The grammar of northern Welsh English: progressive verb phrases. In: Juhani Klemola, Merja Kytö, and Matti Rissanen (eds.), *Speech Past and Present: Studies in English Dialectology in Memory of Ossi Ihalainen*, 308–342. Frankfurt am Main: Peter Lang.
Pitkänen, Heli. 2003. Non-standard uses of the progressive form in Welsh English: an apparent time study. In: Hildegard L. C. Tristram (ed.), 111–128.
Poppe, Erich. 2002. The 'expanded form' in Insular Celtic and English: Some historical and comparative considerations, with special emphasis on Middle Irish. In: Markku Filppula, Juhani Klemola, and Heli Pitkänen (eds.), *The Celtic Roots of English*, 237–270. Joensuu: University of Joensuu.
Poppe, Erich. 2003. Progress on the progressive? A report. In: Hildegard L.C. Tristram (ed.), 65–84.
Poussa, Patricia. 1990. A contact-universals origin for periphrastic *do*, with special consideration of OE-Celtic contact. In: Sylvia Adamson, Vivian Law, Nigel Vincent, and Susan Wright (eds.), *Papers from the 5th International Conference on English Historical Linguistics, Cambridge, 6–9 April 1987*, 407–434. Amsterdam/Philadelphia: John Benjamins.
Preusler, Walther. 1956. Keltischer Einfluss im Englischen. *Revue des Langages Vivantes* 22: 322–350.
Preuß, Martina. 1999. *Remaining Lexical and Syntactic Borrowings from Manx Gaelic in Present Day Manx English, Master of Philosophy Thesis*. Liverpool: University of Liverpool.
Prince, Ellen F. 1978. A comparison of WH-clefts and it-clefts in discourse. *Language* 54: 883–906.
Sabban, Annette. 1982. *Gälisch-Englischer Sprachkontakt*. Heidelberg: Julius Groos.
Śmiecińska, Joanna. 2002/2003. Stative verbs and the progressive aspect in English. *Poznań Studies in Contemporary Linguistics* 38: 187–195.
Thomas, Alan R. 1994. English in Wales. In: Robert Burchfield (ed.), *The Cambridge History of the English Language*, 94–147. Cambridge: Cambridge University Press.
Thomason, Sarah G. 2001. *Language Contact: An Introduction*. Edinburgh: Edinburgh University Press.
Thurneysen, Rudolf. 1975. *A grammar of Old Irish*. Dublin: Dublin Institute for Advanced Studies.
Traugott, Elizabeth Closs. 1992. Syntax. In: Richard M. Hogg (ed.), *The Cambridge History of the English Language*, Vol. 1: *The Beginnings to 1066*, 168–289. Cambridge: Cambridge University Press.
Tristram, Hildegard L.C. (ed.). 1997. *The Celtic Englishes*. Heidelberg: Universitätsverlag C. Winter.
Tristram, Hildegard L.C. 1999. *How Celtic is Standard English?* St. Petersburg: Nauka.
Tristram, Hildegard L.C. (ed.). 2000. *The Celtic Englishes II*. Heidelberg: Universitätsverlag C. Winter.

Tristram, Hildegard L.C. 2002. Attrition of inflections in English and Welsh. In: Markku Filppula, Juhani Klemola, and Heli Pitkänen (eds.), 111–149.
Tristram, Hildegard L.C. (ed.). 2003. *The Celtic Englishes III*. Heidelberg: Universitätsverlag C. Winter.
Vennemann, Theo. 2001. Atlantis Semitica: Structural contact features in Celtic and English. In: Laurel Brinton (ed.), *Historical Linguistics 1999: Selected Papers from the 14th International Conference on Historical Linguistics*, 351–369. Amsterdam/Philadelphia: John Benjamins.
Visser, Fredericus Th. 1963–73. *An Historical Syntax of the English Language*. 4 vols. Leiden: E. J. Brill.
Wagner, Heinrich. 1959. *Das Verbum in den Sprachen der Britischen Inseln: ein Beitrag zur geographischen Typologie des Verbums*. Tübingen: Max Niemeyer.
Wehr, Barbara. 2001. Ein westlich-atlantischer Sprachbund: Irisch, Französisch, Portugiesisch. In: H. Eichner, P.-A. Mumm, O. Panagl, and E. Winkler (eds.), *Fremd und Eigen. Untersuchungen zu Grammatik und Wortschatz des Uralischen und Indogermanischen in memoriam Hartmut Katz*, 253–278. Wien: Edition Praesens.
Williams, Malcolm. 2000. The pragmatics of predicate fronting in Welsh English. In: Hildegard L. C. Tristram (ed.), 210–230.
Willis, David W.E. 1998. *Syntactic change in Welsh: A study of the loss of verb-second*. Oxford: Clarendon Press.

Robert McColl Millar
Chapter 12:
Scots

1   Modern Scots and Scottish English —— 231
2   External history —— 232
3   Present and future prospects for Scots —— 242
4   References —— 242

Abstract: Scots is unique in being an "English" dialect other than Standard English which was used as the early modern language of state (in Scotland) and of high literature. It also demonstrates how a language can be dialectalized without losing features associated with languages. This chapter gives the historical background to these developments: the spread of Old English into what is now Scotland; its triumph over Gaelic; the foundation of the burghs with northern English immigrants; the presence of Low German speakers; the French alliance. The language's decline was caused by changes in religious affiliation, the unions of 1603 and 1707 and the embrace of (spoken) English by the middle classes. High literature continued to be written in Scots, although the concentration on rural dialects when most Scots are urban provoked identity issues for many speakers. Political recognition for Scots at the start of the 21st century appears ineffectual.

1 Modern Scots and Scottish English

The present linguistic ecology of Scotland is more complicated than most other regions in the English-speaking world. It is an English-speaking country, in the sense that the main working language in writing, and for many people in speech, is Scottish Standard English (SSE), discussed in Section 2.5 below. But a Q-Celtic language, Scottish Gaelic, is also spoken, by fewer than 60,000 people out of a population of around 5.2 million. This is a disastrous decline from even a hundred years ago, however, when possibly a million people could speak the language. In 2005, Gaelic was given special legal status in Scotland by an act of the Scottish Parliament. This suggests a bipolar relationship between Gaelic and SSE in Scotland similar to that between Irish and English in Ireland. This is not the case.

Robert McColl: Aberdeen (Scotland)

DOI 10.1515/9783110525045-012

In non-Gaelic Scotland, several highly distinctive dialects are spoken. The normal sociolinguistic rules partially apply: rural and older speakers are more likely to speak traditional dialects than are either urban working class people (who speak modified local dialects which differ from the standard more in phonology than in lexis or structure) or middle class speakers. But these dialects do not fit the routine patterns of dialects in the English-speaking world entirely, however.

Firstly, the dialects involved are in many senses those least like Standard English of any in the "English"-speaking world (with the exception of English-lexified creoles). It is difficult for outsiders to understand dense (McClure 1979) southern or central dialects without considerable exposure. The northern and insular varieties are almost impenetrable; in the case of the dialects of Shetland, even other Scottish people have some difficulty following conversations without practice (see, for instance, Millar 2007). But, despite the differences between the dialects, all speakers agree that their varieties shared more with each other than any non-Scottish dialects (with the exception of the Scots dialects of the northern counties of Ireland).

But there are many highly distinctive groups of English dialects. The Germanic variety of Scotland goes further than this: it has a long written history which includes near-standardization and a continuation – unique among the "English" dialects – as a language of state and literature well into the age of print. Despite its displacement by Standard English in many domains in the early modern period, Scots has continued to be used in literature, not merely, as is the case with many other dialects, in sentimental or comic verse, but in "high" literature, including prose. At the same time, however, traditional rural varieties are considered by many to be in terminal decline. This chapter will describe how the present situation came about. In the following, I will attempt an external history of Scots. Many points have been covered by scholars in the past (I would particularly recommend Macafee [2002] for the early period; the essays contained in Jones [1997] also present a great deal and evidence and analysis of different aspects of the language); many interpretations are mine, however.

2 External history

2.1 The early period

Speakers of Anglian dialects first began to infiltrate south-east Scotland in the 6th century CE. At the time, most of the inhabitants of northern Britain spoke P-Celtic languages (Forsyth 1997). At around the same time as Old English began to be spoken in Scotland, however, a people called the *Scotti* by Roman writers, speaking a Q-Celtic language, gradually shifted their center of gravity from northeast Ireland to the southern islands and mainland of Scotland. These Gaelic speakers became associated early on with a form of Christianity which was transported into the Pictish heartland. Gaelic, for whatever reason, followed so that, in the union of the kingdoms of Picts and Scots in the mid-9th century, while it was the Picts who assimilated the Scots' territory, it was Gaelic which eventually overcame Pictish and the northern British dialects of south-west Scotland (Smyth 1984).

Thus the binary linguistic nature of Scotland – Gaelic and Scots; Celtic and Germanic – has been present for centuries. In a sense, the linguistic history of Scotland is the history of the geographical and social conquest of originally Celtic territory and linguistic domains by Germanic.

The Anglian dialects carried north in the 6th and 7th centuries were probably already somewhat different from those spoken in more southern areas. In its earliest records, Northumbrian, the ancestor of Scots, appears archaic in comparison with southern dialects. A flavor of this can be sensed in the only Old English inscription found in Scotland, a runic version of part of *The Dream of the Rood*, carved on a cross at Ruthwell, near Dumfries. This conservatism was largely obliterated by the effects of the Scandinavian invasions of the 8th to 11th centuries, however.

2.2 The incorporation of northern Bernicia into Alba

Northumbria had a natural tendency in times of stress to divide into two regions: Deira, roughly equivalent to modern Yorkshire and County Durham; and Bernicia, the Northumbrian lands north of the Tyne. Deira was hit severely by the Viking invasions. Bernicia, where the effects of the Norse invasions and settlements were rather more limited, was somewhat cut off from the rest of the English-speaking world for a significant period. Certainly it only marginally participated in the construction of a new "England" under the control of the West-Saxon monarchy, whose center of gravity was the Thames Valley, in the course of the 10th century. Bernicia north of the river Tweed gravitated towards the Kingdom of Picts and Scots, Alba.

Alba had also been affected by the Scandinavian incursions. Indeed, the original Gaelic-speaking heartland of the western and southern isles was removed from Scottish control for a number of centuries: many among the Gaelic-speaking aristocracy gradually focused on the lands to their east and south. By the middle of the 11th century this move was complete, with royal power remaining thereafter in the hands of a family whose power base was centered on the southern valleys of the central highlands. Inevitably, northern Bernicia, with its fertile soils and relatively dry and sunny climate, would have been attractive to the northerly kingdom (Barrow 1989).

It was not inevitable, however, that the Anglian dialects of Bernicia should have overcome Gaelic. Indeed, some Bernician landholders, such as the Douglas family, adopted Gaelicized or Gaelic names. What guaranteed the success of Scots throughout the Lowlands was a combination of this Bernician dialect and one from an unexpected source.

2.3 Anglicization and Normanization

In the early 11th century, the previously stable English monarchy came under attack from both internal and external forces. In 1066, King Edward was succeeded not by the legitimate heir, his great-nephew Edgar Atheling, a boy at the time, but by his brother-in-law, Harold Godwinsson. Following William of Normandy's usurpation of the throne that year, Edgar and his sister Margaret fled to Scotland.

This was by no means unprecedented. The King of Scots, Malcolm III, had spent a number of years in exile at the English court and is likely to have been both Anglophile and Anglophone. Margaret eventually married Malcolm. Their children could speak Gaelic; English was their mother tongue. It was during the reigns of Margaret and Malcolm's sons that Edinburgh, situated in Anglian-speaking Lothian, became increasingly important as a royal center. Inevitably, this change in linguistic and cultural associations by the monarchy would have encouraged similar changes in those near the center of power.

As Kings of Scots, and legitimate claimants to the English throne, it is strange that the Margaretsons and their descendants should have become such great advocates of the innovations in governance and war technology brought by the Normans to England. But this was indeed the case, with good reason. In order to compete with more developed states, Scotland had to create a cash-based economy associated with trade. Moreover, the relatively diffuse nature of government in Scotland in comparison to the rigid hierarchies of Norman feudalism meant that royal power was circumscribed. For both personal and national reasons the king wished to redress this perceived imbalance.

There was no Norman Conquest of Scotland, but there was an infiltration. Norman and other noblemen, largely settled in the northern counties of England, were invited into Scotland by the monarchy, in order, among other things, to set up *burghs*, fortified markets – later, market towns – upon which the transformation to a cash economy was to be based.

Inevitably, these French-speaking nobles and gentry did not come alone. They brought their servants and potential citizens for the burghs: people who understood the economic necessities. Most of these immigrants were from the north of England, and would have spoken heavily Norse-influenced Anglian dialects. Modern Scots is the result of the combination of the original Bernician dialects of Lothian and these new colonial dialects.

Thus, although Scots has a considerably greater Norse element in its lexis than has Standard English – *kirk* for 'church', *gar* 'to make, do, impel', *speir* 'ask (an impolite question)' – this is not as overwhelming as is the case with the dialects of, say, Yorkshire, where words like *lake* 'play', unknown in Scotland, are commonplace. Primary contact between Old English and Old Norse took place in Deira (Samuels 1989); only secondary contact, with people bringing Scandinavian borrowings from their own primary contact regions, took place in Scotland (the Scots dialects of Caithness, Orkney, and Shetland are primary Norse contact dialects. But this represents a much more recent contact – Shetland Norn only died out in the mid 18th century [Knooihuizen 2006]).

2.4 Spread and development

When the burghs were first set up, largely in the more fertile lowlands, most Scots would have been monolingual Gaelic speakers. But because of the economic and social clout, which the people of the burghs had, along with the forging of Scottish nationhood during the Wars of Independence in the 13th and 14th centuries, the Anglian dialect, at the time called *Inglis*, gained considerable prestige. It is likely that, in the hinterlands of the burghs, unequal bilingualism would have quickly developed. The Inglis-speaking inhabitants of the towns (as we can now begin to term them) might have been able to understand and speak some Gaelic (perhaps a form of "kitchen Gaelic"), but the Gaelic-speaking peasantry would inevitably have had to know more Inglis. Gaelic-speakers who wanted to get on (or were ambitious for their children) would have switched to the dominant language as much as they could. In these areas Gaelic was, in a sense, colonized. By the 15th century, very few, if any, speakers of that language would have remained in the Central Belt, although the language was preserved rather longer in the uplands of Fife and Galloway, and in the country north of the Tay (Millar 2009).

Given that Scots and Gaelic have been spoken in close proximity for a millennium and a half, we might expect there to be considerable Gaelic influence upon Scots. This is not the case, however. With the partial exception of the Northern dialects, most Scots varieties have only a smattering of Gaelic vocabulary, largely dealing with topographical features – such as *loch* 'substantial body of standing fresh or salt water' or *glen* 'narrow valley, defile' – or cultural peculiarities, such as *tocher* 'bride-price' (the money, goods or estate that a woman brings to a marriage). Some dialects spoken on the fringe of the formerly Gaelic-speaking region, such as the west central one, have a few more Gaelic words, such as *taunel* 'bonfire', but these are not numerically striking.

We could compare this to the situation in other colonial or post-colonial environments. The colonizer generally feels no need to learn much of the language of those being dispossessed, with the exception of words for environmental or cultural peculiarities. This is particularly striking in the case of Scotland because the people choosing not to use Gaelic words in their new language were themselves mainly descendants of Gaelic speakers.

To function properly, the new burgh economies required trade specializations. Trained workers were in short supply and the patrons of the burghs – whether local landowners or the crown – regularly looked outwards from Scotland for potential skilled immigrants. In the later Middle Ages, many were Low German and Dutch speakers. Surnames such as *Bremner* 'native of Bremen', and *Fleming* 'native of Flanders', still common in Scotland, demonstrate the length and depth of this connection. Their dialects were also relatively near relatives of Scots, sharing many basic vocabulary elements. At the same time, the great cities of northern Germany – such as Bremen, Hamburg, Lübeck, and Danzig (modern Gdansk) – had formed themselves into the Hanseatic League, probably the first multinational corporation. Hanseatic influence is omnipresent on the east coast of Scotland – in the style of architecture, in the food, even in the leisure activities. But the language of the League, Low German, also contributed to the distinctiveness of these dialects.

Low German or Dutch words found in all or almost all Scots dialects include *puggie* 'a "kitty" where money is kept', *bonspiel* 'curling match', *cruisie* 'oil lamp', and *gowf* 'golf'. On the east coast, we still find words such as *loon* 'boy, young man', as well as the habit, particularly in the dialects of the north-east, of adding a diminutive *-ie* to almost all nouns, a trait similar to that found in the dialects of particularly northern Holland.

Because of the generally poor relationship Scotland had with England in the 14th and 15th centuries, it was inevitable that the former found itself in the same political camp as France. Naturally, this meant that Scots was influenced by the highly prestigious French language. Like Standard English, Scots contains many Norman French words borrowed as that language died out in Britain. Scots, however, is the only British dialect of "English" which has borrowed French words independently of Standard English due to this *Auld Alliance*. The words borrowed during this period were generally Central French, particularly Parisian, in character, unlike the earlier Norman borrowings. This can be illustrated by the name of a street in Old Aberdeen. In Standard English, a senior priest in a cathedral is known as a *canon*. The street in Old Aberdeen which leads to St Machar's Cathedral is *The Chanonry*, with the archetypal Norman /k/ dispreferred for late medieval Central French /tʃ/. French borrowings peculiar to Scots include *peirie* 'child's whipping top', *asphet* 'large dish' and perhaps even *Hogmanay*, the Scottish New Year festival.

2.5 Scots an independent language

During the same period, Inglis gained status within the kingdom, replacing French and to some extent Latin as the main working language of government. The first major literary works began to appear, including John Barbour's *Brus*, an epic life of King Robert I, written two generations after the liberation of Scotland as a call to arms and national unity. In the last decades of the 15th and the first of the 16th century, Scots went through a particularly productive literary phase, producing *makars* of the caliber of Robert Henryson, William Dunbar, and Gavin Douglas. It was the last of these, in his outstanding translation of Virgil's *Aeneid*, who self-consciously declared independence for Scots, using the term *Scottis* (previously largely used for Gaelic) for his own language, using *Inglis* for the language of England. At the same time, a number of ambassadors to Scotland noticed the distinction between Scots and English, comparing the difference as being similar to that found between Catalan and Castilian (Spanish), for instance.

The language began to go through circumstantial standardization (Joseph 1987) towards the metropolitan norm of Edinburgh, using a highly distinctive spelling system which was at least as systematic as that used at the time for English. As befitted a national language, many words were borrowed from Latin and Greek into high register usage. A number of these, such as *propone* instead of *propose*, are still found in the language of Scots Law.

2.6 Decline and dialectalization

But social, economic and political currents were already at work in Scotland which meant that Scots would be dialectalized (Kloss 1984) under Standard English by the end of the 17th century at the very latest. For most writers from around 1600 on, Standard English was the default written variety, with Scots being used largely for effect (see the discussion in, for instance, by Macaulay 1991: 185–6) or due to a momentary loss of concentration, as the present writer can attest. Why should this have happened?

In the first place, Scotland went through a series of political and economic disasters in the course of the 16th century. Scottish armies were annihilated by the English at Flodden (1513) and a generation later at Solway Moss (1542). On both occasions, a large part of the Scottish aristocracy was destroyed; King James IV was killed in the first battle; King James V died not long after the second. Both battles caused long-term minorities in a country with a powerful and independent aristocracy. These were merely the most destructive of a number of unlucky encounters between the countries. Inevitably, social cohesion suffered. Equally inevitably, the precocious literary renaissance of the court of James IV was largely stifled. In an age when the effects of printing were only beginning to make themselves itself felt, writers could not survive without aristocratic patrons; these were now in short supply.

Moreover, when the Protestant Reformation arrived rather late in Scotland, it arrived in a radical Calvinist form. This of itself might not have had any deleterious effect on Scots at all; indeed the Reformation held as a central tenet that the Bible should be available in the language of the "common man", a view which undoubtedly helped some vernaculars become national languages. But an English Bible was used as a vernacular text in Scotland. Why should that have been the case?

In the first place, Bible translations, even bad Bible translations, need a period of relative social and economic stability to complete. This was not possible in Scotland. Moreover, a number of the early reformers, most notably John Knox, had lived with English speakers for a large part of their adult life either in Geneva or England. Finally, the economics of text production meant that someone writing in Scots could not hope to have the same size of audience as someone writing in English. This meant that most, probably all, literate Scots speakers were also able at least to read and probably to write English. Those who were writing in the Protestant cause would also have been tempted to use English in order to reach a range of people otherwise unavailable.

In 1603 King James VI became King of England. Too much can be made of the effect the Union of the Crowns had upon Scots; the removal of the Court from Edinburgh to London did inevitably lead to a further lessening in the number of patrons for writers. Thus we can state that, by the mid-17th century, most Scottish people who did not speak Gaelic wrote largely or solely in English, but spoke almost exclusively in their local dialect of Scots, except when reading Standard English aloud (see Meurman-Solin 1993 for evidence). This situation, not dissimilar to the *diglossia* found in German-speaking Switzerland or the Arabic-speaking world today, lasted for some 100 to 150 years in Scotland.

In 1707, the parliaments of Scotland and England united; while the Scottish Church and Law were protected by the Union settlement, practically all governmental functions for Scotland were carried out in Westminster. A significant part of the urban middle classes, particularly in Edinburgh, began to trim their linguistic sails towards this new order. Throughout the 18th century, English was taught as essentially a second language throughout Scotland. Self-help manuals abounded, listing *Scotticisms* to be avoided. These were largely lexical, but also included a considerable number of grammatical and morphological features (Dossena 2005). By the end of the century, a new variety, Scottish Standard English (SSE), had come into being. Standard English in grammar, morphology, and (largely) lexis, speakers of this variety generally use a (sometimes altered) version of their local accent (there is no standard accent in Scotland), although with a basic representation of the southern English rather than Scots phonological pattern. In SSE there are both *overt Scotticisms*, words associated with Scottish culture and heritage, used consciously to mark identity, and *covert Scotticisms*, words which the speaker thinks are English, but are actually Scots, or merely a Scots word which has been Anglicized phonologically (Aitken 1981).

Thus a wedge was forced into the Scots-speaking population, with the rural and the poor (the overwhelming majority, of course) using Scots, while the upper middle classes used English. Since these upper middle classes were the arbiters of literary style and controlled both publishing and education to a considerable degree, it was their views on the national vernacular which were carried into print and action: Scots was associated with old and barbaric times, English with a progressive future (Millar 2003). As an urban lower middle class developed through industrialization, they largely assimilated these views. It is striking that while those areas of Gaelic Scotland which were Scotticized in the early modern period, such as the North-East, have retained forms of Scots as a local vernacular, those areas where Gaelic culture was attacked in the wake of the rebellion of 1745–1746 took on a form of SSE as their new variety: Highland English.

2.7 The "vernacular revival"

It might seem strange, therefore, that it was precisely during this period, when Scots appeared to be in decline as a spoken variety and irretrievably dialectalized, that literature in Scots of considerable quality began to reappear. Robert Burns (1759–1796) is only the most famous of a number of 18th and early 19th century poets using Scots. But how he wrote that variety was unlike how it was used in its heyday:

> *I doubt na, whyles, but thou may thieve;*
> *What then? poor beastie, thou maun live!*
> *A daimen-icker in a thrave*
>   *'S a sma' request:*

> *I'll get a blessin wi' the lave,*
> *And never miss't!*
> (http://www.robertburns.org.uk/Assets/Poems_Songs/toamouse.htm; last accessed 14 April 2017)

Note the use of apostrophes in particular. In a sense they were an economic necessity, telling English-speaking readers where Scots and English phonology diverge. But they also have the unfortunate side effect of making Scots look like "deformed English". With a few exceptions in the last fifty years, this is the way that Scots has been portrayed ever since, encouraging the idea that it is an imperfect variant of Standard English.

More important, however, is the way that Burns uses Scots in relation to subject matter. In the previous passage he is referring to emotional concerns; in this passage, however, he is discussing a philosophical point:

> *I'm truly sorry Man's dominion*
> *Has broken Nature's social union,*
> *An' justifies that ill opinion*
> *Which makes thee startle*
> *At me, thy poor earth-born companion*
> *An' fellow-mortal!*
> (http://www.robertburns.org.uk/Assets/Poems_Songs/toamouse.htm)

On this occasion, the language he uses is, with a couple of exceptions, mainstream Augustan Standard English. Scots is the language of high emotion, often framed in terms of the traditional countryside (Burns's native landscape, of course). It is only a very small step from this use to an association of the language with sentimentality.

From the third quarter of the 18th century, Scotland went through rapid social and political change. A movement towards capitalist agriculture coupled to the economic exploitation of the country's considerable coal and iron ore deposits led to exponential growth in the size of urban areas. By the end of the 19th century, the overwhelming majority of Scottish people lived in these centers.

Naturally, along with the opportunities came many problems caused by the industrialization and urbanization process: poverty, crime, pollution, and disease. But the political radicalism which the changes engendered among the newly educated working classes probably scared the Scottish middle classes most. Many of the latter yearned for a rural, conservative utopia where everyone knew their place but where relations between the classes were friendly and perhaps even to some extent fluid. In this vision, local working people were seen as (rural) Scots-speaking *worthies* who were given the privilege of speaking in a direct and free manner to their "betters", since what they had to say was both humorous and apposite. It could be argued that the fact that this advice and commentary was delivered in Scots made the speakers seem honest and homespun. A literary genre, the *kailyard*, 'cabbage garden', grew out of these dreams: sentimental to the point of mawkishness and often (not always) ill-written (Millar 2004). But although Scottish literary tastes changed rapidly in the early 20th century, the overwhelming majority of written Scots available to the general public was, and remains, of this type. We need only look at a highly popular Scottish newspaper, *The Sunday Post*, where conservative (social) values are tied to an "honest" use of Scots to see how much this is still the case.

2.8 Scots in the modern era

All this leaves Scots speakers in something of a bind. Until recently, speakers of rural dialects were officially encouraged to maintain their speech in appropriate places at school, for instance. Those who spoke urban dialects – the majority – were mocked for their "corrupt" and "slovenly" English. I have seen children physically punished for using local words and phrases in the classroom. Many rural speakers would agree with this judgement upon the urban dialects.

As with all other dialects of English, Scots has not maintained its vocabulary as well as its phonology. In a study of the language use of Glasgow's East End, Macafee (1994) found that, while older informants had a fair knowledge of traditional dialect vocabulary, younger people were less confident in distinguishing between Scots vocabulary and non-standard colloquial usage and "slang".

In those areas which are relatively remote from the Central Belt or where traditional occupations have been the primary source of employment until relatively recently, however, traditional dialects are being passed on to children (Macafee 1997). This is particularly the case in Shetland, where many young Shetlanders take great pride in their local identity and speech. Yet even there, large-scale immigration, particularly associated with the recent exploitation of local oil deposits, has meant that many children of primary school age do not come from Shetland-speaking households. In many places English has become the language of the playground. The Scots language appears to be in terminal decline, at least as an entity separate from Scottish English.

Scots has continued to be used in literature. Indeed, in the figure of C.M. Grieve (alias Hugh McDiarmid, 1892–1978), Scotland produced one of the truly great literary modernists, actively avoiding – if not actually abusing – the kailyard tradition: yet Grieve rarely used the urban experience of most Scots as his primary stimulus (he himself came from a rural background). It was only from the 1960s on that "serious" urban writers began to use their own speech patterns in their writing, a process which was crystallized in the considerable commercial success of Irvine Welsh's *Trainspotting* (1994).

3 Present and future prospects for Scots

From the 1930s on, there have been attempts at language planning for Scots. These have been generally unsuccessful. Indeed, at present there are two spelling systems being touted by different groups. Central government has become gradually less opposed to Scots since the 1970s, probably part of the general move towards Scottish autonomy. Indeed, as part of its ratification of the Council of Europe's Charter for Regional or Minority Languages in 2001, the United Kingdom Government has recognized Scots as a language worthy of preservation. The practical results of this recognition have been extremely limited, however (Millar 2006). Scots continues to be dialectalized and homogenized. As this proceeds, its position as a separate language will become increasingly questionable.

4 References

Aitken, Adam J. 1981. The good old Scots tongue. Does Scots have an identity? In: Einar Haugen, J. Derrick McClure, Derick Thomson, and Adam J. Aitken (eds.), *Minority Languages Today*, 72–90. Edinburgh: Edinburgh University Press.

Barrow, G.W.S. 1989. *Kingship and Unity: Scotland, 1000–1306*. 2nd edn. Edinburgh: Edinburgh University Press.

Dossena, Marina. 2005. *Scotticisms in Grammar and Vocabulary*. Edinburgh: John Donald.

Forsyth, Katherine. 1997. *Language in Pictland*. Utrecht: de keltische Draak.

Jones, Charles (ed.). 1997. *The Edinburgh History of Scots*. Edinburgh: Edinburgh University Press.

Joseph, John Earl. 1987. *Eloquence and Power. The Rise of Language Standards and Standard Languages*. London: Frances Pinter.

Kloss, Heinz. 1984. Interlingual communication: danger and chance for the smaller tongues. *Scottish Studies* 4: 73–77.

Knooihuizen, Remco. 2006. The Norn to Scots language shift: another look at the evidence. *Northern Studies* 39: 5–16.

Macafee, Caroline I. 1994. *Traditional Dialect in the Modern World: A Glasgow Case Study*. Frankfurt am Main: Lang.

Macafee, Caroline. 1997. Ongoing change in modern Scots. In: Charles Jones (ed.), *The Edinburgh History of Scots*, 514–548. Edinburgh: Edinburgh University Press.

Macafee, Caroline. 2002. A history of Scots to 1700. In: *A Dictionary of the Older Scottish Tongue* 12, xxi–clvi. Oxford: Oxford University Press.

Macaulay, Ronald K.S. 1991. *Locating dialect in discourse: the language of honest men and bonnie lasses in Ayr*. Oxford: Oxford University Press.

McClure, J. Derrick. 1979. Scots: Its ranges and uses. In: Adam J. Aitken and Tom McArthur (eds.), *Languages of Scotland*, 26–48. Edinburgh: Edinburgh University Press.

Meurman-Solin, Anneli. 1993. *Variation and Change in Early Scottish Prose*. Helsinki: Suomalainen Tiedeakatemia.

Millar, Robert McColl. 2003. "Blind attachment to inveterate custom". Language use, language attitude and the rhetoric of improvement in the first Statistical Account. In: Marina Dossena and Charles Jones (eds.), *Insights into Late Modern English*, 311–330. Bern: Peter Lang.

Millar, Robert McColl. 2004. Kailyard, conservatism and Scots in the Statistical Account of Scotland. In: Christian J. Kay, Carole Hough, and Irené Wotherspoon (eds.), *New Perspectives on English Historical Linguistics*. Vol. II: *Lexis and Transmission*, 163–176. Amsterdam/Philadelphia: John Benjamins.

Millar, Robert McColl. 2006. "Burying alive": unfocussed governmental language policy and Scots. *Language Policy* 5: 63–86.

Millar, Robert McColl. 2007. *Northern and Insular Scots*. Edinburgh: Edinburgh University Press.

Millar, Robert McColl. 2009. The origins of the Northern Scots Dialects. In: Marina Dossena and Roger Lass (eds.), *Proceedings of the Second International Conference on English Historical Dialectology*, 191–208. Bern: Peter Lang.

Samuels, M.L. 1989. The Great Scandinavian Belt. In: Margaret Laing (ed.), *Middle English Dialectology. Essays on Some Principles and Problems*, 106–115. Aberdeen: Aberdeen University Press.

Smyth, Alfred P. 1984. *Warlords and Holy Men. Scotland AD 80–1000*. Edinburgh: Edinburgh University Press.

Jeffrey L. Kallen
Chapter 13:
English in Ireland

1   Introduction —— 244
2   Establishing an Irish English —— 246
3   History and variation in Irish English —— 249
4   Summary —— 259
5   References —— 260

Abstract: This chapter examines the English language in Ireland by looking both at the spread of English in relation to Irish from the 12th century onwards and at the changes which English has undergone in the context of language contact and bilingualism with Irish. The linguistic focus is largely on traditional dialects as described in the 19th and 20th centuries, yet attention is also paid to medieval Irish English and to more standardized forms of the contemporary language as evidenced in the International Corpus of English (ICE-Ireland). Structural evidence from syntax and phonology, as well as lexical development, suggests that Irish English shows a complex mix of influence from British English dialects, Scots, and Irish, as well as participating in linguistic standardization and occupying a position as a national variety of English which can be compared to other English varieties.

1 Introduction

The historical analysis of the English language in Ireland (here referred to as Irish English, though sometimes also known as Hiberno-English or Anglo-Irish) relies on two complementary approaches. One, usually referred to as external history, traces the use of Irish English from its introduction as the relatively low-status language of a small but powerful group of colonists in the 12th century to its present-day use as the mother tongue of the vast majority of the Irish population. The rise in the status and usage of English in Ireland since that time has not been a steady, uniform process, but rather one which has been influenced both by settlement and population movements that have favored the establishment of

---

Jeffrey L. Kallen: Dublin (Ireland)

English (and, to a lesser degree, Scots), and by native-language speakers of Irish who, especially in the 19th century, adopted the English language. If we see this history as a struggle between two languages for dominance at the levels of prestige and everyday language usage, we could see English as the ultimate 'victor' in the struggle. Yet in today's Republic of Ireland, Irish retains a special place as the constitutionally-designated 'first official language', with an established position in education and official usage, support for *Gaeltacht* areas where Irish is retained as a community language, and a population of first- and second-language speakers who use Irish on a daily basis for a variety of purposes. Language relations in Northern Ireland have favored English much more, yet here too we can find Irish-language education, official use at certain levels of government, and communities of speakers. For many mother tongue speakers of Irish English, the Irish language retains a special position as a medium of expression and national heritage. Thus, in what may seem paradoxical at first, any history of the English language in Ireland must also examine the historical relation with Irish, since the changing relationships between the two languages have provided the social, political, and demographic context for the development of a uniquely Irish English.

A second approach, which we may call the internal history of Irish English, looks at the structure of the language itself and takes account of two interacting factors: the role of dialects of British English and Scots in providing a linguistic basis for English as transplanted to Ireland, and the role of the Irish language, through language contact and over varying periods of Irish-English bilingualism, in giving a specific shape to Irish English. The first of these factors shows Irish English as relatively conservative in relation to many developments in British English, and demonstrates strong (though not exclusive) links with English in Scotland and the North of England. The dominant theme from the second factor is the possibility not only of contact-based structural change (influencing phonological systems as well as grammar), but of large-scale lexical borrowing which often reflects important cultural elements. Though these factors weigh heavily in any linguistic account of Irish English, it would be wrong to focus on these two exclusively. Not only do innovations occur in Irish English independently of antecedents in British English or Irish, but we can also find cases which prove to be too complex for analysis in terms of one language or the other. In Kallen (1997a: 145–146), for example, I have argued that Irish English *gombeen*, which now includes meanings as diverse as 'usurer', 'fool', and 'lump, especially of tobacco', represents a convergence of word formation from both English and Irish with origins going back over several centuries. In recent years, too, it has become realistic to understand Irish English not just in terms of the traditional dialects which inspired most research in the 19th and 20th centuries, but as a national standard language, different from, but sharing features with, other national Englishes. The *International Corpus of English for Ireland* (ICE-Ireland), compiled by Kirk et al. (2011) is based on this assumption, and will be discussed below.

With the foregoing concerns in mind, Section 2 of this chapter examines the external history of Irish English, giving an overview of the initial contacts between Irish and English and examining the ultimate rise of English as the dominant language in Ireland. Section 3 examines the internal history at the levels of lexicon, syntax, and phonology. While it is beyond the scope of this chapter to give definitive answers to complex questions of historical origin for specific features, a variety of evidence is considered to give a picture of the linguistic development of Irish English.

2 Establishing an Irish English

2.1 The introduction of English

It is impossible to know when the first contacts with English speakers took place in Ireland, but it is customary to attach particular importance to the arrival of a small and socially mixed group of people in the 12th century, described by Richter (1986: 41–42) as "Cambro-Normans, that is descendants of Norman nobles who had settled in Wales" and their associated forces from Wales and the southwest of England. The arrival of this socially mixed and linguistically diverse group, first in a short temporary visit in 1167, but in full force in several ships during the year 1169, initiated what is usually referred to as the Anglo-Norman period in Irish history. An abrupt dating of this kind, however, exaggerates the discontinuity entailed by the arrival of Anglo-Norman forces. As Richter (1985: 329) also points out, "small though significant groups" of clerics and aristocrats were already involved in "horizontal loyalties" that drew them into European society as a whole; Martin (1987: 53), too, notes the development of "substantial trade between Dublin and the Normans in Wales, England, and France" beginning in the late 11th century. These and other political and religious connections (on which see also Flanagan 1989), underline the point made by Ó Cróinín (1995: 287), that "the arrival in 1170 of Robert FitzStephen [...] marks a new era in Irish history, though contemporaries could scarcely have seen it that way".

We can best understand the first centuries after the coming of the Anglo-Normans in terms of what Fasold (1984: 53) calls "extended diglossia". For the relatively small but politically powerful Anglo-Irish colony, Latin and French occupied the high-prestige or H domains of language use. Anglo-Irish law of the

12th and 13th centuries shows the predominance of Latin, with French appearing in legal documents of the 14th century (see Gilbert 1889). Literary, legal, and administrative material in French from this period is also detailed by Picard (2003). As in England, English occupied the low-prestige or L domains of ordinary speech, though as McIntosh et al. (1986: 270–279) document, miscellaneous Irish legal, literary, and private materials in English can also be found from the 14th to the 16th centuries. A small body of poetry dating from the early 14th century is the most substantial of these works; these poems, found in the British Library MS Harley 913 and sometimes referred to as the *Kildare Poems*, have been most recently edited by Turville-Petre (2015). For the much larger native Irish society of the time, a standard literary form of Irish existed alongside Latin in the H domains, while it can only be assumed that a non-standard Irish, of which we have no record, occupied the L domains of everyday language use.

Though the status of English rose in the 14th and 15th centuries, this development coincided with concern in the Anglo-Irish colony that English was on the verge of extinction due to an overly-close association between colonists and the native Irish majority. This fear is expressed as early as 1297 (Berry 1907: 211), and legislation at various points in the 14th century was aimed at arresting this trend. Ethnographic insight into close communication between the Anglo-Irish community and native Irish speakers, which could only have arisen in conditions of bilingualism, is seen in a statute which forbids any "Irish minstrels, that is to say, tympanours, pipers, story tellers, babblers, rhymers, harpers, or any other Irish minstrels" to "come amongst the English" (Berry 1907: 447). Ordinances of this kind, discussed in Kallen (1997b: 10–11) and Crowley (2005: 4–5), are significant for the insight which they offer into the maintenance of social boundaries: exhortations to use English apply not to the native Irish population, but to those of English descent.

2.2 Social change and the rise of English

Henry VIII showed a particular interest in Irish affairs, and when a picture of the "state of Ireland" was presented to him in 1515 (State Papers 1834: II, iii: 8), it portrayed a country in which only six counties could be counted as loyal to the King. Even in these counties, it was alleged, disloyalty was widespread among ordinary people. The bill of kingship by which Henry VIII was designated as King of Ireland at the Irish Parliament of 1541 is part of what Bradshaw (1979: 238) describes as "a milestone in Irish constitutional history". The Parliament is of interest for linguistic historians, because a statement in praise of Henry, as well as the bill of kingship, was read out in Irish by the Earl of Ormond to the assembled House of Lords. Most modern observers (e.g. Cahill 1938; Ó Cuív 1951; Hickey 2007) are in accord with the position, as Ó Cuív (1951: 13) puts it, that the use of Irish at this event "was [...] sheer necessity, for it seems that the Earl of Ormond alone of the Anglo-Irish lords knew English". Contemporary records, reviewed in Kallen (1994: 153–154), however, do not support this interpretation. There is no evidence that Irish was used for any other purpose during the Parliament of 1541; there is ample evidence that Irish had national significance for the Irish nobility to whom this reading of the proclamation was addressed; and there are signs from this time of a growing awareness among some of the native Irish nobility of political advantages to be gained from knowing at least some English. The events of 1534, then, are not a demonstration of the complete Gaelicization of the Anglo-Irish nobility, but, rather, a political recognition of the importance of the Irish language for sections of Irish society in the effort to bring about what Maginn (2007: 955) terms "the eventual incorporation of Ireland's English and Gaelic populations into an expanding English state".

The 16th century can thus be seen as pivotal in the establishment of Irish English. The so-called Tudor plantations, which were designed to subdue and anglicize parts of the country, had limited success relative to their objectives, but brought new contacts with English. Plantation schemes in today's Counties Laois and Offaly under Queen Mary in the middle 16th century, and in parts of Munster beginning in 1587 under Elizabeth I, brought English into parts of the countryside in new political and social arrangements. Plantations in Ulster had more far-reaching consequences, settling large numbers of people from Scotland and England in Counties Antrim and Down in 1605; after the Irish "flight of the Earls" in 1607, more settlers came to other parts of Ulster in plantation schemes that were established from 1609 onwards.

By the middle of the 17th century, the social and demographic upheavals of the Cromwellian Commonwealth had settled new English speakers in different parts of the country and dislocated many Irish speakers to poorer lands in the west. The Census of 1659 (Pender 2002 [1939]), though not a modern census and not intended as a language census *per se*, gives a glimpse of the perceived language loyalties of much of the country at the time. This evidence reviewed in Kallen (2013: 25–27) shows a network of urban areas with an English-speaking nucleus, surrounded by suburban districts where Irish is dominant, leading into rural districts where, apart from Ulster, Irish greatly outweighs English (for detailed discussion of the census and its value as a source of data, see also Smyth 1988). Within the model of diglossia, English was increasingly established in most of the H domains in the newly-emergent society. Even within the Irish literary tradition, as documented by Mac Mathúna (2007), there is at this time a growing reflection, through loanwords, code-switching, and inter-language wordplay, of the increasing importance of English in Irish life.

While the 17th and 18th centuries saw continued growth of Irish-English bilingualism and the use of English in many geographical areas and social domains (Crowley 2005), the 19th century provides the turning point in the popular shift to English. A parish-by-parish study of, among other things, language habits in many parts of Ireland was published by Mason (1814–19); this report shows language shift already in progress, demonstrated in a pattern of transitional bilingualism in which the younger generations turn to English with increasing frequency (see Mac Aodha 1985–86 and Kallen 1994: 160–161 for analyses). This language shift was further accelerated by events such as the establishment of the National School system in 1831 and the Famine of the late 1840s. English was used almost exclusively in the national schools, and the death and emigration arising from the Famine had a disproportionate effect in the Irish-speaking west and south of Ireland.

Modern census data provide an overview of the outcome of language shift in Ireland. Fitzgerald's (1984) analysis of the 1881 census estimates, for example, that while 45% of the generation of people born in Ireland between 1771 and 1781 were Irish speakers, this figure declined successively to as little as 13% for those born in the 1861–1871 period. In counties Kerry in the southwest and Mayo in the northwest, the percentage of Irish speakers in the 1771–1781 period is as high as 93% and 95% respectively, dropping to 45% and 60% at mid-century. Current estimates in the Republic suggest that no more than 5% of the population "use Irish as their first or main language" (Ó Riagáin 2007: 229), though Census data show that slightly more than 40% of the population over the age of three are returned as being able to speak Irish (Central Statistics Office 2007: 12). In Northern Ireland, where official policy has been much less supportive of Irish and where the 17th century Plantation brought in large numbers of speakers of English and Scots, the use of Irish is considerably lower. Nevertheless slightly more than 10% of the population are reported in the 2001 census as having some knowledge of the Irish language (NISRA 2000–03).

3 History and variation in Irish English

3.1 Lexicon

The Irish English lexicon has, since the earliest records, exemplified the mixture of Irish-language material, retentions, and developments from earlier and dialectal sources of English, and local innovations which form the main themes in studying Irish English more generally. The Viking presence in Ireland, which dates roughly from the 9th to the 11th century, played a significant linguistic role. The Norse and Danish influence on Irish was not overwhelming, but, as detailed in Ó Muirithe (2010), words such as *haggard* 'stackyard' and many placenames (e.g. *Skerries* and *Ireland's Eye*, both near Dublin) are based on loans from these languages. Irwin (1935: 205–330) identified nearly 200 words which have special significance in the study of early Irish English. Of these, the largest category is that of Irish loanwords, some of which reflect local institutions, conditions, or practices. Examples include *galloglass*, referring to mercenary soldiers, for which Irwin cites an example from 1496, thus predating the *Oxford English Dictionary*'s (OED) earliest usage in 1515; *cosher* (from Irish *cóisir* 'feasting'), which in the 16th century denotes feasting and hospitality as an important social institution; and *bog* 'wet spongy ground', for which Irwin (1935: 286) cites an Irish usage from 1450, well before the earliest citation in the OED. The review by Lucas (1995: 41–42) shows few such loanwords in the poems of MS Harley 913, though examples such as *capil* 'horse', which is the earliest-noted use of this word in the OED, and *tromchery* 'liver' may be cited. Irwin (1935: 224–234) also notes words from this period which appear to have Old English etymologies but which are only found in Irish writings of this time, e.g. *alewyk* 'alehouse' and *bredwik* 'breadshop', based on Old English *wick* 'dwelling'. It is difficult to know if particular words of Old English or French etymology, which are first recorded in Irish English texts, came into being in Ireland, or if their only or first appearance in Irish material is simply a matter of chance. Words of this kind, though, include *folkmele* 'indiscriminately', *horyness* 'filth' (based on *hory* 'foul, filthy', but only cited in the nominal form by the OED from a 15th century Irish English text), and *tripes* 'entrails' (occurring in MS Harley 913, in this form much earlier than the first English citation in the OED, from Caxton, c.1480).

A continuation of the mix in medieval Irish English is suggested by analyses of the archaic dialect of Forth and Bargy in Co. Wexford. The Forth and Bargy dialect attracted antiquarian interest from the late 18th century, and the 19th century glossary compiled by Jacob Poole (edited by Dolan and Ó Muirithe 1996) demonstrates both an archaism and language mixture that make the dialect unique. As Ó Muirithe (1990) and Kallen (2013: 176–179) demonstrate, some salient features are retained in the local English of the present day. Words treated in the OED as archaic and found in Poole's glossary include *attercop* 'a spider', hence also a 'small, insignificant person', *hachee* 'cross, ill-tempered', and *poustee* 'power, ability, bodily strength'. Innovations cited by Poole include *paughmeale* 'the harvest home' (derived from Irish *póg* 'kiss' and *mael* Old English 'time', hence literally 'kissing time') and *craueet* 'danger of choking for want of a drink in eating', for which no etymology has been suggested.

The Ulster vocabulary which derives from Scottish and Northern English dialects and from Scots is surveyed by Macafee (1996), though Braidwood's (1964) historical introduction and the more recent survey of Smyth et al. (2006) are also particularly relevant. Some elements of Ulster vocabulary are specific to Ulster, e.g. *diamond* 'town square' (not necessarily diamond-shaped), yet a larger proportion of the Ulster lexicon reflects more general affiliations to Scotland and Northern England (e.g. *ferntickles* 'freckles' and *skelf* 'splinter'). Gregg (1972: 113) pays particular attention to the differentiation between Ulster Scots and Ulster English, suggesting, for example, a contrast between Ulster Scots *bag* and Ulster English *elder*, both meaning 'udder'.

The separation between Ulster dialect and that of other Irish English varieties, however, is by no means abrupt or absolute. ICE-Ireland (Kirk et al. 2011) provides a database of English usage in Northern Ireland and the Republic of Ireland which facilitates cross-border comparisons (see Kallen and Kirk 2008 for details). Kallen and Kirk (2007: 137) point out that these two dialect zones show significant, though not necessarily categorical, differences on the use of Scottish features in the corpus. The word *aye* 'yes', for example, occurs 354 times in the face-to-face conversations of ICE in Northern Ireland, and 15 times in comparable material from the Republic of Ireland. Such a difference, while not absolute, would be highly salient for members of both speech communities. For further discussion of Scottish influence in ICE-Ireland, see Kirk and Kallen (2010).

Irish-language material in Irish English is dealt with in several recent dictionaries, notably those of Dolan (2004) and Ó Muirithe (1996). Much of this lexicon reflects the absorption of Irish vocabulary into English in the absence of any competing English term: words such as *curach*, a traditional type of boat; *duileasc* (anglicized as *dillisk* or *dulse*, with cognate forms in Scotland and Wales), a type of edible seaweed; and *poitín* (anglicized as *poteen*), a traditional illicit distilled alcoholic drink, are long-established words of this type. Many other words do not fill such lexical gaps, but instead form part of a broader linguistic repertoire that includes, to various degrees, active codeswitching by bilingual speakers; an inventory of what Wigger (2000: 187) terms "interlingual lexemes" which are neither strictly English nor Irish for speakers but demonstrate the "coexistence and mutual infiltration" of the two languages; and long-term linguistic transfers comparable to Allsopp's (1980: 93) concept of *apports*, i.e. "slips, shifts, and innovations" which reflect "intimate [...] cultural survivals" in situations of language contact. Though it is hardly possible to do justice to this vocabulary here, we note certain common themes: (a) the use of Irish-based words for close observations of people (e.g. *ciotóg* 'left handed person'; *straoill* (anglicized as *streel*) 'slovenly girl' (noun), 'trail about' (verb); and *flaithiúlach* 'generous, good-hearted'), (b) aspects of conversation (e.g. *canran* 'complain, grumble', *cogar* 'whisper', *plámás* 'smooth talk, flattery'), and (c) other aspects of everyday life (e.g. *cruibín*, anglicized as *crubeen*, 'small foot, hoof', frequently used in English to refer to boiled pig's trotters prepared for eating; *glantóir* 'duster' used for cleaning blackboards in school; and *grá* 'love, affection').

The English dialect lexicon is also well represented in Ireland. Some common terms, e.g. *press* 'cupboard'; *mot* 'girlfriend, girl'; *cog* 'cheat in school, examinations'; *delph* 'china, crockery'; *grogram* 'a coarse fabric', extended in meaning to refer to a shade of grey; and *airy* 'lively, fond of pleasure' have a well-established history in English, but are either dialectally restricted or more generally obsolete in British English. Other words represent innovative meanings relative to their antecedents, including the long-established *yoke* 'a thing in general', also used as a mildly derogatory term for a person; *hames* 'mess [of something]'; and *tallyman*, referring in the Republic of Ireland specifically to observers in the counting of election ballots. Slang vocabulary, documented, for example, by Beecher (1991), Share (2003), and Ó Muirithe (2004), shows even more possibility for lexical development. Irish vernacular words for which no clear etymology can be demonstrated include *cat* 'bad, terrible'; *gur cake*, a kind of cake made of fruit and bread scraps baked between two layers of pastry; *bazzer* 'a blow, act of striking', particularly associated with Cork; and *grush, grushie* 'scramble for money, food, or other small items or gifts'. For a review of these and other aspects of the Irish English lexicon, see Kallen (2013: 126–176).

3.2 Syntax

3.2.1 Introduction

The grammar of Irish English before the 16th century has not attracted much scholarly attention. Much of what remains from this period is of a formal or legalistic nature, and the relative insulation of the Anglo-Irish colony allowed for less distinctive influence from Irish than might have been the case in lexicon or phonology. The material discussed in this section thus focuses on particularly salient features of traditional dialect and the standard language. Material from spoken language which is not otherwise attributed comes from my data files, based on observed language in use, or from the ICE-Ireland corpus (Kirk et al. 2011).

3.2.2 Clause-level syntax

Complex sentences pose questions about the distinctiveness of Irish English. Here we may consider two features: (a) the structure commonly referred to as "subordinating *and*", as in *They got married there and the house not finished yet* (Hickey 2007: 65), and (b) auxiliary inversion in embedded clauses, seen in *I don't know are they getting the lads from the town to do the band* (Kirk et al. 2011). Filppula (1999: 196–208) reviews historical and linguistic evidence on the origins of subordinating *and*, concluding that while Irish has had an influence on the development of the Irish English pattern, it is "of the reinforcing rather than the direct kind, since none of the H[iberno] E[nglish] patterns appears to be unique to HE" (Filppula 1999: 217). Commenting on inversion in clauses introduced by *ask, don't know, see,* and *wonder,* Kirk and Kallen (2006: 108) show a stark contrast between ICE-Ireland and ICE-GB, in that the ICE-Ireland sample under analysis contains 24 examples of inversion, with only three such examples in ICE-GB. Arguments can be adduced in favor of an Irish origin for such constructions, especially with the lexical patterning found illustrated here, but the precise origins of this pattern and its relation to inversion in other varieties of English have yet to be established.

3.2.3 The verb system

The verb phrase is without a doubt the topic that features most prominently in treatments of Irish English. First we consider the existence of a generic or habitual category, exemplified using (a) *do* alone, as in *He does come when he hears the noise* (Henry 1957: 171), (b) inflected *be*, shown in *We get, Mrs Cullen to leave us in ... She be's going, and she leaves us in, too* (Filppula 2004: 79), and (c) *do* plus *be*, where the latter is either a main verb or an auxiliary, e.g., *The grapefruits do be in full bloom in Israel in September* (Kallen 1986: 135).

Debate on this verbal category centers on the history and geographical distribution of forms with *do* versus those using *be* alone. The dialectal uses cited above are all of a type that does not become clear in our existing records until the 19th century. As discussed in Kallen (1986: 139), the evidence of an Irish grammar from 1815 in which *do be*, etc. is used to translate habitual meaning in Irish is equivocal, as is that of the only *do be* combination in Bliss's (1979) collection of texts up to 1750. Hickey (2007: 224–225) turns to 19th century dialect literature to show the first clear evidence of *do be* constructions, while Montgomery and Kirk (1996: 316) also date the earliest clear evidence of inflected habitual *be* to the middle of the 19th century. The late emergence of this form may be surprising, given that the two commonly-adduced sources for it – the aspectual distinction between punctual vs. extended or habitual categories in Irish and the use of what is generally referred to as periphrastic *do* in English – are of long standing. Filppula's (1999: 136–150) review of the evidence concerning periphrastic *do* in dialects of the southwest of England, universal grammatical features, and the existence of such forms in other Celtic Englishes (cf. Filppula and Klemola, Chapter 11) suggests multiple causation for the patterns of Irish English.

Various categories of verbal use which may be roughly grouped under the notion of perfect aspect have featured prominently in discussions of Irish English since the 19th century: overviews can be found in, for example, Harris (1984), Kallen (1989), Filppula (1999), Hickey (2000, 2007), Corrigan (2010), and Amador-Moreno (2010). In this section, we will consider three particular elements of the system: the *after* perfect, the "medial object" or pseudo-perfect, and the use of past tenses with current relevance.

The *after* perfect (e.g. *A man came over to us and said "Oh, he's after falling"*) has long attracted attention as a distinguishing feature of Irish English. Recent debate has focused on two main issues: (a) understanding uses of the form in earlier literature which refer to events in the future rather than to events in the non-remote past, and (b) accounting for the modern use of this form according to semantic, grammatical, and social factors. Bliss's (1979) collection of texts contains many examples of *after* used with temporal reference, yet Bliss (1979: 300) noted that only one of these resembles the *after* perfect as it is known today: all the others, as in *You vill [will] be after being damn'd* and *Well, fat [what] will you be after Drinking?* refer to events in the future. *After* in English generally can sometimes denote desire or prospective intent (as *Yee shall not goe after other gods* in a Biblical translation from 1611 cited by the OED), but, bearing in mind the satirical nature of many of the Bliss (1979) texts, it is tempting to dismiss these future references as inaccurate representations of the *after* perfect. McCafferty (2003: 311–316), however, has demonstrated a wide range of such uses in literary sources stretching into the 18th century. McCafferty (2006) further demonstrates an overlapping period of usage, so that forms with future reference (*Och then, whisht with you, if you've no more to say, you'll be after killing her intirely, honey!* from 1885) co-exist with the modern perfective functions. McCafferty's (2006: 147) view that the older future references died out in favor of perfective uses during the later stages of the shift to English is given additional support by Ó Corráin's (2006: 157–166) study of comparable material in Irish. Ó Corráin (2006) points out that *iar* or *ar* 'after' had relatively extensive verbal reference in Early Modern Irish, including future, subjunctive, and perfective uses, but became more focused towards stative perfect reference from the 16th century onwards; later developments saw the displacement of *iar* by markers such as *tar éis* 'after', which lack future reference. The evidence thus suggests that the change from early Irish English prospective readings of *after* to the later perfective uses, while perhaps incorporating an element of ambiguity inherent in English *after* generally, reflect a contemporaneous development in Irish grammar.

The second of these issues concerns the development of semantic restrictions on the use of *after*. Harris's (1984) adaptation of the phrase "hot news past" to denote the semantic domain of the *after* perfect provides a significant point of debate. In Kallen (1989: 10–11) it is argued that while a Dublin-based sample of spontaneous speech does provide examples which can be classed as "hot news" (e.g. as quoted above), other examples could not be so described, since they refer to states of affairs which are extended in time (e.g. *We're after bein' livin' there for the past 21 years*), involve significant distance between the time of the event and the moment of speaking (e.g. a university lecturer referring to his university's decision to grant staff concessions, *We're just after – in Nottingham – granting this*), and refer to the existence of events, rather than to their immediacy (e.g. *He's after carrying down a bloody urn*, referring to an earlier event whose existence is used to justify giving a reward to the man who has carried down a coffee urn). McCafferty (2006: 135–139) also argues that in historical usage from 1670 to 1800, "hot news" uses of the *after* perfect, while comprising 44 of 72 examples, also share in the distribution with existential, resultative, and other uses. Ronan (2005: 262–263) provides further reason not to equate *after* perfects with "hot news", noting, for example, that while "hot news" uses of *after* perfects are the most common, at 12%, in her sample of 37 tokens from 28 speakers, "resultative" and "experiential" uses are also common. Adding a new dimension, Ronan (2005: 264–265) further suggests that the use of standard *have* perfects interacts with the semantics of *after* perfects, such that those speakers in her sample who only use *after* perfects for hot news are also those who use the standard *have* perfect in other functions; for those who do not use standard *have* forms in the regular present perfect, *after* perfects take on a wider range of semantic functions. Pragmatic effects are also attributed to the *after* perfect: Kallen (1991) notes frequent occurrences of the *after* perfect in chastising within family or friendly circles, while Hickey (2000: 107) sees the reproaching use of the *after* perfect as an "extension of the relevance element". O'Keeffe and Amador-Moreno (2009) go so far as to see uses of the *after* perfect largely in terms of pragmatic functions which include (in addition to the marking of immediacy) narration, "news marking", and "scolding". Thus the precise historical relationship between *after* perfects as markers of the recent past and their more extended uses remains a question for research.

Further complications in the Irish English perfect are seen in examples such as *Have you your tea taken?* (Henry 1957: 177) and *I have it already drawn on a piece of yellow crepe paper* (Kirk et al. 2011). The sequence of elements in the Irish English construction – *have* + object + v *-en* – leads Filppula (1999: 107–116) to refer to it as the "medial object perfect". Not all analyses, however, see the form as a monoclausal perfect verb form. Henry (1957: 177–179), for example, argues that this form shows "a clear preoccupation with state", in which "the sense of action is practically absent from the participial form", while Harris (1985: 50) maintains that this construction is not a re-ordering of the general English perfect sequence *have* + v *-en*, but represents "a looser expression consisting of two underlying subjoined clauses". In this way of thinking, *have* is seen as the main verb, and the construction as a whole focuses on the state which results from the action referred to in the second clause. This analysis is used by Kirk and Kallen (2007: 278–282), who call the construction a "pseudo-perfect" which resembles the English perfect, but has a fundamentally different structure. This analysis is partly motivated by data in ICE-Ireland, in which some sentences resemble perfects because the subject of the main (*have*) clause is also the agent of the conjoined clause (e.g. *I thought I had them paid for*), yet others differ in structure because the main clause subject is not the agent of the second clause. Examples include (a) *I've two daughters married today and they are carrying on that tradition* and (b) *the Taoiseach hadn't the full information requested*. The Kirk and Kallen (2007: 282) analysis invokes reference to the "stative and possessive nature of comparable forms in Irish", complementing Filppula's (1999: 116) conclusion that despite the superficial similarity between the Irish English form and historical English models, the phasing out of the English "split perfect" and the strong similarity of Irish resultative constructions give "evidence for a significant, and not merely reinforcing, role played by Irish".

The relationship between past and perfect forms in English also provides a comparative note for Irish English. Citing uses of the past tense in Irish English such as *I never saw a gun in my life nor never saw a gun fired*, Harris (1984: 313) lists the preterit as an Irish English marker of "indefinite anterior" time, contrasting with a "standard English" system which requires the perfect in such cases. The form-based approach in Kallen (1989), however, treats preterits as a separate category from the perfect, and Hickey (2007: 195) gives only a brief consideration of the "indefinite anterior" category, suggesting that it is better seen as "just one means of expressing the past". Filppula (1999: 91–98), however, pursues the issue by looking at the examples of reference to indefinite anterior time in his material and noting (Filppula 1999: 95) that, of 487 references to indefinite anterior situations, 430 (88.3%) use the past tense, as opposed to a mere 57 using the *have* perfect. In a diachronic perspective, Kortmann (2006: 607–608) observes that the distinction between past and perfect is "increasingly getting blurred" in English around the world, both by the use of simple past forms to refer to events in the recent past and by the increasing use of perfects with definite time adverbials. We may therefore suggest that while use of the past tense form to refer to states of affairs holding at an indefinite time in the past but viewed with current relevance is not a distinctive feature of Irish English, it may be more statistically frequent, and may occur with a wider range of adverbials and other temporal markers, than in some other varieties.

3.3 Phonology

3.3.1 Consonants

Labial consonants in Irish English show intra-linguistic variation and contrast with British English since the earliest records. McIntosh and Samuels (1968: 5) cite spellings such as *yewe* 'give' and *ewill* 'evil' in Irish Middle English as characteristic departures from Middle English in England at the time. The modern dialectological record gives us a more precise phonetic insight into this area of variation: Henry's (1957: 60) study of traditional dialect in Roscommon attests forms such as [ɸɑr] 'for', [ˈkɑɸən] 'coughing', and [loːɸ] 'loaf' and notes that since [ɸ] is also used for /hw/, homophones arise in words such as [ɸoit] 'fight, white' and [ɸoil] 'file, while'. By the same token, Henry (1957: 60) notes the use of [β] (or a palatalized variant) rather than [v] in [βɑːis] 'voice' and [ˈbreːβɪʃt] 'bravest' and reports (Henry 1957: 36) that forms such as [tβelβ] 'twelve' and [dβelː] 'dwell' "have been occasionally heard from good dialect speakers". Though Henry (1957: 59) observed that much of the bilabial pattern noted here was at the time receding among the younger generation, Ó Baoill (1990: 160) notes the continued use of [ɸ] rather than /hw/ in Irish-speaking districts.

Dental and alveolar sounds also display a lengthy history of variation in Irish English, leading into modern developments in traditional dialect and vernacular speech. Middle English in Ireland shows spellings such as *tis* 'this', *tred* 'third', *set* 'seethe', and *dynge* 'thing' alongside *thyme* 'time', *rathel* 'rattle', and *onther* 'under', while early modern sources include *trone* 'throne' and *wordy* 'worthy' but *oathes* 'oats' and *thell* 'tell'. In traditional dialects of the modern era, the use of phonetic [θ] or [ð] is often seen as diagnostic of the North-South dialect split, with fricatives only used regularly in Ulster English. Alternatives to [θ] or [ð] are phonetically varied, including alveolar stops, pure dental stops, and dental stops which include a secondary non-strident fricative element, as in [t̪θ] and [d̪ð]. For a detailed sociolinguistic variationist treatment of this variable in Galway English, see Peters (2016).

The phonetic realization of /t/ and /d/ provides a rich source of variation in Irish English. Traditional dialects often use dental stops, particularly in the environment of unstressed vowels followed by /r/, as in ['splɪnd̪ər] 'splendor' and ['mad̪əʀn̩] 'modern' (Henry 1957: 57). More distinctive in Irish English is the use of alveolar fricative realizations of alveolar stops in syllable-final positions. The voiceless fricative, sometimes referred to as "lenited /t/" or a "slit fricative" has been described phonetically by Pandeli et al. (1997), who note approximately 20 different transcription symbols for it. Following Ó Baoill (1990: 161), the sound is treated here as a lowered version of /t/ and transcribed as [t̞]. Though it is difficult to read the literary record with certainty in any attempt to date the origins of [t̞], a review of dialectal evidence in Ireland, Newfoundland (Clarke 1997), and elsewhere suggests that it is a long-standing feature of many, though not all, traditional dialects outside the Ulster dialect zone. Yet [t̞] is not the only realization of /t/ that has significance for variation in Irish English: the full range of sounds includes [h], [ʔ], and [ɾ], as well as [tˢ] and [θ] (which can also occur in syllable onsets). Henry's (1958: 123–127) picture of traditional dialects in the mid-20th century captures the variation well, citing examples such as [sθrᵊɑː] 'straw', [buṱər], [buhər] 'butter', ['nɔhəʈɔːl] 'not at all', and [sutˢ] 'soot'. Though the patterns of contemporary urban vernaculars are not identical to those of traditional dialects, the data files from the urban working class study reported in Kallen (2005) include examples such as [æʔ eɪʔəklɑk] 'at eight o'clock', [gərˈɪnt̞ə] 'get into', ['wantɪrə] 'wanted to', [nɑh] 'not', [aˈbaʊh] 'about', and [strih] 'street'. As discussed in Kallen (2005), the search for the origins of this variation can lead in many directions: convergence with Irish (where the sound [t̞] does not exist, but where the occurrence of [h] in syllable-final position is well-formed), convergence with other English dialects which use [ʔ], [ɾ], and [tˢ], and universal features may all be implicated.

3.3.2 Vowels

The most salient features of the syllabic phonology of Irish English taken as a whole are those associated with the division between Ulster dialects and those found elsewhere. Ulster English displays many affinities with Scottish English and Scots, particularly in the use of central or front vowels in the GOOSE and FOOT lexical sets as defined by Wells (1982). The precise realization of categories in Ulster can be quite variable, but Harris (1985: 150–151), for example, defines three distinct classes in Belfast vernacular English: BOOT, categorically taking [ʉ] as in *boot, food, goose*; BUT, categorically taking a central rounded vowel [ɵ] as in *cut, blood, fuss*; and PUT/FOOT, which alternates between [ʉ] and [ɵ] on the basis of lexical and sociolinguistic features. Outside of the Ulster dialect zone, the picture is different: GOOSE words are a well-defined class with [u], but the boundaries between the FOOT and STRUT groups are less clear, where [ʊ], [ʌ], and intermediate vowels such as [ɤ] can occur in words such as *bush, push, pudding, foot, love, soot, stood,* and *cushion.*

We may also note alternations between [ɛ] and [ɪ] in words of the DRESS set. Henry (1958: 111) cites raised realizations such as [bɪnʃ] 'bench', [nɪkst] 'next', [tɪn] 'ten', and [kɪtl] 'kettle' from a range of data points, noting in mid-Ulster, however, a contrary tendency of lowering as in [nak] 'neck'. The history of English shows fluctuation on this point, with raising especially common before nasals, as seen in <gintleman> 'gentleman' and <sincible> 'sensible' cited by Wyld (1927: 189–190); Ó Baoill (1990: 159), however, points out that similar patterns are also shown in Irish-language variations such as *teine ~ tine* 'fire'.

The gradual participation of Irish English in what Wells (1982: 194–195) calls the FLEECE merger, by which words with Middle English /ɛː/ merged with /eː/ words and came to be realized with /iː/, is well documented, in part because it is still in progress. Patterson (1860) noted over 100 words from Belfast (such as *leave, grease,* and *scheme*) in which [eː] was commonly used instead of the later [iː]; representations of [eː] in words such as *beast, meat, please,* and *speak* also feature prominently in 19th century literary depictions of Irish English. Henry (1958: 110) lists a variety of such words, as in [teˑ] 'tea', [kreˑm] 'cream', [bɛˑət] 'beat', [hweˑət] 'wheat', and [meˑlz] 'meals'. Harris (1985: 149) notes the decline of these realizations in Belfast since Patterson's day, but nevertheless lists 21 words of this type in which [eː] is available as a variant. Despite the pace of phonological change, some unshifted realizations have taken on an independent existence: *bate* (<*beat*) can be used to refer to "something which exceeds something else" (as in *Did you ever hear the bate of that?*), the exclamation *Jaysus* is lexically distinct from the religious figure *Jesus,* and *spake* (<*speak*) refers to the act of speaking, as in the common phrase *Now's the time to get your spake in,* i.e., 'to speak up'.

4 Summary

The discussion here has had the aim of demonstrating salient features in the development of Irish English: the long period over which English and Irish occupied different positions in affecting linguistic loyalty and language use, the interaction between the Irish language and English (including varieties of British English and Scots) in determining unique linguistic features within Irish English, and the continuing development of Irish English in the spread of English as a global language. Further questions remain with the changing role of Irish in Irish society, with changing linguistic contacts and normative views of what constitutes 'standard' English in a globalizing world, and with new roles for Irish English provided by literature, film, and other media. Empirical studies concerning ongoing change in Irish English and the adoption of Irish English by new speakers are included in the volume edited by Migge and Ní Chiosáin (2012). What we have explored in this chapter is intended as a picture that is influenced by traditional dialect but which looks at developments in the standard of today: further work on Irish English and globalization, the rise of urban vernacular speech, dialectal convergence and divergence, and the role of other languages in the more multilingual Ireland of today remain for further study.

5 References

Allsopp, Richard. 1980. How does the creole lexicon expand? In: Albert Valdman and Arnold Highfield (eds.), *Theoretical Orientations in Creole Language Studies*, 89–107. London: Academic Press.
Amador-Moreno, Carolina P. 2010. *An Introduction to Irish English*. London: Equinox.
Beecher, Seán. 1991. *A Dictionary of Cork Slang*. 2nd edn. Cork: Collins Press.
Berry, Henry F. (ed.). 1907. *Statutes and Ordinances, and Acts of the Parliament of Ireland. King John to Henry V.* Dublin: Stationery Office.
Bliss, Alan J. 1979. *Spoken English in Ireland: 1600–1740: Twenty-Seven Representative Texts Assembled & Analysed*. Dublin: Dolmen Press.
Bradshaw, Brendan. 1979. *The Irish Constitutional Revolution of the Sixteenth Century*. Cambridge: Cambridge University Press.
Braidwood, John. 1964. Ulster and Elizabethan English. In: George Brendan Adams (ed.), *Ulster Dialects: An Introductory Symposium*, 5–109. Cultra Manor: Ulster Folk Museum.
Cahill, Edward. 1938. Norman French and English languages in Ireland. *Irish Ecclesiastical Record* 5th ser. 51: 159–173.
Central Statistics Office. 2007. *Census 2006: Vol. 9: Irish Language*. Dublin: Stationery Office.
Clarke, Sandra. 1997. The role of Irish English in the formation of New World Englishes: the case of Newfoundland. In: Jeffrey L. Kallen (ed.), *Focus on Ireland*, 207–225. Amsterdam/Philadelphia: John Benjamins.
Corrigan, Karen P. 2010. *Irish English*, Vol. 1: *Northern Ireland*. Edinburgh: Edinburgh University Press.
Crowley, Tony. 2005. *Wars of Words: The Politics of Language in Ireland 1537–2004*. Oxford: Oxford University Press.
Dolan, Terence P. 2004 [1998]. *A Dictionary of Hiberno-English*. 2nd edn. Dublin: Gill and Macmillan.
Dolan, Terence P. and Diarmaid Ó Muirithe. 1996. *The Dialect of Forth and Bargy, Co. Wexford, Ireland*. Dublin: Four Courts Press.
Fasold, Ralph. 1984. *The Sociolinguistics of Society*. Oxford: Blackwell.
Filppula, Markku. 1999. *The Grammar of Irish English*. London: Routledge.

Filppula, Markku. 2004. Irish English: morphology and syntax. In: Bernd Kortmann, Kate Burridge, Rajend Mesthrie, Edgar W. Schneider, and Clive Upton (eds.), *A Handbook of the Varieties of English*, Vol. 2: *Morphology and Syntax*, 73–101. Berlin/New York: Mouton de Gruyter.
Fitzgerald, Garret. 1984. Estimates for baronies of minimal levels of Irish-speaking among successive decennial cohorts. *Proceedings of the Royal Irish Academy 84, Section C*: 117–155.
Flanagan, Marie Therese. 1989. *Irish Society, Anglo-Norman Settlers, Angevin Kingship: Interactions in Ireland in the Late Twelfth Century.* Oxford: Clarendon Press.
Gilbert, John T. 1889. *Calendar of Ancient Records of Dublin.* Vol. 1. Dublin: Municipal Corporation.
Gregg, Robert J. 1972. The Scotch-Irish dialect boundaries in Ulster. In: Martyn F. Wakelin (ed.), *Patterns in the Folk Speech of the British Isles*, 109–139. London: Athlone Press.
Harris, John. 1984. Syntactic variation and dialect divergence. *Journal of Linguistics* 20: 303–327.
Harris, John. 1985. The Hiberno-English 'I've it eaten' construction: what is it and where does it come from? In: Dónall P. Ó Baoill (ed.), *Papers on Irish English*, 36–52. Dublin: Irish Association for Applied Linguistics.
Henry, Patrick L. 1957. *An Anglo-Irish Dialect of North Roscommon.* Dublin: University College Dublin.
Henry, Patrick L. 1958. A linguistic survey of Ireland: preliminary report. *Lochlann* 1: 49–208.
Hickey, Raymond. 2000. Models for describing aspect in Irish English. In: Hildegard L. C Tristram (ed.), 97–116.
Hickey, Raymond. 2007. *Irish English: History and Present-day Forms.* Cambridge: Cambridge University Press.
ICE-GB. 1998. *ICE-GB: The International Corpus of English: The British Component.* CD-ROM. London: Survey of English Usage.
Irwin, P. J. 1935. *A study of the English dialects of Ireland, 1172–1800.* Unpublished Ph.D. thesis, University of London.
Kallen, Jeffrey L. 1986. The co-occurrence of *do* and *be* in Hiberno-English. In: John Harris, David Little, and David Singleton (eds.), *Perspectives on the English Language in Ireland*, 133–148. Dublin: CLCS, Trinity College Dublin.
Kallen, Jeffrey L. 1989. Tense and aspect categories in Irish English. *English World-wide* 10: 1–39.
Kallen, Jeffrey L. 1991. Sociolinguistic variation and methodology: *after* as a Dublin variable. In: Jenny Cheshire (ed.), *English around the World: Sociolinguistic Perspectives*, 61–74. Cambridge: Cambridge University Press.
Kallen, Jeffrey L. 1994. English in Ireland. In: Robert Burchfield (ed.), *The Cambridge History of the English Language,* Vol. V, 148–196. Cambridge: Cambridge University Press.
Kallen, Jeffrey L. 1997a. Irish English and world English: lexical perspectives. In: Edgar W. Schneider (ed.), *Englishes Around the World: Studies in Honour of Manfred Görlach*, Vol. I, 139–157. Amsterdam/Philadelphia: John Benjamins.
Kallen, Jeffrey L. 1997b. Irish English: context and contacts. In: Jeffrey L. Kallen (ed.), *Focus on Ireland*, 1–33. Amsterdam/Philadelphia: John Benjamins.
Kallen, Jeffrey L. 2005. Internal and external factors in phonological convergence: the case of English /t/ lenition. In: Peter Auer, Frans Hinskens, and Paul Kerswill (eds.), *Dialect Change: Convergence and Divergence in European Languages*, 51–80. Cambridge: Cambridge University Press.

Kallen, Jeffrey L. 2013. *Irish English Volume 2: The Republic of Ireland*. Berlin: De Gruyter Mouton.
Kallen, Jeffrey L. and John M. Kirk. 2007. ICE-Ireland: local variations on global standards. In: Joan C. Beal, Karen P. Corrigan, and Hermann Moisl (eds.), *Creating and Digitizing Language Corpora*, Vol. 1: *Synchronic Databases*, 121–162. London: Palgrave.
Kallen, Jeffrey L. and John M. Kirk. 2008. *ICE-Ireland: A User's Guide*. Belfast: Cló Ollscoil na Banríona.
Kirk, John M. and Jeffrey L. Kallen. 2006. Irish standard English: how Celticised? How standardised? In: Hildegard L. C. Tristram (ed.), 88–113.
Kirk, John M. and Jeffrey L. Kallen. 2007. Assessing Celticity in a corpus of Irish Standard English. In: Hildegard L. C. Tristram (ed.), *The Celtic Languages in Contact*, 270–298. Potsdam: Potsdam University Press.
Kirk, John M. and Jeffrey L. Kallen. 2010. How Scottish is Irish Standard English? In: Robert McColl Millar (ed.), *Northern Lights, Northern Words. Selected Papers from the FRLSU Conference, Kirkwall 2009*, 178–213. Aberdeen: Forum for Research on the Languages of Scotland and Ireland.
Kirk, John M., Jeffrey L. Kallen, Orla Lowry, Anne Rooney, and Margaret Mannion. 2011. *International Corpus of English: Ireland Component. The ICE-Ireland Corpus*. Version 1.2.2. [1st version 2006.] CD-ROM. Belfast: Queen's University Belfast and Dublin: Trinity College Dublin.
Kortmann, Bernd. 2006. Syntactic variation in English: a global perspective. In: Bas Aarts and April McMahon (eds.), *The Handbook of English Linguistics*, 603–624. Oxford: Blackwell.
Lucas, Angela M. 1995. *Anglo-Irish Poems of the Middle Ages*. Blackrock: Columba Press.
Mac Aodha, Breandan S. 1985–86. Aspects of the linguistic geography of Ireland in the early nineteenth century. *Studia Celtica*, 20(1): 205–220.
Mac Mathúna, Liam. 2007. The growth of Irish (L1) / English (L2) literary code-mixing, 1600–1900: contexts, genres and realisations. In: Hildegard L. C. Tristram (ed.), *The Celtic Languages in Contact*, 217–234. Potsdam: Potsdam University Press.
Macafee, Caroline I. 1996. *A Concise Ulster Dictionary*. Oxford: Oxford University Press.
Maginn, Christopher. 2007. "Surrender and regrant" in the historiography of sixteenth-century Ireland. *Sixteenth Century Ireland*, 38: 955–974.
Martin, Francis X. 1987. Diarmait Mac Murchada and the coming of the Anglo-Normans. In: Art Cosgrove (ed.), *A New History of Ireland*, Vol. II, 43–66. Oxford: Oxford University Press.
McCafferty, Kevin. 2003. 'I'll be after telling dee de raison ...': *Be after* V-*ing* as a future gram in Irish English, 1601–1750. In: Hildegard L. C. Tristram (ed.), *The Celtic Englishes III*, 298–317. Heidelberg: Universitätsverlag Winter.
McCafferty, Kevin. 2006. *Be after* V-*ing* on the past grammaticalisation path: how far is it after coming? In: Hildegard L. C. Tristram (ed.) 130–151.
McIntosh, Angus and Michael L. Samuels. 1968. Prolegomena to a study of mediaeval Anglo-Irish. *Medium Aevum*, 37: 1–11.
McIntosh, Angus, Michael L. Samuels and Michael Benskin. 1986. *A Linguistic Atlas of Late Mediaeval English*. Vol. 4. Aberdeen: Aberdeen University Press.
Mason, William Shaw. 1814–19. *A Statistical Account, or Parochial Survey of Ireland*, Vol. 3. Dublin: Graisberry and Campbell.
Migge, Bettina and Máire Ní Chiosáin (eds.). 2012. *New Perspectives on Irish English*. Amsterdam: John Benjamins.
Montgomery, Michael and John M. Kirk. 1996. The origin of the verb be in American Black English: Irish or English or what? *Belfast Working Papers in Language and Linguistics* 11: 308–333.

NISRA. 2000–03. *Census 2001 Output, Northern Ireland Level*. http://www.nisranew.nisra.gov. uk/census/Census2001Output/CASTables/cas_tables_ni.html#irish%20language; last accessed 14 April 2017.

Ó Baoill, Dónall P. 1990. Language contact in Ireland: the Irish phonological substratum in Irish-English. In: Jerold A. Edmondson, Crawford Feagin, and Peter Mühlhäuser (eds.), *Development and Diversity: Language Variation Across Time and Space*, 147–172. Dallas: Summer Institute of Linguistics.

Ó Corráin, Ailbhe. 2006. On the 'after perfect' in Irish and Hiberno-English. In: Hildegard L. C. Tristram (ed.), 152–172.

Ó Cróinín, Dáibhí. 1995. *Early Medieval Ireland 400–1200*. Longman History of Ireland. London: Longman.

Ó Cuív, Brian. 1951. *Irish Dialects and Irish-speaking Districts*. Dublin: Dublin Institute for Advanced Studies.

Ó Muirithe, Diarmaid. 1990. A modern glossary of the dialect of Forth and Bargy. *Irish University Review* 20(1): 149–162.

Ó Muirithe, Diarmaid. 1996. *A Dictionary of Anglo-Irish*. Dublin: Four Courts Press.

Ó Muirithe, Diarmaid. 2004. *A Glossary of Irish Slang and Unconventional Language*. Dublin: Gill and Macmillan.

Ó Muirithe, Diarmaid. 2010. *From the Viking Word Hoard: A Dictionary of Scandinavian Words in the Languages of Britain and Ireland*. Dublin: Four Courts Press.

Ó Riagáin, Pádraig. 2007. Irish. In: David Britain (ed.), *Language in the British Isles*, 218–236. Cambridge: Cambridge University Press.

O'Keeffe, Anne and Carolina P. Amador-Moreno. 2009. The pragmatics of the *be + after* + V-*ing* construction in Irish English. *Intercultural Pragmatics* 6: 517–534.

Pandeli, Helen, Joseph F. Eska, Martin J. Ball, and Joan Rahilly. 1997. Problems of phonetic transcription: the case of the Hiberno-English slit-*t. Journal of the International Phonetic Association* 27: 65–75.

Patterson, David. 1860. *The Provincialisms of Belfast and the Surrounding Districts Pointed out and Corrected*. Belfast: Alex Mayne.

Pender, Séamus (ed.). 2002 [1939] *A Census of Ireland, circa 1659*. 2nd edn. Dublin: Irish Manuscripts Commission.

Peters, Arne. 2016. *Linguistic Change in Galway English: A Variationist Sociolinguistic Study of (th) and (dh) in Urban Western Irish English*. Frankfurt am Main: Peter Lang.

Picard, Jean-Michel. 2003. The French language in medieval Ireland. In: Michael Cronin and Cormac Ó Cuilleanáin (eds.), *The Languages of Ireland*, 57–77. Dublin: Four Courts Press.

Richter, Michael. 1985. The European dimension of Irish history in the eleventh and twelfth centuries. *Peritia* 4: 328–345.

Richter, Michael. 1986. The Norman Invasion of 1169. In: Liam De Paor (ed.), *Milestones in Irish History*, 41–51. Cork: Mercier Press.

Ronan, Patricia. 2005. The *after*-perfect in Irish English. In: Markku Filppula, Juhani Klemola, Marjatta Palander, and Esa Penttilä (eds.), *Dialects across Borders*, 253–270. Amsterdam/Philadelphia: John Benjamins.

Share, Bernard. 2003. *Slanguage: A Dictionary of Irish Slang*. 2nd edn. Dublin: Gill and Macmillan.

Smyth, Anne, Michael Montgomery, and Philip Robinson (eds.). 2006. *The Academic Study of Ulster Scots: Essays for and by Robert J. Gregg*. [Belfast]: National Museums and Galleries of Northern Ireland and Ulster Folk and Transport Museum.

Smyth, William J. 1988. Society and settlement in seventeenth century Ireland: the evidence of the '1659 Census'. In: William J. Smyth and Kevin Whelan (eds.), *Common Ground: Essays on the Historical Geography of Ireland Presented to T. Jones Hughes*, 55–83. Cork: Cork University Press.

State Papers. 1834. *State Papers Published under the Authority of his Majesty's Commission*, Vol. III, part iii. London.

Tristram, Hildegard L. C. (ed.). 2000. *The Celtic Englishes II*. Heidelberg: C. Winter.

Tristram, Hildegard L. C. (ed.). 2006. *The Celtic Englishes IV*. Potsdam: Potsdam University Press.

Turville-Petre, Thorlac. 2015. *Poems from BL MS Harley 913: 'The Kildare Manuscript'*. Early English Text Society O. S. 345. Oxford: Oxford University Press.

Wells, John. 1982. *Accents of English*, Vol. I. Cambridge: Cambridge University Press.

Wigger, Arndt. 2000. Language contact, language awareness, and the history of Hiberno-English. In: Hildegard L. C. Tristram (ed.), 159–187.

Wyld, Henry Cecil. 1927. *A Short History of English*. 3rd edn. London: John Murray.

Colin H. Williams
Chapter 14:
English in Wales

1 Introduction —— 265
2 Demolinguistics —— 274
3 Sociolinguistic variation in Welsh English —— 274
4 Literature —— 279
5 Education —— 281
6 Language promotion and group dynamics —— 282
7 Official policy on language equality —— 282
8 Summary —— 283
9 References —— 284

Abstract: The relationship between the English and Welsh languages in Wales is a rich experience of language contact, conflict, shift, and inter-penetration of cultures, mores, ideas and, to some extent, the joint venture of promoting the notion of Britishness within a unifed UK Crown and Polity. However, as England's first colony the Welsh experience is replete with strategic, military, political, legal, and socio-economic patterns and processes which were transposed elsewhere as the reach of England and of the English language became more robust in geo-strategic and commercial terms. This essay considers the historical context of this relationship together with a specific focus on language, sociolinguistics, literature, education, language promotion, and group dynamics, official policy on language equality and legislation and a conclusion which emphasizes that the current attempt to promote an official bilingual society has to take cognisance of the increasingly plural and multicultural reality of contemporary Wales.

1 Introduction

Wales has a long experience of language contact, conflict, and shift. Today Wales is seen as a reasonable model of bilingualism, but in earlier successive eras, the Romano-British (43–c.410 CE), early medieval (c.410–c.1100 CE) and later medieval period (c.1100–c.1500 CE), invasion, resistance, and conquest have had a

---

Colin H. Williams: Cardiff (Wales)

profound linguistic impact on the patchwork of kingdoms, territories, and fealties owed by the Welsh landed classes.

Many have claimed that Wales was largely defined, if not created, by external forces and legitimizing narratives. Anglo-Saxon settlement, particularly in northeast Wales resulted in Old English being spoken along the margins of Offa's Dyke (built in 778 CE, to demarcate the western extent of Mercia) and the incorporation of several loanwords into Welsh such as *llidiart* 'gate', *bwrdd* 'board' and *capan* 'cap' long before the Norman Conquest (Davies et al. 2008: 260). Old orthodoxies about the residual Brythonic Celts being driven westward by successive hordes of Saxon invaders are now being challenged on both historical-linguistic and genetic grounds. The indigenous people called themselves *Cymry* 'compatriots' and their country *Cymru*, while the Germanic population east of Offa's Dyke called them *Wealas*, a term denoting Romanized outsiders. The modern English descriptors, 'Welsh' for the people and their language, and 'Wales' for the country derive from this appellation (Löffler 2008).

What is not in dispute is the emergence of a remarkable indigenous culture which had to cope with Anglo-Saxon penetration, Viking incursions, the Norman suzerainty, and subsequent Anglo-French conquest together with the emergence of an English hegemony. Throughout these power struggles the Welsh language, its literature, legal conventions, and social mores were challenged and transformed so that what emerged at the end of the late medieval period was an enriched, relatively robust, and distinct national culture operating within a dependent political context. The twin anchors of this Welsh high culture were learning and religion which maintained the centuries-old link between Church affairs and the native literary tradition.

However, the English language was introduced into Wales in a systematic manner following the post-colonial conquest, and it is no exaggeration to say that Wales was the first stage in the process of global English expansion and thus reflects the oldest experience of varieties of English outside England.

Following the Norman Conquest of 1066, Anglo-Norman barons constructed fortified settlements in key locations through which they could dominate coastal and riverine patterns of communication. Small market towns and garrisons were populated by English craftsmen, traders, and soldiers. In a classic demonstration of colonialism the "foreign" burghers in these "English boroughs" were granted generous privileges while the indigenous population was often forcibly moved to different locations. Moreover, Welshmen were forbidden to acquire land in the English boroughs, to carry weapons there, or to marry into borough families. Baronies were often divided into an 'Englishry' and a 'Welshry' in which different laws and customs prevailed (Jenkins 1997: 54). In the Vale of Glamorgan, Gower, southern Gwent, and southern Pembrokeshire the colonial settlement patterns introduced Flemish weavers and farmers, and although they were soon assimilated into stronger English networks their impact in terms of the place names, land holding, farming patterns, and vernacular architecture is still evident today.

The Edwardian colonial conquest of Wales after 1282–1283 CE resulted in the annexation of Wales into England and was sealed in law by the First Statute of Westminster (1284). The gradual incorporation of the landed gentry throughout the later Middle Ages had transformed Wales from a rebellious periphery to a fairly conservative, if not quite domiciled, border region of England. The impressive Edwardian castles are a permanent reminder that Wales is a conquered territory, where a re-settled "alien" population dominated the urban hierarchy and sought to diminish the differences between the Welsh and the English. Despite the conquest and partial re-settlement, Welsh laws, Welsh local administration and religious customs prevailed, such that the anticipated erosion of national differences between the native Welsh and foreign English was not progressing sufficiently quickly. Mann (2005: 58) reports how that in 1509 the English burgesses of Conway, a plantation garrison town, petitioned for more discrimination against the Welsh. They complained "it is no more meete for a Welshman to bears any office in Wales – than it is for a frinchman to be Officer in Calis [Calais], or a skotte in Barwicke [Berwick]". Their petition was sent to the first of the Tudors, Pembroke-born King Henry VII, whose accession in 1485 had sealed a long process of aristocratic lateral assimilation and inter-marriage between English and Welsh lords.

His son, Henry VIII, enacted the Acts of Union 1536 and 1542, which formally incorporated Wales into the legal and political realm of England, imposing one administration, one law, and one language. The Act's most significant clause in terms of the gradual growth of English was to exclude Welsh from official life and require all public officialdom that was transacted in the principality to be in English. Thus "all Justices [...] shall kepe the sessions [...] in the Englisshe Tongue" and no one who commanded only "the Welsshe spech shall have or enjoy any manner of offices or fees within this realm." (Hansard 1993). These Acts are often interpreted as a turning point in Welsh history when both state incorporation and linguistic exclusion dealt a double blow to the Welsh people. Yet as Mann (2005: 58) observes, "while about 90 per cent of the Welsh monolingual population were now officially disqualified from holding public office, *they never held public office*. As in England, 90 per cent of the population did not count in politics", and they would not have held office anyway, with or without the injunction. What mattered were the remaining ten per cent: the nobility, gentry, merchants, and guildsmen. Along with Latin and French, English had become an increasingly important language of officialdom and bureaucracy and the anglicized ruling cohorts in Wales had acquired English as a second language in order to prosper in the ascendant Tudor state.

What operated was an early example of colonial language policy, reminiscent of imperial India and parts of Africa and in more subtle, less formal terms, analogous to the impact which English hegemony has today as a result of globalization and advanced capitalism. But to see all this in terms of national displacement is to give undue emphasis to the nationalist vision of world order. Mann is correct in repeating that what was involved in this institutional coercion was in part colonial exploitation by the English, in part class betrayal by Welsh elites.

In 1563 the Anglican Church recognized that to convert Welsh people to Protestantism required a Bible in Welsh, the only language understood by the masses. Agitation and support for this policy came from the Welsh Gentry. Thus an Act of Parliament required that a copy of the English Bible and the Book of Common Prayer be placed alongside the Welsh versions in every church, so that the people might "the sooner attain the knowledge of the English tongue" (Morgan 1988). This project also encouraged literacy in Welsh, and the translation of the Bible into Welsh in 1588, under the oversight of Bishop William Morgan, created a standardized and elegant written form of the language, while the smaller editions available from the 1630s facilitated the official and private use of the Welsh language in the religious domain (Löffler 2008).

Within the Established Church both Welsh and English were used to varying degrees depending upon location, the Bishop's injunctions and the predisposition of the local priests (Pryce and Williams 1988). Some degree of autonomous cultural reproduction was encouraged in the 17th century by the emergence of new religious movements, such as the Independents (Yr Annibynwyr) and the Baptists (Y Bedyddwyr), which paved the way for non-established religious affiliations with their own social organizations, networks and denominational presses. Calvinistic Methodism dominated the next century with its emphasis on order, sobriety, piety, and learning. The Methodist Church gained influence as the dominant religious force in large parts of the country. However, several religious leaders encouraged the establishment of English-medium denominations as an antidote against the perceived decline of the Welsh causes. Thus the Wesleyans had circuits in Pembrokeshire, Breconshire, and Cardiff, the Congregationalists were gaining strength in the urban market towns of Glamorgan and Monmouthshire, the Baptists established their English Assembly of Monmouthshire and the Calvinistic Methodists paralleled their Welsh-medium chapels by opening some 43 English medium chapels by the turn of the 19th century.

In the succeeding decades, despite discrimination and persecution, dissenting religious groups flourished and encouraged a Trans-Atlantic, Welsh-medium network of correspondents, journalists, teachers, social, and spiritual interpreters that culminated in a period of late-19th-century liberal radicalism and laid the foundations for a more conscious national identification.

However, it was during the latter part of the 19th century that systematic Anglicization occurred as a result of industrialization and urbanization, consequent to the development of the primary, extractive minerals such as iron, coal, slate and their utilization in the production of copper, tin, and steel products. This, together with the associated developments within rail and port construction, created a new dynamic set of urban-industrial spaces and catapulted Wales into the forefront of the British economy. The simplest explanation for the emergence of English as a dominant language are the unprecedented waves of in-and-out migration in the period 1875 to 1914, mainly to and from England, but also elsewhere. Between 1881 and 1891 the population of eight of the 13 Welsh counties declined sharply as thousands migrated to England (228,000 Welsh born residents), to the USA (where 100,000 native born were recorded in the 1890 census) and to Glamorgan and Monmouth, where in the decade 1881–1891, 87,200 had migrated from the depression-hit rural areas of Wales (Morgan 1970). Added to this was the massive immigration from England which, according to the 1911 Census account for the Glamorgan coalfield, indicated that some 49% of the coalfield population had been born in England and the remainder in Scotland, Ireland, or elsewhere. The proportion born in Monmouthshire (excluding Newport County Borough) stood at 59%, that of Welsh-born 33%. The eastern coal valleys tended to anglicize while the western ones tended to withstand the pressure of language shift. In Glamorgan the percentage decline in Welsh speaking dropped from 44% in 1901 to 20% by 1951, while even in Carmarthenshire it dropped from 90% to 77% by 1951. The scant evidence that exists also suggests that those migrants from Italy, Poland, and elsewhere in Europe who tended to work in the service and construction sectors also assimilated into the English rather than the Welsh sociolinguistic networks.

For the first time in Welsh history bilingualism became a mass phenomenon creating novel, if relatively unstable sociolinguistic patterns. New codes of worship, work, leisure, and political beliefs were transmitted to an increasingly literate work force by a mass media created by print capitalism. The Welsh language was undoubtedly strengthened by the redistribution of a growing population consequent to industrial expansion. As industrialization generated internal migration, the Welsh, unlike the Scots or the Irish, did not have to abandon their language and homeland for employment abroad, particularly by emigrating to the New World (Thomas 2000; Williams 1994). Consequently the large-scale rural-urban shift which took place within Wales was capable of sustaining a new set of Welsh institutions, which gave a fresh impetus to the Welsh language and culture, institutionalizing them within new, modernizing industrial domains. This may be the principal reason why modern Welsh identity is more closely linked to the maintenance of language than any other Celtic case. Perforce Welsh culture was less reliant on the political and formal national institutions and has been reflected more through popular involvement in chapel-based social activities, choral festivals, *Eisteddfodau* competitions in music, drama, and poetry, a brass band tradition, miners' libraries, and early national sporting federations. These manifestations were as much a redefinition of indigenous Welsh culture as they were the sharpening of a distinctly Anglo-Welsh identity and tradition. However, this mutually-dependent Welsh and Anglo-Welsh popular culture has heavily influenced the nature of urban Welsh-medium culture, for, unlike rural Wales, such changes were operative within a set of formal, English-medium public sector and commercial domains.

At the beginning of the 20th century English had emerged as the dominant language in Wales, primarily as a result of in-migration and state policy. Imperial economic advances and state intervention following the Education Act of 1870 and the Welsh Intermediate Education Act of 1889, bred a new awareness of English values, culture, and employment prospects and gave a powerful institutional fillip to the process of Anglicization, which encouraged the transmission of Welsh identity through the medium of English. The standardization of education and local government encouraged closer economic and administrative association with the rest of the UK. Modernization reinforced English and denigrated Welsh. Refusal to speak Welsh with one's children was a common enough reaction to the status differential which developed between the languages. How the masses welcomed this "liberation" from traditionalism and conservatism is best evidenced by the wholesale generational language shift in the period 1914–1945 (Pryce and Williams 1988). English was perceived as the language of progress, of equality, of prosperity, of commerce, of mass entertainment, and pleasure. The previous experience of Empire-building, understandably, had made acquisition of English a most compelling feature and the key to participation in the burgeoning British-influenced world economy. Added to the refusal or inability of many parents to transmit the Welsh language to their children was the failure to use Welsh in the wide range of newer speech domains which developed in all aspects of the formal and social life of the nation. These trends intensified during the first half of the 20th century, especially within the densely populated coalfield settlements of south and north-east Wales, together with major ports along the Bristol Channel, so much so that a sharp contrast occurred between the gwerin/folk relatively conservative Wales and the new international consciousness mediated mainly by English.

A prime vehicle of modernization was the rapidly expanding communication network, which intensified in the late 19th century and reached its apogee in the inter-war years. Relative inaccessibility had provided some basis for cultural differentiation both within and between the socio-linguistic communities. However, the relative isolation was overcome by the development of an externally derived transport and communication system designed to facilitate through traffic from England to Ireland via Wales. The main railway routes ran east-west through the center and along the northern and southern coasts respectively, with branch lines penetrating the resource-rich hinterland allowing the exportation of slate, coal, iron, and steel products. Between 1839 and 1870 some 2,300 km of railway track had been built (an investment of £20 million in mid-19th century prices). In 1885 the Severn Tunnel was opened which had the effect of quickening the economic integration of South Wales with London, the Bristol region, and the Midlands while North Wales was linked more directly through Chester and Crewe to the Lancashire conurbations focused on Manchester and Liverpool and the Potteries district. The extensive rail network also encouraged the age of mass tourism to Welsh coastal resorts and the workers' annual holiday to Llandudno, Rhyl, Tenby, Aberavon, Porthcawl, and Barry contributed to their development as significant nodes in the Welsh urban hierarchy. They were also, by and large, far more exotic and multicultural in their makeup and have been seen by many as representing the face of modern, English Wales.

Yet the communication revolution also enabled entrepreneurs to develop new public spaces and domains wherein Welsh could be used, such as a dynamic Welsh-medium press (Jones 2000), and to encourage national cultural events, such as the network of *Eisteddfodau*, which culminated in the strengthening of a national consciousness and did so much to establish the basic parameters of contemporary culture (Löffler 2008). Wales lacked a metropolitan tradition and in effect, London, Birmingham, and Liverpool fulfilled these functions. Welsh societies in these major conurbations, particularly London, were extraordinarily influential in determining events at home (Jones 2001).

As a consequence of both industrialization and modernization, political life in Wales reflected the radicalism of a working class mass struggling for representation, equality of opportunity and decent working and living conditions for themselves and their dependants. At the turn of the 20th century the majority of voting males supported the Liberal Party. It was dedicated to social justice, to educational and health improvements under statutory regulation, to the disestablishment of the Church of England in Wales, and to Home Rule all round for the Celtic nations, particularly in Ireland. Under its charismatic, Welsh-speaking Prime Minister, David Lloyd-George, the Liberal Party was arguably the most influential political party on the world stage reflecting British Imperial power and interests. At the local level, the main conduit for spreading the Liberals' message of social reform and democratic representation was the Free Church or Nonconformist Chapel System which pervaded almost every settlement in Wales. The spectacular growth of the Nonconformist denominations following on from the Great Religious Revival of 1905 not only made Wales an outwardly more Christian society than hitherto, but also influenced nearly every aspect of public behavior and private life. Both in literary and scholarly terms, the increasingly bilingual popular culture owed a great deal to the opportunities for self-expression and publication afforded by the various denominations.

Counter movements to resist Anglicization were formed by intellectuals such as the Reverend Michael D. Jones, who in 1865 established a wholly Welsh migrant community in Patagonia (Argentina) (Williams 1992). The Reverend Emrys ap Iwan was the first minister of religion to appear before a court of law and insist on the primacy of the Welsh language in legal proceedings in Wales. Dan Isaac Davies, the HMI (Her Majesty's Inspector) for Schools, advocated a greater use of Welsh-medium education. Thomas Gee, the publisher of such ambitious multi-volume encyclopaedias as *Gwyddoniadur* was an advocate of mass circulation periodicals in Welsh. O. M. Edwards, university teacher, writer, publisher, and first Chief HMI for schools in Wales, tried to establish a more tolerant approach to bilingualism by attacking the injustice associated with the Welsh Not within the school system (a practice to punish pupils for using Welsh). His son, Sir Ifan ab Owen Edwards, established Urdd Gobaith Cymru (The Welsh League of Youth) in 1922; it has become the largest mass movement in Wales encouraging children and young adults to develop skills, competence, and leadership qualities in a variety of contexts, principally community work, *Eisteddfodau*, and sporting achievements.

In the liberal heyday, Wales established a set of national institutions that paralleled those in Scotland and Ireland. These include the overwhelmingly English-medium federal University of Wales (established 1883), the National Library of Wales at Aberystwyth and the National Museum of Wales at Cardiff which were established in 1907, and the Church in Wales which was created following the Act of Disestablishment in 1920.

The growing institutional strength of English as the language of commerce, public administration, and formal politics led to a counter-movement to protect Welsh culture. Plaid Genedlaethol Cymru (The Welsh National Party) formed in 1925 at Pwllheli, was dedicated to the promotion of Welsh-medium cultural and spiritual values, primarily through the maintenance of a small-scale, predominantly rural, Welsh language communitarian lifestyle. Plaid Cymru also railed against British imperialism and state nationalism. Under Gwynfor Evans, who became President of Plaid Cymru in 1945, the party grew and was active in the promotion of Welsh language rights, pacifism, and the defence of communities threatened by capital intensive projects initiated by English local governments anxious to develop hydro-electric power schemes and construct reservoirs, by drowning Welsh valleys, to provide water for English cities.

However, starting with the slump and depression of the period 1925–1936 the economy's over dependence on extractive industries was laid bare and Wales hemorrhaged thousands of its workers in search of work in the more prosperous manufacturing parts of industrial Britain. In the 50s and 60s this trend was continued and it is only rather recently that Wales has managed to restructure its economy to fashion a post-industrial society which prizes the knowledge economy and the widespread adoption of IT. Clearly the population's fluency in English gives Wales an advantage in attracting international organizations and companies, but on the down side the relatively high wage and social costs tend to mitigate against a full restructuring of the workforce and has led to several instances of relocation of capital and plant to less expensive locations in Eastern Europe and South East Asia.

Today the majority accepts that bilingualism is a distinct feature of society, of whom a significant proportion see it as advancing their children's education, social, and employment prospects. But there is also evidence of quite significant divergences, both within the adult and school-aged populations. Coupland et al. (2005) demonstrate considerable variability in the manner in which secondary school pupils perceive the value of Welsh, but the overall trends reinforce the salience of English which dominates the landscape and socio-economic sectors. So much so that outside of the specific metacultural domain, such as Welsh-medium education, the small and struggling Welsh language media sectors, national institutions, and some public sector organizations through which Welsh and bilingualism are being promoted, English is the functional default language of society.

The modern relationship between the Welsh and English languages can be interpreted in terms of five significant contexts. First the demographic transition and geographical distribution of speakers. Secondly, how either language influences the speech pattern, grammar, or morphology of the other. Thirdly the extent to which the two literatures conflict, engage in a "dialogue of the deaf" or coalesce. Fourthly how both languages and their related cultures are acquired and represented in the education system. Fifthly how interests related to language promotion and competition influence political culture and key issues within civil society.

2 Demolinguistics

The first language census of 1891 recorded that 898,914 people spoke Welsh (54.4%). Ten years later, in 1901, 929,824 (49.9%) were so recorded. At its census peak in 1911, the Welsh-speaking population numbered 977,366 (43.5%) of whom 190,300 were monoglot Welsh. Continuous decline throughout the century resulted in a 1981 Welsh-speaking population of 503,549 speakers (c.17.5%), of whom 21,283 recorded themselves as monoglot. By 1991 the Welsh-speaking population had declined to 496,530, a fall of some 1.4% (Aitchison and Carter 1993). The long trend of decline had finally slowed, compared with the acute fall of 17.3% between 1961 and 1971, and the fall of 6.3% for the period 1971–1981. By the 1980s English had become universal in Wales, so much so that the census ceased asking how many Welsh monoglots there were. In 2001 Wales was home to 2,903,085 residents, 71.57% of these declared that they had no skills in Welsh, while of those born in Wales this proportion reduced to 66%. Only 16.32% of the total population declared that they could speak, read, and write Welsh and 20.8%, (some 582,000), declared that they could speak the language. However, the increasingly multicultural population, containing some 5,436 Bangladeshi, 6,500 Somali and other non-European migrants, should caution us against assuming that all other residents are comfortable in using English in public life. Wales is an increasingly multilingual society.

3 Sociolinguistic variation in Welsh English

3.1 Phonology

Overviews of regional and social variation in English as spoken in Wales are provided by Wells (1982: 377–393) and Penhallurick (2007); see also the listings in Crystal (2003: 335). Variation in Welsh English broadly reflects historical tendencies of Anglicization, with some eastern varieties of English being perceived as "not Welsh", while other varieties are strongly resonant of Welsh identities. Vernacular English spoken in north-east Wales, in a zone including Rhyl, Prestatyn, Mold, and Buckley, is systematically influenced by Liverpool norms, for example with affricated final /t/ and /k/ in *great, like*, etc., hypercorrect-sounding realizations of *know, cold*, etc. (where the onset to the diphthong is schwa) and north-of-England-type realizations of *bath* (with short /a/) and *blood* (with 'uh' rather than the wedge vowel found in Received Pronunciation). A much smaller zone in the extreme south-east, east of Newport, shares features with south-west (of England) speech, most notably its rhotic characteristic (pronouncing /r/ in *farm, guard, first*, etc.). Other longstanding English areas (cf. Awberry 1997: 86–88) are southern Pembrokeshire and Gower (Penhallurick 1994) where rhotic pronunciation is also found as a relic feature.

The populous south-eastern conurbations of Barry, Cardiff (the capital city), and Newport developed a distinctive and again perceptibly rather "un-Welsh" vernacular variety during their rapid growth as industrial port cities. Successive studies by Parry (1977, 1978, 1979a, 1979b, 1990b), Penhallurick (1991), Mees and Collins (1999) and Coupland (1988) have shown that the English spoken in urban south-east Wales shows few signs of Welsh-language influence, and bears traces of the dialects of its principal donor communities. These include neighboring areas of England, especially the South West and West Midlands (Awberry 1997: 94–95; Jenkins 1997: 55), but also Liverpool and Ireland. A regularized pattern of present-tense verb morphology with *-s* in vernacular Cardiff speech produces utterances such as *They squeaks when I walks*, and this feature is common in many areas of southern and south-western England, but not in Wales outside the south-east. Similarly, the compound adverbial in *Where to is it?* is common both in south-east Wales and in south-west England, but not elsewhere in Wales. The compound adverbials *by here* (meaning simply 'here') and *by there* ('there') are much more widespread, although in the south-east they tend to be pronounced in their full forms, but reduced (to *by'ere* and *bu'there*) further west.

Coupland (1988) comments on pronunciation variables that distinguish Cardiff speech (reinterpreted by him in Graddol et al. 1996: 326; Viereck 1984). The most robust stereotype of vernacular Cardiff pronunciation is fronted and raised long 'a' sound in words such as *dark* and *park*, and indeed in *Cardiff*. The written form 'Kairdiff' is one attempt to capture the quality of Cardiff long /a:/ in newspaper discussions of accent. Words that have short 'a' in most varieties of English speech, for example in *cat* and *bag*, are also prone to fronting and raising in Cardiff, so that both short and long 'a' forms can be salient markers of local speech. Many other features regularly distinguish vernacular Cardiff speech from Received Pronunciation. Some local variants are shared by many other urban British vernaculars, including alveolar variants of the /ŋ/ nasal variable (*runnin'* versus *running*), zero realizations of /h/ (*'appy* versus *happy*) and the reduction of consonant clusters (*don' ey* versus *don't they*). /t/ between vowels is particularly prone to being realized as a tap or flap in Cardiff vernacular speech (e.g. in *better* or *lot of*) and, more unusually, /r/ between vowels is also liable to be flapped rather than continuant (in *very, sorry*, etc.). Whereas words with /ai/, such as *like* and *time*, tend to have centralized, schwa-like onsets in most varieties of Welsh English, in the urban south-east they tend to have rounded and retracted onsets, making the word *tie* resemble *toy*. Diphthongs with /ou/ can be lengthened, producing disyllabic pronunciations of *goal, coal*, as 'go-al' and 'co-al', etc.

Across the remainder of Wales, English speech has a large number of distinguishing characteristics, most of them influenced by the Welsh language, either concurrently (in the English speech of speakers who also speak Welsh) or historically (when community norms have developed under the influence of Welsh). Some clear variation exists, all the same, between northern and southern heartland varieties of English, and the former mining communities of the South Wales Valleys are generally distinguished from those of the rural south-west. Detailed descriptive studies are still sparse, but the phonology of English spoken in the Rhondda Valley has been analyzed by Walters (1999, 2001, 2003a, 2003b); and Tench (1990) and Connolly (1990) offer descriptions of English spoken in Abercrave and Port Talbot, respectively. In sources cited above, Penhallurick is able to draw from the findings of the *Survey of Anglo-Welsh Dialects* (Parry 1977, 1978, 1979a, 1979b, 1990a, 1990b).

One reliable marker of Welshness through English in most areas of Wales is the pronunciation of words such as *Tuesday* and *cure* (cf. Penhallurick 2007: 159), which have /iu/ (best captured in the written form 'iw'). This means that the pronunciation of *blue* regularly differs from that of *blew*, while *cure* has two syllables, 'iw' plus 'er' (Connolly 1990: 122–125). Most Welsh people outside of the south-east, whether they speak Welsh or not, pronounce Welsh place-names and other forms with a reasonable approximation to Welsh phonology, meaning that they have the sounds represented in writing by <ll> (the lateral fricative) and <ch> (the velar fricative) in their speech repertoires. Although the situation in Cardiff is changing with the growth in the number of fluent Welsh residents, speakers there have tended to pronounce place-names like *Llantrisant* and *Llandaf* with initial /l/, for example. Walters (2003a, b) analyzes the 'sing-song' intonation and stress patterns of Rhondda Valley English, which are replicated in other areas. Key features in this speech style are a considerable degree of pitch movement around stressed syllables, and the lengthening of consonants at the end of such syllables, which Walters argues are patterns directly transferred from Welsh speech (see also Penhallurick 1991, 2007: 163–164; Connolly 1990: 126). An interesting but idiosyncratic feature of some south-western rural varieties is the dropping of /w/ in word-initial position, so that, for example, *wood* is pronounced like 'ood'. A much more widely used feature is the use of full vowels in unstressed position, where standard English reduces those vowels to schwa (e.g. in *better* and *letter*).

The use of clear /l/ in all word-positions distinguishes English speech in much of southern and mid Wales, when most other varieties of English distinguish between clear and dark (or velar) forms of the phoneme /l/ (for example in the two realizations of /l/ in the words *leaf* and *feel*, respectively). In north-west Wales, however, and particularly in Gwynedd, very dark, pharyngealized /l/ predominates. Welsh English often has monophthongs where Received Pronunciation has diphthongs, particularly in words such as *great, made* (which can have /eː/) and *goat, nose* (which can have /oː/). This makes word-contrasts available in Welsh English which are not available in Received Pronunciation, such as *nose* versus *knows* and *made* versus *maid*. Particular patterns of distribution are complex, and some varieties in the south-west and north-west have monophthongs also in words in the *knows* and *maid* sets, but the general pattern of variation is explained by the Welsh language again having no /ei/ or /ou/ diphthongs (Penhallurick 2007). North Wales pronunciation of English is distinctive for its 'throaty' (pharyngealized) high vowels, also for the use of /s/ where most other varieties have voiced /z/, for example in *thousand* and *cheese* (Penhallurick 2007). This pattern of de-voicing results from Welsh lacking /z/, and similarly, the lack of affricates in Welsh results in identity between word-pairs such as *chin* and *gin*, both sounding like *chin* in North Wales.

3.2 Grammar and vocabulary

In terms of grammar, invariant use of the tag *isn't it*, whatever the grammatical form of a preceding statement, is held to be characteristic of Welsh English. It probably features more in stereotypical parodies than in actual usage, although it is entirely plausible as a transfer from colloquial Welsh question tag-forms such as *yntefe*. So-called "periphrastic *do*" constructions are found in southern Welsh English, as in *I do do it* and *They do like it*, where, unlike in Standard English, *do* is unstressed and the meaning is not contrastive. Predicate fronting is widely attested, where the fronted item is stressed, as in *Awkward it was* or *Fresh I wanted it*. Of these two grammatical features, the first (periphrastic *do*) is unlikely to be sourced from Welsh, while the second (predicate fronting) can safely be assumed to be so (Penhallurick 2007: 164–169). Many lexical items are transferred into English from Welsh, although it is difficult to gauge their status – whether they should be considered as relatively spontaneous lexical code-switches or as more fixed incorporated loans into English. Examples include *crachach* 'posh people', *cwtch* 'a cuddle', *eisteddfod* 'the competitive arts and performance festival', *Duw* 'God' (as an exclamation), and *bach* 'little', *del* 'dear' and *fy nghariad* 'my loved one' as terms of endearment. There are also less common items such as *venter* 'bet' which also have their roots in Welsh, in this case in the verb *mentro*, to venture (Connolly 1990: 127–128).

Because Welsh English has many distinctive features, many of them regularly used by "educated" people in formal situations, it is possible to argue that a Standard Welsh English exists. Garrett et al. (2003) argue on the basis of findings from extensive attitudinal research that English speech associated with rural south-west Wales, centered on Carmarthen, has the strongest profile as a putative standard variety. Even so, outside of the south-eastern conurbations, Wales tends not to have fully stratified class structures consistent with the attribution of standard and non-standard speech. Coupland (1990: 243–252) also makes the point that different varieties of Welsh English have been used to signify ideologically different political stances, rather than marking class or status *per se*. In her consideration of the field, Löffler (2008) has cautioned that although the "Welsh Englishes" are an acknowledged feature of the sociolinguistic situation in Wales, their social role is neither clear-cut nor simple.

Borrowings from Welsh into English from the 17th century onwards relate mainly to aspects of Welsh culture and an illustrative list will suffice here. They include *tad* or *dad*, father; *cromlech* an 'arched stone' a megalithic chamber tomb or *dolmen; englyn*, a four-lined stanza of prescribed from written in *cynghanedd* metre; *flummery*, a pudding made with coagulated wheatflour or oatmeal, which has come to mean flattery or nonsense; *Gorsedd*, a 'throne' a meeting of bards and druids; *cynghannedd*, a complex form of alliterative metre; *cwm*, a valley; a deep rounded hollow with a steep side formed by ice action; a cirque; *eisteddfod*, 'session' a festival of poetry, singing, music the arts and increasingly technology; *hwyl*, emotional fervor, characteristic of poetry recitation, and *corgi*, 'dwarf-dog' short-legged dogs from either Cardigan or Pembroke as favored by the British Royal Family (Helcion 1998).

Finally, it is important not to over-compartmentalize Welsh and English in Wales, because code-switching is a common characteristic of bilingual usage. Research by Deuchar (2006) and Deuchar et al. (2007, 2016, 2017) for example, has evaluated universal and conditional models of code switching. Stammers and Deuchar (2007) have analyzed English verbs in Welsh speech by reference to generic hypotheses suggested by Poplack and Meechan (1998) and Myers-Scotton (1993) and concluded that frequency may be more important than contrast between switches and loans. Deuchar (2006) also argues that Welsh-English speakers in her data tend to maintain a Welsh-language matrix in their code-switched speech, and consequently that they are comparable to Spanish-English speakers in the USA, or Arabic-Dutch speakers in the Netherlands. This in turn suggests a pattern of bilingual communication typical of relatively stable bilingual contexts, rather than one that presages language shift or language death. Musk (2010) takes a different perspective, providing evidence that Welsh-English bilinguals tend to blend their codes into a relatively syncretic and flexible communication system. Codes are kept separate only for specific discursive purposes, such as quoting other people's utterances.

4 Literature

John Hughes (1924) advanced the study of Wales and the Welsh in English Literature while sustained critical attention to Welsh writing in English (as opposed to occasional reviews and essays) began in the 1930s with the founding of the literary magazine *Wales* by Keidrych Rhys. This coincided with the so-called "first flowering" of Anglo-Welsh writers (Webb 2013) such as Glyn Jones, Dylan Thomas, Gwyn Jones, Lewis Jones (Prys-Williams 2004), and Bert Coombes (Jones and Williams 1999). The prominence of Dylan Thomas in the 1940s and 1950s also meant that English magazines and critics increasingly paid more attention to Welsh writing. Thus Thomas's characters in *Under Milk Wood* voice clear influences of Welsh alliterative patterns in their speeches and in his descriptive passages about "streets rocked to sleep by the sea" (Thomas 1995: 17).

In 1975 Gwyn Jones, published his *The First Forty Years: Some Notes on Anglo-Welsh Literature* which is a seminal statement by a scholar and writer who himself published key creative works in the 1930s, such as the novel, *Times Like These*. This was in part a riposte to Saunders Lewis's 1939 largely negative polemical essay *Is there an Anglo-Welsh literature?* (Harris 2000: 451–452). It reflected the increasing tension between Welsh medium and Anglo-Welsh literature which revolved around questions of authenticity, originality of subject matter and the difficult question "Who should speak for the Welsh nation and in which language(s)?". Some early attempts to bridge the gap between both traditions were made, witness the work of Jones ([1968] 2001), *The Dragon has Two Tongues*, which is an important critical statement by a participant in the flowering of Anglo-Welsh writing from the 1930s onwards. Jones gives informed evaluations of the work of his own contemporaries, as well as providing a revealing autobiographical account of his own growth as a writer.

Critical too was the founding of "second flowering" journals such as *Poetry Wales, Dock Leaves* and *The Anglo-Welsh Review* (Garlick 1972). The critics of this period often adopted an overtly nationalist agenda and a positive attitude towards the Welsh language. By the 1970s, the Writers of Wales series was established by the University of Wales Press; the emphasis of this series and of the criticism more generally was decidedly biographical. Raymond Garlick (1972) and Roland Mathias (1985, 1986) were prominent figures in the 1970s and 1980s, their criticism being scholarly, perceptive but basically Leavisite in its aesthetic assumptions (if not in its politics). Tony Conran and Raymond Williams brought more challenging, theoretically-inflected approaches to Welsh writing in English during the late 1970s and 1980s. Conran's work (1982 and 1997) has been described as "idiosyncratic, opinionated, brilliant analyses of the Welsh poetic tradition by a scholar and translator who knows the Welsh-language tradition very well indeed and traces the influence of Welsh on English in his theory of 'seepage' from one poetic tradition to the other" (Gramich 2007). Raymond Williams's (1979) *The Welsh Industrial Novel*, derived from the inaugural Gwyn Jones lecture given at Cardiff University College, is a seminal Marxist-inflected analysis, where the foremost cultural critic of his day turns his attention to Welsh material.

Other theoretical approaches came to be adopted increasingly by critics in the 1980s and 1990s, as discussed in Hooker (2001) along with more comparative perspectives. The best recent articulator of the comparative approach is M. Wynn Thomas (1992, 1999, 2002, 2003), whose literary criticism is superb, being both accessible and grounded in a thorough understanding of the interaction between English and Welsh cultures. Consequently he is a seminal figure who is equally well respected and active in both traditions.

A conscious promotion of Welsh writing in English was reflected in the establishment of CREW (The Center for Research into the English Literature and Language of Wales) at Swansea University and in the publication of authoritative reference works such as M. Stephens' (1998) *The New Companion to the Literature of Wales*, his 2007 *Poetry 1900–2000* and the founding of the refereed *Yearbook of Welsh Writing in English* (now called *Almanac*) which reflected the dynamism associated with the critical idiom. In the later 1990s and in the first decade of the new millennium, feminist and postcolonial approaches have dominated critical writing in the field. Thus Knight (2004) and Bohata (2004) provide contrasting surveys of the literary field from a sustained post-colonial viewpoint, while Aaron and Williams (2005) provide a parallel critique in terms of social and political perspectives.

Given that bilingualism is an increasingly prevalent norm in Welsh society, it is no surprise that the integrative and bridge-building synthesis of earlier decades has become a more common starting point for literary criticism and interpretation. Thus Jane Aaron (2007) offers a pioneering history of 19th-century Welsh women's writing; covering work in both languages while Katie Gramich (2007) has constructed the first history of 20th-century Welsh women's writing, again covering work in both languages and deploying feminist and spatial theory. This third generation consciously avoid the term Anglo-Welsh and prefer to use the descriptor "English-language poetry/fiction/literature in Wales" or "Literatures of Wales", or as deployed in the Welsh Literature Abroad catalogue *Turning Tides: Contemporary Writing from Wales* (Minhinnick 2004) This includes the full panoply of authors such as Angharad Price, Mihangel Morgan, Gillian Clarke, and Robert Minhinnick. Several notable authors translate their own work, such as Gwyneth Lewis and see no inherent contradiction or conflict in working in both languages simultaneously, in keeping with the national leitmotif of inhabiting "the bilingual nation".

5 Education

Between 1870 and 1950 statutory education in Wales was conducted almost entirely through the medium of English and the school was the most important socialization agency in spreading proficiency in English. From the early 50s onwards a minority of parents agitated for Welsh-medium education. Labour Party controlled Local Education Authorities, especially Flint and Glamorgan, developed pioneering bilingual educational policies in anglicized Wales, and established several Welsh medium primary and secondary schools in the period 1952–1965. The growth of an alternative and competitive Welsh-medium education system offered a certain amount of choice to parents, but it also threatened to reproduce "a dialogue of the deaf" between the two language communities and was not universally popular. A common national curriculum was introduced following the reforms of the 1988 Education Act which made Welsh a foundation subject. By April 1994 all schools were now obliged to teach Welsh within the curriculum. This has had profound consequences for the relationship between the Welsh and English languages. For the first time ever, all children are now exposed to the formal teaching of Welsh. Prior to the 1988 Reforms some 244 (14.2%) of primary schools did not teach any Welsh at all and many of the others did not teach it in a systematic fashion. As a result of a more pluralistic mix of languages of instruction being used, Welsh is seen more as an additional skill for many pupils from non-Welsh speaking homes and some of the old antagonism born of group resentment and lack of exposure to Welsh has been reduced. At the Further and Higher Education level English predominates as a medium of instruction, despite periodic attempts to broaden the range of subjects and qualifications available to students desirous of a Welsh medium education. A promising development is the *Coleg Cymraeg Cenedlaethol*, a Welsh-medium option for university-level instruction which has already appointed a number of Welsh-medium lectureships in Social Science, Humanities, and Science disciplines at many Welsh universities.

A fundamental consequence of both educational and political changes of late has been the growth of national consciousness and self-confidence, and this has been reflected in the dynamism of the media, theatre, popular culture, and entertainment in both languages. Sport and the media have long had a distinct Welsh organizational structure; to this we may add newer formal, institutional, and professional networking opportunities to serve lawyers, accountants, medics, public servants, and trade unionists. All of these new national organizations evince a bilingual code of practice and several operate a robust bilingual policy where Welsh and English operate as co-equal languages in formal settings.

6 Language promotion and group dynamics

Throughout the 20th century attempts to counter the hegemony of English and to promote a Welsh language revival included the establishment of Welsh-medium education (1939), the formation of Cymdeithas yr Iaith Gymraeg (The Welsh Language Society) in 1963, the creation of Welsh-language radio stations (1974) and a television channel (1982, 1998), and the Welsh Language Act of 1993, which made Welsh an official language in Wales alongside English and established the Welsh Language Board to oversee language policy and engage in language revitalization efforts (Williams 1986; Philips 1998; Löffler 2000).

More recently, Welsh language organizations have focused on the preservation of *Y Fro Gymraeg* 'The Welsh Speaking Heartland' including attempts to bilingualize English-speakers and to strengthen the rural economy. Movements such as *Cymuned* 'Community' dedicated to the strengthening of Welsh language communities, have been caricatured by the popular press as vehicles for anti-English racism and this has reconfigured the debate as an ethnic minority-state majority conflict which renders the Welsh discourse illegitimate by branding it as race hatred (Brooks 2006). In several parts of Wales, movements such as English First represent the demands of English medium parents to have their children educated mainly in English within local education authorities which have an officially bilingual policy, such as Gwynedd, Môn, and Carmarthen.

Within the English-Welsh relationship there is a form of double helix paradox or bind. For some, their activism in support of Welsh can be interpreted as an attempt to deprecate or deny the hegemony of English. Consequently their attempt to preserve a distinct Welsh identity can also include a conscious attempt to move away from the Received Pronunciation that would have been emphasized in their education and in civil society. For others, who are largely non-Welsh speaking working class, it is their accent which marks them and perhaps inevitably, the politics of Welsh versus English social identities are often played out within the resources of the English language, and this undermines the validity of the concept of Welsh Wales, as if non-Welsh speaking Wales has no means of expressing its Welshness.

7 Official policy on language equality

British constitutional change established a 60 member National Assembly for Wales in 1999 and has thus enabled language, education, and cultural issues to be debated and formulated within a Welsh national context for the first time ever in modern history. The current government, since the spring of 2011, is formed by the Labour Party which remains committed to the construction of a fully bilingual nation.

Language issues received a great deal of attention in the first terms of the Assembly's deliberations and in 2003 the Assembly Government published its language policy, *Iaith Pawb: A National Action Plan for a Bilingual Wales*. This was revised in 2010 with the publication of *A Living Language: A Language for Living*. The original and new policies confirm that individuals should have the right to use the language of their choice and that organizations should exercise a responsibility to acknowledge and facilitate the individual's right to do so. Welsh language activists interpreted this as a coming of age of government policy whereby at long last the right of speakers to use the language as 'a matter of choice' was enshrined in official policy. In February 2011 additional legislation was passed as the Welsh Language (Wales) Measure whereby such choices would be enframed within law, and a new regulatory system, employing national standards of bilingual service delivery, overseen by a Language Commissioner would be put in place during the period 2011–2014. Significantly the new Welsh Language Measure, which ushers in a period of legislative devolution, has shied away from formulating a set of fundamental language rights, and this will doubtless be a new battleground which threatens to repoliticize the language issue in the future.

Increasingly the Welsh population is characterized by having full fluency in a major world language, with all the opportunities which English offers for engagement in a world economy, and varying degrees of fluency in Welsh, which has extended its remit and purchase within a wider set of contemporary domains.

8 Summary

The development of a bilingual society remains a huge challenge. If the current promotional and regulatory efforts succeed in forming the contours of a bilingual society within an increasingly multicultural context, then such efforts will counter the predictions of doom mongers who interpret the inexorable dominance of English as being both hegemonic and pernicious to the interests of the smaller nations with which it interacts. It could be argued that an undue emphasis on the promotion of Welsh has overshadowed and underplayed the fundamental distinctiveness of the role of English in shaping Wales. It could also be argued that the conventional Welsh-English divide masks the contribution of a more subtle, nuanced, and diverse multilingual and multicultural population, whose interests are not best served by an official discourse and accompanying set of policies which tends to privilege the majority, at the expense of a range of minorities, hardly any of whom are mobilised on a set of common demands or operate with a united front within civil society.

Acknowledgements: I am especially grateful to Nik Coupland for his advice and to Marion Löffler and Katie Gramich for their willingness to share their work and offer constructive criticisms of this entry.

9 References

Aaron, Jane. 2003. *The Welsh Survival Gene*. Cardiff: Institute of Welsh Affairs.
Aaron, Jane and Christopher Williams (eds.). 2005. *Post Colonial Wales*. Cardiff: University of Wales Press.
Aaron, Jane. 2007. *Nineteenth-Century Women's Writing in Wales: Nation, Gender and Identity*. Cardiff: University of Wales Press.
Aitchison, John and Harold Carter. 1993. The Welsh language in 1991 – A broken heartland and a new beginning. *Planet* 97: 3–10.
Awbery, Gwen. 1997. The English language in Wales. In: Hildegard C. Tristram (ed.). *The Celtic Englishes*, 86–100. Heidelberg: Universitätsverlag C. Winter.
Bohata, Kirsti. 2004. *Postcolonialism Revisited*. Cardiff: University of Wales Press.
Brooks, Simon. 2006. The Idioms of Race: the "Racist Nationalist" in Wales as Bogeyman. In: Robin Chapman (ed.), *The Idiom of Dissent: protest and propaganda in Wales*, 139–165. Llandysul: Gomer Press.
Collins, Beverly and Inger M. Mees. 1990. The Phonetics of Cardiff English. In: Nikolas Coupland (ed.), *English in Wales: Diversity, Conflict and Change*, 87–103. Clevedon: Multilingual Matters Ltd.
Conran, Anthony. 1982. *The Cost of Strangeness: Essays on the English Poets of Wales*. Llandysul: Gomer.
Conran, Anthony. 1997. *Frontiers in Anglo Welsh Poetry*. Cardiff: University of Wales Press.
Connolly, John H. 1990. Port Talbot English. In: Nikolas Coupland (ed.), 121–129.
Coupland, Nikolas. 1988. *Dialect in Use: Sociolinguistic Variation in Cardiff English*. Cardiff: University of Wales Press.
Coupland, Nikolas. 1990. 'Standard Welsh English': a variable semiotic. In: Nikolas Coupland (ed.), 232–257.
Coupland, Nikolas (ed.). 1990. *English in Wales: Diversity, Conflict and Change*. Clevedon: Multilingual Matters Ltd.
Coupland, Nikolas and Martin J. Ball. 1989. Welsh and English in contemporary Wales: sociolinguistic issues. *Contemporary Wales* 3: 7–40. Cardiff: University of Wales Press.
Coupland, Nikolas, Hywel Bishop, Angie Williams, Betsy Evans, and Peter Garrett. 2005 'Affiliation, engagement, language use and vitality: Secondary schools students' subjective orientations to Welsh and Welshness. *International Journal of Bilingual Education and Bilingualism* 8(1): 1–24.

Crystal, David (ed.). 1997. *The Cambridge Encyclopaedia of Language*. Cambridge: Cambridge University Press.
Crystal, David (ed.). 2003. *The Cambridge Encyclopaedia of the English Language*. Cambridge: Cambridge University Press.
Crystal, David. 2004. *The Stories of English*. London: Penguin.
Davies, John, Nigel Jenkins, Menna Baines, and Peredur I. Lynch (eds.). 2008. *The Welsh Academy Encyclopaedia of Wales*. Cardiff: University of Wales Press.
Deuchar, Margaret. 2006. Welsh-English code-switching and the Matrix Language frame model. *Lingua* 116(11): 1986–2011.
Deuchar, Margaret and Jonathan Stammers. 2016. English-origin verbs in Welsh: Adjudicating between two theoretical approaches. *Languages 2016*, 1 (1), doi 10.3390/languages1010007.
Deuchar, Margaret, Kevin Donnelly, Caroline Piercy. 2017. "Mae pobl monolingual yn minority": Factors favouring the production of code-switching by Welsh-English bilingual speakers. In: Mercedes Durham and Jonathan Morris, J. (eds), *Sociolinguistics in Wales*, 209–239. Basingstoke: Palgrave MacMillan.
Evans, Caradoc. 1987. *My People*. Edited by John Harris. Bridgend: Seren.
Garlick, Raymond. 1972. *An Introduction to Anglo-Welsh Literature*. Cardiff: University of Wales Press.
Garrett, Peter, Nikolas Coupland, and Angie Williams. 2003. *Investigating Language Attitudes: Social Meanings of Dialect, Ethnicity and Performance*. Cardiff: University of Wales Press.
Graddol, David, Dick Leith, and Joan Swann (eds.). 1996. *English: History, Diversity and Change*. London: Routledge.
Gramich, Katie. 2007. *Twentieth-Century Women's Writing in Wales: Land, Gender, Belonging*. Cardiff: University of Wales Press.
Harris, John. 2000. The war of the tongues: Early Anglo-Welsh responses to Welsh literary culture. In: Geraint H. Jenkins and Mari A. Williams (eds.), 439–461.
Hansard. 1993. *House of Lords Debate 02, February 1993* Vol. 542. CC: 136–216.
Hooker, Jeremy. 2001. *Imagining Wales: A View of Modern Welsh Writing in English*. Cardiff: University of Wales Press.
Hughes, W. John. 1924. *Wales and the Welsh in English Literature*. Wrexham: Hughes and Son.
Helcion. 1998. *The Hutchinson Factfinder*. Oxford: Helicon.
Jenkins, Geraint (ed.). 1997. *The Welsh Language Before the Industrial Revolution*. Cardiff: University of Wales Press.
Jenkins, Geraint H. and Mari A. Williams (eds.). 2000. *'Let's Do Our Best for the Ancient Tongue': The Welsh Language in the Twentieth Century*. Cardiff: University of Wales Press.
Jones, Aled. 2000. The Nineteenth-Century Media and Welsh identity. In: Laurel Brake, Bill Bell, and David Finkelstein (eds.), *Nineteenth-Century Media and the Construction of Identities*, 310–325. Basingstoke: Palgrave.
Jones, Bill and Christopher Williams. 1999. *B. L. Coombes*. Cardiff: University of Wales Press.
Jones, Emrys (ed.). 2001. *The Welsh in London*. Cardiff: University of Wales Press.
Jones, Gwyn. 1975. *The First Forty Years: Some Notes on Anglo-Welsh Literature*. Cardiff: University of Wales Press.
Jones, Glyn [1968] 2001. *The Dragon Has Two Tongues*. Cardiff: University of Wales Press.
Klaus, Gustav H. and Stephen Knight (eds.). 2000. *British Industrial Fictions*. Cardiff: University of Wales Press.

Knight, Stephen. 2004. *A Hundred Years of Fiction*. Cardiff: University of Wales Press.
Löffler, Marion. 2000. The Welsh language movement in the first half of the twentieth century: an exercise in quiet revolutions. In: Geraint H. Jenkins and Mari A. Williams (eds.), 181–216.
Löffler, Marion. 2008. The English Language in Wales. In: Michael Matto and Haruko Momma (eds.), *A Companion to the History of the English Language*, 350–357. Oxford: Blackwell Publishing.
Mann, Michael. 2005. *The Dark Side of Democracy: Explaining Ethnic Cleansing*. Cambridge: Cambridge University Press.
Mathias, Roland. 1985. *A Ride Through the Wood: Essays on Anglo-Welsh Literature*. Bridgend: Poetry Wales Press.
Mathias, Roland. 1986. *Anglo-Welsh Literature – An Illustrated History*. Bridgend: Poetry Wales Press
Mees, Inger M. and Beverley Collins. 1999. Cardiff: A real-time study of glottalisation. In: Paul Foulkes and Gerard Docherty (eds.), *Urban Voices: Accent Studies in the British Isles*, 185–202. London: Arnold.
Minhinnick, Robert. 2004. *Turning Tides: Contemporary Writing from Wales*. Cardiff: Wales Arts International.
Morgan, Kenneth O. 1970. *Wales in British Politics, 1868–1922*. Cardiff: University of Wales Press.
Morgan, Prys. 1988. *A Bible for Wales-Beibl I Gymru*. Aberystwyth: National Library of Wales.
Musk, Nigel. 2010. Code-switching and code-mixing in Welsh bilinguals' talk: Confirming or refuting the maintenance of language boundaries? *Language, Culture and Curriculum* 23(3): 179–197.
Myers-Scotton, Carol. 1993. *Duelling Languages: Grammatical Structures in Codeswitching*. Oxford: Clarendon Press.
National Assembly for Wales. 2011. *Welsh Language (Wales) Measure*. Cardiff: National Assembly for Wales.
Parry, David. 1977. *The Survey of Anglo-Welsh Dialects*. Vol. I: *The South-East*. Swansea: University of Wales Swansea.
Parry, David. 1978. *Notes on the Dialect of Gwent*. Swansea: University of Wales Swansea.
Parry, David. 1979a. *The Survey of Anglo-Welsh Dialects*. Vol. II: *The South-West*. Swansea: University of Wales Swansea.
Parry, David. 1979b. *Notes on the Glamorgan Dialects*. Swansea: University of Wales Swansea.
Parry, David. 1990a. The conservative English dialects of North Carmarthenshire. In: Nikolas Coupland (ed.), 142–150.
Parry, David. 1990b. The conservative English dialects of south Pembrokeshire. In: Nikolas Coupland (ed.), 151–161.
Penhallurick, Robert. 1991. *The Anglo-Welsh Dialects of North Wales*. Frankfurt am Main: Peter Lang.
Penhallurick, Robert. 1994. *Gowerland and its Language: A History of the English Speech of the Gower Peninsula, South Wales*. Frankfurt am Main: Peter Lang.
Penhallurick, Robert. 2007. English in Wales. In: David Britain (ed.), *Language in the British Isles*, 152–175. Cambridge: Cambridge University Press.
Philips, Dylan. 1998. *Trwy Ddulliau Chwyldro*. Llandysul: Gomer Press.
Poplack, Shana and Marjory Meechan. 1998. How languages fit together in codemixing. *International Journal of Bilingualism* 2(2): 127–138.

Pryce, W. T. Reece and Colin H. Williams. 1988. Sources and methods in the study of language areas: a case study of Wales. In: Colin H. Williams (ed.), *Language in Geographic* Context: 167–237. Bristol: Multilingual Matters.
Prys-Williams, Barbara. 2004. *Twentieth Century Autobiography*. Cardiff: University of Wales Press.
Stammers, Jonathan and Margaret Deuchar. 2007. *English Verbs in Welsh Speech*. Presentation at ISB6 Hamburg, June 2007.
Stephens, Meic (ed.). 1998. *The New Companion to the Literature of Wales*. Cardiff: University of Wales Press.
Stephens, Meic. 2007. *Poetry 1900–2000: One Hundred Poets from Wales*. Cardigan: Parthian.
Tench, Paul. 1990. The pronunciation of English in Abercrave. In: Nikolas Coupland (ed.), 130–141.
Thomas, Brynley. 2000. A cauldron of rebirth: population and the Welsh language. In: Geraint H. Jenkins (ed.), *The Welsh Language and its Social Domains, 1801–1911*, 81–100. Cardiff: University of Wales Press.
Thomas, Dylan. 1995. *Under Milkwood: the Definitive Edition*. London: Everyman.
Thomas, M. Wynn. 1992. *Internal difference: Studies in modern Welsh writing in English*. Cardiff: University of Wales Press.
Thomas, M. Wynn. 1999. *Corresponding Cultures: The Two Literatures of Wales*. Cardiff: University of Wales Press.
Thomas, M.Wynn. 2002. *Kitchener Davies*. Cardiff: University of Wales Press.
Thomas, M.Wynn. 2003. *Welsh Writing in English*. Cardiff: University of Wales Press.
Viereck, Wolfgang. 1984. *Varieties of English Around the World. Focus on England and Wales.* Amsterdam: John Benjamins.
Walters, J. Roderick. 1999. *A Study of the Segmental and Suprasegmental Phonology of Rhondda Valleys English*. Unpublished PhD thesis, Pontypridd: University of Glamorgan.
Walters, J. Roderick. 2001. English in Wales and a Welsh Valleys accent. *World Englishes* 20(3): 285–304.
Walters, J. Roderick. 2003a. Celtic English. Influences on a South Wales Valley Accent. *English World-Wide* 24(1): 63–87.
Walters, J. Roderick. 2003. On the intonation of a South Wales Valleys accent of English. *Journal of International Phonetics Association* 33(2): 211–238.
Webb, Andrew. 2013. *Edward Thomas and World Literary Studies: Wales, Anglocentricism and English Literature*. Cardiff: University of Wales Press.
Wells, John. 1982. *Accents of English,* Vol. 2*: The British Isles*. Cambridge: Cambridge University Press.
Welsh Government. 2010. *A Living Language: A Language for Living*. Cardiff: Welsh Government.
Williams, Christopher. 1998. *Capitalism, Community and Conflict*. Cardiff: University of Wales Press.
Williams, Colin H. 1986. Language planning and minority group rights. In: Iain Hume and W.T.R. Pryce (eds.), *The Welsh and Their Country*, 253–272. Llandysul: Gomer Press.
Williams, Colin H. 1994. *Called Unto Liberty*. Clevedon, Avon: Multilingual Matters.
Williams, Colin H. 2008. *Linguistic Minorities in Democratic Context*. Basingstoke: Palgrave.

Williams, Glyn. 1992. *The State and the Ethnic Community*. Cardiff: University of Wales Press.
Williams, Raymond. 1979. *The Welsh industrial novel: The inaugural Gwyn Jones lecture*. Cardiff: University College Cardiff Press.

Marianne Hundt
Chapter 15:
Australian/New Zealand English

1   Introduction —— 290
2   Accent —— 292
3   Lexicon —— 296
4   Grammar —— 301
5   Dialects —— 302
6   Summary —— 305
7   References —— 306

Abstract: The chapter provides a comparative overview of the external histories, the development of the regional accents, vocabulary, and grammar in Australia and New Zealand. Both language contact with the indigenous languages as well as dialect contact amongst the original input varieties play a role in the evolution of the two Englishes. Social, ethnic, and regional varieties of the two southern-hemisphere Englishes are also of relevance to the history of New Englishes as their development represents an important step in the developmental process (Schneider 2007). The settlement period is treated, but more recent developments (i.e. the question of an ongoing Americanization) are also discussed. Evidence on the evolution of Australian and New Zealand English comes from demographic data, meta-linguistic comments, historical dictionaries, corpora and – for New Zealand English – even some recordings of the first New Zealand-born speakers of the variety. The comparative approach to the history of the two southern-hemisphere Englishes confirms that the two varieties are closely connected. Not surprisingly, there are also some local developments, mostly in their vocabulary and accent. The chapter further shows that the development of the local lexicon and accent has received much broader treatment whereas differential grammatical change in the two varieties is still largely uncharted territory.

Marianne Hundt: Zürich (Switzerland)

1 Introduction

The concept of a joint chapter on Australian (AusE) and New Zealand English (NZE) is controversial, especially to New Zealanders who might justly object to being treated simply as an appendix to Australia. Initially, the description of NZE lagged behind that of the variety across the Tasman: in the early 1990s, there was a more substantial body of research on AusE; the situation has been rectified, however, and NZE is no longer "the dark horse of World English regional dialectology" (Crystal 1995: 354) but one of the most researched varieties worldwide (see Bell and Kuiper 2000). In fact, as far as the evolution of the regional accent is concerned, much better evidence is available for NZE (see Section 2.2). The history of the two varieties receives separate treatment in volume 5 of the *Cambridge History of the English Language* (Burchfield 1994). The histories of Australia and New Zealand are closely connected, however (see Section 1.1), and the following account will not treat the development of the two varieties separately. Instead, the historical account of their accents, lexicon, grammar, and dialects will take a comparative approach in order to tease out the common ground and differences in the development of the two inner-circle varieties in the south Pacific.

1.1 English in Australia and New Zealand

A brief sketch of the external history of AusE and NZE gives a first indication as to why the two varieties are closely connected. English arrived in Australia and New Zealand in the late 18th century. However, large-scale settlement affected Australia about 50 years earlier than New Zealand. In Australia, large numbers of people started arriving from the 1790s onwards; in New Zealand, substantial migration happened from the 1840s, after the Treaty of Waitangi had been signed, in which the Maori chiefs yielded sovereignty to the British crown. Furthermore, European colonization of Australia began as a penal colony in 1788, with non-convict settlers arriving in greater numbers after 1820, whereas settlement of New Zealand was exclusively by free settlers, spearheaded by the New Zealand Company in the early colonial period. Initially, this resulted in a more marked social divide in Australia than in New Zealand which, to the present day, has a reputation of being an exceptionally egalitarian society, even by Western standards (see Bell and Kuiper 2000: 13; note that similar beliefs have also developed in Australia, see for instance Downie n.d.). Another difference between the two countries was that, prior to European settlement, Australia had been a highly multilingual country with hundreds of (at times unrelated) Aboriginal languages whereas language contact in New Zealand involved dialects of a single Polynesian language.

One explanation why AusE and NZE developed similarities is that they derive from a similar input of English, Scottish, and Irish dialects, with a predominance of south-eastern English dialects (note that this also applies to White South African English, see Gordon and Sudbury 2002). Migration from Australia to New Zealand and vice versa contributed to the maintenance of close socio-political ties. New Zealand even started out as colony of New South Wales, but gained independent colonial status in 1841. At the same time, migration in the other direction, from New Zealand to Australia, was only outnumbered by immigrants from the British Isles during the colonial period, as Gunn (1992: 220) points out. Gold rushes in New South Wales, Victoria, and Otago in the 1850s and 1860s were one reason for migration across the Tasman; they also attracted fortune seekers from other colonies, amongst them North America. After World War I, both countries gained independence with the signing of the Treaty of Versailles. Soldiers from Australia and New Zealand fought alongside British (and American) troops in both world wars. The political and economic ties with Britain weakened considerably, however, after it had joined the European Economic Community; at the same time, this development increased trans-Tasman ties. The relations between New Zealand and the US (but not between Australia and the States) cooled somewhat after New Zealand's withdrawal from the ANZUS treaty (a security treaty linking Australia, New Zealand, and the United States), largely due to the very decided anti-nuclear politics of New Zealand. This might also have had repercussions on attitudes towards both American English (AmE) and AusE as reference varieties for New Zealanders. The second half of the 20th century saw substantial migratory movements from Europe and (South) Asia to both countries, resulting in growing multi-culturalism and increased language contact.

1.2 Evidence

The evidence on the development of AusE and NZE comes from demographic sources (migration records, census data), metalinguistic comments from visitors or school inspectors and early written documents (on the limitations of reconstructing the accent of a variety from written evidence, see Gordon 1998); authentic spoken data is hardly ever available (for an exception, see Section 2). Historical text corpora are not publicly available for either Australian or New Zealand English, but Fritz (2007) uses a corpus of early Australian English (COOEE) for his study, covering the period 1788–1900. Electronically available texts were collected into a pilot corpus of early New Zealand English at the University of Zürich

(Hundt 2012; note that historical texts are available electronically in some cases but they are not corpora in the strict sense of the word); for developments in the 20th century, Macalister has collected a larger corpus (see Macalister 2006). The comparative description of the vocabulary is facilitated by the historical dictionaries of the varieties. Meta-linguistic comments are a valuable source for reconstructing features of early colonial varieties, but they also provide a window on peoples' attitudes to emerging varieties. Changing attitudes are part of the history of new Englishes. Gunn (1992: 220–221) points out that "an important distinguishing feature was the emergence of nationalism, strong and early in Australia, whereas New Zealand maintained firm, long-lasting ties, both emotional and linguistic, with the mother country". This claim is still supported by fairly recent evidence on attitudes towards the local accent in Australia and New Zealand: Bradley and Bradley (2001: 282) show that "Australians are feeling progressively more positive about Australian as opposed to other varieties of English speech" whereas Bayard (2000: 321) finds that "New Zealanders still are uneasy about their own voices, and clearly prefer overseas accents not only in terms of the power dimension [...] but also in terms of solidarity and mateship" (see also Bayard and Green 2003).

1.3 Outline

In writing a historical account of English in Australia and New Zealand, one of the choices to be made is whether to focus on the development of standard English, or whether to include non-standard varieties. The focus in this chapter will not be exclusively on standard English but also include information on social and regional dialects as well as ethnic varieties. Within the scope of this chapter, non-standard varieties cannot be treated in depth, however. The remainder of the chapter will review the state of the art on the history and development of the local accent, vocabulary, grammar and dialects in Australia and New Zealand.

2 Accent

The AusE and the NZE accent share some characteristic features, such as the raised short front vowels in the lexical set TRAP, DRESS and KIT; the similarities often make it difficult for outsiders to distinguish between the two accents (for the history of these pronunciations in NZE, see Woods 2000). However, the two accents differ in the realization of the KIT vowel. New Zealanders are commonly stereotyped as pronouncing *fish and chips* as *fush and chups*, a popular meal that Australians refer to as *feesh and cheeps* (see Bell 1997). These eye-dialect renderings try to capture the fact that the New Zealand KIT vowel is slightly lower and more centralized while the Australian realization approximates [i]. For a more detailed description of the phonetics and phonology of AusE and NZE, see e.g. Wells (1982).

Initially, the main controversy in studies on the origin of the Australian and New Zealand accents revolved around single-origin vs. mixed-origin explanations, i.e. whether the accents were essentially transported Cockney or East Anglian English, for instance, or whether they were the result of dialect mixing (and where this mixing occurred). For the New Zealand accent, the additional question arises as to whether it developed parallel to the Australian accent or with direct Australian input, a position favored by Bauer (1994, 1997, 1999). The best overview of theories on the origin of the New Zealand (and Australian) accent is provided in Gordon et al. (2004), even including lay theories such as hay fever as a cause for some nasal sounds (Gordon et al. 2004: 68).

The main difference between historical accounts of the two accents lies in the availability of material. With the exception of ongoing research by Cox (2009), studies on the origin of the Australian accent have had to rely mainly on demographic evidence and meta-linguistic comments.

For the origins of the New Zealand accent, a unique set of data are available in the form of recordings made throughout rural New Zealand in the 1940s, among them some of the first New-Zealand-born speakers of English which allowed people on the Origins of New Zealand English Project (ONZE n.d.) to document the embryonic stages of the New Zealand accent (see Gordon et al. 2004 for a description of the data or the project's homepage at http://www.nzilbb.canterbury.ac.nz/onze.shtml; last accessed 14 April 2017.)

2.1 Australian English

The hypothesis that the Australian accent had its origins in Cockney English (on Cockney, see Fox, Chapter 10) is a persistent one that goes back to the colonial period when people observed, for instance, that Australians were prone to pronounce *very* with an initial semivowel instead of a labio-dental fricative (see Turner 1994: 283; Moore 2008: 69 or Gordon et al. [2004: 71, 81–82]). Other correspondences were seen in the vowel inventory of Cockney and AusE (see Turner 1960: 35–37 or Hammarström 1980). On closer analysis, AusE phonology is obviously not identical with Cockney English (and never was). The more likely story is one in which dialect mixing took place. For a detailed account, the evidence on NZE in Gordon et al. (2004) probably sheds light on the kind of process that also took place in Australia (see also Section 2.2).

Here, the focus will be on the emergence of the tripartite distinction into broad, general, and educated AusE, originally introduced by Mitchell (1965) into the discussion of extra-territorial Englishes in the southern hemisphere. Yallop (2001) is a posthumous summary of Mitchell's position on the origins of the Australian accent division (see also Mitchell 2003). Mitchell uses demographic evidence to counter the common stereotype that the early colony was made up of "coarse intellectual clay" (Yallop 2001: 292–294). He does not endorse the mixing bowl theory. Instead, he claims that the typical Australian accent developed mostly from the attempts of speakers to accommodate to the largest dialect group in the colony, namely the emergent urban dialect of the London area. This accommodation process, together with the emergence of the Australian-born children as a significant group of speakers, led to the development of the earliest form of Broad Australian by about 1830. General Australian, according to Mitchell, evolved with the second wave of free immigrants. This new accent is said to have become the majority accent between 1870 and 1890 (Yallop 2001: 297). The cultivated end of the spectrum, finally, Mitchell sees as arising from external influences during the first half of the twentieth century when "educated Australians felt a need to imitate RP or adapt their speech to it" (Yallop 2001: 300; for a similar view that also involves a second wave of migration, see Leitner [2004: 312–329]).

2.2 New Zealand English

The idea that NZE, like AusE, was a transplanted form of 19th-century Cockney English does not find support in the linguistic facts of the ONZE project. Gordon et al. (2004: 256) conclude that "we can eliminate the Cockney hypothesis once and for all".

Initially, Gordon (1989) argued for an Australian origin of the NZE accent, instead, just like Bauer (1997: 428) who claimed that "the hypothesis that New Zealand English is derived from Australian English is the one which explains most about the linguistic situation in New Zealand". Gordon et al. (2004: 299), on the basis of their ONZE data, can neither confirm nor refute the hypothesis that Australia had a major impact on the development of the New Zealand accent; but they also point out that "it is unlikely that New Zealand English is purely a transported version of Australian English" (Gordon et al. 2004: 230).

In a similar vein, the development of the New Zealand accent shows close affinities with south-eastern English dialects, but the ONZE data do not provide conclusive evidence on how this regional connection developed. It is certainly not simply the result of the fact that the early settlers came mainly from the south-eastern dialect areas of England (an assumption underlying the "founder principle" and the notion of "colonial lag"). Gordon et al. (2004: 258) ultimately argue for multiple factors, namely input from settlers who came via Australia and swamping effects from large-scale immigration in the 1870 in addition to the founder principle, whereas Trudgill (2004: 158–160), on the basis of the same data, makes an argument for largely independent (but to a certain extent parallel) dialect formation.

2.3 Recent developments

One of the most conspicuous features of the AusE and NZE accent is the use of a rising intonation with declarative sentences, a phenomenon that has been labeled "High Rising Terminal" (HRT). The question whether it originates in NZE or AusE has been a controversial subject in the literature. Wells (1982: 604) mentions HRTs as a characteristic intonation pattern of AusE, but not of NZE, whereas the data discussed in Allan (1992) suggest that HRTs are more common in NZE than in AusE. Britain (1992: 97) maintains that "we cannot conclude with any certainty that HRTs are a New Zealandism that has crossed the Tasman Sea to Australia. Particularly as HRTs are also found in Canada and the United States, HRTs may well be an independent innovation in each country". For an earlier meta-linguistic comment on the absence of HRTs in Australia vis-à-vis America and a possible chronology of the development, see Turner (1994: 296–267). The vocalisation of post-vocalic /l/ in words such as *will* is an ongoing change in both varieties in which, according to Horvath and Horvath (2001a), NZE is more advanced than AusE.

There is evidence of some degree of Americanization in both AusE and NZE accents. T-flapping (the voicing of intervocalic /t/) is an example of such influence on NZE, supported by the results of Bayard (1999: 154) who found that the frequency of t-flapping correlated with a preference for AmE lexical items. Leitner (2004: 204) speculates that t-flapping in Australia might be attributed to contact with speakers of AmE during World War II (for other potential dialect contact features with AmE accents, see Leitner 2004: 203–206).

Recent phonological change may also lead to regional differences: the New Zealand merger of the diphthong in words such as *ear* and *air* is not shared with AusE. The merger is clearly an innovative feature in NZE, which was once heavily stigmatized but it is "rapidly establishing itself as a new norm" (Holmes 1997: 116).

3 Lexicon

Two dictionaries provide historical information on the words used in Australia and New Zealand, namely *The Australian National Dictionary* (AND), edited by Ramson and published in 1988, and *The Dictionary of New Zealand English* (DNZE), edited by Orsman and published in 1997. Unlike these dictionaries on historical principles, general dictionaries like the *Macquarie Dictionary* (Delbridge et al. 1997) or *The New Zealand Oxford Dictionary* (Deverson and Kennedy 2005) may give a wider coverage of words used in the two countries but do not include the first attestations.

3.1 Regional origins and developments

Bauer (2000) investigates the dialectal origin of NZE on the basis of lexical evidence recorded in the DNZE and comparative evidence from the AND, again in an attempt to verify whether NZE originated mainly in South-Eastern English dialects or derived from Australian English. One of the reasons that it is difficult to ascertain the English dialectal origins of words in NZE, he concludes, is that they have often been mediated by AusE (Bauer 2000: 51–52). Trudgill (2004: 9–10) points out that lexical evidence on the Australian origin of NZE is the least likely to provide a convincing argument, as dialects frequently borrow words and meanings from each other (see Trudgill 2004: 10 on lexical influence of American on British English). The minutiae of such borrowing paths are investigated in Peters (2009). On the basis of evidence from the AND and the DNZE, she reviews the parallel development of shared Australian and New Zealand lexis and semantics. As far as lexical items are concerned, loanwords from Aboriginal languages and Aboriginal English are of particular interest, such as *cooee* 'a bush call used to attract attention', which is attested in Australia as a noun in 1790 and as a verb in 1824, and thus considerably antedates their New Zealand uses (1838 and 1843, for the noun and verb, respectively). For a potential semantic influence of AusE on NZE, transfers of words from the convict and underworld repertoire to farming are of great significance, such as *mob* which is attested in its extended meaning to farm animals in AusE in 1828 whereas its use for sheep and cattle in NZE dates from 1842.

Peters (2009: 115) concludes that "the shared items [...] are demonstrably Australian in origin, and indicative of AusE inputs to NZE in the 19th century". Her argument obviously hinges on the reliability of the diachronic data.

Deverson (2000: 27) refutes the common claim that NZE lexis, in general, differs only minimally from that of its Australian neighbor. An overall comparison of the DNZE and AND shows that less than 10% of the entries overlap (Deverson 2000: 27).

3.2 External influences

Apart from a few shared items (see Section 3.2), borrowings from indigenous languages are the most likely source of differences between AusE and NZE. As Schneider (2003, 2007) points out, toponymic borrowings from the indigenous language(s) and loans for flora and fauna are amongst the first in the development of new Englishes.

3.2.1 Loans from Aboriginal languages

The most comprehensive study of loans from Australia's indigenous languages is Dixon et al. (2006, 2nd edn.) who estimate the amount of lexical material in mainstream AusE at about 400 words, but they also point out that "[i]t would be wrong to think that the Aboriginal contribution to Australian English, because relatively small, was insignificant. In fact it provides the most distinctive Australian words of all" (Dixon et al. 1990, 1st edn.: 219). According to Schneider (2007: 120), "Australia's toponymy is strongly indigenous in character: a very large number of place names were taken over from the Aboriginals, e.g. *Wagga Wagga, Wodonga, Mundabullangana, Mungallala, Youangarra*"; to this list we could add numerous more, such as *Allawah*, (Lake) *Burrendong, Ringarooma* (River), or (Mount) *Dandenong*. More recently, there has been a movement for double naming, i.e. to use the Aboriginal place name alongside (and ultimately instead of) a more established English name, the most famous landmark probably being *Uluru* for *Ayers Rock* (see Walsh forthc. for more examples and the details of the political minefield that this linguistic process has to negotiate). Moore (2001: 145) points out that there is ongoing shift from the *Olgas* to *Kata Tjuta* and variation between, for instance, *Katherine Gorge National Park* and *Nitmiluk National Park*.

Kurrajong (1793) and *waratah* (1788) are Aboriginal names for native trees (figures in brackets give the year of the first attested occurrences in the AND). An obvious borrowing from Aboriginal languages is the word *kangaroo* (on its early history in AusE and variant spellings, see Turner 1994: 279); other examples of loans for native fauna are *dingo* (1798), *budgerigar/budgie* (1840/1935), *kookaburra* (1834), *koala* (1798), and *wallaby* (1798). But native Australian languages have also given rise to popular loans such as *cooee* (1790) which, according to the AND (Ramson 1988: 166), was originally "a call used by an Aboriginal to communicate (with someone) at a distance; later adopted by settlers and now widely used as a signal, esp. in the bush [...]". Among the cultural terms, the most widely known is probably *boomerang* (1790); a less common term *is coolamon/kooliman* (1845) (a container for liquids). Leitner and Sieloff (2003) provide an in-depth account on the familiarity of Australians with Aboriginal loanwords, based on questionnaire data. They conclude that "Dixon et al.'s (1990) evaluation of Aboriginal influence, viz. that loans were the most distinctive characteristic of mAE [mainstream Australian English, MH], must be treated with caution. [...] we established that the expressions are not widely known" (Leitner and Sieloff 2003: 166). While it may be true that some of the borrowings in Dixon et al. ([1990] 2006) are specialized or obsolete and therefore not widely known, loanwords such as *kangaroo, koala, wallaby, boomerang*, etc. certainly are borrowings that are amongst the most distinctively Australian words. Moore (2001) looks at more recent loans from Aboriginal languages and culture, and words that relate to the Aboriginal rights movement which, according to him, "reflect significant changes taking place in Australian society" (Moore 2001: 136). The lexical changes he focuses on apparently show how "AusE is registering a profound change of attitude towards its indigenous peoples, just as those indigenous peoples are asserting their place in the lexicon of AusE" (Moore 2001: 148).

3.2.2 Loans from Maori

Of the 6,000 main headwords in the DNZE, about 12 per cent are of Maori origin (Orsman 1997: viii). In the following, the figure in brackets refers to the earliest attested occurrence in the DNZE. Examples of toponymic loans are *Aotearoa* (1855) the Maori name for New Zealand, literally 'Land of the Long Twilight' according to the DNZE (Orsman 1997: 13), or *Ngauruhoe* and *Ruapehu*, two volcanoes in the North Island. As part of the Maori renaissance, places which also have English names are increasingly referred to by the original Maori designation, such as *Mount Taranaki/Egmont* (the word is first attested as referring to Maori people from the region in 1863). Examples of typical Maori tree and plant names are *kauri* (1817), *matai* (1831), *rimu* (1820), *manuka* (1826–27), and *pohutukawa* (1820), the New Zealand Christmas tree. Maori loans for indigenous birds are *kiwi* (1820), *korimako* (1820), *kea* (1862), and *tui* (1815). Cultural terms (like *Maoritanga* [1843], the traditional term for Maori traditions, beliefs and cultural practices including things like the *marae* [1769] 'meeting house', *hongi* [1793] a greeting that involves the pressing or touching of noses, *ngati* [1856] 'tribe, clan', *kai* [1840] 'food' cooked in the *hangi* [1820], an earth oven, but also *te reo Maori* [1878] 'the Maori language') are examples of such words where Maori has left its mark on

NZE. The impact of borrowings from Maori has been much greater in the last four decades, though, as a result of the Maori renaissance (see Deverson 1994). Kennedy and Yamazaki (1999) provide a systematic review of the evidence on Maori loans in the DNZE; Macalister (2006), on the basis of a historical corpus (newspaper texts, parliamentary debates, and the School Journal), takes a different approach, but also finds that there were two main phases of borrowing, namely during the colonial period (lasting until 1880) and a second from about 1970.

3.2.3 Americanization?

In the more recent history of the two varieties, influence from American English (AmE) is a factor to take into account. Butler (2001) looks at the impact of American lexical items on AusE. The recent influx of lexical Americanisms such as *schmooze, schlep, smick, dreck*, and *zine* (Butler 2001: 154) lead her to hypothesize that Australians might be having an identity crisis (some of these might also be of a different origin, see Section 5.2 below). She claims that the "trickle of Americanisms has now grown into a flood" (Butler 2001: 153). This does not mean that Australians take over all of the American neologisms, though. Butler claims that typical Australianisms such as *bush* and its derivatives, or words like *mate* and *grouse* (meaning 'cool') "will remain an essential part of what is seen as quintessentially Australian" (Butler 2001: 161).

In a similar vein, studies by Bayard (1989) and Meyerhoff (1993) provide some evidence that the influence of AmE on the New Zealand lexicon is growing. At one stage, Bell (1992: 254) even feared that NZE was "in danger [...] of falling out of the British frying pan into the American fire". A study by Vine (1999), however, shows that New Zealanders are neither consciously endorsing nor avoiding lexical Americanisms. They are sometimes not even aware of their AmE origin. Vine also found that her informants often used the AmE word when they wanted to make a semantic distinction, e.g. between *serviettes* (made from paper) and *napkins* (made from cloth) or between *biscuits* (bought) and *cookies* (home-made).

3.3 Internal developments

In addition to loanwords, local coinages and semantic change also contributed to the development of distinct varieties of English in the southern hemisphere. They once again provide for shared ground between AusE and NZE.

3.3.1 Coinage

One of the most distinct patterns of word formation to be found in AusE and NZE are hypocoristics such as *brekkie* for 'breakfast' and *arvo* for 'afternoon'. Peters (2009: 115) points out that the use of hypocoristics in *-ie* is associated with children's talk in Britain but that it "is greatly extended into a general marker of familiarity and social belonging among adults" in Australia and New Zealand. Again, she traces the first attestation of most hypocoristics to Australia rather than New Zealand, and argues that they provide another example of influence from AusE onto NZE, even though individual items (*bullocky* for 'bullock-driver') are first attested in New Zealand and some appear very soon after they are first attested in Australian written sources. Seeing that hypocoristics of the *bushie* ('bushman') and *smoko* ('cigarette break') type are colloquialisms in both varieties, which are typically used in the spoken medium long before they are recorded in written usage, one could easily argue for parallel developments in both varieties rather than New Zealand borrowings from across the Tasman. Bardsley and Simpson (2009: 50–52) confirm that some formations are shared between the varieties because "Australian and New Zealand shepherds, shearers, and sheep-breeders traveled freely across the Tasman in the 1850s and 1860s [...]" (Bardsley and Simpson 2009: 51). But they paint a slightly different picture of the development of hypocoristics on both sides of the Tasman: they are able to show that some New Zealand coinages go back as far as 1800, and they also provide examples like *woollie/wolly* that are attested first in NZE and later in AusE, i.e. some hypocoristics that could have been adopted from NZE by Australian farmers (Bardsley and Simpson 2009: 51). In other words, studies such as Peters (2009) and Bardsley and Simpson (2009) confirm the (likely) influence that AusE has had on NZE, but at the same time they highlight the fact that NZE did not have its origin exclusively in AusE.

3.3.2 Semantic change

As pointed out in the introduction to this section, lexical items often developed local meanings in Australia and New Zealand. Alongside *mob*, a typical example is *bush*, which is used to refer to the indigenous rain forest in New Zealand and wooded areas or, more generally, non-urban areas in Australia. However, in the colonial context, the word is also used to refer to a way of life. The importance of the bush in the early days of the colonies is reflected in phrases like *take to the bush* 'revert to less civilized ways' and *go bush* (of a Maori) 'revert to traditional tribal ways' or compounds like *bush baptist* 'religious radical' and *bush-philoso-*

pher 'rural moralizer given to expressing often crass opinions' (see Orsman and Orsman 1994: 40–41; Delbridge et al. 1997: 297–299; Ramson 1988: 112–124; Deverson and Kennedy 2005: 106–121). *Bush philosopher* is a compound typical of NZE whereas AusE has *bush parson* as a regional coinage (see Peters 2009: 111). A particularly interesting case is *bushranger* which meant 'runaway convict' or 'armed robber' (especially on country roads) in Australia but lacked the convict sense in New Zealand where it was, among other things, also used to refer to a volunteer member of the militia engaged in bush-fighting during the New Zealand wars against the Maori (Orsman and Orsman 1994: 44).

4 Grammar

Grammatically, AusE and NZE are very similar to each other and often also to British and American English. Differences between the national varieties are a question, largely, of preferences for one grammatical construction over another (i.e. a matter of frequencies, see Hundt 1998 and Peters et al. 2009). A striking difference between the two southern hemisphere varieties is the more frequent use of the progressive in present-day NZE, for instance. So far, however, there is a lack of longitudinal, real-time studies on the development of Australian and New Zealand English grammar, also with respect to their divergence from British patterns of usage (e.g. on the basis of evidence from ARCHER, A Representative Corpus of Historical English Registers, Biber et al. 1994). Fritz (2007: Chapter 4.2) provides evidence from his historical corpus of 19th-century Australian texts, but the composition of his corpus does not allow for easy comparison with studies based on ARCHER. In addition, he mostly gives results for his corpus as a whole (comparing it with previous studies of Present-day Australian and New Zealand English) and only rarely includes information on the development of a grammatical feature from one sub-period to the next. Another problem for a comparative study of early New Zealand texts and the evidence provided in Fritz might be differences in the definition of the syntactic variables: for instance, he includes the *going-to* construction in his overall figure of progressives (Fritz 2007: 231). As mentioned previously, a corpus of early New Zealand texts is currently being compiled at Zürich University (Hundt 2012). First, explorative studies on the progressive indicate that its popularity in New Zealand is a development of the late 20th century. Another small case study based on newspaper evidence from *The Dominion* and *The Times* (Ainsworth 1992: 19) suggests that NZE was more advanced in the spread of the *s*-genitive to place names than British English (BrE) in the 1920s. Hundt and Szmrecsanyi (2012) found that animacy was a determinant of grammatical variation that can be found in early New Zealand texts but that affects the development of progressives and the genitive alternation differently. But apart from such isolated studies, very little has been done on the historical development of Australian and New Zealand grammar. In other words, there is ample scope for further research on differential grammatical change in AusE and NZE and comparison with available evidence for British and American English. The likely picture to emerge from such studies is one that goes beyond the simple dichotomy of colonial lag and innovation (see Hundt 2009 on differential change in American and British English).

5 Dialects

In Schneider's (2003, 2007) dynamic model of new dialect formation, internal stratification only develops at stage 5, i.e. when a "new English" has fully developed and thus ceases to be "new". The new local identity is firmly established at this stage, and this allows for the development of internal diversification under the umbrella of a unifying national identity.

5.1 Social

The focus in this section is on the socio-historical dimension in the two varieties rather than the complex picture of social variation (e.g. in ongoing sound change) that has emerged from numerous studies on both sides of the Tasman.

The social accent or "Dagg to Dougal" (Bayard 2000: 298) continuum in Australia and New Zealand has been classified as ranging from "educated" over "general" to "broad" accents (see Section 2.1 for Mitchell's account of its development in Australia).

Evidence on social variation in the history of New Zealand English comes from the ONZE project and provides a much more fine-grained picture, allowing to account for the overlap between social, gender and ethnic variation, as well. Gordon et al. (2004: 276) found, for instance, that "for all but one change, the women are ahead in the changes that we have documented that are leading towards modern New Zealand English". This fact also holds for variants which later came to be stigmatized within New Zealand (Gordon et al. 2004: 276). The evidence from the ONZE project thus confirms Holmes' (1997: 135) findings for ongoing change in New Zealand: "women lead changes which could be described as prestige changes, as well as changes which are undoubtedly vernacular changes".

5.2 Ethnic

Malcolm (2001: 202) describes the socio-historical circumstances leading to the ongoing indigenisation of Aboriginal English (AbE) in Australia. One of the functions of this variety, namely the maintenance of Aboriginal cultural identity (especially in the face of ongoing death of indigenous languages), is likely to contribute to the continued use of AbE as a separate variety in Australia. Furthermore, AbE as such is not a homogeneous variety but rather a series of Aboriginal Englishes, as Arthur (1996: 2) points out.

Apart from indigenous varieties of English in Australia, the label "ethnic" variety has also been applied to the English spoken by migrant groups in Australia. Clyne et al. (2001), for instance, look at the ethnolects of German, Greek, Hungarian, and Jewish immigrants, describing their lexical, semantic, phonological, and syntactic features. These ethnolects enable second and later generations to express their dual identity as Australians with a different ethnic background (Clyne et al. 2001: 225 and also Warren 1999). More recent studies have also looked at Lebanese speakers (Kiesling 2005 and Tabar 2007).

While language contact in Australia undoubtedly led to pidginization and creolization (see Shnukal 2001 for one of the contact varieties with English), clear linguistic evidence is missing for a similar process to have taken place in New Zealand. Clark (1990) discusses the question whether the contact between English settlers and Maori in New Zealand led to a pidgin variety in the early days of the colony. According to him, a substantial number of Maori spoke educated English by the beginning of the 20th century. "At the same time, however, there appears in print a 'Maori Pidgin English' in the form of a stereotyped literary dialect" (Clark 1990: 109). He concludes that this literary dialect might simply reflect negative racial attitudes and that Maori pidgin English was probably the fabrication of the European (Pakeha) settlers.

Maori English, on the other hand, is a well established ethnic variety in New Zealand (see Bell 1997 or Holmes 1997). On the basis of evidence on final consonant cluster reduction in the ONZE data, Schreier (2003: 386–88) is able to show that late 19th-century Maori-NZE was characterized by substratum influence typical of L2-varieties (English as a second language) of English but converged early in the twentieth century to the native speaker model provided by Pakeha speakers.

5.3 Regional

Both Australian and New Zealand English have been described as being regionally homogeneous (see Bernard 1969 or Bauer 1994), an outcome of the earlier koinéization process (see Trudgill 1986). Hickey (2003: 236) claims that the absence of regional variation in present-day New Zealand is not simply due to accommodation and subsequent dialect leveling during new dialect formation. Instead, he postulates that it arose from supra-regionalization, i.e. "the adoption of the focused variety of New Zealand English from areas of high density, varied settlement to areas of lower, less varied settlement" (Hickey 2003: 236) which resulted in the removal of minority, non-prestige features of local speech in the accents, e.g. of late 19th-century Irish immigrants. Trudgill et al. (2000: 307) see focusing (i.e. the reduction of the original variants) as the main reason for the absence of regional variation in the two southern hemisphere varieties. Gordon et al. (2004: 254) point at internal migration (i.e. a high degree of regional mobility) as an additional factor. Britain (2005: 164–165) holds that network ties in NZ prevented the development of regional variation.

There are some studies, however, that attempt to show (developing) regional variation within both AusE and NZE. Once regional variation has been established in both countries, they have reached what Schneider (2003, 2007) refers to as stage 5 in his dynamic model of the evolution of new Englishes, i.e. the stage of internal differentiation (both socially and regionally) and they would then cease to be "new" Englishes.

For Australian English, Horvath and Horvath (1997, 2001b) have substantiated regional variation of two variables, short *a* and vocalization of /l/ with empirical research: in Brisbane, speakers for instance favor short or flat /æ/ in words such as *bath* whereas Mount Gambier and Adelaide are places where broad or long /a/ is the preferred variant (Horvath and Horvath 2001b: 349–350). Despite the fact that working class speakers show a slight preference for short /æ/, the authors maintain that variation with the BATH vowel "is a geolectal rather than a sociolectal one" (Horvath and Horvath 2001b: 352). They conclude, however, that further research needs to be done before the regional dialects of AusE can be delimited with any certainty. One could argue that beyond a statistically significant correlation between certain variants and a particular geographical area, speakers of AusE would also need to be able to recognize certain regional dialects. There is no evidence so far that this will happen in the near future. Overviews of AusE regionalisms can be found in Bradley (2004) and Moore (2008: chapter 12). The latter also includes an overview of regional lexis. With respect to regional grammatical variation, Moore (2008: 166) points out that it coincides with other sociolinguistic variables, such as ethnicity (i.e. grammatical regionalisms occur where speakers from a particular migrant group are concentrated in a particular region). This falls outside the realm of grammatical variation in standard AusE and therefore outside the scope of this chapter.

For NZE, Bartlett (2002) has investigated the Southland variety: his data show that what has traditionally been associated with the Southland area, namely postvocalic /r/, is a recessive feature, whereas a rhotic vowel in words such as *nurse* is on the increase. More importantly, the shibboleth of a New Zealand regionalism is not simply the result of local Scottish influence: "the nature of the rhoticity found in SldE [Southland English, M.H.] does not match that found in ScotE" (Bartlett 2002: 143); Bartlett attributes it to dialect mixing and leveling, a hypothesis that seems to be supported by data from the ONZE project (Gordon et al. 2004: 172–174). Data from this project add to the picture of the historical development in other areal phenomena: Schreier et al. (2003) show that the distinction between *which* (with initial /hw/) and *witch* was maintained longer in areas with substantial Scottish dialect input at the beginning of the 20th century.

Incipient regionalization in the New Zealand lexicon has been studied by Bauer and Bauer (e.g. 2000, 2002, 2005) on the basis of questionnaire data distributed to primary schools across the country, which indicates the development of a northern dialect area in the North Island and differences between the North and South Island. As is to be expected, regionalization in the North shows overlap with social and ethnic variation (see Bauer and Bauer 2000). Another study (Ainsworth 2004) found regional variation in intonation patterns within New Zealand (i.e. between the Taranaki and Wellington regions).

In a globalized world, migration continues to affect both Australia and New Zealand and it is therefore questionable whether substantial and stable regional variation is likely to develop.

6 Summary

Historical linguistics of English in Australia and New Zealand has largely concentrated on accent and vocabulary, so far. Grammatical regionalisms (in the form of preferences for options also available in other varieties of English) have mainly been studied synchronically. Future research will have to map the minutiae of differential grammatical change in the two varieties. But even the large body of available evidence for the development of the distinctive AusE and NZE accents and lexicon is far from conclusive (see the unresolved controversy on the origins of the NZE accent). The main lesson to be learnt from previous studies on the development of AusE and NZE is that rather simple hypotheses on the origin (such as AusE and NZE are "transported Cockney") and development (colonial Englishes have a tendency for fossilization) can nearly always be proved false.

7 References

7.1 Printed resources

Ainsworth, Helen. 1992. The mark of possession or possession's mark? A case study. *New Zealand English Newsletter* 6: 17–20.

Ainsworth, Helen. 2004. *Regional Variation in New Zealand Intonation: Taranaki versus Wellington*. Unpublished PhD thesis. Victoria University of Wellington.

Allan, Scott. 1992. The rise of New Zealand intonation. In: Allan Bell and Janet Holmes (eds.), 115–128.

Arthur, Jay Mary. 1996. *Aboriginal English. A Cultural Study*. Melbourne: Oxford University Press.

Bardsley, Dianne and Jane Simpson. 2009. Hypocoristics in New Zealand and Australian English. In: Pam Peters, Peter Collins, and Adam Smith (eds.), 49–70.

Bartlett, Christopher. 2002. *The Southland Variety of New Zealand English*. Unpublished PhD thesis. Dunedin: University of Otago.

Bauer, Laurie. 1994. English in New Zealand. In: Robert Burchfield (ed.), 382–429.

Bauer, Laurie. 1997. Attempting to trace Scottish influence on New Zealand English. In: Edgar W. Schneider (ed.), 257–272.

Bauer, Laurie. 1999. On the origins of the New Zealand English accent. *English World-Wide* 20(2): 287–307.

Bauer, Laurie. 2000. The dialectal origins of New Zealand English. In: Allan Bell and Koenraad Kuiper (eds.), 40–52.

Bauer, Laurie and Winifred Bauer. 2000. The influence of the Maori population on NZ dialect areas. *Te Reo: Journal of the Linguistic Society of New Zealand* 43: 39–61.

Bauer, Laurie and Winifred Bauer. 2002. Can we watch regional dialects developing in colonial English? The case of New Zealand. *English World-Wide* 23(2): 169–193.

Bauer, Laurie and Winifred Bauer. 2005. Regional dialects in New Zealand children's playground vocabulary. In: Allan Bell, Ray Harlow, and Donna Starks (eds.), 196–216.

Bayard, Donn. 1989. Me say that? No way!: The social correlates of American lexical diffusion in New Zealand English. *Te Reo: Journal of the Linguistic Society of New Zealand* 32: 17–60.

Bayard, Donn. 1999. Getting in a flap or turning off the tap in Dunedin? Stylistic variation in New Zealand English intervocalic (-T-). *English World-Wide* 20(1): 125–155.

Bayard, Donn. 2000. New Zealand English: Origins, relationships, and prospects. *Moderna språk* 94(2): 160–166.

Bell, Allan. 1997. The phonetics of fish and chips in New Zealand: marking national and ethnic identities. *English World-Wide* 18(2): 243–270.

Bell, Allan and Janet Holmes (eds.). 1992. *New Zealand Ways of Speaking English*. Clevedon: Multilingual Matters Ltd.

Bell, Allan and Koenraad Kuiper (eds.). 2000. *New Zealand English*. Amsterdam/Philadelphia: John Benjamins.

Bell, Allan, Ray Harlow, and Donna Starks (eds.). 2005. *Languages of New Zealand*. Wellington: Victoria University Press.
Bernard, John R. 1969. On the uniformity of spoken Australian English. *Orbis* 18: 62–73.
Biber, Douglas, Edward Finegan, and Dwight Atkinson. 1994. ARCHER and its challenges: Compiling and exploring a Representative Corpus of Historical English Registers. In: Udo Fries, Gunnel Tottie, and Peter Schneider (eds.), *Creating and Using English Language Corpora. Papers from the Fourteenth International Conference on English Language Research and Computerized Corpora*, 1–13, Amsterdam: Rodopi.
Blair, David and Peter Collins (eds.). 2001. *English in Australia*. Amsterdam/Philadelphia: John Benjamins.
Bradley, David. 2004. Regional characteristics of Australian English. In: Bernd Kortmann, Edgar W. Schneider, Kate Burridge, Rajend Mesthrie, and Clive Upton (eds.), Vol. 1, 645–655.
Bradley, David and Maya Bradley. 2001. Changing attitudes to Australian English. In: David Blair and Peter Collins (eds.), 271–285.
Britain, David. 1992. Linguistic change in intonation: the use of High Rising Terminals in New Zealand English. *Language Variation and Change* 4: 77–104.
Britain, David. 2005. Where did New Zealand English come from? In: Allan Bell, Ray Harlow, and Donna Starks (eds.), 156–193.
Burchfield, Robert (ed.). 1994. *The Cambridge History of the English Language,* Vol. V: *English in Britain and Overseas: Origins and Development*. Cambridge: Cambridge University Press.
Butler, Susan. 2001. Australian English – an identity crisis. In: David Blair and Peter Collins (eds.), 151–161.
Clark, Ross. 1990. Pidgin English and Pidgin Maori in New Zealand. In: Alan Bell and Janet Holmes (eds.), 97–114.
Clyne, Michael, Edina Eisikovits, and Laura Tollfree. 2001. Ethnic varieties of Australian English. In: David Blair and Peter Collins (eds.), 223–238.
Crystal, David. 1995. *The Cambridge Encyclopedia of the English Language*. Cambridge: Cambridge University Press.
Delbridge, Arthur, John Bernard, David Blair, Susan Butler, Pam Peters, and Colin Yallop (eds.). 1997. *The Macquarie Dictionary*. Sydney: Macquarie Library.
Deverson, Tony. 1994. New Zealand English past and present. In: Elizabeth Orsman and Harry Orsman (eds.), vi–xxviii.
Deverson, Tony. 2000. Handling New Zealand English lexis. In: Allan Bell and Koenraad Kuiper (eds.), 23–39.
Deverson, Tony and Graeme Kennedy (eds.). 2005. *The New Zealand Oxford Dictionary: the ultimate guide to New Zealand English*. South Melbourne: Oxford University Press.
Dixon, Robert M.W., William Stanley Ramson, and Mandy Thomas [1990] 2006. *Australian Aboriginal Words in English. Their Origin and Meaning*. Melbourne: Oxford University Press.
Fritz, Clemens W. A. 2007. *From English in Australia to Australian English. 1788–1900*. Frankfurt: Peter Lang.
Gordon, Elizabeth. 1989. That colonial twang: New Zealand speech and New Zealand identity. In: David Novitz and Bill Willmott (eds.), 77–90.
Gordon, Elizabeth. 1998. The origins of New Zealand speech: The limits of recovering historical information from written records. *English World-Wide* 19(19): 61–85.
Gordon, Elizabeth and Andrea Sudbury. 2002. The history of southern hemisphere Englishes. In: Richard Watts and Peter Trudgill (eds.), 67–86.

Gordon, Elizabeth, Lyle Campbell, Jennifer Hay, Margaret MacLagan, Andrea Sudbury, and Peter Trudgill. 2004. *New Zealand English: Its Origins and Evolution*. Cambridge/New York: Cambridge University Press.

Gunn, John S. 1992. Social contexts in the history of Australian English. In: Tim W. Machan and Charles T. Scott (eds.), 204–229.

Hammarström, Göran. 1980. *Australian English: Its Origin and Status*. Hamburg: Helmut Buske Verlag.

Hickey, Raymond. 2003. How do dialects get the features they have? On the process of new dialect formation. In: Raymond Hickey (ed.), 213–239.

Hickey, Raymond (ed.). 2003. *Motives for Language Change*. Cambridge: Cambridge University Press.

Hoffmann, Thomas and Lucia Siebers (eds.). 2009. *World Englishes – Problems, Properties and Prospects*. Amsterdam/Philadelphia: John Benjamins.

Holmes, Janet. 1997. Setting new standards: sound changes and gender in New Zealand English. *English World-Wide* 18(1): 107–142.

Horvath, Barbara M. and Ronald J. Horvath. 1997. The geolinguistics of a sound change in progress: /l/ vocalization in Australia. In: Miriam Meyerhoff, Charles Boberg, and Stephanie Strassel (eds.), 105–124.

Horvath, Barbara M. and Ronald J. Horvath. 2001a. A multilocality study of a sound change in progress: the case of /l/ vocalisation in New Zealand and Australian English. *Language Variation and Change* 13: 37–57.

Horvath, Barbara M. and Ronald J. Horvath. 2001b. Short a in Australian English: a geolinguistic study. In: David Blair and Peter Collins (eds.), 241–355.

Hundt, Marianne. 1998. *New Zealand English Grammar – Fact or Fiction? A Corpus-Based Study in Morphosyntactic Variation*. Amsterdam/Philadelphia: John Benjamins.

Hundt, Marianne. 2009. Colonial lag, colonial innovation, or simply language change? In: Günter Rohdenburg and Julia Schlüter (eds.), 13–37.

Hundt, Marianne. 2012. Towards a corpus of early New Zealand English – news from *Erewhon*? *Te Reo: Journal of the Linguistic Society of New Zealand* 55.

Hundt, Marianne and Benedikt Szmrecsanyi. 2012. Animacy in Early New Zealand English. *English World Wide* 33(3).

Kennedy, Graeme and Shunji Yamazaki. 1999. The influence of Maori on the New Zealand lexicon. In: John Kirk (ed.), 33–44.

Kiesling, Scott F. 2005. Variation, stance and style: word-final *-er*, high rising tone, and ethnicity in Australian English. *English World-Wide* 26(1): 1–42.

Kirk, John (ed.). 1999. *Corpora Galore: Analyses and Techniques in Describing English*. Amsterdam: Rodopi.

Kortmann, Bernd, Edgar W. Schneider, Kate Burridge, Rajend Mesthrie, and Clive Upton (eds.). 2004. *A Handbook of Varieties of English*. Berlin/New York: Mouton de Gruyter.

Leitner, Gerhard. 2004. *Australia's Many Voices. Australian English – The National Language*. Berlin/New York: Mouton de Gruyter.

Leitner, Gerhard and Inke Sieloff. 2003. Aboriginal words and concepts in Australian English. *World Englishes* 17(2): 153–169.

Macalister, John. 2006. The Maori presence in the New Zealand English lexicon, 1850–2000: evidence from a corpus-based study. *English World-Wide* 27(1): 1–24.

Machan, Tim W. and Charles T. Scott (eds.). 1992. *English in Its Social Contexts: Essays in Historical Sociolinguistics*. Oxford: Oxford University Press.

Malcolm, Ian G. 2001. Aboriginal English: Adopted code of a surving culture. In: David Blair and Peter Collins (eds.), 201–222.
Meyerhoff, Miriam. 1993. Lexical shift in working class New Zealand English: Variation in the use of lexical pairs. *English World Wide* 14(2): 231–248.
Meyerhoff, Miriam, Charles Boberg, and Stephanie Strassel (eds.). 1997. *Working Papers in Linguistics: A Selection of Papers from NWAVE 25.* Philadelphia: University of Pennsylvania.
Mitchell, Alexander G. 1965. *The Pronunciation of English in Australia.* Sydney: Angus & Robertson.
Mitchell, Alexander G. 2003. The story of Australian English: Users and environment. (A public lecture delived at Macquarie University on 12 October 1993). *Australian Journal of Linguistics* 23(2): 111–128.
Moore, Bruce. 2001. Australian English and indigenous voices. In: David Blair and Peter Collins (eds.), 133–149.
Moore, Bruce. 2008. *Speaking Our Language: The Story of Australian English.* Melbourne: Oxford University Press.
Novitz, David and Bill Willmott (eds.). 1989. *Culture and Identity in New Zealand.* Wellington: GP Books.
Orsman, Elizabeth and Harry Orsman (eds.). 1994. *The New Zealand Dictionary.* Educational edition. Auckland: New House.
Orsman, Harry W. 1997. *The Dictionary of New Zealand English: A Dictionary of New Zealandisms on Historical Principles.* Auckland: Oxford University Press.
Peters, Pam. 2009. Australian English as a regional epicenter. In: Thomas Hoffmann and Lucia Siebers (eds.), 107–124.
Peters, Pam, Peter Collins, and Adam Smith (eds.). 2009. *Comparative Studies in Australian and New Zealand English Grammar.* Amsterdam/Philadelphia: John Benjamins.
Ramson, William Stanley (ed.). 1988. *The Australian National Dictionary: A Dictionary of Australianisms on Historical Principles.* Melbourne: Oxford University Press.
Rohdenburg, Günter and Julia Schlüter (eds.). 2009. *One Language, Two Grammars? Differences between British and American English.* Cambridge: Cambridge University Press.
Schneider, Edgar W. (ed.). 1997. *Englishes Around the World: Studies in Honour of Manfred Görlach.* Vol. 2. Amsterdam/Philadelphia: John Benjamins.
Schneider, Edgar W. 2003. The dynamics of New Englishes: from identity construction to dialect birth. *Language* 79(2): 233–281.
Schneider, Edgar W. 2007. *Postcolonial English: Varieties Around the World.* Cambridge: Cambridge University Press.
Schreier, Daniel. 2003. Convergence and language shift in New Zealand: Consonant cluster reduction in 19th century Maori English. *Journal of Sociolinguistics* 7(3): 378–391.
Schreier, Daniel, Elizabeth Gordon, Jennifer Hay and Margaret Maclagan. 2003. The regional and sociolinguistic dimension of /hw/ maintenance and loss in early 20th century New Zealand English. *English World-Wide* 24(2): 245–269.
Shnukal, Anna. 2001. Torres Strait English. In: David Blair and Peter Collins (eds.), 181–200.
Tabar, Paul. 2007. "Habibs" in Australia: Language, identity and masculinity. *Journal of Intercultural Studies* 28(2): 157–172.
Trudgill, Peter. 1986. *Dialects in Contact.* Oxford: Blackwell.
Trudgill, Peter. 1999. A window on the past: 'Colonial lag' and New Zealand evidence for the phonology of nineteenth-century English. *American Speech* 74(3): 227–239.

Trudgill, Peter. 2004. *New Dialect Formation: The Inevitability of Colonial Englishes*. Edinburgh: Edinburgh University Press.
Trudgill, Peter, Elizabeth Gordon, Gillian Lewis, and Margaret Maclagan. 2000. Determinism in new-dialect formation and the genesis of New Zealand English. *Journal of Linguistics* 36: 299–318.
Turner, George W. 1960. On the origin of Australian vowel sounds. *Journal of the Australiasian Universities Modern Language Association* 13: 33–45.
Turner, George W. 1994. English in Australia. In: Robert Burchfield (ed.), 277–327.
Vine, Bernadette. 1999. Americanisms in the New Zealand English lexicon. *World Englishes* 18(1): 13–22.
Warren, Jane. 1999. "Wogspeak": transformations of Australian English. *Journal of Australian Studies* 62: 86–94.
Watts, Richard and Peter Trudgill (eds.). 2002. *Alternative Histories of English*. London: Routledge.
Wells, John Christopher. 1982. *Accents of English*. Vol. 3. Cambridge: Cambridge University Press.
Woods, Nicola J. 2000. Archaism and innovation in New Zealand English. *English World-Wide* 21(1): 109–150.
Yallop, Colin. 2001. A.G. Mitchell and the development of Australian pronunciation. In: David Blair and Peter Collins (eds.), 287–302.

7.2 Internet resources

Downie, David n.d. *Class in Australia*. Brisbane, Australia. http://www.australianbeers.com/culture/class.htm; last accessed 14 April 2017.
Bayard, Donn and James Green. 2003. *Evaluating English Accents worldwide: Introduction*. https://www.researchgate.net/publication/286023670_Evaluating_English_accents_worldwide; last accessed 14 April 2017.
Cox, Felicity. 2009. Research Page of Macquarie University, Sydney/Australia. http://www.mq.edu.au/about_us/faculties_and_departments/faculty_of_human_sciences/linguistics/linguistics_staff/associate_professor_felicity_cox/; last accessed 14 April 2017.
ONZE n.d. *The Origins of New Zealand English (ONZE)*. University of Canterbury, New Zealand. http://www.nzilbb.canterbury.ac.nz/onze.shtml; last accessed 14 April 2017.
Walsh, Michael forthc. Political issues in Australian Aboriginal toponyms. In Wolfgang Ahrens, Sheila Embleton and André Lapierre, *Names in Multi-Lingual, Multi-Cultural and Multi-Ethnic Contact: Proceedings of the 23rd International Congress of Onomastic Sciences August 17–22, 2008, York University, Toronto, Canada*. https://yorkspace.library.yorku.ca/xmlui/handle/10315/2901; last accessed 14 April 2017.

Devyani Sharma
Chapter 16:
English in India

1   The early presence of English in India (17th–18th century) —— 312
2   Colonial language ideologies (18th–19th century) —— 313
3   English and the independence movement (19th–20th century) —— 317
4   English in independent India: planning and use (20th century) —— 319
5   Variation in Indian English —— 322
6   References —— 328

Abstract: English has existed in India for at least 400 years but its place in the Indian linguistic ecology has always been conflicted. It arrived as a tool of colonialism but became one of resistance; it is used widely in the country but remains a second language for most speakers; it transcends regional divides yet continues to underscore socioeconomic disparities. An adequate history of English in India must therefore accommodate a wide diversity of ideologies, functions, and forms of the language. The present chapter outlines the establishment and development of English in India through four historical segments: early presence, colonial ideologies, the independence movement, and independent India. Each section links structural linguistic changes to historical and sociopolitical dynamics. Both British and Indian varieties of English in India are examined in the colonial segments, as these constitute two markedly different outcomes of contact: British English in India – temporarily a "settler" variety, in Schneider's (2003) terms – is an example of light lexical borrowing in a prolonged but highly asymmetric contact situation; Indian English – an "indigenous" variety – is an example of moderate first language interference in a contact situation, with limited access to the target variety and limited language shift (Thomason and Kaufman 1988). In closing, the chapter describes contemporary variation in Indian English as a window into diachronic processes and theoretical debates.

Devyani Sharma: London (UK)

1 The early presence of English in India (17th–18th century)

1.1 Historical developments

English was established in India with Queen Elizabeth's Royal Charter of 1600, granting the East India Trading Company exclusive rights to pursue trade in the Indian subcontinent for two decades. This led to two centuries of economic and military expansion by the Company, culminating in the assumption of direct British rule in 1858. In the early years of British India, the main domains of English use were trade, military, and missionary work. The initial practice was for men to take up temporary posts in India without their families. They were frequently encouraged to learn the vernacular in order to communicate with local groups. At first, then, contact between English and vernacular languages was functional, each group incompletely acquiring fragments of the other's language for trade, revenue collection, and other officialdom. Only later did missionary schools, established from the early 18th century onwards, become the first institutionalized source of diffusion of English into the indigenous population.

1.2 Linguistic structure

Both early Indian and early British varieties of English in India were affected by these superficial and functional modes of contact. Bilingualism among Indians was limited at first and the systematic *Indianisation* (Kachru 1983) of English did not develop until later. Nevertheless, early superficial English use among Indians did give rise to *Butler English* (Hosali 2005), also called *Bearer English* or *Kitchen English*, a pidginized variety used between Indian domestic staff and their British employers. Hosali (2005: 34) countered Hugo Schuchardt's characterization of Butler English as a disappearing variety in 1891 by collecting original recordings (1980–82, domestic servants working in former colonial clubs) that strongly resemble a late 19th century example of Schuchardt's. The example below (Hosali 2005: 36) is from a 67-year-old, old enough to have worked under the British: "Working the bearer... just I going six month ago–dining-hall [...] attend after the drink – any sahibs coming. Morning-morning's 8 to 4. One time one week like that. One one week night." The extract retains the British Indian terms *sahib* and *bearer* and uses some typical Indian English features (reduplication with distributive meaning: *one one*; progressive with habitual meaning: *sahibs coming*) but also many strikingly non-Indian English features (null copula: *I going*; noun reduplication: *morning-morning*; lack of plural marking: *six month*). A number of these features are shared with other English pidgins.

British English began to adopt Indian terms during this period as well. Many were ephemeral loans and coinages; others were transported back to Britain and remain in British English today. In the earlier decades of British rule, words for trade, social rank, and Asian cultural objects and practices were adopted. The following examples of Indian loans, attested from the 17th and 18th century and remaining in English today, reflect a rich diversity of pre-British layers of language contact, including the early Portuguese colonial trading presence in India: *bungalow* (Hindi [H.], Bengali [B.] *bangla* 'Bengali'), *juggernaut* (Sanskrit [S.] > H. *jagannath* 'lord of the world'), *jungle* (S. > H. *jangal* 'uncultivated land'), *mogul* (Mongolian *mongol* > Persian [P.] *mugul* > Urdu [U.] *mughal* 'member of Indian Muslim dynasty'), *palanquin* (S. *palyanka* > H. *palaki* > Portuguese [Pg.] *palanquim* 'bed, litter'), *shawl* (P. > U. *shal* 'cloth wrap'), *shampoo* (H. *champo* 'press, massage', imperative verb), *sepoy* (U. *sipahi* > Pg. *sipae* 'Indian soldier or horseman under European command'). In later centuries, the semantic domains of borrowing shifted along with changes in the colonial relationship.

2 Colonial language ideologies (18th–19th century)

2.1 Historical developments

During the 18th century the expansion of the East India Company created a base of power for British dominion. This included increased monopolistic control of trade and revenue (e.g. the Treaty of Allahabad, 1765, which designated the Company as chief revenue collector of the weakened Mughal Emperor's Eastern provinces) and greater military command of Indian provinces (e.g. the Battle of Plassey, 1757, in which the Company exerted control over Bengal through military conquest). The resulting tensions culminated in the Indian Mutiny of 1857 and the immediate assumption of direct rule by the British crown in 1858, with continued central administration by the East India Company. Language ideologies and language practices were profoundly affected by this elaboration of British rule, as it extended deeper into intellectual and cultural dominion. Colonial language ideologies grew more complex, crystallising into an opposition between what were then termed "Orientalist" and "Anglicist" stances.

The term *Orientalist* applied to the styles of engagement favored by British governors and scholars during the 18th and early 19th century, which tended to condone the retention of indigenous knowledge structures and languages (as opposed to Western learning and English), with motivations ranging widely from pure strategy to intellectual appreciation.

Warren Hastings, the first British Governor General of India (1773–1785), promoted a tactical acceptance of extant commercial, judicial, military, and cultural systems in order to better cooperate with intermediaries. He was known to express respect for Indian culture and ancient scripture, spoke Bengali, and founded the Calcutta Madrassa on the old Persian Islamic model. Hastings brought Orientalist scholars to India, most notably William Jones, founder of the Royal Asiatic Society of Bengal. In a historic address to the newly founded Society in 1786, Jones hypothesized a shared origin for Indo-Aryan languages and Greek and Latin, an Aryan link that formed the foundation of a particular Orientalist affection for Indic study and that tended to restrict the infiltration of the English language and Western education into India. Indeed, even ancient Indic language debates over which vernacular to promote were enthusiastically revived among British Orientalists. The second Governor General, Charles Cornwallis (1786–1793), continued the Orientalist practice of leaving internal social structures broadly in place, but his stance was rooted in a fear that Western education and the English language would foment a dangerous rationality and autonomy among overseas subjects.

In the early 19th century, a countervailing Anglicist ideology promoting Western cultural and linguistic intervention emerged. Two domestic developments in British political and religious philosophy drove this change: the Evangelical movement and utilitarianism. The Evangelical movement fought to strengthen missionary work in British India and forge a new moral obligation: the "enlightenment" of native populations. The English language played a pivotal role in these ideals. Charles Grant, Evangelist chairman of the East India Company (1746–1823), saw the imposition of English as a means to "silently undermine, and at length subvert, the fabric of error" in Hindu culture (Zastoupil and Moir 1999: 6). Nineteenth century advocates of utilitarianism arrived at a similar colonial policy, viewing rational socioeconomic progress (rather than Christian faith) as a modernizing and civilizing force.

The provision of a small amount of funds by the Charter Act of 1813 for "the revival and improvement of literature, and the encouragement of the learned natives of India, and for the introduction and promotion of a knowledge of the sciences" (Zastoupil and Moir 1999: 91) ignited a protracted Orientalist-Anglicist debate to define this mission. The Orientalists argued for the indigenous revival of traditional learning, the Anglicists for exogenous renewal with Western learning.

The Anglicist view that ultimately prevailed was implemented in an ordinance passed by the Governor General Lord Bentinck in 1835, decreeing that

English be the medium of all higher education in India. The ordinance was based on a recommendation by an ardent Evangelist, Thomas Babington Macaulay (member of the Supreme Council of India, 1835–1839). Macaulay's opinion, entitled *Minute on Indian Education*, illustrates the dramatic reversals in language attitudes among 19th century British colonists in India:

> What then shall that language be? One-half of the Committee maintain that it should be the English. The other half strongly recommend the Arabic and Sanscrit [sic]. The whole question seems to me to be, which language is the best worth knowing?
> I have no knowledge of either Sanscrit or Arabic, – I have never found one among them [Orientalists] who could deny that a single shelf of a good European library was worth the whole native literature of India and Arabic. It is, I believe, no exaggeration to say, that all the historical information which has been collected from all the books written in the Sanscrit language is less valuable than what may be found in the most paltry abridgments used at preparatory schools in England.
> We have to educate a people who cannot at present be educated by means of their mother-tongue. We must teach them some foreign language. The claims of our own language it is hardly necessary to recapitulate. It stands preeminent even among the languages of the West. ... We must at present do our best to form a class who may be interpreters between us and the millions whom we govern; a class of persons, Indian in blood and color, but English in taste, in opinions, in morals, and in intellect. (Macaulay, cited in Zastoupil and Moir 1999: 166)

The striking failure of several expert and persuasive Orientalist rebuttals suggests that the tide of British missionary zeal was already with Macaulay, and his personal standing in British society sealed the transition (Cutts 1953). Furthermore, the Indian response was not one of monolithic resistance: a number of Hindu intellectuals, most notably Raja Rammohun Roy, adopted the view that Western learning and the English language could be beneficial in such areas as political and religious reform (Zastoupil and Moir 1999).

2.2 Linguistic structure

This period witnessed significant developments in Indian English, mostly due to greater bilingualism, the establishment of more convent schools, and further employment of Indians under the British. Changes in social relations also affected the domains from which the British borrowed Indian loanwords.

A particularly distinctive Indian community that formed during this period was the Anglo-Indian community, mostly Christian and of mixed Indian and British ancestry. Although Anglo-Indians are among the very few Indians who count English as their native language, their variety and community tended to be marginalized by both the British and the Indians. A derogatory term at the time for this variety was *Chee-Chee English*, possibly from the Hindi term of disapproval *chhi*. Anglo-Indian English shares many general features with contemporary Indian English but also has striking traits that derive from late 18th century British English dialects, largely due to early nativization and greater British input. For instance, the variety retains h-dropping and r-lessness from British English. It also reserves [oː] for the words *four, bored, course, force, pork* and [ɔː] for words such as *north, stork,* and *fork*; contemporary British English speakers no longer distinguish between these lexical sets but did until recent decades (Coelho 1997). The distinction appears in the speech of some general Indian English speakers as well, possibly transmitted through convent education.

Another type of Indian English that may have developed as early as the 18th century was *Babu English*; this term is often conflated with *Butler English* and *Bearer English* but, as Widdowson (1979) clarifies, the term *babu* was derogatorily ascribed at the time to obsequious or officious Indian junior clerks who used a hyper-elaborated bureaucratic style of English. As such uses continue today, the term is occasionally used to describe any Indian English of intermediate proficiency (Hosali 2005: 38).

The barracks continued to be a primary site of Indian loanword infiltration into British usage, e.g. *durbar, afghan, coolie, lascar, peon, khaki, babu*. The strict class hierarchy of Indian British society is reflected in the domains and trajectories of loanwords. British intellectuals brought esoteric loans into higher registers of English, e.g. *avatar, sandhi, Buddha, pundit, guru, karma*. By contrast, 19th century barracks loans frequently ended up in Cockney usage in Britain, e.g. *blighty* (Arabic > U. > H. *bilayati, wilayati* 'foreign'), *mufti* ('civilian clothes', from U. *mufti* 'Muslim cleric' or 'freedom'), *dekko* (H. *dekho* 'see', imperative verb), *cushy* (H. *khushi* 'comfort, pleasantness'), *doolally* ('crazy', from Deolali, site of a British Indian transit camp) (Yule and Burnell 1886). Across classes, the arrival of British officers' families and the establishment of convent schools led to a massive increase in contact between colonists and Indians. Indian loans into British English extended to domains such as domestic items, food, export items, social personae, religion, clothing, and architecture, e.g. *bearer, bazaar, verandah, chintz, chutney, loot, thug, bangle, bandana, saffron, polo, jute, indigo, cummerbund* (Lewis 1991).

With the increased scale of contact, inexpert uses of Indian languages by lower class British residents in India even became a recognized discourse style, mocked by the domestic British public. A novel from 1900 parodies this style, mixing working class British dialect with inexpert, fragmented use of Hindi: "*Decko*, you want this *admi abhi*, but you ain't goin' to get 'im. *Tumhara nahin.* He's mine, *mehra admi, sumja?* If you want to *lurro*, come on." ('*Look*, you want this *man now*, but you ain't goin' to get 'im. *Yours not.* He's mine, *my man, understood*? If you want to *fight,* come on.') (Lewis 1991: 12). Remarkably, the widespread British use of imperative orders such as *decko* and *lurro* during this period may well have formed the basis of the most productive loan template for contemporary Hindi-English code-switching among Indian English speakers, namely use of the imperative as a base form for verbs with code-switched inflection: e.g. *College principal ghera-o-ed*. ('surround-IMPERATIVE-ed', headline from *The Hindu*, 12 January 2008). Native Hindi-English bilinguals consulted on variants of this construction rejected alternatives, such as use of the infinitival stem: **College principal ghera-ed.*

3 English and the independence movement (19th–20th century)

3.1 Historical developments

The comprehensive implementation of English in India via Macaulay's *Minute* was a transformative moment in India's linguistic history. The 19th century witnessed a steady increase in English use in education, press, printing, and bureaucracy. However, particularly after World War I, the National Swadeshi ('self-reliance') Movement emerged as an opposing force, bringing with it ideologies of vernacular resistance such as Mahatma Gandhi's argument that "real education is impossible through a foreign medium" (Mehrotra 1998: 5).

As with his knowledge and exploitation of British law, Gandhi's uses of the English language were skilful, calculated inversions of a norm. He used English to make the case for independence to British and Indian audiences but always promoted vernacular medium education as central to his policies of non-cooperation and self-rule:

> The only education we receive is English education [...] I hold it to be as necessary for the urban child as for the rural to have the foundation of his development laid on the solid work of the mother tongue. It is only in unfortunate India that such an obvious proposition needs to be proved. (Gandhi, cited in Ramanathan 2006: 236)

Nehru's landmark words at the moment of Indian independence were nevertheless in English, using the metaphor of speech for freedom.

Gandhi and Nehru as individuals embody the conflicted place of English in early 20th century India. Gandhi, born in a small Gujarati town in 1869, initially struggled with English at school and in early public speaking. It was only when he was studying law in London that he recognized the political benefits of a command over English rhetoric and style and began to take elocution lessons and read widely (Khilnani 2003). Gandhi's first book, *Hind Swaraj* (1909), was written in Gujarati en route to South Africa but translated by Gandhi into English (*Indian Home Rule*) and published in 1910. An immediate British ban on grounds of sedition remained in place until 1938, but this and subsequent writings by Gandhi – some in English, some in Gujarati, and some translated – nevertheless formed the key texts for the independence movement in the intervening period. Nehru, born 20 years after Gandhi into a powerful family in the colonial administrative center of Allahabad, received English tuition very early and spent years at Harrow and Cambridge. Unlike Gandhi's works, Nehru's three major books and collections of letters were all written in English, in prison. Writings by these two leaders, more than any other in the independence movement, represent the transformed role of English in India by the 20th century: "English made the empire, but they showed how it could be used to unmake it – how the language could be a tool of insubordination and, ultimately, freedom" (Khilnani 2003: 136).

The political equivocation over whether a new nation should eschew or exploit the colonial language is apparent in the final decades of the independence movement. During the 1920s and 1930s a critical stance was widely adopted, and Gandhi amended the Indian National Congress party constitution in 1925 to reduce the role of English. Nehru too suggested that continued reliance on the language would cause Indians to "remain slaves to British thought". However, once independence (which came in 1947) was imminent, more pragmatic views resurfaced, with Gandhi acknowledging "the rule of the English will go because it was corrupt, but the prevalence of English will never go" (Khilnani 2003: 154).

Despite the persistence of English, by the mid-20th century many Indians no longer aspired to a British acrolectal standard. This is the crucial point at which endonormative stabilization of a variety in a multilingual setting takes root and progresses, leading to a divergence of stable, indigenized, non-native Englishes from regular second-language speech (Schneider 2003).

3.2 Linguistic structure

Detailed historical analyses dating the origins of Indian English features do not yet exist and are complicated by second language variability; however, Mehrotra (1998) shows that many contemporary Indian English features, discussed later, appear in 19th century letters and other texts. By the late 19th and early 20th century many contemporary features of Indian English are evident in newspaper texts and lexical loans from Hindi into Indian English are already becoming unmarked in press usage. A leading English-language newspaper, *The Hindu*, uses quotation marks to signal a loan in the headline "A general 'hartal' was observed in the town to-day" (1 July 1950), yet the resumed story lower on the same page states "A hartal was being observed in the town markets to-day", with no quotation marks around the word *hartal* ('strike'), a word used freely in Indian English today.

4 English in independent India: planning and use (20th century)

4.1 Historical developments

The languages of India today form a complex multilingual hierarchy of local, state, regional, and national codes, within which Hindi and English are the two major languages of wider communication in the country, despite extremely low numbers of native English speakers. A conservative estimate of the number of languages in India is 415 (Gordon 2005). The Indian Constitution, written in 1950 with subsequent amendments, currently lists 22 official major regional languages and designates Hindi as the official language of central government with English as a co-official language. The North Eastern states of Meghalaya, Manipur, and Nagaland designate English as their state language. The Constitution lists slightly different official roles for Hindi and English: for instance, both are official languages of parliamentary proceedings and national administration, but English is the official language of the Supreme Court and of laws. Extensive provisions for exceptions and translation are provided and states are given the authority to regulate official language designations at the state level.

Immediately after independence, Indian languages were initially favored as the medium of instruction, and the Congress party supported efforts to re-introduce them at the university level. English was seen as a necessary presence, but one that might soon be phased out: "The English language shall continue to be used for a period of 15 years from the commencement of this Constitution for all official purposes of the Union for which it was being used immediately before such commencement" (Indian Constitution, 1950, Article 343). "It shall be the duty of the Commission to make recommendations to the President as to: (I) the progressive use of the Hindi language for the official purposes of the Union; (II) restrictions on the use of the English language for all or any of the official purposes of the Union" (Indian Constitution, 1950, Article 344).

However, pragmatic and political concerns arose almost immediately. In pragmatic terms, ceasing widespread English use in newspaper production, universities, and government was unfeasible. Politically, the choice of the Northern, Indo-Aryan lingua franca Hindi as a national language was far from neutral. Antagonism to the imposition of Hindi and to potential benefits to Hindi speakers was fierce, particularly in the South, where Dravidian languages are spoken. Tamil Nadu eventually witnessed language riots in the 1960s in which 70 people were killed and Hindi and English were both temporarily banished from the state (Kachru 1983: 90). Very early in the debate, the government was forced to offer a more generous re-interpretation of the post-independence role of English:

> We do not recommend that any restriction should be imposed for the present on the English language for any of the purposes of the Union [...] It is not suggested that English be rejected merely because it is a foreign language for we entirely agree that a language is not the property of any particular nation, and obviously it belongs to all who can speak it. (Official Language Commission, 1956)

In the field of education, distinct pressure groups emerged early in the debate, variously championing English, Hindi, or regional languages. The Council for Secondary Education (1956) ultimately settled on a three-language formula for education, still in place today, whereby non-Hindi speakers would learn Hindi, English, and their mother tongue, while Hindi speakers would learn Hindi, English, and another Indian language. A modified version in 1966 proposed that the mother tongue or regional language would be studied for 10 years, the official language (Hindi or English) for a minimum of 6 years, and a modern Indian or foreign language for a minimum of 3 years.

Ambiguities in the three-language formula were left open to determination by each state, and these have been resolved very differently. Hindi states frequently fill the modern Indian language slot with Sanskrit, while some non-Hindi states (e.g. West Bengal) have sometimes replaced the Hindi slot with Sanskrit. In contentious non-Hindi regions, the three-language formula has often been reduced to two languages or even one. In others, in which minority languages are not identical to the regional language, there is an effective four-language policy in place (see Khubchandani 1978).

English is taught as a subject in almost all schools, and English-medium education exists in private schools as well as via government initiatives in state schools. State governments change English-medium teaching provisions regularly; for example, West Bengal abolished English-medium teaching in government schools in 1984 but were forced through popular protest to bring back and expand the provision from 1992 onwards. Aside from perceived economic benefits, English-medium schools are sought after as preparation for university study, which is largely in English.

Along with other major languages such as Hindi and Tamil, English now dominates domains such as administration, law, national politics, the armed forces, business, entertainment, mass media, and publishing. English newspaper production began in Calcutta in the 1780s, at the same time that newspapers were first being established in Britain; the current top-selling English daily in India, *The Times of India*, was founded in 1838. The figures in terms of print media have shifted in recent decades: in 1978, out of 16,000 newspapers and magazines, 27% were Hindi and 20% English (Mehrotra 1998: 10). In 2006, the Registrar of Newspapers for India (RNI) recorded 62,000 total registered newspapers and magazines, of which 2,130 were daily newspapers, 44% Hindi and 9% English.

These figures indicate the central position of the two languages in India, but also the faster growth of Hindi. Despite its popularity, English has not displaced indigenous languages extensively. In 1971, the Indian Census reported 192,000 mother tongue speakers for English and 202 million for Hindi. Thirty years later, the 2001 Census reported a similar absolute number for English – 227,000 – but a doubled figure of 422 million for Hindi. As the population of India also doubled during this time, the relative proportion of Hindi speakers has remained steadily close to 40%. By contrast, the lack of change in the extremely low numbers of native English speakers suggests a decrease in reporting of English as a native language. These numbers do not accurately reflect regular English use, however, which is true for a much larger proportion of the population (Pingali 2009).

At present, English in India is best described as existing alongside other languages playing an awkward, functional role; certainly at this stage Hindi has greater replacive potential in relation to minority languages than English. However, census figures belie the dramatic change taking place in urban areas such as Delhi and Bombay, where intensive code-switching by balanced bilinguals has become the norm among many segments of the younger generation, possibly presaging language shift for some. English has thus become an indigenized element – an Indian language in some sense – yet still remains an alien code at the very top of the scale, supporting class asymmetries (Dasgupta 1993).

4.2 Linguistic structure

As English has filtered into informal genres, the range in bilingual competence and indigenized uses has continued to expand. The contemporary newspaper extracts below illustrate some widespread uses and ongoing changes, discussed in more detail in Section 5:

- loanwords: '*A dais was erected, from which, the **safai netas** using hailers, did their best to incite the safai **karamcharis** to keep up their **dharna**'* (safai 'cleaning', netas 'leaders', karamcharis 'workers', dharna 'strike', *Times of India*, April 2003)
- article use: '*On the economic affairs, the party now has virtually endorsed the 1991 reforms but clarifies that it remains committed to Ø mixed economy; Mr. Kapoor said the applications were being scrutinised on Ø priority basis.*' (*The Tribune*, September 1998).
- verb and modal usage: '*The Foreign Secretary-level talks **had bogged down** after the third round*' (past perfect form with simple past meaning; *Hindustan Times*, September 1998); '*We believe they **would be taking** instructions from their leader*' (modal would with simple future meaning; *The Tribune*, September 1998).

Despite continuing indigenization of the variety, pedagogical norms for the type of English taught in schools remain conservative except in pronunciation, where indigenous norms have prevailed for some decades.

5 Variation in Indian English

While political decisions and language planning have played a key role in determining the uses of English in India, organic social and cognitive processes have over time determined the precise traits of the transformed language. A few features of English in India are conservative retentions from British source dialects – e.g. non-rhoticity in acrolectal varieties (many varieties of Indian English are rhotic), [a] in the PATH lexical set, archaic phrasing, and idioms (see also Anglo-Indian English, discussed in Section 2.2) – but none of these are entirely consistent across regions. Native substrate languages are a much greater influence in Indian English, which today forms a "cline of bilingualism" (Kachru 1983), exhibiting a dramatic range of variation determined by the key factors of first languages, region, socio-economic positioning, mode of acquisition, register of use, and attitude.

After an overview of variation in contemporary Indian English and its sources, this final section concludes with a review of changing theoretical orientations towards the analysis of this variation.

5.1 Regional and social variation in speech

Phonetic variation in Indian English varieties takes markedly different forms according to region and is sensitive to first language systems (Wiltshire and Harnsberger 2006; Pingali 2009). Typical phonetic characteristics of Northern Indian English varieties, many of which are shared with South Indian varieties, include:
- inventory substitutions (e.g. substitution of retroflex consonants for the alveolar series, monophthongs for diphthongs, dental stops for interdental fricatives, trilled /r/ for approximant or silent /r/)
- phonemic differences (e.g. lack of phonemic difference between /v/ and /w/)
- phonotactic differences (e.g. repair of sC- clusters with vowel epenthesis, e.g. [ɪskul] 'school')
- addition or loss of allophonic rules (absence of stop aspiration, absence of vowel reduction in unstressed positions, absence of /l/-velarization)
- prosodic differences (e.g. syllable-timed rather than stress-timed prosody, idiosyncratic lexical stress often driven by spelling or analogy).

South Indian English, influenced by substrates such as Tamil and Malayalam, has certain distinct features such as glide epenthesis in vowel-initial words (e.g. [jɛvəri] 'every') and unaspirated stop replacement of voiceless interdental fricatives (e.g. [t̪ɜːd̪] as opposed to North Indian [t̪ʰɜːd̪] for British English [θɜːd]). Wiltshire and Harnsberger (2006) note differences in aspiration between Northern and Southern varieties based on differences in phonemic contrast in the L1 systems. Similarly, varieties in Western India have selected regional features; for instance, the Bengali English phonemic inventory replaces English /v/ variably with /bʰ/ rather than the /w/ substitute in North Indian varieties.

Grammatical divergence in Indian English is less regionally variable, possibly due to greater convergence in substrate systems in the domain of morphosyntax. Some commonly observable grammatical features in Indian English varieties include (see Bhatt 2008):
- invariant tags (*You're English, isn't it?*)
- lack of auxiliary inversion (*Where she's going?*)
- innovative verb-particle constructions (*They dismissed off any objections.*)
- reduplication (*We had four four mangoes.* 'We had four mangoes each.')
- innovative discourse markers (*She was there only.* 'She was in fact there.')
- stative progressives (*He is knowing science very well.*)
- extension of *would* and *could* (*I would be sending it to you tomorrow.* 'I will send it to you tomorrow.')

- extension of perfect to simple past contexts (*Last week my parents had visited me.*)
- variable article omission and insertion (*I need to get license.*)
- count use of mass nouns (*I have passed on the informations.*)

The source of most of these features is transfer from the first language systems (e.g. reduplication, focus *only*, lack of auxiliary inversion) but can also be system-internal regularization (e.g. count use of mass nouns) or an emergence of cognitively unmarked systems (e.g. verb-particle constructions). The latter two sources may account for the occurrence of these features across unrelated dialects. The first source accounts for regional differences; for instance, *this*, *that*, and *some* are used more frequently by South Indian speakers in place of English articles *a* and *the* as Dravidian languages permit the use of demonstrative and quantifier forms in these contexts. Similarly, particular pragmatic choices (e.g. *Will you give me water?* with polite rather than direct meaning) can be traced to a mapping from parallel constructions in the first languages of speakers (see Sridhar 1991).

Lexical indigenization can also range from region-specific to cross-regional, depending on the source and register of the form. Lexical change in Indian English has derived historically from a number of distinct processes, including the following (see Kachru 1986: 42, 152–153):
- register-specific loanwords: *lathi* ('stick, police baton'), *bandh* ('strike', lit. 'closed')
- hybrid loans: *lathi charge* ('armed charge for mob control'), *goondaism* ('hooliganism'), *policewala* ('police person')
- loan translations or calques: *open hair* ('hair worn down or untied'), *to stand on someone's head* ('to supervise closely')
- innovations: *eve-teasing* ('euphemism for sexual harrassment'), *prepone* ('bring forward'), *revert back* ('respond to a message')
- archaisms: *donkey's (y)ears, evil-doers, dastardly deeds, thrice, stepney* ('spare tyre')
- reduplication (with genericizing function): *acting-wakting* (based on the Hindi reduplication template), *court-kacheri* (hybrid reduplication, similar to historical Old English-Norse contact doublets such as *kith and kin*)

Media usage facilitates the transmission of these forms across communities, but lexicon can also vary regionally (e.g. *military hotel* 'restaurant' in South India) or culturally (e.g. *zakat* 'alms-giving' in Muslim communities).

Indigenous sociolinguistic norms have not stabilized in India to the extent that they have in native colonial varieties, particularly from a pedagogical point of view. No single standard variety is shared across the country, but educated bilingual speech in urban centers have begun to focus towards regional norms to some extent (Sedlatschek 2009). Many upper class, and increasingly middle class, urban families are balanced bilinguals and many of the best known Indian writers in English represent a relatively focused Northern variety, with a highly distinctive set of indigenized phonetic norms but relatively few grammatical divergences from British English (e.g. invariant tags, focus *only*). Most such speakers command a native-like style range and code-switch regularly, a practice widely referred to as "Hinglish", or "Tamlish", "Benglish", and other regional variants (Krishnaswamy 2009). This tiny proportion of highly educated, fluent English users have constituted a recognizable group since long before independence. On hearing a speech by the politician Krishna Menon in the 1930s, H. G. Wells reported, with a note of irony: "A very eloquent man! I can't speak as well as he does, I am a mere Kentish man; once a haberdasher's assistant; learnt to speak and write English the hard way. But you fellows speak very clearly, and for all to hear. We mumble, bumble, grumble" (Skinner 1998: 33).

Social class broadly determines an individual's mode of acquisition, which may range from exclusively formal educational settings to exclusively informal spoken interaction, or any combination. The prominence of British-influenced school curricula and the high prestige of functional literacy in English (without language shift) perpetuates a characteristic conservatism, formal style, spelling pronunciations, and widespread prescriptivism in Indian English. The high prestige of British English in relation to American English has waned slightly in recent years however, with evidence of American style markers (e.g. rhoticity and idioms) in popular media, call centers, and casual speech (Cowie 2007; Chand 2009; Pingali 2009; Sedlatschek 2009).

5.2 Register variation in texts

Recent American influences notwithstanding, British-influenced conservatism has long defined the style of written prose in Indian English, which often tends towards a dense bureaucratic style or a highly elaborated style.

The bureaucratic style favors acronyms, passives, nominalizations, and the omission of function words (e.g. *CT3 certificate is required to be obtained from the Range Superintendent of Central Excise*, Indian government tax website, http://www.cbec.gov.in/htdocs-cbec/faq; last accessed 14 April 2017). The central role of the government in English use in India and seepage among registers has caused this bureaucratic style to influence journalistic and other prose as well (e.g. *The Gautam Budh Nagar district Congress has demanded CID enquiry, Hindustan Times*, 4 September 1998).

Indian English writing can also favor a highly wordy style, marked by a lack of contracted forms, frequent Latinization (e.g. *demise* rather than *death*), and florid phrasing (e.g. *most respected sir, for your kind attention, your good self*). This may derive from bookish prescriptivism and conservatism, but also draws on traditional Indian textual genres which involve elaborate politeness and honorific marking.

Despite considerable formality, even relatively standard written registers are firmly indigenized in certain respects. All the grammatical and lexical traits described in the previous section are prevalent in the *Kolhapur Corpus of Indian English* (1 million words of written Indian English; created in 1971, see Shastri 1996), existing comfortably alongside British archaisms and highly standard style. This balance between convention and change is particularly apparent in Indian literature in English.

As in many former colonies, the presence of English has profoundly affected the literary world as well, and India has developed a rich tradition of English writing, beginning as early as the 18th century. While some early Indian prose and poetry mimicked the British canon, from the very beginning Indian writers have experimented with Indian imagery and meanings. Some writers have specifically employed vernacular lexicon and rhythm in their English (e.g. Mulk Raj Anand, R. K. Narayan, Raja Rao) and almost all rely on indigenous cultural knowledge and postcolonial experience, built into linguistic choices, narrative styles, and actors' voices (e.g. Salman Rushdie, Vikram Seth, Amitav Ghosh). For example, in Rushdie's (1995: 165–166) *The Moor's Last Sigh*, a drunken monologue uttered at the moment of Indian independence articulates the awkwardness of English speakers in India: "bleddy Macaulay's minutemen! […] Bunch of English-medium misfits, the lot of you. Minority group members. Square-peg freaks. *You don't belong here.*" (see discussions in Mehrotra 2003; Skinner 1998).

5.3 Theoretical debates

The diversity in types of English used in India, varying according to regional language, education, nativeness, and register, raises the question of whether a single entity – either "Indian English" or "standard Indian English" – exists at all, and if so, what its status is. In practical terms, "Indian English" tends to be used to refer to acrolectal or mesolectal Indian English, but certainly no single variety or standard is shared across the North or the South, much less across the entire country. However, given the long history of English in India, the shared move away from a British standard, and the clear lectal continuum of uses, many favor the use of the term "Indian English" as a useful umbrella term for these related varieties.

Kachru (1986: 19) was among the first to characterize Indian English as a variety in its own right and characterizes it as a type of "non-native institutionalized variety". Others (e.g. Mufwene 2001: 108) view the term "non-native" as disenfranchising and favor "indigenized". This terminological debate fundamentally addresses the more important question of how to classify Indian English. The variety is cited in a number of early typologies of language contact and change. Fishman (1967) considered English in India to be a case of diglossia without bilingualism, arguing that access to English is reserved for urban elites. Thomason and Kaufman similarly focused on elite usage:

> especially where use of the target language is confined to educated people who write it regularly, interference is very slight or nonexistent in the morphosyntax but more extensive in the phonology [...] The English spoken by Indians in India is a classic example, with Standard English syntax but phonological features. (Thomason and Kaufman 1988: 129)

In fact English use has spread far more broadly than Fishman or Thomason and Kaufman's descriptions suggest (see D'Souza 2001), and English in some parts of India has moved towards a state of diglossia with bilingualism. Individuals are tied into personal networks based in local languages, but they participate daily in English-based institutional or informal domains composed of other bilingual speakers.

In a parallel debate over classification, opinion has been divided on the theoretical question of whether the "divergences" described in Section 5.1 constitute learner errors or dialect innovations. Early studies of Indian English tended to be restricted to prescriptive or pedagogical descriptions based on deficiency- or error-oriented approaches. This early work was founded on the exo-normative principle that appropriate norms for use were to be determined by a variety outside the context of use, such as British English (Quirk 1990). More recently, endo-normativity has been argued to distinguish postcolonial varieties from incomplete second language learning (see Kachru's 1991 rebuttal to Quirk 1990). Factors such as the absence of a native target, heterogeneous modes of transmission, and a stable, functional role for English have led to attitudinal shifts in the direction of indigenization: Sahgal (1991) has shown evidence of a developing preference among Indians for "Ordinary Indian English" accents over American or British English, in contrast to Kachru's findings 20 years earlier that a majority of English users in India favored a British model. Sharma (2005) also offers quantitative evidence that stable "indigenized" features – both structural and attitudinal – can indeed be distinguished from generic non-native learner features in Indian English.

It is becoming clear that English in postcolonial regions can neither be straightforwardly subsumed under models of individual second language learning nor under models of native variation. Evidence from patterns of linguistic variation as well as attitudinal behavior both indicate that Indian English is still at an intermediate stage of nativization. A detailed understanding of the sociohistory of this variety is still hampered by a lack of historical studies of Indian English and the complications of studying a second language variety. Nevertheless, recent research suggests that, under Schneider's (2003) dynamic model of the formation of New Englishes, Indian English falls between Stage 3 and Stage 4 (depending on the region and social class of a given sub-community), undergoing a shift from exonormative to endonormative stabilization but not as fully nativized and diversified as native varieties.

6 References

Bhatt, Rakesh M. 2008. Indian English: Syntax. In: Rajend Mesthrie (ed.), *Varieties of English: Africa, South and Southeast Asia*, 546–562. Berlin/New York: Mouton de Gruyter.
Chand, Vineeta. 2009. [v]at is going on? Local and global ideologies about Indian English. *Language in Society* 38(4): 393–419.
Coelho, Gail. 1997. Anglo-Indian English: A nativized variety of Indian English. *Language in Society* 26(4): 561–589.
Cowie, Claire. 2007. The accents of outsourcing: the meanings of 'neutral' in the Indian call center industry. *World Englishes* 26(3): 316–330.
Cutts, Elmer H. 1953. The background of Macaulay's minute. *The American Historical Review* 58(4): 824–853
Dasgupta, Probal. 1993. *The Otherness of English: India's Auntie Tongue Syndrome*. New Delhi, India: Sage Publications.
D'Souza, Jean. 2001. Contextualising range and depth in Indian English. *World Englishes* 20(2): 145–159.
Fishman, Joshua. 1967. Bilingualism with and without diglossia; diglossia with and without bilingualism. *Journal of Social Issues* 23(2): 29–38.
Gordon, Raymond G. Jr. (ed.) 2005. *Ethnologue: Languages of the World, Fifteenth edition*. Dallas, Tex.: SIL International. http://www.ethnologue.com/; last accessed 14 April 2017.
Hosali, Priya. 2005. Butler English. *English Today* 21(1): 34–39.
Kachru, Braj. 1983. *The Indianization of English: The English language in India*. Oxford: Oxford University Press.
Kachru, Braj. 1986. *The Alchemy of English: The Spread, Functions, and Models of Non-Native Englishes*. London: Pergamon Press.
Kachru, Braj. 1991. Liberation linguistics and the Quirk concern. *English Today* 7(1): 3–13.
Khilnani, Sunil. 2003. Gandhi and Nehru: The uses of English. In: Arvind Krishna Mehrotra (ed.), *A History of Indian Literature in English,* 135–156. London: Hurst and Company.
Khubchandani, Lachman M. 1978. Language planning processes for pluralistic societies: A Critical Review of the Indian Scene. *Language Problems and Language Planning* 2(3): 141–161.

Krishnaswamy, Subashree. 2009. *Mind it! We are in Chennai, Machan!* Paper presented at Chutnefying English Conference, 10–11 January 2009, Mumbai, India.

Lewis, Ivor. 1991. *Sahibs, Nabobs and Boxwallahs: A Dictionary of Words of Anglo-India*. Oxford: Oxford University Press.

Mehrotra, Arvind Krishna (ed.). 2003. *A History of Indian Literature in English*. London: Hurst and Company.

Mehrotra, Raja Ram. 1998. *Indian English*. Amsterdam/Philadelphia: John Benjamins.

Mufwene, Salikoko. 2001. *The Ecology of Language Evolution*. Cambridge: Cambridge University Press.

Pingali, Sailaja. 2009. *Indian English*. Edinburgh: Edinburgh University Press.

Quirk, Randolph. 1990. Language varieties and standard language. *English Today* 6(1): 3–10.

Ramanathan, Vaidehi. 2006. Gandhi, non-cooperation, and socio-civic education in Gujarat, India: Harnessing the vernaculars. *Journal of Language, Identity, and Education* 5(3): 229–250.

Rushdie, Salman. 1995. *The Moor's Last Sigh*. New York: Random House.

Sahgal, Anju. 1991. Patterns of language use in a bilingual setting in India. In: Jenny Cheshire (ed.), *English Around the World*, 299–308. Cambridge: Cambridge University Press.

Schneider, Edgar. 2003. The dynamics of New Englishes: From identity construction to dialect birth. *Language* 79(2): 233–281.

Sedlatschek, Andreas. 2009. *Contemporary Indian English: Variation and Change*. Amsterdam/Philadelphia: John Benjamins.

Sharma, Devyani. 2005. Dialect stabilization and speaker awareness in non-native varieties of English. *Journal of Sociolinguistics* 9(2): 194–225.

Shastri, S. V. 1996. using computer corpora in the description of language with special reference to complementation in Indian English. In: R. J. Baumgardner (ed.), *South Asian English: Structure, uses, and users*, 70–81. Urbana: University of Illinois Press.

Skinner, John. 1998. *The stepmother tongue: An introduction to new Anglophone fiction*. New York: St. Martin's Press.

Sridhar, K. K. 1991. Speech acts in an indigenised variety: sociocultural values and language variation. In: Jenny Cheshire (ed.), *English Around the World*, 308–318. Cambridge: Cambridge University Press.

Thomason, Sarah G. and Terrence Kaufman. 1988. *Language Contact, Creolization, and Genetic Linguistics*. Berkeley: University of California Press.

Widdowson, H. G. 1979. *Explorations in Applied Linguistics*. Oxford: Oxford University Press.

Wiltshire, Caroline and James Harnsberger. 2006. The influence of Gujarati and Tamil L1s on Indian English: A preliminary study. *World Englishes* 25(1): 91–104.

Yule, H. and A. C. Burnell. 1886. *Hobson-Jobson: A Glossary of Colloquial Anglo-Indian Words and Phrases, and of Kindred terms, Etymological, Historical, Geographical, and Discursive*. London: J. Murray.

Zastoupil, L. and M. Moir (eds.). 1999. *The Great Indian Education Debate: Documents Relating to the Orientalist-Anglicist Controversy, 1781–1843*. Richmond: Curzon Press.

Rajend Mesthrie
Chapter 17:
English in Africa – a diachronic typology

1 Introduction – many shapes and sizes —— 331
2 Pidgins —— 333
3 Creoles —— 334
4 Contemporary language mixing —— 336
5 L1 Englishes —— 336
6 L2 Englishes in Africa —— 341
7 Summary —— 345
8 References —— 345

Abstract: Although the historical linguistics of English in Africa is not a heavily studied area, this overview attempts to show that it is not without considerable interest in its own right. Moreover, for two L1 varieties comparisons with similar varieties outside the continent can be historically illuminating. The first is White South African English, for which the main debates in the field are covered, showing some large scale recent changes in the era of globalization, notably a reverse chain shift of the short front vowels. The other L1 variety with a rather different history is Liberian English, which is discussed in relation to syntactic retentions from early times in this repatriated creole, which still shares similarities with AAVE and Afro-Caribbean creoles. Even pidgin Englishes appear by virtue of their historicity in Africa to be amenable to study via appropriate modifications of the traditional family tree or wave models of relations. Finally the chapter shows how the L2 English syntaxes and phonologies lend themselves to internal African comparisons from which future developments can be monitored.

Rajend Mesthrie: Cape Town (South Africa)

1 Introduction – many shapes and sizes

English is an important but far from homogeneous language in Africa as in any other terrain. The form and functions of English on the continent have long diversified depending on the history of particular regions and the nature of the contacts with speakers of English. Those contacts become even more interesting if islands off the mainland of Africa are included: Mauritius, Tristan da Cunha, and St Helena. Africa evinces the full gamut of historical variation in English from pidgin to L2 to creole and "transplanted" L1. On the mainland the earliest significant presence of English is in West Africa, then Southern Africa, next East Africa and North Africa. English is to be found in all inhabited parts of the continent, with areas that were under French, Portuguese, or German influence now all finding it hard to resist the linguistic globalization of the planet via English. The historical account in this section is a summary and modification of Mesthrie and Bhatt (2008: 1–17), with special focus on Africa.

According to Spencer (1971: 8) English (in its Elizabethan form) was probably first heard in Africa in the 1530s when William Hawkins the Elder passed there on his way to Brazil. This was not the first European language to be used there, that honour going to Portuguese and its simplified contact varieties. A regular trade in spices, ivory, and slaves began in the mid 1500s when British ships sailed along the Guinea coast (Schmied 1991: 6). European forts were built along the West African coast. As British supremacy in trade gradually grew, English became established. During this time West Africans were taken in small numbers to Europe to be trained as interpreters. An account in Hakluyt (1927 [1598–1600]: Vol. VI) cited by Spencer (1971: 8) suggests that by 1555 five West Africans had been taken to England for over a year for this purpose. In South Africa a similar development took place centuries before the formal settlement of the English. The Cape was seen as a stopping place for European ships en route to the East Indies before the 17th century. Trade and barter with the local coastal Khoesan inhabitants led to a small lexicon of words developing that included Dutch, Portuguese, and English words (Den Besten 1989). Moreover a few Khoesan people were taken to England to learn English; others were taken on ships bound for the East with the intention of being forced to learn English and serve as interpreters (Malherbe 1990). The earliest recorded English sentence (in 1613) uttered by a South African was probably *Couree home go*, by one such person in England, showing Khoekhoe SOV syntax ('Couree wants to go home'; Den Besten 1989).

It is of linguistic significance that in Africa as elsewhere, these earliest contacts between English speakers and the locals were informal and sporadic. There was no expectation of a permanent settlement or of colonization (and therefore formal education) until centuries later. In this early phase pidgins and "broken English" (i.e. early-fossilized interlanguages) were the outcomes of contact (cf. Romaine, Chapter 20). These would not necessarily be ephemeral: West African Pidgin English whose roots lie in the 17th and 18th century is today more widespread (in the Cameroons, Ghana, and Nigeria) than is English as a second language. Pidgin English was not the only code used, as the African interpreters returning from training in England would probably have used a variety that was an L2 rather than pidgin.

St. Helena English, described by Schreier (2008: xi) as the oldest variety of Southern Hemisphere English, has its roots in the 17th century when the East India Company began its reign there, taking over from the Portuguese and Dutch. The island, up till then unpopulated, was soon stocked with English settlers, West African and Malagasy slaves, French Huguenots, and still other settlers, and served as a stopping point in mid-Atlantic for ships traversing half the world. In a careful and detailed assessment of the status of English on the island, Schreier (2008: 246) proposes that "when taking everything into consideration [i.e. history of contacts and typological features], it is not exaggerated to say that St. Helena English is an English-based creole after all".

Two varieties that gained significance in west Africa (from about 1787 onwards) were the forms of creole English spoken by manumitted slaves who were repatriated from Britain, North America and the Caribbean. Krio was the name given to the English creole of slaves freed from Britain who were returned to Sierra Leone, where they were joined by slaves released from Nova Scotia and Jamaica. Liberia was established in 1821 as an African homeland for freed slaves from the U.S. The creole English that the returnees brought with them was most likely related to African American Vernacular English (Hancock and Kobbah 1975: 248, cited by Todd 1982: 284; cf. Lanehart, Chapter 5). Today, American rather than British forms of English continue to dominate in Liberia (see Singler 2004a, 2004b). Todd describes four types of English in West Africa today: pidgin; ESL; standard West African English (mostly oriented to the UK, with the exception of places like Liberia) and francophone West African English.

English settlement in East Africa was different. English ships began making trips along the east coast of Africa by the end of the 16th century, prior to the formation of the British East Africa Company. An alliance was formed with the British government in India in 1810, resulting in Mombasa becoming a protectorate of the Crown. Whereas in West Africa local people had very little exposure to native speakers of English, giving prominence to pidgin English, in east Africa "native speakers were present in considerable numbers, had great influence in government and filled a higher percentage of teaching posts" (Hancock and Angogo 1983: 306).

North Africa was generally less under Anglophone English, with Arabic being the language that dominated. However, given that places like Egypt had "protectorate" status in the British Empire, English was not entirely foreign even here, and with globalization continues to spread after the age of empire. South Africa provides the largest mother-tongue base for English in Africa, though even here the percentage was never more than 10%. The settlement was relatively late, first of administrators and military personnel in 1795 (in Cape Town) and then of a civilian population in the Eastern Cape, called the 1820 Settlers.

2 Pidgins

There are many reasons why pidgin Englishes in Africa should be taken seriously, and not as mere transient forms, associated with incomplete mastery of a target language. As suggested in Section 1, pidgins in Africa have historicity, going back to the era of contacts with European traders, sailors, and slavers. For example, trading contacts in the Gold Coast (later called Ghana) go back to 1471, and this phase lasted for almost 400 years before formal colonization by Britain in 1844 (Huber 2004: 842). Menang (2004: 903) states that by the 18th century Pidgin English was firmly established throughout the West African coast. Some pidgins appear to have been influenced in their vocabulary by the English-lexified creoles brought back by manumitted slaves from the Caribbean and US South (in the 18th and 19th century). Another reason to take pidgins seriously is that they fulfill a range of functions. One of these is as a lingua franca when no other language is available for the purpose. Thus pidgin can play a vital role in the multilingual urban marketplaces of West Africa (see Menang 2004: 905 for Cameroon). Where new plantations were established within Africa, a pidgin variety proved useful in uniting a diverse labor force. It is also an important medium when young people gather, especially in schools and now at universities (Huber 2004: 869–870). Menang elaborates four functions for Pidgin English (a.k.a. Kamtok) in the Cameroons: an ecclesiastical function (in evangelization and liturgy), a commercial function (as in the marketplaces), a technical function (for technological and knowledge transfer), and a lingua franca function. For the latter he reminds us that in highly multilingual countries (like Cameroon with over 200 languages), it is important to analyse the territory in terms of lingua franca zones. Of the four lingua franca zones in the country (French, Fulfulde, Pidgin English, and possibly a Fang-Beti zone), Pidgin English is a major player, "matched only by the French zone in the size of its population" (Menang 2004: 905). Although Pidgin English is often associated with lack of an advanced education in English, it carries an increasing symbolism of youth, especially maleness and urban modernity. Not being able to speak pidgin in Ghana makes one not "one of the boys". Huber (2004: 870) proposes that Pidgin English is slowly becoming more acceptable within the universities of Ghana, where previously it was proscribed: "This is because unlike their senior and linguistically more conservative colleagues, young male Ghanaian lecturers did speak Pidgin at the time they were students". All of these considerations mean that pidgins are likely to grow in West Africa, in a kind of complementary functional allocation to languages associated with traditional culture, formal education and higher echelons of employment. Finally, it is necessary to stress that the boundary between pidgin and creole is not very clear-cut since (a) the creoles of the area (like Krio) exerted an influence on the growth of pidgins, (b) pidgins are becoming acceptable as one of the languages of the home in territories like Nigeria and Ghana, and (c) there is considerable overlap between pidgins in extended use and a creole in the sense of an L1.

For reasons of space it is not possible to discuss structural features of pidgins and their historical evolution. However, my impression is that whereas West African pidgins show great overlaps phonologically with the L2 English in their area, this is less true of the syntax (see Mesthrie 2004a, 2004b).

3 Creoles

Two later influential varieties in West Africa (from about 1787 onwards) were the forms of Creole English spoken by manumitted slaves who were repatriated from Britain, North America, and the Caribbean. Krio was the English Creole of slaves freed from Britain who were returned to Sierra Leone, where they were joined by slaves released from Nova Scotia and Jamaica. Liberia was established in 1821 as an African homeland for freed slaves from the US. The Creole English that the returnees brought with them was most likely related to African American Vernacular English (Hancock and Kobbah 1975: 248, cited by Todd 1982: 284; Singler 2004a, 2004b). Today, American rather than British forms of English continue to dominate in Liberia. Singler (2004a, 2004b) distinguishes between modern developments of Liberian Settler English and Vernacular Liberian English. The former is the language of the Settler ethnic group in which the role of formal education is discernible. Nevertheless, it can still be considered a direct descendant of 19th century African American Vernacular English (AAVE) that the immigrants brought to Liberia. The latter, Vernacular Liberian English, "had at first been a variety of the pidginized English that developed along the West African coast more generally, the influence of Settler English upon it caused it to diverge sharply from pidgin English in the rest of West Africa" (Singler 2004a: 875).

Singler shows how an analysis of the Settler variety can illuminate debates about the early history of AAVE. The debates revolve around an Anglicist position that the core features of AAVE can be found in British English dialects of earlier times (McDavid and McDavid 1951) and the Creolist position that AAVE began as a creole evolving features that were maximally distinct from the superstrate (Rickford 1975) – cf. Lanehart, Chapter 5. The Anglicist position appears to be reinforced from two independent approaches. Poplack and Tagliamonte (2001) studied two expatriate African American communities in the Dominican Republic and two Afro-Nova Scotian communities in Canada. They conclude that the language of these two varieties is closer to White varieties of North American English than is AAVE, which they propose has diverged gradually since its inception. Likewise Myhill (1995) presented features of AAVE that he proposed were relatively recent, i.e. post-Civil War: omission of verbal -s and possessive -s; copula absence, *ain't* for 'didn't' and forms like *be done*, semi-auxiliaries *come* and *steady* and stressed *been*. Singler's studies (see 1994a, 1994b) of the Sinoe Settler community show that all these features occur in Liberian Settler community of Sinoe. A small selection follows:

(1) *Because that one I* ain't *see with my own eye*. (*ain't* for 'didn't').

(2) *You* be done *crack you palm nut [...] then you make you palm butter [...]* (use of *be done*).

(3) *We talking about ending the war, and you* come *talking about Sinoe Defense force*. (semi-auxiliary *come* to express disapproval).

(4) *[...] When the teacher beat me, I run, man, I* (be) steady *holling all the way home*. (auxiliary *steady*; [*holling* = 'hollering']).

Singler distinguishes positive features of AAVE from negative features: the former involve non-standard forms, the latter involve the absence of a standard form. He concludes (Singler 2004b: 893) "Inasmuch as the positive features occur in Liberian Settler English and AAVE but do not occur in Samaná English, the most parsimonious account is that they are old and Samaná English has either lost them or never had them". Singler explains the differences between Samana and Sinoe in terms of origins in the US: whereas the Sinoe settlers emigrated directly from the Lower South of the US, the Samaná settlers had come from Philadelphia, which was an important city in post-emancipation movements. Furthermore Singler is able to posit that Liberian Settler English is more conservative than AAVE even, given that the frequency of the diagnostic features is greater in Liberia.

4 Contemporary language mixing

There is another aspect to the ontology of English in Africa, viz. its intertwining with local languages. Two types of contact effects are relevant here: (a) code-switching and (b) relexicalization in language mixing. The use of English in H(igh) contexts in colonial times over local languages has resulted in a new resource in many African contexts. The seminal work of Carol Myers-Scotton (1993) has shown how code switching is strategically used in East Africa to negotiate power relations between speakers. Notions like status versus solidarity, rights versus obligations of interlocutors, and the marked versus unmarked use of different languages come into play as speakers uses their multilingual resources in delicate ways. English is often used in code-switched discourse to stress status and education, rather than local solidarity (see Myers-Scotton 1993). For urban youth English tends to be a good source for slang lexis, and there are claims that new urban varieties have arisen based on the syntax of a local language (like Swahili in East Africa) and salient lexis from English. Sheng is the name given to this variety, and Engsh, to its polar opposite that draws on English syntax with salient Swahili slang (Kiessling and Mous 2004). While these are vibrant forms of expression amongst young peoples, and hence labeled "youth languages", hard evidence that these are fully fledged languages used in autonomous contexts (rather than anti-linguistic ones) has yet to be produced. Whether the youth language will grow up or continue to live an age-graded existence is a fascinating issue.

5 L1 Englishes

The main L1 English in Africa is the variety spoken by descendants of 19th century English settlers in South Africa, though the speech community has obviously diversified considerably beyond this base. This variety, called White South African English, is an important one on the continent, since it provided the input or was an influential model to L1 varieties that gelled in neighboring countries in southern Africa (Zimbabwe, Zambia, Namibia, etc.) and East Africa (especially Kenya). As Lass (2002) observed, although the origins of 19th century British settlers in South Africa was diverse, the variety that emerged in South African showed the influence of the southern majority: in being largely non-rhotic, in distinguishing TRAP from BATH, and STRUT from FOOT, and having lengthened [æ] before voiced stops, including /m/ and /n/ (as in *bad, bag, man*). Within South Africa there were originally three strands that merged into a continuum: (a) Cape Town English dating to 1795, spoken by largely an administrative, sailing and military segment; (b) Eastern Cape English dating to 1820, spoken by a class of settlers of mainly upper-working class origins from the Home Counties (Buckinghamshire, Hampshire, Essex, etc.); and (c) Natal English dating to the 1840s, comprising a mixture of origins with a middle class segment perhaps dominating and a mixture of people from the North and South (Lanham and Macdonald 1979). The Eastern Cape variety would have been the most similar to other Southern Hemisphere varieties in the Antipodes: the 1820 settlement was a mere 32 years after the first British settlements in Australia and 20 years before formal British colonial rule in New Zealand. The Natal variety is perhaps closer to the other "Southern variety" – that of the USA (settled from the 17th century on), with which it shares some prominent phonological rules: glide weakening of PRICE, fronting of the nucleus of the MOUTH diphthong, fronting and lowering of the nucleus of the GOAT diphthong, and lowering and retraction of the nucleus of the FACE diphthong – see Tillery and Bailey (2004: 333) for the Southern US values; Lass (2002) and Bowerman (2004) for the South African ones. To these can be added prominent GOOSE fronting, which within the US may have originated in the south and which has long been present in South African English (Hopwood 1928: 22).

Lanham and Macdonald (1979) argued that whilst they were once initially distinct, the Eastern Cape and Natal varieties have become more similar because of the opening up of the mines in the northern interior of the country, which drew people from the coastal provinces (and from other territories world-wide). This resulted in the rise of the more prestigious Natal variables (like PRICE weakening) as a counterforce (or substitute in Lanham's thinking) for the more prestigious, but less available RP-like varieties in the mining houses and elsewhere. And as White English speakers returned to the coastal areas a more homogeneous South African English spread, which today remains hard to describe purely in terms of regional variation. Bekker (2008) provides a recent acoustic study with a detailed historical overview and an important new historical account of the dialect around Johannesburg, arguing – contra Lanham – for its relative autonomy from other centers in the country both historically and currently. I focus on three chain shifts discernible in some varieties of South African English.

5.1 Chain shift 1

South African English shares with other Southern Hemisphere varieties, especially New Zealand, a front vowel shift. As in New Zealand (cf. Hundt, Chapter 15) the BIT vowel is centralized (with some complications with the KIT allophone in velar environments), DRESS is accordingly raised to a position just short of high front and TRAP is raised to a position closer to mid-front. Lass and Wright (1986) argued convincingly that this was a systemic selection from a range of variants found in working-class Victorian English. The complications with the KIT allophone have been called the KIT-split (Wells 1982). The realization of /ɪ/ in the environment of velars and /h/ remains a short front vowel [ɪ] in South African English.

In a preliminary account, Schreier (2008: 243) notes that St. Helenian English also has variation in this short front vowel set, whose "places of articulation tend to be closer rather than more open". South Africa is not as "advanced" as New Zealand in the chain shift, where to South African ears the degree of raising of DRESS and TRAP is greater, and where front allophones of KIT are rare (Bauer and Warren 2004: 586). In fact there is evidence that some South Africans might now be reversing the shift, as I discuss below.

5.2 Chain shift 2

Since around the year 2000 young, middle class White South Africans have been showing signs of adopting features that go contrary to the front short-vowel chain shift (see Chevalier 2016). At first sporadic and "experimental" versions of TRAP lowering and retraction appeared, in my experience mainly among young middle-class female speakers. It had been my impression at the time that these were ephemeral tokens, but since then more and more attestations have turned up amongst young teenage children and young women in "expressive" styles within peer groups and in the media, mainly television. Bekker and Ely (2007) and Bekker (2008), show that the phenomenon was quite widespread among White females in Johannesburg; but it appears to go beyond this as a big city phenomenon, judging from its appearance in Cape Town and Durban in the last decade. I have not encountered them in my ongoing fieldwork in the smaller cities of Port Elizabeth and Kimberley.

Bekker (2008) has in fact linked TRAP lowering in South Africa with developments in London and south east England (Torgersen and Kerswill 2004), where a reverse chain shift is evident with the fronting of FOOT, the extreme fronting of KIT, and lowering of DRESS and TRAP. This is a reversal and opposing trajectory to an older Cockney tendency of vowel raising (*keb, kittle* and *git* spellings occur in 19th century spellings for standard *cab, kettle* and *get*) that was the pre-cursor to Southern Hemisphere raising. Although Bekker (2008: 63) ties TRAP lowering in South Africa to this vernacular-driven shift in the south of England by invoking colonial lag, it is more likely to be a change from above, since as noted previously there is a middle-class, prestigious, experimental, or innovative aspect to it. Bekker (2008: 437) in fact also raises this as a possibility. In Cape Town DRESS is also lowering incipiently (to [ɛ]) and KIT is being lowered and retracted (to a centralized [ë]), especially in velar and glottal environments (in words like *kit* and *hit*). Again these are variants found in young middle-class female "expressive" styles. Whereas around 2000, it was customary in my undergraduate second-year sociophonetics class to find many White students with vowel raising and almost none with the counter shift, by my class of 2009 the numbers were dramatically reversed. A word of caution is necessary, though, that these were in citation, rather than vernacular, styles.

In considering the origins of (incipient) chain shift 2, the comparative method is illuminating. Here the options are embarrassingly rich, and both supported by external historical considerations. The first possible solution arises from recent social history. Although these lowered values had been noted by Lass (1990) they have only taken off around 2000. This date is not arbitrary. It is the time about which political uncertainty and increased global (rather than local) opportunities for White South Africans saw many young, middle-class, White South Africans take a gap year between school and university to travel to England and live for a year, earning a modest living and achieving a degree of independence before returning to South Africa. They would have been immersed in an environment in which non-raised tokens for DRESS and BIT were common and in which RP itself was indulging in TRAP lowering and backing, as is reasonably well established now. This is how Upton describes the TRAP vowel in RP:

> Associated with the general tendency of the modern RP front vowels to lower articulation (see also KIT and DRESS), the movement by younger speakers from traditional RP [æ] to RP [a] is arguably one of the most striking changes that has taken place in the accent group in recent years. (This "classical" chain shift, it should be noted, is being recognized in the accents of some non-standard dialects too, as in Ashford, by Kerswill [2002: 201].) It is also undoubtedly a most controversial matter. This is seemingly at least in part because the newer form corresponds with what is perceived by many to be a "Northern" sound [...]. (Upton 2004: 222)

Lowered TRAP can be heard among "posh" newsreaders (now of diverse backgrounds) on South African television, probably in imitation of RP. However, there are competing sources of origin. I first cite two phenomena that are unlikely to have influenced South Africa, but which must be considered important parallel developments: Australia and Canada. Horvath (2004: 640) lists lowered and retracted TRAP as one of several changes that occurred in Australian English between 1960 and 1990. The Canadian Shift was first described by Clarke et al. in 1995, involving the KIT, DRESS, and TRAP sets being lowered and/or retracted to respectively [ɛ], [æ] and [a]. It would appear that chain shift 2 in South Africa, TRAP lowering in Australia and the Canadian Shift are parallel responses to some earlier prime mover. That prime mover might for the first two appear to be RP, but as RP is less likely an influence in Canada, it is time to look for a new source. For this we turn to Gordon's account of the lowering of lax front vowels in California:

> In California, the vowels of KIT and DRESS may undergo lowering, and the vowel of TRAP may undergo both lowering and backing which results in realizations near [ɛ], [æ] and [a] respectively. Impressionistic descriptions of this trend suggest *six* sounds like *sex, sex* sounds like *sax,* and *sax* like *socks*. This lowering appears to be a recent development and may be a change in progress. It was not noted in earlier studies of California English and seems to have come to the attention of linguists only in the mid-1980s. It is reported to be especially characteristic of the speech of young urban women – a pattern that is consistent with its interpretation as an active change. The geographical extent of this lowering is not known, but it has been documented in both Southern California and the San Francisco Bay area [references omitted – RM]. (Gordon 2004: 347)

Chain shift 2 is thus an intriguing phenomenon for the historical linguist. To bring the discussion back to Africa, California is a more likely source for influencing young people via the popularity of Hollywood and Valley-speak sitcoms, which far outnumber RP or other-British accented programs. However, if we are to accept Chambers's (1998) conviction that sounds do not pass from one dialect to another via television, then we may have to accept a multiple influence scenario. Chain shift 2 in South Africa may well show colonial lag, not from below as suggested by Bekker (2008: 195) but from above (see Chevalier 2016). More intriguingly we can conjecture that the direction of influence could well be from Hollywood to RP, though if we take the datings seriously then it could just as intriguingly be from RP to Hollywood.

5.3 Chain shift 3

A third chain shift occurs not so much in White communities of South Africa as in its "colored" communities, who speak a variety of L1 or L2 English that has features inherited from the more broad White varieties (Wood 1987) and many innovations including those arising out of bilingualism with Afrikaans (Finn 2004). My fieldnotes as a student in 1978 indicate salient vowel raising, this time of the long back vowels. Here are some transcriptions of words from natural conversations that I have noted over the years in Cape Town:

[wuːtə] ~ [wo̝ːtə]   'water'
[bruːdə] ~ [bro̝ːdə]   'broader'
[kuːl] ~ [ko̝ːl]   'call'
[spɔːks]   'sparks'
[kɔ̝ːnt]   'can't'

(Note: [̝] indicates vowel raising)

Data such as that above shows a chain shift of /ɑː/ > /ɔː/ > /o̝ː/ ~ /uː/. Such systematic raising is a chain shift probably initiated by the raising of BATH (which is particularly backed in this sociolect, and slightly rounded and raised), which probably triggers the raising of THOUGHT. The encroachment on GOOSE has not yet been studied, and GOOSE has in fact remained a back vowel among working class speakers of the sociolect. The chain shift has not been carried to fruition, it is most perceptible among young working-class children, but is subject to less-raised values in other subgroups and styles.

For reasons of space it is not possible to discuss other changes in South African English phonetics: the standard sources are Lanham and Macdonald (1979) and Lass (2002), with Bekker (2009) being an important new voice.

6 L2 Englishes in Africa

The second language varieties of English in sub-Saharan Africa (SSE) have been studied mostly from a synchronic perspective, within the paradigm of language contact and transfer from the substrates, which are mostly languages of the Niger-Congo family. As with their syntax, these varieties share significant structural similarities in their phonologies. These phonological similarities are discussed in this section.

6.1 Effects of contact in SSE phonology

Among the salient phonetic/phonological tendencies in Bantu languages that are relevant to SSE phonetics and phonology is the prevalence of five or seven vowel systems in which length is not distinctive and diphthongs absent (Clements 2000: 135). Furthermore, African languages tend to have few instances of vowel reduction to schwa. Accordingly, most of the varieties of SSE, especially those spoken by people with lower levels of formal education and fewer contacts with native speakers, display a five vowel system, with few or no diphthongs and few traces of schwa. There is internal differentiation in the three broad areas of SSE: East Africa, West Africa and Southern Africa, shown in Figures 17.1 to 17.4 below, using Wells's (1982) lexical sets for monophthongs.

At this stage, taking into account vowel-length neutralization, we have the following monophthongal systems:

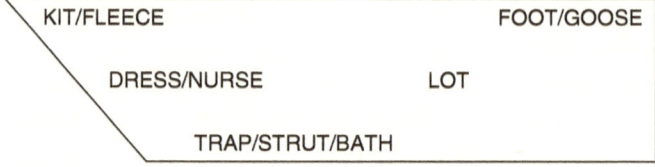

Figure 17.1: 5-vowel system – type 1 (Southern Africa – idealized)

Figure 17.2: 5-vowel system – type 2 (East Africa)

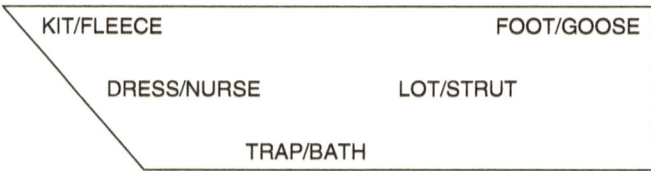

Figure 17.3: 5-vowel system – type 3 (West Africa)

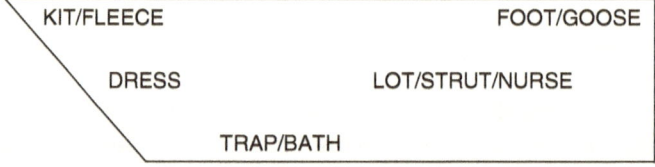

Figure 17.4: 5-vowel system – type 4 (Cameroons, Central Africa)

Type 1 is Southern African; Type 2 is East African and Type 3 is West African. In the Cameroons (the western edge of Central Africa) we have a further type, distinguished by the treatment of NURSE, which is usually [ɔ], though some words in this set take [ɛ] (Simo Bobda 2004).

Despite the broad similarities owing to neutralization of length, the four types are distinguishable as follows: East Africa has [a] for NURSE in contrast to the others; West Africa has [o] for STRUT, unlike the others; Southern Africa has [e] for some realizations of TRAP (i.e. a TRAP split between [e] and [a]); while Cameroons has [o] for NURSE, unlike the others. Taking Black South African English data as an example of the TRAP split, TRAP$_1$ (a raising to [e] or [ɛ]) can be found in words like *have*, *trap*, *fat*, *back*, *happy*, and *bat*. Words of this subset tend to be monosyllables or occasionally disyllables. On the other hand, the following polysyllabic words of Well's TRAP set have TRAP₂ (a central low [a]): s*a*laries, *a*nalyst, *a*dam*a*nt, *a*cademic, etc.

The diphthongs of SSE lend themselves to fewer generalizations. A noticeable tendency is to monophthongize FACE and GOAT. These are given as [e] and [o] respectively in East and West Africa, the Cameroons, and South Africa. It would be interesting to see whether these are phonemically distinct as /e/ and /o/ from the other sets which might be conceived of as /ɛ/ and /ɔ/. This appears to be the case in Southern Nigeria (Gut 2004: 819), and for South Africa (Van Rooy 2004: 947). Finally, although vowel length is not a distinctive feature in SSE, there is a regular phonological rule that lengthens vowels in heavy final syllables (CVC or VCC) or else in the penultimate syllable (see Van Rooy 2004: 950).

6.2 Effects of dialect input in SSE phonology

This substrate driven vowel typology might not give much leeway for observations of a more traditional historical linguistic nature. However, there are some relevant diachronic facets. Two scholars who have taken such a historical perspective are Harris (1996) and Simo Bobda (2003), proposing that not all influences are automatically attributable to substrate influence. Some of the variation in realizations of individual lexical sets might have been due to differential input. Simo Bobda (2003) provides a long list of possible phonetic links between SSE and British English dialects that are masked if one were to use the modern standards (or prestige varieties – RP or "General American") as the yardstick. Some of his examples are convincing: the monophthongal realizations of the FACE and GOAT diphthongs may well be linked to the older forms of these diphthongs ([e] and [o]) in Northern English, the Celtic Englishes and the Caribbean.

Harris (1996: 7–8) points out that even where interlingual phonemic identification between substrate and L2 English appears to indicate substrate influence "lock, stock, and barrel", the very fact that the L2 lexis comes almost entirely from the superstrate means that "on the basis of shared lexical stock, it is still possible to establish regular phonological correspondences between the contact variety and its lexical donor". He proposes that the realization of TRAP and STRUT as [a] and [ɔ] respectively in West Africa and [e] or [ɛ] and [a] in Southern Africa is due to such differences in superstratal values in the 17th century for West Africa and 19th century for Southern Africa. This is a plausible argument, except that the Southern African realizations of TRAP are (as pointed out in Section 6.1) more complex than an examination of just the (monosyllabic) token *trap* indicates. A large number of tokens in the set have [a] which is more likely to favor the substrate pattern, rather than the shape of the superstrate in 19th century South Africa (showing raising of the TRAP vowel).

As Simo Bobda points out, there is also a convincing case that links the realization of STRUT as a rounded back vowel in West Africa and the Caribbean, two territories whose historical connections in the era of slave trading are strong. Other examples of parallels that Simo Bobda (2003) cites (e.g. *l*-vocalization, fronted variants of NURSE) are less compelling, though his overall position that these parallels should not be entirely ignored is a valid one.

6.3 Contact in L2 SSE syntax

My assessment that contact between substrates and superstrate played a far larger role in the phonologies of L2 Englishes in Africa is reinforced by findings regarding the syntax. Here, there is large-scale agreement about the influence of the substrates and the effects of psycholinguistic processing in second language acquisition. For reasons of space only a sketch list is provided, and a selection at that: for further details see Mesthrie (2004b), which is an overview of the recurrent features of L2 varieties in Africa and Asia.

(a) Tendency to use resumptive pronouns inside relative clauses: *This is the kind of person that I would like to give an award to them.*
(b) Extension of the progressive into stative contexts, thus allowing *be + -ing* with verbs like *love, understand, know, have.*
(c) High use of left dislocation in topic-focus constructions: *The children – they are facing many challenges.*
(d) Occasional conflation of gender in pronouns, especially among less advanced speakers of the L2: *My wife hurt himself.*
(e) A different system underlying presupposition concerning and responses to yes/no questions couched in the negative: *Q: Aren't you a doctor? A: Yes (I'm not a doctor).*
(f) Tendency to extend plural -s to non-count or mass nouns (*staffs, machineries, luggages*).
(g) Regularization of comparative and superlative forms (*He is one of the radical students that you can ever find; He loves his car than his children*).
(h) Use of prepositions with verbs like *mention (about), discuss (about).*

Here the claims for historical continuity are slim, even though one might come across occasional similarities in the history of English: e.g. resumptive pronouns in Chaucerian English (*He was a man that he loved chivalrye* – *Prologue* to the *Canterbury Tales*). On the other hand, contact with substrates is alone not a convincing explanation, since many of these features – all the above except (d) and (g) – are in fact also reported in Asian L2 varieties of English. The case for universals of L2 psycholinguistic processing is therefore strong.

7 Summary

The historical linguistics of English in Africa is not a heavily studied area; but it is hoped that this overview shows that it is not without interest in its own right. This applies to the ways in which the L2 English syntaxes and phonologies lend themselves to internal African comparisons from which future developments can be monitored. Moreover, in two areas comparisons with similar varieties outside the continent can be historically illuminating. This was shown by the significance of Liberian English syntactic retentions and in chain shifts in South African Englishes. Even pidgin Englishes would appear by virtue of their historicity to be amenable to study via appropriate modifications of the traditional family tree or wave models of relations.

8 References

Bauer, Laurie and Paul Warren. 2004. New Zealand English: phonology. In: Edgar W. Schneider (eds.), Vol. 1: 580–602.

Bekker, Ian. 2009. *The Vowels of South African English*. Unpublished PhD thesis, North-West University, Potchefstroom, South Africa.

Bekker, Ian and Georgine Ely. 2007. An acoustic analysis of White South African English monophthongs. *Southern African Journal of Linguistics and Applied Language Studies* 25(1): 107–114.

Boberg, Charles. 2004. English in Canada: phonology. In: Edgar W. Schneider (eds.), Vol. 1: 351–365.

Bowerman, Sean. 2004. White South African English: phonology. In: Edgar W. Schneider (eds.), Vol. 1: 931–942.

Chambers, Jack K. 1998. Myth 15: TV makes people sound the same. In: Laurie Bauer and Peter Trudgill (eds.), *Language Myths*, 123–131. Harmondsworth: Penguin.

Chevalier, Alida. 2016. *Globalisation versus internal development: the reverse short front vowel shift in South African English*. Unpublished PhD. University of Cape Town.

Clarke, Sandra, Ford Elms, and Amani Youssef. 1995. The third dialect of English: some Canadian evidence. *Language Variation and Change* 7: 209–228.

Clements, George N. 2000. Phonology. In: Bernd Heine and Derek Nurse (eds.), *African Languages – an introduction*, 123–160. Cambridge: Cambridge University Press.

Den Besten, Hans. 1989. From Khoekhoe foreigner talk via Hottentot Dutch to Afrikaans: the creation of a novel grammar. In: Martin Pütz and Rene Dirven (eds.), *Wheels within Wheels*, 207–254. Frankfurt: Peter Lang.

Elugbe, Ben. 2004. Nigerian Pidgin English: phonology. In: Edgar W. Schneider, Kate Burridge, Bernd Kortmann, Rajend Mesthrie, and Clive Upton (eds.), Vol. 1: 831–841.

Finn, Peter. 2004. Cape Flats English: Phonology. In: Edgar W. Schneider (eds.), Vol. 1: 964–984.

Gordon, Matthew. 2004. The West and Midwest: phonology. In: Edgar W. Schneider (eds.), Vol. 1: 338–350.

Gut, Ulrike. 2004. Nigerian English – phonology. In: Bernd Kortmann and Edgar Schneider (eds.), *A Handbook of Varieties of English*, 813–830. Berlin/New York: Mouton de Gruyter.

Hakluyt, Richard. 1927 [1598–1600] *The Principal Navigations, Voyages, Traffiques and Discoveries of the English Nation*. London: Dent and Sons.

Hancock, Ian F. and Rachel Angogo. 1983. English in East Africa. In: Richard W. Bailey and Manfred Görlach (eds.), *English as a World Language*, 306–323. Ann Arbor: University of Michigan Press.

Hancock, Ian F. and Piayon E. Kobbah. 1975. Liberian English of Cape Palmas. In: Joey L. Dillard (ed.), *Perspectives on Black English*, 248–271. The Hague: Mouton.

Harris, John. 1996. On the trail of short *u*. *English World Wide* 17: 1–40.

Hopwood, David. 1928. *South African English Pronunciation*. Cape Town: Juta and Co.

Horvath, Barbara. 2004. Australian English: phonology. In: Edgar W. Schneider (eds.), Vol. 1: 625–644.

Huber, Magnus. 2004. Ghanaian Pidgin English: phonology. In: Edgar W. Schneider (eds.), Vol. 1: 866–873.

Kiessling, Roland and Maarten Mous. 2004. Urban youth languages in Africa. *Anthropological Linguistics* 46(3): 303–341.

Lanham, Leonard W. and Carol Macdonald. 1979. *The Standard in South African English and its Social History*. Heidelberg: Julius Groos Verlag.

Lass, Roger. 1990. How to do things with junk: exaptation in language evolution. *Journal of Linguistics* 26: 79–102.

Lass, Roger. 2002. South African English. In: Rajend Mesthrie (ed.), *Language in South Africa*, 104–126. Cambridge: Cambridge University Press.

Lass, Roger and Susan Wright. 1986. Endogeny versus contact; 'Afrikaans influence' on South African English. *English World Wide* 7(2): 201–223.

Malherbe, Vertrees C. 1990. *Krotoa called 'Eva' – a Woman Between*. Cape Town: UCT African Studies.

McDavid, Raven and Virginia McDavid. 1951. The relationship of the speech of American Negroes to the speech of Whites. *American Speech* 26: 3–17.

Menang, Thaddeus. 2004. Cameroon Pidgin English (Kamtok): phonology. In: Edgar W. Schneider (eds.), Vol.1: 902–917.

Mesthrie, Rajend. 2004a. Synopsis: the phonology of English in Africa and South and Southeast Asia. In: Edgar W. Schneider (eds.), Vol. 1: 1099–1110.

Mesthrie, Rajend. 2004b. Synopsis: morphological and syntactic variation in Africa and south and southeast Asia. In: Bernd Kortmann (eds.), Vol. 2: 1132–1141.

Mesthrie, Rajend and Rakesh M. Bhatt. 2008. World Englishes – the study of New Linguistic Varieties. Cambridge: Cambridge University Press.

Myers-Scotton, Carol. 1993. *Social Motivations for Code-Switching: Evidence from Africa*. Oxford: Clarendon Press.

Myhill, John. 1995. The use of features of present-day AAVE in the ex-slave recordings. *American Speech* 70: 115–147.

Poplack, Shana. 2000. *The English History of African American English*. Oxford: Blackwell.

Poplack, Shana and Sali Tagliamonte. 2001. *African American English in the Diaspora*. Oxford: Blackwell.

Rickford, John. 1975. Carrying the new wave into syntax: the case of Black English been. In: Ralph W. Fasold (ed.), *Analyzing Variation in the Form and use of Languages*, 162–183. Washington: Georgetown University Press.

Schmied, Josef. 1991. *English in Africa: an Introduction*. London: Longman.

Schmied, Josef. 2004. East African English (Kenya, Uganda, Tanzania): phonology. In: Edgar W. Schneider (eds.), Vol. 1: 918–930.

Schneider Edgar W., Kate Burridge, Bernd Kortmann, Rajend Mesthrie, and Clive Upton (eds.). 2004. *A Handbook of Varieties of English*, Vol. 1: *Phonology*. Berlin/New York: Mouton de Gruyter.

Schneider Edgar W., Kate Burridge, Bernd Kortmann, Rajend Mesthrie, and Clive Upton (eds.). 2004b. *A Handbook of Varieties of English*, Vol. 2: *Morphology and Syntax*. Berlin/New York: Mouton de Gruyter.

Schreier, Daniel. 2008. *St. Helenian English: Origins, Evolution and Variation*. Amsterdam/Philadelphia: John Benjamins.

Simo Bobda, Augustin. 2000. Research on New Englishes: a critical review of some findings with a focus on Cameroon. *Arbeiten aus Anglistik und Amerikanistik* 25: 53–70.

Simo Bobda, Augustin. 2001. East and southern African English accents. *World Englishes* 20(3): 269–284.

Simo Bobda, Augustin. 2003. The formation of regional and national features in African English pronunciation – an exploration of some non-interference factors. *English World Wide* 24(1): 17–42.

Simo Bobda, Augustin. 2004. Cameroon English: phonology. In: Edgar W. Schneider (eds.), Vol. 1: 885–901.

Singler, John. 2004a. Liberian Settler English: phonology. In: Edgar W. Schneider (eds.), Vol. 1: 874–884.

Singler, John. 2004b. Liberian Settler English: morphology and syntax. In: Edgar W. Schneider (eds.), Vol. 1: 879–897.

Spencer, John. 1971. West Africa and the English language: In: John Spencer (ed.), *The English Language in West Africa*, 1–34. London: Longman.

Tillery, J. and G. Bailey. 2004. The urban south: phonology. In: Edgar W. Schneider (eds.), Vol. 1: 325–337.

Torgersen, Eivind and Paul Kerswill. 2004. Internal and external motivation in phonetic change: dialect leveling outcomes for an English vowel shift. *Journal of Sociolinguistics* 8(1): 23–53.

Todd, Loreto. 1982. The English language in West Africa. In: Richard W. Bailey and Manfred Görlach (eds.), *English as a World Language*, 281–305. Ann Arbor: University of Michigan Press.

Upton, Clive. 2004. Received Pronunciation. In: Edgar W. Schneider (eds.), Vol. 1: 217–230.

Van Rooy, Bertus. 2004. Black South African English: Phonology. In: Edgar W. Schneider (eds.), Vol. 1: 943–952.

Wells, John Christopher. 1982. *Accents of English. Vol. 1: Introduction*. Cambridge: Cambridge University Press.

Wood, Tahir. 1987. *Perceptions of, and attitudes towards, varieties of English in the Cape Peninsula, with particular reference to the 'Coloured Community'*. Unpublished M.A. thesis. Grahamstown: Rhodes University.

David Britain
Chapter 18:
Diffusion

1   Introduction —— 349
2   Terminology —— 350
3   Diffusion at the micro-level: the role of local social networks —— 351
4   Diffusion at the macro-level: geographical pathways —— 353
5   The linguistic consequences of diffusion —— 359
6   Summary —— 361
7   References —— 361

Abstract: The diffusion of innovative linguistic forms is discussed at three levels. Firstly, the chapter deals with terminological issues. What is the difference between an innovation and a change? How do we (and, indeed, should we) distinguish between changes diffused because of speaker migration, and those spread because of everyday human contact? Secondly, the chapter considers the spread of features from one individual to another. Is it possible to socially locate those who diffuse linguistic changes? Here, we consider competing arguments concerning the embedding of diffusers in local social networks of different strengths and structures. Finally, the geographical diffusion of changes is examined. By what routes do changes spread from place A to B? In this section, the different models of innovation diffusion are compared and critiqued. Throughout, studies on Englishes past and present are used to exemplify the arguments, models, and critiques.

1 Introduction

This chapter examines, both at the level of a person's social network ties and at a broader spatial scale, how new linguistic items – new sounds, new grammatical forms – are diffused from one speaker to another and one community to another. It begins with some necessary terminological clarifications, before proceeding to an inspection of the (rather contested) role of social network strength in the spread of new forms. This is followed by an examination of the various models of

David Britain: Bern (Switzerland)

innovation diffusion in the literature that have attempted to grasp how innovations spread spatially across the speech community, and applies the rather incisive critiques of innovation diffusion models in the human geographical literature to the models generally used in dialectology. The chapter concludes with an examination of the multiple possible outcomes of linguistic innovation diffusion.

2 Terminology

It is important to firstly and briefly address here the relationship between "innovation", "diffusion", and "change", as well as between different types of diffusion. Milroy (1992) argues forcefully that we should distinguish between "innovations" – novel linguistic outputs by speakers that may or may not be adopted by others – and "changes" – effects on the linguistic system caused by speaker innovations being adopted beyond the original innovator. Milroy suggests that we cannot observe change until it has already begun to spread from innovator to early adopters, but that we might (accidentally) be able to spot an innovation (without knowing whether it will, one day, be successful and be adopted by other people). From the social (-linguistic) point of view, then, the study of diffusion plots the paths by which innovations spread from the innovator to early adopters and beyond, but we must recognize that we've been more successful at understanding the diffusion from early adopters to later ones, than from innovators to early adopters.

The study of diffusion is interested in the socio-geography of interaction, in who speaks to whom, in what sorts of people are linguistically influential and whose innovations seem to be successful, and how those innovations reach different social groups (or not) and different geographical locations (or not). These issues form part of Weinreich et al.'s (1968) "embedding problem", one of five "problems" that they argued had to be addressed in order to fully comprehend language change. From the more purely linguistic point of view, the study of diffusion plots the path by which changes spread through the language: in which linguistic environments is the change found first and most frequently? Is the speed of its adoption in the linguistic system steady or is it rapid at certain stages and slower at others? Are changes abrupt or gradual? – and so on, thereby addressing elements of Weinreich et al.'s "transition" as well as "embedding" problems. The study of diffusion, then, reaches to the very heart of the sociolinguistic dialectological enterprise, addressing questions identified as core to understanding language change as a whole. In this section on Varieties of English and dialect contact, however, I focus on the socio-geography of diffusion, on the spread of new linguistic forms across the social and geographical dialect landscape, drawing on both historical and present-day examples.

Some authors (e.g. Gerritsen 1988) divide diffusion into two types: "relocation diffusion" and "expansion diffusion", depending on how the innovation moves from A to B. Relocation diffusion, it is argued, is the result of the actual movement of speakers from A to B, carrying the innovation with them from A, and "implanting" it in the new location of B. Expansion diffusion, meanwhile, is the result of everyday contacts and interactions passing innovations on from one speaker to another. Whether the distinction is a fruitful one or not is questionable, since even expansion diffusion involves mobilities, albeit perhaps rather mundane, everyday, routine ones (though see Britain 2012a for an examination of the power and intensity of mundane mobilities in late modernity), some of these mobilities are hard to tease apart (e.g. long distance commuting [presumably a trigger for expansion diffusion] and urban to rural counterurbanization [relocation diffusion] are often engaged in by the very same people [Champion et al. 2009]) and the linguistic outcomes, although possibly less radical than those triggered by long-distance migrations, are nevertheless typologically very similar. Here, I will not be examining international migrations as a diffusion mechanism, but intranational, intra-regional, and local ones instead.

3 Diffusion at the micro-level: the role of local social networks

There has been a certain amount of disagreement in the literature over the relationship between the nature of speakers' social networks and innovation diffusion. It is fairly well established that network strength plays an important role in determining the speed and likelihood of innovation adoption:

> the idea that *relative strength of network tie* is a powerful predictor of language use is implicit in the theoretical model we have used [...] Many studies, both urban and rural, have shown that a close-knit network structure functions as a conservative force, resisting pressures for change originating from outside the network; conversely those speakers whose ties to the localized network are weakest approximate least closely to localized vernacular norms, and are most exposed to external pressures for change. (J. Milroy 1992: 176–177, emphasis in original; see also L. Milroy 1980; J. Milroy and L. Milroy 1985; Lippi-Green 1989)

Lesley Milroy (1980) found, for example, in her Belfast study that those with stronger network integration into the local Belfast speech community were more likely to retain traditional local dialect forms in the face of competition from dialect forms external to the community. Yet researchers disagree somewhat about the transmission of dialect forms into and between strong networks. James Milroy argues forcefully that the key to understanding the spread of dialect forms is understanding the weak ties that link together different strong networks. Drawing on Granovetter (e.g. 1973), he proposes that

> weak ties between groups regularly provide bridges through which information and influence are diffused […] these bridges cannot consist of strong ties; the ties *must* be weak […] Thus weak ties may or may not function as bridges, but no strong tie can […] the important point […] that follows from all this is that weak inter-group ties are likely to be critical in transmitting innovations from one group to another, despite the common-sense assumption that *strong* ties fulfil this role. (Milroy 1992: 178–179, emphasis in original)

This assumption has been adopted more widely in other parts of the related sociolinguistic literature, for example in contact dialectology, where it has been argued that typologically different types (and rates) of change are adopted in high-contact, mobile, typically weak-networked communities when compared with low-contact, relatively static, typically strong-networked communities.

Others think differently, however. Labov's work in Philadelphia (e.g. 2001) led him to argue that innovations diffuse through the influence of people who have strong ties both inside and outside the local group: "the leaders are people who are not limited to their local networks, but have intimate friends in the wider neighborhood" (Labov 2001: 360). His research pinpointed a small number of "leaders" of linguistic change, whose use of vigorous and recent innovations was the most advanced in the community studied. What they had in common, according to Labov, was central roles in local community networks, as well as "the highest proportion of friends off the local block" (Labov 2001: 344). One leader discussed in detail by Labov is "Celeste S.",

> someone who unites several sub-groups through symmetric linkings, and is automatically mentioned by everyone […] We can then add the property of centrality to the characterization of leaders of linguistic change. Celeste's central position indicates that people look to her as a point of reference, and are likely to be influenced by her actions, behavior and opinions […] local social networks of this kind allow leading figures to exert linguistic influence on others […] the leaders of linguistic change who have emerged from the Philadelphia study show an unusual combination of centrality with a high frequency of social interaction outside of their immediate locality […] leaders of linguistic change are centrally located in social networks which are expanded beyond their immediate locality. (Labov 2001: 351, 364)

Milroy is not convinced, suggesting that Labov's innovator

> is a person who is sociable and outgoing, and who has many friends both inside and outside the local group […] it seems very likely that information of all kinds […] can be diffused by such persons, for the reason that they have many contacts. But, according to our account,

such individuals could not be near the center of a close-knit group, and at the same time have many strong outside ties. (Milroy 1992: 183)

The literature on historical change has provided support for both proposals. Both Conde-Silvestre and Hernández-Campoy (2004) and Nevalainen (2000) have argued for the pivotal role that lawyers and other legal professionals played in the promotion of changes (in, of course, the written language), suggesting that, just as Celeste S. was an important and influential central figure in her neighborhood in Philadelphia, lawyers played crucially important roles as language brokers in the written linguistic marketplace in early modern England. Furthermore, drawing on evidence from the *Helsinki Corpus of Early English Correspondence*, Raumolin-Brunberg (2006) was able to suggest that both the Labovian and Milroyian approaches to finding the social locus of the diffusers of change may be accurate, sometimes. For a number of different features, she examined the rates of change at different stages of progress, and was, thereby, able to shed light on the strength of innovators' network ties at those different stages. When changes were in their infancy, she found that it was those individuals who were highly mobile and who had social profiles characterized by many weak social networks that were leading the change. When the changes were somewhat more advanced, however, it was individuals who were influential central "pillars" of their communities, with strong multiplex social ties, that were leading. She was able to conclude, therefore, that the two positions are perhaps not mutually exclusive, but simply reflect the position at different points along the life-cycle of a change.

Both Labov and Milroy did agree, but coming to the position from different angles (see Britain 2012b for a discussion), that it is the *central* classes of society who tend to lead language change – the upper working and lower middle classes. Extensive evidence from earlier stages of English agrees with this view, with Raumolin-Brunberg (2006: 131), for example, arguing that change is led by "interior social groups" and "middle ranking people".

4 Diffusion at the macro-level: geographical pathways

Sociolinguistic models of the geographical spread of innovations have largely been influenced by developments in economic geography – how, for example, novel products, technological inventions, fashions, and healthcare treatments come to be adopted or not across geographical space. These developments have provided us with a number of diffusion paths that have come to be adopted in investigations of dialect change, too. Perhaps the most iconic model of the diffusion of an innovation is the *wave model*, whereby innovations spread out in waves from a central point, in a manner similar to that by which ripples spread out from the point where a stone is dropped into water. Nearby places are affected before places further afield, and the order of adoption is one purely determined by as-the-crow-flies distance. Despite its iconicity, however, relatively few studies have been able to persuasively demonstrate that actual linguistic innovations have diffused (approximately) in this way. Such a model depends entirely on a perfectly geographically even distribution of interactions and mobilities and a perfect pattern of denser interactions in locations geographically near to the origin of the innovation and evenly sparser interactions at ever greater distances from the core, regardless of terrain. Trudgill (1986), investigating linguistic innovations spreading from London into East Anglia in Southern England, showed that, although approximate, the wave model accounted best for the gradual geographical diffusion of fronted (i.e. [ɐ]) variants of /ʌ/ (in words such as *cup* and *fun*). Such fronting was found most in locations physically nearer to London, but was increasingly less likely the further the settlement was from the capital (see also Bailey et al. [1993] and Labov [2003] for further examples of innovations apparently diffused in a wave-like way). From a historical perspective, Nevalainen and Raumolin-Brunberg (2003: 170) have argued, in a discussion of the ways in which features of Northern English diffused to the "magnet" of London in the period between the 15th and 17th centuries, that the use of the indicative present plural form *are* of the verb BE gradually diffused southwards in a wave-like manner, reaching East Anglia before London.

Better attested is the *Urban Hierarchy Model* of diffusion, sometimes labeled "cascade diffusion". This model suggests that diffusing innovations usually begin in large urban centers and spread down an urban hierarchy of large city to smaller city, to large town, to smaller town, village and may, eventually, reach the deep countryside. It is an extension of the wave model, in that distance is still shown to play an important role. To a certain extent, though, and unlike wave model diffusion, urban hierarchy models reflect an understanding that the landscape is not evenly populated, nor evenly resourced with transportation networks and service infrastructure and builds on the idea that such infrastructure (and therefore the facilitation of interaction between geographically distant locations) largely connects urban with urban at the national and regional levels, with each urban area having its own sphere of economic and social influence into the surrounding suburban and rural landscape, reinforced by infrastructure that perpetuates that influence. Urban to urban, then, is seen as a particularly well-trodden path, guiding future mobilities to re-entrench those same geographical routes of influence.

Two examples will suffice here. First, we can look to Kerswill's (2003) nationwide picture of the adoption of the fronting to [f] and [v] of /θ/ and non-initial /ð/ respectively in Britain. He shows, by plotting the size of a number of urban centers against the dates of the first reports of the adoption of [f v], that the spread of this (rather unmarked) innovation cannot be accounted for by geographical distance alone – though clearly distance plays a role – but also important is the size of the urban center receiving the innovation. Contrasting three urban centers in his survey, all roughly the same distance from London, he demonstrates that Derby (population 230,000, 210 km from London) adopted the innovation before Norwich (135,000 and 190 km), which in turn received it before Wisbech (20,000 and 170 km). Although slightly more distant from London, Derby is quicker to reach by public transport than either Norwich or Wisbech.

A somewhat different example of cascade diffusion in action comes from Hernández-Campoy's (2003) research examining the diffusion of standard forms of Castilian Spanish into the Region of Murcia in South-Eastern Spain, an area with a well-recognized non-standard dialect of Spanish. He showed that the standardization of a number of linguistic variables was most prevalent in the city of Murcia, the capital and by far the largest city of the region, with other larger urban areas showing more standardization than smaller towns in the region.

These examples suggest that a combination of population size and distance help account for the route of diffusion, and this combination was formalized in so-called gravity models, which quantitatively simulate the likelihood of one location influencing another. Trudgill (see esp. 1983) successfully applied such gravity models (and recognized the potential problems with them) to the diffusion of innovations in urban East Anglia in the east of England, and to the Brunlanes peninsula of Southern Norway. In both, gravity model projections accurately predicted the hierarchy of linguistic influence – which towns were more likely to be linguistically influenced by the main urban center – that the largest urban center (London and Larvik, respectively) would have on others in the region.

Whilst they found that some forms appeared to have spread from Northern England in a wave-like manner, Nevalainen and Raumolin-Brunberg (2003: 178) found rather more changes in the *Corpus of Early English Correspondence* had spread hierarchically from the North to London, reaching urban London before the geographically nearer rural East Anglia. The use both of *my* and *thy* in place of *mine* and *thine* and of third person singular present tense -*s* appears to have spread hierarchically in their data.

Another possible model was proposed by Barbara and Ron Horvath (1997, 2001, 2002) in their investigations of the vocalization of /l/ in urban Australia. They found that /l/ vocalization was used most in both urban and more rural areas of southern Australia and that it wasn't until the innovation had gained a solid foothold across the region around Adelaide that /l/ vocalization began to spread significantly to urban centers beyond South Australia. They labeled this pattern the *Cultural Hearth* model, recognizing that urban centers will indeed influence their nearby hinterlands before reaching (esp. in the Australian context) cities that are a significant distance from the center of the innovation.

Rare are *counterhierarchical* diffusions, features that spread from rural areas to more urban ones. Examples provided in the literature include Trudgill's (1986) demonstration that smoothing processes (turning triphthongs into diphthongs or long vowels) in East Anglia began in rural Norfolk and are spreading southwards and to more urban areas and Bailey et al.'s (1993) research showing the spread of *fixing to* from rural to urban in Oklahoma.

All of these models are supposedly reflections of the geographies of interaction, of who speaks to whom where – indeed Hägerstrand, probably the diffusion geographer that has had the most influence on sociolinguistic dialectology because of Trudgill's early (e.g. 1974) engagement with his work, argued that "the diffusion of innovation is by definition a function of communication" (Hägerstrand 1966: 27). But Hägerstrand's models of innovation diffusion have undergone severe and incisive critique in the human geographical literature in the last 40 years. Gregory (1985, 2000) is perhaps one of the most critical (see also Blaikie 1978). Some of the more important criticisms are presented below.

There is an implicit understanding that the central focus of enquiry in diffusion studies is how one conservative form is replaced by another innovative form. "This is supposed to consist of a cascade of systematic spatial regularities: local concentrations of initial acceptances; radial dissemination and the rise of secondary concentrations; saturation [...] the explanation then is a strictly morphological one" (Gregory 1985: 303). Innovation diffusion has thus largely (and this is as true in the diffusionist geographical work as in the sociolinguistic) been treated as the replacement of one traditional form by another new form. This is problematic for sociolinguistics in (at least) two respects: firstly it ignores the fact that innovation diffusion leads to contact (between old and new), and contact has a fairly well-known set of linguistic outcomes (see Trudgill 1986; Kerswill 2002; Britain 2012a), including linguistic hybridity and simplification (see below). Secondly, there has largely been an assumption that the innovation will remain intact as it diffuses and won't have mutated en route. Linguistic examples of mutations will be discussed in greater depth below, but there is good evidence also that very often even the social evaluation of innovations may change as they diffuse. Glottal stops in England, stereotypically 'stigmatized' as characteristic of working class speech in the South-East have been found *more* among middle class (female) speakers than working class speakers in both Cardiff (Mees and Collins 1999) and Newcastle (Watt and Milroy 1999), upsetting the expected social stratification of a vernacular linguistic change. In Cardiff, Mees and Collins (1999: 201) argued that the adoption of London's glottal stops represented a shift to "more sophisticated and fashionable speech".

The spatial reach of a diffusing innovation is portrayed as being a function of the strength and influence of its promoting urban center (Wells 1982, for example, claimed that London was probably the most linguistically influential city in the Anglophone world), rather than being determined by resistance or acquiescence by speakers. As Gregory (1985: 322–323) argues:

> In even the most developed version [of Hägerstrand's diffusion theory – DB] it is axiomatic that 'resistance levels' will eventually diminish, and these are supposed to be a function of insufficient information – of ignorance – rather than of conscious collective action. There is a strong presumption that innovations are *pro bono publico*, therefore, and that their adoption is as uncontentious as it is unproblematic.

Diffusion theory, it is argued, has proceeded on the assumption that non-adoption of the innovation is a "passive state where the friction of distance applies a brake to innovation […] rather than 'an active state arising out of the structural arrangements of society'" (Gregory 1985: 319). Resistance to an innovation, he argues, "connotes a process of sustained struggle: considered and collective action on the part of people whose evaluation of the available information may be strikingly different to that of the 'potential adopters'" (Gregory 2000: 176). One innovative dialect feature which now appears to be remarkably stable, if not retreating, is the BATH /ɑː/ – TRAP /a/ split of Southern England. Britain (2001) showed that at least along the Eastern end of the isogloss between areas with the split, to the south, and those without it (where both BATH and TRAP have /a/), to the North, the split is not advancing northwards, and speakers to the North of the isogloss have been leveling away occasional uses of the /ɑː/ form to become more categorically 'northern'. Is this because the innovation has 'run out of steam', or because speakers reject the innovation? Wells (1982: 354), after all, did suggest that even middle class people in the north of England "would feel it to be a denial of their identity as northerners to say BATH words with anything other than short [a]".

Gregory argues that diffusion theory has demonstrated a fixation with the spatial, such that it has been insensitive to the social structure of communities affected by innovations. Gravity models, based on population and distance, used in the dialectology of diffusion assume that everyone who uses the innovation has an equal chance of transmitting it to non-users and that everyone in the geographical path of the innovation has an equal chance of adopting it. However, we live in a socially differentiated world, where access to the resources facilitating mobility and interaction are unevenly and unequally distributed (see Britain 2009a, 2010a, 2012a). That gravity models ignore the complexity of social structure led Gregory (1985: 328) to argue that they "failed to cut through the connective tissue of the world in such a way that its fundamental integrities are retained" and that there has been "no serious discussion of the structures of social relations and systems of social practices through which innovations filter" (Gregory 1985: 304). Few attempts have been made to enrich linguistic applications of spatial diffusion models with meaningful social information about the speakers involved.

There is also little sensitivity in such models to the historical geographies of interactions, and the fact that space is a process, always, to cite Pred (1985), in a state of "becoming". Gregory claims that

> diffusion theory [...] is seen to be rooted in a stable rural environment where friction of distance is immensely high and the projects related to human action are on the whole strongly repetitive and restricted to compact space-time bubbles which are elongated in time but very narrow in space [...] the casting and recasting of webs of interaction is clearly not independent of the production and reproduction of the locational structures which contain them. These are not constants. (Gregory 1985: 312–315)

The geographies of our mobilities, our contacts and our interactions change over time and in different social contexts, but the model building in studies of diffusion has not been sensitized to this (see, for example, Bergs [2006: 28] for a plea in historical sociolinguistic studies of diffusion to examine "the actual way(s) and path(s) of travelling speakers"). In England, for example, the 19th century was demographically marked by (largely working class) urbanization, but the 20th (and beyond) by (largely middle class) counter-urbanization; the invention of railways and cars has facilitated mundane mobility that was previously much slower and more local, and it has facilitated longer distance commuting; more and more young people are leaving their homes for higher education; more and more enterprises are in the spatially flexible tertiary sector, demanding a mobile and skilled workforce. But these mobilities are both a product of our time, and could change, and are highly socially differentiated (see Britain 2012a). Diffusion models, then, need to keep pace with and be sensitive to the actual mobilities and interactions that speakers engage in. Urban hierarchy models, for example, are inadequate to deal with the linguistic consequences of middle class counter-urbanization – an ongoing demographic trend of at least the past half-century – to (traditional dialect speaking) deep rural areas in Southern England. In so far as physical, attitudinal, social, economic, and political barriers cause barriers to interaction, so the ability of innovations to diffuse is likely to be affected (see, for example, Boberg 2000; Britain 2014).

In general, then, the weaknesses of contemporary spatial diffusion models can be seen to result from their failure to adopt a richly socialized and interactional perspective on the spaces across which features diffuse. Society in diffusion models, Gregory (1985: 328–329) argues, needs to be conceived as a "multidimensional structure and not 'squashed into a flat surface, pock-marked only by the space-time incidence of events'".

5 The linguistic consequences of diffusion

As mentioned above, diffusion does not (always) result in the simple adoption of the innovative form. In many ways, diffusion can be best conceptualized, as Trudgill strongly argued (see Trudgill [1986: 42–82] for a detailed account of the different outcomes of diffusion), as one form of dialect contact, and in adopting this conceptualization, we can be open to the possibility of a number of typologically different linguistic outcomes from the diffusion process, outcomes typical of dialect contact in general (see also Britain 2010a).

One of the most prominent and likely outcomes is victory of the innovative form over other conservative variants, where the victor is often (but not always) unmarked, or used by a majority of speakers, or salient, relative to the loser. But even such apparently simple outcomes can lead to (possibly temporary and minor) complexification of the system. One such example is the diffusion of labiodental variants [f] and [v] of the English interdentals (θ) and (ð) in England (and beyond) (see Kerswill 2003 for an overview). On the surface, this appears to be a system-simplifying change. Two rather marked phonemes, acquired late in child language acquisition, succumb to less marked forms, and merge with them. The change appears not to be proceeding so straightforwardly, though. Despite being a vigorous innovation, spreading rapidly across the country as Kerswill shows, linguistically there is complexity in the detail. Generally, whilst the change affects (θ) in every phonological environment, word initial (ð) is not affected, retaining its interdental quality. Two parallel pairs of sounds have been replaced, then, not by just one, as would be the case in a straightforward merger, but by one merger and one partial, incomplete merger with a (rather frequently used, in words such as *the, this, that* etc.) residue. Similar stories can be told for other variables. The diffusion of a merged GOAT vowel (at the expense of the traditional split system of [ʌʊ] and [ʊu] deriving from ME /ɔu/ and /ɔː/ respectively) into East Anglia in England has triggered a wide variety of contact phenomena (see also below), one of which is the relic use across a wide area of the region of the traditional [ʊu] variant solely in the (frequent) word *go* (and *goes, going* etc.) (Britain 2005), with, for many speakers, the merger successful in all other respects.

A further outcome of the arrival of an innovation is the emergence of hybrid inter-dialect forms rather than the simple victory of the innovation. Both Trudgill

(1986) and Britain (2005), for example, discuss the hybrid outcomes of the diffusion of the merged and also fronted GOAT vowel mentioned just above. These include merged interdialect forms (i.e. phonologically similar to the innovation – a merger – but phonetically different) (Trudgill 1986) and the retention of the split, with fronting only affecting the lexical set of Middle English /ou/ (Britain 2005), and not that of [ɔː].

Simplification is another possible outcome of innovation diffusion. This possibility has been examined most recently by Labov (2007). He showed how the New York system of tensing and raising of short /a/, determined by complex phonological, grammatical, lexical, and stylistic constraints has been simplified as it diffused to Albany, Cincinnati, and New Orleans. The simplifications triggered by the diffusion to the three cities are presented in Table 18.1.

Table 18.1: Simplification and the consequences of diffusion: the tensing and raising of /a/ in New York City, Albany, Cincinnati, and New Orleans (based on Labov 2007) (see also Britain 2010b).

Tensing contexts	New York	Albany	Cincinnati	New Orleans
Before: /b d m n g f s θ dʒ ʃ/	✓	✓	Not before /g/, but also before /v z/	Also before /v z/
Not in function words with simple codas	✓	✗	✗	✗
Not in open syllables without a morpheme boundary	✓	✗	✗	✓ (but weakened among younger speakers)
Not word-initially, except in frequent words (e.g. 'ask', 'after')	✓	✓	✓	Not in 'after'
Lexical exceptions (e.g. 'avenue')	✓	?	?	?
Other conditions (e.g. not in abbreviations, acronyms, learned words)	✓	?	?	?

Labov showed that the tensing and raising of /a/ is ongoing, but some of the more marked constraints on tensing have been lost in the diffusion process. He specifically contrasts these simplifying tendencies with the small but perceptible incrementations in changes that take place as a result of parent to child transmission in relatively stable communities (but see Britain 2016), and accounts for the difference between diffusion and transmission by arguing that contact across communities involves learning, primarily by adults, who acquire the new variants of the originating community in a somewhat diluted form [...] Adult learning is not only slower, but it is also relatively coarse: it loses much of the fine structure of the linguistic system being transmitted [...] these contact phenomena share the common marks of adult language learning: the loss of linguistic configurations that are reliably transmitted only by the child language learner. (Labov 2007: 380–382)

One final possibility that, of course, cannot be ruled out here is the active rejection of the innovation through the use of hyperdialectalisms – dialect forms which, apparently diverging from the incoming innovation, overextend the traditional conservative form, often to linguistic contexts where it had not been historically attested. One often mentioned example is the hyper-rhoticity on the rhotic side of the rhotic/non-rhotic border in the south and west of England (see, for example, Britain 2009b), whereby [r] is inserted into words such as *wash* and *last*, as non-rhoticity spreads.

Trudgill (1986) mentions other, further, possible outcomes of diffusion, clearly demonstrating a wide array of possibilities beyond simple eradication of the conservative variant.

6 Summary

This chapter has examined innovation diffusion at the scale of individual social networks and from the perspective of changes across space, showing examples of a range of different outcomes of diffusion. A number of points of disagreement and conflict in the literature have been witnessed, notably concerning the locus of the social network embedding of innovators and the incisive criticism of diffusion models in human geography (a criticism that has largely not reached dialectological research). There is still a lot to be done and a lot to be understood about the diffusion of linguistic innovations at all scales and it is to be hoped that the recent revival of interest in the geography-dialectology interface (see, for example, Auer and Schmidt 2009; Lameli et al. 2010) will lead to these issues, fundamental to our understanding of language change, receiving further attention.

7 References

Auer, Peter and Jürgen Erich Schmidt (eds.). 2009. *Language and Space. An International Handbook of Linguistic Variation*. Vol. 1: *Theories and Methods*. Berlin/New York: Mouton de Gruyter.

Bailey, Guy, Tom Wikle, Jan Tillery, and Lori Sand. 1993. Some patterns of linguistic diffusion. *Language Variation and Change* 5: 359–390.
Bergs, Alexander. 2006. Spreading the word: Patterns of diffusion in historical dialectology. In: Markku Filppula, Juhani Klemola, Marjatta Palander, and Esa Penttilä (eds.), *Topics in Dialectal Variation: Selection of papers from the Eleventh International Conference on Methods in Dialectology*, 5–30. Joensuu: University of Joensuu Press.
Blaikie, Piers. 1978. The theory of the spatial diffusion of innovations: a spacious cul-de-sac. *Progress in Human Geography* 2: 268–295.
Boberg, Charles. 2000. Geolinguistic diffusion and the U.S.-Canada border. *Language Variation and Change* 12: 1–24.
Britain, David. 2001. Welcome to East Anglia!: two major dialect 'boundaries' in the Fens. In: Jacek Fisiak and Peter Trudgill (eds.), *East Anglian English*, 217–242. Woodbridge: Boydell and Brewer.
Britain, David. 2005. Innovation diffusion, 'Estuary English' and local dialect differentiation: the survival of Fenland Englishes. *Linguistics* 43: 995–1022.
Britain, David. 2009a. Language and space: the variationist approach. In: Peter Auer and Jürgen Schmidt (eds.), *Language and space: an international handbook of linguistic variation*, 142–162. Berlin/New York: Mouton de Gruyter.
Britain, David. 2009b. One foot in the grave?: Dialect death, dialect contact and dialect birth in England. *International Journal of the Sociology of Language* 196/197: 121–155.
Britain, David. 2010a. Conceptualisations of geographic space in linguistics. In: Alfred Lameli, Roland Kehrein, and Stefan Rabanus (eds.), *Language and Space: An International Handbook of Linguistic Variation*. Vol. 2: *Language Mapping*, 69–97. Berlin/New York: Mouton de Gruyter.
Britain, David. 2010b. Contact and dialectology. In: Raymond Hickey (ed.), *Handbook of Language Contact*, 208–229. Oxford: Wiley Blackwell.
Britain, David. 2012a. The role of contact and mobility in dialect birth and dialect death. In: Daniel Schreier and Marianne Hundt (eds.), *English as a contact language*, 165–181. Cambridge: Cambridge University Press.
Britain, David. 2012b. Innovation diffusion in sociohistorical linguistics. In: Juan Manuel Hernández-Campoy and Juan Camilo Conde-Silvestre (eds.), *Handbook of Historical Sociolinguistics*, 451–464. Oxford: Wiley.
Britain, David. 2014. Where North meets South? Contact, divergence, and the routinisation of the Fenland dialect boundary. In: Dominic Watt and Carmen Llamas (eds.), *Language, borders and identity*, 27–43. Edinburgh: Edinburgh University Press.
Britain, David. 2016. Sedentarism, nomadism and the sociolinguistics of dialect. In: Nikolas Coupland (ed.), *Sociolinguistics: Theoretical Debates*, 217–241. Cambridge: Cambridge University Press.
Champion, Tony, Mike Coombes, and David L. Brown. 2009. Migration and longer-distance commuting in rural England. *Regional studies* 43: 1245–1259.
Conde-Silvestre, Juan Camilo and Juan Manuel Hernández-Campoy. 2004. A sociolinguistic approach to the diffusion of Chancery written practices in late fifteenth century private correspondence. *Neuphilologische Mitteilungen* 105: 133–152.
Gerritsen, Marinel. 1988. Sociolinguistic developments as a diffusion process. In: Ulrich Ammon, Norbert Dittmar, and Klaus J. Mattheier (eds.), *Sociolinguistics: an International Handbook of the Science of Language and Society*, 1574–1591. Berlin/New York: Mouton de Gruyter.

Granovetter, Mark S. 1973. The strength of weak ties. *American Journal of Sociology* 78: 1360–1380.
Gregory, Derek. 1985. Suspended animation: the stasis of diffusion theory. In: Derek Gregory and John Urry (eds.), *Social Relations and Spatial Structures*, 296–336. London: Macmillan.
Gregory, Derek. 2000. Diffusion. In: Ron Johnston, Derek Gregory, Geraldine Pratt, and Michael Watts (eds.), *The Dictionary of Human Geography*, 175–178. 4th edn. Oxford: Blackwell.
Hägerstrand, Torsten. 1952. *The Propagation of Innovation Waves*. Lund: Gleerup.
Hägerstrand, Torsten. 1966. Aspects of the spatial structure of social communication and the diffusion of information. *Papers and Proceedings of the Regional Science Association* 16: 27–42.
Hernández-Campoy, Juan Manuel. 2003. Exposure to contact and the geographical adoption of standard features: two complementary approaches. *Language in Society* 32: 227–255.
Horvath, Barbara and Ron Horvath. 1997. The geolinguistics of a sound change in progress: /l/ vocalisation in Australia. In: Charles Boberg, Miriam Meyerhoff and Stephanie Strassel (eds.), *A selection of papers from NWAVE 25. Special issue of University of Pennsylvania working papers in linguistics*, 4: 109–124. Philadelphia: University of Philadelphia Press.
Horvath, Barbara and Ron Horvath. 2001. A multilocality study of a sound change in progress: the case of /l/ vocalisation in New Zealand and Australian English. *Language Variation and Change* 13: 37–58.
Horvath, Barbara and Ron Horvath. 2002. The geolinguistics of /l/ vocalisation in Australia and New Zealand. *Journal of Sociolinguistics* 6: 319–346.
Kerswill, Paul. 2002. Koineization and accommodation. In: Jack K. Chambers, Peter Trudgill, and Natalie Schilling-Estes (eds.), *The Handbook of Language Variation and Change*, 669–702. Oxford: Blackwell.
Kerswill, Paul. 2003. Dialect levelling and geographical diffusion in British English. In: David Britain and Jenny Cheshire (eds.), *Social Dialectology: In Honour of Peter Trudgill*, 223–244. Amsterdam/Philadelphia: John Benjamins.
Labov, William. 2001. *Principles of Linguistic Change: Social Factors*. Oxford: Blackwell.
Labov, William. 2003. Pursuing the cascade model. In: David Britain and Jenny Cheshire (eds.), *Social Dialectology: In Honour of Peter Trudgill*, 9–22. Amsterdam/Philadelphia: John Benjamins.
Labov, William. 2007. Transmission and diffusion. *Language* 83: 344–387.
Lameli, Alfred, Roland Kehrein, and Stefan Rabanus (eds.). 2010. *Language and Space. An International Handbook of Linguistic Variation*. Vol. 2: *Language Mapping*. Berlin/New York: Mouton de Gruyter.
Lippi-Green, Rosina. 1989. Social network integration and language change in progress in a rural alpine village. *Language in Society* 18: 213–234.
Mees, Inger and Beverley Collins. 1999. Cardiff: a real-time study of glottalisation. In: Paul Foulkes and Gerry Docherty (eds.), *Urban Voices*, 185–202. London: Arnold.
Milroy, James. 1992. *Linguistic Variation and Change*. Oxford: Blackwell.
Milroy, James and Lesley Milroy. 1985. Linguistic change, social network and speaker innovation. *Journal of Linguistics* 21: 339–384.
Milroy, Lesley. 1980. *Language and Social Networks*. Oxford: Blackwell.
Nevalainen, Terttu. 2000. Processes of supralocalisation and the rise of Standard English in the early Modern period. In: Ricardo Bermudez-Otero, David Denison, Richard Hogg, and

Chris McCully (eds.), *Generative theory and corpus studies: a dialogue from 10 ICEHL*, 329–371. Berlin/New York: Mouton de Gruyter.

Nevalainen, Terttu and Helena Raumolin-Brunberg. 2003. *Historical Sociolinguistics*. London: Longman.

Pred, Allan R. 1985. The social becomes the spatial, the spatial becomes the social: enclosures, social change and the becoming of places in the Swedish province of Skåne. In: Derek Gregory and John Urry (eds.), *Social Relations and Spatial Structures*, 337–365. London: Macmillan.

Raumolin-Brunberg, Helena. 2006. Leaders of linguistic change in early modern England. In: Roberta Facchinetti and Matti Rissanen (eds.), *Corpus-based Studies of Diachronic English*, 115–134. Bern: Peter Lang.

Trudgill, Peter. 1974. Linguistic change and diffusion: description and explanation in sociolinguistic dialect geography. *Language in Society* 3: 215–246.

Trudgill, Peter. 1983. *On Dialect*. Oxford: Blackwell.

Trudgill, Peter. 1986. *Dialects in Contact*. Oxford: Blackwell.

Watt, Dominic and Lesley Milroy. 1999. Patterns of variation and change in three Tyneside vowels: Is this dialect levelling? In: Paul Foulkes and Gerry Docherty (eds.), *Urban Voices*, 25–46. London: Arnold.

Weinreich, Uriel, William Labov, and Marvin Herzog. 1968. Empirical foundations for a theory of language change. In: Winfred Lehmann and Yakov Malkiel (eds.), *Directions for Historical Linguistics*, 97–195. Austin: University of Texas Press.

Wells, J. 1982. *Accents of English*. Cambridge: Cambridge University Press.

Raymond Hickey
Chapter 19: Supraregionalization

1   Introduction —— 365
2   The process of supraregionalization —— 367
3   Other scenarios for supraregionalization —— 374
4   Summary —— 381
5   References —— 382

Abstract: Supraregionalization is an historical process whereby varieties of a language lose specifically local features and become less regionally bound. The upper limits of supraregionalization depend on a number of external factors, such as the boundary of the state in which the set of varieties is spoken. Furthermore, if the state historically derives from a colony of another state, then there may be an (unconscious) wish within that state to maintain some linguistic distinctiveness *vis à vis* the varieties of the former colonizing country. As a type of language change supraregionalization is subject to the phases of actuation, propagation and termination. Actuation is probably triggered by a consciousness of the provinciality of one's own language and the presence of more mainstream varieties, be these extranational or not. In the case of Irish English we can see that in the course of the 19th century a number of features are filtered out so that reports on Irish English at the beginning of the 20th century make no allusion to them. This chapter is concerned with just what type of features are removed during the process of supraregionalization and by comparison with other varieties' attempts to offer reasons for the disappearance of certain features and the retention of others.

1 Introduction

The process to be discussed in this chapter is one which has occurred frequently in many regions and countries of the Anglophone world, but which has not received due attention from scholars. There are a number of reasons why this is the case, chief of which is the location of the process between new dialect

---

Raymond Hickey: Essen (Germany)

formation (Hickey 2003a) and vernacular varieties on the one hand and standardization (Milroy and Milroy 1999: 18–23) on the other. There has been a lack of recognition that these processes form two ends of a scale which involves other intermediary developments. The name for the process in question is "supraregionalization" and reasons for the choice of this term are given in the following.

Supraregionalization (Hickey 2013) is an historical process whereby varieties of a language lose specifically local features and become less regionally bound. The upper limits of supraregionalization depend on a number of external factors, such as the country in which the set of varieties is spoken. If this country was historically a colony of another, then there may be an (unconscious) wish within this country to maintain some linguistic distinctiveness *vis à vis* the varieties of the former colonizing country (Hickey 2007: 309–315). Such "extranational" forms of a language are significant in a country although they stem from outside its borders. In a way they act as a brake on supraregionalization because structural distance must be maintained from them. Common examples of extranational varieties of languages in Europe would be German for the Austrians, French for the Walloons and Dutch for the Flemings.

A region within a state may also show supraregionalization, often a region which has a geographical and cultural identity of which speakers are aware. The north of England (Wales 2006) is just such a case. There is clearly a northern type of accent in England and this arose through a set of local features being used across the subregions of the north and maintained by non-local speakers for identification purposes *vis à vis* the south of England.

Table 19.1: Supraregionalization in Northern England

Supraregional	(non-local) features	[a] in BATH lexical set
		[ʊ] in STRUT lexical set

Apart from features which are found across a region there may well be features which are confined to either a subregion within a larger one or which are associated with strong vernaculars across the entire region and hence not part of a supraregional variety. In the case of north England, the unshifted long vowel – /uː/ – in the MOUTH lexical set would be one such example. It is furthermore typical of supraregional varieties that they tolerate vernacular features in lexically confined instances, for example the unshifted vowel in *the town* [tuːn] as a local reference to the city of Newcastle with supraregional speakers who otherwise have /au/ in the MOUTH lexical set.

1.1 Suppression and selection

Supraregionalization is achieved by the twin processes of *suppression* and *selection*. These show a certain overlap with processes during standardization, as formulated in the well-known table by Einar Haugen.

Table 19.2: Criteria for standard languages (Haugen 2003 [1964]: 421)

	Form	Function
Society	Selection	Acceptance
Language	Codification	Elaboration

What is missing in supraregionalization is codification, because the supraregional variety does not generally have a codified written form used for official purposes.

It is obvious that suppression is the opposite of selection. Although one could say that with standardization there is passive suppression (by the avoidance of local features), during supraregionalization suppression is a much more active process and may consist of additional sub-processes such as the deliberate relegation of local features to vernacular modes to which supraregional speakers may switch by conscious decision (see example of /uː/ in MOUTH referred to above).

If countries in which supraregional varieties have arisen develop into independent states then such varieties can form the basis for a standard of the new state. After this has happened, codification usually takes place, e.g. in the United States in the 19th century. Whether this kind of codification occurs depends on external factors, such as the relationship with the former colonial power. Where this relationship has been fairly close codification may not take place to anything like the same degree as in the case of Canada.

In order to illustrate how supraregional varieties arise (Hickey 2003b) examples from Irish English will be offered below. Such instances can presumably be replicated across the Anglophone world, although differences in local conditions mean the manifestation of supraregionalization varies.

2 The process of supraregionalization

A consideration of the history of English in Ireland shows that there was not only influence from Irish during the long period of language shift from the 17th through to the 19th century (Hickey 2007: Chapter 4) but also a large degree of superimposition or adoption of more standard forms of English due to exposure to forms of British English. This superimposition has led to layering in Irish English where remnants of former distributions have become confined to certain registers and/or are indicative of strongly localised varieties. This is true of unshifted ME /eː/ in the MEAT lexical set or /ʊ/ in the STRUT lexical set (in local Dublin English).

Superimposition of more standard forms has led in its turn to the process of supraregionalization. Part of this process is, for instance, the ironing out of non-standard vowel features among earlier forms of Irish English, e.g. the replacement of /uː/ by /au/ in words like *down, crown, about*, etc. It is important to grasp that the appearance of /au/ in the MOUTH lexical set is not the result of internal change in Irish English. Rather it is due to the adoption of a pronunciation from British English, i.e. it is due to the superimposition of a pronunciation variant from outside the country.

Supraregionalization must be carefully distinguished from dialect leveling or the formation of compromise forms. For instance, in late medieval Irish English there is some evidence that a middle way was chosen among competing morphological forms from different dialect inputs of British origin: the quantifier *euch(e)* 'each' was seen by Samuels (1972: 108) as a hybrid between *ech(e)* and *uch(e)* both of which were probably represented in the initial input to Irish English.

2.1 Reduced variation in supraregional varieties

Because a supraregional variety is not locally bound it can never serve the identity function which the vernacular fulfils for members of social networks (L. Milroy 1976; J. Milroy 1991). For that reason supraregional varieties tend not to show the degree of phonological differentiation present in the vernaculars to which they are related. For instance, in local forms of Irish English, both urban and rural, there is a distinction between short vowels before historic /r/, i.e. the vowels in *term* and *turn* are distinguished: *term* [tɛɹm] versus *turn* [tʌɹn]. In the supraregional variety, however, a single vowel is found in both cases, namely schwa [ə].

Another feature, which shows that supraregional varieties are less differentiated than their related vernaculars, is so-called *t*-lenition (Hickey 1996). In supraregional Irish English *t*-lenition is nearly always realized by the apico-alveolar fricative [t̞]. But in local Dublin English, there is a range of realizations, from [t̞] through [ɹ, h, ʔ] to zero (Hickey 2009).

2.2 How supraregionalization is triggered

In Ireland, and presumably in other European countries, the main trigger for supraregionalization in the late modern period was the introduction of general schooling and the rise of a native middle class during the 19th century. The Catholic Emancipation Act of 1829 was passed after political agitation under the leadership of Daniel O'Connell (Connolly 1998: 75; 399–400). Shortly afterwards, in the 1830s, so-called "national schools", i.e. primary schools (Dowling 1971: 116–118), were introduced and schooling for Catholic children in Ireland became compulsory and universal. The experience of general education for the generation after this increased their acceptance in the higher classes of Irish society (Daly 1990). A native middle class came into existence with all that this meant in terms of linguistic prejudice towards vernacular varieties of English. It is thus no coincidence that the disappearance of certain features of Irish English is located in the mid to late 19th century (Hickey 2008). These features were largely replaced by the corresponding mainland British pronunciations. An instance is provided by unshifted Middle English /aː/ which was a prominent feature up to the 18th century. For instance, George Farquhar in his play *The Beaux' Stratagem* (1707) has many of the stereotypes of Irish pronunciation, including this one: *Fat sort of plaace* (= [plaːs]) *is dat saam* (= [saːm]) *Ireland?* 'What sort of place is that same Ireland?'. Somewhat later, Jonathan Swift used end-rhymes which indicate that for him words like *placed* and *last* rhymed. At the end of the century, Thomas Sheridan criticized the Irish use of /aː/ in *matron, patron*, etc. But by the mid 19th century there are no more references to this. Dion Boucicault (1820–1890), who does not shy away from showing phonetic peculiarities in his dramas, does not indicate unshifted ME /aː/ when writing some eighty years after Sheridan. This kind of development can be shown to have applied to a number of features. For instance, SERVE-lowering – the realization /saːrv/ rather than /sɜːrv/ – appears to have died out during the 19th century and by the beginning of the 20th century the feature had all but disappeared. The same is true of ASK-metathesis which is attested in many representations of vernacular Irish English in the 19th century.

2.3 How supraregionalization proceeds

Supraregionalization is a type of language change. It too is subject to the phases of actuation, propagation, and conclusion. Actuation is probably triggered by a consciousness of the provinciality of one's own language and the presence of more mainstream varieties, be these extranational or not.

For the propagation phase there are two competing views of how the process takes place. The elimination of local features may be lexically abrupt with the substitution of local feature X by supraregional feature Y in all words in which it occurs. This corresponds to the Neogrammarian view of change. But equally a scenario is conceivable in which a local feature is replaced by a supraregional feature, if not word by word, at least not across the entire lexicon at once. Lexical replacement of this kind would correspond to lexical diffusion as conceived of in studies like Wang (1969).

An example of this would be the following: in the south of Ireland remnants of the previously widespread diphthongization of former /oː/ before velar [ɫ] + /d/ are found with *old* [auɫd] and *bold* [bauɫd]. But historically, this pronunciation is recorded for many other words, like *cold, hold, sold*. The pronunciation would seem to have applied previously to all words which matched the phonetic environment. The replacement of [-aulC] by [oːlC] would appear to have proceeded by a process of lexical diffusion. The same would seem to have applied in the north of Ireland to Belfast (J. Milroy 1981: 28). Furthermore, the words with the /au/ pronunciation (with deleted final /-d/) have retreated into more colloquial forms of speech so that now there is a lexical split between *old* /aul/, /oːld/ and *bold* /baul/, /boːld/: the form /aul/ for *old* implies a degree of affection and /baul/ for *bold* a sneaking admiration as in *Nothing beats the* /aul/ *pint; The* /baul/ *Charlie is some crook* (the adjectives in these senses only occur attributively).

The conclusion of supraregionalization is somewhat difficult to pinpoint. In the case of Ireland it cannot be the complete adoption of English pronunciation norms. Indeed, differential linguistic features *vis à vis* extranational varieties of English are maintained, not just in Ireland, consider Scotland and its supraregional variety Scottish Standard English (Abercrombie 1979; Stuart-Smith 2008; McColl Millar, Chapter 12) which, for instance, shows a clear non-prevocalic /-r/ in strong contrast to southern British English.

Speakers would seem to be unconsciously aware of supraregional varieties, that is there is unconscious consensus about what features are characteristic of them. An essential part of being a native speaker lies in knowing which features are part of the supraregional variety and which are not. For instance, native speakers of Irish English are aware that *t*-lenition, as in *city* [ˈsɪt̞ɪ], is permissible in the supraregional variety but that the extension of lenition to a glottal stop, as in *city* [ˈsɪʔɪ], is not. A case from grammar would be the *after*-perfective, as in *He's after breaking the glass*, which is acceptable in the supraregional variety, whereas the *do(es) be* habitual, as in *He does be mending cars in his spare time*, is not.

The features of a supraregional variety are not immutable but at any given time speakers know what belongs to it: features may be added, such as the raised back vowels or retroflex /r/ of recent Dublin English (see Section 3.5). Equally, speakers know what does not belong to the supraregional variety (of Irish English): *h*-dropping, or syllable-final deletion of /r/, for instance.

2.4 The paths taken by supraregionalization

Apart from the question of actuation, propagation, and conclusion, the paths which supraregionalization can take are of linguistic interest. In the Irish English context the following paths are attested.

2.4.1 Entire replacement of vernacular features

A number of archaic pronunciations are to be found in early modern documents of Irish English. For instance, the word for *gold* still had a pronunciation with /uː/ (as did *Rome*) in late 18th century Ireland: *goold* /guːld/, a pronunciation criticized by the prescriptivist John Walker (1791). The word *onion* /ʌnjən/ had /ɪnjən/, an older pronunciation mentioned by P. W. Joyce at the beginning of the 20th century (Joyce 1979 [1910]: 99). This was recorded by the lexicographer Nathan Bailey in 1726 (*Universal Etymological English Dictionary*) but was not typical of mainstream pronunciations as Walker notes at the end of the 18th century.

Vowels before /r/ provide further instances where Irish English was out of step with developments in England. *R*-lowering did not occur in words like *door* /duːr/, *floor* /fluːr/, *source* /suːrs/, *course* /kuːrs/, *court* /kuːrt/ which, according to the Appendix to Thomas Sheridan's *Rhetorical Grammar* (1781: 137–155), were typical Irish pronunciations. This means that the southern mainland English lowering of back high vowels before /r/ had not occurred in Ireland by the late 18th century but was introduced in the following century by lexically replacing those pronunciations which conflicted with mainland British usage.

2.4.2 Restriction to a specific phonetic environment

When a local feature is being removed from a supraregional variety then there may be a phase in which the feature goes from being unconditional to conditional. This is clearly recognizable if the conditional realization is still attested. Consider the case of short E-raising in Irish English. This is recorded in many environments in historical documents but later texts show a restriction to pre-nasal environments (as found nowadays in south west and mid-west varieties). Another instance is the metathesis of a vowel and /r/. In the 19th century and earlier it is attested in stressed syllables but later only in unstressed ones.

Table 19.3: Restriction of vernacular features in the 20th century

Feature	Pre-20th century	20th century and later
1) /e/ to /i/ raising	unconditional *togither, yis, git*	only before nasals (south west) *pen* [pɪn], *ten* [tɪn]
2) metathesis	in stressed syllables *purty* [ˈpɜːɹti] 'pretty'	only in unstressed syllables *modern* [ˈmɒdrən]

One explanation for the survival of features as conditional variants is that these are less salient (Hickey 2000a; Kerswill and Williams 2002) than unconditional ones. If a feature like short e-raising is restricted to a pre-nasal position, a phonetically preferred environment for this raising, then it is automatic (for the variety which has this raising) and so less salient for speakers. Similarly, if metathesis is confined to unstressed syllables then it is less acoustically prominent and again less salient and hence less likely to be removed by supraregionalization.

2.4.3 Relegation to colloquial registers

Although the supraregional form of English is the native style of many speakers in Ireland, they may deliberately manipulate salient features and adopt a vernacular pronunciation, for example for the purpose of caricature or when style-shifting downwards (Labov 2001). Simple instances of this are the replacement of *you* by *youse*, the use of [lɛp] for *leap* [liːp] or the high vowel in *get* as in *Get* [gɪt] *out of here!*, all typical of colloquial registers of Irish English.

In the course of its development, Irish English has evolved a technique for attaining local flavoring. This consists of maintaining two forms of a single lexeme, one a standard British one, adopted during supraregionalization, and another an archaic or regional pronunciation which differs in connotation from the first (see also the discussion of *old* and *bold* in Section 2.3). The second usage is always found on a more colloquial level and plays an important role in establishing the profile of vernacular Irish English. The following are some typical examples to illustrate this phenomenon:
- *Eejit* [ˈiːdʒət] for *idiot* (Dolan 2004: 83–84) has adopted the sense of a bungling individual rather than an imbecile.

- *Cratur* [ˈkreːtəɹ] shows a survival of the older pronunciation and denotes an object of pity or commiseration. Indeed for the supraregional variety of the south, unraised /eː, eː/ automatically implies a vernacular register. Other words which, colloquially, still show the mid vowel are *Jesus, decent, tea* (represented orthographically as *Jaysus, daycent, tay*). In these cases the replacement of an older pronunciation by a more mainstream one has led to the retreat of the former into a marked style, here one of local Irishness.
- *Fellow* has final /ou, oː/ in the supraregional standard. But a reduction of the final vowel to /ə/ is historically attested in Irish English as in *yellow* [jɛlə]. There is now a lexical split with the first word such that the pronunciation [fɛlə] means something like 'young man, boyfriend' in colloquial Irish English.

2.5 Further issues in supraregionalization

Mergers: sociolinguistic research on vernacular forms of English in Belfast (see J. Milroy 1981) has shown that non-standard phonology is more complex than standard phonology and that mergers are more common in standard and koiné varieties. At first sight this might seem to hold for southern Irish English as well. For instance, there is no distinction between historically different short vowels before /r/. Hence one has a single rhotacized vowel [ɚ] in the supraregional variety but in vernacular forms /ɛ/ and /ʌ/ are kept distinct before /r/ as in *girl* [gɛrəl] and *burn* [bʌrən].

There is an apparent contradiction here because with dental stops in the THIN (and THIS) lexical sets, a shift to an alveolar articulation is found in many vernacular varieties. This leads to a merger with the alveolar stops in the TWO lexical set (cf. *thinker* and *tinker*, both [ˈtɪŋkəɹ]) which is stigmatized in Irish English. However, stigma or acceptance of mergers in vernacular varieties depends crucially on whether the merger is unconditional or not. With the single rhotacized vowel [ɚ] one is dealing with a merger in a specific phonological environment, namely before tautosyllabic /r/. With dental vs. alveolar stops on the other hand one finds that it is the unconditional merger, leading to noticeable homophony, which is stigmatized.

Hypercorrection: in the Ireland of the 18th and early 19th centuries, when many of the pronunciations discussed above were not confined to specific styles, hypercorrection was common. Both Sheridan (1781) and Walker (1791) remark on the fact that the Irish frequently say *greet* 'great', *beer* 'bear', *sweer* 'swear', unaware of the fact that these words had /eː/ rather than /iː/, although by the 18th century the majority of words in the MEAT lexical class already showed the /iː/

vowel. However, before tautosyllabic /-r/ and in a few lexicalised cases like *great, break, steak*, the shift to /iː/ had not taken and was not to take place. This fact was not recognized by speakers shifting from their native mid front vowel to the presumedly universal /iː/ in the MEAT lexical class, hence the instances of hypercorrection just quoted.

In his *Rhetorical Grammar*, Sheridan (1781) also has /ʌ/ in the words *pudding* and *cushion*. This could be explained, not only as hypercorrection *vis à vis* mainstream English, but also with regard to local Dublin English which now, and certainly then, had /ʊ/ in these and all words with early modern English /ʊ/. The situation in Belfast where [ʌ] in words like *pull, bush, would* can be found is separate from that in Dublin and derives from an overgeneralization of the lowering of early modern English [ʊ] to [ʌ]. Indeed, according to Sheridan, /ʌ/ was found in *foot, bull, bush, push, pull, pulpit*, all but the last of which have /ʊ/ in (southern) Irish English today.

Hypercorrection would appear to die away with supraregionalization. This stands to reason: if local features are replaced by more standard ones then later generations master the correct distribution of sounds immediately.

Unaffected features: supraregionalization does not appear to be something which speakers are aware of, e.g. no comments on how it was occurring in Irish English are recorded. There is no possibility of it being a planned process and so some features, which might have been affected, are not involved. An example of non-participation in the process is provided by the shortening of late modern English /uː/, seen in words like *took* and *look*, which now have short /ʊ/, despite the spelling which suggests a former /uː/. In supraregional Irish English, a long /uː/ before /k/ has been retained in some words where this was later shortened in British English, e.g. *cook* [kuːk] and sometimes *book* [buːk].

The shift from long to short vowel probably took place in England by lexical diffusion and in Ireland not as many words have been affected by this process. It is most likely that Irish English speakers did not proceed with the shift to the same extent as those in England because the long /uː/ was not stigmatized, i.e. a pronunciation like *cook* [kuːk] was, and is, not used in Ireland to assess a speaker socially.

3 Other scenarios for supraregionalization

The discussion so far has been of supraregional varieties which have arisen through the suppression of vernacular features leading to forms of a language in which there is less variation than in local speech. There is, however, not just one source of supraregional varieties. A supraregional variety can arise through the adoption of a geographically confined variety by sections of a population spread over a much larger area. In such cases the variety which triggers this process stems from a source which has prestige in the society in question. A clear example of this type of development can be seen in the Republic of Ireland over the past 15 years or so where changes in Dublin English have spread to the entire country.

3.1 Varieties of Dublin English

Before discussing details of change, a few basic groupings of speakers in Dublin must be made. The first group consists of those who use the inherited popular form of English in the capital. The term "local" is intended to capture this and to emphasize that these speakers are those who show strongest identification with traditional conservative Dublin life of which the popular accent is very much a part. The reverse of this is "non-local", a label which refers to sections of the metropolitan population who do not wish a narrow, restrictive identification with popular Dublin culture. This group then subdivides into a more general section, labeled "mainstream" and an increasing significant group which rejects a confining association with low-prestige Dublin. This group can be simply labeled "new".

Table 19.4: Divisions of Dublin English

1) *local* Dublin English	
2) *non-local* Dublin English	a) *mainstream* Dublin English
	b) *new* Dublin English

A central issue in contemporary Dublin English is the set of vowel shifts which represent the most recent phonological innovation in Irish English. This is not surprising as Dublin is a typical location for language change given the following facts:
a) the city has expanded greatly in population in the last three or four decades. The increase in population has been due both to internal growth and migration into the city from the rest of the country and from abroad.
b) it has undergone an economic boom in the last 15 years or so. The increase in wealth and international position has meant that many young people aspire to an urban sophistication which is divorced from strongly local Dublin life. For this reason the developments in new Dublin English diverge from those in local Dublin English, indeed can be interpreted as a reaction to it.

This type of linguistic behavior can be termed *local dissociation* as it is motivated by the desire of speakers to hive themselves off from vernacular forms of a variety spoken in their immediate surroundings (Hickey 2000b).

3.2 How dissociation works

Speakers of both mainstream and new Dublin English generally avoid local features. What distinguishes the latter from the former group, however, is that it has developed strategies for a maximization of the phonetic difference between realizations typical of their own variety and that of local Dublin English. This has been achieved by moving away – in phonological space – from the realizations found locally. The following list gives some indication of what is involved here:
a) local Dublin English has a distinction between historic back and front short vowels before /r/, in the NURSE and GIRL lexical sets, [nʊː(ɹ)s] and [gɛː(ɹ)l] respectively. But because the open front realization is so typical of local Dublin English, there has been a migration in new Dublin English of historically front long vowels to the central rhotic type as seen in words from the SQUARE lexical set like *carefully* [kɜːɹfəli] and *daring* [dɜːɹɪŋ]. This realization has no precedent in the history of southern Irish English.
b) connected with the previous feature is the strict avoidance of schwa retraction before /r/ in NURSE words such as *third* [t̪ɜːɹd], *purse* [pɜːɹs], not [tʊː(ɹ)d] and [pʊː(ɹ)s].
c) the local back rounded vowel /u/ in the STRUT lexical set is replaced by an unrounded front vowel which is almost /i/, as in *Sunday* [sɨnde].
d) a syllable-final retroflex /r/, [ɻ], is used which has the advantage of marking the /r/ even more clearly *vis à vis* the popular forms of Dublin English which, if at all, have only a weak syllable-final /r/.

Apart from the above features there has also been a shift of vowels (Hickey 2005: 45–91), the most important part of which is the raising of low back vowels and the retraction of diphthongs. The raised realization of vowels in, say, the THOUGHT lexical set – [tɒːʔ] in local Dublin English and [t̪ɔːt̪] in new Dublin English – illustrates this particularly well as do other instances of vowel raising such as that in the CHOICE lexical set, e.g *toy* [tɒɪ] in local Dublin English and [tɔɪ], [toɪ] in new Dublin English.

3.3 Local Dublin English features in the new supraregional variety

Although the motivation for the shifts in Dublin English has been dissociation from local speech, there are a number of common features found in both local and new varieties. These have all become part of the supraregional variety of Irish English which has arisen in recent years due to the spread of new Dublin English.

MOUTH-*fronting:* in Dublin English the vowel in the MOUTH lexical set has a front starting point. A realization as [au] is more conservative in Dublin and in rural areas it has been traditionally typical of the south west and west of Ireland. The fronted onset of the /au/ diphthong has not been the subject of sociolinguistic censure in Dublin and so has migrated into the new pronunciation where it is regular for words of the MOUTH lexical set.

SOFT-*lengthening:* here one is again dealing with a traditional feature of Dublin English. Recall that the vowels of the CLOTH and BATH lexical sets, i.e. low and low back vowels before voiceless fricatives, showed lengthening which started in the early modern period. In England the lengthening was retained in the BATH set (Wells 1982: 203–206) but reversed in the CLOTH set. Earlier Dublin English adopted and kept the lengthening in both these cases so that today words like SOFT show a long vowel, i.e. *soft* = [sɒːft]. The long vowel in the SOFT group did not spread to the entire country previously but is doing so now due to the adoption of new Dublin English by speakers outside the capital.

L-*velarization:* traditionally, Irish English has an alveolar [l] in all syllable positions. A velarized [ɫ] is really only a feature of contact Irish English, i.e. of the English of native speakers of Irish, and of local Dublin English. However, new Dublin English show a definite velarization of /l/ in this position: [fiːəɫd]. This velarized [ɫ] has become all but universal in young people's speech in Ireland.

3.4 Loss of distinctions in the new pronunciation

When comparing new Dublin English with conservative mainstream Irish English it is remarkable that a merger has occurred, the lack of which has hitherto been a prominent feature of Irish English. This is the *for/four*-merger where the formerly distinct vowels /ɒː/ and /oː/ have collapsed before /-r/ due to the raising of the former to [ɔː] and then to [oː], its realization in new Dublin English today.

Another merger which is found in new Dublin English is that of /hw-/ [ʍ] and /w-/ [w] as in *which* and *witch* respectively. Irish English has traditionally maintained the distinction between these sounds, as have other conservative varieties of English, such as Scottish English (in various forms). This merger is found in many other varieties of English, indeed would seem to be characteristic of standard varieties of English world-wide (Chambers 2002: 370).

This loss of phonetic distinctiveness in new Dublin English and by extension in the emerging supraregional variety is not of any sociolinguistic consequence, given that supraregional speakers generally belong to weak-tie social networks which do not place any store on strongly vernacular norms (L. Milroy 1976). This means that phonetic distinctions which could be instrumental in the maintenance of such norms are not necessary for such speakers. For further instances of a loss of distinctions, see Section 2.1 above.

3.5 The spread of the shift

Because of the status of Dublin, non-vernacular speech of the capital acts as a guideline for the rest of the country when others, outside of Dublin, are seeking a non-local, generally acceptable form of Irish English. This has meant, for instance, that the retroflex [ɻ], used by fashionable speakers in Dublin, is spreading out of the capital, especially with younger urbanites from different parts of the country.

The spread of features of new Dublin English has accelerated considerably in the past few years. Whereas for studies by the present author in the early and mid 1990s a pattern of lexical diffusion of new pronunciations – that is, for certain key words – was much more common (Hickey 1998), in the early 2000s this sporadic distribution became recessive and a general adoption of fashionable Dublin English features could be observed.

Given that supraregionalization is a type of language change, it is not surprising that young female speakers have most readily adopted the new Dublin pronunciation outside the capital. For instance, the use of a retroflex /-r/ is most common among young female speakers as the recordings for Hickey (2004) show conclusively. In fact for all female speakers under 25 this pronunciation has become the norm, irrespective of what part of the country they come from. The same is true for the raised vowels in the THOUGHT and CHOICE lexical sets as well as for velarized, syllable-final [ɫ].

It should be mentioned that not all features of a donor variety, such as new Dublin English, are adopted into an emerging supraregional variety. Where there is internal variation in the source variety, a feature involved in this variation may not be sufficiently salient to be perceived by outsiders as part of the new variety. For instance, the rounding of the SQUARE vowel (see Section 3.2 above) or the retraction of /ai/ to [ɑi] are not found with all speakers of the new pronunciation and have not established themselves in the new supraregional variety.

3.6 Spread of features in present-day Britain

The spread of features from a leading urban variety can be seen elsewhere, e.g. in contemporary Britain. Here the vernacular varieties which stem from London and the Home Counties show glottalization of /t/, typically in intervocalic and word-final position, e.g. *water* [ˈwɒːʔə] and *cut* [kʌʔ]. This has been picked up by supraregional speakers in northern Britain (Milroy et al. 1994) where the glottal stop has been incorporated into "supra-local norms". Even though it is true that there is an independent origin for glottalization in the north of Britain (Beal 2007: 39–40) the perception of it for present-day speakers as a feature of southern Britain remains. These remarks also apply to other features which have generally been assumed to have a southern origin in Britain, e.g. TH-fronting as in [fɪŋk] for *think* (Beal 2007: 37–38).

3.7 Supraregionalization and heteronymy

The notion of heteronymy has been employed by linguists (Chambers and Trudgill 1999: 10–14) to refer to the fact that similar dialects in a geographical area can often be related to different standard languages, especially when a national border runs through the area in question. A well-known example for this is the German-Dutch border. Rather than just specifying the relationship of a dialect to a standard, one can express the relationship as one between a dialect and a supraregional variety. This captures the insight that speakers can shift away from their dialect by the adoption of less regionally bound features without necessarily switching to the codified standard of a country. Supraregionalization would then exercise a pull in two opposite directions depending on what the heteronymic relation is in the dialects of an area as show in the following map.

In the context of the current chapter, one can consider examples of heteronymic pull in varieties of Irish English. A good example for this can be found in south east Ulster, an area which straddles the divide between Northern Ireland and the Republic of Ireland and which consists of counties Monaghan (Republic of Ireland), Armagh and south Down (the latter two in Northern Ireland). For speakers north of the border, the supraregional variety they gravitate towards is Northern Irish English whereas for those south of the border their guideline supraregional variety is that of the south of Ireland.

Local varieties of English in south east Ulster share certain features, for instance an off-glide after the vowel in the FACE lexical set and the use of a dental stop and front [æː] in the BATH lexical set. Speakers of the supraregional variety north of the border retain the offglide in their speech because this is part of

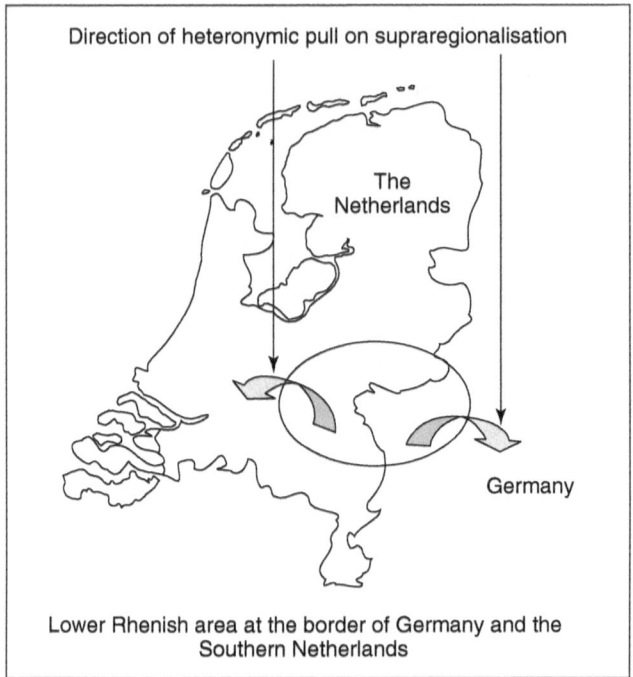

Map 19.1: Direction of heteronymy on the German-Dutch border

northern supraregional speech. Those south of the border drop the offglide as supraregional Irish English does not have this. In the BATH lexical set, supraregional speakers south of the border retain the [bæːt̪] pronunciation whereas those north of the border use a more central vowel followed by an (inter)dental fricative.

Table 19.5: South east Ulster local and supraregional pronunciations

South east Ulster local pronunciations		
FACE lexical set:	[feːəs]	
BATH lexical set:	[bæːt̪]	
Southern supraregional variety		
FACE lexical set:	[feːs]	(without off-glide)
BATH lexical set:	[bæːt̪]	(front vowel + dental stop)
Northern supraregional variety		
FACE lexical set:	[feːəs]	(with off-glide)
BATH lexical set:	[baːθ]	(mid vowel + dental fricative)

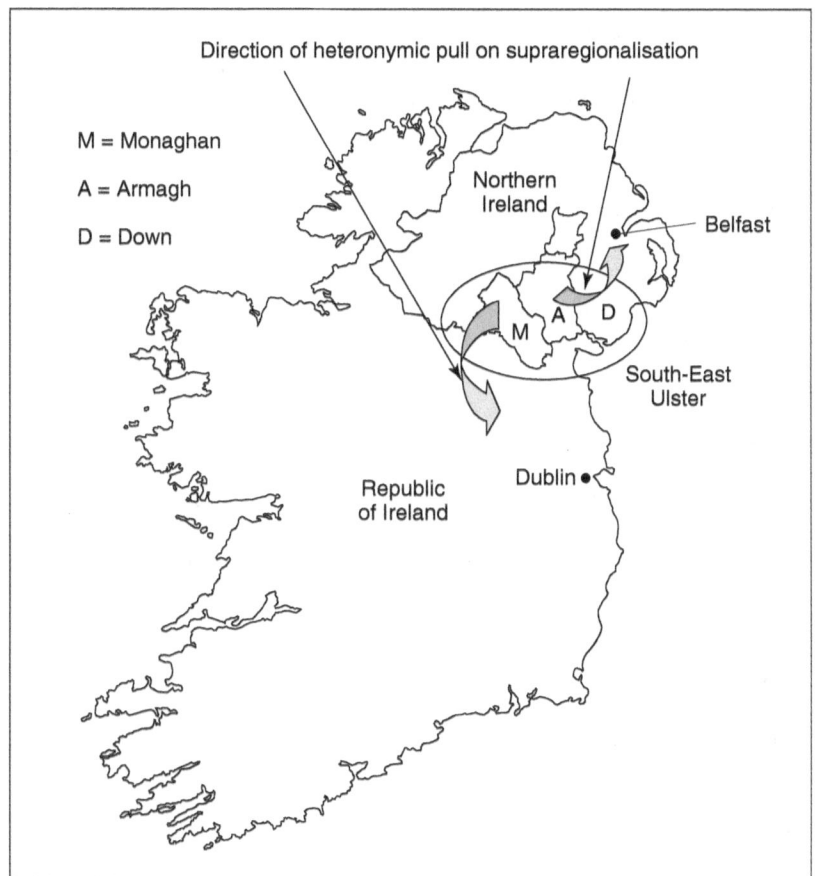

Map 19.2: Direction of heteronymy on the North-South Irish border

4 Summary

The consideration of supraregionalization in this chapter has shown that it refers to both a historical process of the late modern period and a state which has been attained in countries like Ireland or Scotland and in regions of Britain such as northern England. The rise of these varieties is triggered by such factors as general education and the appearance of a middle class. The latter group then avoids features indicative of vernacular varieties by a process of suppression and selection. This generally leads to reduced variation in supraregional varieties, something which also shows that they are essentially different from vernacular varieties which maintain phonological complexity as a linguistic correlate of intricate social networks. At the opposite end of the social scale one finds a standard of a language with which a supraregional variety is not identical. The codification and the functional elaboration is missing with supraregional varieties. Frequently a country has a supraregional variety in phonological terms but avails of the standard in writing and largely in morphosyntax.

Supraregional varieties are not static and can alter under appropriate social circumstances. The recent changes in Dublin English show this: the features of a leading urban variety have in this case spread out from the capital to the rest of the country and have shaped a new supraregional variety which is fast replacing the established one.

5 References

Abercrombie, David. 1979. The accents of Standard English in Scotland. In: Adam J. Aitken and Tom McArthur (eds.), 68–84.

Aitken, Adam J. and Tom McArthur (eds.). 1979. *Languages of Scotland*. Edinburgh: Chambers.

Beal, Joan. 2007. 'To explain the present': nineteenth-century evidence for 'recent' changes in English pronunciation. In: Javier Pérez-Guerra, Dolores González-Álvarez, Jorge L. Bueno-Alonso, and Esperanza Rama-Martínez (eds.), 25–46.

Bolton, Kingsley and Helen Kwok (eds.). 1991. *Sociolinguistics Today. International Perspectives*. London: Routledge.

Chambers, Jack K. 2002. Patterns of variation including change. In: J. K. Chambers, Peter Trudgill, and Natalie Schilling-Estes (eds.), *The Handbook of Language Variation and Change*, 349–372. Malden, MA: Blackwell Publishing.

Chambers, Jack K. and Peter Trudgill. 1999. *Dialectology*. 2nd edn. Cambridge: Cambridge University Press.

Connolly, Sean J. 1998. *The Oxford Companion to Irish History*. Oxford: Oxford University Press.

Daly, Mary. 1990. Literacy and language change in the late nineteenth and early twentieth centuries. In: Mary Daly and David Dickson (eds.), 153–166.

Daly, Mary and David Dickson (eds.). 1990. *The Origins of Popular Literacy in Ireland: Language Change and Educational Development 1700–1920*. Dublin: Anna Livia.

Dolan, Terence P. 2004 [1998]. *A Dictionary of Hiberno-English. The Irish Use of English*. 2nd edn. Dublin: Gill and Macmillan.

Dossena, Marina and Charles Jones (eds.). 2003. *Insights into Late Modern English*. Frankfurt: Peter Lang.

Dowling, Patrick J. 1971. *A History of Irish Education*. Cork: Mercier.

Eckert, Penelope and John R. Rickford (eds.). 2001. *Style and Sociolinguistic Variation*. Cambridge: Cambridge University Press.

Fisiak, Jacek and Marcin Krygier (eds.). 1998. *English Historical Linguistics 1996*. Berlin/New York: Mouton de Gruyter.

Haugen, Einar. 2003 [1964]. Dialect, language, nation. In: Christina Bratt Paulston and G. Richard Tucker (eds.), 411–422.

Henry, Alison, Martin Ball, and Margaret MacAliskey (eds.). 1996. *Papers from the International Conference on Language in Ireland*. Belfast: University of Ulster.

Hickey, Raymond. 1996. Lenition in Irish English. In: Alison Henry, Martin Ball, and Margaret Mac-Aliskey (eds.), 173–193.
Hickey, Raymond. 1998. The Dublin Vowel Shift and the historical perspective. In: Jacek Fisiak and Marcin Krygier (eds.), 79–106.
Hickey, Raymond. 2000a. Salience, stigma and standard. In: Laura Wright (ed.), 57–72.
Hickey, Raymond. 2000b. Dissociation as a form of language change. *European Journal of English Studies* 4(3): 303–315.
Hickey, Raymond. 2003a. How do dialects get the features they have? On the process of new dialect formation. In: Hickey, Raymond (ed.), *Motives for Language Change*, 213–239. Cambridge: Cambridge University Press.
Hickey, Raymond. 2003b. How and why supraregional varieties arise. In: Marina Dossena and Charles Jones (eds.), 351–373.
Hickey, Raymond. 2004. *A Sound Atlas of Irish English*. Berlin/New York: Mouton de Gruyter.
Hickey, Raymond. 2005. *Dublin English. Evolution and Change*. Amsterdam/Philadelphia: John Benjamins.
Hickey, Raymond. 2007. *Irish English. History and Present-day Forms*. Cambridge: Cambridge University Press.
Hickey, Raymond. 2008. Feature loss in 19th century Irish English. In: Terttu Nevalainen, Irma Taavitsainen, Päivi Pahta, and Minna Korhonen (eds.), *The Dynamics of Linguistic Variation: Corpus Evidence on English Past and Present*, 229–243. Amsterdam/Philadelphia: John Benjamins.
Hickey, Raymond. 2009. Weak segments in Irish English. In: Donka Minkova (ed.), *Phonological Weakness in English. From Old to Present-day English*, 116–129. Basingstoke: Palgrave Macmillan.
Hickey, Raymond. 2013. Supraregionalisation and dissociation. In: J. K. Chambers and Natalie Schilling-Estes (eds.), *Handbook of Language Variation and Change*, 537–554. 2nd edn. Malden, MA: Wiley-Blackwell.
Jones, Mari and Edith Esch (eds.). 2002. *Language Change: The Interplay of Internal, External and Extra-Linguistic Factors*. Berlin/New York: Mouton de Gruyter.
Joyce, Patrick Weston 1979 [1910]. *English as we Speak it in Ireland*. Dublin: Wolfhound Press.
Kerswill, Paul and Ann Williams. 2002. 'Salience' as an explanatory factor in language change: evidence from dialect levelling in urban England. In: Mari Jones and Edith Esch (eds.), 81–110.
Kortmann, Bernd and Clive Upton (eds.). 2008. *Varieties of English*. Vol. 1: *The British Isles*. Berlin/New York: Mouton de Gruyter.
Labov, William. 2001. The anatomy of style-shifting. In: Penelope Eckert and John R Rickford (eds.), 85–108.
Milroy, James. 1981. *Regional Accents of English: Belfast*. Belfast: Blackstaff.
Milroy, James. 1991. Social network and prestige arguments in sociolinguistics. In: Kingsley Bolton and Helen Kwok (eds.), 146–162.
Milroy, Lesley. 1976. Phonological correlates to community structure in Belfast. *Belfast Working Papers in Language and Linguistics* 1: 1–44.
Milroy, James, Lesley Milroy, and Sue Hartley. 1994. Local and supra-local change in British English: the case of glottalisation. *English World-Wide* 15: 1–33.
Milroy, James and Lesley Milroy. 1999. *Authority in Language*. 3rd edn. London: Routledge.
Paulston, Christina Bratt and G. Richard Tucker (ed.). 2003. *Sociolinguistics: The Essential Readings*. Oxford: Blackwell.

Pérez-Guerra, Javier, Dolores González-Álvarez, Jorge L. Bueno-Alonso, and Esperanza Rama-Martínez (eds.). 2007. *Of Varying Language and Opposing Creed*. Frankfurt: Peter Lang.
Samuels, Michael. 1972. *Linguistic Evolution*. Cambridge: Cambridge University Press.
Sheridan, Thomas. 1781. *A Rhetorical Grammar of the English Language Calculated Solely for the Purpose of Teaching Propriety of Pronunciation and Justness of Delivery, in that Tongue*. Dublin: Price.
Stuart-Smith, Jane. 2008. Scottish English: phonology. In: Bernd Kortmann and Clive Upton (eds.), 48–70.
Wales, Katie. 2006. *Northern English. A social and cultural history*. Cambridge: Cambridge University Press.
Walker, John. 1791. *A Critical Pronouncing Dictionary of the English Language*. Reprint. Menston: The Scolar Press.
Wang, William. 1969. Competing changes as a cause of residue. *Language* 45: 9–25.
Wells, John. 1982. *Accents of English*. Cambridge/New York: Cambridge University Press.
Wright, Laura (ed.). 2000. *The Development of Standard English 1300–1800. Theories, Descriptions, Conflicts*. Cambridge: Cambridge University Press.

Suzanne Romaine
Chapter 20:
Pidgins and creoles

1   Introduction —— 385
2   Defining pidgins and creoles —— 387
3   Classifying pidgins and creoles —— 389
4   Theories of origin and structural features of pidgins and creoles —— 391
5   Sociolinguistic dimensions of pidgins and creoles —— 396
6   References —— 401

Abstract: Pidgins and creoles are the outcome of diverse processes and influences in circumstances where speakers of different languages have to work out a common means of communication. Although no one knows how many pidgins and creoles there are, millions of people around the world speak these languages every day. As some of the newest languages on earth, pidgins and creoles present many fascinating challenges to linguists because they raise fundamental questions about the evolution of complex systems and historical change. There is still no consensus on the relationship between pidgins and creoles, or on the extent to which creoles form a structurally well-defined language type, or whether they can be defined only with respect to the special socio-historical circumstances that give rise to them. The focus of this chapter is the so-called English-based (or English-lexicon) pidgins and creoles, whose lexicons are predominantly derived from English.

1 Introduction

Pidgins and creoles are the outcome of diverse processes and influences in circumstances where speakers of different languages have to work out a common means of communication. Although no one knows how many pidgins and creoles there are, millions of people around the world speak these languages every day. For a long time many linguists ignored pidgins and creoles in the belief that they were not "real" languages. Puristic attitudes worked against the study of language contact and contact languages because linguists were interested in "pure"

Suzanne Romaine: Oxford (UK)

languages rather than ones that were mixed, and therefore difficult to classify in genetic terms. There are still many problems in drawing firm boundaries between pidgins and creoles as well as between them and different kinds of contact varieties such as the so-called New Englishes widely spoken in places such as India, Singapore, and elsewhere, or mixed languages such as Media Lengua, a mix of Quechua and Spanish spoken in Ecuador.

As some of the newest languages on earth, pidgins and creoles present many fascinating challenges to linguists because they raise fundamental questions about the evolution of complex systems and historical change. Many pidgins and creoles emerged around trade routes in the Atlantic or Pacific during the 17th to 19th centuries, and subsequently on plantations, where a multilingual labor force comprising slaves or indentured immigrant laborers needed a common language. Tok Pisin ('talk pidgin'), for instance, spoken by more than four million people in Papua New Guinea, owes its origins to a pidgin that developed during the 19th century on sugar plantations in Queensland, Australia. Workers recruited from various parts of the Pacific speaking mutually unintelligible languages found themselves living and working together and needing a means of communicating with one another as well as with their English-speaking plantation managers.

When the Pacific Labor Trade came to an end in 1905, most of the workers went back to their home countries, taking with them knowledge of this Queensland Plantation Pidgin. In highly multilingual countries such as Papua New Guinea with more than 800 languages, this pidgin served useful internal functions in communicating across ethno-linguistic boundaries. Social conditions were thus ripe not just for the retention and spread of pidgin but also for its stabilization and subsequent nativization. Today Tok Pisin is used across the whole social spectrum, by villagers and government ministers alike. It is the most frequently used language in the House of Assembly, the country's main legislative body and the constitution recognizes Tok Pisin as one of the national languages.

In other parts of the world, however, pidgins were short-lived because local conditions did not sustain their further development for various reasons. Chinese Pidgin English, for example, was a crucial element in 19th century trade based at the port of Canton (today Guangzhou) between European merchants and Chinese selling commodities such as silk and tea. Due to its limited domains of use, Chinese Pidgin English was a more rudimentary pidgin than Tok Pisin. It fell out of use in the 20th century as more and more Chinese learned English. However, the language left its legacy in the form of the word *pidgin*, derived from English *business* rendered through Cantonese pronunciation. The term *pidgin* occurred as early as 1807, where it appeared in the diary of missionary Robert Morrison (Baker and Mühlhäusler 1990: 93). By contrast, the term *creole* was used in reference to a non-indigenous person born in the American colonies, and later used to refer to customs, flora and fauna of these colonies. The history of these terms reflects the typical circumstances of origin and contexts of use for many pidgins and creoles. Although European colonial encounters during the 17th to 19th centuries produced the most well known and studied languages, there are numerous examples of indigenous pidgins and creoles predating European contact such as Mobilian Jargon, a now extinct pidgin based on Muskogean, and widely used along the lower Mississippi River valley for communication among native Americans speaking Choctaw, Chickasaw and other languages. There were probably many more such languages that have disappeared, and/or have not been documented.

2 Defining pidgins and creoles

Although the study of pidgin and creoles (sometimes called creolistics) has become an established area of linguistic research since the latter part of the 20th century, linguists are still not agreed about how to define pidgins and creoles or where they come from. Likewise, there is no consensus on the relationship between pidgins and creoles, or on the extent to which creoles form a structurally well-defined language type, or whether they can be defined only with respect to the special socio-historical circumstances that give rise to them (Mufwene 1986; McWhorter 2005; Ansaldo et al. 2007). Nevertheless, after years of treating pidgins and creoles as parasitic (and often debased) versions of other languages, most scholars now agree that there is such a group of languages with recognizable structures of their own independent of the languages involved in the original contact. This chapter will rely on the following working definitions for the moment, but will point out later some of the reasons why they pose problems.

A pidgin is a contact variety restricted in form and function and native to no one, which is formed by members of at least two (and usually more) groups of different linguistic backgrounds. Pidgins are simplified languages characterized by a minimal lexicon, little or no morphology, and limited syntax. Although not all linguists agree that creoles need to have a prior pidgin stage, the term "creole" is generally applied to pidgins which have expanded in form and function to meet the communicative needs of a community of native speakers.

The conventional view of pidgins and creoles and their relationship to one another found in a variety of introductory texts (e.g. Romaine 1988) therefore assumes a two stage development. The first involves rapid and drastic restructuring resulting in a reduced and simplified language variety. The second consists of elaboration as the functions of this variety expand and it becomes nativized or serves as the primary language of most of its speakers. The reduction in form characteristic of a pidgin follows from its restricted communicative functions. Pidgin speakers, who have another language, can get by with a minimum of grammatical apparatus, but the linguistic resources of a creole must be sufficient to fulfill the communicative needs of its users.

The degree of structural stability varies, depending on the extent of internal development and functional expansion the pidgin has undergone at any particular stage in its life cycle. Creolization can occur at any stage in the development continuum from rudimentary jargon to expanded pidgin. The term "jargon" refers to a speech variety with a minimal linguistic system and great individual variation used for communicating in limited situations between speakers of different languages, e.g. trade, while a pidgin has a certain degree of stability. If creolization occurs at the jargon stage, the amount of expansion will be more substantial than that required to make an expanded pidgin structurally adequate. In some cases, however, pidgins may expand without nativization. Where this happens, pidgins and creoles may overlap in terms of structural complexity, and there will be few, if any, linguistic differences between an expanded pidgin and a creole that develops from it. Varieties of Melanesian Pidgin English (a cover term for three English-lexicon pidgins/creoles in the southwest Pacific comprising Tok Pisin, Solomon Islands Pijin, and Vanuatu Bislama) are far richer lexically and more complex grammatically than many early creoles elsewhere. Their linguistic elaboration was carried out primarily by adult second language speakers who used them as lingua francas in urban areas. A similar scenario has taken place in parts of West Africa in languages such as Cameroon Pidgin English (also called Kamtok), which has been a lingua franca in Cameroon since the 1880s, and Krio spoken in Sierra Leone by about 90% of the population as a second language, as well as by a small group in and near the capital Freetown who use it as their mother tongue.

Creolization is thus not a unique trigger for complexity, and the "same" language may exist as both pidgin and creole. Debate continues about the role of children vs. adults in nativization and creolization. Once creolization has occurred, however, the evolutive changes that take place thereafter may make it impossible to identify a prior creole or pidgin stage, as in the case of African American English in the United States, which some linguists believe to be a creole in the late stages of decreolization (cf. Lanehart, Chapter 5). The term "decreolization" is used to refer to changes that bring a creole closer to its superstrate language, i.e. the language contributing most of its vocabulary.

3 Classifying pidgins and creoles

Although there are numerous ways in which pidgins and creoles could be classified genetically, typologically, geographically, and sociolinguistically, the standard view of them as mixed languages with the vocabulary of the superstrate (also called the lexifier or base language) and the grammar of the substrate (the native language(s) of the groups in contact) has provided the conventional primary basis for classifying them according to their lexical affiliation. Thus, in the case of Tok Pisin, English is the superstrate and the indigenous languages of Papua New Guinea are the substrate. It is customary practice to label pidgins and creoles with a three-term formula including their location and their principal lexifier language, e.g. Chinese Pidgin English, Berbice Creole Dutch, Haitian Creole French, etc. These groupings based on lexical affiliation, are, however, distinctly different from the genetically-based language families established by applying the comparative historical method. Pidgins or creoles as a group are not genetically related among themselves, although those with the same lexifier usually are.

The focus of this chapter will be the so-called English-based (or English-lexicon) pidgins and creoles, whose lexicons are predominantly derived from English. This group includes, for instance, in addition to languages already mentioned such as Tok Pisin, Kamtok, Krio, and Chinese Pidgin English, numerous others such as Jamaican Creole English, spoken by millions in Jamaica. It will already be evident that linguists' names for pidgins and creoles are not always widely used by the speakers of the languages themselves, who often have no special name for their languages other than "pidgin" or "creole". This can cause confusion at times. Tok Pisin has sometimes been referred to by linguists as Neomelanesian or New Guinea Pidgin English, while its speakers call it Tok Pisin, or simply pidgin. Speakers of Torres Strait Creole English call their language "Broken" (i.e. broken English), while speakers of Australian Creole English call their language "Kriol", speakers of Jamaican Creole English call their language "Patois", and speakers of Hawai'i Creole English call their variety "Pidgin", etc. Sranan, spoken in Suriname along the northern coast of South America, is sometimes also called "Sranan Tongo" ('Suriname tongue') or "Taki-Taki" ('talktalk').

Creoles with an English lexical affiliation are more numerous than those related to any other language, attesting to the greater spread of English than any other metropolitan European language. Britain's three and a half centuries of imperialism spread not just varieties of standard and regional English, but also resulted in the creation of hundreds of English-lexicon pidgins and creoles. Holm (1989: xxii) lists 35 contemporary pidgins and creoles lexically affiliated to English, but different sources give different figures due to the lack of unanimity in defining which languages count as pidgins or creoles. This group of languages is sometimes further subdivided into two major geographic groupings: Atlantic and Pacific. The Atlantic creoles were established primarily during the 17th and 18th centuries in the Caribbean and West Africa, while the Pacific group originated primarily in the 19th. The earliest known text of an English-based creole dates from 1718 and is written in Sranan.

3.1 Atlantic pidgins and creoles

The Atlantic pidgins and creoles, comprising the largest number, and now spoken by more than 20 million people, were mainly products of the slave trade in West Africa, which dispersed large numbers of West Africans to the Caribbean. These languages share a common substrate in the Niger-Congo languages of West Africa and display many common features. Holm (1989: xxii) identifies 27 English creoles spoken along the west African Coast, throughout the Anglophone Caribbean islands, along the northern coast of South America, in central America, and in coastal areas of South Carolina and Georgia. The largest group is located in the Anglophone Caribbean with a population of around six million, comprising those territories having English as an official language: in practice, these are countries that are current or former colonies of Britain, i.e. Antigua, Barbados, Barbuda, the Bahamas, Belize, Dominica, Jamaica, Trinidad and Tobago, St. Vincent, St. Lucia, St. Kitts, Nevis, the U.S. Virgin Islands, The Turks and Caicos islands, Grenada, and Guyana (Devonish 2006).

The majority of the population uses an English-related creole as the everyday medium of communication. The term "Caribbean English creoles" is widely used to refer to these languages, the three largest of which are Jamaican Creole English, Trinidad and Tobago Creole English, and Guyanese Creole English. The West African English-based creoles include Kamtok (Cameroon Pidgin English), Nigerian Pidgin English, and Krio (Sierra Leone Creole English). The so-called Suriname creoles spoken in what was formerly the Dutch part of the Guianas in northern South America include Sranan, Saramaccan, and Ndjuka. Finally, Gullah (Sea Island Creole English) is spoken in the coastal plains of Georgia and South Carolina and the Sea Islands of South Carolina by African-American descendants of slaves.

3.2 Pacific pidgins and creoles

Historians interested in tracking the spread of English in the Pacific are fortunate in that the much shallower time depth of pidgin formation here compared to the Atlantic, furnishes a more or less continuous chain of documentation extending from the late 18th century through to the present. By the latter part of the 19th century contacts between English speakers and Pacific islanders had led to the formation of English-based pidgins spoken in various forms and with differing degrees of stability in almost the entire Pacific basin from New Guinea to Pitcairn island, from the Marshall Islands and Hawai'i to New Caledonia and New Zealand. Today, however, pidgins and creoles are found only in those parts of Melanesia, Polynesia, and Australia, where early pidgins stabilized and subsequently creolized (Romaine 2004). Holm (1989: xxii) lists eight pidgin and creole languages lexically related to English in the region, including Chinese Pidgin English, Tok Pisin, Bislama (Vanuatu Pidgin/Creole), Solomon Islands Pidgin English, Torres Strait Creole English, Australian Creole English, Norfolk Creole English, and Hawai'i Creole English. The linguistic as well as socio-historical and cultural conditions out of which these languages arose were also somewhat different than in the Atlantic. Obviously, different languages formed the substratum. Although the plantation setting was crucial for pidgin formation in both areas, in the Pacific laborers were recruited and indentured servants rather than slaves. While this traditional grouping is geographically convenient, it may obscure a far more complex picture of interrelationships and interactions between Atlantic and Pacific.

4 Theories of origin and structural features of pidgins and creoles

Questions regarding genetic and typological relationships between pidgins and creoles and the languages spoken by their creators continue to generate controversy. Pidgins and creoles challenge conventional models of language change and genetic relationships because they appear to be descendants of neither their superstrate languages from which they took most of their vocabulary, nor of the diverse substrate languages spoken by their creators. Scholars have proposed a variety of theories to explain why the structures of pidgins and creoles show more similarities to one another than they do to their lexifiers. It is in the area of syntax that the boldest claims have been made for the distinctiveness of creoles.

Some time ago scholars noted that the most striking differences between the deepest varieties of Jamaican Creole and those closest to English lay not so much in phonology and vocabulary as in grammar. Creoles typically display a range of varieties, and speakers' competence usually spans several varieties, as illustrated in Figure 20.1 for the Jamaican Creole English continuum. More basilectal varieties (i.e. the "deepest" varieties furthest from the superstrate) are often more typically found in rural areas and among the less educated, while the acrolectal varieties closer to the superstrate are more frequent among the more educated and higher social classes. Mesolectal varieties are intermediate.

basilect	mesolect	acrolect
mi a nyam	*mi a eat*	*I am eating*
	mi eatin	
	a itin	
	a is eatin	

Figure 20.1: "I am eating" across varieties of the Jamaican creole continuum

The ordering of the varieties presented here makes no claim about their diachronic development since it seems likely that in many cases mesolectal and acrolectal varieties were present even in the earliest phases of creole formation and do not always develop after creolization in adaptation to the superstrate. Thus, acrolectal varieties cannot be regarded as necessarily "later" than basilectal ones. Indeed, some scholars have claimed that early plantation slaves acquired a normally transmitted variety of the lexifier directly from Europeans, but this imperfectly acquired variety was subsequently diluted over time or "basilectalized" as successive generations of slaves learned from other slaves rather than from Europeans (Chaudenson 1992). According to this view, sometimes referred to as the superstrate theory, creoles represent gradual continuous developments with no abrupt break in transmission from their lexifiers. This perspective eliminates the assumption of a prior pidgin history and accepts creoles as varieties of their lexifiers rather than as special or unique new languages. That is, there are no particular linguistic evolutionary processes likely to yield (prototypical) creoles; they are produced by the same restructuring processes that bring about change in any language. Creoles are neither typologically nor genetically unique, but are instead "advanced varieties" of the lexifiers.

Nevertheless, the gap between basilectal and acrolectal Jamaican Creole English led other scholars to conclude quite the opposite; namely, that ordinary evolutionary processes leading to gradual divergence over time may not be applicable to creoles. From this perspective basilectal Jamaican Creole could not be regarded simply as a dialect of English, but was instead a new and different language, "born again" via a break in transmission and radical restructuring.

Creoles are thus non-genetic languages that emerge abruptly (Thomason and Kaufman 1988).

One explanation offered for the non-English character of basilectal creole was that its grammar had African origins. Indeed, African influence can clearly be seen in the word *nyam* 'eat' commonly found in West African languages such as Twi and Wolof. As far as grammar is concerned, however, early scholars such as Hugo Schuchardt (1842–1927), generally regarded as the founding father of creole studies, noted striking similarities across creole tense-mood-aspect (TMA) systems. Creoles tend to express the categories of tense, mood, and aspect by means of three preverbal free-standing particles appearing in a fixed order, whose semantics are highly constant (one for completed action, one for durative, and one for futurity/irrealis) as are their etymologies in their respective superstrates. For example, the irrealis mood or future marker typically comes from a verb meaning 'go', e.g. Hawai'i Creole English *I go leave om outside for you* 'I will leave it outside for you', the completive marker from a past form of *be*, e.g. Sranan *mi brada ben go* 'my brother went', and the aspect marker from a word meaning 'there' or 'to be located in a place', e.g. Saramaccan *mi tá nyán* 'I am eating'. Compare Portuguese, which has heavily influenced the lexicon of Saramaccan, where the verb *estar* is used to express location (e.g. *a manteiga está na mesa* 'the butter is on the table') and as an auxiliary in the formation of the progressive (e.g. *eu estou comendo* 'I am eating').

These similarities in TMA marking became a focal point of debate as a result of the bioprogram hypothesis (Bickerton 1984), which suggested that creoles held the key to understanding how human languages originally evolved many centuries ago. In this scenario children created the first creoles from the inadequate pidgin input supplied by their parents by relying on universal grammar. Although most creolists reject the bioprogram hypothesis in its strongest form (Singler 1990: ix), it led not only to an increase in research on creoles, but also a great deal of attention from scholars in other fields of linguistics such as language acquisition and related disciplines such as cognitive science.

Many linguists now find the concept of a common "creole syntax" or "creole prototype" uncontroversial, even though there might still be disagreements about exactly which features are included and why such similarities exist. Do pidgins and creoles share so many common characteristics because they are descended from a common historical ancestor, or did they arise independently but develop in parallel ways because they used common linguistic material and were formed in similar socio-historical circumstances? Was syntax diffused in a way similar to some of the words such as *savvy* (< Portuguese/Spanish *sabir/saber* 'to know'), found in both the Atlantic and Pacific languages? Or do the common elements perhaps reflect biological and cognitive constraints on what constitutes a minimal human language? Substrate influence is clearly responsible for some properties of pidgins and creoles, but it is still unclear why some substrate features appear in some languages and not others, and why some creoles appear to have more substrate features than their pidgin predecessors.

Each of these ideas has had its main proponents, but few scholars believe that one theory can explain everything satisfactorily. Most now accept that the various theories of origin are complementary, with each source of influence (i.e. diffusion, substrate, superstrate, and language universals) contributing something to the overall complex picture. Although it is possible to trace the origins of some vocabulary items such as *savvy* to the movements of people (Baker and Huber 2001), the existence of so many common syntactic features is not so easily explained by diffusion theories. For example, how do we explain the fact that a number of creoles use the same word to mark the grammatical functions of both possession ('have') and existence ('there is/are')? In most English-lexicon creoles a form of the word *get* serves this function. Compare, for example, how one would say in Guyanese Creole English, Hawai'i Creole English and Tok Pisin: "There is (existence) a woman who has (possession) a daughter" (Figure 20.2).

	Existence 'there is'	indefinite noun 'a woman'	Relative 'who'	Possession 'has'	indefinite noun 'a daughter'
Guyanese Creole	get	one uman	we	get	gyal pikni
Hawai'i Creole	get	wan wahine	shi	get	wan data
Tok Pisin	i gat	wanpela meri	0	i gat	wanpela pikinini meri

Figure 20.2: "There is (existence) a woman who has (possession) a daughter" in Guyanese Creole English, Hawai'i Creole English and Tok Pisin

The common syntactic structure is immediately apparent, with only minor differences. Tok Pisin, for instance, requires a so-called predicate marker *i* to precede certain verb forms, and does not require a relativizer to connect the two clauses. Similarly, Hawai'i Creole English uses the third person pronoun *she* to introduce the second clause, while Guyanese Creole English uses *we* (English 'where') as a relativizer. Most of the lexicon is drawn from English, with the exception of Hawai'i Creole English *wahine* (Hawaiian 'woman'), Guyanese Creole English *pikni* and Tok Pisin *pikinini* (Portuguese/Spanish *pequenho/pequeño or pequeniño* 'small'). In addition, the word *meri* 'woman' in Tok Pisin may represent a convergence of influence from English 'Mary' and Tolai (one of the indigenous languages of Papua New Guinea) *mari* 'love/pretty'.

This sentence also illustrates another of the many similarities in the source words used to express grammatical distinctions. The indefinite article in English lexicon creoles is usually derived from the numeral "one". Appealing to substrate or superstrate influence cannot satisfactorily explain the existence of the same grammatical patterns because different substrate languages are involved. Although these three languages have a common superstrate, they have not borrowed this grammatical pattern from English. Moreover, French- and Portuguese-based creoles show a similar construction not found in their respective superstrates French and Portuguese. Compare Papiá Kristang (Malaccan Creole Portuguese) spoken by a community of mixed Malay-Portuguese descent in Malacca (Malaysia) and Singapore, where forms of the verb *tem* 'to have' are used for both possession and existence, as in (1) and (2):

(1) irmang   machu   teng   na   rua
    sibling   male   have   in   street
    'my brother is in the street'

(2) yo teng   irmang   machu
    have   sibling   male
    'I have a brother'

Note also how the grammatical category of gender is often expressed analytically in phrases such as *pikinini meri, gyal pikni, irmang machu*, rather than as in the superstrate languages. In Portuguese, for instance, the source for Papiá Kristang *irmang* 'sibling', all nouns are classified grammatically as masculine or feminine; gender is lexicalized in two separate words, *irmão* 'brother' and *irmã* 'sister', which fuse the meanings of 'sibling' + 'male'/'female' into one word form. Although English no longer has grammatical gender, there are gender-differentiated sets of terms such as *sow/boar, cow/bull, mare/stallion*, but these are idiosyncratic formations, as compared to the regular Tok Pisin expressions *pik meri/pik man, bulmakau meri/bulmakau man, hos meri/hos man*, where gender is expressed by means of a separate word meaning male or female. Compare also Jamaican Creole *man hag/uman hag* 'boar/sow', and Kamtok *man pikin got/wuman pikin got* 'billy kid (goat)'/ 'nanny kid (goat)'.

Generally speaking, creoles are more regular and do not mark grammatical categories such as gender, case, or number by means of inflectional morphology as their superstrates often do. The more analytical and transparent structure of creoles tends toward expressing one meaning with one form.

5 Sociolinguistic dimensions of pidgins and creoles

The sociolinguistic dimensions of pidgins and creoles are also the subject of much debate and scholarly research, especially problems arising from the communication gap between the elite, who speak metropolitan European languages and the masses, who are creole-speaking. Despite many years of scientific research validating the linguistic status of these languages, Alleyne's (1994: 8) remarks about what might be called the double marginalization of creoles are unfortunately still true.

One of the general problems that continues to affect creole linguistics in several ways is the extreme marginalization of creole languages relative to the class of natural languages. For instance, creole languages have been ranked with baby talk, child language, foreigner talk, and with other instances of non-natural language that do not serve normal societal communicative needs nor the full cognitive needs of the human species. Consequently, it is not surprising that they have been the most stigmatized of the world's languages. All this has inhibited any programs that would standardize these languages and lead to the elevation of their status and role in the societies where they are spoken.

The advent of political independence from the 1960s onwards in many pidgin and creole-speaking territories around the world was not automatically accompanied by linguistic independence. Most pidgins and creoles are still not written and remain undeveloped for use in public and official domains such as government and education. For example, none of the Caribbean English Creoles has achieved official or public recognition as a language in its own right. In the Pacific only Tok Pisin and Bislama have received some official recognition as national languages of their respective countries, but English is still the most widely used medium of education. Paradoxically, Bislama is actually forbidden in the schools, making Vanuatu perhaps the only country in the world which forbids the use of its national language! Although most people in the Caribbean speak creole languages in their everyday lives, the majority of children throughout the territory continue to be educated in metropolitan languages rather than in their own native creole languages. The disparity between home and school language has contributed to a high rate of educational failure and low rates of literacy. Moreover, many of these problems and the debates surrounding them have impacted the educational systems of Britain and North America due to large-scale ongoing migration from the Anglophone Caribbean, which has brought an influx of Caribbean English-speaking students into schools. As many as 20,000 children from the Anglophone Caribbean enter the school system in New York state every year

(Devonish 2006: 2092). Most Caribbean students consider themselves speakers of English, and are surprised and embarrassed when sent to remedial English or English as a second language classes. In some cases, however, recognition of the creole in question as a language distinct from English results in the children's entitlement to bilingual education.

While linguists have generally been strong advocates for standardization, especially in the promotion of vernacular literacy, many pidgin and creole speakers still believe it is not possible to write their languages. This is one of the paradoxes posed by the very notion of writing in pidgins and creoles: for many people only "real" languages are written, and so the written form of a language is assumed to be the "real" language as it should be. Many pidgin and creole speakers write a language they don't speak and speak a language they don't write. When asked whether students should be allowed to write in Hawai'i Creole English in the classroom, one woman replied: "That's why you go to school for, so you don't write pidgin English" (Romaine 1999: 291). A teacher said that Hawai'i Creole English should not be written because it had no grammar (Romaine 1999: 293). One Bajan speaker explained her discomfort at seeing Bajan (Barbados) creole in print by likening it to the experience of looking at a face disfigured by an accident:

> They say there was this Christ Church woman who face got mash up in a car accident. She looking so ugly they took away al the mirrors so the woman kyaan (could not) see she face. Well, when we see this Bajan writing and thing is like we see [our] language in a broke-up mirror [...]. (Fenigsen 1999: 78)

Her reaction can be interpreted at least partly in terms of the almost complete hegemony that standard English exerts over print in Barbados, so that readers almost never see the creole written in any serious context. Fenigsen observes, for instance, that if you wrote someone's death certificate in Bajan people would think you were joking. The reaction in Hawai'i to such a text would probably be similar. In newspapers, Bajan creole might occasionally appear in isolated phrases in political cartoons or humorous columns. Although politicians may be heard using some Bajan in heated debates on the radio, in print they are represented as if they had spoken in the standard form.

The existence of continua between many creoles and their lexifiers poses the question of which variety to choose as the basis for standardization. In Papua New Guinea the standard was based on rural Tok Pisin, which at the time was the variety most widely spoken. This contrasts with the route to standardization followed by the lexifiers, where the varieties of the elite in capital cities such as London and Paris, provided the basis for codification of a standard. Devonish's (1986: 115) solution for the Anglophone Caribbean creoles is to recognize a range of intermediate forms in wide use as acceptable forms of Creole. This democratic approach attempts to avoid imposing a single variety on everyone in the society. Otherwise, the language planning process is adopting the very model of intolerance and negative attitudes towards the Caribbean creoles that it is trying to reject.

Although some have argued for recognition of Jamaican Creole as an official language, public attitudes still tend to be largely negative, particularly among the elite. The late Morris Cargill, for example, opined that "corruption of language is no cultural heritage. Corrupt people speak corrupt languages and that's that" (Cargill 1989: 8A). Such statements illustrate the way in which negative stereotypes about people are projected onto the language they speak. For most speakers of pidgin and creoles languages it is a revelation that their languages can be regarded as legitimate and that the study of pidgin and creole languages constitutes a recognized academic discipline. Nevertheless, the situation is rendered complex by what has been called the paradox of power and solidarity (Rickford and Traugott 1985). Creoles, like other minority languages and non-standard varieties, are symbolic of familiar, intimate, and solidary relations among in-group members as opposed to the more formal, public, and distant connotations of the colonial or standard language. Although basilectal speech is typically highly stigmatized due to its association with people of low social status and lack of education, at the same time, it is the basilectal and mesolectal varieties that are used to assert Caribbean identity. Across the Caribbean the absence of a high culture expressed through an indigenous language has meant that the voice of the masses and popular culture have generally been expressed through creoles, in both spoken and written forms.

Although Devonish (1986: 87) has rightly observed that in the Commonwealth Caribbean the "language question never became an important issue in the anti-colonial struggles, in Jamaica, in particular, a strong, black national identity has gone hand in hand with nationalist politics to foster a powerfully vibrant creative arts movement, whose influence has extended far beyond Jamaica and the Caribbean". Rejecting the term *dialect* because it suggested inferiority, Edward Kamau Brathwaite (1984) argued for the use of what he called "nation language" (Jamaican Creole English) in poetry as a way of capturing the sounds and rhythm of oral traditions of performance. The very act of writing in a marginalized language whose status as a language is denied by the mainstream is symbolic of the appropriation of the power vested in the written word. Writing in Jamaican Creole English becomes, in Le Page and Tabouret-Keller's (1985) terms, "an act of identity". Brathwaite was one of the founders of the Caribbean Artists Movement in 1966 in London, who fostered the development of a West Indian literature rooted in the languages and experiences of the islands. Through the commercial success of performers such as Bob Marley, Mikey Smith, Linton Kwesi Johnson, Benjamin Zephaniah or Mutabaruka, whose music and sound poems were on the British reggae music charts in the late 1970s and early 1980s, the once historically devalued Caribbean popular culture has become part of multicultural Britain.

These artists did much to elevate the status of Jamaican Creole. As early as 1942 Jamaican poet Louise Bennett (Miss Lou) became a household name and icon of popular Jamaican culture. A number of her poems challenged prevailing stereotypes of Jamaican language and culture as inferior, such as this one, where she satirized the prejudice and irony in the colonial perspective that regards Jamaican Creole as a "corrupt" form of English, but English as a language derived from other languages it has borrowed from (Bennett 1993: 1):

> My Aunty Roachy seh dat it bwile her temper
> and really bex her fi true anytime she hear anybody
> a style we Jamaican dialec as 'corruption of the
> English language'. For if dat be de case, den dem
> shoulda call English Language corruption of
> Norman French and Latin and all dem tarra
> language what dem seh dat English is derived
> from.
> Oonoo hear de wud? 'Derived.' English is a
> derivation but Jamaican Dialec is a corruption!
> What a unfairity!
> No massa, noting no go so. We not 'corrupt', an dem 'derive.'
> We derive to.
> Jamaica derive.

Gloss: My Aunty Roachy says that her temper boils and that
> it really makes her angry anytime she hears anyone
> describe our Jamaican dialect as a 'corruption of the
> English language'. If that's the case, then they
> should call the English language a corruption of
> Norman French and Latin and all those other
> Languages they say English is derived from.
> Did you (plural) hear the word? 'Derived.' English is a
> derivation but Jamaican Dialec is a corruption!
> How unfair!
> No sir, that's not how it is. We're not 'corrupt', and they 'derived.'
> We derive too.
> Jamaica derives.

By contrasting the ways in which terms *corrupt* and *derived* are applied to the two languages, Bennett establishes parity for Jamaican Creole English as a legitimate language with a respectable, albeit mixed lineage, similar to English. Any language that is closely related to another in vocabulary or structure could be said to be a debased or corrupted form of that language when looked at from the perspective of that other language (Romaine 1988: 13). Indeed, English and other European languages were once regarded as corrupted forms of Latin. Sir Thomas Bodley (1545–1613), founder of Oxford University's Bodleian Library, one of the oldest libraries in Europe, would not allow works of English literature in it, dismissing them as "idle bookes and riffe raffes" at a time when the only serious books were in Latin, and a few books in the vernacular languages of Europe such as Italian.

Comparisons between pidgins and creoles and their lexifiers are inevitably biased due at least partly to the fact that the former typically have a rather shorter history than their lexifiers and most still remain unwritten. Tok Pisin, one of the handful of pidgins and creoles to be standardized, has been written for only about 100 years (Romaine 1996). By contrast, English has been written for centuries. It can easily be overlooked that highly elaborated languages have been centuries in the making. English was still in many respects stylistically limited in the 16th century by comparison with Latin, and it was not until the end of the 17th century that English replaced Latin as the language of science. The 17th century saw concerted efforts on the part of lexicographers, grammarians, and writers to remedy the perceived inadequacies of English to enable it to meet a continually expanding range of functions. The continuing expansion of standard English into domains once occupied by Latin and French was accomplished partly by heavy borrowing. It would take even longer before people were confident enough about English to deem it worthy of study as a subject for teaching and research. Now that English is so well established as a discipline, we tend to forget that even as late as the 19th century it was not recognized as a legitimate subject.

This brings us back to the position that the only thing special about creoles is the socio-historical situation of language contact in which they emerge. Yet even that may not be so special when we consider the history of so-called "normal" languages, most of which are hybrid varieties that have undergone restructuring and borrowing to various degrees depending on the circumstances. Scholars such as Bailey and Maroldt (1977: 21), for example, have suggested that English is a creole because the outcome of mixing was substantial enough to result in a new system separate from the antecedent parent systems, i.e. French and English. They depict Middle English as a language of mixed parentage with Old French acting as a superstrate on an Anglo-Saxon substrate, with additional input from Norse. Linguistic evidence offered in support of the creolization hypothesis consists of a number of grammatical changes that eliminated a great deal of the inflectional morphology of English. Ultimately, the validity of the creolization hypothesis depends on how we define creoles. If all we mean by creole is a mixed language, then most of the world's languages are creoles and the term creole is rendered useless. There are no clear criteria for determining how much mixture or restructuring there must be in any given case of language contact before deciding that we are dealing with pidginization or creolization as distinct from the effects of borrowing or interference. It may be useful to distinguish between the processes of pidginization and creolization on the one hand and pidgins and creoles as outcomes of such processes on the other. That is, many language varieties may at various points in their evolution be affected by processes typical of pidginization and creolization, but not all such varieties result in pidgins or creoles.

6 References

Alleyne, Mervyn C. 1994. Problems of standardization of creole languages. In: Marcyliena Morgan (ed.), *Language and the social construction of identity in creole situations*, 7–18. Los Angeles: Center for Afro-American Studies, University of California.
Ansaldo, Umberto, Stephen Matthews, and Lisa Lim (eds.). 2007. *Deconstructing creole*. Amsterdam/Philadelphia: John Benjamins.
Baker, Philip and Peter Mühlhäusler. 1990. From business to pidgin. *Journal of Asian Pacific Communication* 1(1): 87–115.
Baker, Philip and Magnus Huber. 2001. Atlantic, Pacific, and world-wide features in English-lexicon contact languages. *English World Wide* 22(2): 157–208.
Bailey, C.J. and Karl Maroldt. 1977. The French lineage of English. In: Jürgen M. Meisel (ed.) *Langues en contact – Pidgins – Creoles*, 21–53. Tübingen: Narr.
Bennett, Louise. 1993. *Aunty Roachy seh*. Kingston: Sangster's Book Stores, Ltd.
Bickerton, Derek. 1984. The language bioprogram hypothesis. *Behav Brain Sci* 7: 173–221.
Brathwaite, Edward Kamau. 1984. *The history of the voice: The development of nation language in anglophone Caribbean poetry*. London: New Beacon Books.
Cargill, Morris. 1989. Corruption of language is no cultural heritage. *Sunday Gleaner*, 29 October 1989.
Chaudenson, Robert. 1992. *Des îles, des hommes, des langues*. Paris: L'Harmattan.
Devonish, Hubert. 1986. *Language and liberation: Creole language politics in the Caribbean*. London: Karia Press.
Devonish, Hubert. 2006. The anglophone Caribbean. In: Ulrich Ammon, Norbert Dittmar, and Klaus J. Mattheier (eds.), *Sociolinguistics: An international handbook of the science of language and society*, Vol. III, 2083–2095. 2nd edn. Berlin/New York: Mouton de Gruyter.
Fenigsen, Janina. 1999. 'A Broke-up Mirror': Representing Bajan in print. *Cultural Anthropology* 14(1): 61–87.
Holm, John. 1989. *Pidgins and Creoles*. 2 vols. Cambridge: Cambridge University Press.
Le Page, Robert B. and Andrée Tabouret-Keller. 1985. *Acts of identity. Creole-based approaches to language and ethnicity*. Cambridge: Cambridge University Press.
McWhorter, John. 2005. *Defining creole*. Oxford: Oxford University Press.
Mufwene, Salikoko S. 1986. Les langues créoles peuvent-elles être définiés sans allusion à leur histoire?*Etudes créoles* 9: 135–150.
Rickford, John R. and Elizabeth C. Traugott. 1985. Symbols of powerlessness and degeneracy or symbol of solidarity and truth? Paradoxical attitudes towards pidgins and creoles. In: Sidney Greenbaum (ed.), *The English language today*, 252–262. Oxford: Pergamon.

Romaine, Suzanne. 1988. *Pidgin and Creole Languages*. London: Longman.
Romaine, Suzanne. 1996. Pidgins and creoles as literary languages: Ausbau and *Abstand*. In: Marlis Hellinger and Ulrich Ammon (eds.), *Contrastive Sociolinguistics*, 271–289. Berlin/New York: Mouton de Gruyter.
Romaine, Suzanne. 1999. Changing attitudes towards Hawai'i Creole English: Fo' get one good job, you gotta know ho fo' talk like one haole. In: John R. Rickford and Suzanne Romaine (eds.), *Creole genesis, attitudes and discourse. Studies celebrating Charlene J. Sato*, 287–301. Amsterdam/Philadelphia: John Benjamins.
Romaine, Suzanne. 2004. The English input to the English-lexicon pidgins and creoles of the Pacific. In: Raymond Hickey (ed.), *Legacies of colonial English. Studies in transported dialects*, 456–499. Cambridge: Cambridge University Press.
Singler, John V. (ed.). 1990. *Pidgin and creole tense-mood-aspect systems*. Amsterdam/Philadelphia: John Benjamins.
Thomason, Sarah G. and Terrence Kaufman. 1988. *Language contact, creolization and genetic linguistics*. Berkeley: University of California Press.

Index

adjective 27, 133, 134, 136, 137, 222, 370
– comparative 27, 136
– superlative 27, 136
adverb 133, 134, 136, 137
Africa 21, 59, 103, 190, 390, 393
African American 24, 63, 128, 390
– Language 68, 106, 330–345, 338
– (Vernacular) English 80–92, 332–335
alliteration 278, 279
allophonic variation 164, 323
analogy 15, 16, 123, 124, 323
Anglo-Saxon (language), see also 211, 217, 266, 400
– Old English
aspect 83–86, 142, 251, 252, 254, 393
auxiliary, see also do 83–85, 142, 143, 253, 323, 324, 335, 393
Australia 18, 26, 103–106, 128, 289–306, 339, 355, 356, 389–391

BBC 107, 108, 151, 180
– BBC English, see Received Pronunciation (RP)
borrowing
– lexical 99, 219, 235, 245, 296–299, 311
– syntactic 99
– morphological 99, 236, 237

Canada 33, 45–48, 54–72, 103, 104, 295, 335, 339, 367
Caribbean 10, 59, 68, 83, 87–89, 106, 108, 205, 332–334, 343, 344, 390, 396–399
Celtic 6, 132, 210–227, 231–233, 270, 343
– Celtic Hypothesis 210–227, 232, 233, 254, 343
chain shift 46, 47, 337–341
– Canadian Shift 54, 67, 68, 339
– Northern Cities Chain Shift 47–49, 67
– See also Great Vowel Shift
Cockney 129, 170–173, 179, 187–208, 293, 294
– Rhyming slang 205–208
codification 100, 111, 367, 397
collocation 112

comparative, see adjective
consonant inventory, changes in 123–126, 198–201, 323
contact, language 12, 64, 67, 86, 88, 90, 146, 190, 204, 210–227, 235, 245, 246, 251, 265, 291, 303, 312, 313, 316, 327, 331, 333, 336, 341, 344, 345, 385, 387, 400, 401
corpus/corpora 55, 62, 63, 112, 221, 301
Creole 87–92, 144, 215, 334–336, 385–401
– creolization 303, 388, 400, 401

determiner 142
dialect(s) 11, 13, 19, 20, 24, 32–49, 55, 59, 70, 72, 88, 92, 98, 107, 131, 132, 159, 172–176, 187, 213–218, 224, 232–237, 241, 245, 250–252, 257, 291, 302–305, 337, 343, 344, 350–352, 359, 360, 379
– dialect atlas 33–39, 45–49, 56, 61
– dialect features 57, 107, 121, 122, 135, 136, 140–147, 250, 251, 258, 275–276, 295, 335, 357, 379
dictionary
– Oxford English Dictionary (OED) 2, 28, 42, 103, 115, 153, 250
– Dictionary of Canadian English 65
– Johnson's Dictionary 10, 102, 110, 154, 157
– Webster, Noah 17, 32, 109, 110, 115
diffusion 349–361, 370, 378, 394
discourse
– analysis 3, 25, 112, 114, 156, 184, 316, 323, 336
– courtroom, see also register, legal 238, 272, 319
– news 107, 112, 115, 117, 171, 180, 299, 301, 318, 319, 321, 322, 397
– science, see also register, scientific 82, 98, 100, 102, 153, 400
– internet/media 107, 108, 115, 123, 180, 181, 206, 269, 273, 281, 321, 324, 325, 338
do, auxiliary 83, 253, 323
– development of 214, 253, 254, 277
Dutch 216, 226, 236, 331, 366, 379, 380, 390

education 23, 34, 44, 97, 99, 102, 109, 152–159, 165, 180, 239, 270, 273, 281, 282, 314–320, 333–336, 341, 381, 396, 397, 398
Early Modern English 3, 14, 97, 98, 112, 123, 125, 215, 232, 374
Estuary English 107, 123, 124, 130, 131, 152, 161, 164, 169–184

folk linguistics 6, 183
French 13, 98, 102, 216, 223, 224, 235–237, 246, 247, 250, 267, 333, 366, 389, 395, 400

gender
– as sociolinguistic variable 43, 158, 159, 174–178, 302
– grammatical 344, 395
genre 19, 20, 101, 157, 241, 321, 326
– letters 18, 26, 98, 224, 318
– and language change 11, 19, 39, 45, 100, 101, 114, 241, 281, 321, 322, 350, 353, 378
German (Modern) 9, 21–23, 33, 223, 226, 303, 331, 366
Germanic 1, 13, 131, 216–219, 222, 223, 226, 227, 233, 266
grammar, prescriptive 101, 102, 109, 112, 113, 156, 400
grammaticalization 146, 221
graphology, see orthography
Great Vowel Shift 3, 67, 126, 130
Greek 216, 218, 303, 314

Hindi 312–321
hypercorrection 373, 374

idiom/idiomaticity/idiomaticization 108, 205
India 59, 104–106, 108, 117, 161, 190, 268, 311–328, 386
inkhorn 99, 100
Irish 12, 16, 26, 58–60, 68, 69, 106, 125, 132, 140, 143, 152, 155, 212, 214, 215, 222–224, 231, 244–260, 269, 291, 365–381

L1 varieties 105, 116, 121, 122, 132–140, 323, 226–341

L2 varieties 116, 117, 135, 136, 303, 332, 334, 341–345
Late Modern English 374
Latin 98–100, 216, 218, 221, 224, 237, 246, 247, 267, 283, 314, 326, 400
lexicon 7, 49, 246, 249–252, 290, 296–299, 305, 324, 326, 331, 370, 385, 387–389, 393–395
literacy 21, 92, 101–103, 268, 325, 396–399

Middle English 2, 3, 67, 98, 125–130, 216, 257, 259, 260, 369, 400
modal 62, 68, 84, 112–114, 141, 142, 214, 322
morphology 98, 110, 111, 239, 273, 275, 387
– inflectional 27, 211, 395, 400
– derivational 127, 204
– stem-based 84, 110

names 234, 267, 276, 297, 298, 301
negation 68, 85, 107, 112, 134–137, 202, 203
New Zealand 7, 26, 105, 106, 125, 289–306, 337, 338, 391
Norman Conquest 266
norms, see standardization
noun 25, 27, 65, 141, 142, 215, 216, 226, 296, 312, 394

Old English 231–235, 250, 266, 324
orthography 17, 98
– standardization 109, 110, 117
orthoepists 110

periphrasis 3
phoneme 16, 45–48, 67, 122–131, 164, 173, 257–260, 274–277, 323–325, 341–343, 359–361, 367–378
phonotactics 123, 323
Pidgin 105, 106, 135, 136, 303, 312, 313, 330–334, 345, 385–401
politeness 70, 71, 141, 326
pragmatics 70, 71
pragmatic markers 204, 205
prescriptivism 25, 101, 155, 158, 160, 325–327, 371

prestige 11, 14, 24, 107, 152, 156, 158, 160, 184, 245–247, 302, 325, 343, 375
– overt 156, 165
– covert 40, 81, 162, 165
printing (press) 98, 238
pronouns 84, 85, 113, 133, 134, 137, 138, 141, 142, 222, 344
– relative, see relativizer
progressive 6, 133, 135, 142, 143, 210, 212, 216–219, 226, 239, 301, 302, 312, 323, 344, 393
prosody 223, 323

Received Pronunciation (RP) 23, 104, 123, 129, 130, 151–166, 170–173, 178–180, 183, 184, 191, 193–197, 274–277, 282, 339, 340, 343
register
– legal see also discourse, courtroom 27
– scientific 27, 98, 100
– see also discourse, science
relativizer/relativization 133–135, 137, 139, 142, 144, 145, 204, 394

semantic change, lexical 66, 298–301, 324
Spanish 21–23, 88, 278, 355, 386, 393, 394
speaker, individual 203, 283, 325, 327, 349
sociolect 130, 304, 341
– social rank 34, 39, 55, 103, 107, 109, 152, 158, 162, 171, 174, 177–180, 278, 302, 316, 325, 353, 356, 392
social network 7, 57, 349–353, 361, 368, 378, 382
sound change(s) 39, 45–49, 125, 201, 302, 339–344, 359
spelling 71, 110, 111, 116, 117, 156, 199, 237, 242, 257, 297, 338, 374
– see also standardization
– reform 15, 16, 103
spoken language 63, 107, 113, 160
standard, English 4, 5, 40, 97, 98, 125, 127, 146, 155, 231, 232, 235–237, 343, 368, 378, 379, 389
– American English 9–28, 83, 115–117, 133

– British English 96–117, 201–204, 212
– Canadian English 54–68
– Scottish English 239
standardization 3, 110, 156, 232, 237, 244, 355, 367, 396, 397, 400
stress 84, 110, 124, 125, 142, 153, 157, 173, 200, 220–221, 224, 258, 276, 277, 323, 335, 372
style 5, 99, 100, 113, 130, 174, 177–181, 239, 276, 316, 325, 326, 338, 339, 341, 373
subject, category of 85, 113, 133, 134, 136, 137, 138, 139, 141, 142, 143, 144, 202, 204, 215, 222, 256
superlative, see adjective
substrate 89, 322, 323, 341–345, 389–391, 394, 395, 400
superstrate 335, 343, 344, 388, 389, 391–395, 400
syllable 15, 110, 125, 154, 164, 173, 194, 258, 276, 343, 360, 371, 372, 376–378

tense 18, 68, 83–85, 112, 133–144, 202, 203, 212, 217, 254, 256, 257, 275, 355, 393
Tudor (English) 98, 110

usage guides 18

verb 6, 138, 139, 142–144, 213, 253, 256, 275, 278, 317, 322, 335, 344, 354, 395
see also auxiliary, modal, progressive, tense
vernacular (varieties) 1, 18, 19, 90, 98, 101, 102, 135, 136, 147, 179, 180, 212, 214, 224, 238, 239, 252, 257, 258, 260, 274, 275, 302, 312, 314, 317, 326, 334, 338, 339, 351, 357, 366–369, 371–381, 397, 400

Wales 4, 6, 102, 107, 163, 212, 215, 246, 265–284
word formation 66, 83, 84, 245, 300
word order 133, 134, 222, 225, 393

www.ingramcontent.com/pod-product-compliance
Lightning Source LLC
Chambersburg PA
CBHW030104010526
44116CB00005B/90